DELACROIX
IN MOROCCO

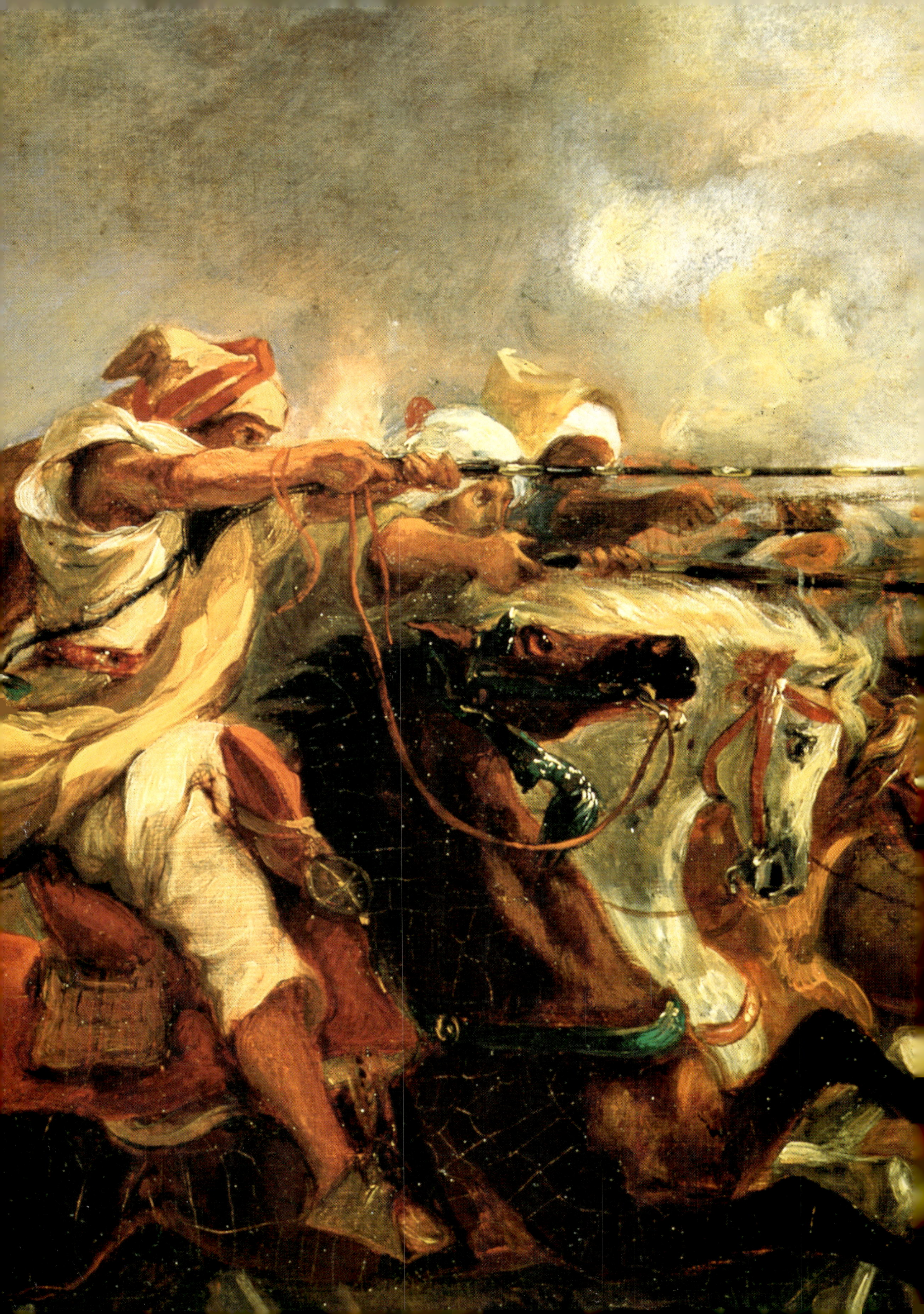

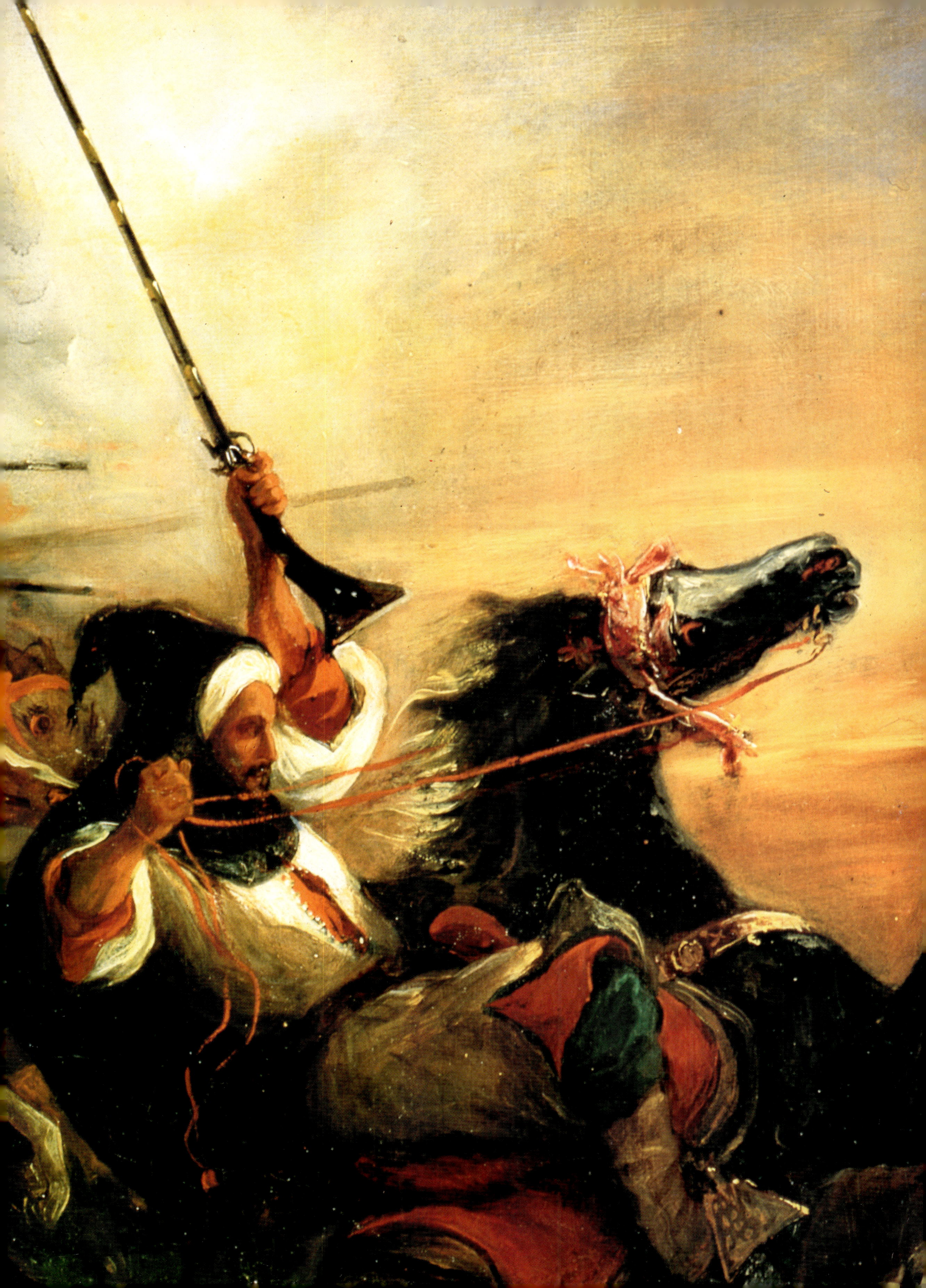

DELACROIX
IN MOROCCO

Exhibition organized by the Institut du Monde Arabe
1, rue des Fossés-Saint Bernard, 75005 Paris
27 September 1994–15 January 1995

INSTITUT
DU MONDE
ARABE

Flammarion
Paris - New York

The catalogue was prepared by the Institut du Monde Arabe and Flammarion

Conception of the catalogue: **Brahim Alaoui**
Picture research and co-ordinator, I.M.A.: **Eric Delpont**
Editorial co-ordinator, Flammarion: **Delphine Le Cesne**
Editorial secretary: **Caroline Boulay**
Copy-editing and lay-out (French edition): **Béatrice** and **Frédéric Vignals**

Translated from the French by **Tamara Blondel**
Copy-editing and additional research for the English edition by **Sophy Thompson**

Designed by **Sandra** and **Christian Gamby**
assisted by **Caroline Dubuc**
Photoengraving by Euresys, Baisieux
Typsetting by Octavo Editions, Paris
Printed by Clerc, Saint-Amand-Montrond
Bound by Brun, Malesherbes

Pages 2 and 3:
Moroccan Military Exercises, or **Fantasia**, *detail, 1832. Musée Fabre, Montpellier.*

Flammarion
26, rue Racine
75006, Paris

ISBN: 2-08013-572-4
N° édition: 0843
Dépôt légal: September 1994
Printed in France

Contents

DELACROIX IN MOROCCO

This exhibition has been organized under the patronage of:

His Majesty Hassan II King of Morocco	***François Mitterrand*** President of the French Republic

COMMITTEE OF HONOUR

Abdellatif Filali Prime Minister Minister of State for Foreign Affairs and Cooperation	***Edouard Balladur*** Prime Minister
Allal Sinaceur Minister of Cultural Affairs	***Philippe Séguin*** President of the Assemblée Nationale
Serge Berdugo Minister of Tourism	***Alain Juppé*** Minister of Foreign Affairs
Abbès El-Fassi Moroccan Ambassador to France	***Jacques Toubon*** Minister of Culture
André Azoulay Adviser to the King	***Jacques Chirac*** Mayor of Paris
Mohamed Mekouar President of the Fondation Connaissance du Maroc	***Michel Laclotte*** Director of the Louvre

This exhibition has been organized by the Institut du Monde Arabe

President: **Edgard Pisani**   Director General: **Mohamed Bennouna**

Exhibition Committee

Chairman

Maurice Sérullaz
Honorary Inspector General for French Museums

Executive Steering Commitee

Arlette Sérullaz
General Curator at the Département des Arts graphiques, Louvre, Chief Curator of the Musée Eugène Delacroix

Brahim Alaoui
Responsible for the Plastic Arts, Musée de l'Institut du Monde Arabe

Advisory Scholar: **Maurice Arama**
Art Historian

Administration

Administrator: **Badr-Eddin Arodaky**

Production

Responsible for collections and exhibitions: **Noha Hosni-Maillard**
assisted by: **Eric Delpont**
Marielle Dupont
Islamic Art: **Joëlle Lemaistre**
responsible for textile collections
Exhibition Secretary: **Caroline Boulay**,
assisted by: **Amal Keddeh**
Kébira Alami El-Idrissi, **Sandrine Viboud**

Exhibition space

Installation: **Vincen Cornu** and **Benoît Crepet**
Architects DPLG
Engineer: **Alain Kronenberg**
Assistant, Building Maintenance and Security: **Guy Lebegue**
Technician: **Jalal Alami El Idrissi**

Communications

Thierry Fabre
Director of Communications
Khémaïs Khayati
Press Office
Sylvie Laurens Aubry and **Frédéric Plumas**
Press Attachés

Acknowledgements

This exhibition was made possible by the various museums, institutions, galleries and collectors who have offered us their support and assistance.

We wish to thank in particular Françoise Viatte, Chief Curator of the Département des Arts graphiques, Louvre, for the numerous works loaned to us and the department's assistance from the outset of the project.

We also wish to thank:

United States: *Albright-Knox Art Gallery, Buffalo:* Douglas G. Schultz, Laura Catalano, Daisy Stroud. *The Art Institute of Chicago:* Suzanne Folds McCullagh, Mary Mulhern. *The Baltimore Museum of Art:* Melanie F. Harwood, Jay M. Fisher. *The Fine Arts Museums of San Francisco:* Steven A. Nash, Robert Flynn Johnson, Ted A. Greenberg, Sonya Knudsen. *The Metropolitan Museum of Art, New York:* Helen B. Mules, Minora Pacheco. *Milwaukee Art Museum:* Dr Russel Bowman, Leigh Albritton. *Minneapolis Institute of Arts:* Dr Evan M. Maurer, George Keyes, Peggy Tolbert. *Philadelphia Museum of Art:* Joseph Rishel, Nancy S. Quaile. **France**: *Musée des Beaux-Arts, Bordeaux:* Francis Ribemont. *Musée des Beaux-Arts, Dijon:* Emmanuel Starcky, Pierre Granville. *Musée archéologique municipal, Laon* : Caroline Jorrand. *Musée Fabre, Montpellier:* Michel Hilaire. *Musée des Beaux-Arts, Nantes:* Henry-Claude Cousseau. *Musée des Arts décoratifs, Paris:* Pierre Arizzoli-Clémentel, Marie-Noëlle de Gary. *Bibliothèque nationale de France, Paris:* Jean Favier, Laure Beaumont Maillet. *Musée Carnavalet, Paris:* Jean-Marc Léri, Rosine Trogan. *Musée Eugène Delacroix, Paris:* Arlette Sérullaz. *Musée du Louvre, Paris:* Pierre Rosenberg. *Musée d'Orsay, Paris:* Françoise Cachin. *Musée Sainte-Croix, Poitiers:* Michel Rerolle, Jeanne Villeneuve. *Musée des Augustins, Toulouse:* Denis Milhau, Monique Rey-Delqué. *Musée des Beaux-Arts, Tours:* Jacques Nicourt. **Hungary**: *Szépmüvészeti Muzeum, Budapest:* Miklos Mojzer, István Szönyi, Brigitta Cifka. **Japan**: *Hiroshima Museum of Art:* Osamu Hashiguchi, Koichiro Morikawa. **Morocco**: Ali Amahan, Director of Museums, Rabat. **Holland**: *Museum Boymans-Van Beuningen , Rotterdam:* Dr J.R. ter Molen, A.W.F.Meij, Maartje De Haan. **United Kingdom**: *The British Museum, London:* Anthony V. Griffiths, Janice Reading. *National Gallery of Scotland, Edinburgh:* Michael Clarke, Julia Lloyd William, Anne Buddle, Janice Slater. **Russia**: *Musée de l'Ermitage,* **St Petersburg:** Boris Piotrovsky, Mr Vilinbakhoff. **Switzerland**: *Kunsthaus, Zurich:* Dr Felix Baumann, Dr Christian Klemm. **Sweden**: *Nationalmuseum, Stockholm:* Olle Granath, Görel Cavalli-Björkman, Ulf Cederlöf, Lillie Johansson.
Private Collectors: Timothy Bathurst, Artemis Group, Huguette Bérès, Hector Brame and Jean Lorenceau, Paul L. Herring, Jan Krugier, Manuel Schmit, Eugene V. Thaw
And all those who have preferred to remain anonymous.

We wish to thank the following for their help and co-operation in our research :

Jacques Chaban-Delmas, Deputy-Mayor of Bordeaux, fomer President of the Assemblée nationale, Jean-Marc Ayrault, Deputy-Mayor of Nantes, Dominique Baudis, Deputy-Mayor of Toulouse, Jean Royer, Deputy-Mayor of Tours, Robert Poujade, Mayor of Dijon, Georges Frêche, Mayor of Montpellier.

Farid Britel, President of the O.N.A. Foundation, Zouhair Mehaji, Director of the Fondation Connaissance du Maroc, Ahmed Nemar, of Royal Air Maroc, Paris, Issam Lamdouar, Director of the Moroccan National Tourism Office, Paris, Tawfik Bennani Smires, Director General of 2M, Casablanca, Morocco, Mr Touri, Director of National Heritage, Ministry of Cultural Affairs, Rabat, Morocco.

Ms Allaire, Cultural Acvisor at the French Embassy, Budapest, Hungary, Alain Nahoum, Cultural Advisor at the French Embassy, Tokyo, Japan.

and also: Maître Catherine Charbonneaux, Maître Pierre-Yves Lefèvre, Maître Jacques Tajan, Farida Belyazid, Danuta Krammer, Antonia Yasmina Filali, Faten Safieddine Melehi, Pascale Pavageau, Jane Roberts, Margret Stuffmann, Patricia P. Tang, Daniela Tobler, Gérard Barralis, Christian de Pourtales, Georges Bousquet, Jean-Louis Scherrer, Harald Szeeman, Gérard Turpin, Yves Vidal.

at the Bibliothèque nationale de France: Françoise Jestaz, François Fossier.

at the Louvre: Christine André, Marie-Thérèse Genin, Anne Giroux, Clarine Guillou, Linda de Lépine, Ghislaine Millioud, Brigitte Scart and the documentation service of the Department of Graphic Arts, Bruno Alet, Pierre Coural, Jacques Foucart, and the documentation service of the Paintings Department, André Le Prat, Cyrille Patrick et Jean-François Sainsard.

the Réunion des musées nationaux: Catherine Bossis and Annie Madec.

the Service de restauration des Musées nationaux: Nathalie Volle and Christiane Naffah.

the Institut du Monde Arabe: Laurence Fruitier, Laila Hazaz, Annie Hull, Meriam Kettani, Jeanne Mouliérac, Faten Mourad, Arlette Posty, Nicole Thévenin, Magda Wassef, Yannick Bennet, Bernard d'Aste, Philippe de la Salle, Malek Fallouh, Mohamed Metalsi, Mahieddine Roumili.

Our thanks to all above.

We would like to take this opportunity to express our profond gratitude to Patti Cadby Birch, who did so much to assist the exhibition in the United States.

Preface

Several months before the opening of the exhibition of Delacroix's Moroccan drawings and paintings, the Institut du Monde Arabe and the Centre National de la Photographie put on an exhibition of historical photographs illustrating the Western world's perception of the Orient. The detailed images portrayed the fantasies of the former rather more than the reality of the latter. Times have changed, however, and a project is already taking shape for an exhibition devoted to the modern Arab world seen through the eyes of Arab photographers, an exhibition designed to illustrate these changes, the evolution of reality and of its perception.

The exhibition devoted to Delacroix in Morocco will have no sequel, for the image that he portrays in each brushstroke, in each scene, is inimitable. It is marked by his genius for the expression of form and light, by his sense of precise detail and by the majesty or intimacy of a way of life which he seems to have grasped in its essence.

What is surprising in this phase of Delacroix's work, is not only the stylistic difference between his rapid sketches made from life and the resulting vast and elaborate paintings, but also the considerable length of time which elapsed between his voyage and the actual execution of the greater part of this work. Many people will no doubt wonder whether they prefer the often intimate improvisations or the bold reconstructions with their dazzling light. Why choose? It is the same Delacroix, portraying the same Morocco, with the same genius; something would necessarily be sacrificed if a choice were made.

If one considers his overall work, leaving aside what might appear out of fashion, one discovers that Delacroix comes close to an essential truth (which the trail of his Moroccan itinerary still reveals today) and which is indeed the privilege of the artist: in capturing the fleeting moment he renders it immortal.

Edgard PISANI
President of the Institut du Monde Arabe

Foreword

A voyage, a coincidence, a combination of circumstances . . . And then a cascade of new sensations, flavours, perfumes, and a procession of confused, violent and tender images, details which suddenly appear in a blinding light and then fade. Here are faces with expressions that are serene, mocking, aggressive, passionate, timeless. In this country time itself has ceased to exist and no-one remembers when it last moved forward; it has lost itself in the dried out river beds, in the everyday, in the lavish rituals. But maybe it can be found in the secret irony of a woman's glance, met at the corner of a dark and mysterious alleyway.

The foreigner, fascinated, invokes tradition, an ageless and carefree woman, welcoming and generous, ready for adventure if it holds no risk of her losing herself or her soul.

The artist tries to control the flood of memory, he accepts the challenge of these images which haunt him; he gives them life and movement in the rhythm of his palette of colours, free from the modesty of yester-year. Alchemy, or miraculous encounter, the artist is reborn, he discovers a new light. Undreamt-of perspectives open out before him.

The land of the setting sun indulges and watches over this privileged witness; henceforth they are irrevocably bound, and their union has been transformed, by others throughout the world, into a legend.

Mohamed BENNOUNA
Director General of the Institut du Monde Arabe

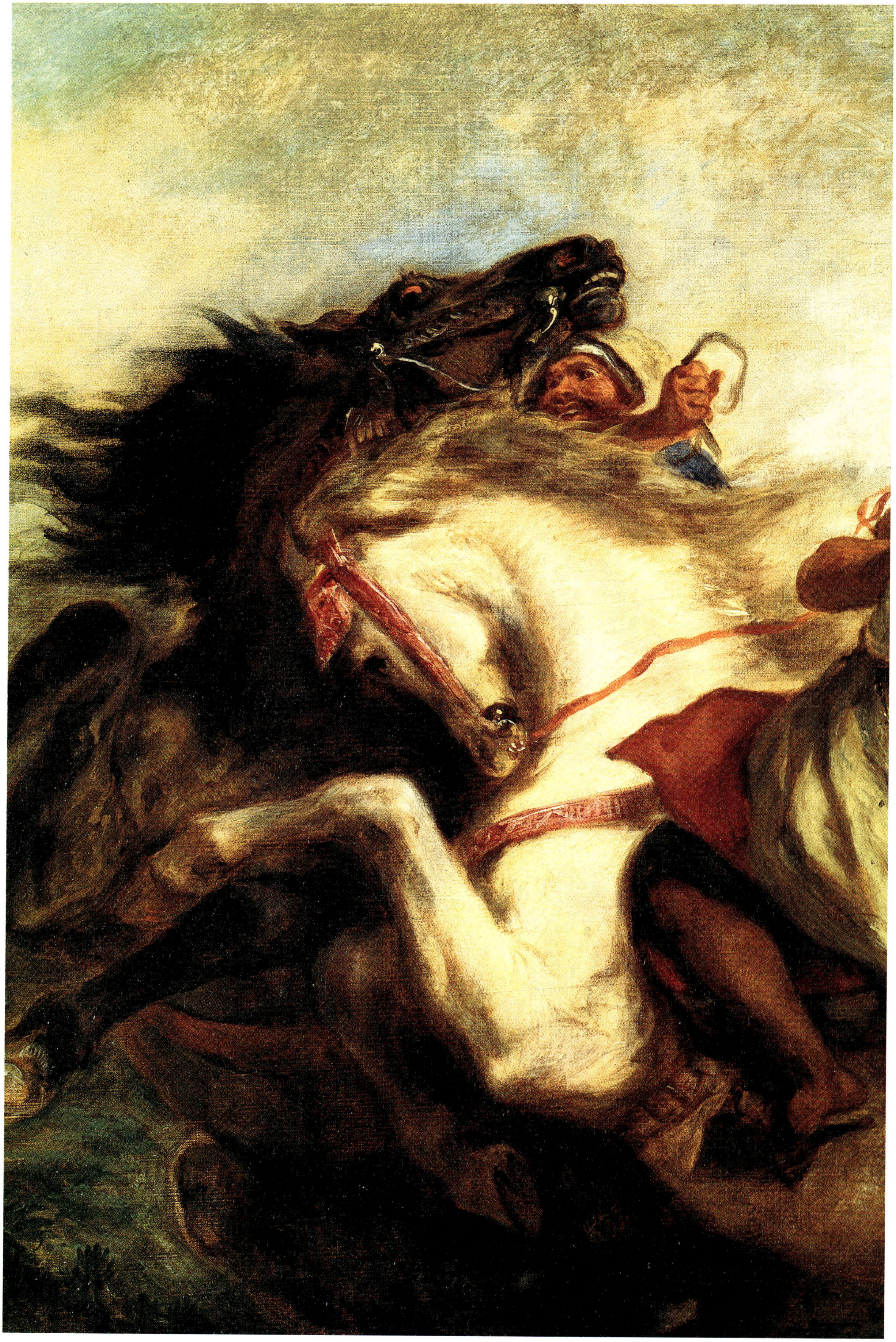

Delacroix and the Arabian Horse: a Tribute to the Son of the Wind

'At the moment I am like a man in a dream, seeing things he's afraid will vanish from him.' The language of one in love, for when Delacroix set foot on Moroccan soil his heart received a shock, like an encounter which one instinctively knows will prove decisive, if not fatal. Will the vision fade? maybe disappear? 'I am quite bewildered', he admits. Where should he start? He finds the women admirable. Especially the Jewish women: 'They are real pearls of Eden.'[1]

Delacroix arrived in Tangier on 25 January 1832, and in the space of three months Morocco won him over. In a letter to his elder brother, he writes: 'Farewell, good brother, your African sends you his love . . . '. He describes himself as African. He would willingly have envisaged prolonging his stay and even not returning to France: 'If it weren't for one's friends at home, one would willingly leave the north and emigrate.'[2] However, like all persons who are prey to a devouring passion he goes from one extreme to another, from total certitude to the gravest doubts. One day he accumulates everything he sees in his sketch-book: colours, costumes, festivities and landscapes, not wanting to miss a single detail. Morocco becomes a part of his life. Morocco, he states to himself, nothing but Morocco. . . . France is so far away! He speaks of France with detachment and says clearly that it is no more his country than Morocco. But the next day he trembles with doubt: 'Supposing this state of mind does not last?' He fears that once back in France his precious notebooks, with their multitude of sketches and notes, might prove to be of no more use to him than 'trees torn from their native soil', mere souvenirs, despised, useless, soon to be forgotten. His fears were empty . . . In fact he was to consult his notebooks until his dying day.

The six months Delacroix spent in North Africa and all the brief outlines and thumbnail sketches he brought back, resulted in more than one hundred paintings which portray an Orient liberated of its habitual trappings and clichés. Delacroix, unlike others, did not use this Islamic land as an excuse for his fantasies. His Morocco is a country which is real, and in this reality there figure real horses and horsemen. Many of his Moroccan paintings portray Arab riders, charging horses, a man saddling his horse, another, his foot in

Collision of Arab Horsemen (detail),
1843–4,
oil on canvas.
The Walters Art Gallery, Baltimore.

1 *Letter to Jean-Baptiste Pierret, Tangier, 25 January 1832, Louvre. Quoted by Maurice Arama in* Le Voyage au Maroc. *Sagittaire, p. 181 (The translations of the extracts from Delacroix's letters are from* Eugène Delacroix: Selected Letters, 1813–1863, *edited and translated by Jean Stewart. London, 1971, p.181)*

2 *Letter to General Charles Delacroix. Private collection. Ibid., p. 211.*

the stirrup ready to mount, a farrier with hammer in hand, a bivouac where a *moghazni* takes a rest with his mount, a cemetery where a kaid mourns by a grave while his horse, with the burned chestnut coat so highly prized by the Arabs, his neck bent as if to bow down, gazes at his master desperately, sadly, as if to share his sorrow. Here Delacroix reveals the specifically Arab relationship between man and horse. For let there be no mistake, in Delacroix's works the function of the horse is never decorative, nor is the horse an element of ostentation. Its function is so complex that one may speak of the sacred. It is not an equestrian spirit that motivates Delacroix and still less the love of riding. He is not a horseman in the way his friend Géricault was at the time when Delacroix met and admired him so much. Unlike Géricault, he was not an *habitué* of riding stables, of the high-up places where silent laws are decreed, which tend to force the horse into submission, to break its rebellious spirit. Delacroix had never taken an interest in training horses, nor did he frequent the imperial stables or those circles where the initiated discuss the performances of thoroughbred racehorses. He shares Géricault's romantic ardour for the fieriness of the rearing horse ready to bolt, he marvels at the animal's fighting spirit, his muscular energy and the majesty of his gallop, but Delacroix's admiration does not stop there. The horse which he portrays in his Moroccan paintings is, as the Arabs say, the companion, the friend that 'no man living by his spurs', be he a high-ranking or simple rider, can do without. Admittedly we are talking about a companion who submits to the will of his master and, in a way, the horse is a slave, but a slave through love and by God's will. Very rapidly Delacroix became aware of what is usually very difficult for a European to understand and that is the Arab's understanding of the role of horses. The almost religious complicity between them becomes apparent on reading a letter that the Emir Abd-el-Kader wrote to General Daumas, in 1857, on the origin of Arabian horses.[3] He explains: 'We believe that God created the horse out of the wind, as he created Adam out of clay. This is irrefutable. Several prophets—a blessing on their souls!—proclaimed: "When God wanted to create the horse, he said to the South Wind: *Out of you I wish to bring forth a creature, condense yourself*. And the wind condensed itself. Then the angel Gabriel took a handful of this substance and presented it to God who fashioned it into a burnt chestnut horse and cried: I name you *horse*, I create you *Arabian*." This letter teaches us that God created nothing more dear to himself than man and horse and that 'He who looks after and trains a horse for God's cause shall be rewarded; his sins shall be forgiven him and fear will never dishonour his heart.' The horse as object of the quest for spirituality is the essence of Abd-el-Kader's letter and constitutes the symbolic value of Delacroix's equestrian works. He had come a long way from the traditional subjects and yet how easy it would have been to have limited himself to those traditions! The beauty of the *courses de poudre*, the splendour of the fantasias, the mystery

3 Les chevaux du Sahara. *General Daumas, Calmann-Levy, Paris, 1887. The Emir's letter is quoted in full on p. 8.*

of the shadowy stables where the horses affront each other in 'the fiercest battle you can imagine', make the artist exclaim: 'all the furies invented by Gros and Rubens are tame in comparison' (Stewart, p. 183), even at the risk of giving the impression that Arabs understood nothing about looking after horses, that they were in fact torturers who considered their mount merely as the instrument of their force. This is why Delacroix's spontaneous watercolours or intimist paintings often offer a true illustration of what no-one but he has succeeded in portraying: the reality of a nation who associate all aspects of life with religion. There is such serenity in *Arabs and Horses near Tangier* and in the bivouac scenes where men and horses stay close together even in sleep. As the renowned saint, Ben-el-Abbas affirmed: 'I include the horses in the family circle. I share my children's bread with them. My wives decorate them with their veils.' There is no clearer way of demonstrating how well-loved they are. How else can one account for the calm watchfulness of the *Arab Soldier seated by his Horse*, if not by the proximity of one of those chargers, so swift that they are called 'drinkers of air'? The horse, the incarnation of tension and power, proudly raises its head and, alert, it watches a point on the far horizon. But the Arabs maintain that 'nothing is far for a horse' and indeed it seems as though nothing can escape the intensity of that look. The horse is there to protect its master and to surprise the enemy. The master can sleep in peace and benefit from his stop while the horse keeps watch. The magic rippling of its mane is simply the breath of its father, for the horse is the son of the wind, a symbol of all that is good, the link between humanity and God.

Edmonde CHARLES-ROUX
of the Académie Goncourt

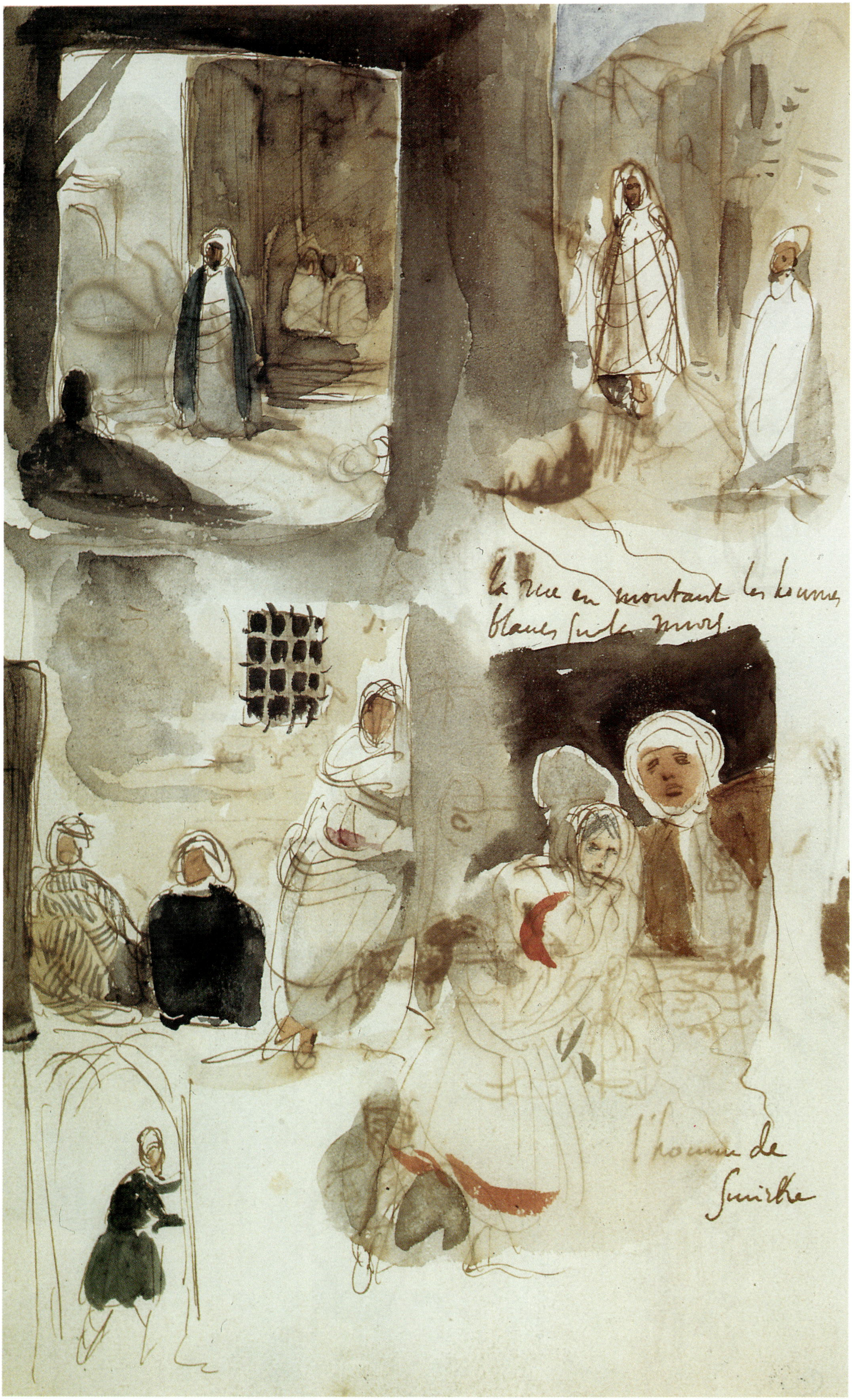

Prologue

The Orient is a misunderstanding, a mirage, a promise that appeases an over-excited, impatient imagination weary at times of the pallor of the sky or of human pettiness.

The Orient exists because great artists invented and transformed it. Some thought they found it in the turmoil of an open-air market, or in the sensuality of a veiled woman crossing the patio of a beautiful mansion.

The Orient is an idea, a way of life, a way of honouring the dead and of believing in the sky and the trees, a mania for bringing a little madness and magic into everyday life, a habit of adding colour to the hues of the climate, to the voluptuous waves of the dunes and the sea, and to the eyes of unruly children.The Orient is a dream which grows up in childhood memories and which pursues the artist and the poet who finds 'beauty to be bitter' but invents the colour of vowels before leaving for the desert, 'the burnt orchard' offering itself to the sun, the 'god of fire'.

Perhaps this is why Eugène Delacroix describes the shock he received on his arrival in Morocco, on 25 January 1832, in the following terms: 'I am like a man in a dream, seeing things he's afraid will vanish from him.'[1]

What is so overwhelming is of course the light, the strange duplicity of the light in Tangier and Meknes, light from an intangible and distant past, made of subtle colours which, as Goethe said, act on the soul. And Delacroix's soul needed fresh air, the inimitable influence of the sun and to mingle with a different, even strange race.

What does he discover? Quite simply the sublime, and for an artist who is not afraid of words, that is surely the appropriate term. In a letter dated 29 February 1832, he mentions the 'striking sublimity that lies all about one here'. At the same time this sublimity, which fascinates and excites him, imposes a bitter reality: 'At every step one sees ready-made pictures!' He learns to observe without haste, without causing inconvenience, how to be admitted into the privacy of the local family circles and he even attends a Jewish wedding in Tangier. He learns that form of laziness which enables one to register the minutest details and to work in depth; he learns to live with the intensity of someone who is convinced that he will be radically changed by

North African and Spanish Album,
1832.
Département des Arts graphiques, Louvre, Paris (fol. 26v).

1 The translations of the extracts from Delacroix's letters are from Stewart, 1971.

his journey. He confides to his friends: 'I am gradually insinuating myself into the customs of the country, so as to be able to draw many of these Moorish figures quite freely. . . . I enjoy moments of delicious idleness in a garden by the city gates, under a profusion of orange trees in full bloom and covered with fruit. Amid these lush natural surroundings I experience feelings like those I had in childhood.'

With time he realizes that the Orient he had come to find in Morocco, the most western region of the Orient, had not changed since antiquity. He exclaims 'It is beautiful. It is like the age of Homer!' It is a return to a primitive world which has been preserved in all its simplicity and originality. He is so attracted by the colours, by the elegant and natural movement of the Moroccans and the grace and dignity of their women, that he draws away from the picturesque to concentrate on the essence, the heart of the country, the intimacy of the landscape, the soul of a proud and modest nation.

What impresses him the most is the vivid and omnipresent 'antiquity' as he calls it, in other words the origin of things, the memory of the world and of humanity. This revelation enables him to penetrate into the heart of inanimate objects and of living persons. His enchantment and well-being explains the disorder of his notes and sketches made during the voyage. He lives his dreams which, like those of Baudelaire, are filled with 'magnificent forms which vibrate in this wonderful vast picture, in itself a dream'.

Land of welcome and of legends, land of diversity and intoxicating colours, with its mysteries and its passions, Morocco invaded the works of the great artists who learned to love, respect and portray it. Some of Delacroix's written phrases were clumsy, but it is the paintings that he accomplished on his return to France which count. His commentaries and letters express a confusion of emotions and sensations. But Morocco, the land, the sky and its people, its light and its music, its spices and perfumes are present in the colours, in people's movements, in dream-like expressions, in the magic of an eternity burned to infinity by the sun, in a perception which eliminates the exotic, in the ardent spirit of a poet who is not afraid of the audacity of a dazzling lyricism.

It took only one voyage and its various encounters, notably with Moulay Abd al-Rahman, for Morocco to invade Delacroix's works, not merely as a souvenir, but as a universe which was to nourish and enrich his creativity. His technique and his aesthetic sense were changed. The Morocco he portrayed exists because he came and sought out the soul of the country. It is a Morocco which first of all astonishes the Moroccans themselves, for it reveals a country of an amplitude and beauty they are aware of, but are unable to express. It is like a subtly distorting mirror reflecting unadorned nature, movements of horsemen and their mounts, facial expressions sketched with rapidity and precision, colours which do not correspond to reality. But what does reality signify in the case of a country whose roots are buried deep in the earth and whose history is like a fascinating novel?

The 'specialists' also, those who had always included North Africa in Orientalism, were surprised by Delacroix's Morocco because he never fell into the trap of the picturesque. Moroccan life at that time was neither exotic nor quaint and Delacroix looked further, behind the landscapes, behind the faces, deep into the soul of a welcoming but not always readily open country.

Delacroix understood that Moroccan reality is elusive. No exact copy is possible, any pretension of portraying it in precise detail is doomed to failure. A creative artist does not copy life, he does not portray reality. How can one represent light? How can one capture a passing facial expression? Delacroix never stopped working, his vision and his emotions also worked, too fast and too much. In the profusion of sensations which submerged him, he sketched constantly. There was no time to stop, to put down his pencils and think. He accumulated everything his vision could retain.

For these reasons his Morocco is our heritage, never final, but eternal in its movement and in its capacity to surprise and overwhelm us.

Tahar BEN JELLOUN

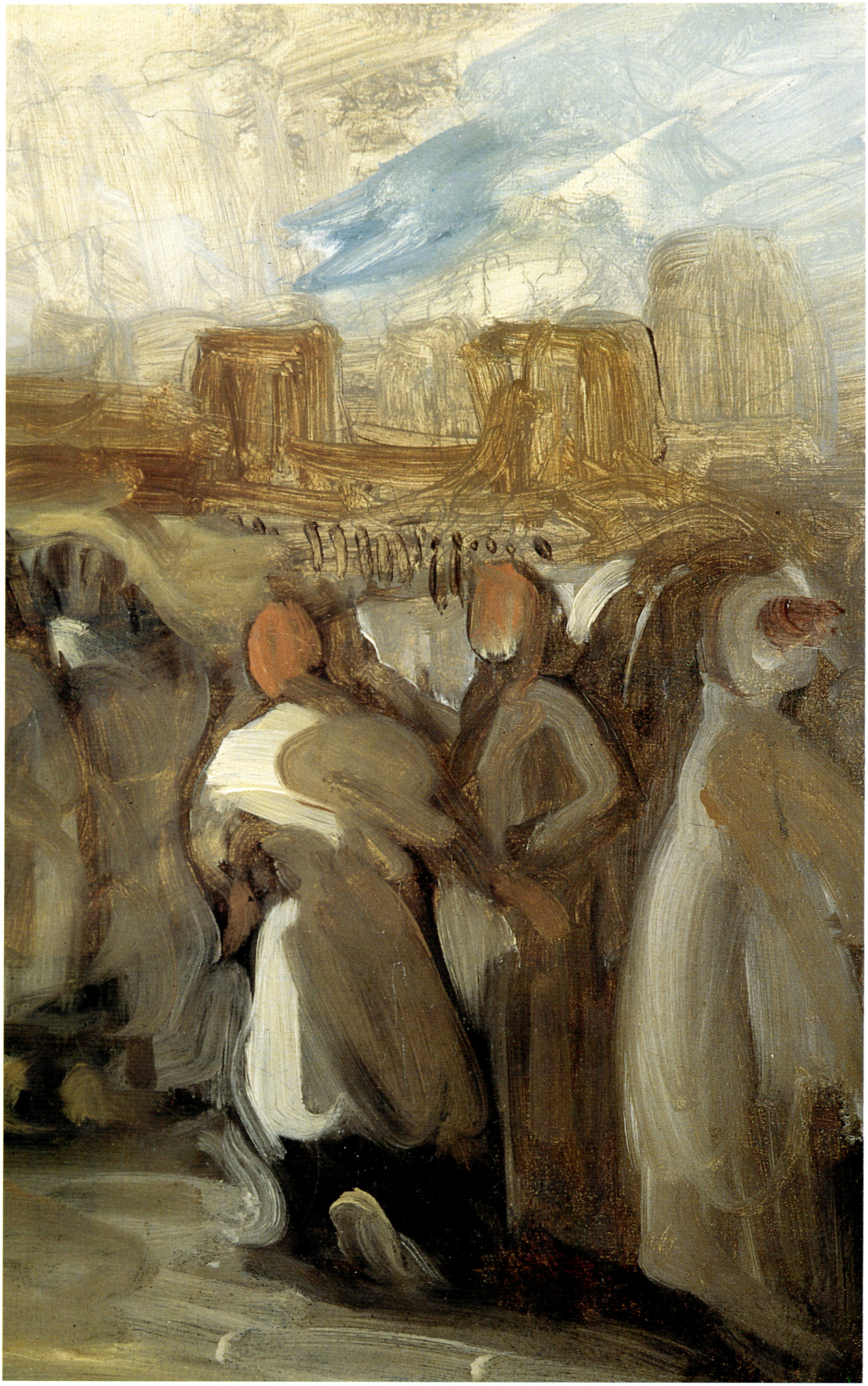

Introduction

It is impossible to speak of Eugène Delacroix without evoking his Moroccan voyage, a unique venture which tore him away from his Parisian studio and which was to play a decisive role in his artistic life.

When Delacroix landed in Tangier in January 1832, at the age of thirty-four, he had already produced several masterpieces of oriental inspiration, such as *The Massacre at Chios* (1824) and *The Death of Sardanapalus* (1827).

Yet, once in Morocco, the Orient of his dreams came to life before his very eyes, and he concentrated all his talent into making sketches to record his new surroundings. Delacroix discovered Morocco in the company of the Count de Mornay, who was sent by the French king, Louis-Philippe, to meet the Sultan Moulay Abd al-Rahman. The object of the diplomatic mission was to ensure Moroccan neutrality along the new frontier created by the French occupation of Algeria. During the course of his six-month stay, from January to July 1832, Delacroix accompanied the delegation on a journey from Tangier to Meknes where they were ceremoniously received by the King of Morocco.

The Sultan of Morocco (detail),
Musée des Beaux-Arts, Dijon,
Donation Granville.

While in Morocco, Delacroix proved to have a great eye for observation. The country came to life in his incredibly rapid pencil strokes, and he accumulated sketch after sketch, not missing a single detail, his keen vision recording colours and movement, light and shade. He was astonished to find, 'At every step . . . ready-made pictures, which would bring fame and fortune to twenty generations of painters'. [1]

He went in search of humanity, and by mixing with a population whose daily existence seemed to him imbued with humility and tolerance, he freed himself of his former prejudices. Similarly, from an aesthetic point of view, he lived for the moment, capturing the fleeting instant with a new freedom of expression, responsible for the impression of modernity one now experiences when looking through Delacroix's travel notes.

On his return to France, and for the next thirty years, Delacroix found inspiration in the hundreds of sketches he had executed in Morocco. They were transformed into luminous, colourful paintings, which testify to the impact that the image of the Moroccan landscapes and people had made on the artist.

1 *Letter to Armand Bertin, Meknes, 2 April 1832; Stewart, p. 192*

Beyond the aesthetic discovery, Delacroix lived his Moroccan visit as an encounter with the culture and nature of a 'new-found humanity', an encounter also with a different light which was to enhance his works and brighten his palette. His Moroccan paintings established him as an innovator and the forerunner of a new aesthetic, which was to inspire the Impressionists and modern artists alike. His paintings heralded a fundamental reappraisal of the conventions of western art, which, defined by the Italian Renaissance, had remained unchanged for four centuries.

From Delacroix on, North Africa was to penetrate the visual universe of the avant-garde, and it offered artists working at the beginning of this century, such as Matisse, Klee and Kandinsky, both the idea of a new world and aesthetic elements which corresponded to or stimulated their artistic preoccupations.

When Matisse landed in Tangier eighty years later, he was astounded and exclaimed, 'I found the Moroccan landscapes exactly as they are described in Delacroix's paintings.' [2]

In the current exhibition, the Institut du Monde Arabe presents Delacroix's exceptional, but paradoxically little-known, Moroccan works. There have, in fact, been no exhibitions on this subject since that of 1933, held in the Orangerie des Tuileries, more than sixty years ago.

The hundred or so major works—paintings, watercolours, drawings and engravings—which are exhibited here, were executed either during or after Delacroix's voyage in 1832. Among them, visitors will find works from public or private collections which are being shown to the public for the first time, such as *Mule-drivers from Tetuan* (cat. no. 66), an *Arab Soldier by a Grave* (cat. no. 71), and *View of Tangier from the Seashore* (cat. no. 101).

The exhibition is centred around the large painting of the *Sultan of Morocco,* lent by the Musée de Toulouse. Various studies in pencil and watercolour help trace the origins of this masterpiece, which was highly praised by Baudelaire.

Ample space has, however, been reserved for the numerous drawings and watercolours which reveal the brilliance of the sketches the artist made from life. Delacroix experienced an intense desire to note down all the new facts, events and sensations which astounded him day after day. These remarkable works on paper have been placed near the paintings which they later inspired in order to underscore their relationships.

Facsimiles of Delacroix's travel notes, in diary form, constitute the first part of the exhibition and provide a vivid illustration of the various stages of the journey and its numerous revelations.[3] These pages, which form a sort of journalistic report of the day-to-day events and different surroundings which Delacroix encountered, contain the artist's first rough impressions, which were later transformed by his immediate or distant memory into the pictures presented in this exhibition.

2 *Quoted by Elderfield,* Matisse in Morocco, *Paris 1990, p. 188*

3 *Edited by* Le Sagittaire *under the direction of Maurice Arama, Paris, 1992*

The last part of the exhibition is devoted to a display of Moroccan *objets d'art*, some actually brought back by the artist himself, which correspond to the highlights of this voyage, the Jewish wedding, the fantasias and the interior decoration and costumes, which Delacroix never ceased to admire.

Brahim ALAOUI

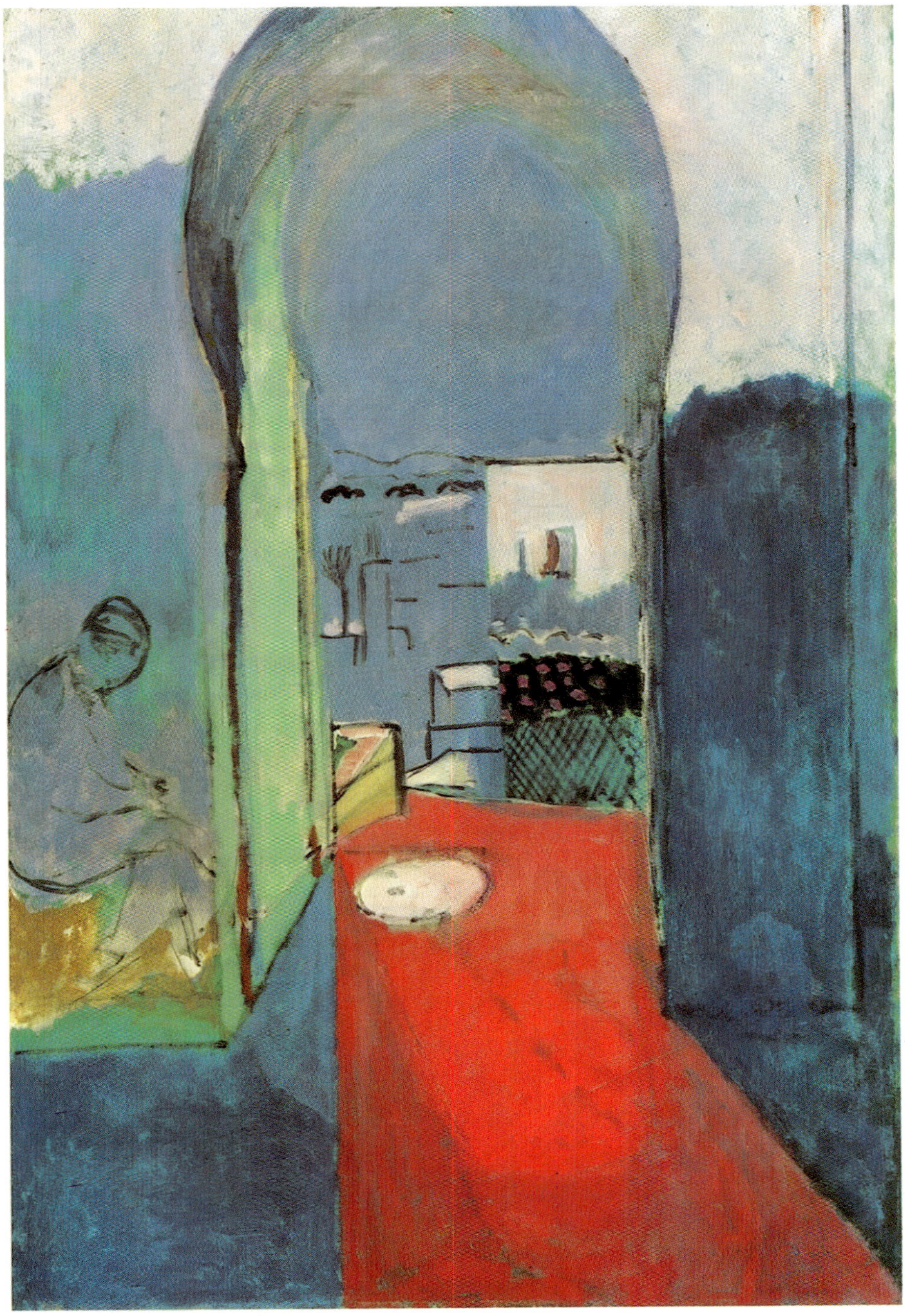

Henri Matisse
Tangier, the Kasbah Gate,
1912.
Pushkin Museum, Moscow.
© Succession Henri Matisse

Delacroix and the Orient

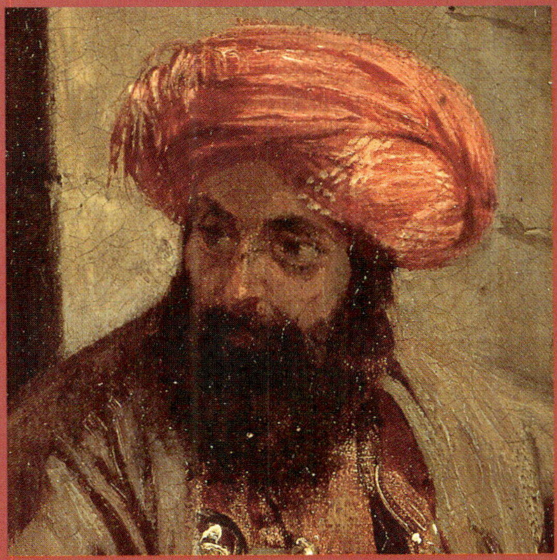

Delacroix and the Orient

Many a nineteenth-century artist dreaming of mysterious, unknown horizons was inspired by that magic and evocative word invented by the romantics—the Orient. Each portrayed it in their own individual way, guided by their fancy, and the fruits of this 'orientalism' left an indelible mark on the French imagination. Although the countries generally associated with the Orient in Delacroix's time were those of the Ottoman Empire—Turkey, Syria and Egypt, not to mention Greece which became partially independent in 1829—from the seventeenth to the nineteenth century, the Orient was a mythical space, a land of ever-changing frontiers.

As early as the seventeenth century the Jesuits introduced the Chinese and Japanese languages and culture to the western world. During the same period, Jean-Baptiste Colbert (1619–83) founded a school for young linguists, the 'École des jeunes de langues', to train interpreters for the Levant. The *Compagnie des Indes orientales* was founded by Colbert in 1664 and renamed the *Compagnie des Indes* in 1719; its activities greatly influenced commercial and artistic circles. The style of the renowned 'Grand Degré', the Ambassador's Staircase at Versailles—designed by Charles Le Brun (1619–90) and used by foreign envoys on their way to attend audience at the court of Louis XIV—is a perfect example of this extension of frontiers. Working from plans by Le Vau, François d'Orbay supervised the building in collaboration with Le Brun, who executed the paintings on the ceiling and first-floor walls, representing the five continents, Europe, Asia, Africa, America and Oceania, as figures dressed in national costume. The entire work was completed in 1679 and admired by all Europe. It was destroyed, however, in 1752 and only drawings and engravings remain to remind us of its splendour (Département des Arts graphiques, Louvre, Paris).

During that century many great authors looked to the Orient for inspiration, or more precisely to Turkey, and from this point on French culture was marked by an increasing attraction to an imaginary Orient. In 1641 Scudéry and his sister published a novel entitled *Ibrahim* or *L'Illustre Bassa* which invoked the land of Turkey in pure fantasy, while in Rotrou's comedy *La Sœur*, written in 1645, one of the characters spoke in Turkish. In 1660 Jean-Baptiste Lully

Page 29:
Turk with Saddle (detail).
Louvre, Paris.

1 - Armed Indian of Gourka-kree,
oil on canvas,
40 x 32 cm.
Kunsthaus, Zurich,
Vereinigung Zürcher Kunstfreunde.
See p. 44.

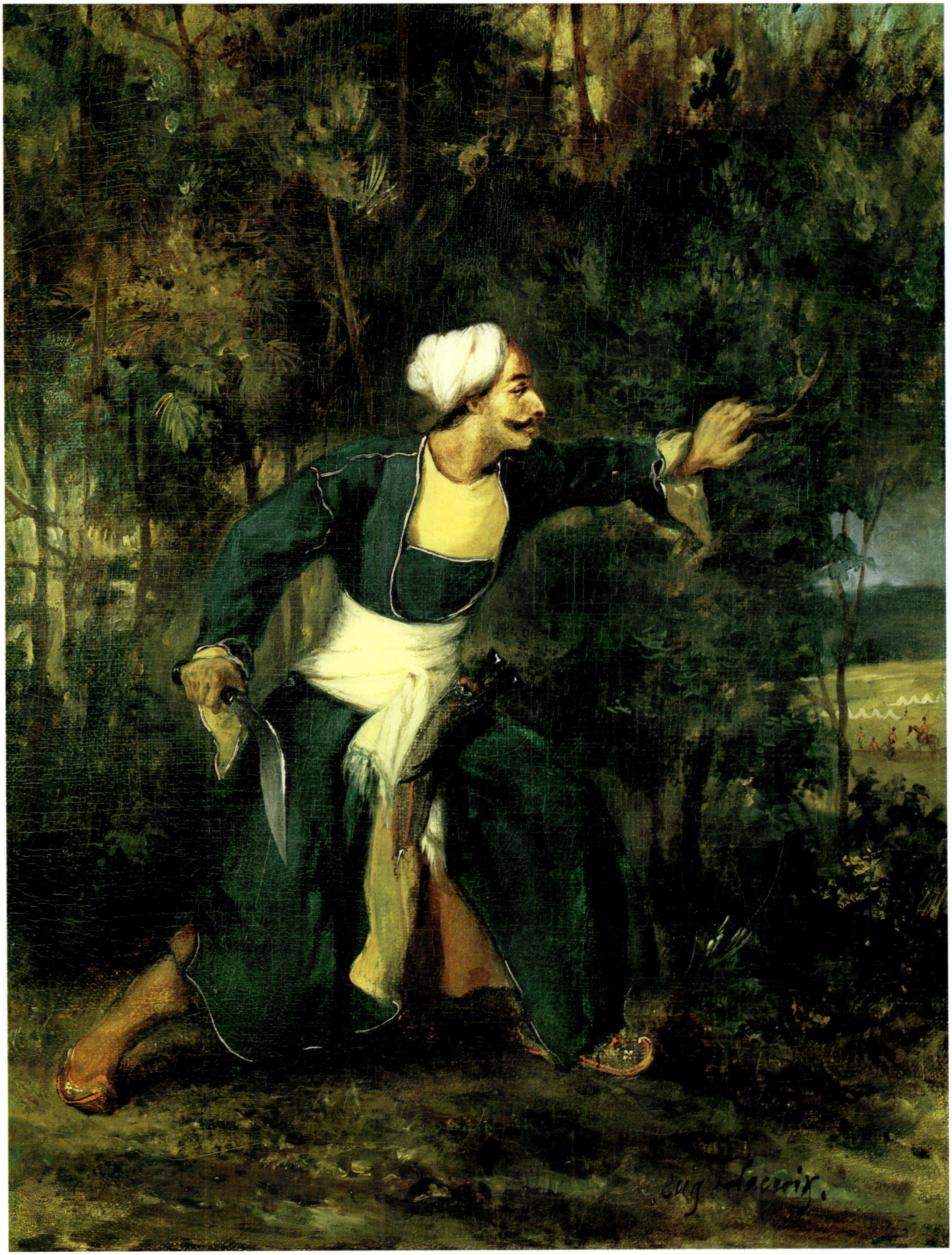

presented a Turkish-style narrative to the court which found great favour with Louis XIV, and in 1672 Racine based his tragedy *Bajazet* on a court intrigue set in Constantinople. Due to this popularity of all things Turkish, Molière's troupe decided to adapt a Turkish ceremony for the 'royal entertainment'. Under Lully's guidance, the broad outlines gradually emerged for the plot of the *Bourgeois gentilhomme*, a comic ballet performed for the court at Chambord on 14 October 1670 as a tribute to the 'Turkish ballets'. Shortly after, in 1685, another ballet, the *Carrousel des galants Maures*, confirmed the interest in a little-known Orient, as did the expressive 'orientalist' sketches and engravings by the prodigious graphic artist, Jacques Callot.

It was, however, in the eighteenth century—at the end of Louis XIV's reign, during the Regency and finally under Louis XV—that a veritable obsession with exoticism emerged, marked by a particular inclination towards the fantastic and the picturesque. Oriental tales became fashionable and the famous orientalist Antoine Galland (1646–1715) translated *The Arabian Nights* (1704). Scheherazade's enchanting stories provided endless room for fantasy, and met with great success. In 1699 Dufresnoy published a novel entitled *Amusements sérieux et comiques,* and in 1684, J.P. Marana wrote the *Espion du grand seigneur* in which the hero Mehemet comments on European current events in a series of letters. Therein lies, without doubt, the inspiration for Montesquieu's celebrated *Persian Letters,* published in 1721, in which the alliance of the magical and the baroque evokes an Orient which is both colourful and mysterious. Lastly, Voltaire published *Zaire* in 1732 and *Candide* in 1759.

In 1714 the French ambassador to Constantinople, Charles de Ferriol published a book on the costumes of the Ottoman Empire which was to prove very popular. It was illustrated with engravings by Le Hay which were inspired by paintings by J.B. Vanmour, a fashionable artist who had made himself a specialist in portraits of Europeans in Turkish dress.[1] Henceforth not only the Turks and Chinese were in vogue, but also the Persians and the Indians. On 7 February 1715, Louis XIV received a formal delegation from the Persian ambassador to Paris, Mehemet Riza Beg 'Calender' d'Erivan. Several engravings evoke this historic event and Watteau made five studies, in red chalk and charcoal, of Persians (fig. 2), one of whom is thought to have been a leading figure at the Embassy (Département des Arts graphiques, Louvre). The strengthening of diplomatic relations between France and certain 'oriental' countries was at the origin of the proliferation of Turkish, Persian and Chinese themes which invaded French art and literature in the first quarter of the eighteenth century. In 1721 and in 1742, two large Turkish delegations known as the 'Sublime Porte' were received in Paris with as much ceremony as d'Erivan's earlier Persian delegation.[2] This infatuation for Turkey spread increasingly, not only among artistic circles but throughout the general public, even reaching beyond the French borders.

1
Recueil de 100 estampes représentant différentes nations du Levant . . . 1714 *(Bibliothèque Nationale, Paris, Estampes, Od 11 fol).*

2
The 1721 delegation was led by Mehmed Efendi. The splendid procession was portrayed by Charles Parrocel in a series of sketches while the reception at the Invalides was painted by Pierre d'Ulin (1669–1748). The 'formal' delegation which the Ottoman Sultan sent to the French court in 1741 constituted the final episode of the Treaty of Belgrade, the only treaty which favoured the Turks due to the role played by the French ambassador to Constantinople, Louis-Sauveur de Villeneuve. Louis XV received them in Versailles in the Grand Gallery on 11 January 1742. Readers of the Mercure de France *were informed in great detail of the progress of the ceremony and were thus able to appreciate the quality of the gifts exchanged. 30 years later art lovers were able to admire an equally accurate illustration from the engraving, executed in 1774 by N.J.B. de Poilly from a drawing by Cochin the younger (1715–90; Département des Arts graphiques, Louvre).*

The Genevan artist Jean-Étienne Liotard (1702–89) stayed in Constantinople from 1738 to 1742 and was requested by Lord Sandwich to 'draw the costumes worn in every region he visited'. The numerous drawings in red chalk and in charcoal that he brought back from his long journey via Malta, Milo, Paris, Chios, Smyrna and Constantinople, prove that the artist never tired of painting portraits of the various classes of the cosmopolitan population living under Ottoman rule. *Turkish Seamstresses at Work, European Woman with her Slave in the Hammam* (fig. 3), *The English Merchant, Mr Levett in Tartar Dress* and *Turkish Musician*, all feature models who agreed to pose for Liotard, not to mention the various dignitaries of the Empire and ambassadors to foreign countries who also sat for the artist: *Sir Everard Fawkener, the British Ambassador; Madame Gaspard de Pelleran, Wife of the French Consul in Smyrna; Richard Pococke* etc.[3] It was after this trip that Liotard took to wearing Turkish dress, which brought him great notoriety in Europe. In 1761, the tremendous success of Favart's comedy *Les trois Sultanes*, induced Liotard to paint a miniature depicting Madame Favart, the actress who played the lead role in the original production, wearing a costume specially made in Constantinople (Hermitage Museum, St Petersburg).

3
cf. exhibition catalogue, Dessins de Liotard, *Musée d'Art et d'Histoire, Geneva; Louvre, Paris, 1992.*

Aside from Liotard, two Frenchmen also visited Constantinople, Chevalier Antoine de Favray (1706–92) and Jean-Baptiste Hilair (1753–after 1822). Favray was the official painter of the Order of Malta. He stayed in Constantinople from 1762 to 1771, where he painted *Eastern Women with Hairstyles for Indoors* and *Eastern Women with Hairstyles for the City* (Musée des Augustins, Toulouse) as well as portraits of *The French Ambassador Vergennes in Turkish Dress* and of *Madame de Vergennes in Oriental Dress* (1766; private collection). Hilair, meanwhile, brought back several detailed scenes made during his visit to Constantinople: *The Rivers of Asia* (Musée des Beaux-Arts, Strasbourg) and *A Seraglio* (Musée de Peinture et de Sculpture, Grenoble), and a whole series of drawings of oriental costumes from various regions of Turkey (1776; Louvre).

'Turcomania' spread rapidly through Paris, capturing the imaginations of members of fashionable society and influencing the theatre, the opera, interior decoration, fashion, sentimental novels and art. Many French artists inspired by pashas, sultans, harems, chinoiseries and oriental fantasies, transposed their inspiration onto canvases where the picturesque and anecdotal tended to prevail over anything that might be considered 'realistic'. Amongst these artists, special mention should be made of François Boucher (1703–70), along with Jean-Baptiste Leprince, Amédée and Carle Van Loo and Jean-Honoré Fragonard, not omitting their contemporaries, the engravers François-Antoine Aveline and Jean-Jacques Flipart, and Gabriel Huquier the elder and the younger. In 1736 Boucher was commissioned, along with Jean-François de Troy and four other artists, to collaborate on a series of six *Foreign Hunts*—Boucher himself painted *The Leopard Hunt* (fig. 4)—and in around 1738, he

Antoine Watteau
2 - The Persian,
graphite and red chalk,
30.2 x 19.9 cm.
Département des Arts graphiques,
Louvre, Paris.

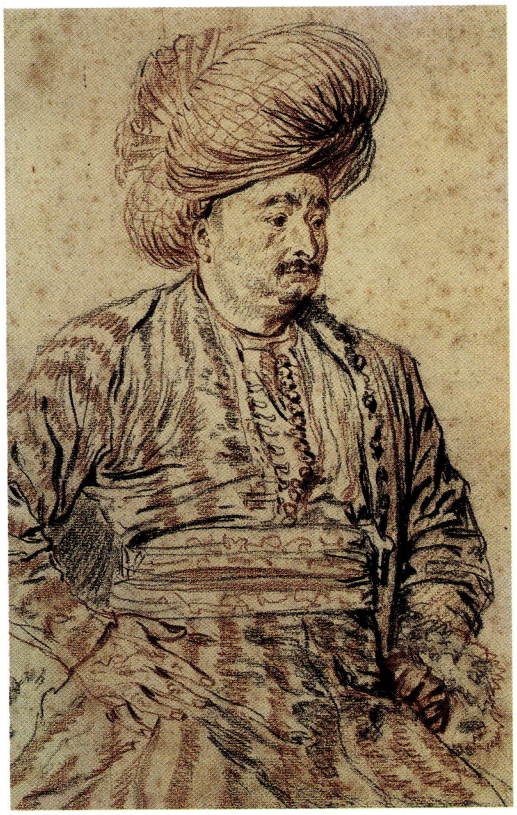

was again commissioned—this time to work in collaboration with Jean-François de Troy, Carle Van Loo, Nicolas Lancret, Jean-Baptiste Pater and Charles Parrocel—to paint a new series of exotic hunting scenes (*The Crocodile Hunt*, Musée de Picardie, Amiens). It was some years later, however, at the Salon of 1742, that Boucher dazzled the public with a series of ten paintings given evocative titles such as *Audience of the Chinese Emperor*, *Chinese Fair*, *Chinese Garden*, *Fishing in China* etc., all sketches for Beauvais tapestries. At the peak of his career, Boucher gave free rein for several years to his passion for Chinese subjects, which can be found in his paintings as well as in designs for tapestries, theatre sets and in engravings. By orientating his work in this direction, Boucher actively promulgated a style which dated from Watteau's Chinese figures decorating Claude Audran's grotesques at the Château de la Muette in France. And as Pierre Rosenberg notes, if Boucher supplied the Beauvais tapestry manufactory with sketches for weaving, it was because at the end of the seventeenth century this workshop had produced a series of tapestries from Guy-Louis Vernansal's popular Chinese-style cartoons.[4]

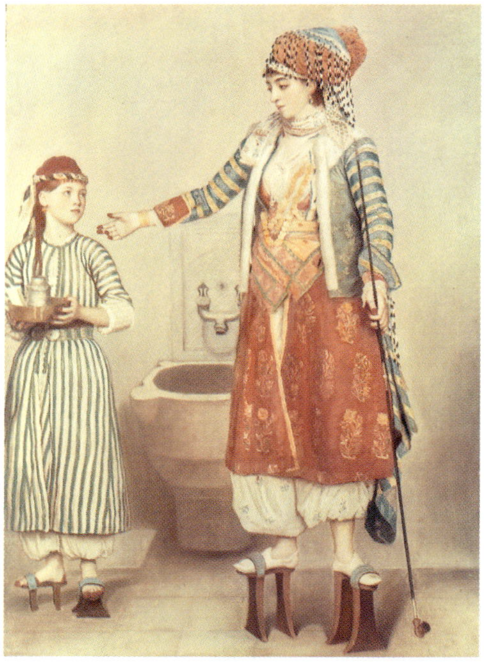

Jean-Etienne Liotard
3 - European Woman with her Slave in the Hammam,
pastel,
71 x 53 cm.
Musée d'Art et d'Histoire, Geneva.

Between 1773 and 1775 it was for the Gobelins manufactory that Amédée Van Loo (1719–95) created his cartoons for the *Tapestry of Turkish Dress*. The subjects which most clearly characterize this oriental tendency are without doubt *Sultana giving orders to Odalisques* and *A Sultana at her Toilette* (Louvre).

During this period, Carle Van Loo (1705–65) was one of the first artists to paint his sitters in fanciful Turkish costumes, for example, *Gentleman giving a Concert for his Mistress* (1737; Wallace Collection, London) and *Gentleman having a Portrait painted of his Mistress* (Museum of Fine Arts, Richmond, Virginia). He also painted various 'Turkish' works for Madame de Pompadour: *Sultana taking Coffee*; *Two Sultanas working on a Tapestry* (the 1755 Salon; Hermitage Museum, St. Petersburg), as well as *Sultana playing a Tchegour*, destined to decorate the bedroom of his patroness in the Château de Bellevue (private collection, Paris).

At the same time, Jean-Honoré Fragonard (1732–1806) also succumbed, in a moderate fashion, to the Turkish vogue, as can be seen in two studies in the Louvre: *Head of an Oriental Man*, directly inspired by the first series of *Studies of Heads* by Giovanni Battista Tiepolo, edited by Giandomenico his son, and a work in brush and brown wash entitled *The Pasha*, executed in a strikingly free style. Finally, closely resembling the paintings of Amédée Van Loo, are two fantasy figures, *The Small Sultana* and *Sultana with Flowers*, both charming illustrations of an attractive exoticism (Ball State University Art Gallery, Muncie; private collection, New York).

We also owe several official portraits in Turkish dress to Jacques Aved (1702–66). His most famous work is the *Portrait of Said Mehemed Pasha*, the ambassador of the Turkish delegation received by Louis XV in Versailles in 1742 (Musée de Versailles).

4
cf. exhibition catalogue, François Boucher *1703–1770, The Metropolitan Museum of Art, New York; Museum of Art, Detroit; Grand Palais, Paris, 1986–1987, pp. 205–10.*

During carnival time 'oriental masquerades' became highly fashionable at the French Academy in Rome. The first took place in 1735, while the second, the 'Chinese masquerade', was organized in 1744 to celebrate the recovery of the King, who had been in poor health. These were followed by the famous 'Turkish masquerade' in 1748 which was popularized by a series of thirty-two drawings engraved by the organizer of the ceremony, Joseph-Marie Vien (1716–1809). In the same year, Vien painted three portrait studies for *The Mogul Ambassador*, *The Black Sultana* and *The Queen Sultana* (the drawings and paintings are now in the collection of the Petit Palais, Paris). Another masquerade followed in 1751, this time given in honour of the Marquis de Marigny.

It was, however, one man, the nation's hero, Napoleon Bonaparte, who revealed the real living Orient to French artists. His campaigns, especially the Egyptian campaign of 1798 (the year of Delacroix's birth), were commented in detail almost daily and created the impression that Egypt was just outside the gates of Paris. Napoleon gave the French nation a completely new vision of an unfamiliar universe and it was during this legendary era that Romanticism was born. Baron Dominique Vivant Denon (1747–1825) followed Napoleon to Egypt and played a strategic role by sketching Pharaonic ruins and Egyptian costumes, not however without incurring certain personal risks. In 1802, three years after his return to France, he published two volumes entitled *Voyage dans la Basse et la Haute Égypte, pendant les campagnes du Général Bonaparte,* dedicated to Napoleon, and some time later the important collective work *Description de l'Égypte* which was to be of considerable scientific and iconographic importance to the period (fig. 6). During the thirteen months he spent in Egypt (3 July 1798–23 August 1799), Denon made a collection of notes and sketches which he knew would have considerable repercussions. Jean-Marcel Humbert, recently commenting on the publication of the *Voyage*, writes that, 'by combining the account of a topical military campaign with the description of a beautiful country, [Denon] gave an opportunity to compare this original civilisation with that of classical Greece. Furthermore, it was impossible not to appreciate the quality of the text which was rivalled only by the originality of the presentation. . . . The importance attached to the illustrations and the size and quality of the engravings constituted yet another novel element.' [5]

François Boucher
4 - The Leopard Hunt,
oil on canvas,
1.74 x 1.29 m.
Musée de Picardie, Amiens.

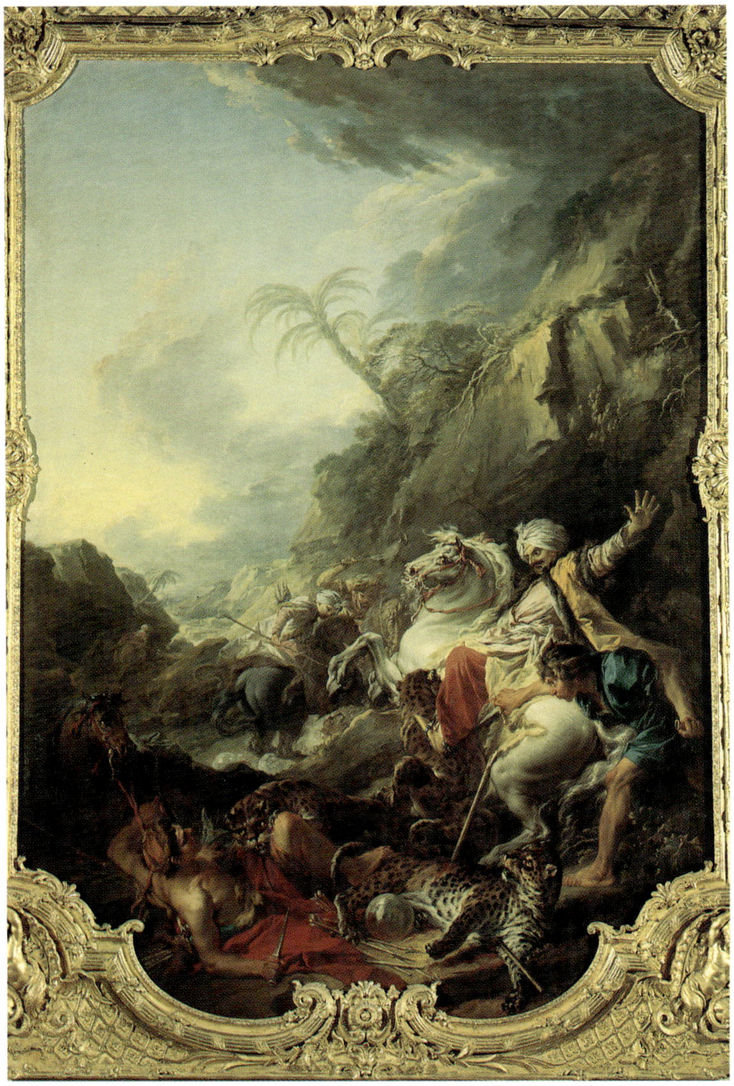

As soon as Jean-François Champollion (1790–1832) had deciphered the mystery of hieroglyphics, progress could also be made in developing the understanding of this highly refined civilisation. A young artist, Nestor L'Hôte (1804–42), assisted the scholar in his task, and was dazzled by the beauty, harmony and colours of the Nile Valley, taking the time to record his impressions in the pages of his albums. On his return to France, L'Hôte took an active part in the publication of *Monuments d'Égypte et de Nubie*. We are also indebted to him for *Notice historique sur les obélisques égyptiens et en particulier sur l'obélisque de Louqsor*, which was published in 1836 when the obelisk in question was erected on the Place de la Concorde.[6]

Aside from this documentary information, artists also found inexhaustible subject-matter in the accounts of Napoleon's accomplishments which tended to become idealized in their imaginations. Cleverly organized propaganda insistently whetted the appetite of their ambitions, but the rules and traditions of history painting and the demands of a somewhat dominating 'patronage' constituted a handicap to the artists' freedom of expression. This is more than apparent in the career of Baron Gros (1771–1835), the first French romantic orientalist. Nominated official historian to Napoleon Bonaparte, Gros, who

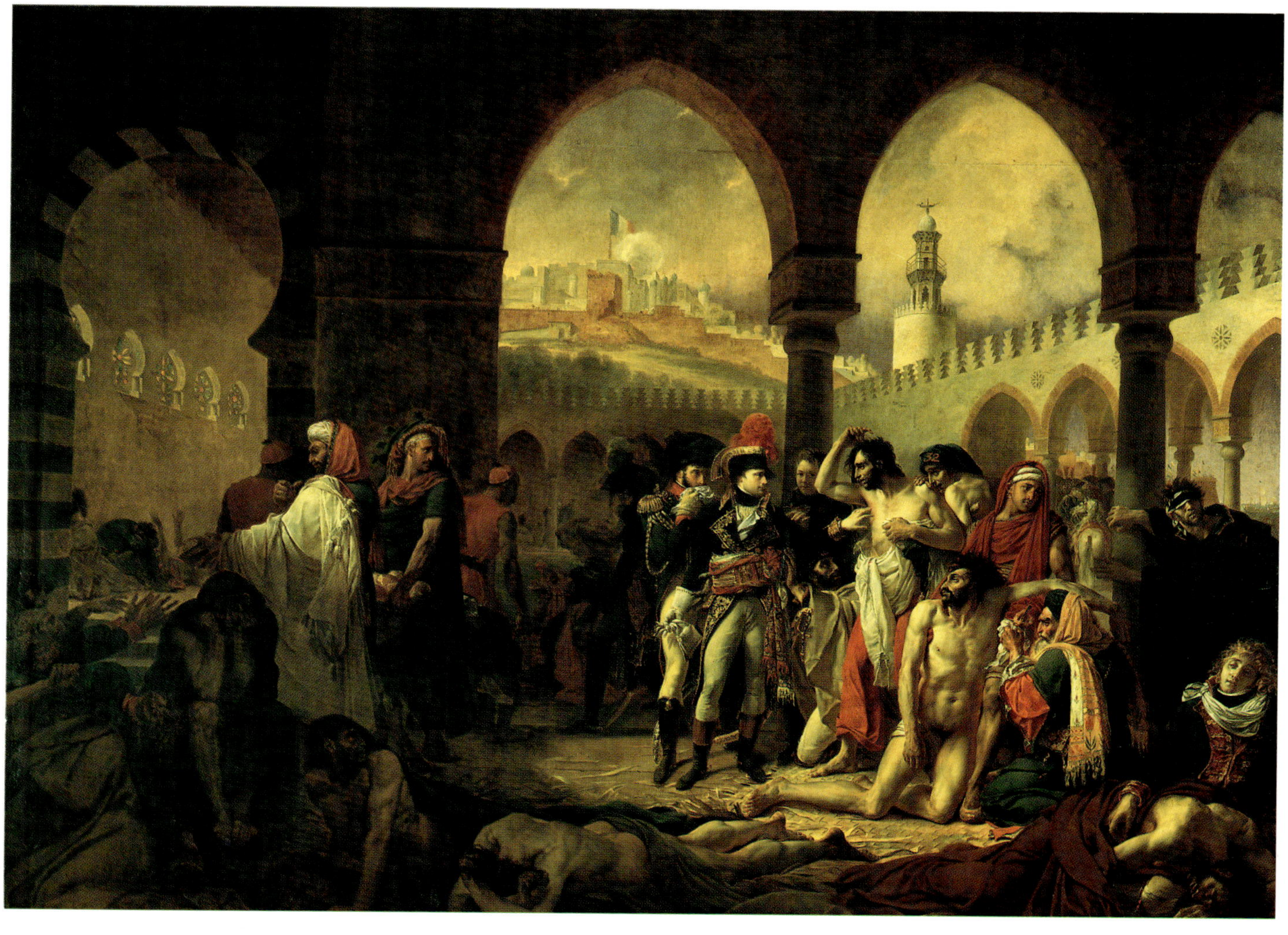

Baron Antoine-Jean Gros
5 - The Pest-house at Jaffa,
oil on canvas,
5.23 x 7.15 m.
Louvre, Paris.

had never set foot in the Orient, proved himself to be the greatest painter of oriental battle scenes of his day. As early as 1801 his taste for exoticism emerged with his sketch of *The Battle of Nazareth* (Musée de Nantes) which took place in the year AD 9.

The winner of the competition instituted at Napoleon's request to commemorate General Junot's victory on Mount Tabor on 8 April 1799, Gros chose to depict the end of the battle and the routing of the Mamelukes. But Napoleon substituted another subject, this time to commemorate the carefully calculated heroism of his visit to the plague-stricken population of Jaffa on 11 March 1799. The enormous painting (fig. 5), which was exhibited at the 1804 Salon, depicts Napoleon touching the running sores of a bare-chested victim of the plague. The scene takes place under a brick archway in a mosque courtyard, the right-hand side of which is open to the sea. The ramparts and houses of Jaffa rise in tiers in the background and on the right stands a minaret. This work is undeniably the artist's masterpiece, executed with great élan in broad, sweeping brushstrokes. The viewer's attention is drawn by the realism of the figures, costumes and scenery and above all by the contrast between the bright sunlight and the large areas of shadow. Here was the revelation of a new world which Gros had in fact never seen. But despite this considerable handicap, inspiration and a powerful imagination enabled him to reproduce the magical atmosphere, which Delacroix was later to discover in 1832. Significant in this respect is the following remark, made by Delacroix some twenty years later while painting *The Massacre at Chios* (1824 Salon; Louvre): 'I didn't clean Gros's palette very well!'

To satisfy Murat, who wished to perpetrate the memory of a battle won mainly on his own personal initiative, Gros exhibited another large work at the Salon in 1806, entitled *The Battle of Aboukir* (Musée de Versailles). Although the General is proudly portrayed, the viewer's attention is irresistibly drawn to the Mamelukes and the Pasha, not only because of their exotic costumes, but because they are the symbols of an Orient which Gros may never have witnessed, but which he recreated with the same passion that Delacroix would later express in his painting of Chios.

In 1809 Gros was commissioned by the Imperial Senate to paint *The Battle of the Pyramids* as decoration for the senate room. First exhibited at the 1810 Salon, this work is now in the Musée de Versailles. Once again, the subject-matter of the painting was chosen deliberately to enable Napoleon, the principal figure in the battle, to be seen by all to good advantage—and there can be no doubt that this was one of the Emperor's foremost preoccupations. After all, in 1800 he had already commissioned François-André Vincent (1746–1816), through the offices of Lucien Bonaparte, then Minister of the Interior, to paint an enormous canvas, the required dimensions of which (nearly 8 metres by 5) probably explain why the artist was unable to carry out his task. As for Gros, he did not encounter the same difficulties. Of more

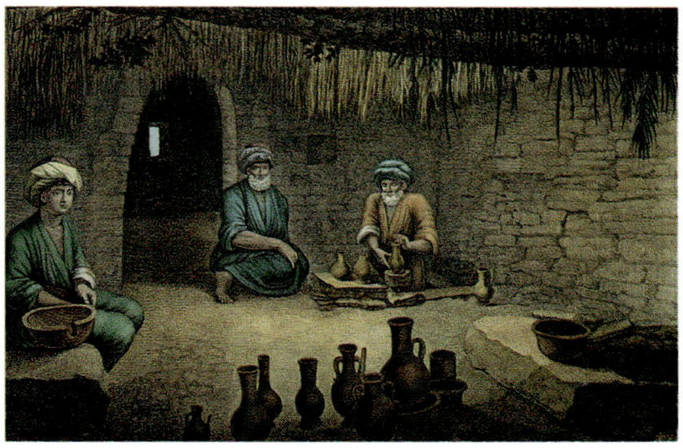

Drawing by Nicolas-Jacques Conté, engraved by Letellier
6 - Interior of a Potter's Studio,
in Description de l'Egypte, Vol. II, État moderne, *1817.*

5
J.M. Humbert, Egyptomania, *exhibition catalogue, Louvre, Paris, 1994, p. 204. Denon's* Voyage en Egypte *was featured on a list made by Delacroix of works he almost certainly wished to consult (album RF 6736; Louvre, Paris; c. 1818–21).*

6
For further information on this little-known artist, see the work recently published by Diane Harlé and Jean Lefebvre, Sur le Nil avec Champollion. Lettres, journaux et dessins inédits de Nestor L'Hôte. Premier voyage en Egypte—1828–1830, *Orléans–Caen, 1993.*

moderate dimensions (only 3 metres by 5!) his work commemorates the famous episode when Napoleon addressed his troops crying 'Soldiers! From the top of these pyramids forty centuries are watching you!' At the same 1810 Salon, Anne-Louis Girodet-Trioson (1767–1824) exhibited a painting entitled *The Cairo Revolt* (Musée de Versailles) alluding to the rebellion of the Egyptian population on 21 October 1788, scarcely two months after Napoleon's arrival. Both the preparatory studies in pastel (Louvre) and the final composition reveal the artist's fascination for the romantic Orient. Girodet apparently 'worked surrounded by Mamelukes who more or less lived in his house and whose beauty stimulated him'. He executed this painting with assurance and speed, without making any preliminary oil sketches. Two years previously, at the 1808 Salon, Pierre-Narcisse Guérin (1774–1833), Delacroix's teacher, chose to present a work entitled *Napoleon Pardoning the Cairo Rebels, 23 October 1798* (Musée de Versailles), in other words, the event immediately following the one painted by Girodet: after the revolt had been suppressed, Napoleon gathered the rebels together in El-Bekir square and granted them a general pardon.

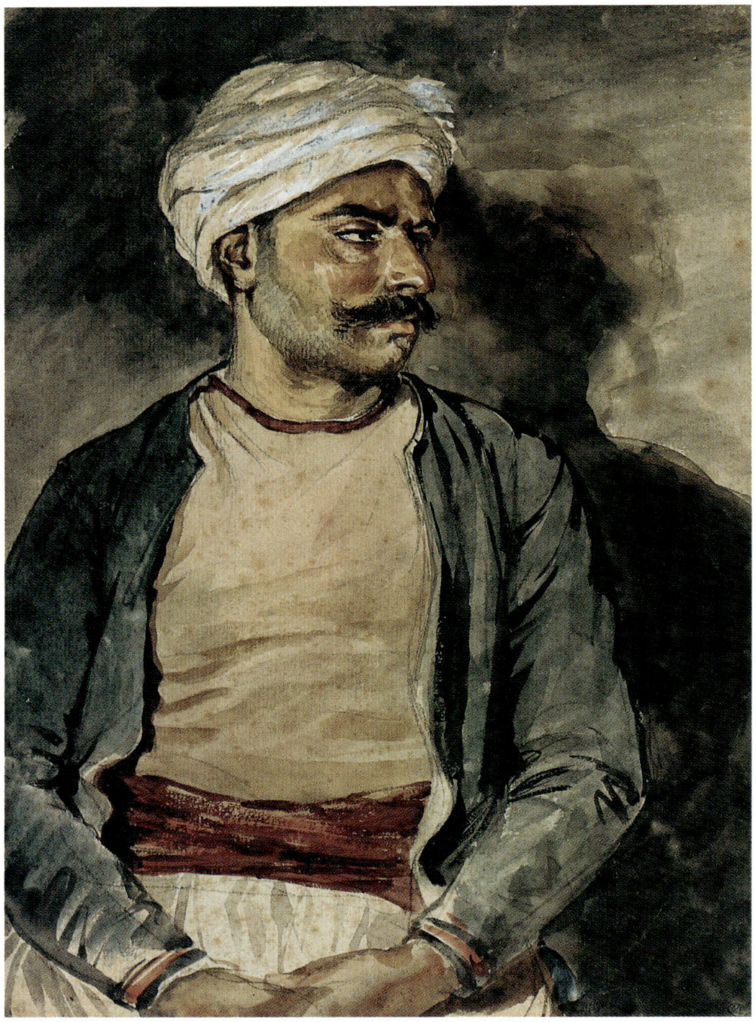

Théodore Géricault
7 - Portrait of an Oriental, known as Mustapha,
watercolour,
30 x 22 cm.
Département des Arts graphiques, Louvre, Paris.

The above works, plus some of his friend Géricault's creations and especially paintings by Gros, are at the origin of young Delacroix's first visions of the Orient, which was to attract him and mark his work right from the beginning of his career and more particularly after his voyage in 1832.

Compared to Guérin, to Girodet and even to Gros, the 'oriental' part of the work of Théodore Géricault (1791–1824) possesses a rare force and originality. In the confrontation between soldiers and Mamelukes, the artist exalts violent effort and intense combat (*Mameluke thrown from his Horse; Battle of the Cavalry*, Louvre). All his oriental figures, inspired by the same model—no doubt the notorious Mustapha, his Turkish servant—wear the traditional turban and tunic (*Head of an Oriental*, Musée de Besançon; *Portrait of an Oriental, known as Mustapha*, (fig. 7)) but in no way do they resemble the quaint images of the previous centuries. There is a recurring focus on black models in his paintings, drawings and engravings, the origin of which is perhaps to be found in the colonial wars such as the Haitian revolution (1801–03); examples of this tendency are to be found in *A Black Standard-bearer*, a drawing now in the Stanford University Museum of Art and in *Black on a Rearing*

Horse (private collection, Paris). Géricault decided to condemn the traffic of slaves in a single ambitious work, *The Black Slave-Trade*, and it is again a black who dominates the composition of *The Raft of the Medusa* (1819 Salon; Louvre). One should not forget, also, that Géricault and Delacroix first met and worked together in Guérin's studio.

When evoking Delacroix's early works, it is customary to point out his humanistic education at the Lycée Louis-le-Grand and his classical training with Guérin. For the purpose of this study, however, his early background is of relatively slight importance. Nevertheless, his early love of Persians and Indians, so favoured by eighteenth-century artists, should be emphasized, even if technically speaking his lithographs such as *The Persian Ambassador* and *The Persian Ambassador's favourite Slave* reveal his extreme youth (Delacroix was nineteen years of age at the time!). In around 1823, Delacroix made a series of *Studies of Indians in Calcutta Dress* sold posthumously in 1864.[7]

Delacroix, like all young romantic Europeans, could not help but react strongly to the Greek uprising against the Turks in the 1820s, but it was in fact the poets, not the artists, who first rallied to the Greek cause. From 1818–22 Casimir Delavigne (1793–1843) wrote his *Douze Messéniennes*, one of which in particular, *Aux Ruines de la Grèce payenne*, dealt with the Greek tribulations under Turkish domination. Denouncing his contemporaries, he cried:

'Guerre, guerre aux tyrans! Nochers, fendez les flots! Du haut de son tombeau Thémistocle domine sur ce port qui l'a vu si grand; Et la mer à vos pieds s'y brise en murmurant le nom sacré de Salamine.'[8]

In England, Byron, as we shall see further on, shared this same concern for the Greek cause. A little later, in 1824, Népomucène Lemercier (1771–1840) published a volume of heroic Greek songs translated into French, (*Chants héroïques des montagnards et matelots grecs, traduits en vers français*), followed a year later by *Suite des chants héroïques et populaires*. In 1828 Victor Hugo wrote his *Orientales* which contain some of the most important poems inspired by the Greek uprising: *Canaris*; *Les Têtes du Sérail*; *L'Enfant*; *Lazzara*; *Vœu* and *Enthousiasme*, which begins with the impassioned exhortation:

En Grèce! en Grèce! adieu, vous tous! il faut partir!
Qu'enfin, après le sang de ce peuple martyr,
Le sang vil des bourreaux ruisselle!
En Grèce! ô mes amis! vengeance! liberté!
Ce turban sur mon front! ce sabre à mon côté!
Allons! ce cheval, qu'on le selle![9]

7 Numbered 183–6 in the sale and designated as the work of Delacroix, a few of these sketches have sometimes been attributed to the artist Alexandre Decamps (1803–60), whose reputation as an orientalist was established at the Salon of 1831.

8 'War, war to the tyrants! Sailors, plough the seas!/From his grave Themistocles watches this port that once knew his greatness; And the waves break at your feet, murmuring the sacred name of Salamis!'

9 'To Greece! To Greece! farewell to all! it is time to leave'/The blood of this martyred people should no longer flow/but the vile blood of their murderers!/To Greece! O, my friends! vengeance! liberty!/Turban on my head! Sabre at my side!/Come! Saddle my horse!'

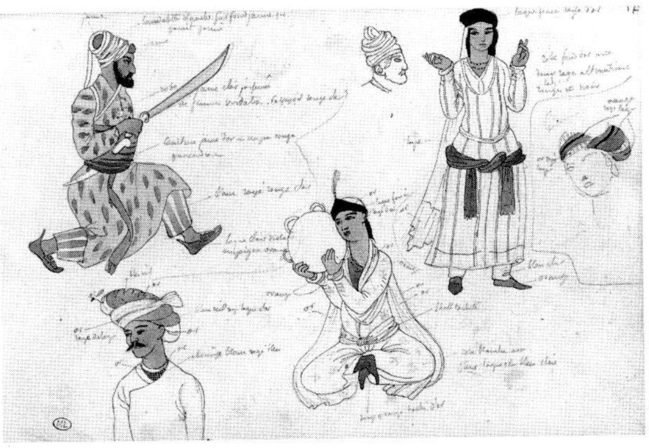

8 - Studies after Persian miniatures depicting Indians,
pen and watercolour,
13 x 20.5 cm.
Département des Arts graphiques,
Louvre, Paris (Album RF 9145, fol. 17r).

A letter dated 15 September 1821 from Delacroix to his friend Charles Soulier, then in Naples, shows the young artist's early interest in the Greek cause: 'I am thinking of painting for the coming Salon a picture whose subject I shall take from the recent wars between the Turks and Greeks. I think that under the circumstances, and provided the work is well done, this would be a way to attract some attention', (*Correspondance*, I, p. 132). He abandoned his project in favour of *The Barque of Dante*, exhibited at the 1822 Salon, but as early as May 1823 he took up the idea again in his *Journal* (I, p. 32): 'On Saturday I decided to paint scenes from the massacre at Chios for the 1824 Salon', and on Sunday 9 November of the same year (I, p. 35): 'This week I completed my painting of Chios' (fig. 9). On 1 December he wrote to his friend Félix Guillemardet: 'There is a large new blank canvas which has been in my studio for several days now and I shall need all the faculties I possess to cover it!' (A. Dupont, *Lettres intimes*, 1954, p. 148.) Finally, on Monday 12 January 1824, he wrote: 'Appointment this morning with Raymond Verninac to meet M. Voutier, just back from Greece where he has held an important post. He is returning there.[10] M.Voutier is a fine-looking man, a Greek type. He has small, bright eyes and seems full of energy. Over and over again he has been struck with admiration for the Greek soldiers, whom he has seen overcoming their enemies and trampling them underfoot, shouting *Zito Eleutheria!* ('Long live Liberty!'). During the siege of Athens, when the Greeks carried their attack to within pistol-shot of the city walls, he was so much impressed by the magnificent head of a Turk who appeared on the battlements that he prevented a soldier from shooting at him. The massacre at Chios lasted for a month. It was at the end of the month that Captain Georges d'Ipsara with, I think, one hundred and forty men, set fire to the Turkish flagship. The Captain-pasha and the senior Turkish officers perished, but the Greeks escaped safe and sound. A ship bearing the head of Balleste, the gallant French officer, as a gruesome trophy, put into port at Chios on its way from Candia to Constantinople. The ship was set on fire and the head of the heroic Balleste was buried with suitable honours. . . . Went to the Luxembourg after lunching with Raymond Verninac and M. Voutier. Came back to the studio bursting with enthusiasm and Hélène [one of his models], arriving shortly afterwards, I made a series of studies for the picture . . . Today, Monday 12, I am really beginning my picture.' (*Journal*, I, pp. 43–5; Wellington, pp. 20–1.)

On re-reading these confidential lines, one may suppose that Voutier's narratives and the conversations between Delacroix and his brother-in-law, Raymond de Verninac, ex-ambassador to the Sublime Porte who was sent to Constantinople in 1795 and 1796, stimulated the artist's interest in the subject on which he now had a clearer idea than in 1821. Several weeks before the Salon, Delacroix borrowed some oriental costumes, or sketches of costumes (the phrase in the *Journal* is not clear), from his artist friend Jules Robert Auguste. On 30 June he wrote 'At M. Auguste's. Saw some splendid paintings

10

Olivier Voutier, colonel of artillery, is one of the finest figures of French philhellenism. He played a decisive role as Mavrocordatos' aide-de-camp. In 1823 he published Mémoires du colonel Voutier sur la guerre actuelle des Grecs *and in 1826,* Lettres sur la Grèce, notes et chants populaires.

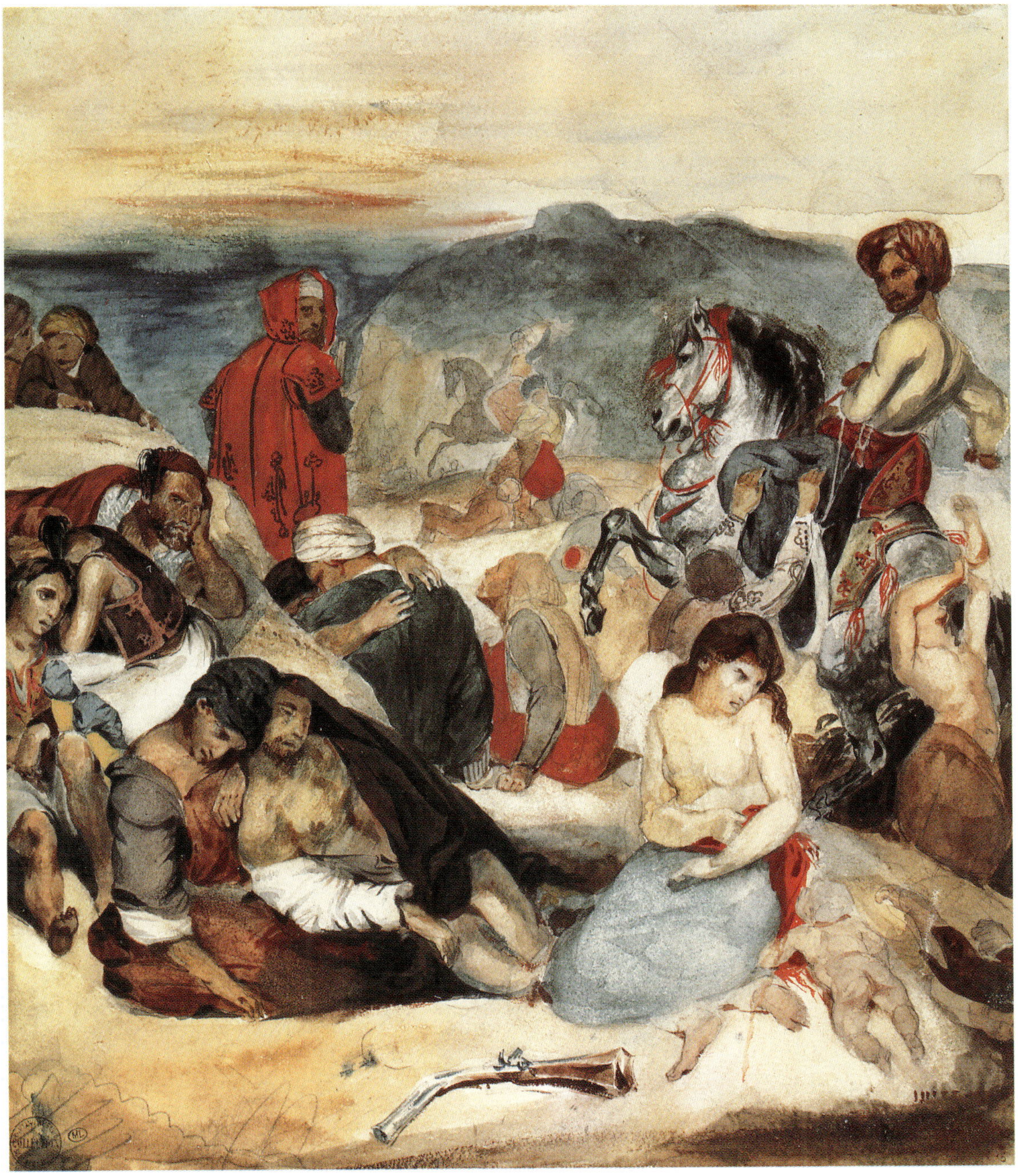

9 - Study for The Massacre at Chios,
watercolour,
33.8 x 30 cm.
Département des Arts graphiques, Louvre, Paris.

after the masters; costumes, and especially horses—admirable beyond anything Géricault ever did. It would be a great advantage to have some of these horses to copy, as well as the costumes, Greek, Persian, Indian etc.' (*Journal* I, p. 116; Wellington, p. 48) (fig. 8). On 7 July he noted 'M. Auguste came to the studio today; he seemed delighted by my pictures. Felt much encouraged by his praise. Time is getting on. Tomorrow I'll go to Auguste's and collect some costumes.' (*Journal*, I, p. 117; Wellington, p. 48). It is possible that Delacroix used these costumes for *The Massacre at Chios*, but in this respect one should not underestimate the iconographic research he carried out in the Bibliothèque Nationale which is mentioned in his notebooks at the time.[11] If *The Massacre at Chios* (fig. 10) attracted interest at the Salon, it

11
In a notebook used from about 1820–5 (Département des Arts graphiques, Louvre, RF 9152), Delacroix mentions the work of Claude-Étienne Savary, Lettres sur la Grèce, *published in 1788. Several sketches from this notebook prove that Delacroix had consulted Rosset's book* Mœurs et coutumes turques et orientales dessinées dans le pays en 1790.

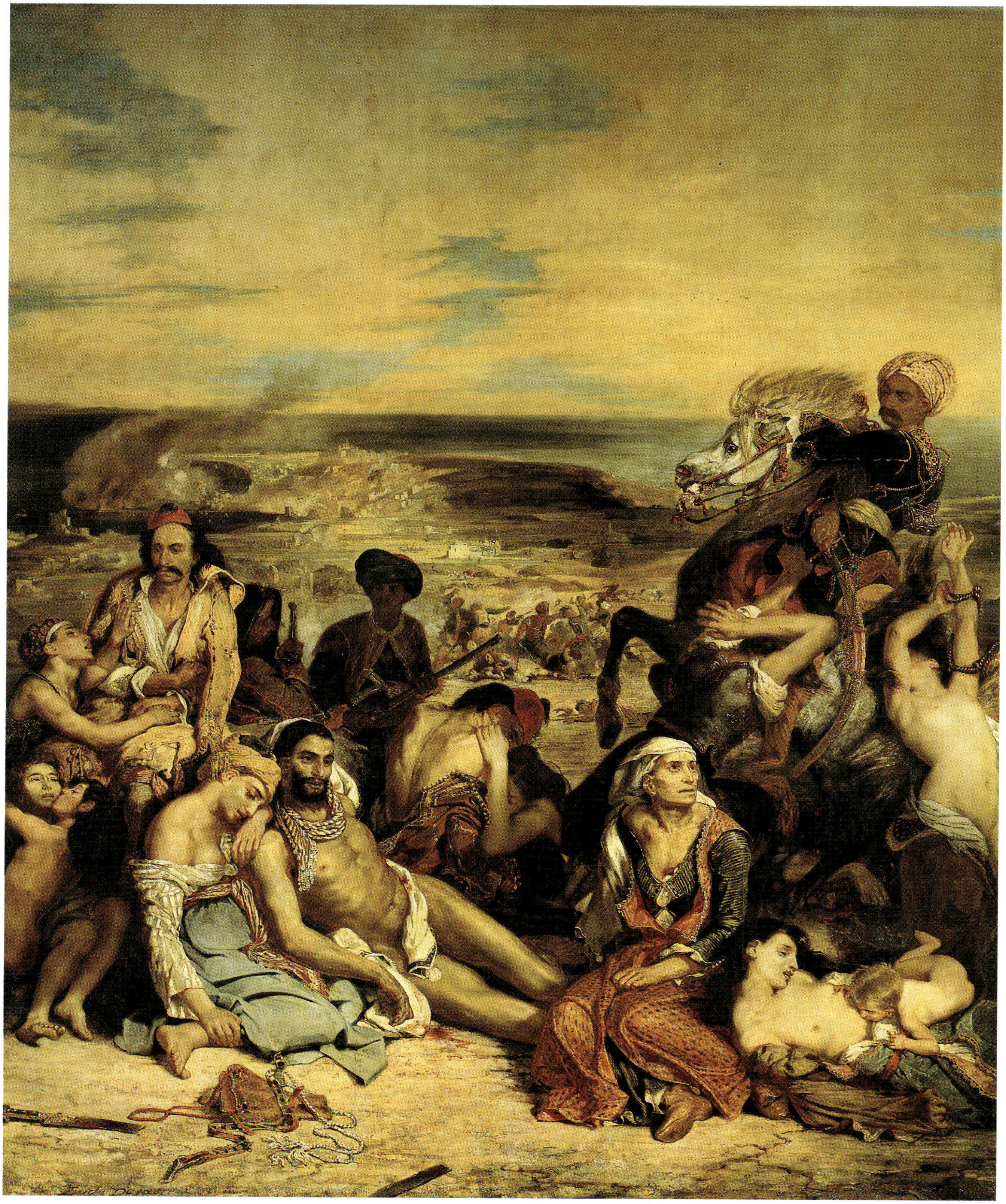

was nevertheless very severely judged not only by the critics, but by most artists and the public.[12] Signing himself A.., Stendhal wrote in the *Journal de Paris et des Départements* (1824): 'M. Delacroix's *Massacre at Chios* is to painting what Messrs Guiraud and de Vigny are to poetry, an excess of sorrow and gloom. The public is so bored, however, with the traditional academic style . . . that the visitors all tend stop in front of the spectacle of livid, unfinished corpses that M. Delacroix's picture offers . . . '. 'Furthermore,' adds Stendhal, 'the figures are actually in movement . . . ', and Delacroix shows himself to be ' . . . a student of Tintoretto'. Gros, who had praised *The Barque of Dante,* manifested his displeasure by stating: 'It is the massacre of art!' Thiers on the other hand, concluded his article in *Le Constitutionnel,* 1824, with the following phrase: 'M. Delacroix . . . proves he has great talent and has dissipated any doubts on that point with this Greek painting which follows his *Dante.*' In retrospect, the lack of comprehension on the part of his contemporaries can only find justification in the revolutionary character of his painting, which deliberately breaks with so-called 'history painting' and springs from a very personal conception of orientalism. Instead of following his predecessors, Girodet, Guérin and even Gros, who all used the canvas widthways, Delacroix's used it lengthways, making his composition tall rather than wide. This unusual presentation allowed him to give the subject more space and depth and to paint other battle scenes in the middle distance behind the main figures, the whole in a vast, colourful landscape dominated by a luminous sky of intense blue with translucent clouds. As for the dead or dying figures grouped in the foreground, some possess the macabre realism of those painted by Géricault in his *Raft of the Medusa,* and others bear a haggard expression accentuated by the bright red rings circling their eyes. This group makes a striking contrast with the one on the right portraying a Turkish officer forcefully capturing a young, half-naked Greek, who clings to his rearing horse. The savagery opposing these two characters heightens the violence and brutality of the scene.

10 - The Massacre at Chios,
oil on canvas,
4.19 x 3.54 m.
Louvre, Paris.

This particular Orient is certainly very romantic, but compared to his contemporaries and even to Gros, Delacroix had no hesitation in giving free rein to his prolific imagination, not just regarding the main subject but for the whole conception of the work. Other artists also let themselves be carried away, but with less intensity, by accounts of the brutalities inflicted on the inhabitants of the Greek islands. *Souliote Women* by Ary Scheffer (1795–1858), portrays Greek widows, whose husbands had been massacred by the troops of the Pasha, throwing themselves into an abyss to escape further violence (1827 Salon; Louvre).

Jules-Robert Auguste (1789–1850), mentioned above, and whom his friends called with respect, Monsieur Auguste, showed a less impassioned reaction to this savage conflict. Nevertheless, he remains one of the most curious figures in this small world of romantic artists, among whom his talent,

12
Gérard, who had seen the painting just before the opening of the Salon was, according to Delacroix, the only one to have expressed real praise.

taste and fortune were an important driving force. Meanwhile his complete indifference to fame or even simple recognition left him in almost total oblivion for more than half a century. After a stay in Rome, Auguste travelled to Greece, Egypt, Asia Minor and Morocco. When back in Paris he often kept open house to artists and writers, such as Mérimée, Balzac, Géricault, Bonington and Poterlet, not to mention Delacroix himself, who visited occasionally and always praised the studies Auguste had executed during his trips to the Orient, notably the watercolours and delicate pastels (fig. 11). Auguste also owned a collection of oriental objects which he had brought back with him: clothes, costumes, weapons and various objects, some of which, as we have seen, he lent to Delacroix for his *Massacre at Chios*. Auguste, generally considered as the instigator of a certain French exoticism, left a fairly large collection of colourful works of great sensuality: *Studies of Arabs*; *Two Women, one of them Black, in a Landscape*; *Two Creole and a White Woman in a Landscape*; (Musée des Beaux-Arts, Orléans), or again *The Friends* and *The Black Amazon* (Louvre). Certain of these works were sometimes attributed to Delacroix, yet the 'orientalism' of this fine artist, although certainly inspired by authentic sources, mainly found expression in small, colourful paintings which have a discreet charm but remain anecdotal and picturesque in comparison with the dramatic grandeur of a Delacroix. At the Salon of 1824, Delacroix exhibited two other paintings (listed together under no. 451 in the Salon catalogue) entitled *Head of an Old Woman* and *Young Orphan Girl in a Cemetery*, both directly related to *The Massacre at Chios*. The first is a study for the haggard elderly woman seated on the right in the foreground of the picture and the second a study for the young man on the far left.

Although the dramatic events on the island of Chios monopolized Delacroix's attention for a while, it was at this time that he dreamt of portraying the courage and daring of Marcos Botzaris (1788–1823), one the heroes of the Greek struggle for independence. In the spring of 1821, Botzaris began the campaign against the Turks with a series of victories, but the Greeks were later forced to withdraw as far as Missolonghi. The Turks had received considerable troop reinforcements, but Botzaris, along with with three-hundred volunteers, invaded their camp at night. The brave leader slaughtered everyone in his path as far as the Pasha's tent, but just as he reached it he fell, shot through the forehead. Impressed by this heroic act, Delacroix notes in his *Journal* (I, p. 76) on 12 April 1824: 'I must make a large sketch of Botzaris with the confused and terrified Turks falling on one another.' Several studies, including a beautiful watercolour (fig. 12), prove that the artist did more than just dream of depicting the subject. It was not until the end of his career, however, in about 1862, that he seems to have entertained the idea of executing a really large painting for which there remains the unfinished sketch, *Botzaris surprises the Turkish Camp at Dawn and falls fatally wounded* (private collection).

Jules-Robert Auguste
11 - Greek Soldier,
pastel,
38 x 24 cm.
Département des Arts graphiques
Louvre, Paris.

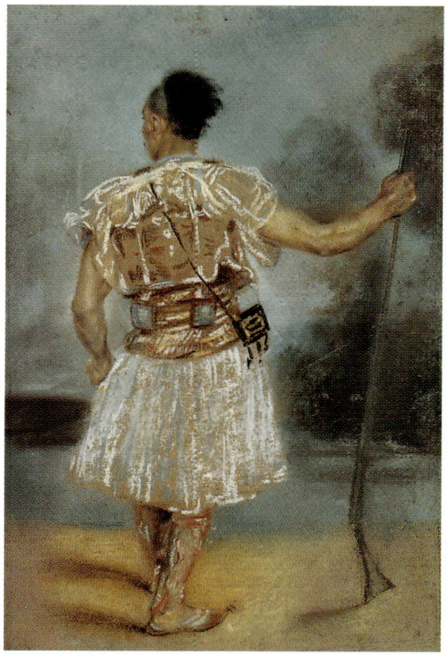

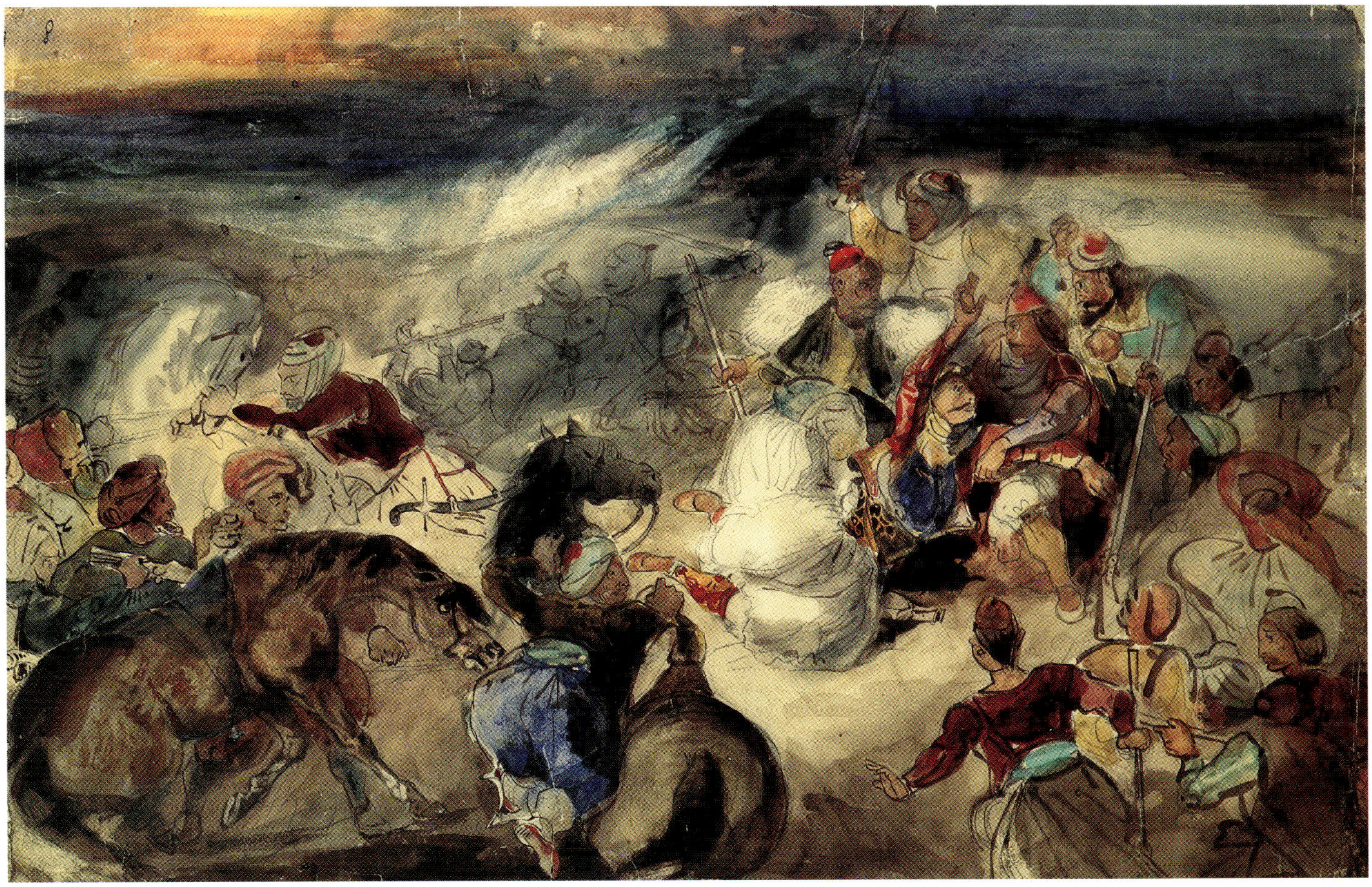

12 - Battle between Greeks and Turks,
watercolour,
34 x 51.7 cm.
Département des Arts graphiques,
Louvre, Paris.

The impact caused by the efforts of the Greek population in their struggle for freedom continued to have effect from 1823 to 1826 when Delacroix painted a whole series of figures in Greek (Suliote or palikar), or in Turkish and Indian dress.

In addition to portraits of two of his female models, *Aspasie the Moor* and *Aline the Mulatto* (Musée Fabre, Montpellier; private collection) (fig. 13), Delacroix painted four studies of *Figures in Greek Dress* (two are in the Louvre (fig. 14), the third in the Gothenberg Museum; the whereabouts of the fourth remains unknown). Also in the same style, special mention must be made of the *Portrait of Count Palatiano in Souliote Dress,* exhibited at the 1827–8 Salon (Cleveland Museum of Art), for which Delacroix made a whole series of preliminary drawings (Département des Arts graphiques, Louvre).[13]

Parallel with these Greek works, the artist painted seven studies of figures in Turkish dress: *Figure of a Seated Turk*, where the model is perhaps J.B. Pierret (private collection); *Seated Turk*, known as *Turk with Saddle* (Louvre); *Turk seated on a Sofa Smoking* (fig. 15); *Standing Turk in a Red Cape* (private collection); *Young Turk grooming his Horse* (Musée J.P. Pescatore, Luxemburg); *Turkish Horseman at the Gallop* (whereabouts unknown) and finally *Body of a Turkish Officer in the Mountains* (1826) (fig. 17). Mention should also be made of a *Portrait presumed to be of the Singer Baroilhet in Turkish Dress* (fig. 16). Delacroix also painted two studies of figures in Indian dress: *Indian Warrior with his Horse tied*

13
The Count Demetrius de Palatiano (1794–1849), born in Corfu, visited Paris in 1825 before travelling to London where he stayed for nine years. Sharing Delacroix's studio during the winter of 1825–6, the English artist Bonington also painted the count's portrait.

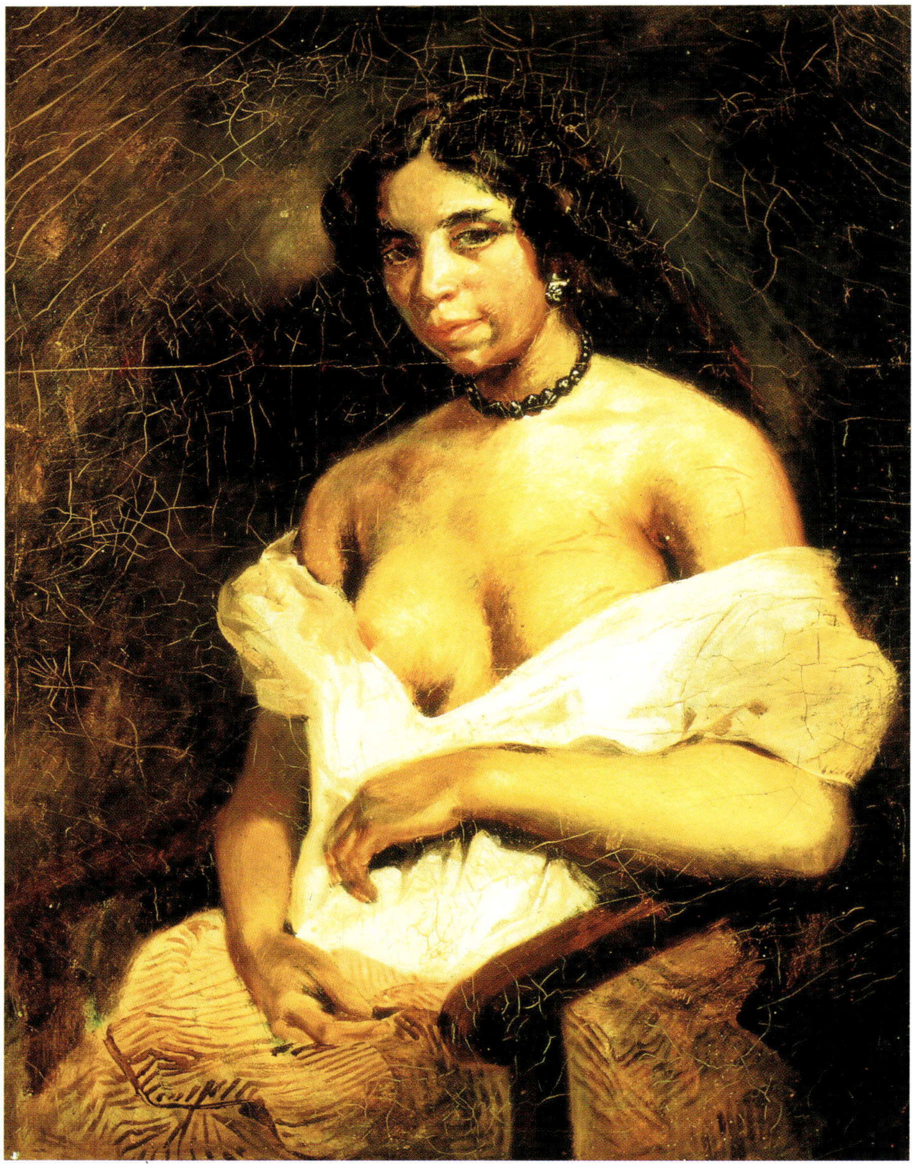

13 - **Aline the Mulatto,**
oil on canvas,
81 x 65 cm.
Musée Fabre, Montpellier.

14 ____
The exhibition held in the Galerie Lebrun in 1826 comprised no less than 198 pictures, some of which were considered to be among the masterpieces of the greatest Empire and Restoration artists. In addition to Greece Expiring on the Ruins of Missolonghi *(ex catalogue), Delacroix exhibited* Marino Faliero, Don Juan *and* Body of a Turkish Officer in the Mountains. The Battle of Nazareth *and* The Pest-house at Jaffa *by Baron Gros were hung next to David's* The Death of Socrates. *Horace Vernet sent four canvases including one* Naval Battle between Greeks and Turks, *Ary Scheffer sent five, including* Portrait of Colonel Fabvier *who had fought with the Greeks, while Bonington presented* A Seated Turk. *Géricault, Prud'hon, Achille and Eugène Devéria, Louis Boulanger and many others were also among the exhibitors.*

to a Post (private collection) and *Armed Indian of Gourka-kree* (fig. 1), exhibited at the 1831 Salon. All the figures are clothed in richly coloured, embroidered costumes, with finely decorated slippers (fig. 20), sparkling turbans and highly polished arms; they are, in other words, variations on the infinite theme of orientalism which at the time attracted the still romantic Delacroix, who found therein a pretext for expressing his immense talent as a colourist.

Delacroix participated in an exhibition of works by French artists held in Paris in 1826 at the Galerie Lebrun, 4 rue du Gros-Chenet, in order to collect funds to support the Greek cause.[14] The work he showed was destined to have quite a different impact to these colourful portraits. It was no longer a question of proudly portraying a precisely documented event, but of addressing a vehement message to the public (the French government was trying to observe a strict neutrality). Missolonghi, after fifteen months of heroic resistance, had just fallen (22 April 1826).

In choosing an allegorical symbol for this composition, entitled *Greece Expiring on the Ruins of Missolonghi* (fig. 18), Delacroix, admittedly, adopts a form of expression used by all traditional academic artists, but he surpasses this style in his revolutionary use of colour. Aside from Victor Hugo, the critics were unenthusiastic about the painting, no doubt disconcerted by Delacroix's

14 - Two Greek Soldiers Dancing,
oil on canvas,
35 x 46 cm.
Louvre, Paris.

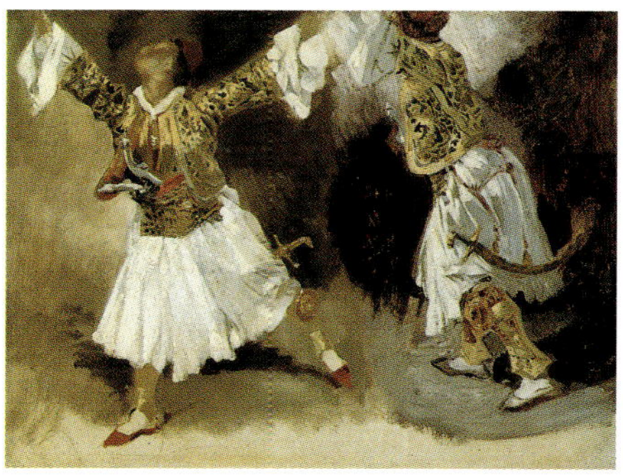

interpretation of the subject. Hugo commented: 'M. Eugène Delacroix has just presented a new painting to the ill-humoured critics and to the enlightened public, which clearly reveals all the qualities of this young and already talented colourist. We do not like allegories, but this one is of profound interest. This woman who symbolizes Greece has such a beautiful attitude and expression! The triumphant Egyptian, the severed heads, the blood-stained stones, all this has a pathetic strain! And there is so much learning and art in the bold work of M. Delacroix!' Was Hugo aware when writing this account, which remained unpublished until 1967, that apart from Delacroix's tribute to the champions of liberty, he was also displaying his admiration for the English poet who died in Missolonghi two years earlier? Byron had expressed his attraction to the Orient since 1813 in poems which were a fundamental and continuing influence in Delacroix's work, such as *Combat between the Giaour and the Pasha* (fig. 19), *The Bride of Abydos*, *The Corsair* and *Lara*.

15 - Turk seated on a Sofa Smoking,
oil on canvas,
25 x 30 cm.
Louvre, Paris.

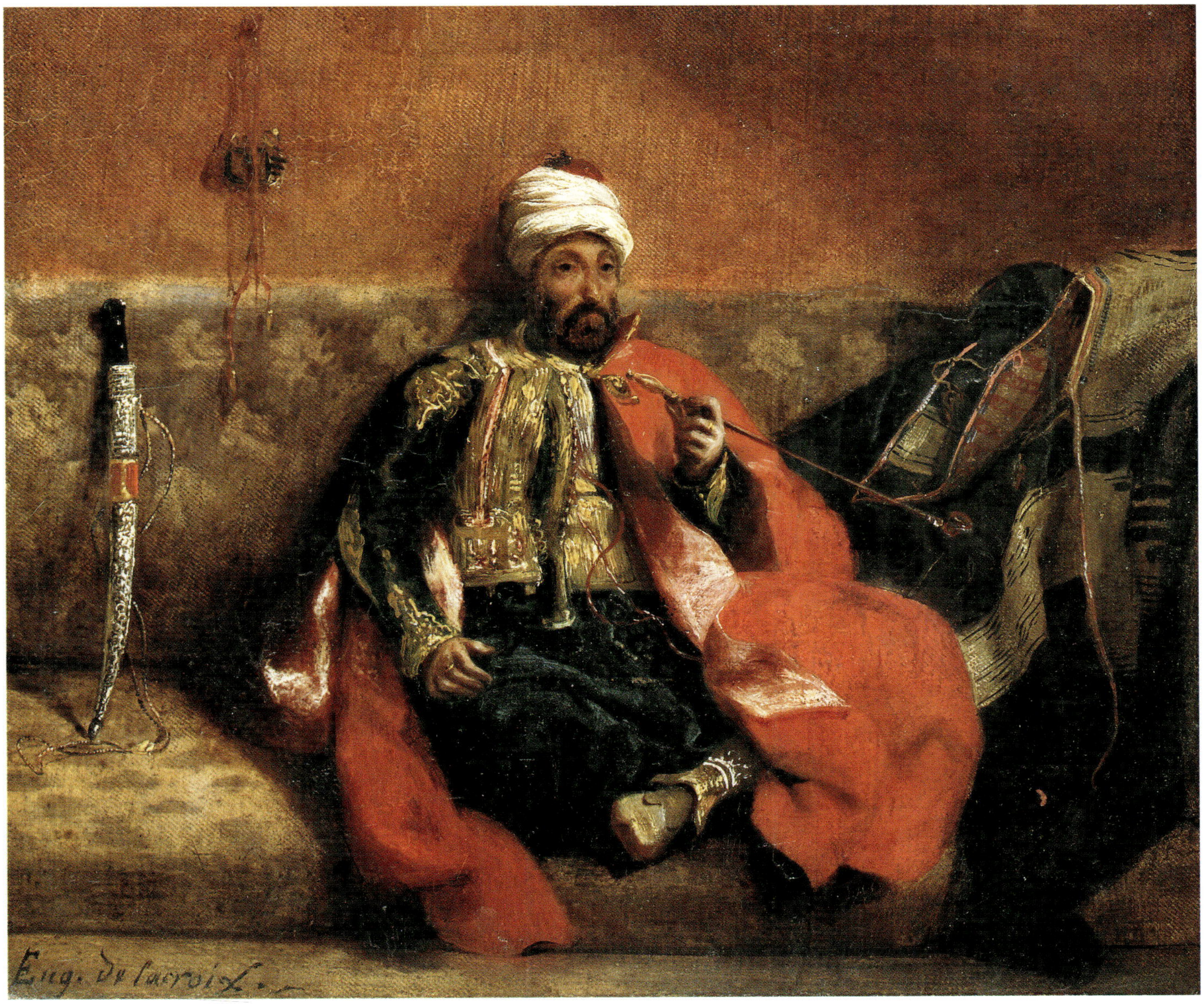

The victory of the powerful allied French, English and Russian fleet over the Turkish and Egyptian vessels at Navarino on 20 October 1827, constituted an initial conclusion to the war which had been raging between the Greeks and Turks since 1820–1. As soon as the news reached Europe, this episode became the subject for numerous paintings and engravings, and in order to obtain a first-hand report, the French government delegated Alexandre Decamps (1803–60) and Louis Garneray (1783–1857) to visit Greece and Asia Minor. On 3 February 1830, by the Treaty of London, Greece was finally declared an independent realm.

From 1820 to 1830, Byron's poems tended to direct Delacroix's imagination towards a sumptuous and fertile Greek-style Orient, whereas another writer, French this time, enabled the artist to discover a new type of exoticism which Bernardin de Saint-Pierre's novel *Paul et Virginie* had made fashionable in as early as 1787. François-René de Chateaubriand (1768–1848) spent five months in America from July to December 1791, returning to France with an enormous quantity of notes and the outlines of the epic prose poem *Les Natchez*. The writer had taken refuge in London in 1773 but returned to France in 1800 after his name had been struck off the list of emigrants. While completing *Les Natchez*, in order to attract attention, he extracted an episode entitled *Atala*, published in 1801.

The resounding success of this text from which Girodet transposed one of the most moving passages onto canvas, *The Funeral of Atala* (1808 Salon; Louvre) did not escape Delacroix, who on 5 October 1822 mentioned in his *Journal*

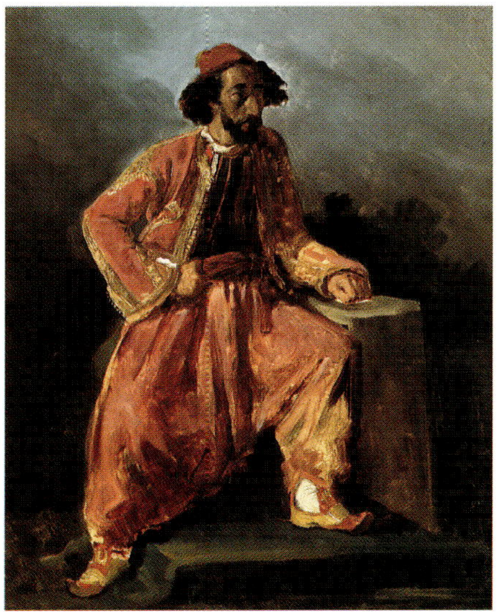

16 - Portrait presumed to be of the Singer Baroilhet in Turkish Dress,
oil on canvas,
46 x 38 cm.
On loan from the Louvre to the Musée Delacroix, Paris.

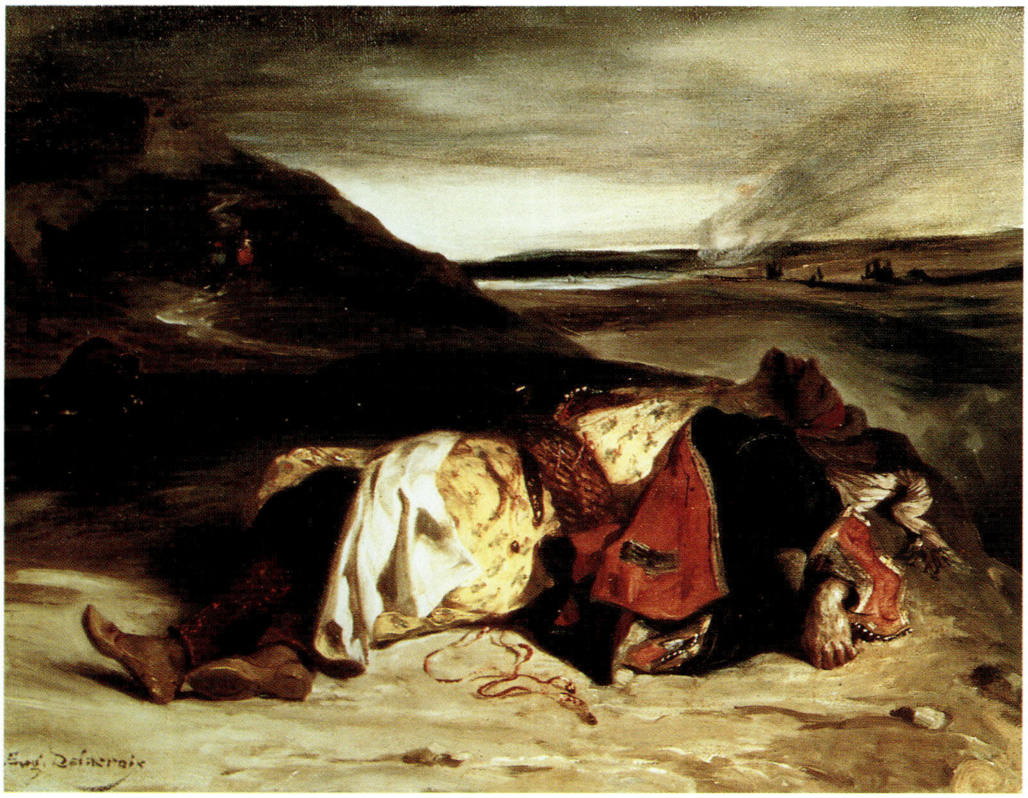

17 - Body of a Turkish Officer in the Mountains
oil on canvas,
33 x 41 cm.
Bührle Foundation, Zurich.

18 - Greece Expiring on the Ruins of Missolonghi,
oil on canvas,
2.09 x 1.47 m.
Musée des Beaux-Arts, Bordeaux.

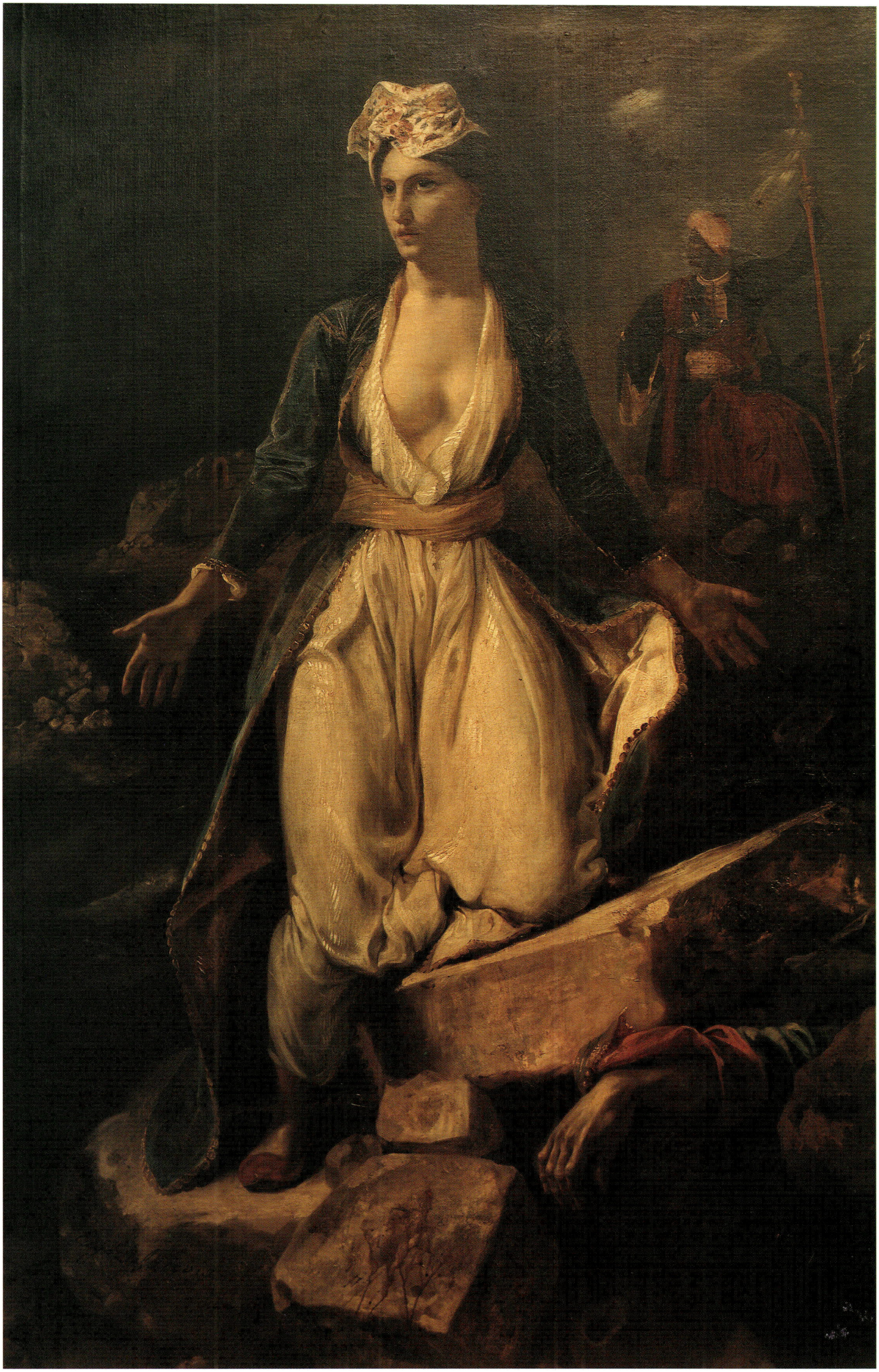

(I, p.15): 'A young Canadian woman crossing the desert with her husband starts labour pains and gives birth; her husband takes the new-born baby in his arms.' The following year on 23 December the artist notes: 'I am working on my natives' (fig. 21). According to Lee Johnson, Delacroix already had the intention to paint a subject taken from the epilogue to *Atala*, when the narrator, having followed the Mississippi, meets the young Indian woman and her husband on the banks of the Niagara with their dead child. The artist's work on *The Massacre at Chios* prevented him from pursuing his idea on the subject and it was only at the 1835 Salon that he was able to exhibit the completed work. The exhibition catalogue clearly explains the composition: 'Fleeing the massacre of their tribe, two young natives go up the Mississippi and during the journey the young woman starts labour pains. The episode chosen by the artist is that of the father taking the new-born baby in his arms while both of them looking at it tenderly (*Chateaubriant* [*sic*]: *épisode d'Atala*)'.

Delacroix's final large work inspired by the Orient before 1832 is *The Death of Sardanapalus* (fig. 21), exhibited at the 1827–8 Salon. The following text was quoted by Delacroix and printed in the Salon catalogue: 'The rebels besieged him in his palace . . . Lying on a magnificent bed on an enormous funeral pyre, Sardanapalus orders his eunuchs and palace officers to cut the throats of his wives, his pages and even his favourite horses and dogs; nothing that had served his pleasure should survive him. . . . Aischeh, a Bactrian woman who couldn't bear to die by the hands of a slave, hung herself from the pillars that supported the dome. . . . Baleah, Sardanapalus's cup-bearer set fire to the funeral pyre and then leapt into it himself.' Was Delacroix the only person to be aware of the literary source of this text with its unfinished phrases? The question remains unanswered to this day. Delacroix might have been inspired by Byron's tragedy published in 1821 which was translated into French shortly after by Amédée Pichot; and no doubt the illustrations of Etruscan, Greek and Roman objects in *Les Antiquités étrusques, grecques et romaines tirées du cabinet de M. Hamilton* supplied him with further references, but nevertheless, the exact identification of the above text, transcribed by the artist, remains a mystery.

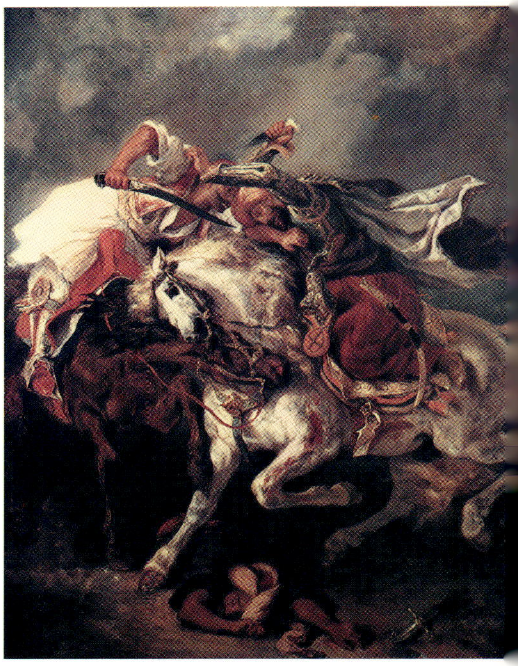

19 - Combat between the Giaour and the Pasha,
oil on canvas,
74 x 60 cm.
Petit Palais, Paris

Dreading the critics' reactions, and with good reason, Delacroix confided to his friend Soulier on 6 February 1828: 'I have actually finished my *second Massacre* . . . They re-opened the Salon this morning. My daub has been hung in the best possible position' (*Correspondance*, I, p. 211). On 22 March another letter addressed to Soulier reflects his confusion: 'They'll end by making me believe that I've had a real fiasco. . . . Some say it's a total failure, that the *Death of Sardanapalus* means the death of the Romantics, since that's what they call us' (*Correspondance*, I, p. 213).

The Death of Sardanapalus, with its dominating tones of red, orange, yellow and brown, is the apogee of Delacroix's romanticism, and it is without doubt his most exuberant and violent work, the one which most faithfully translates the fever which took hold of the artist every time he was carried away by the fantasy of a luxurious and tragic Orient. Baudelaire, who rediscovered the painting in the Galerie Martinet, 26 boulevard des Italiens, late in 1861 or at the beginning of 1862, made no mistake when he remarked: 'No painted figure ever gave a better rendering of an Asiatic despot than this *Sardanapalus*, with his plaited black beard and female attitude, he lies dying on his funeral pyre, draped in muslin. And this harem of radiantly beautiful women and all this *sardanapalesque* luxury which sparkles on the furnishing, clothes, armour, crockery and jewellery. Who inspired the artist with this fire, this freshness and this poetic enthusiasm, who? Who? . . . *Sardanapalus* revisited is youth regained!'[15]

Confronted with this turbulent universe, the oriental world portrayed by Delacroix's rival and leader of classicism, Jean-Auguste-Dominique Ingres (1780–1867) is by contrast one of idle luxury. In his fantasies, Ingres imagined harems full of odalisques and bathing women whose undulating nudity fired the dreams of the sultans and eunuchs. From *La Grande Odalisque,* 1814 (Louvre) to his much later masterpiece of oriental voluptuousness, the *Turkish Bath,* 1862 (Louvre), Ingres unconsciously slid from an 'icy eroticism' into an uneasy sensuality that few of his successors have expressed without falling into an excess of circumstantial exoticism.

In conclusion, it should be mentioned that many of Delacroix's contemporaries offered a rich variety of interpretations of the Orient, fashioned according to the individual nature of the artist and often derived from actual personal experience.

Not one of them, however, managed to equal Delacroix, whose potential genius existed well before 1832, nor did they possess his gift for expressing everything through colour, both rich and terrible. None of them attained the tortured gestures, the vigour or the overflowing pathos that give Delacroix's 'oriental' paintings that incomparable sense of movement which his contemporaries were unable to appreciate: 'Embraces of despair! Precious realm of painting! That silent power that speaks at first only to the eyes and then seizes and captivates every faculty of the soul! Here is your real spirit; here is your own true beauty, beautiful painting, so much insulted, so grievously misunderstood and delivered up to fools who exploit you. But there are still hearts ready to welcome you devoutly, souls who will no more be satisfied with mere phrases than with inventions and clever artifices . . . you have only to be seen in your masculine and simple vigour to give pleasure that is pure and absolute. I confess that I have worked logically [in reference to *The Massacre at Chios*], I who have no love for logical painting. I see now that my turbulent mind needs activity, that it must break out and try a hundred different ways before reaching the goal towards which I am always straining. There is an old leaven working in me, some black depth that must be appeased. Unless I am writhing like a serpent in the coils of a pythoness I am cold. I must recognize

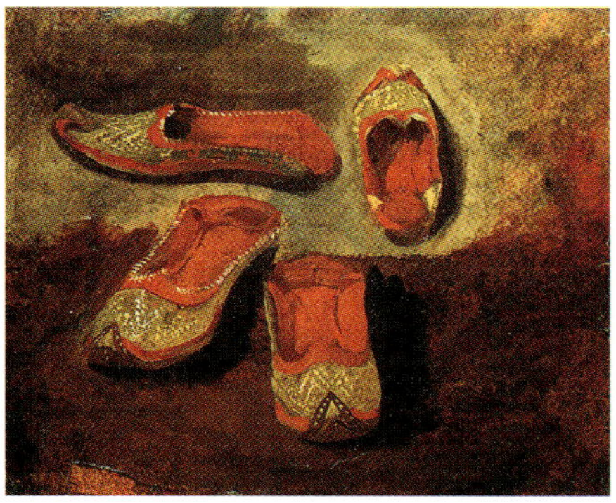

20 - Study of Turkish Slippers,
oil on cardboard,
16.5 x 20.5 cm.
Louvre, Paris.

15 *Translated from the French; Baudelaire,* Œuvres complètes, II, *texte établi, présenté et annoté par Claude Pichois, Editions Gallimard, Paris, 1976, p. 734*

this and accept it and to do so is the greatest happiness. Everything good I have ever done has come about in this way.' (*Journal*, I, p. 96–7; Wellington, p. 37).

In *The Massacre at Chios*, as in *Greece Expiring on the Ruins of Missolonghi*, Delacroix expresses his personal interpretation of an imaginary, tragic Orient, in which his extreme romanticism filters through his fascination for suffering and terror. It was the real, luminous and *classical* Orient that he finally visited in 1832, an Orient 'as beautiful as antiquity'.

Maurice SÉRULLAZ

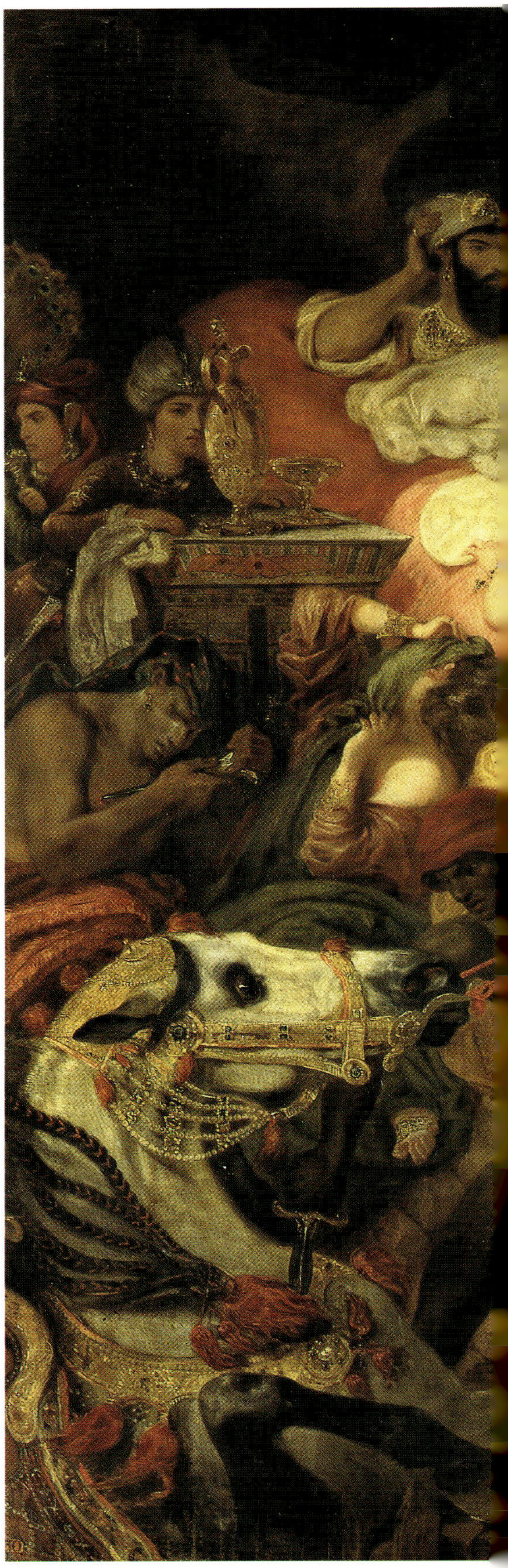

21- The Death of Sardanapalus,
oil on canvas,
3.92 x 4.96 m.
Louvre, Paris.

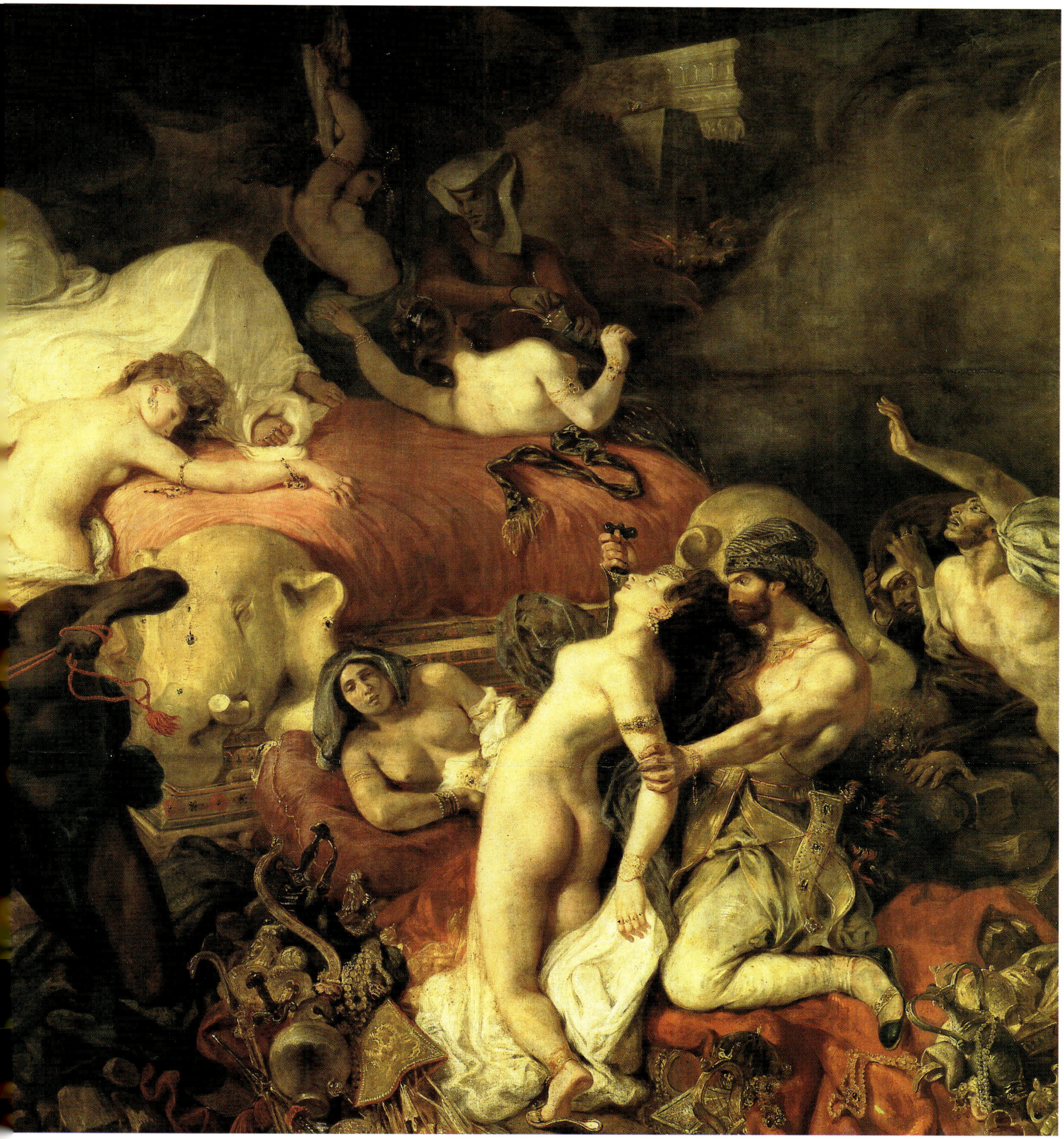

The Journey

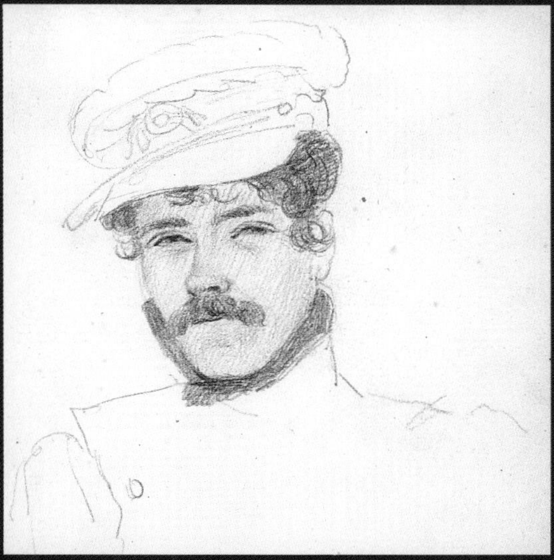

The Journey

The delegation which Louis-Philippe sent to Morocco in 1832 to settle several controversial affairs stemming from France's occupation of Algeria, was expected to follow the usual intricate diplomatic steps which are brought to a halt in a flourish of signatures on parchment. Although certain memorable treaties have changed the course of history, such was not the to be case for Charles de Mornay's mission to Morocco and his negotiations with Moulay Abd al-Rahman.[1] The conflict opposing the two countries was only resolved many years later and only then after military confrontation. Nevertheless, the delegation succeeded in transmitting a favourable image of a country and its inhabitants to a whole continent, and because Eugène Delacroix was a member of the mission, Morocco made a majestic entry into western art (fig. 1), freeing itself from all the clichés accumulated by several generations of authors and artists who had used the 'Orient' as an alibi for exploring an exotic world of fantasy.

Charles Edgar Count de Mornay (fig. 2), the diplomat responsible for bringing the message from Louis-Philippe to the Moroccan ruler, had received his instructions in mid-October, but this gentleman of the King's Chamber and acknowledged lover of the famous actress Mademoiselle Mars, was loath to exchange the warm atmosphere of Parisian social circles for a land reputed to be full of cruel-minded inhabitants and bloodthirsty wild beasts.[2]

The orders were given to sail for the Moroccan coast without delay, as tension was mounting in the district of Oran. Mohammed Belhamri, a Moroccan general, was said to be approaching Tlemcen at the head of his cavalry. There were reports of skirmishes throughout eastern Morocco and appeals for help were becoming pressing. What reply was the Moroccan emperor meant to give to the delegations who came rushing to him from all over the Oran province, urgently requesting troops and arms?

Mornay's mission was threefold: he was to negotiate the restitution of three French brigs, *L'Albine*, *Le Marie-Joseph* and *L'Amitié*, which had been captured by the Algerians and were being held in Moroccan ports; to settle outstanding commercial problems, and to establish an acceptable frontier between the new French colony—the city of Tlemcen included—and the rest of the Muslim empire.

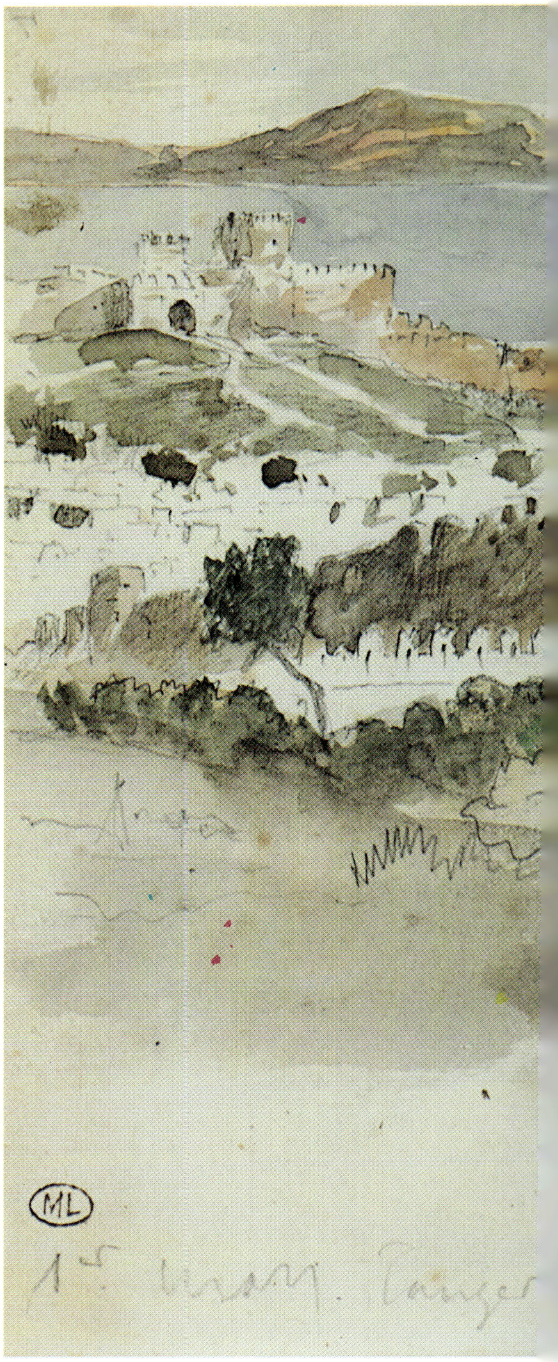

1 - North African and Spanish Album: view of Tangier,
watercolour and pencil drawing.
Département des Arts graphiques, Louvre, Paris (RF 1712 bis, fol. 1r).

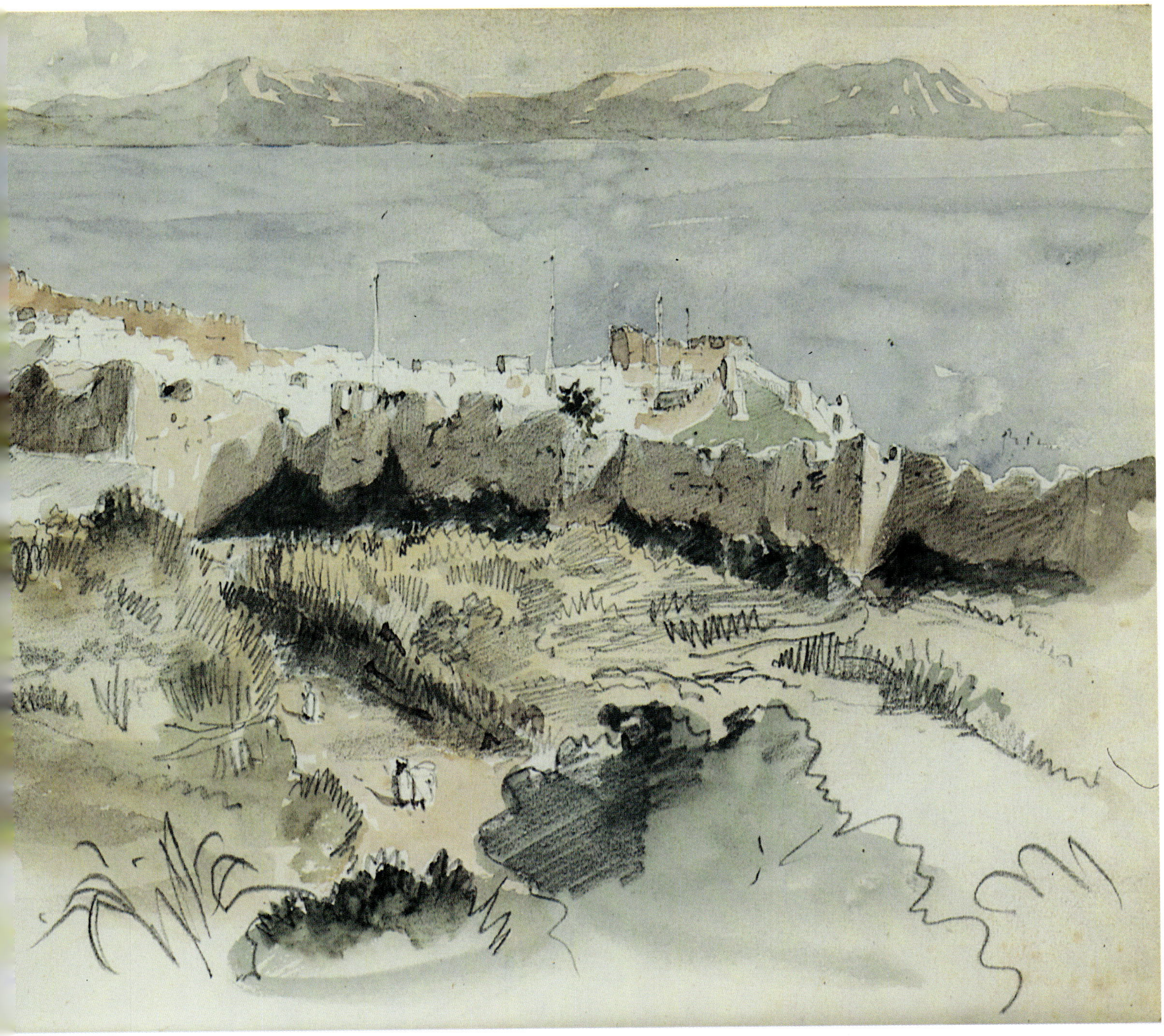

Jacques-Antoine Desgranges, eighteen years his senior, was appointed official interpreter to the ambassador, but Mornay was not entirely pleased by his nomination. Despite the fact that Desgranges had brilliantly accomplished several government assignments from Bassora to Tunis, he hardly seemed the ideal companion for the venture. Mornay, wishing to add prestige to his delegation, requested the presence of an additional person. Eugène Isabey was approached but declined the invitation: the young artist had recently come back from Algeria and rather dreaded the idea of returning to African territory.

Eugène Delacroix attended the opening night, on 21 November 1831, of Meyerbeer's *Robert le Diable*. Music, art and literature were the three pillars of his existence and he was perfectly acquainted with the Parisian operatic, theatrical and literary circles. It was here that important commissions were negotiated, decorations and favours obtained, fashions started and reputations made or broken. Was it the director of the Paris Opera, Charles-Edmond Duponchel, or the head of the influential *Journal des Débats*, Armand Bertin, or perhaps Mademoiselle Mars herself who in fact engaged Delacroix to accompany Mornay to Morocco? The actress was well aware of the hazards of living in close quarters in a restricted community, and was glad to think that her friend might be 'in the company of a talented young artist with a sense of humour and an excellent character, not qualities to be under-estimated when one has to spend four or five months together'. Her wishes were to be fulfilled.

Only one problem remained, however, that of convincing the Ministry of Foreign Affairs to agree to Delacroix joining the delegation, and the case was not an easy one to defend. In order to minimize the inconveniences of a journey in a hostile environment, the ministry agreed to the presence of an additional person, but neither the treasury nor the government were willing to support any supplementary expenses for the expedition. With the occupation of Algeria, France was having to restrict its budget. The decision of Count Horace Sebastiani, Minister of Foreign Affairs, was final. The artist could travel on the vessel transporting the mission to Tangier, but he was to pay his own expenses both on board and during his stay in Morocco.

Delacroix had been dreaming of Italy but, in the December of 1831, it was not Italy but the Orient which came to him. He wrote to his friend Frédéric Villot, 'Next week I shall probably leave for Morocco . . . Don't laugh. It's quite true. I am really quite flabbergasted. . . .'

On **Saturday 31 December**, New Year's Eve, Charles de Mornay and Eugène Delacroix dined with Mademoiselle Mars. The artist was in the habit of seeing the new year in with two close friends, Jean-Baptiste Pierret and Félix Guillemardet, but he could hardly decline the actress's invitation. They were to leave for Morocco from the hotel where she lived in the rue de la Tour-des-Dames. At about three o'clock in the morning, in piercingly cold weather, the

Page 55:
North African and Spanish Album: Self-portrait by Delacroix,
pencil,
Département des Arts graphiques, Louvre, Paris (RF 1712 bis, fol. 89v).

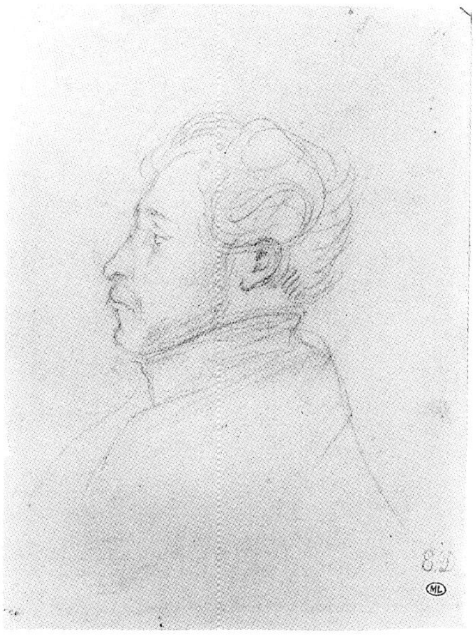

2 - Portrait of Count Charles de Mornay,
pencil,
18.1 x 13.6 cm.
Département des Arts graphiques, Louvre, Paris.

coach started for Fontainebleau, travelling on through Auxerre and Mâcon: 'We have had a great many misadventures on this confounded journey', wrote Delacroix to his friend Pierret.[3] Between Lyon and Avignon it snowed, and the final lap of the journey towards Marseille and Toulon was completed under grey skies with a biting mistral wind.

In Toulon the port admiral was unable to hide his anxiety. As transport for the delegation, the Admiralty had ordered an 'imposing warship to impress the Moroccan inhabitants and facilitate negotiations'. As it happened the greater part of the fleet was already engaged in the Algerian conflict and the port admiral therefore only disposed of a few sailing barges, tenders and two corvettes, one of which, the *Iphigénie*, had raised anchor on 8 January and was heading for Greek waters. All that remained was the corvette, *La Perle*, which was beginning to show signs of wear and tear. Designed by Bretsig and built in 1813 in Cherbourg, it had been overhauled in Bayonne in 1829 and armed with eighteen cannons. The elegant ship's head—a female figure with an advantageous bosom, tucking up her petticoats—hardly disguised the vessel's military allure. The captain, Ange-François Jouglas, had orders to set sail as soon as the distinguished passengers arrived on board. Special consideration was to be accorded to the Count Charles Edgar de Mornay and his interpreter Antoine Desgranges who were both to dine at the captain's table. The other passengers, the secretary François Ferrary and the two valets, Claude Maurignaut and Pierre Boispon, were to take their meals with the members of the crew. No instructions had been received, however, regarding Delacroix, who did not figure on any of the Admiralty's lists.

Six days passed without news of the king's interpreter who was stranded on the icy roads. When Desgranges finally arrived on Tuesday 10 January, the quay resumed its customary feverish activities. The departure was imminent. *La Perle* raised anchor on **Wednesday 11 January** in uncertain weather conditions. Jouglas headed south. The Admiralty had ordered a stopover at either Algeciras or Gibraltar but as soon as the ambassador arrived in Tangier, instructions from Paris could be considered obsolete. For the time being the distinguished guests gathered at the rear of the vessel and watched the contours the Var landscape rapidly disappear into the distance. The first meal was served. The Moroccan voyage had really begun.

After leaving Toulon the corvette ran into squalls. Delacroix wrote of 'Long days and tedious nights of lurching and tossing on the rough sea . . . ', 'We eat and drink too much to make up for the boredom and take no exercise.' Despite his indisposition, the artist nevertheless had the strength to admire a series of 'lovely coasts, Minorca, Majorca', . . . subjects for rapid sketches (Salobrena, 19 January) (fig. 3).

On **Saturday 21 January**, *La Perle*, having passed Malaga and Gibraltar, cast anchor off Algeciras. But the presence of a yellow flag warned ships not to enter the port and sailors not to venture into the town. There was a cholera

1
Moulay Abd al-Rahman Ben Hicham (1778–1859)
Nephew and son-in-law to Moulay Sliman, he succeeded him to the throne in 1822, contrary to the law of succession which was based on direct descent. Moulay Abd al-Rahman ended Morocco's isolation by opening up several of the coastal towns, including Tangier and Mogador, as centres for European trade. This well-calculated policy of openness ensured the kingdom's independence, despite the occupation of Algeria, the Franco-Moroccan war of 1844 and several other conflicts with European nations (Austria, 1828; Spain, 1844).

2
Charles Henri Edgar, Count de Mornay *(1803–1878), former gentleman of the Chamber to Charles X, in October 1831 he was put in charge of the extraordinary mission dispatched by Louis-Philippe to Moulay al-Rahman. The success of this assignment earned him the post of Resident Minister to the Court of Baden (31 December 1832), and later that of Minister Plenipotentiary in Stockholm. A former French peer, he left a contrasting image behind him. The target of the gossip columnists due to his relationship with the actress Mademoiselle Mars (after a scandal in 1825, he became her acknowledged lover), Stendhal considered him 'the only dandy in this country with any spirit', and Alexandre Dumas describes him as 'elegance, aristocracy and gentry personified . . . gifted with a brilliant mind'. Delacroix left a portrait of him, executed in 1837 (collection of Prince Paul of Yugoslavia).*

3
The edition permitting, translations of extracts from Delacroix's letters have been taken from Stewart, 1971. Extracts from Delacroix's Journal *are taken from Wellington, 1980.*

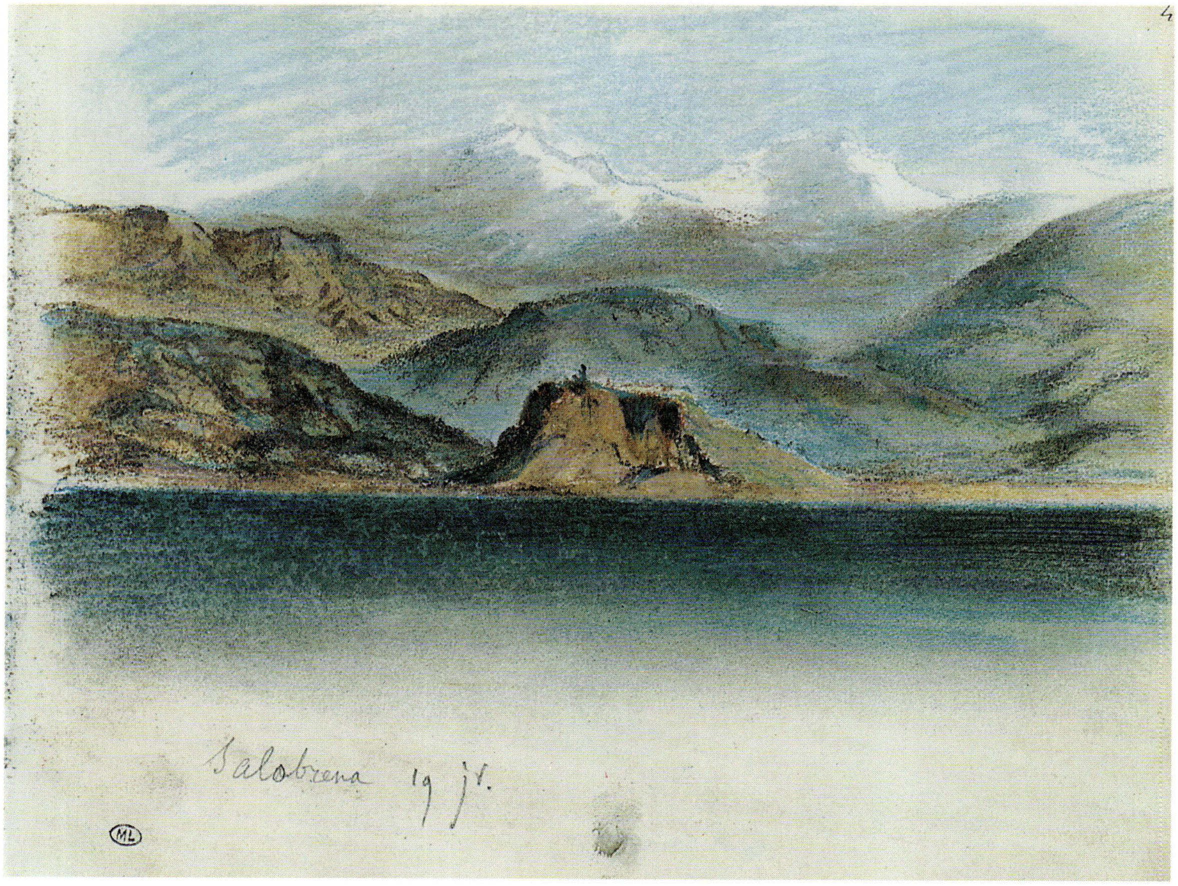

3 - Album: the Spanish Coast at Salobrena,
pastel.
Département des Arts graphiques, Louvre, Paris (RF 9154, fol. 4r).

epidemic in the region which had already claimed thousands of victims all along the Mediterranean coast. After discussion with the port authorities, a rowing-boat was allowed to draw alongside in order to deliver food supplies and to embark Léonce Angrand, the French consul in Cádiz, who brought new instructions from Paris and who wished to travel to Tangier. Delacroix accompanied the rowing-boat passengers: 'Grave Spaniards, dressed *à la Figaro* . . . All Goya was alive around me', he wrote to his friend Pierret.

In order not to offend the population's religious sentiments, on the Sunday *La Perle* remained off the coast of Algeciras. Jouglas was certain that if they raised anchor on the Monday, they could reach Tangier by nightfall. In clement weather the intense blue silhouette of the Moroccan coast can be seen on the horizon. But the weather now turned against them and the vessel was suddenly drawn towards the Atlantic. Delacroix noted: 'Despite all our efforts we were forced to cross the straits and found ourselves in the ocean. We spent a very bad night, but towards morning our bad luck turned and we were able to return.' The captain kept his calm and searched the skies for a break in the clouds in order to locate the Cape of Spartel lighthouse.

After 'an interminable crossing lasting thirteen long days', they finally reached Tangier, perched on its impressive rock. The town was the centre of all transactions between 'the impenetrable kingdom' and the infidel nations. The routes that link the sea with the imperial cities began at the foot of the ramparts of this one time Phoenician, Carthaginian and Roman trading town, domain of the legendary Columns of Hercules. The rivalry between the different trading nations was bitter during this period, and in order to obtain a few privileges with the Muslim court, they endlessly plotted and made accusations against one another. Europeans and Moroccans alike were the prey of denunciations, but the Moroccans possessed an inexhaustible supply of particularly subtle means of discrediting their adversaries.

On **Tuesday 24 January**, the observers, perched on the summit of the kasbah overlooking the calm bay, saw the French vessel emerge from the morning mists, proudly displaying her sails, flags and shining canons. The Moroccan authorities were not in the least flurried by this arrival: *La Perle* was expected. Judah Benoliel, Moulay Abd al-Rahman's watchman in Gibraltar, had been following the progress of the French vessel. His mission was to deal with the grievances aired by the Europeans concerning Morocco, which had been flooding in during the last few months, almost as though they had all agreed amongst themselves to lodge their complaints simultaneously. 'The Emperor had come to terms with the situation . . . he no longer felt the reserve he and his uncle, the deceased emperor, had always manifested towards the powerful Christian nations', who now exerted pressure in the form of a never-ending chain of battleships, especially French, off the Moroccan coast. In the space of a few days *Le Suffren, La Railleuse, La Béarnaise,* followed by *La Ménagère, L'Émulation, L'Algésiras* . . . had all ostentatiously crossed the straits as if in a parade. The armada sailing towards the Mediterranean navigated as close as possible to Tangier in order that the Moroccans crouching in the rocks could see the impressive number of cannons with their own eyes.

The captain Ange Jouglas issued brief orders to the crew, while Mornay and Desgranges stood at the ship's rail in the weak sun trying to dry their clothes, still damp from the 'floating prison'. Delacroix scrutinized Tangier. Was it really there, the Orient which had fired the imaginations of so many artists, including his friend Jules-Robert Auguste? For the time being all he could see was a town emerging from the morning mist and a rowing-boat which drew alongside *La Perle* transporting the French vice-consul surrounded by 'a score of black, green and yellow marabouts, who started climbing over the whole ship like cats.'

Jacques Denis Delaporte, the French vice-consul in charge of the consulate in Tangier since the death of Édouard Sourdeau in 1829, found himself in a delicate situation.[4] He had just been informed that for economic reasons his post was to be suppressed, which put him 'in a very difficult position' with his colleagues in Tangier. In the face of this adversity he strived to maintain 'as much dignity as possible'. Moreover, to make things worse, he had learned of the arrival of a special envoy from his country through a general rumour and had never been officially notified. What attitude should he adopt after so many years of devoted service and efficiency which had earned him the unanimous esteem not only of the Moroccan court but also of the Moors, the Jews and the Christians? The vice-consul kept a brave face: 'Although I have not received any instructions from Your Excellency as to my function during this mission, that will in no way prevent me from offering the Count de Mornay

4
Jacques Denis Delaporte (1777–1861).
A student in Oriental languages, Delaporte was made a member of the 'Committee for the Sciences and the Arts' for the Egyptian expedition in 1798. He was subsequently appointed librarian of the Egyptian Institute from 1800 to 1801. He served for fourteen years in the French consulate in Tripoli, Libya, then became chancellor/interpreter in Tangier in 1816. In 1831, the Ministry terminated his post of vice-consul and advised him to accept a position as translator in Algeria or to take his retirement. Nevertheless, he remained in his post until the arrival of the new consul general, M. Méchain, on 9 March 1833. In 1836, he was nominated consul, 2nd class, to Mogador (Essaouira). Called back to France in 1841, he finally retired in 1842.

any advice from my experience here which might help to contribute to the success of his mission.' He visited *La Perle* at ten o'clock on 24 January, to inform the young ambassador of the customs of the country and of 'all the honours that are due to special envoys sent by the sovereigns of other nations'. Well into his fifties, Delaporte had a sad expression in his eyes and a face darkened by thirty-two years of African sun. The introductions were brief. Mornay reported, 'We agreed that he would immediately return to Tangier to negotiate with the Pasha as to what salute should greet our vessel and to inform him that I wished to disembark the following morning to visit the consulate.'

Mornay was a man of protocol, of which he left no doubt at the fortress: he ordered a seven-gun salute to be fired on Delaporte's departure from *La Perle* and a further nineteen when he reached firm ground. The Tangier authorities were taken unawares by this unusual procedure, but after a moment of confusion, retaliated by firing a nineteen-gun salute which shook the very walls of the kasbah and echoed as far as Cape Spartel. At midday the ambassador ordered an additional twenty-one gun salute to be fired 'in honour of the French and the consular flags'. The kasbah did not return the salute, considering the game to be rather puerile and one which, in the long run, would empty the fort of its arsenal of arms. In Morocco the importance of an envoy was assessed first by the dimensions and armament of the vessel which transported him and second by the sum of money allocated to the emissary, which gave a very good idea of the prestige he enjoyed in his own country. Finally, the quality of the gifts he brought gave a discreet indication of the willingness to facilitate negotiations. Parades and noise were merely the expression of an arrogant and impulsive temperament, so the Moroccan authorities decided to treat the French demonstration in the bay that morning with complete indifference. The consulates on the other hand kept a strict count of the number of salutes. Demonstrations of force announced underlying disagreements, bitter negotiations and requests for special privileges. In this game the various nations had no intention of letting themselves be outdistanced.

On the same **Wednesday 25 January**, all the consuls currently in office in Tangier lined up on the shore in order of seniority. Some arrived in the company of their chancellor or secretary, others were flanked by their dragomen. Hidden behind their apparent discretion and the usual diplomatic veneer, was a devouring curiosity to see the man who, since his arrival the previous day, had been filling the air with cannon fire as if hammering on a door.

At about ten o'clock in the morning, two rowing-boats cast off from the corvette. In the first one, with Charles de Mornay, were Antoine Desgranges, Eugène Delacroix, the captain Ange Jouglas and three of *La Perle*'s officers, Jacques Chéruel, Alexandre Mollière and Auguste Soutoul. In the second boat were Léonce Angrand, the French consul in Cádiz, François Ferrary, who was responsible for the mail and Claude Maurignaut and Pierre Boispon, who, along with a few sailors, were to keep watch over the ambas-

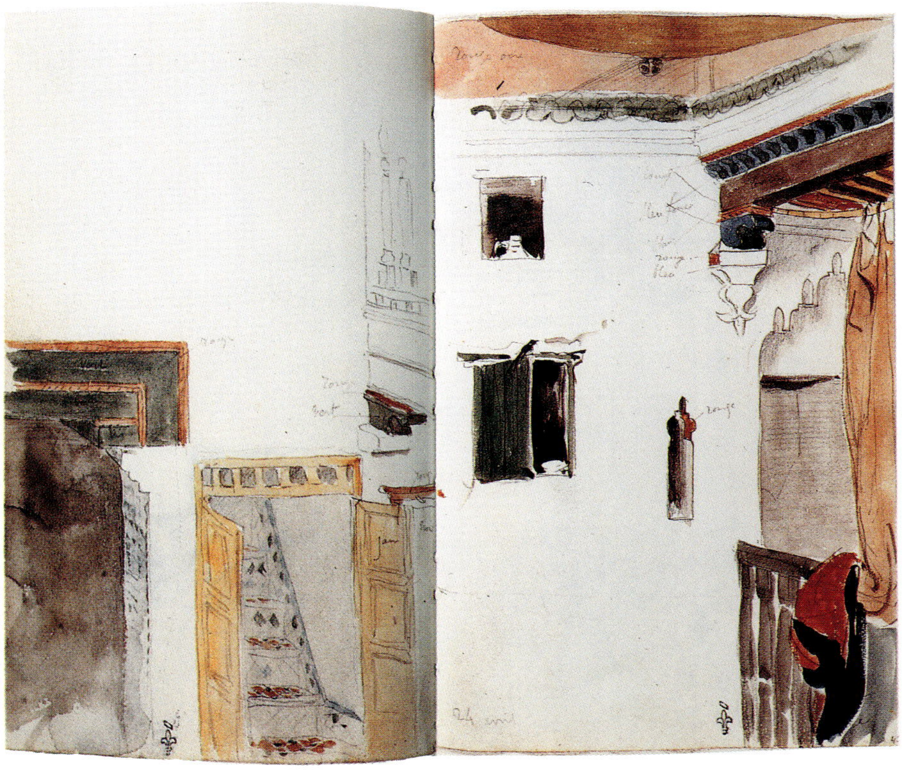

4 - Moroccan Notebook: interior courtyard in Tangier,
pencil and watercolour.
Musée Condé, Chantilly (fol. 48v–49r).

sador's trunks and the gifts for the Moroccan sovereign and important members of his entourage. Delaporte made the introductions while the dragomen busied themselves around the precious luggage trying to guess the contents of the parcels by their size and shape. Their efforts were to no avail, however, and the consuls were only able to make laconic remarks in their reports, summed up by José Rico, the Spanish vice-consul: 'When I know what's in the parcels, I'll let you know.'

Forming a long procession and flanked on both sides by a guard of honour, preceded by a 'military fanfare', the ambassador and his delegation, 'Jouglas and members of his general staff, to make [our] procession look more imposing', the consuls, the customs *amin*, Sidi Ettayeb Biaz, and the town officials in their large white capes, all passed under the porch of the customs office and the Bab el-Mersa to meet Sidi Larabi Saïdi, the Pasha of Tangier, who concluded his message of welcome with the words, 'The Emperor, my master, is a friend of the citizens of France and wishes to remain at peace with them.' His words were addressed to Mornay but were also meant for the ears of the representatives of the other nations who were always interfering with affairs which did not concern them.

After the ceremony, Mornay—still accompanied by his escort of soldiers, military band, consuls and a crowd of inquisitive onlookers—reached the French consulate via several steep, narrow alleyways. It was midday and the elaboration of the text for the official mission document could commence. In the afternoon, the foreign consuls arrived at the French consulate alone, or in groups, and in keeping with an obscure protocol, congratulated Mornay, expressed their hopes for the success of France and left smiling. The English and Swedish consuls concluded their visit with an invitation and a message containing some scathing remarks about diplomats who curried favour with 'the cupidity of the Moroccan court' by offering sumptuous gifts. The remark cut the French emissary to the quick.

Tangier had undeniable charm, each alley was a scene to itself and every doorway the subject for a painting (fig. 4). No coaches or carriages ever congested the hard, dust roads, studded with the occasional cobble-stone. Public lighting was unheard of and the main street a huddle of shacks from which serious-looking Moors in hooded cloaks sold rancid lard. 'I just arrived in Tangier. I have rushed through the town . . . ', Delacroix wrote to his friend Pierret. 'We landed in the midst of the strangest crowd of people. . . . One would need to have twenty arms and forty-eight hours a day to give any tolerable impression of it all.' It is a spontaneous letter, full of joy; he falters between surprise and dream-like wonder in a daze of indescribable happiness.

5 - Moroccan Notebook: studies of Jewish Women,
pencil and watercolour.
Musée Condé, Chantilly (fol. 26v–27r).

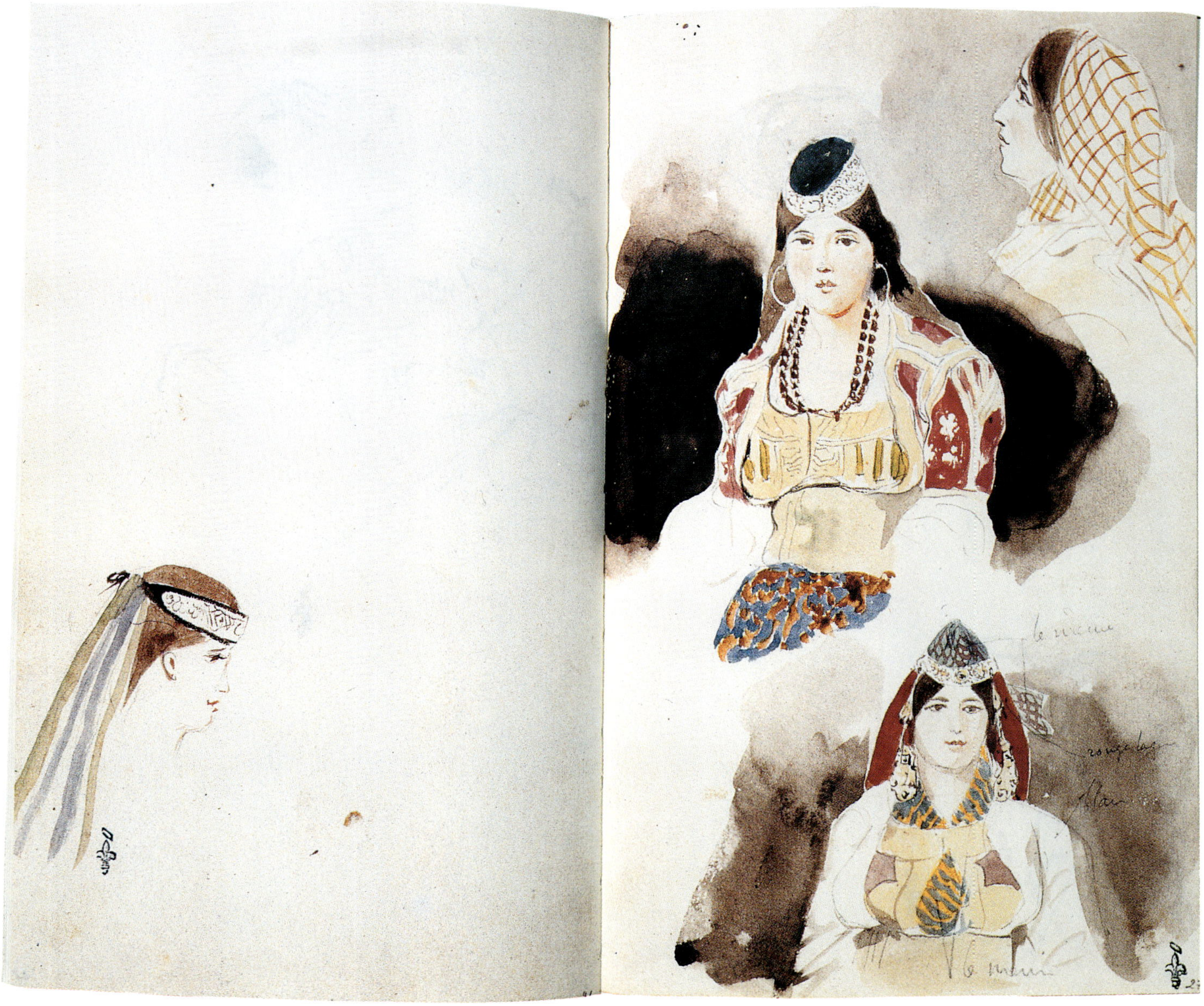

The brilliant receptions, the military music and the Jewesses like 'pearls of Eden' (fig. 5), had no attraction whatsoever for Mornay, in fact what he saw of the local surroundings he found totally depressing. How long was he going to have to stay in this small town, shut away in the consulate which afforded relatively modest comfort, in the midst of a cosmopolitan population who spent their days in petty haggling? He immediately wrote to the ministry: 'My mission being of a specific and temporary nature, I beg to request permission to return to France . . . '. At Mornay's instigation his companions started to sound the alarm. In the circumstances the co-ordination of all the influential parties was essential and letters began arriving from Tangier pleading the cause of the 'poor exiles'.

On **Thursday 26 January** at ten o'clock, Mornay, Jouglas and the officers of *La Perle*, all dressed in their magnificent uniforms, left the French consulate and followed the vice-consul in the direction of the kasbah. The massive fortress which dated from the time of Moulay Ismaël, shortly after the English evacuation of Tangier in 1684, was built on the summit of a hill with a triple view over the Rif mountains, the Rock of Gibraltar and the Spanish coast. The crenellated ramparts enclosed a vast amphitheatre within which the town had gradually spread. The houses were initially built huddled against the walls as a natural protection against old fears, but subsequently construction had become more chaotic and the white cubes began to crop up defiantly on sites overlooking the shore. The fort contained various administrative buildings, Bet el-Mal, the treasury, Dar ech-Cheraa, the lawcourts and Dar el-Maghzen, where on that Thursday morning the Pasha Sidi Larabi Saïdi was waiting to greet his distinguished guests 'with all the honours of which the country was capable'.

Delacroix followed cheerfully. The route to the kasbah took them through a labyrinth of narrow alleyways flanked by storeyed houses. They had constantly to seek refuge in corners or doorways from the groups of mules and donkeys, who scratched the walls with their baskets as they passed. The artist looked up at all the windows for 'some fine Moroccan figures'. He always kept his little green leather sketch-book to hand (fig. 6), ready to capture anything of interest that this town 'born of the earth like Antaeus' had to offer. The Pasha's reception and 'the castle hall. The guardroom in the courtyard. The façade. The alleyway . . . ', all this was promising material.

The *moghaznis*, literally 'pointed bonnet without turban', formed a guard of honour for Mornay and his delegation who, advancing in single file, reached a large patio with 'bad composite capitals' and 'a fountain in the centre'. Several Moroccan notables were assembled in the official reception room around the Pasha, Sidi Larabi Saïdi, to welcome the French visitors (fig. 7). Somewhat apart from the others was Ettayeb Biaz, with his straight beard, bare feet and toes splayed out against a *canoun*. Draped in three large burnouses, one blue over two white, the hood askew over a chalk-coloured

6 - Moroccan Album, first page dated 26 January.
Département des Arts graphiques, Louvre, Paris (RF 39050, fol. 2r).

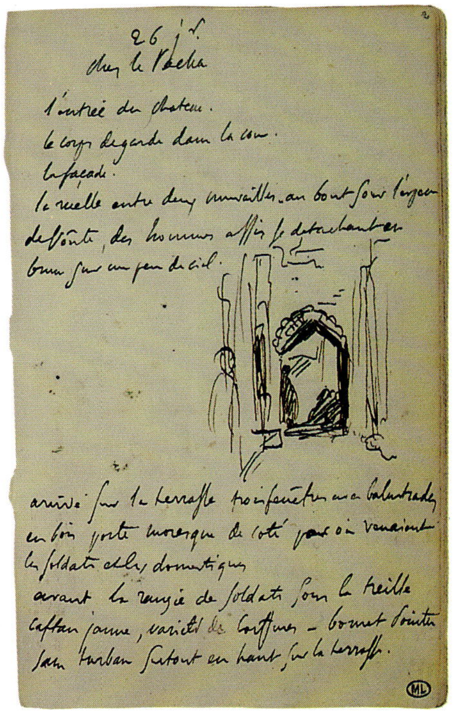

turban from which hung a piece of purple fabric, he quietly scrutinized each new arrival.[5] Biaz, who was the customs *amin*, spoke several languages, held preliminary negotiations with foreign delegations in the name of the emperor, and accompanied to the capital those guests whom the Moroccan monarch wished to honour with an official audience. He was known to be 'very astute' and in describing him to Mornay, Delaporte insisted on his adroitness in the Moroccan court, and added that he was a 'miserly, greedy' man but that France needed his support.

Mulattos served aromatic tea and pastries. Delacroix was granted the privilege of visiting the old palace and of crossing the high-walled garden planted with orange trees. He climbed the steep steps which led to the terrace. From the sentinel's path there was a panoramic view as far as the Spanish coast. Everything was bathed in a soft light which was reflected in the flooded plain below.

Mornay requested a private interview in order to remit a copy of the French grievances to Larabi Saïdi and to fix an early date for his trip to Meknes. The meeting was arranged for the following day, before the midday prayer. 'At your service', the Pasha of Tangier added, with a glint in his eye.

In the afternoon, the French envoy began the courtesy visits that all diplomats were obliged to make to the representatives of the 'Christian nations' present in Morocco. These habits of protocol occupied a prominent place in the city's calendar and had punctuated the lives of the élite for the past century. Delaporte had carefully drawn up the list of visits, the first of which was planned for the British consulate.

Edward William Auriol Drummond-Hay was the most prominent consul in Tangier.[6] His office was the centre of all incoming and outgoing information concerning the country and Moroccan government officials came here to collect salaries or receive orders. The English consul ranked higher than all his colleagues in the Pasha's estimation: the French envoy could not do without such a precious ally. Mornay explained to the Minister, 'The English are alone responsible for practically all the country's internal trade', adding, 'Due to the proximity of Gibraltar, England can survey all our activities. They fear our expansion along the Mediterranean coast. . . . '

The French visitors spent their second Moroccan evening at the British consul's residence. Mornay did not mention their welcome to Edward and Louisa Drummond-Hay but punctuated his conversation with sarcastic remarks about the two-faced nature of British diplomacy.

On **Friday 27 February**, Mornay returned to the kasbah and was glad to see a second French warship, *Le Faucon*, anchored off Tangier. Delacroix was spared a second visit to the fortress: the discussions were confidential. In any case, the diplomatic and military problems scarcely interested the artist, he was not in Morocco to negotiate, but to observe and study, preferably with his sketch-book in hand. This interval gave him a welcome opportunity to

5
Sidi Ettayeb Biaz.
Customs administrator, he was put in charge, by Sultan Moulay al-Rahman, of conducting negociations with foreign delegations. He later became the Governor of Fez but fell into disgrace while in this post. For his portrait, see cat. no. 51.

6
Edward Auriol Drummond-Hay (1785–1845).
Of Scottish origin, he began his career as an officer in the British army, and fought at Waterloo. He assumed his post as British consul general on 25 August 1829, and was to keep it until his death. A man of culture and a fine diplomat, he wrote two essays devoted to the geography of Morocco and Berber grammar. He was succeded by his second son, John, who became British ambassador to Morocco in 1864.

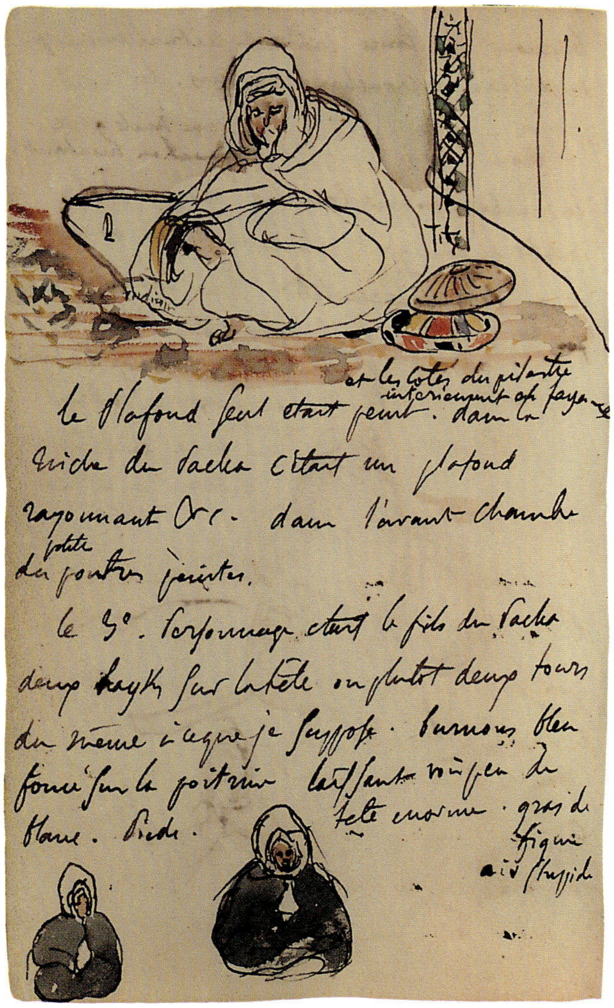

7- Moroccan Album: sketches and notes made during the audience with the Pasha of Tangier,
ink and watercolour.
Département des Arts graphiques, Louvre, Paris (RF 39050, fol. 3v).

familiarize himself with the life here, of which so far he had he had only caught a glimpse.

When Mornay arrived, Ettayeb Biaz and Larabi Saïdi were already waiting for him. He ceremoniously remitted his two-point memorandum to the 'Illustrious and honoured Lords, the Governor and customs administrator'. Desgranges was responsible for translating it. The two Moroccans were at first attentive, but once their initial curiosity had been satisfied, their faces communicated a puzzling range of expressions: seriousness, interrogation, snide looks and stifled laughter gave way to open hilarity. The king's interpreter for oriental languages spoke Arabic, but a rather particular version of the language, the likes of which had never before been heard in the fortress. Desgranges's translations aroused the same open gaiety in the Tangier consular communities where his 'Arabic' was the source of many jokes. A somewhat sardonic, confidential letter, discovered in London, divulges: 'In the course of one of the Count de Mornay's latest visits to the kaid of Tangier, Monsieur Desgranges's 'Arabic' was barely understood by the Moors, and he himself was practically incapable of following the kaid's speech. The Jewish interpreter from

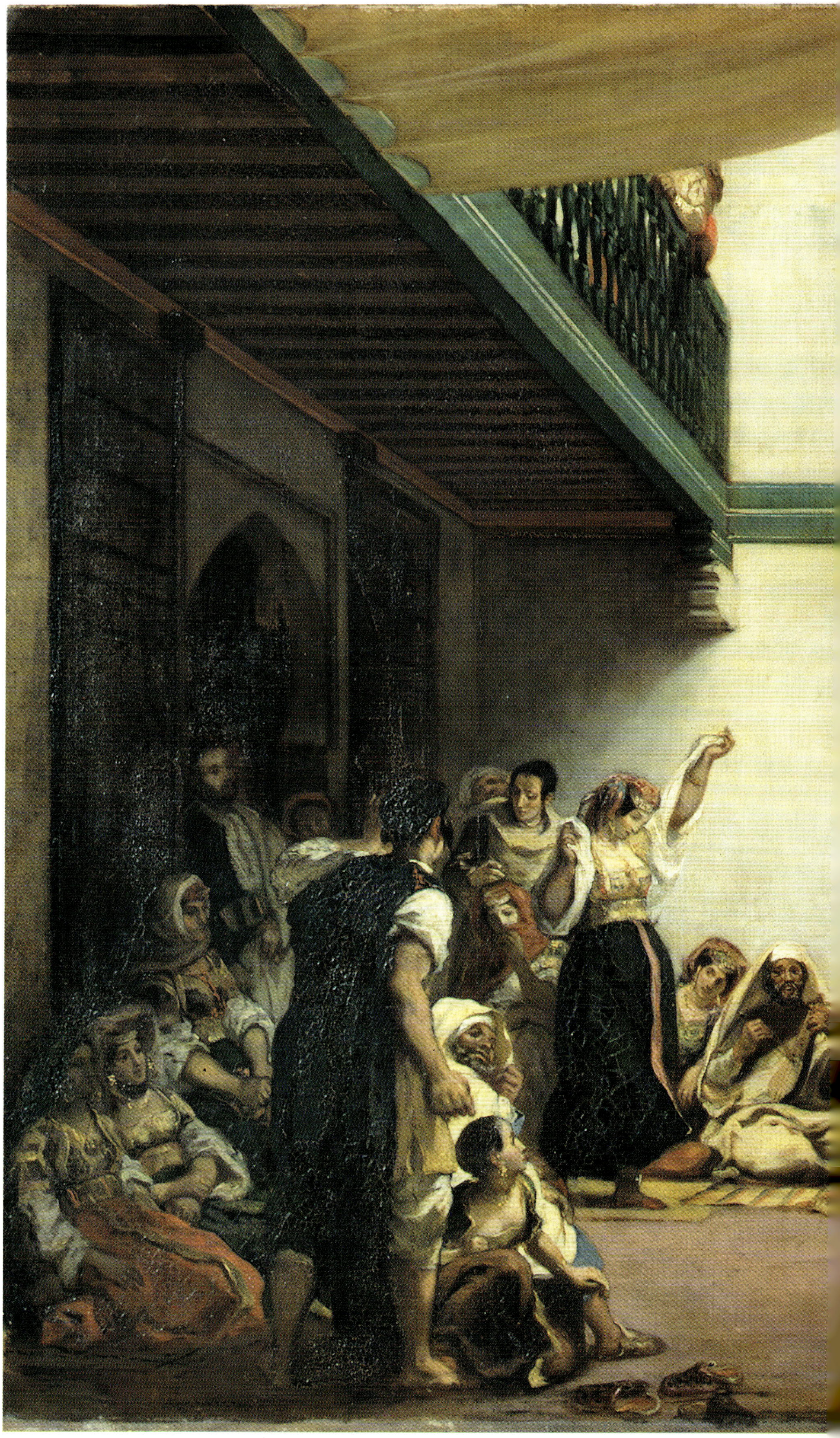

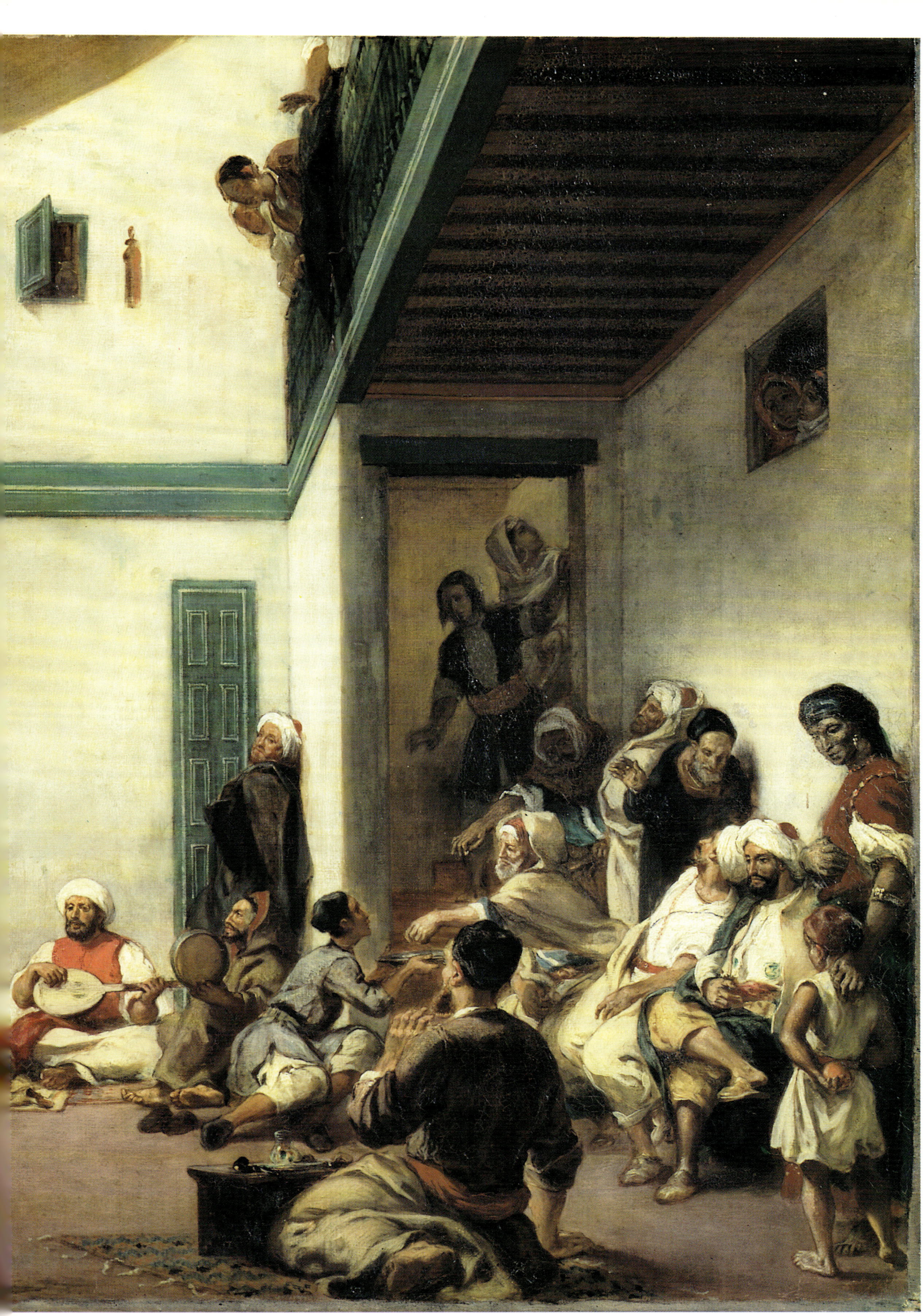

the French consulate had urgently to be sent for.'[7] Confronted with a difficult situation, Mornay nevertheless managed to find a solution. 'The Emperor does not permit a European envoy to speak to him directly and stipulates that a Jew must serve as interpreter, I therefore find myself obliged to bring our Jewish interpreter from the consulate. The presence of Monsieur Desgranges, whose sharpness of mind I admire, will be of great assistace to me.' To Mornay's dismay, Abraham Benchimol was involved in all the negotiations (fig. 8). 'It is normal that I should express to a Prince and an ally all the honours that are due to him, but when one speaks for France, one can not be permitted to adore any person and the Jew will not be in a position to distort what I say.

Like his father Moses before him, Abraham was consulate dragoman, appointed in 1820 after the death of his brother-in-law, Haïm Azencot.[8] The post of interpreter was jealously guarded by families, passed down from father to son, brother to nephew and from cousin to uncle.[9] The post was generally honorary, but it brought prestige and standing to the person that occupied it. Furthermore, the dragomen were placed in an advantageous position to trade with the countries they assisted. They were in charge of purchases, often acted as money-lenders, found the necessary credits for the running of the consulate and saw to it that mules, horses and servants were provided. A close network linked them to the various capitals. The information they gave concerning neighbouring legations and the customs of their tenants provided anecdotes for the news with which the consuls peppered their reports. 'In this country where every consul is obliged to use the services of a Jew for interpreter, the affairs of all the governments are generally common knowledge', affirmed Mornay. Benchimol, this affable, tactful dragoman, though held in high esteem by the Moroccan authorities, always seemed to be in Mornay's way. The French envoy constantly complained about this replacement for 'a secretary/translator of the king', never missing an occasion to snub him or to subject him to his changeable moods. It was only at the end of the voyage that he recognized, 'I have nothing but praise for the zeal of poor Abraham, whom I regularly inconvenienced, often unjustly.'

The dragoman had also been France's creditor for more than four years, despite his repeated requests for reimbursement. The debt amounted to 8,684 Spanish piastres, not taking into account the two and a half point loan rate in Tangier.

Delacroix's attitude was spontaneously quite different to Mornay's. His encounter with the Moroccan Jews was a revelation. He had no preconceived ideas when he first came into contact with them and his journal testifies to this openness of mind. Indifferent to the preoccupations which tormented Mornay, Delacroix enjoyed observing this community. There are hundreds of notes in his writings about his attentive hosts whose lives 'were marked by social events and gestures derived from the most ancient customs . . . . Having

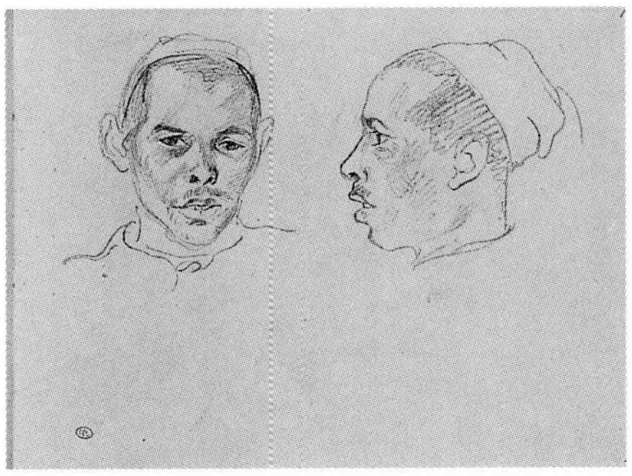

8 - Album: portrait of Abraham Benchimol,
pencil.
Département des Arts graphiques, Louvre, Paris (RF 9154, fol. 14r).

9 - Jewish Wedding,
oil on canvas,
1837/41,
1.05 x 1.40 m.
Louvre, Paris.

7
Antoine Jérôme Desgranges (1784–1864). *The King's secretary interpreter for Oriental languages, he was praised by the Ministry of Foreign Affairs for the satisfactory fulfilment of several missions . . . Bassora (1808), Constantinople (1811 and 1816), Tunis (1824) . . . Unable to understand or translate what the Moroccan authorities said, he was the laughing-stock of consulate circles in Tangier during the Count de Mornay's mission. Delacroix did not paint his portrait.*

8
Abraham Benchimol. *From an important Jewish Moroccan family, Benchimol became dragoman to the French consulate in 1820, following his brother's death from the plague, which he caught while assisting a French ship in quarantine. Working in partnership with the Portugese consul in the running of a tannery, he obtained the monopoly on exporting leather to Marseille. He was Delacroix's host and valuable guide during the artist's stay in Morocco. Before the bombardment of Tangier by a French squadron in 1844, he refused an offer from the Duke de Joinville to take refuge on his ship, and left his post as dragoman. Moulay Abd al-Rahman later nominated him customs* amin. *His nephew, David Azencot, succeeded him as dragoman to the consulate of France.*

come to Morocco at his own expense, the artist found open house in the dragoman's circle of family and friends (fig. 12). He established his quarters at Abraham's house or those of his brothers Jacob, Isaac, David and Haïm, and with their sister Guimol Azencot, mother of David, the auxiliary dragoman. He painted the portraits of Leditia, Abraham's niece, and drew his wife Saada, along with Preciada and Rachel, his daughters. He found several obliging models inside these Jewish homes, but it was in the privacy of the consulate, with the complicity of Madame Delaporte, that he was able to paint timid young Muslim girls whom she had found to pose for him.

Was Benchimol his guide or his host on Tuesday February 21, at one of the celebrations held over a period of seven days that mark every Jewish wedding in Morocco? (fig. 9). Delacroix discovered two ancient civilisations, whose daily alliance seemed bitter but was immersed in a tolerant, biblical coexistence. Entranced, he tried not to forget anything and feverishly accumulated notes and sketches. Morocco mixed ordinary daily work and events with powerful local scenes and customs, which were explained to him by Abraham.

When no outside reception was scheduled, the members of the embassy took up their quarters in the consulate. After dinner, Delacroix often worked on the day's harvest of sketches and drawings, adding luminous touches of watercolour. Then the interrogation session began. The artist wanted to know everything about the life and customs of the country. He carefully noted down the answers in his notebook, and repeated after Delaporte or the dragoman the Arabic names for the objects around him. Not far from the garden of the British consulate, the followers of Sidi Aïssa had set up camp. Once a year during *Aïd el-Kebir*, they gathered around the mausoleum of the blessed one at Meknes. In the town the artist had seen several members of the brotherhood whose mysterious practices, songs, dances and contortions led some of them into trances or convulsions (fig. 11). The descriptions given by the vice-consul and the meeting in Tangier with some members of the sect sufficiently fired Delacroix's imagination to induce him, once back in Paris, to transpose the ecstatic Aïssaoua onto canvas on two occasions (figs 10 and 13).

9

Dragomen working in Tangier in 1832:
Austria and Denmark: Isaac Sicsu; Spain: Salomon de Judah Aboudarham; United States: Isaac Moses Parienté; France: Abraham Benchimol; Great Britain: Isaac Abensour; Holland: Abraham Bendellac; Sardinia: David Hassan; Sweden: Jacob Ben Selloum

The renowned Moroccan hospitality lived up to its reputation. Two dinners were given in the kasbah in honour of the French emissary and his delegation. The Pasha wanted to reassure Mornay about his visit to Meknes. He was assured that 'no other envoy from any nation had received as many honours as himself. . . . I [therefore] agreed to make my preparations. . . . ' A letter was sent to Meknes announcing his arrival. The wait would only be for a few days, the time it would take for the royal authorization to reach them. It finally arrived forty-two days later.

On the evening of **Friday 3 February**, the fortress cannons tore the air with a terrific blast which echoed in the mountains and died away at sea. The heavy silence that followed was short-lived and soon gave way to chants coming from the mosques. An enormous din filled the town: drums, trumpets

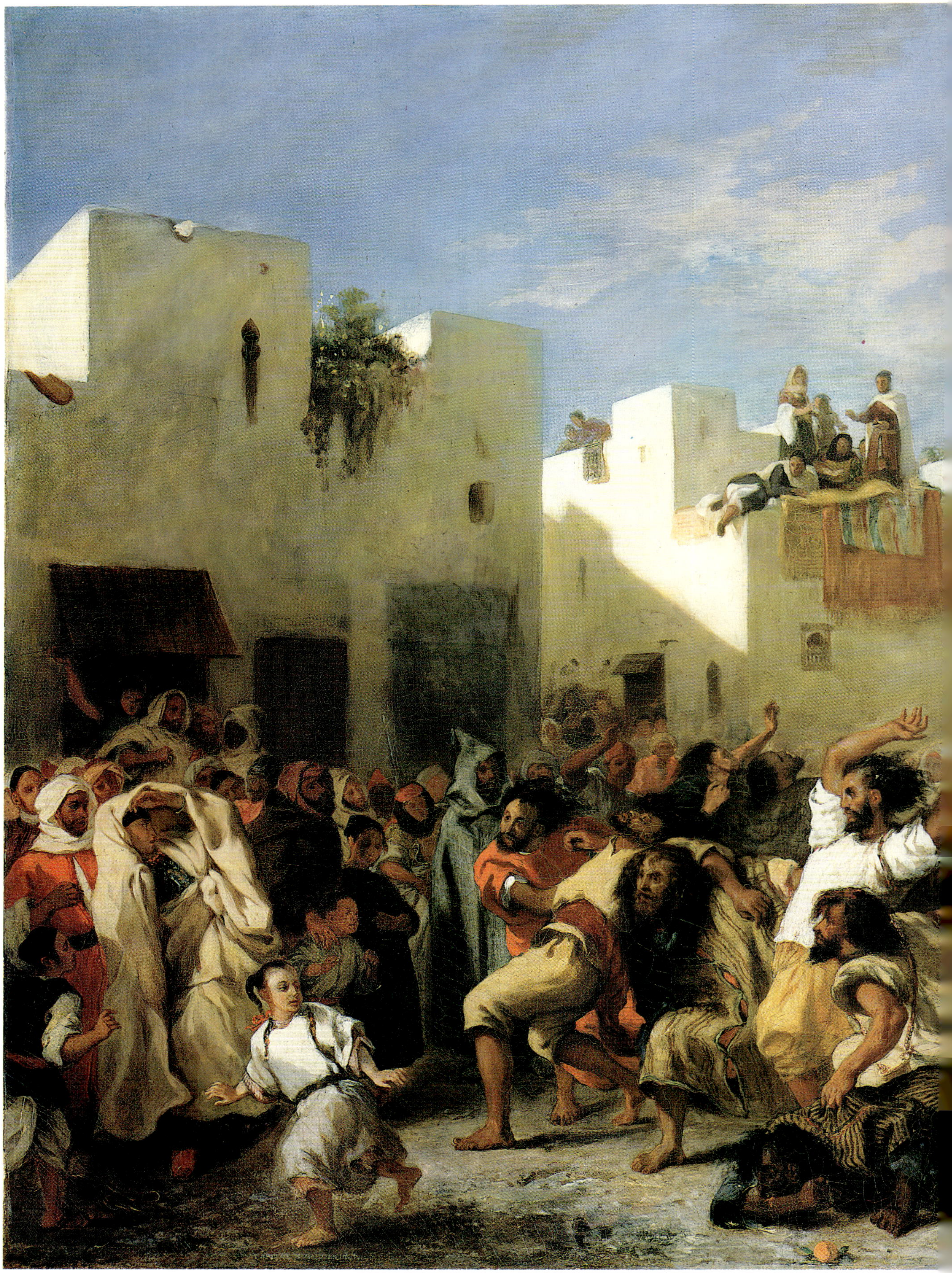

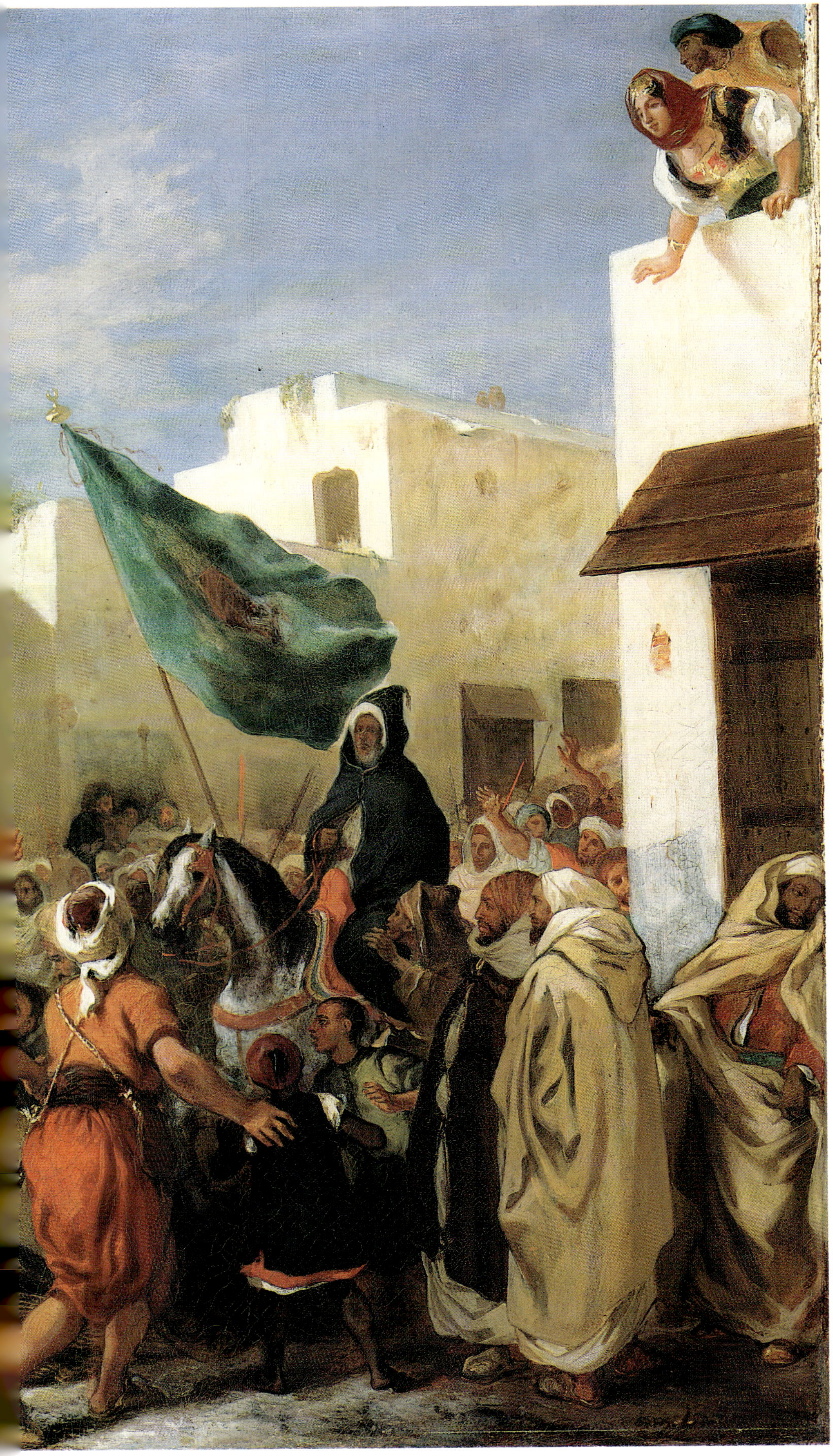

10 - The Aïssaouas,
1838,
oil on canvas,
0.97 x 1.31 m.
The Minneapolis Institute of Arts.
Bequest of J. Jerome Hill.

and rifle shots announced the start of Ramadan to the faithful. A month of fasting and prayer had begun for Moulay Abd al-Rahman. It was impossible for the head of the Moroccan court and the country's spiritual leader to receive the visit of a Christian ambassador during this sacred period. The pause, however, could well prove propitious in calming certain tribes' recriminations against the French and give weight to the demands of the French king. Diplomacy could be suspended for a while.

The authorization had still not arrived. 'I have not yet received a reply to the letter that I dispatched to the Emperor to request audience. They are holding it in Meknes until the departure of the escort who will accompany me. I still do not know the date of my departure. . . .

After the first few weeks in Tangier, however, Mornay started to relax a little. He was treated with great consideration as regards his person and his rank, which he swore did not impress him, and he appeared to condemn in all his letters the 'so-called honours' that the Moroccans paid him. He accepted the invitations of 'the honourable consuls' and in return he organized a reception in their honour in the French consulate.[10] On Sunday 12 February, Delaporte and his wife, *née* Ange Régini, acted as hosts. The French consulate was by no means used to opening its doors for protocol dinners. The budget did not provide for such expenses and since the death of the consul Édouard Sour-

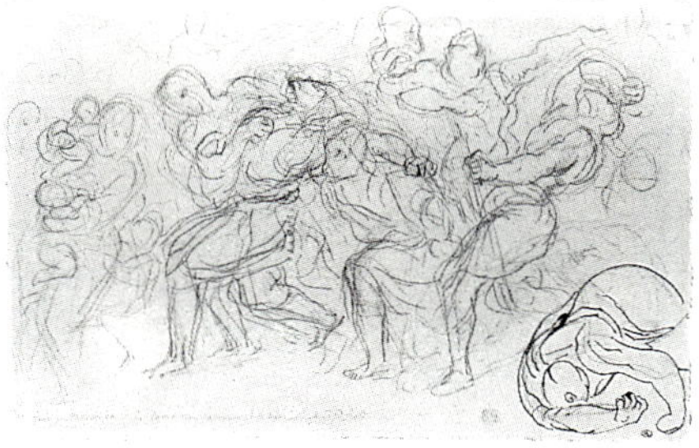

11 - Page of studies for *The Fanatics of Tangier,*
pencil,
23.5 x 36.8 cm.
Département des Arts graphiques, Louvre, Paris.

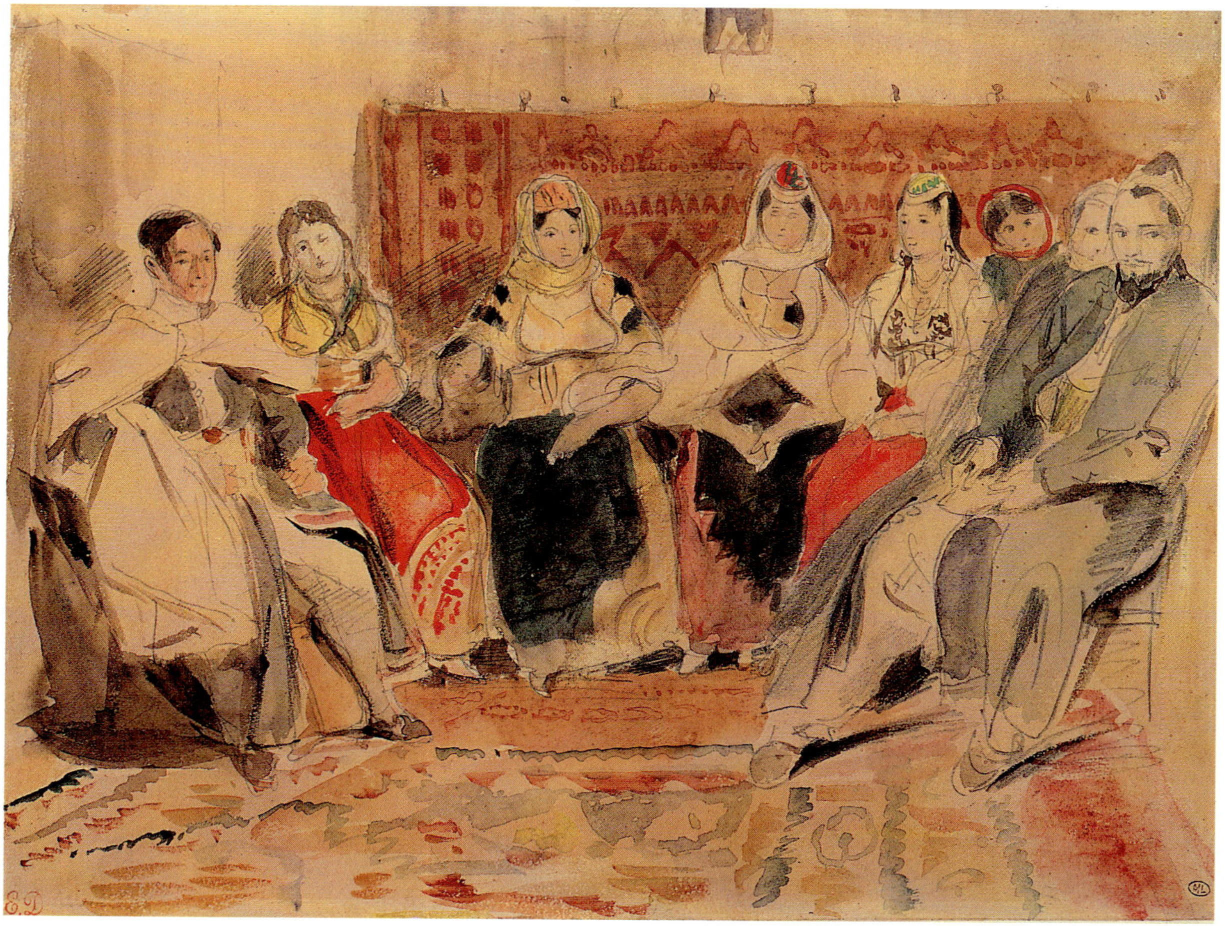

12 - A Man and Woman in an interior (the Bouzaglo home)
pencil and watercolour,
23.7 x 31.8 cm.
Département des Arts graphiques, Louvre, Paris.

deau, funds had been meagre. Mornay decided to include the reception in the mission's budget. He did not yet know under which item he would post the expense, but the account covering gifts for Moroccan dignitaries could, if necessary, be increased without risk. All the ambassadors were obliged to adopt this tactic in the face of administrations who refused to acknowledge the everyday realities of consular activities. Benchimol was in charge of the food. Everything had to be perfect so that 'His Excellency' would recognize the dragoman's efficiency and arrange for the reimbursement of his 8,684 piastres. That evening José Rico sang Spanish songs. As for Delacroix, he was unwell.

When the weather was favourable, Mornay left the French residence and joined Delacroix in the garden of the Swedish consulate. In this privileged spot of about two acres there were orange and lemon trees, enormous aloes, flowering almond trees, Persian lilacs which had grown into tall trees, *Egyptiaca* irises—a variety of cacti, flowers and plants and many new perfumes (fig. 14). The palm trees were over a hundred years old.

By now, Delacroix was familiar with the streets of Tangier. Every day he followed Benchimol or his nephew David, the assistant dragoman, to breathe in the odour of garlic and orange blossom, of kif smoke and burned aloes that hung in the narrow, twisting alleyways. These cobble-stoned alleys, damp

10

Diplomatic Corps in Tangier in 1832: *Austria: Peter Kofoed-Anker Schousboë, general agent († 25.02.1832); Denmark: Marc-Paul Marcussen, assistant general agent; Spain: Antonio Beramendi, consul general, José Rico, assistant consul general; United States: Samuel Carr, consul; France: Jacques Denis Delaporte, assistant consul; Great Britain: Edward Drummond-Hay, consul general, John Bell, assistant consul general; Holland: Jean Freyssinet, consul general; Portugal: José Colaço, consul; Sardinia: Baron Georgio Ermirio, consul general; Sweden: Baron Julios Lagerheim, temporary consul, in the absence of Johan Mathias Ehrenhoff, from May 1831 to October 1832, Frederik Crusentolpe, chancellor.*

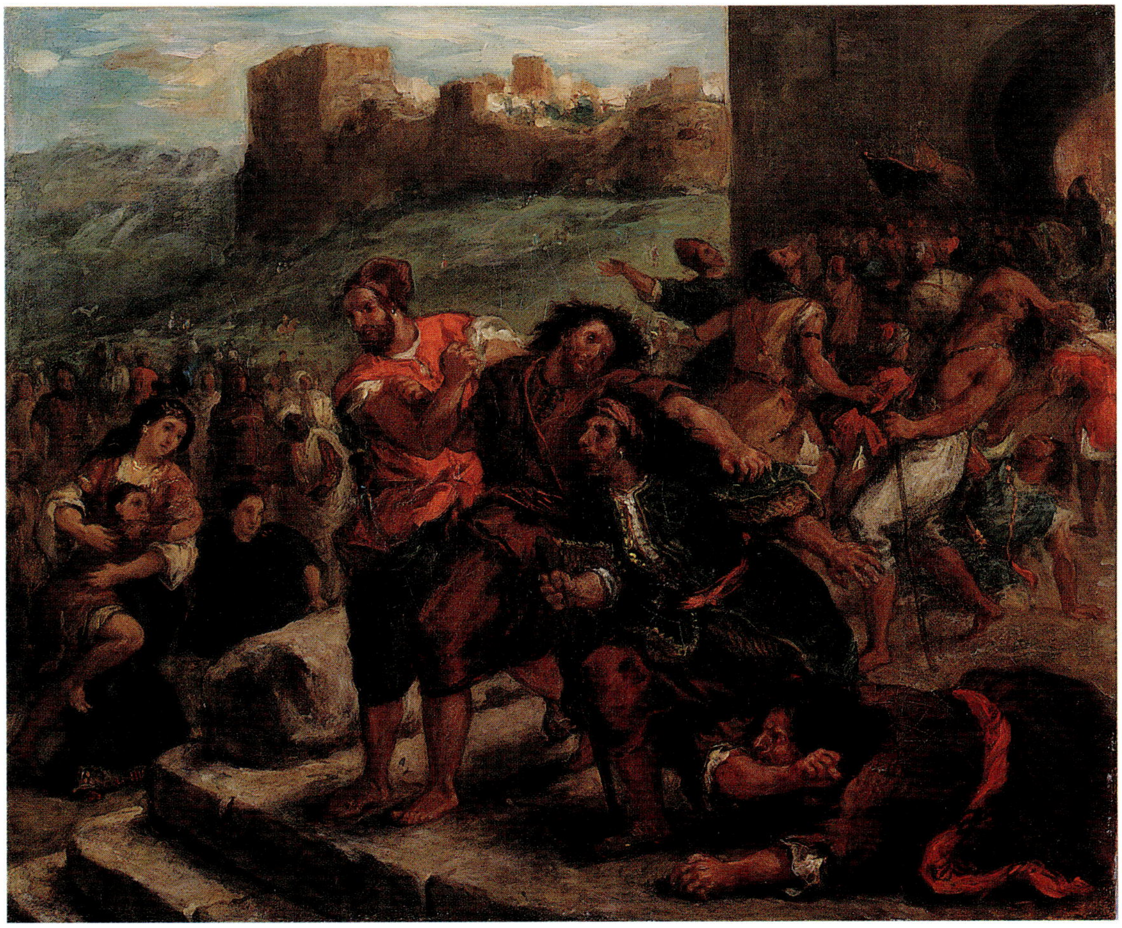

13 - The Fanatics of Tangier,
1857,
oil on canvas,
47 x 59 cm.
Musée des Beaux-Arts, Ontario, Toronto, purchased in 1962.

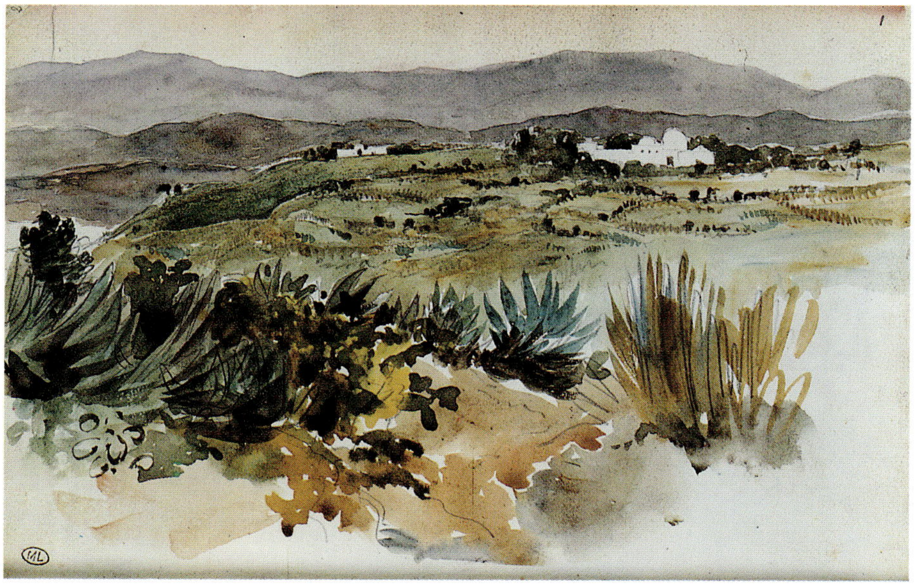

14 - North African and Spanish Album: landscape outside Tangier,
pencil and watercolour.
Département des Arts graphiques, Louvre, Paris (RF 1712 bis, fol. 2r).

and slippery at this time of the year, led to the large market-place, the Socco. He mixed with the local population all wearing hooded cloaks, who walked slowly, jostled only by the enormous loads transported by the donkeys and mules. He was concerned, however, that he might not remember everything he saw, these 'fine Moroccan figures', whose expressions he wanted to capture (fig. 15). Would his notes and drawings have any value on his return to France? 'Away from the land where I discovered them, such particulars will be like trees torn from their native soil', he wrote to his friend Pierret. His presence in the middle of the crowd in the Socco did not seem to impress the passers-by, nor the merchants squatting in their minute shops. Only the sketch-book in which the artist scribbled intrigued the merchants, provoking reproving looks from behind the skilful folds of their haiks. In troubled times, countries invent bad omens and the worried population see spies everywhere. What mysterious signs was the foreigner marking in his sketch-book? Benchimol, aware of the religious prohibitions, the demands of their traditions and the inflexible opposition of these people to the reproduction of an image, warned Delacroix not to draw there. 'They have prejudices against the noble art of painting' sighed the artist.

Mornay and Delacroix shared a passion for horses with the English consul Drummond-Hay, who, as a challenge, used to mount the most difficult thoroughbreds. In a letter to Pierret, Delacroix writes 'I don't think I have written to you since an excursion we made in the neighbourhood of the town with the English consul, who has a mania for riding the most unmanageable horses in the country, and that's saying something, for the gentlest are all absolute devils.' He used to take the painter and the diplomat, who were not averse to these exhilarating outings, on long rides along the beaches and in the mountains. 'They give me infinite pleasure' admitted Delacroix. Drummond-Hay had discovered several magnificent viewpoints in the countryside around

Tangier 'Superb landscapes . . . mountains [of an] extremely mellow hue, dark blue-green sea . . . yellow hedges . . . '.

Sometimes the three men stopped for a while near the Roman bridge whose submerged supports and crumbling arch made it look like it was on the verge of collapse. Then, following the ochre-coloured ramparts at a gentle trot, they regained the town and the British consulate. Sometimes the artist returned there in the afternoons, this time with Benchimol, perched on his mule, as his companion. The artist would take a little wooden board and a sheet paper out of his haversack, give his pencil free rein, then after adding a few touches of watercolour and brown wash, show the finished work to the dragoman. Abraham, dumbfounded, would look from the watercolour to the landscape and puzzle over the missing details; the consulate interpreter had a sharp eye, but his vision was not used to this sort of image.

Meanwhile, Mornay was still waiting for news: 'I am doing everything within my power to obtain an official order from the Pasha . . . I still don't know the date of my departure . . . '.

On the Moroccan side there was confusion. One party advocated the occupation of Tlemcen and its frontier regions, while another, in the name of

15 - View of Tangier,
oil on canvas,
46 x 50 cm.
The Minneapolis Institute of Arts, gift of Georgiana Slade Reny.

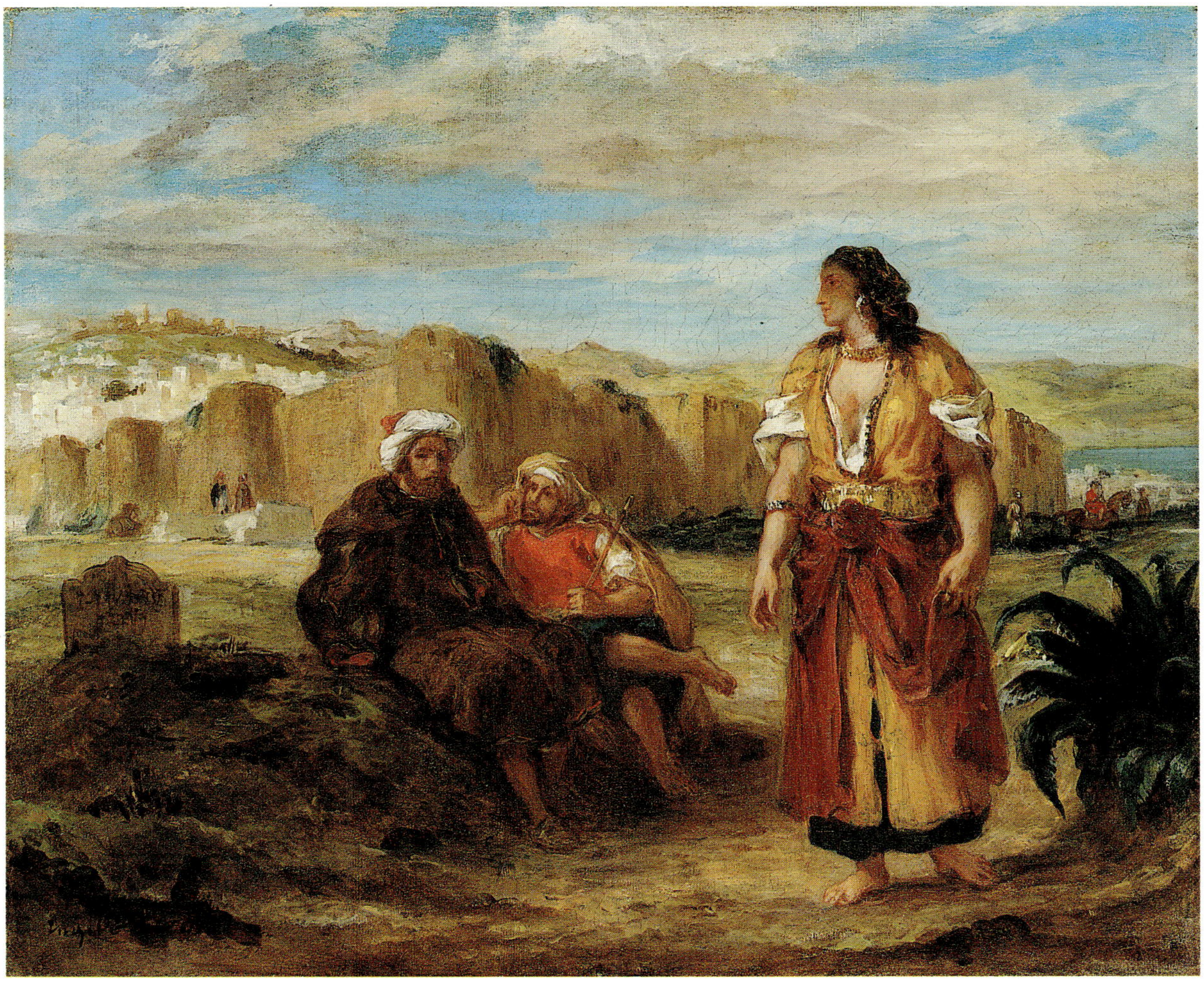

Islam, wanted to offer discreet but efficient support to the Algerian leaders, while at the same time currying favour with the French. The same differences of opinion existed among the monarch's advisers.

This turmoil left Delacroix indifferent and Mornay's political preoccupations soon bored him. In their circle there was too much talk of cannons, cavalry and infantry and, above all, money, which was at the centre of all conversations. The knowledge that the Algerian delegation had arrived with eighty thousand francs in cash as a gift for the Moroccan monarch, had driven the French envoy into a frenzy. He in contrast disposed of only thirty thousand francs, for an assignment that was dragging on indefinitely. He was in charge of six people who had unavoidably been joined by hangers-on. Could he really refuse a place at his table to Delacroix, who was supposed to pay his own expenses, or there again to Delaporte, whose house was always open to him? The consuls had made enquiries through various channels about the amount of money at the disposal of the French embassy. They knew the figure, although the Swedish were somewhat unsure about the currency it was in, 'dollars or French dollars', but on 28 May 1832, Julius Lagerheim finally transmitted the vital clarification to Stockholm . . . the 'dollars' were in fact only French francs.

Turmoil was also provoked by the gifts Mornay had brought. The prestige of an ambassador was judged by the quantity of gifts, that of a foreign monarch by their value. The secret was not divulged until the official audience took place, both to excite the curiosity of the consuls and to awaken the interest of the emperor. There was nothing on the subject in the French documents from the period but in the various consular chronicles, many lines were devoted to the question—the consuls considered these gifts to be the key to the success of all negotiations. What could the French envoy's trunks possibly conceal to warrant such a haughty attitude? In their reports the consuls all used the British consul general's laconic phrase: 'A gift of considerable value, according to rumour, has been brought by the Count of Mornay for the Sultan.' After examining all the information, the Spanish vice-consul addressed a triumphant message, on 29 May, to Madrid: 'According to the latest news, the gifts, valued at four thousand duros, consist of a silver coffee service, brocades, velvets, material from Damascus, Holland and Ireland and loincloths or sheets'. There was nothing exceptional in this list, nothing that could justify the secrecy that the French had maintained since their arrival.

Delacroix had unconsciously detached himself from the course of events to devote himself solely to the pleasures of discovery and creation. He did not share the opinions held by his fellow-travellers and the other consuls. Observation had taught him humility in his assertions and a respect for different customs. What was the point of all these peremptory tirades? Of the mocking terms employed by the French envoy when communicating with the authorities in Paris, which spared neither 'emperors, ministers, dignitaries nor soldiers' . . . ?

He personally found the daily life in Tangier very pleasant. What he saw exalted his spirits but at the same time fed his anxiety: 'Anything I may accomplish will be insignifiant in comparison with what might be done here. Sometimes I feel quite baffled . . . ' (fig.16). In the Tangier of 1832, setting up an easel in the midst of the bustling Moroccans was no easy matter. The artist followed Benchimol, and would position himself in a doorway or follow the paths leading up to the terraces. From there he could see over the town to the vast horizons of the countryside surrounding Tangier. The Moroccan terraces, dazzling white jewel-cases, formed a town apart, the private reserve of women. He watched the Moroccan women, always veiled when he crossed them in the street, here moving freely in their haiks. They hung out washing, relaxed on sofas and carpets, carried on with their secret lives: '. . . ready-made paintings . . . '. Whenever Delacroix did not have the time or the possibility to sketch a scene, he described it in frenzied notes. Brief, scribbled words followed the succession of images, the most insignificant of which seemed nonetheless spectacular. The cosmopolitan city of Tangier was an ever-changing spectacle of animation and colour. Pupils leaving a Koranic school, 'a procession with a band (drums and oboes) . . . A young boy . . . surrounded by singing schoolfellows and his parents and teachers', adults performing their ablutions before entering the mosque for prayers, or even the merchants in their little shops: each scene was a painting that the artist yearned to leave for posterity.

In the meantime Mornay redoubled his cutting remarks about 'the habits, prejudices and character of the Moors'. The tedious delay before his departure was punctuated by his criticisms which were aimed at exonerating him from an eventual failure in the negotiations: 'In this country of ignorance, barbary and conceit, it is very difficult to find any real truth. . . . All the decisions we reach with the Moroccan government subsequently become the subject of interminable negotiations . . . '. These sort of remarks were endless. Delacroix on the contrary saw there 'a unique race' which differed 'from other Mahometan peoples . . . [their] ancient and simple customs take on a certain majesty that, in very grave circumstances, does not exist in our country. . . . In these southern countries life is synonymous with the love of air and light'. . . . 'How peacefully men live here . . . how little they are concerned about the vanities that fret our minds! Fame, here, is a meaningless world . . . nothing suggests that this is not the most desirable state in the world. Beauty lies everywhere about one . . . '.

He was distressed, however, by the lack of letters from his friends. Everything had been arranged for correspondence to transit by the diplomatic pouch, but the department concerned was not in agreement. A threatening letter was received by Delaporte mentioning 'the excessive use of the diplomatic services of the Ministry of Foreign Affairs for private correspondence'. The vice-consul took this note as a personal attack and he retaliated, ironically,

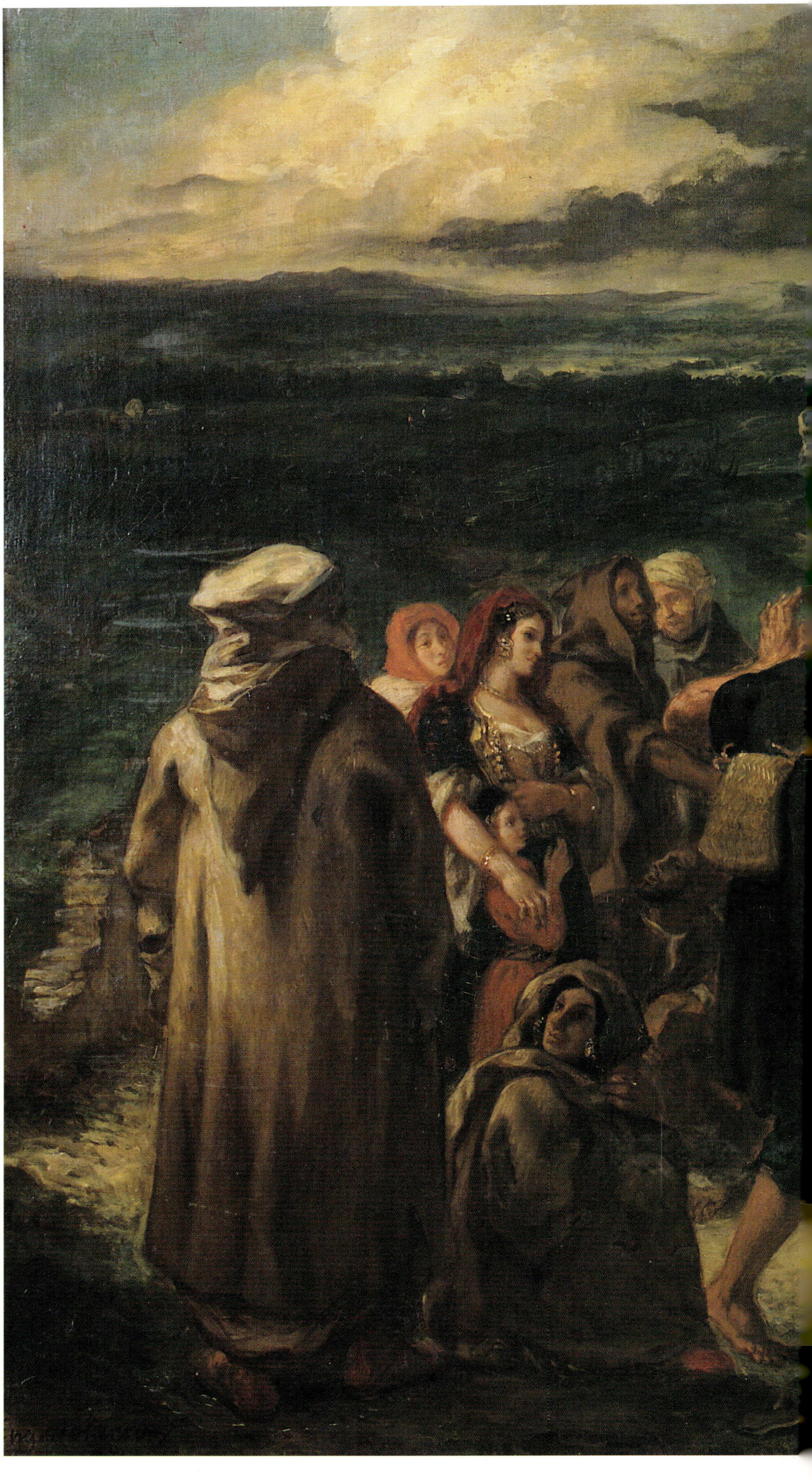

16 - Arab Players,
1848,
oil on canvas,
0.96 x 1.30 m.
Musée des Beaux-Arts, Tours.

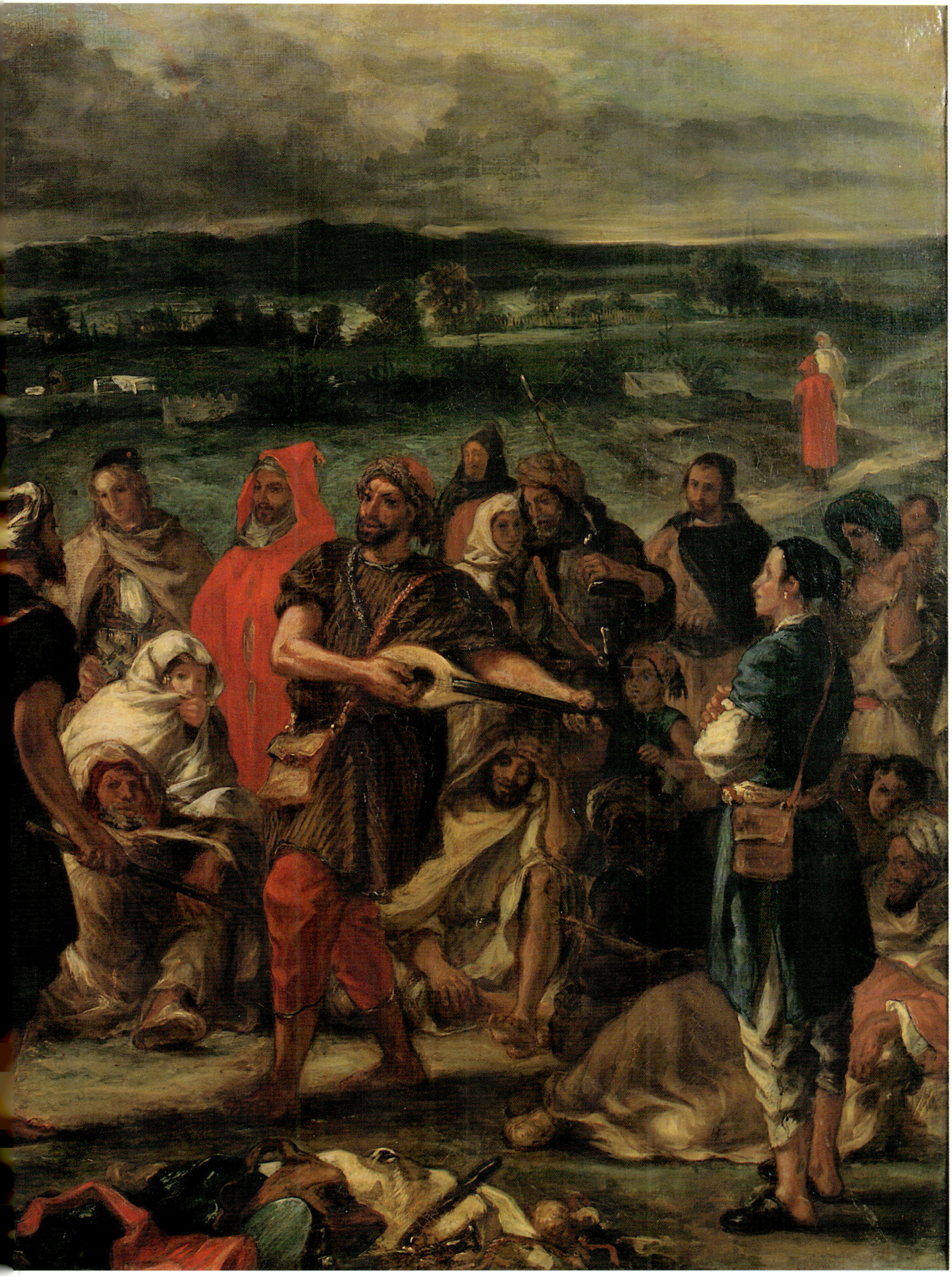

'Despite the circular . . . which forbids consuls to send private mail to France under cover of the Ministry of Foreign Affairs, I thought it in my power to take the liberty of putting my harmless correspondence under your protection . . . Your Excellency will please excuse me if I know of no other means of communication between Meknes and Paris.'

On **Saturday 3 March**, the royal authorization finally arrived. Mornay was at last going to leave Tangier and the restrictive circle of the European consulates to visit Morocco and the Moroccans. What did he know of this country apart from interviews with the Pasha of Tangier and the customs administrator, meetings with individuals who crossed his path and whose names he had not even retained, two receptions in the kasbah and a few exotic and aromatic meals? The French envoy hoped to close the negotiations as soon as possible and then request his return to Paris. An eleven-day journey to Meknes, covering forty-five leagues, was going to be a laborious enterprise. Knowing the protocol that traditionally accompanied such expeditions, Mornay did his utmost to ensure that the display was in keeping with his means. 'These so-called honours always being very costly . . . I requested, but to no avail, that they be reduced by half. . . '.

Delacroix awaited their departure with enthusiasm. He had observed the day-to-day life of the Muslims in Tangier and the movements of the crowd which swept up the onlookers and passers-by in the momentum of its colourful swell. He had seen weddings, street musicians, he had waited for the children to come out of the Koranic school, gravely sheltering from the rain under their parchment manuscripts . . . He had seen men working in the towns, in the fields, quarrelling or trading, or performing their ablutions before prayer . . . A simple life in fact, but from which he had only been able to pluck isolated moments. He was at last going to live whole days in their company. Sketching a female Muslim was quite impossible without the help of the vice-consul's wife. He had attempted to sketch one, unobserved, while she bathed in the river, but the episode had ended in a 'headlong flight' from the fury and the rifle of the jealous husband (see p.180). The real work had not yet started, it remained for him to portray 'the living and striking sublimity that lies all about one here . . . '.

On **Monday 5 March**, an indescribable din filled the consulate courtyard. In the balmy atmosphere, pervaded by the perfume of orange blossom and the odour of horse manure, there was nothing but the whinnying of horses, and the shouting of orders in a cacophony of Arab, French and Spanish accents. The departure for Meknes was imminent. From daybreak they had been loading trunks and baskets onto forty mules 'on loan from the Emperor' and led by mule-drivers from Tetuan (see cat. nos. 65 and 66). After much deliberation, Mornay decided to travel to the Emperor's palace on a mule (fig. 17), Delaporte's mule. The vice-consul could hardly refuse the loan of his mount, even though it was his only possession. On the occasion of the official

The route followed by the delegation led by Count de Mornay.

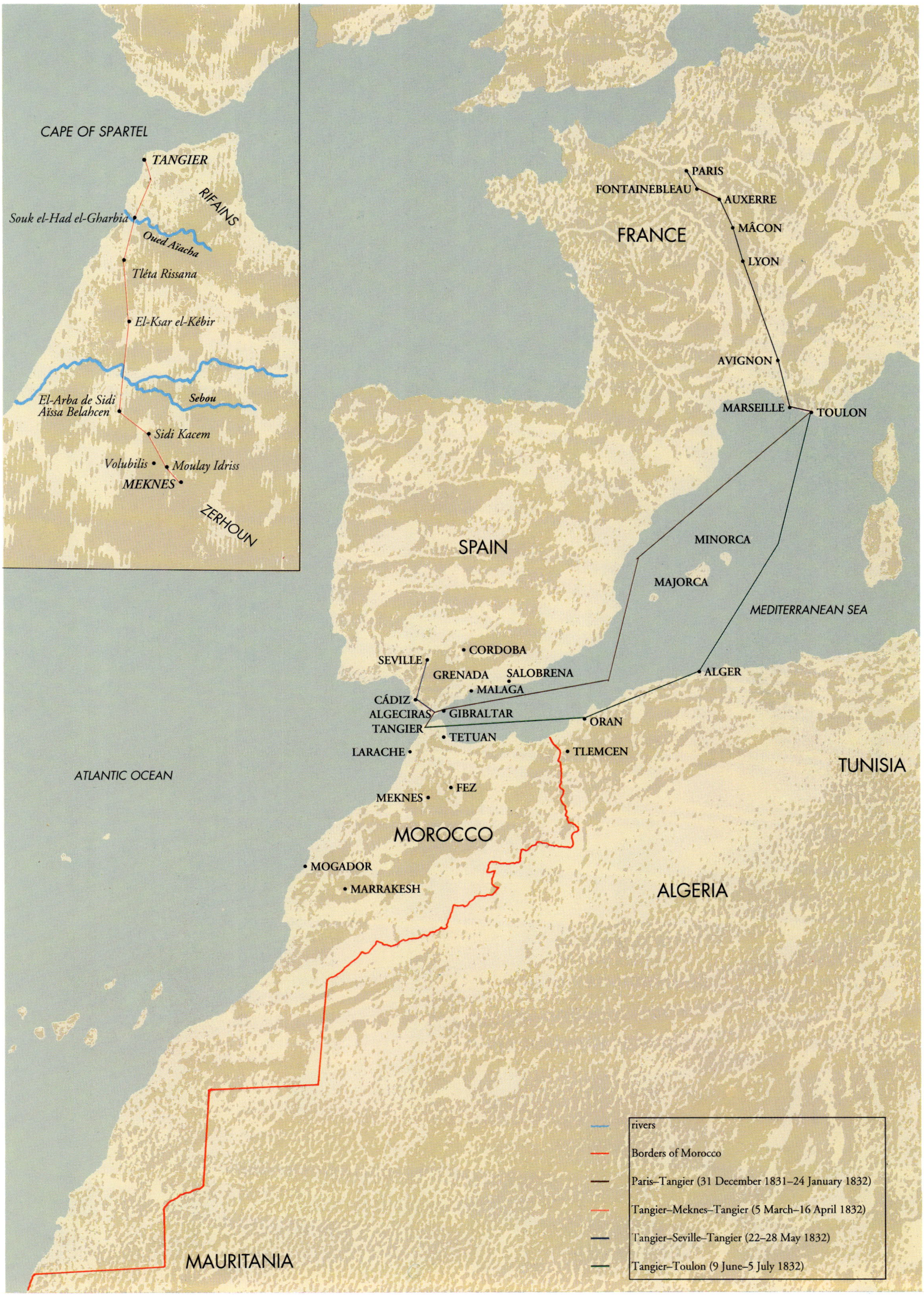
CAPE OF SPARTEL
TANGIER
RIFAINS
Souk el-Had el-Gharbia
Oued Aïacha
Tléta Rissana
El-Ksar el-Kébir
Sebou
El-Arba de Sidi
Aïssa Belahcen
Sidi Kacem
Volubilis
Moulay Idriss
MEKNES
ZERHOUN
PARIS
FONTAINEBLEAU
AUXERRE
FRANCE
MÂCON
LYON
AVIGNON
MARSEILLE
TOULON
SPAIN
MINORCA
MAJORCA
MEDITERRANEAN SEA
CORDOBA
SEVILLE
GRENADA
SALOBRENA
MALAGA
CÁDIZ
ALGECIRAS
GIBRALTAR
TANGIER
ALGER
ORAN
TETUAN
LARACHE
TLEMCEN
ATLANTIC OCEAN
TUNISIA
FEZ
MEKNES
MOROCCO
MOGADOR
MARRAKESH
ALGERIA
MAURITANIA
rivers
Borders of Morocco
Paris–Tangier (31 December 1831–24 January 1832)
Tangier–Meknes–Tangier (5 March–16 April 1832)
Tangier–Seville–Tangier (22–28 May 1832)
Tangier–Toulon (9 June–5 July 1832)

handing over, as is the custom, of the register containing the agreements, treaties and all copies of the official correspondence between France and the Moroccan Court, the vice-consul timidly recommended that Mornay take good care of the beast. The assembly point for the departure was at the Socco el-Bara. The vast square with its scant covering of grass and occasional dwarf palm trees opened out onto Bab Fas. It was here that the traditional *moussems* took place, agricultural fairs, and where escorts for departing caravans assembled.

Draped in wide, blue capes, one hundred and twenty horsemen, under the

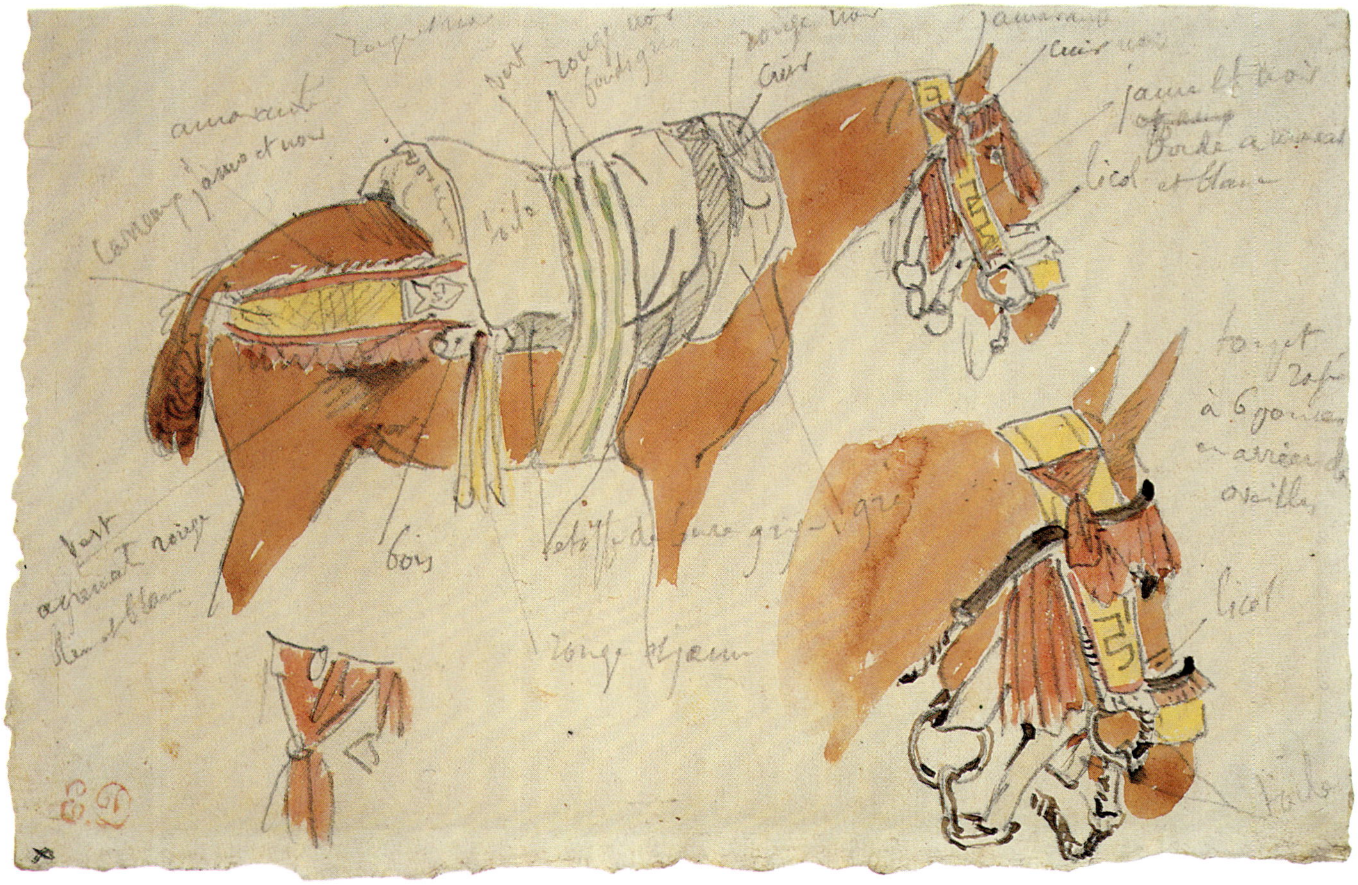

17 - Study of a Mule,
pencil and watercolour,
12 x 18.6 cm.
Département des Arts graphiques,
Louvre, Paris.

orders of the kaid Mohammed Ben Abou, formed two compact squadrons, preceded by about ten standard bearers holding red and green banners honouring the name of Allah in sophisticated gold lettering. Nearby was the colony of foreign consuls who, following protocol, had come to escort the French delegation for the first hour. Comfortably seated astride his grey mule, on a scarlet velvet saddle, Ettayeb Biaz, the customs *amin*, had a proud contented expression on his lined face. The old man was to accompany the ambassador to Meknes and confer with the French in the name of the emperor.

Within the confines of the province of Tangier, the caravan (fig. 18) was under the authority of its Pasha, Sidi Larabi Saïdi, escorted by a squadron of *moghaznis*, with their straight lances, white capes and pointed red bonnets (fig. 20). Benchimol, perched high on his mule, anxiously surveyed the Count's precious trunks and the band of servants on foot. A vast and memorable scene unfurled before Delacroix's eyes.

In the midst of all this cavalry, Mornay felt his equipage to be somewhat lacking. He persistently exaggerated the shortcomings of the mule. Abraham, who still cherished the hope of a reimbursement of the debt France had contracted with his family, seized this favourable opportunity to show his zeal. Hardly an hour had passed before the dragoman proposed to the French envoy the reins of a thoroughbred belonging to Caddour, the guardian at the

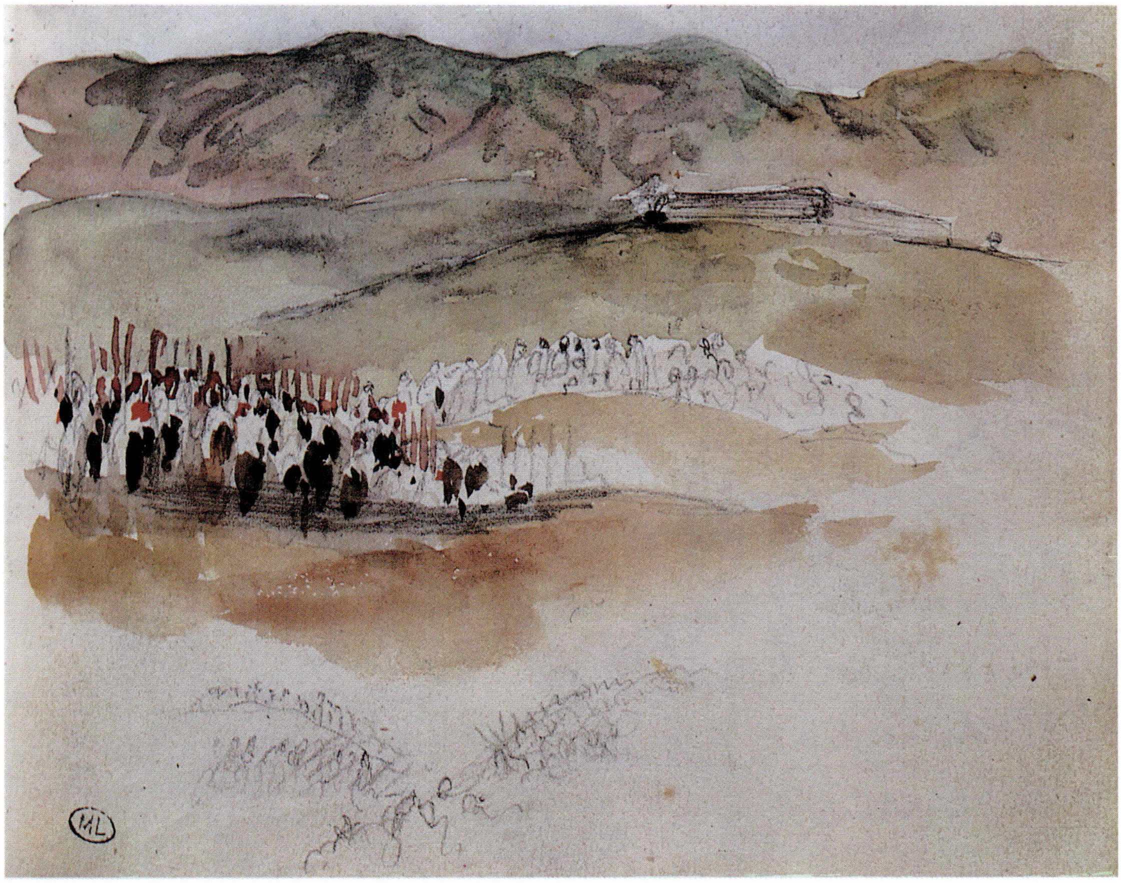

18 - North African and Spanish Album: troop of riders crossing a plain (detail),
pencil and watercolour.
Département des Arts graphiques, Louvre, Paris (RF 1712 bis, fol. 17r).

French consulate, in the hope that 'its beautiful Arabian saddle' might appease the Count.

The route to Meknes followed the old Roman road along which the legions marched to Volubilis. The French were tightly buttoned into inappropriate clothes, and to make the journey more bearable, the convoy made frequent stops. Mornay, who after much hesitation had decided to continue on the vice-consul's mule, trotted behind Biaz. He had written to Paris of his plan to outwit the customs *amin* and to try, during the journey, to find the flaw that would bring the old man round to his point of view, 'I will try to gain his confidence . . . I count on making him feel that any reward depends on the success of my negotiations.' Delacroix, wearing a naval officer's peaked cap lent to him by Jouglas, rode along next to Ben Abou whose pointed beard accentuated his sharp profile (fig. 19).[11] The artist scrupulously noted in his sketch-book, which was propped up against the pommel of his saddle, the various stages of the journey, the incidents which punctuated the itinerary and the Moroccan officer's observations.

A kaid's tent, white with black designs and flying the French flag, awaited Mornay at each of the halts. The first had been fixed at El-Arba Aïn-Dalia, scarcely a stone's throw from Tangier (fig. 21). On **Tuesday 6 March**, the route led them in the direction of Souk-el-Had el-Gharbia across flooded ground, steep paths and rivers that the caravan had to ford.

Four hundred cavaliers led by the brother of Sidi Abdeslam Essalaoui, the Pasha of Larache, awaited the travellers at the entry of the new province with an impressive tournament: *jeux de poudre—Laab el barode* as the Moroccans call them (fig. 22). Here was the dazzling spectacle of a veritable ballet of cavalry with their coloured capes flying in the wind, the riders, glued to their mounts, threw their rifles over their heads, caught them, spun them around and then fired them into the air, into the ground, or behind them. They then let the horses have their rein, disappeared with wild cries

19 - Album: Mohammed Ben Abou,
pencil.
Département des Arts graphiques, Louvre, Paris (RF 9154, fol. 17r)

20 - Studies of Arab Horsemen,
pencil and brown wash,
9.6 x 15.3 cm.
Département des Arts graphiques, Louvre, Paris.

21 - North African and Spanish Album: encampment on the road to Meknes,
pencil and watercolour.
Département des Arts graphiques, Louvre, Paris (RF 1712 bis, fol. 6r).

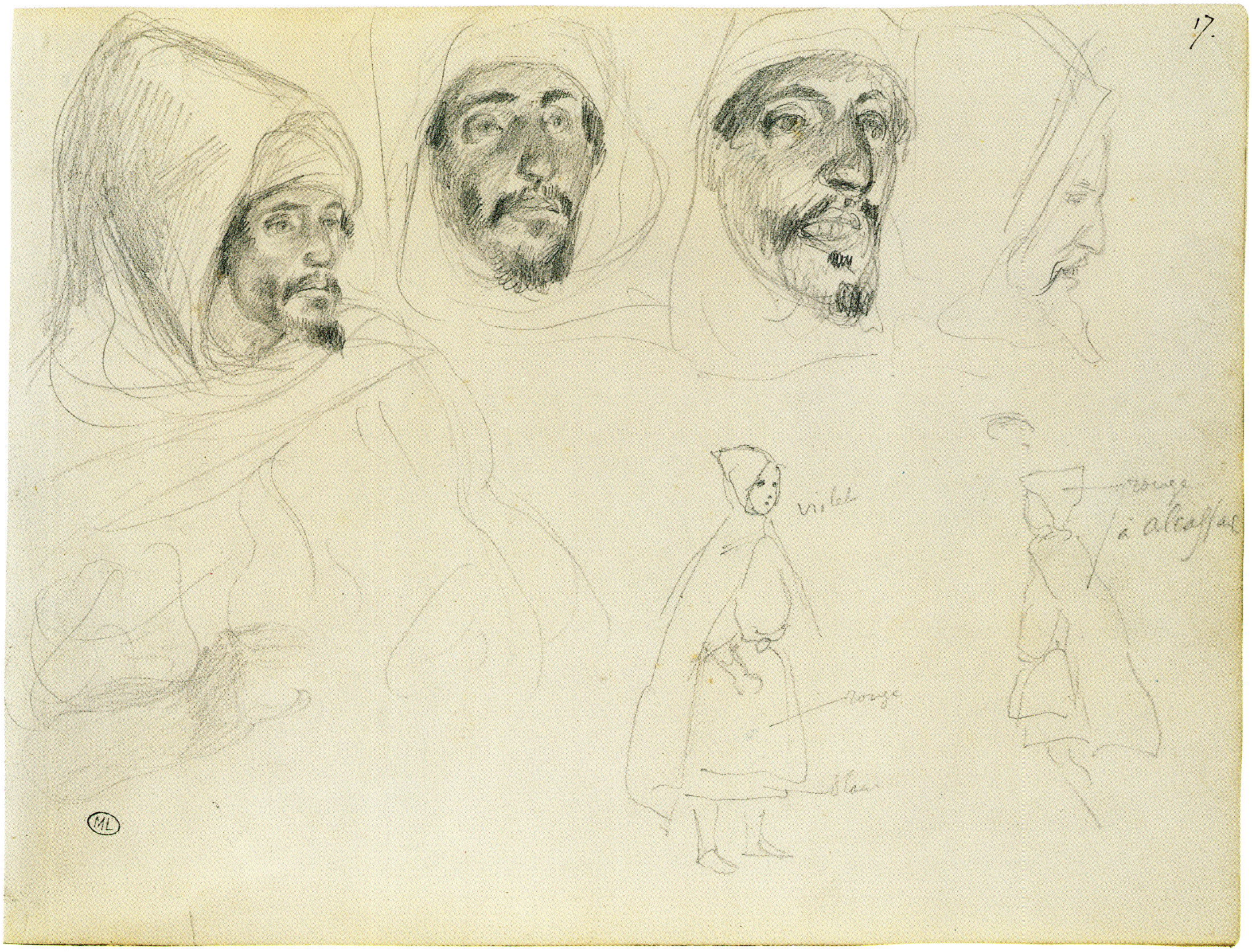

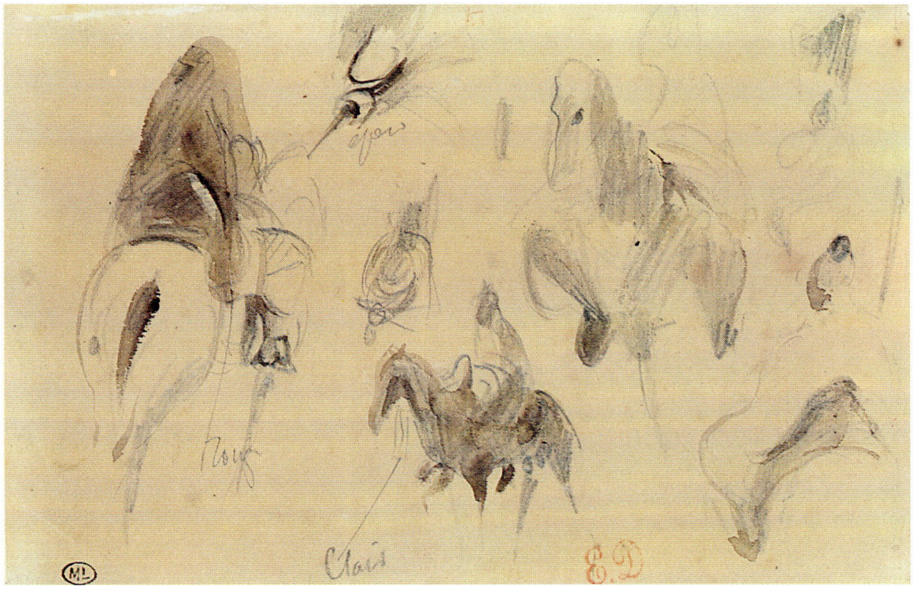

11
Mohammed Ben Abou Ben Abd-el-Malek.
Commander of the Royal cavalery in Tangier, Ben Abou accompanied the French diplomatic mission to Meknes, and on the return journey to Tangier. He is also referred to as having been 'an honourable correspondant' for the British consulate. Delacroix executed several portraits of him: see cat. nos 15, 20, 56, 67, 71 and 83.

and returned with perspiring faces, their stirrups red from the blood that stained the horses bellies. Clods of earth were thrown up by the horses' hooves and flew in all directions, often ricocheted into the river. Even an hour after these virile confrontations had ended, the air was still full of smoke and gunpowder.

At dawn on **Wednesday 7 March** they advanced towards Tleta Rissana and the Aïacha river. The camp (fig. 23) had been set up beyond the mausoleum of Sidi Lamani, near the river in the midst of olive trees, with green mountains and yellow earth 'in the distance'. The food for the troops was prepared on the spot, whereas the distinguished travellers were offered local delicacies and 'couscous in a carpet', brought ceremoniously to them by the inhabitants of neighbouring villages. Sometimes they arrived with extravagant offerings such as oxen, sheep, or cows with their calves; 'ridiculous generosity' which embarrassed the French envoy and obliged him to offer the 'customary gifts' in exchange. The caravan had spread out while crossing the misty green oak forests. Orders were given to regroup before skirting the hills and crossing the wide, damp and deserted plain. Scouts had spotted some horsemen whose suspicious behaviour might cast a slur on the royal guests' journey. A halt was agreed to give the animals a rest on a sacred site, that of the 'Battle of the Three Kings'; on August 4, 1578, forty thousand soldiers and their leaders, don Sebastian, the child king, Moulay Mohammed El Motaouakir, the deposed king, and the victor, Moulay Abd-el-Malek, all lost their lives in this pastoral setting.

On **Friday 9 March**, El-Ksar el-Kebir came into view. 'Trumpets and never-ending gunfire . . . storks on roofs . . . Jews in windows', a whole population waited in the rain by the entrance to the city to greet the French on their arrival. 'One of the poor fellows firing the rifles' got away from the crowd and 'had the sad satisfaction of firing at me . . . '. Mornay, after a moment of

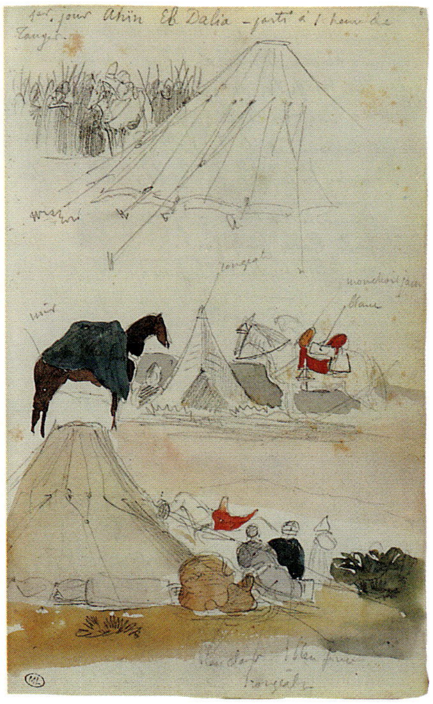

panic, stayed the sabre which was ready to cut the insolent fellow down. Ben Abou redoubled the security measures. 'The dangers affronted on the borders of Barbary' subsequently animated many a Parisian dinner attended by the Count. 'The vast escort which seemed superfluous before we left, was scarcely sufficient to control the multitude . . . ', he remarked. The journey effectively proved more agitated than expected. On several occasions the population showed its hostility towards France. When children threw stones at the troop, the whole village was put under arrest. The previous day men had laid an ambush for the convoy, but the attack was immediately suppressed by Ben Abou's cavalry. Abraham Benchimol's fears increased when they entered the territory of the Beni Snassen. He told Delacroix of the warlike exploits of the emperor's subjects, the most hot-blooded and turbulent race in the Sebou valley, the most thieving also, 'capable of attacking the camps, pashas or

22 - Moroccan Fantasia,
1832,
oil on canvas,
60 x 74 cm.
Städelsches Kunstinstitut, Frankfurt.

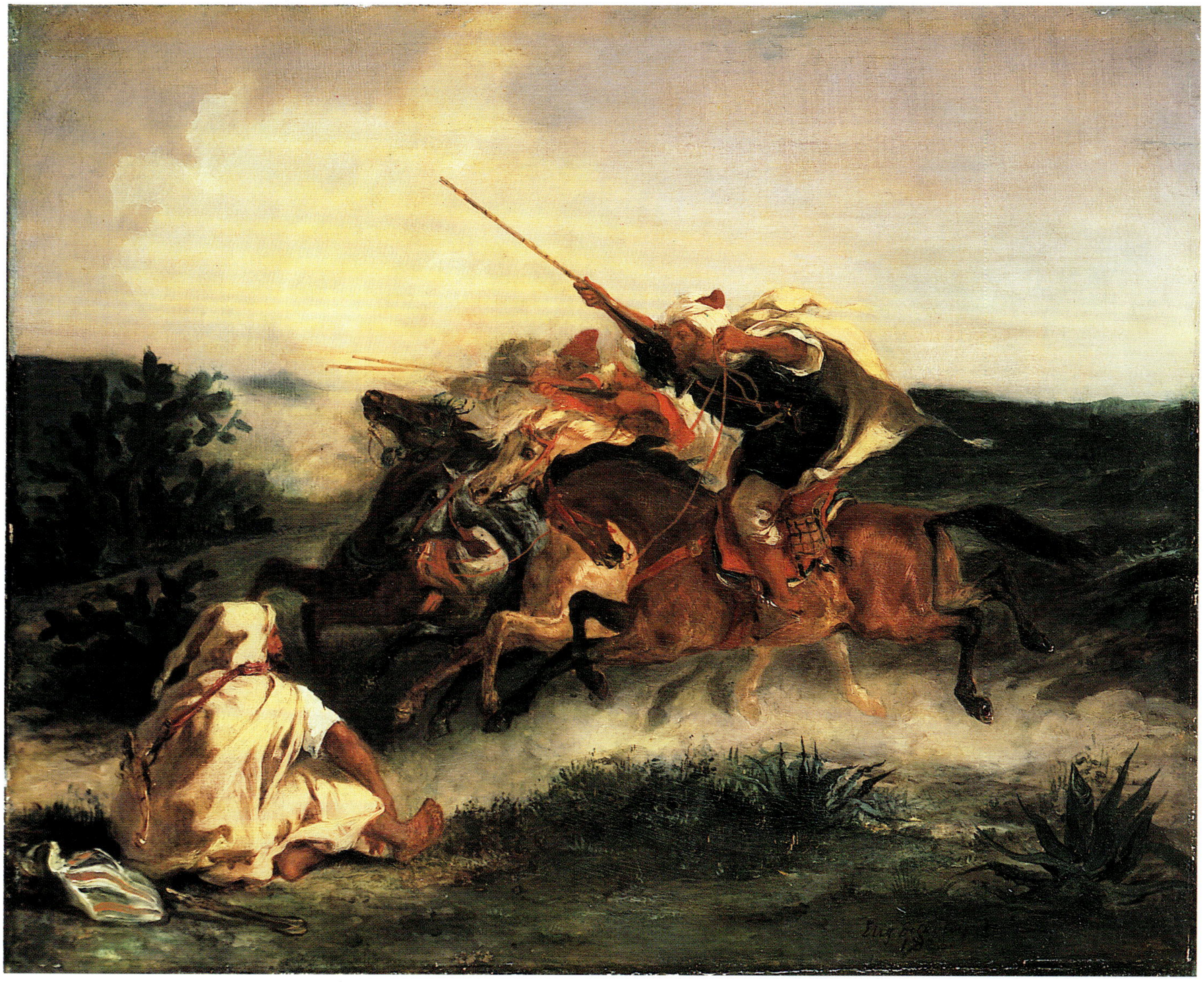

ambassadors', even the most closely guarded. But the following day the population paid Mornay 'all possible tributes'.

In order to reach Sidi Kacem, Moulay Idriss and follow the Zerhoun gorges as far as Meknes, it was necessary to cross Fouarate and the Mda river, **Saturday 10 March**, and on the Sunday, El Arba de Sidi Aïacha Belhacen and Mechra bel Ksiri, and to ford the Sebou (see cat. no. 100). The muddy waters, swelled by the heavy rains, were flowing rapidly and the strong current promised a difficult crossing. Two small, very old boats had been requisitioned which, in their apparent state of dilapidation, even the mules and horses refused to board. Ben Abou's cavalry, knee-deep in mud, pushed, pulled, reassured or screamed at the animals. Half a day later, after alternate coaxing and punishment, and several comical incidents, the entire herd found itself on the opposite bank. It remained only for the men to make

23 - An Arab Camp at Night,
1863,
oil on canvas,
54 x 65 cm.
Szépmüvészeti Muzéum, Budapest.

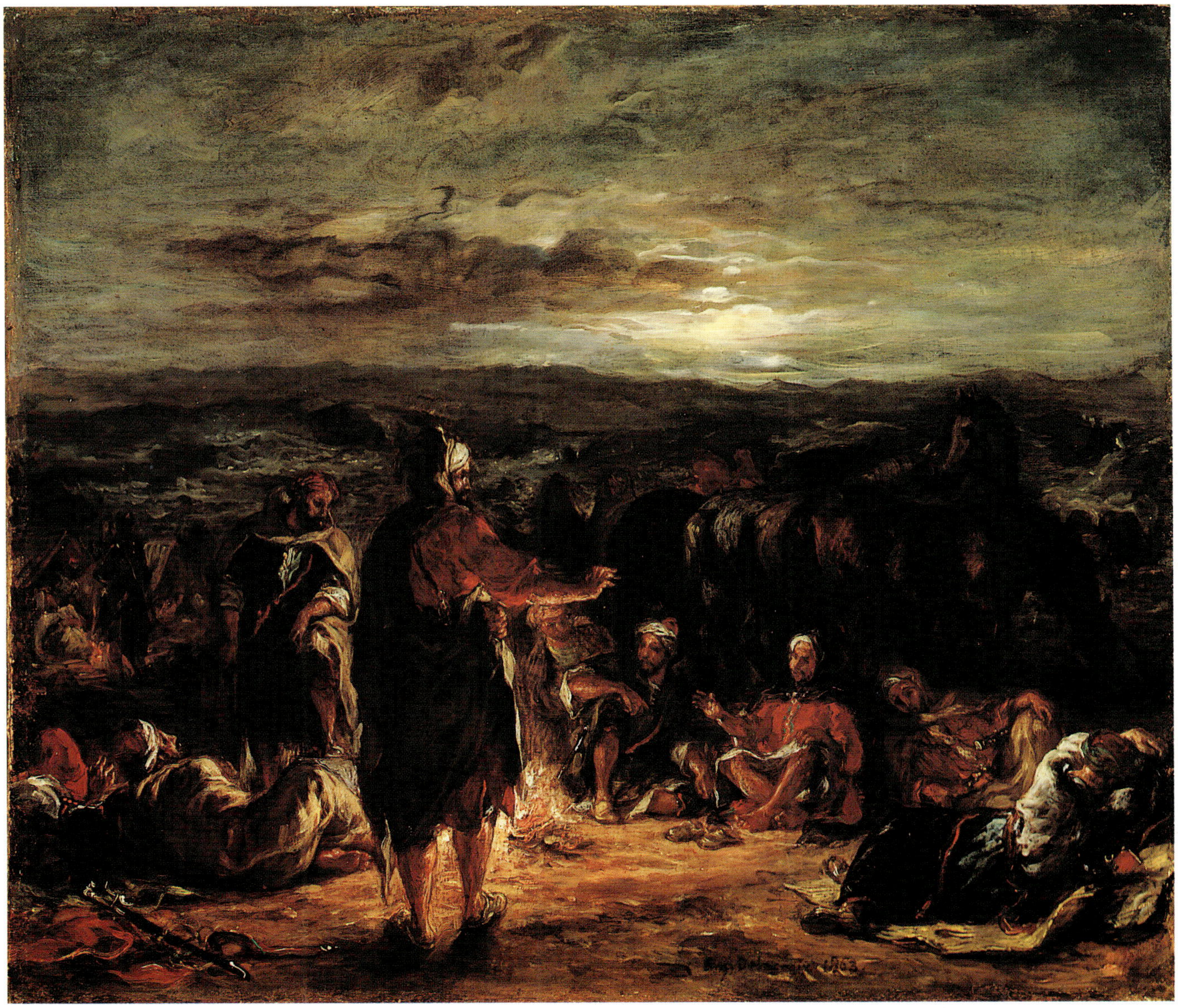

the crossing, some of whom wore courageous expressions, others the mask of self-sacrifice.

On **Wednesday 14 March**, after Sidi Kacem (fig. 24), the sky had drawn an enormous blue veil over a landscape of hills and mountains, which in the distance took on a purple hue. The pleasant weather cheered their route which was carpeted with poppies and buttercups. All nature seemed to be smiling and finally Delacroix's pranks succeeded in putting Mornay in better humour.

The last camp before Meknes was set up at the foot of Zerhoun opposite Moulay Idriss. The town, perched on two different levels, overlooked a host of white houses built into the rock. The delegation was not authorized to climb the winding paths which led to the city, accessible only to Muslims. From the camp Delacroix could make out the alleyways running through the mystic town, renowned in all Islam. At the foot of the hills stood Volubilis, silent keeper of the columns and sculptures dedicated to Jupiter and to the masters of Rome. 'El Kasba de Pharon', the Pharaoh's castle, the artist noted in his sketch-book. This was the name the Moroccans gave to this Roman town, uniting in a single title all the edifices built in honour of the absurd and fleeting phenomenon of human glory.

On **Thursday 15 March**, the road to Meknes transformed into a series of loops between small gentle valleys (fig. 25) and low cultivated hills with knotted olive trees. The delegation was expected at Hamria, the vast, reddish, dusty square which extends as far as Bou Ameir and the gardens of El-Hboul on the banks of the Boufekrane river. An immense crowd was waiting for them: musicians, the royal guard in ceremonial uniform, standard bearers,

25 - Rocks and a Small Valley,
watercolour,
18 x 23 cm.
Musée de Grenoble

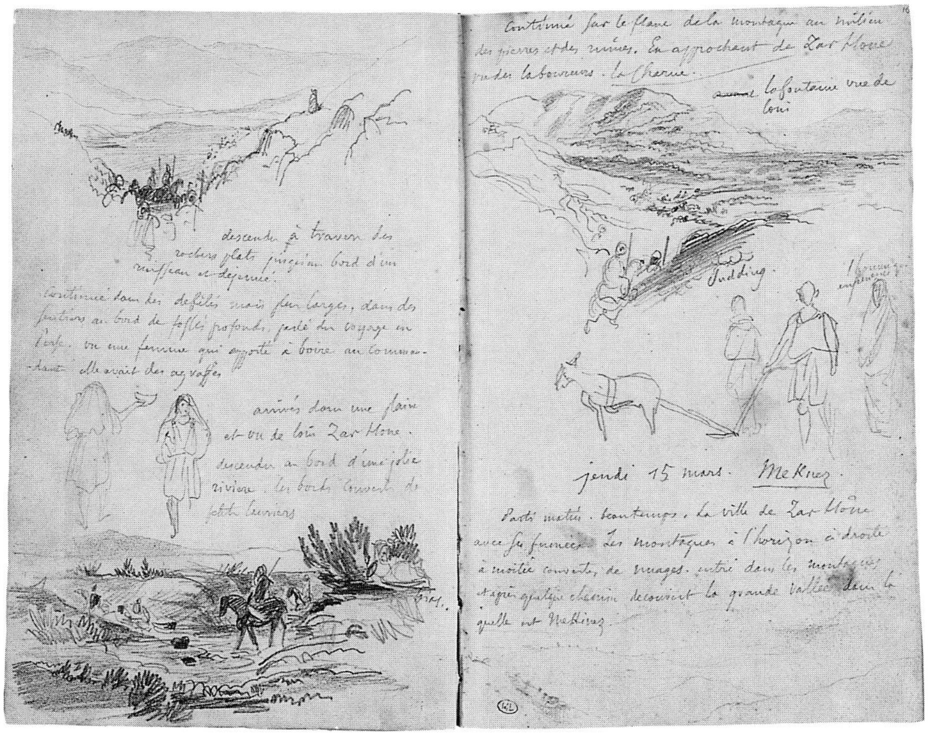

24 - North African and Spanish Album: notes and sketches made on the journey from Tangier to Meknes,
pencil.
Département des Arts graphiques, Louvre, Paris (RF 1712 bis, fol. 15v–16r).

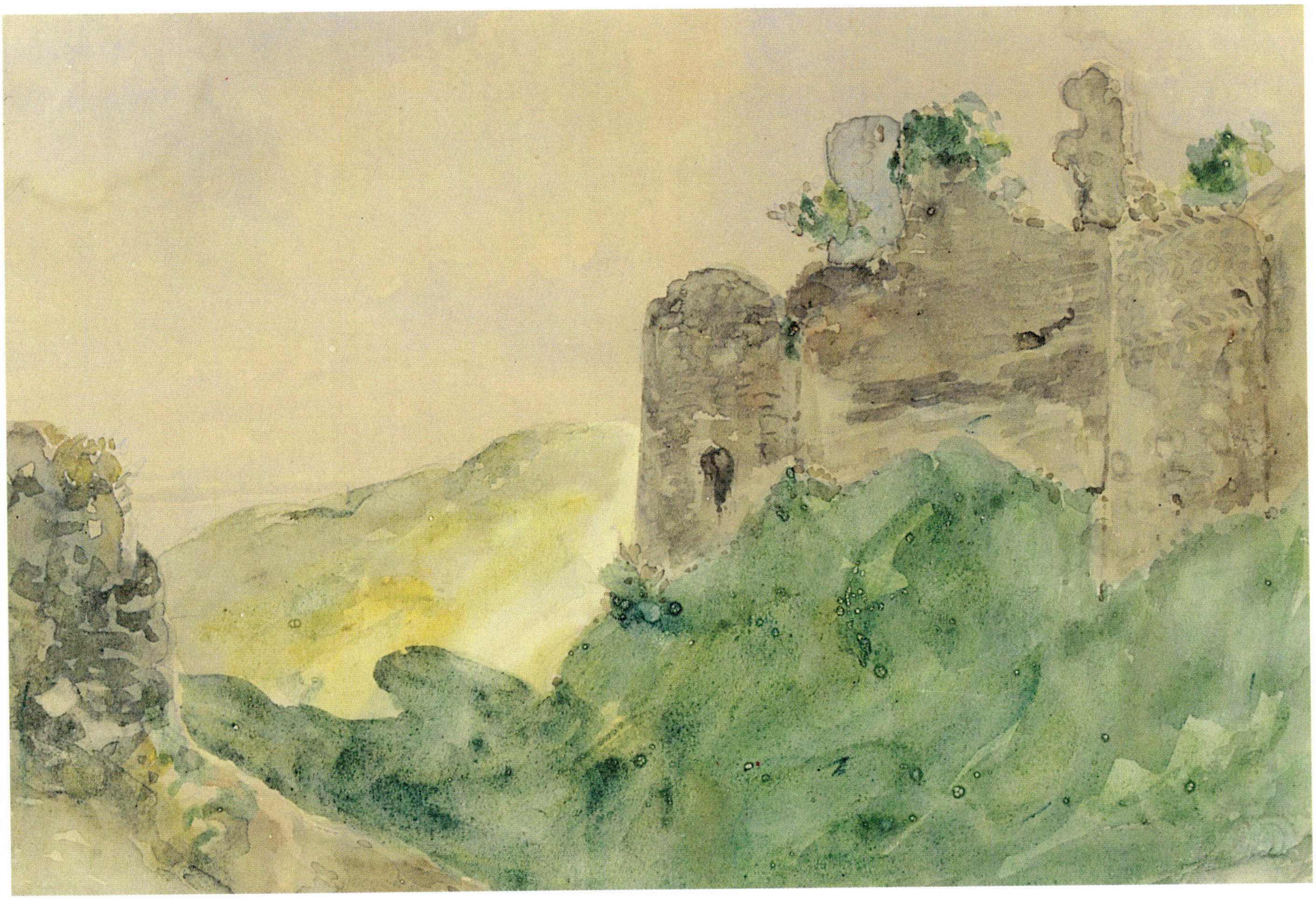

several hundred horsemen, *moghaznis* on foot and a mass of curious onlookers. The day had been declared a public holiday, and the palace had given orders for the people to congregate *en masse* in front of the Embassy, to welcome the French and 'enjoy themselves . . . make the occasion one of celebration . . . If not they would be severely punished'. In the name of the emperor, his spokesman, Mokhtar el-Jamaï had come to pronounce the welcoming speech and conduct the members of the mission to their residence. The reception augured well for the outcome of the negotiations.

Before entering Meknes and going on to their residence, the delegation was taken on a tour of the town. The long procession was to follow the forty kilometres of bastions and enormous walls, which surrounded the capital. The caravan spread itself out to emphasize its strength (fig. 26), then regrouped itself at the foot of the monumental gates of Bab el-Khmis, Bab Berdaïn and Bab el-Mansour (fig. 27) for the serenades and welcoming ceremonies.

'The crowd was enormous and the commotion extreme' (fig. 28), there was nothing but jostling, 'to the extent that our little troop, the sound of thousands of rifle reports ringing in our ears, had great difficulty in keeping together'. Tired, having been glued to his saddle ever since Tangier, Delacroix found this 'triumphal entry . . . to be somewhat of an ordeal'.

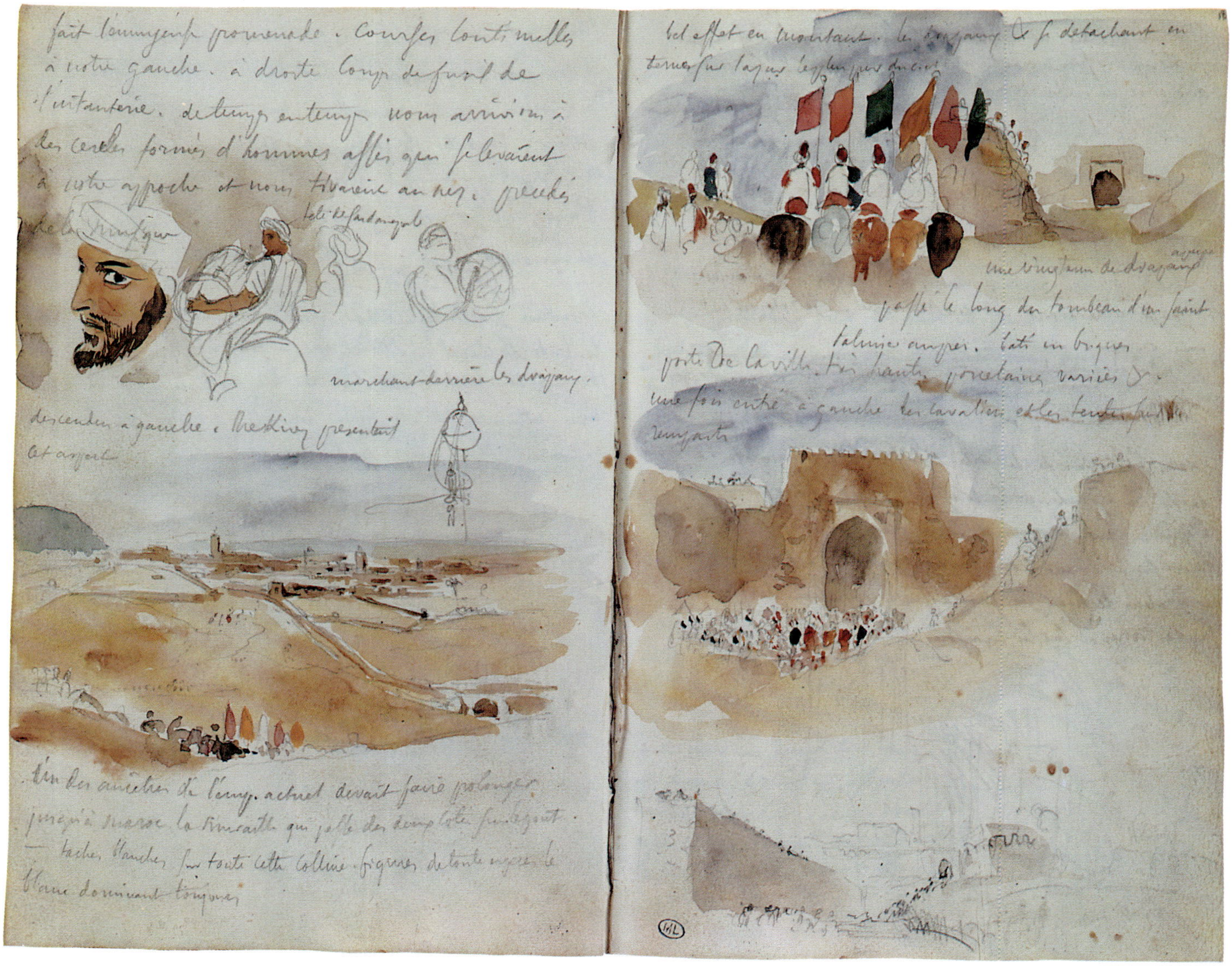

They reached their residence after a three-hour tour. It was a vast property with 'very strange Moorish architecture, like a Grenadian palace'. The house, not far from Jamaa el-Kebir, the large mosque, was in the centre of Berrima, a charming district between the Mellah and the Royal Palace. The French were invited to remain inside the residency for a few days. The presence of a large Algerian delegation, come to pay allegiance to the emperor during the month of Ramadan, had put everyone in a turmoil, which could lead to verbal abuse or even violence and might compromise the laborious attempts at reconciliation.

The presentation of the French delegation was scheduled for the following Thursday at the end of the morning. Mornay had long been waiting for this audience, and he wanted to leave nothing to chance. He checked everything, double-checked the contents of the trunks, re-read his speech and spent the next eight days giving orders.

On **Thursday 22 March**, Meknes was once again invaded by a profusion of men and animals, just as it had been six months earlier during the Austrian visit. Mohammed Ben Abou, who had led the mission from Tangier, was responsible for escorting its members to the Mechouar. At daybreak he had positioned his horsemen along the neighbouring alleys. Meanwhile he waited, one eye on the gifts guarded by the porters, the other on the imposing palace gate. At nine o'clock, the ambassador, in his blue uniform with numerous gold stripes, made a ceremonious exit (fig. 29). Scarcely had Ben Abou raised given the signal for departure, than the news had spread through the onlookers and reached the heart of the palace.

The riders led the French delegation through the crowds. They crossed several alleys bordered with rows of small shops (figs 30 and 31), where the light filtered through the plaited reed roofs of the stalls, 'like the ones in Alcassar', casting dancing shadows. At ten o'clock, they finally reached the immense El-Hdim square. It was seething with people and animals. It seemed as if the whole city had gathered at the foot of the walls of Bab el-Mansour, the 'monumental gate'. The mounts were left in Lalla Aouda square. Ben Abou led Mornay and his followers on foot to the Mechouar, while Benchimol kept a careful eye on the trunks. The imperial guard circled the parade-ground. Following orders, the various dignitaries were all present by delegation, and along with oulemas, counsellors, notables, *amins* and heads of brotherhoods, they formed an impressive crowd which seemed to grow by the minute. The

26 - North African and Spanish Album: the arrival in Meknes,
pencil and watercolour.
Département des Arts graphiques, Louvre, Paris (RF 1712 bis, fol. 17v–18r).

27 - Bab el-Mansour (details),
pencil, ink and watercolour.
Département des Arts graphiques, Louvre, Paris (RF 1712 bis, fol. 25r and RF 10091).

28 - North African and Spanish Album: crowd outside one of the gates of Meknes (detail),
ink and watercolour.
Département des Arts graphiques, Louvre, Paris (RF 1712 bis, fol. 24v).

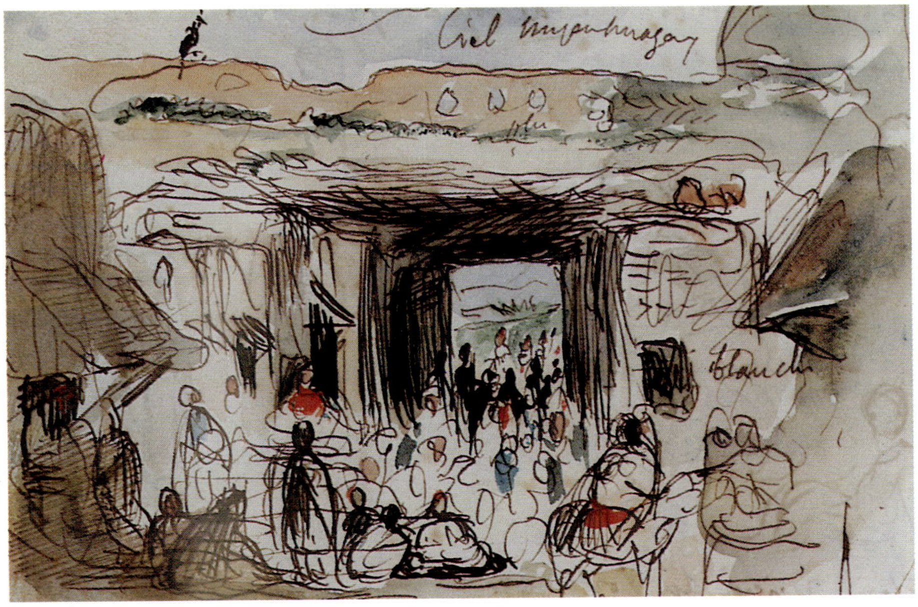

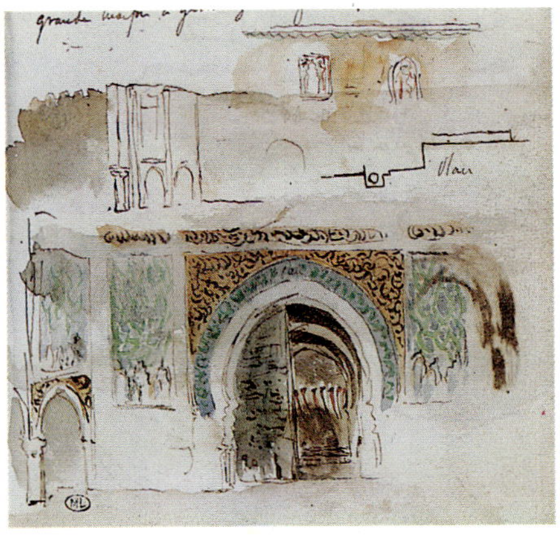

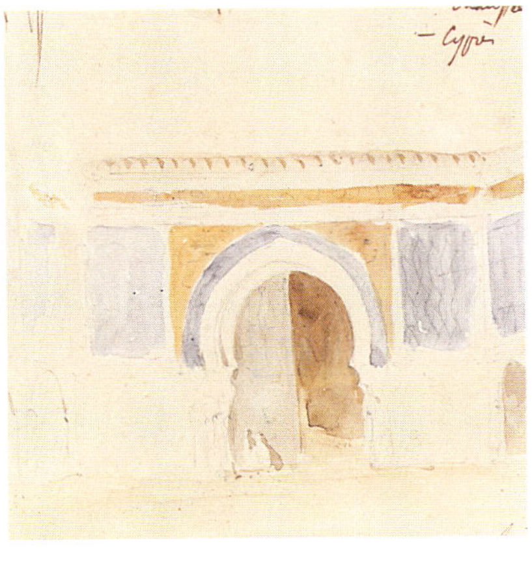

ministers, Taleb Ben Jelloun and Mokhtar el-Jamaï, were waiting at the entrance to the Mechouar. Mornay was pleased to find that Ettayeb Biaz was also there. He hoped to extract information from the customs *amin*, as to the emperor's decisions regarding France's demands.

Suddenly an impressive roll of drums, accompanied by the shrill sound of brass and fife, brought the noisy, fidgety crowd to a standstill. A white wall of burnouses and jellabas reflected the bright glare of the sun, which by now was near its zenith.

The royal guards raised their lances and unfurled their red and green standards, decorated with the name of the Prophet in gold calligraphy. The atmosphere was charged. The eyes of the colourful crowds were firmly fixed on the gateway, 'mean and without ornament', through which the emperor traditionally exited.

Moulay Abd al-Rahman rode out solemnly onto the vast parade-ground. Alone on horseback, he was flanked by his guards on foot, followed by the bearer of a red and green parasol, topped by a golden orb, an emblem of authority, and preceded by two *moghaznis* and a chamberlain, waving 'white handkerchiefs, as long a turban cloths'. The immense clamour of the crowd was accompanied by the *you-you* of the women who had gathered on the surrounding terraces.

High on his thoroughbred horse, 'grey . . . with a hogged mane', with a 'rose and gold-coloured' saddle and 'silver stirrups', the emperor dominated over the crowds, who, at an imperceptible signal given by the chamberlain, bowed down in unison and cried, three times, *Allah I bark amar Sidna!*, 'May God protect our sovereign'.

Delacroix at first tried to find a good place to rest his sketch-book. To no avail. This historical event was unfurling before his eyes at an ever-increasing pace. He was obliged, therefore, to scribble down in ink, in rushed handwriting, the important stages of the ceremony. He would have to rely on his visual memory for the colours, contrasts, the imposing decor, the magic of this unique moment, that no painter other than himself had ever witnessed. He concentrated on the emperor: 'a rather handsome man' . . . 'young . . . thick beard, moderately dark complexion. *Burnous* of fine cloth, almost closed in front. The *haik* beneath it, worn over the upper part of the chest and almost entirely covering the thighs and legs. A string of white beads threaded on blue silk round the right arm . . . Yellow heel-less slippers. . . .'

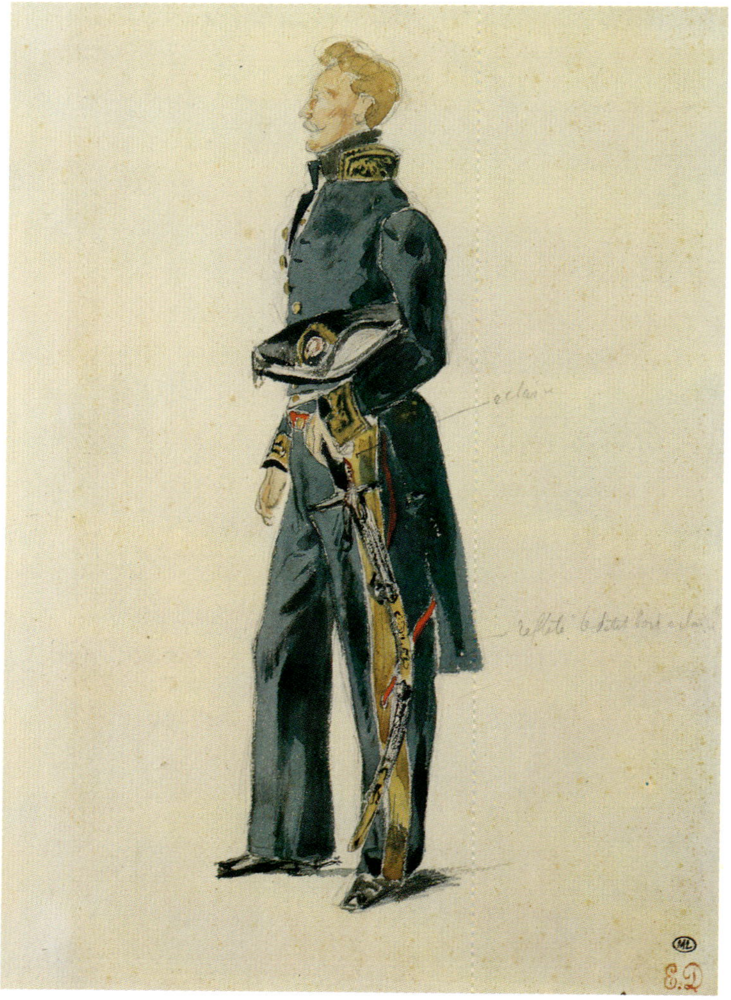

29 - Portrait of the Count de Mornay in Ambassadorial dress,
pencil and watercolour,
24.7 x 18.1 cm.
Département des Arts graphiques,
Louvre, Paris.

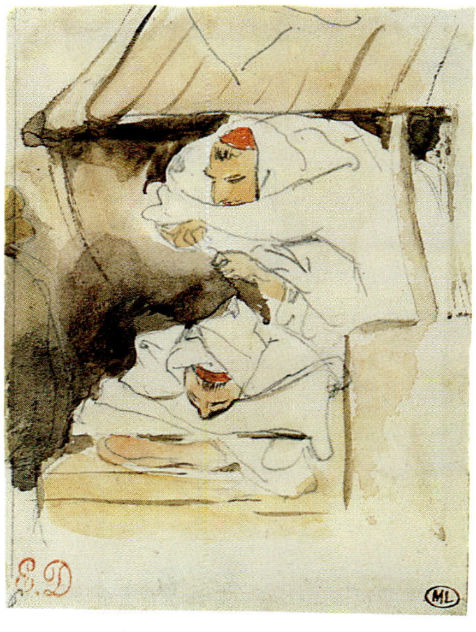

The sovereign stopped to listed to Mornay's message from Louis-Philippe, translated by Benchimol. His eyes met Delacroix's. The painter had momentarily abandoned his notebook in order to make a rough sketch of the figure of the sovereign, who answered the ambassador's speech with the 'expected compliments'. Moulay Abd al-Rahman stayed 'longer than is usual at such receptions', and 'made a sign of farewell' to the French, before returning to his palace. As he turned, he gave a few brief orders, asked the head of protocol to ensure the French were comfortable, glanced at the trunks which had been ostentatiously displayed at the feet of Boispon and Marignaut, then, still preceded by his chamberlain, the bearer of the 'parasol with [an] unpainted wooden handle', and musicians, and followed by 'his state coach, a sort of wheelbarrow driven by a mule', he soon disappeared into the crowd of notables, who tried to kiss his slippers as he passed.

The Count de Mornay was pleased with his performance. Delacroix read through his notes. The tangled mass of words (fig. 32), contained all the ingredients necessary to create a highly memorable work of art (see cat. nos 75 to 84).

The French delegation was granted an 'exceptional' favour: a visit of the royal palace. Built by Moulay Ismaël, the Meknes palace was encircled by a triple wall with high towers. In the middle of orchards, there were a series of white buildings with green-tiled roofs. Sidi Mokhtar, who acted as guide, led his visitors through a suite of rooms, where the walls, decorated with sculpted wood medallions and interlacing, lifted the festooned interweaving of their plaster-work up towards a symphony of ogive arches, ornamental reliefs and sculpted cedar beams on the ceiling. Double-doors, which reached up to the roofs, guarded the various entrances. They often opened onto charming courtyards with tiles, fountains and colourful basins. The rooms seemed to have been deserted by their hosts; only a few nonchalant *moghaznis* were present to enjoy this haven of peace (fig. 33). They wandered along corridors and pathways, admired several pavilions, the four-acre lake of Aguedal, the gigantic arched silos with Cyclopean pillars, followed overgrown paths and crossed a 'more rustic' garden, only finally returning to Berrima at nightfall. Delacroix immediately set to work. He wanted to record the royal audience on paper, before time dimmed his memory. He made numerous sketches in an effort to fill out the sparse notes he had made on the square of the Mechouar. He made several attempts at capturing a face, a pose or the atmosphere of the impressive ceremony, which was the climax of the whole journey (fig. 34).

The emperor had designated three characters already familiar to Mornay, to negotiate with the French: Mokhtar el-Jamaï, Taleb Ben Jelloun and Ettayeb Biaz. 'Three personalities who [are] reputed to be the most subtle, if not the most honest, of all the Moors', wrote Mornay to Delaporte, wondering, also, how he might be able to influence their decisions.

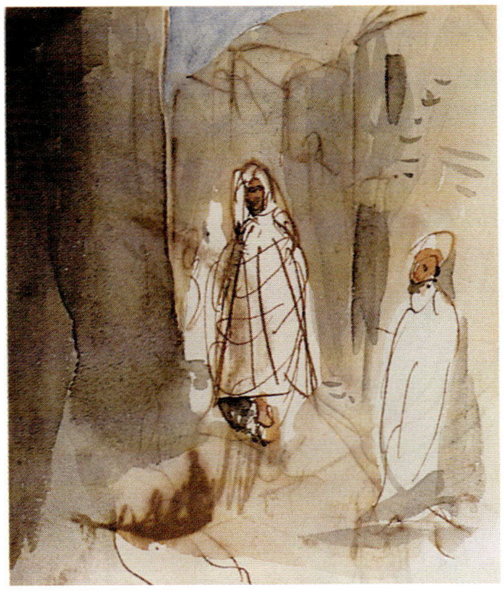

31 - North African and Spanish Album: the streets of Meknes
(details),
ink and watercolour.
Département des Arts graphiques, Louvre, Paris (RF 1712 bis, fol. 26v).

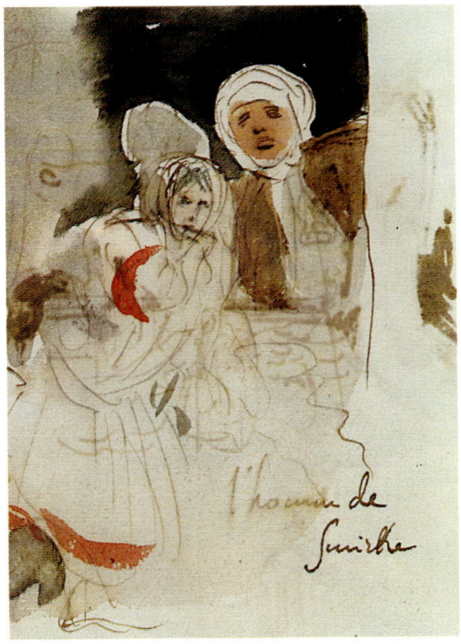

Left:
30 - Two Arabs in a Small Shop,
pencil and watercolour,
10.2 x 80 cm.
Département des Arts graphiques, Louvre, Paris.

Delacroix was anxious to discover the capital, to mingle with the crowds, different from those he had seen in Tangier, to admire the tile-decorated doorways at his leisure, to paint the astonishing scenes he had caught a glimpse of when they first arrived in the town and during the noisy, lively parade organized in their honour. His temper was beginning to fray after eight days confined to the Berrima residence. He was tired of endless futile conversations with his companions; even his exchanges with Mornay had been reduced to meaningless civilities.

On **Friday 23 March**, he finally visited Meknes, in the company of Benchimol, who was once again to be his guide. Surrounded by guards, the two men went first to the El-Hdim market, with its cupboard-size shops. The streets were filled with the sound of laughter and proud riders sitting on top of their mules, already weighed down by excessive loads. The midday call to prayer suddenly emptied the streets, and the painter and the dragoman went to a more lively area, the Mellah, where tobacco, copper, leather and all kinds of objects were traded. In the days to come, Delacroix would make several visits to the Jewish district and to the area around the Bab el-Khemis. The *fellahs* who came to sell their produce there at dawn provided an interesting spectacle. The artist sometimes climbed up onto one of the terraces overlooking the market. From here he could see over the town and he had an exceptional view over the ochre-coloured ramparts that Moulay Ismaël had wanted to build as far as Marrakesh. The artist would stay late into the evening, watching the burning reds and oranges 'in this ever changing, Veronese sky, lightly tinged with blue'. He would return to Berrima only when silence had calmed the frenzied city, and there he would show his latest pictures to his companions.

Sometimes he ventured outside the town gates—'I was the only member of our party to take advantage of this privilege'—and wandered as far as Sidi Saïd. He would note down the important points on his itinerary, thus making it possible for others to retrace his steps (fig. 35). He lingered by the famous gateways which were the pride of the capital: Bab Jama en-Nouar, Bab Berrima, Bab Filala, Bab er-Rih, Bab el-Khemis, Bab Berdaïn, which led to the mausoleum of Sidi Mohammed Ben Aïssa, the patron saint of the Aïssaouas, or Bab el-Mansour el-Aleuj, which stood at the entrance to the road leading to the royal palace. Many of the roads were decorated with fountains and with ceramic-tiled panels, and in the squares there were clearings where hoards of children played. The vines that climbed up the walls offered welcome shade to passers-by, barbers working outdoors (fig. 36), traders, craftsmen and a whole population 'who give thanks to God for [their] bad food and wretched clothing . . .'.

Ettayeb carried out the main negotiations with Mornay. Without being lazy, but without hurrying either, the Tangier customs *amin* deliberately exaggerated the Moroccan recriminations in the hopes of persuading France to

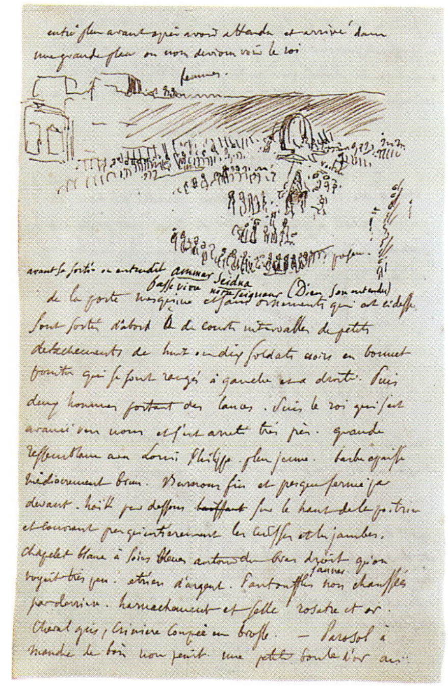

32 - North African and Spanish Album: audience with the Sultan,
ink.
Département des Arts graphiques, Louvre, Paris (RF 1712 bis, fol. 19v).

33- Soldiers Sleeping in a Guardroom,
1846,
oil on canvas,
65 x 54 cm.
Von Der Heydt Museum, Wuppertal.

34 - Study of the two figures who appear to the left of the Sultan in *The Sultan of Morocco*,
pencil,
19 x 12.5 cm.
Département des Arts graphiques, Louvre, Paris.

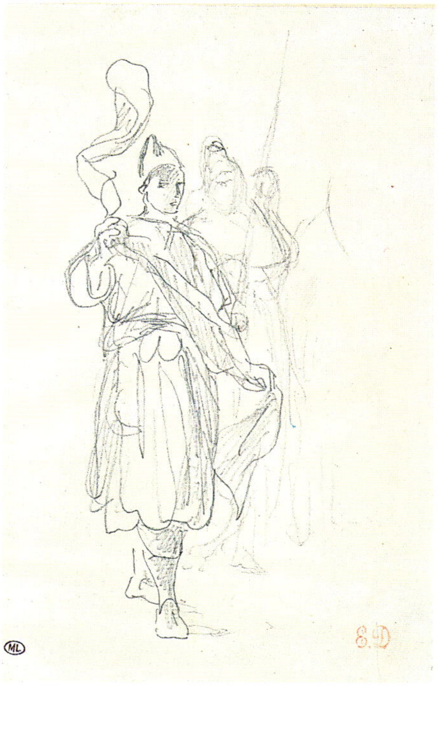

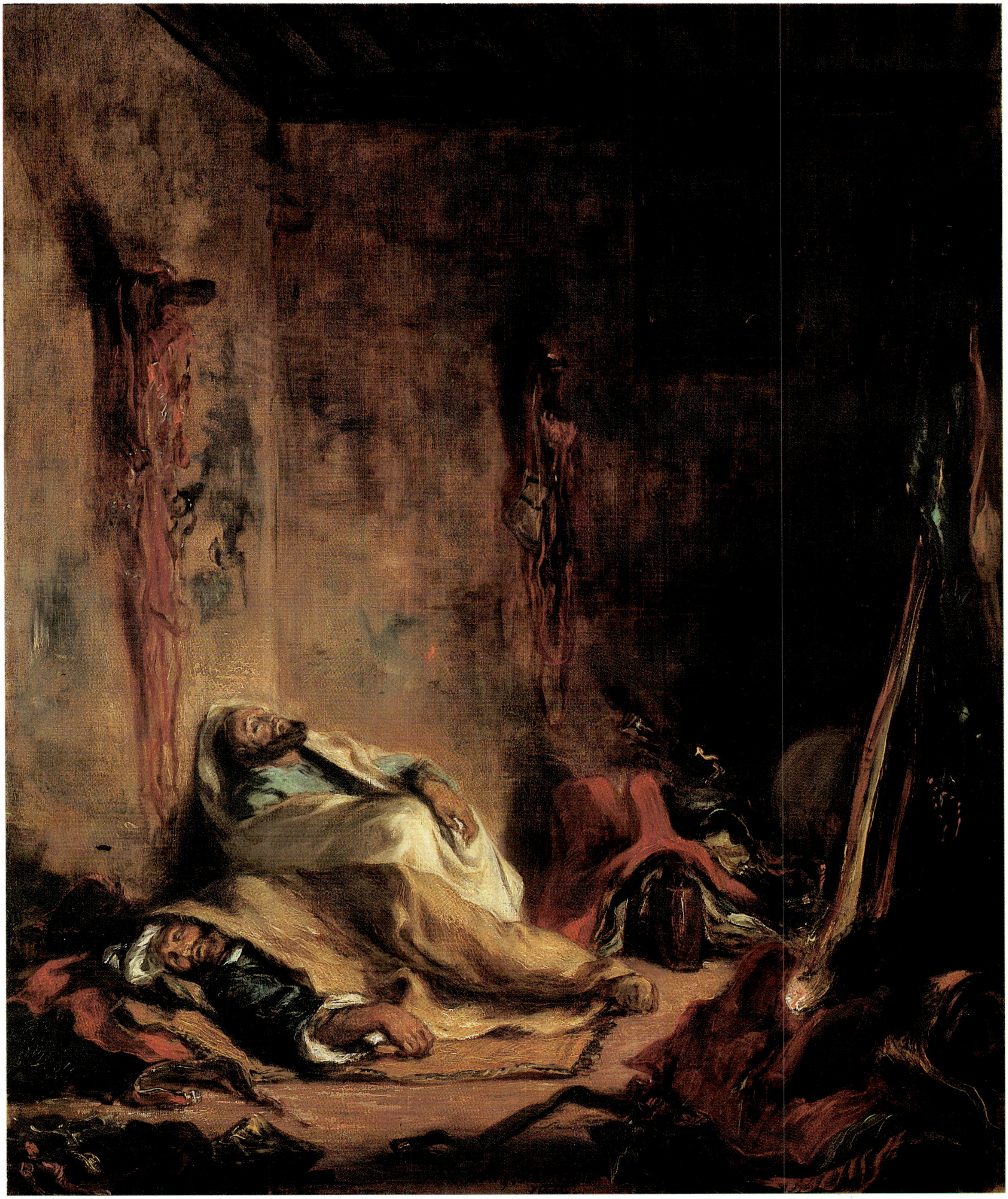

adopt a more flexible attitude. Following the Ministry's instructions, Mornay punctuated his remarks with threats and hinted at the 'misfortunes that could result . . . from a rupture of relations with France'. The two sides finally saw eye to eye. The ministers redoubled their courtesy visits to Berrima while the palace paid even greater attention to their guests. It seemed that it would end happily after all.

On **Thursday 29 March**, at the emperor's request, his personal orchestra came to give a concert in honour of the French visitors. The musicians, 'the best in all the empire', were Jewish and came from Mogador. The simple trio consisted of a *rebec* player, a sort of lute 'of very elegant shape', a tambourine which beat out the rhythm of the hypnotic melodies, and a female singer with a warm voice, who sang tender songs and hymns dedicated to her sovereign (fig. 37), which began, after a while, to grate on the artist's ears; their 'merit' apparently resided in them being shouted.

On **Sunday 1 April**, now that his mission had been successfully concluded, Mornay risked leaving the residence to visit the royal stud-farm to the south of the palace, with its three kilometres of galleries and endless stables, where, in the steam and the odour of horse manure, whole armies of blacksmiths, farriers, saddlers and stablemen worked busily. This one farm boasted over twelve thousand thoroughbreds, horses and mules. Delacroix admired the racing horses which were the pride of the kingdom, and which were forbidden to leave Moroccan territory (fig. 38). He tried to capture their energy and the hue of their coats in few entangled lines in his notebook. The emperor had ordered the head of the stable to choose four thoroughbreds as gifts for the French king, and one for each of the distinguished visitors, Mornay, Desgranges and Delacroix. Benchimol could content himself with a fine, robust mule. The visit extended to the menagerie located next to the royal palace. There a few extra gifts had been assembled for Louis-Philippe: a lioness, a tiger, two ostriches, two gazelles, an antelope and 'a kind of stag which is a savage beast; it took a dislike to one of the poor ostriches and ran it through with its horns . . . .'

On **Wednesday 4 April**, after eleven conferences, Ettayeb Biaz delivered an open letter from Moulay Abd al-Rahman addressed to Louis-Philippe. The letter resolved all the differences that had arisen between the two countries following the French occupation of Algeria, and ended with the words, 'Please be informed that we still observe the treaties concluded between us . . . with the intention of conserving our friendship in all its force and purity . . .' Mornay now had but one wish, and that was to return as soon as possible to Tangier and then finally to Paris.

On **Thursday 5 April**, at around eleven o'clock in the morning, the French diplomat gravely mounted the vice-consul's mule. The convoy had changed its appearance; it was less military than the one which had brought the French to Berrima twenty days earlier. There were fewer horses for the parade but the

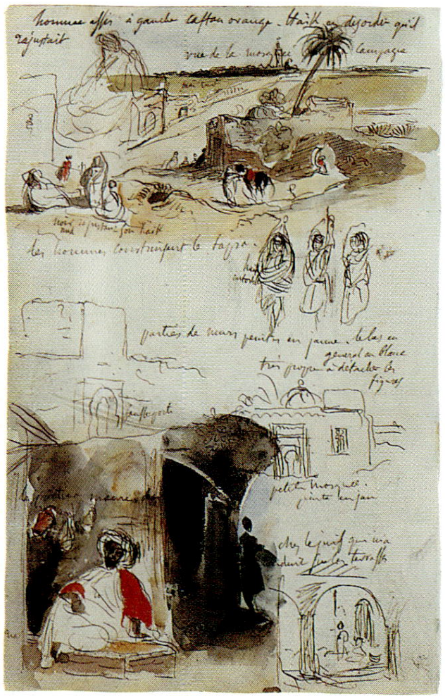

35 - North African and Spanish Album: in the Jewish quarter and in the hills overlooking Meknes (details), *ink and watercolour.*
Département des Arts graphiques, Louvre, Paris (RF 1712 bis, fol. 23v–24r).

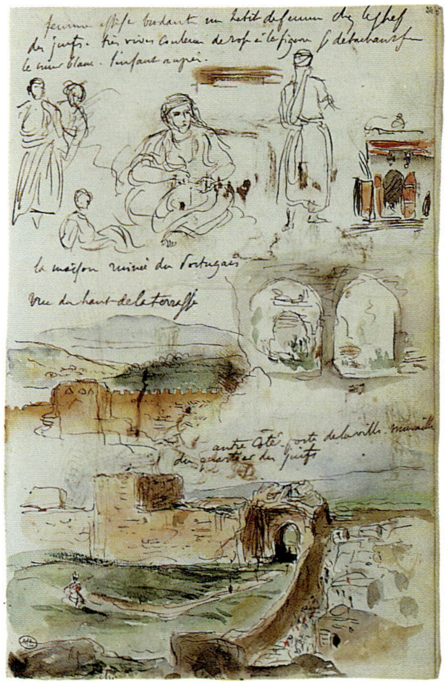

36 - Street Barber,
brown wash,
18.4 x 26.6 cm.
Département des Arts graphiques,
Louvre, Paris.

same number of mules, which had been very carefully loaded with cages full of ostriches and wildcats which terrified the servants. The caravan looked decidedly more exotic. Ben Abou once again joined the convoy while Ettayeb Biaz remained in Meknes: rumour had it that the monarch, highly satisfied with the *amin*'s services in regards to the French mission, wanted to express his compliments to him in public. The kaid's cavalry had opened up the route in the direction of Bab Berdaïn and had regrouped on the hills of Hamria. The caravan had started its march to Sidi Kacem across olive groves and fields; on no account was the ambassador's pace to be slowed. The itinerary skirted Volubilis and Moulay Idriss. Suddenly, at the foot of the holy city, Mornay ordered an unscheduled halt. One of the paragraphs of the agreement could be interpreted in several ways. He had been warned against the Moroccans with whom, 'any point on which a conclusion had not been reached became a subject for interminable negotiations'. The French envoy, who wanted to reach Tangier knowing everything was in order, obliged Benchimol to turn back in order to question Biaz and Ben Jelloun.

The convoy returned along much the same route by which they came. On **Friday 6 April**, they set up camp at Sidi Kacem. The following day,

37 - Jewish Musicians from Mogador,
oil on canvas,
46 x 55 cm.
Louvre, Paris.

they crossed a branch of the Sebou and then the Ouerrha river. The drop in the water level made the fording of the rivers easier. In order to win favour with Mornay and to hasten their return to Tangier, Ben Abou sometimes ordered the troop to cut across the fields. This accelerated pace brought the caravan to the outskirts of Ksar el-Kebir on **Monday 9 April**. There an envoy was waiting for them to retrieve the forty mules on loan from the royal stables to carry the luggage. The emperor was heading a division of his army to quell a rebellion near Marrakesh, and these imperial expeditions literally emptied the stables, even of the weakest animals. Once again it was Benchimol who was charged with bargaining for replacement mules in neighbouring settlements. 'All the work fell on me alone . . .', he complained in a note to Delaporte.

Springtime had coloured the Moroccan countryside with an exuberant new palette. The land was lush with 'carpets of white, pale yellow, dark yellow and purple flowers, as far as the eye could see . . .', which lent a new lyricism to the artist's work. Mornay, meanwhile, moaned quietly. Fatigue and the heat had put a stop to his criticisms and he dozed, opened one eye, closed it again, letting himself be rocked by the regular sway of his mule.

The roads they took were more animated than on the outgoing journey. They were continually passing caravans (fig. 39), merchants, families on the move and squadrons on their way to another province, to collect taxes or to enforce imperial authority (see p. 123). At the sight of the convoy, women came rushing forward bearing jugs of milk as a sign of welcome to Ben Abou and Mornay (see cat. no. 69).

On **Tuesday 10 April**, the caravan halted for lunch on the banks of the river Maghzen, then headed for Tleta Rissana and Aïn Dalia, where they spent the night. The next day they left for Tangier at seven o'clock in the morning. Informed of the success of the mission, various dignitaries, headed by the Pasha, Sidi Larabi Saïdi, hastened to meet the travellers. Amused by all these festivities, the peak of his cap pulled down over his sun-tanned forehead, Delacroix, unruffled, recorded in cramped handwriting in his sketch-book, propped up against the pommel of his saddle, what the discomfort of the situation did not permit him to draw.

At last, Tangier came into view. The last kilometres were a series of welcoming ceremonies and manifestations of goodwill: fantasias, impromptu orchestras, a twenty-one gun salute fired from the kasbah, and the *you-you* of the women who offered poultry, baskets of fruit and earthenware jugs of milk. The Moroccan flag had been hoisted at the entrance of the city. The consuls, chancellors and dragomen, who had formed a welcoming committee at the foot of the ramparts, were surprised by the exceptional reception given to the French. Seemingly insignificant, it was in fact carefully calculated to maintain the balance between two equally powerful neighbours, the English in Gibraltar and the French in Algeria.

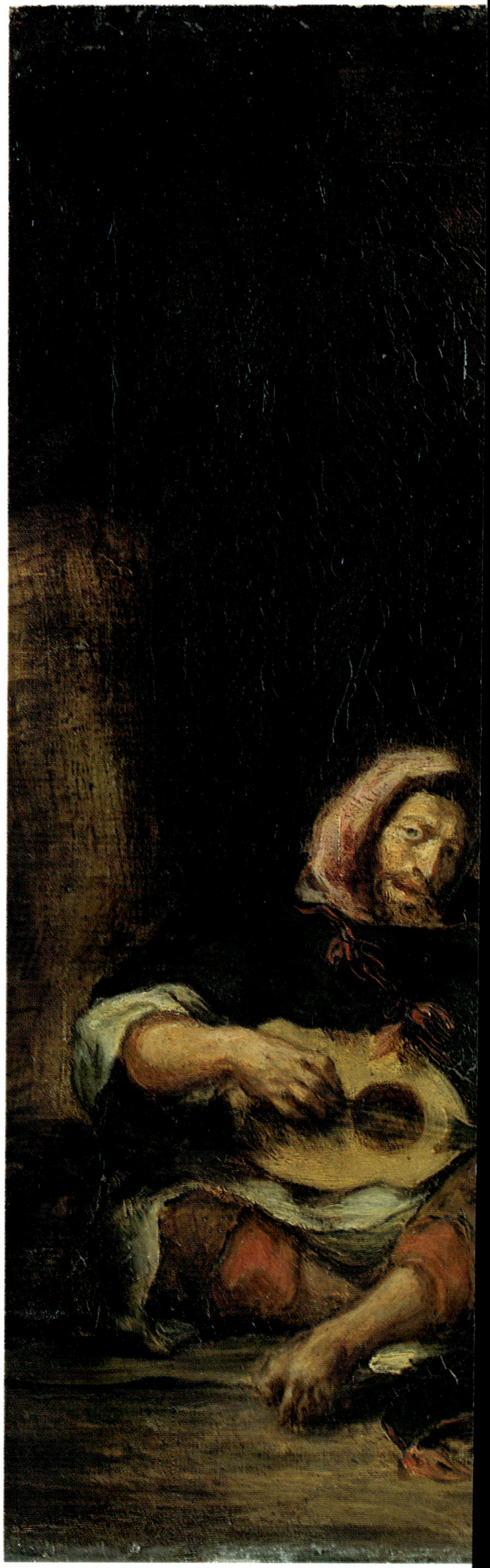

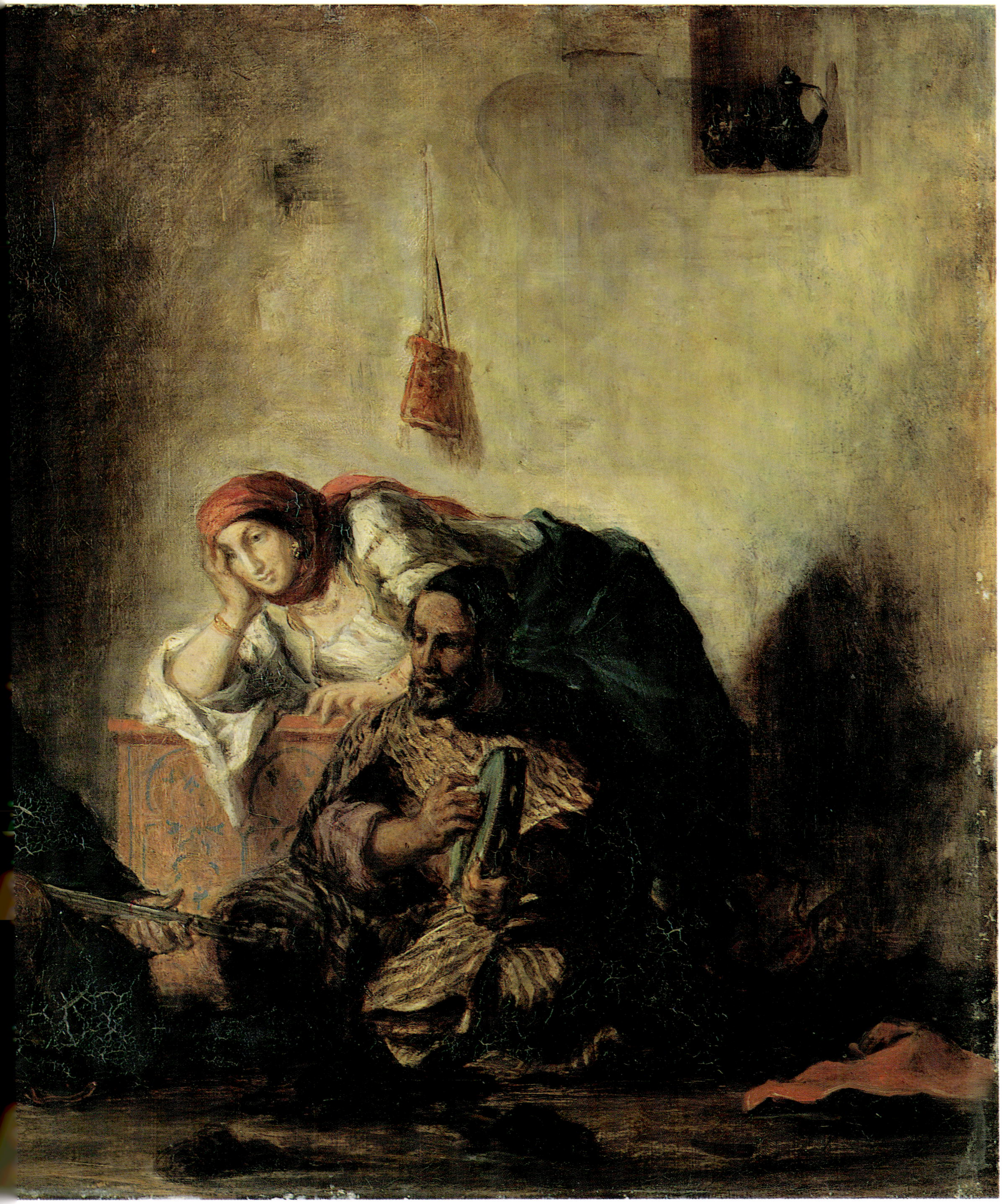

A few final turns in the road and they reached the French residence, where everyone regained his quarters for a welcome rest. Then the delays began once again. Before he could leave the country, Mornay had to wait for the official document of the agreement made in Meknes to be delivered to him, have it approved by Paris and sealed by the emperor.

Delacroix had fallen ill for the third time, and had remained in his room for several days. What did the throbbing fever hide, merely fatigue from the journey, or was it the forerunner of the cholera epidemic that had spread throughout the Mediterranean region? Still weak, Delacroix, accompanied by Delaporte and Freyssinet, enthusiastically returned to the animation of the rue de la Marine, the calm of the Swedish and Danish gardens, and the British Embassy and its charming hosts, Louisa and Edward Drummond-Hay. Abraham still accompanied him on his wanders around the town. The dragoman invited him into friends' houses and led him to spots where the colourful crowds responded ecstatically to religious chants and other music: processions, story-tellers, singers, clowns, actors, marabouts, all encircled by curious spectators. At night, different spectacles filled the streets: torch-lit processions and orchestras leading newly-weds to their husbands' houses . . .

Delacroix had perceived the beauty of this simple life: 'This place is made for artists . . . beauty abounds here; not the over-praised beauty of fashionable paintings', but an image purer than the one offered by the Parisian exhibitions. The artist who had so much wanted to visit Italy, was constantly finding in Morocco a living antiquity: ' . . . figures like Roman consuls, like Cato or Brutus . . . [who] look as satisfied as Cicero must have been in his curule chair . . . All of them in white, like Roman senators or Greeks at the Panathenaean festival . . .' (fig. 40).

Mornay, however, had yet again to arm himself with patience: Moulay Add al-Rahman had left for Rabat to celebrate *Aïd el-Kebir*. How could he pleasantly occupy himself in the meantime? The dinners and visits to notables, such as Jacob Bouzaglo on 29 April, were no longer sufficient to break the boredom of these idle days. Mornay's reports lost their spark. Only Delacroix was still entranced with Morocco. He watched the sky which set the landscape ablaze and which brought him echoes of the scenes he had witnessed in this land. He kept a careful list of themes to paint on his return, which grew longer every day. He would draw inspiration from the list until the end of his life.

La Perle had dropped anchor in the bay of Tangier. A rapid excursion was planned on **Thursday 10 May** along the neighbouring coast, to visit Cádiz, Gibraltar and Seville. The Spanish consul in Tangier pleaded on behalf of the French who wanted their entry into Spanish territory to be discreet as possible, 'The Count de Mornay . . . has concluded his mission and while awaiting the replies from his government, has decided to leave today to visit Cádiz on an unofficial visit . . . '. The secret arrival of the French was soon public

38 - Album: stallion galloping,
pencil.
Département des Arts graphiques, Louvre, Paris (RF 9154, fol. 40r)

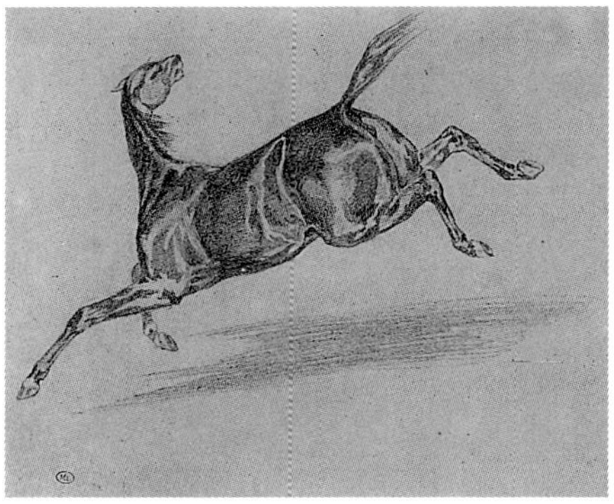

39 - Moroccans travelling,
1855,
oil on canvas,
54 x 65 cm.
Museum of Art, Rhode Island School of Design, Providence.

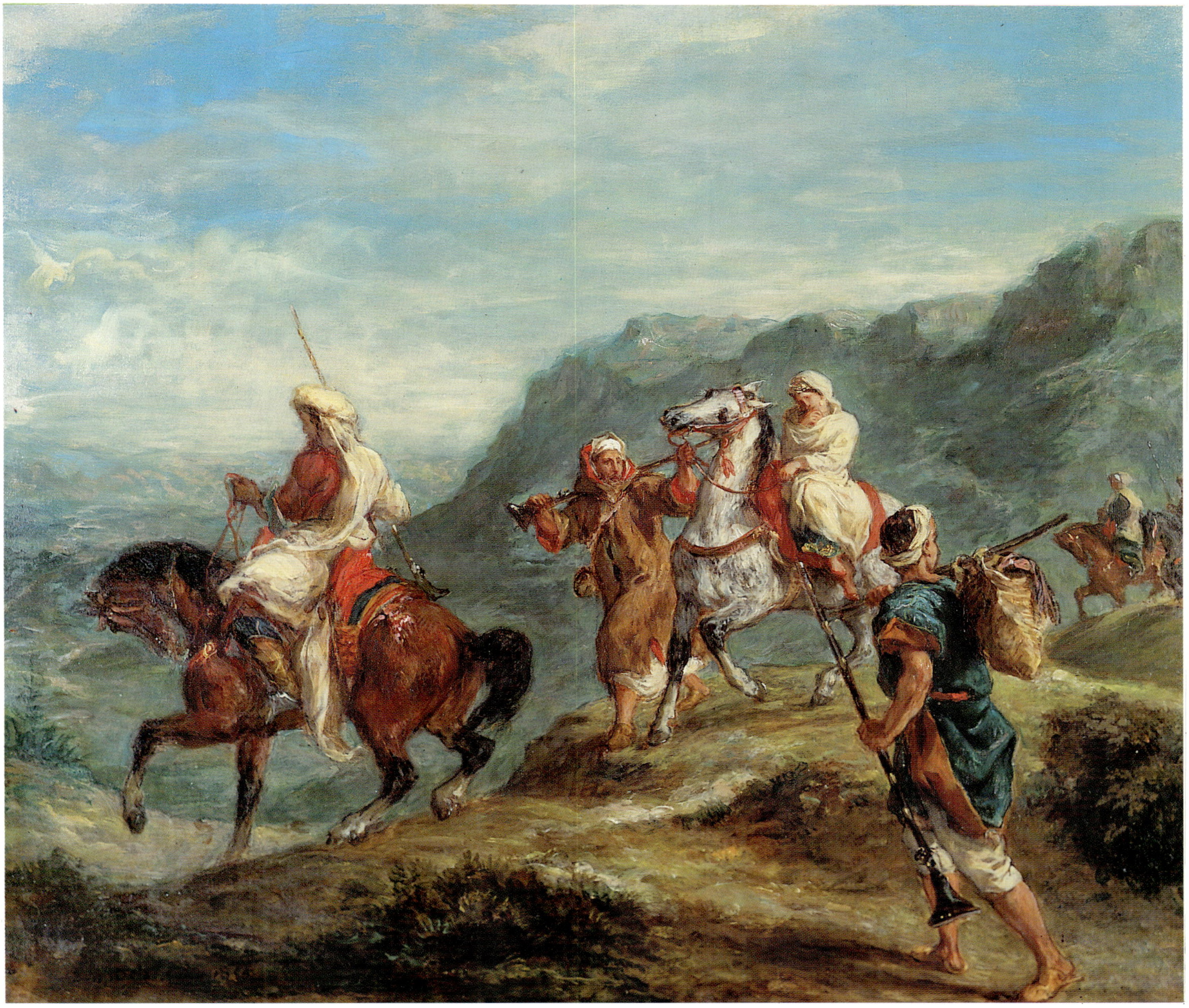

knowledge throughout Andalusia. Moreover, the corvette was unable to circumvent the health regulations and because of the publicity their presence had aroused, they were unable to experience the usual pleasures and escapades enjoyed by men of their age. The week's quarantine had limited Mornay's sightseeing programme and the 'monks, bullfights and even the ardent Spanish women' no longer found favour with the Count who, in the company of Desgranges, went discreetly to Gibraltar. Meanwhile, on **Monday 21 May**, Delacroix set off alone for Seville.

The two diplomats returned to Tangier on **Monday 4 June**. *La Perle*, with Delacroix on board, had arrived three days earlier. A special emissary from Moulay Abd al-Rahman awaited Mornay with the official document. The precious manuscript, complete with the emperor's seal, marked the end of the mission. There was nothing further to retain the delegation on Moroccan soil.

There was, however, the question of the wildcats and horses offered to Louis-Philippe—the animals were the object of much discussion and admiration. The menagerie completely occupied the courtyard of the French residence, filling it with its odours and din. Mornay was beside himself. Finally, on **Tuesday 29 May**, the cages and the fettered thoroughbreds were transferred to the hold of the English vessel the *John-Edward*, under the supervision of François Ferrary. The mystery remains unsolved as to the fate of the three thoroughbreds offered by the emperor to Delacroix, Mornay and Desgranges. They were not registered on the *John-Edward*, so it would seem that they were sold on the spot. Was it Delaporte, Benchimol or Ben Abou who played the role of horse dealer, and how much did the transaction bring to each of the accomplices? There can surely be no doubt that Delacroix's purchases were financed by the sale of his race-horse.

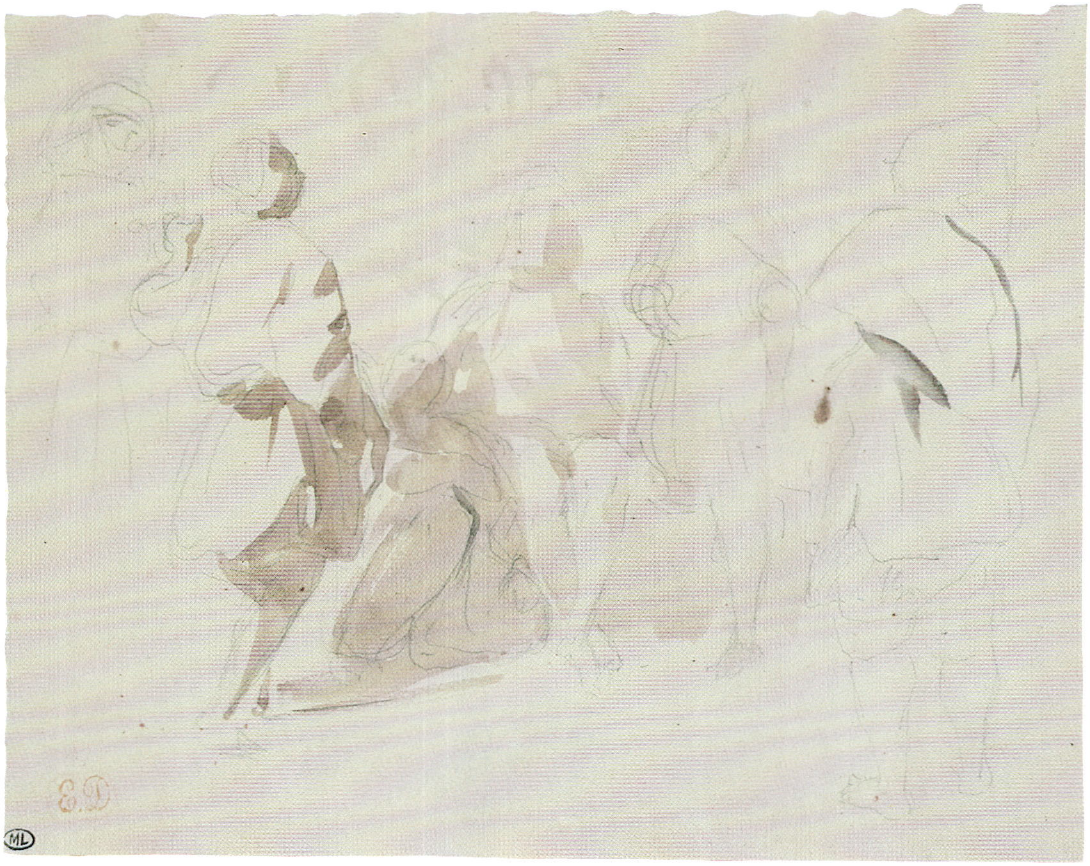

Prior to departure, Benchimol was responsible for making the purchases that would impress Parisian friends, while Claude Maurignaut and Pierre Boispon were in charge of finding space in the trunks for all the clothes, copperware and leather goods obtained by the dragoman's bargaining. Delacroix begged space in everyone's luggage for his purchases, 'long johns, caftans, spurs, a pointed bonnet, morocco leather for Bertin, clasps for Monsieur Auguste and cushions for R.C. . . .' . Mornay, who had never ceased to scoff at the Moroccans and their taste in gifts in his reports, was bringing back one present, given to him by the emperor: on Sunday 1 April, the palace had delivered to the Count a cherry-coloured, velvet saddle with gold embroidery, silk harnesses worked with silver and gold-plated stirrups, all wrapped in a 'metal-studded horse blanket' (fig. 41). The gift, judged by Delacroix to be of inestimable value, was rapidly entrusted to Benchimol who hid it carefully away.

For two whole days a constant flow of mules and rowing-boats went back and forth loading luggage, food and water onto *La Perle*. It had been agreed that they would set sail for Oran on **Saturday 9 June** at the latest. Few consuls came to take leave of the French delegation; since January their interest had somewhat waned.

An unexpected display of protocol nevertheless awaited the passengers of *La Perle* just as they raised anchor. The English royal yacht, the *Procris*, which had put in at Tangier three days earlier, accompanied the French vessel far out in the bay. She then hoisted the French colours and fired a fifteen-gun salute in in honour of Mornay and his delegation which was greatly amplified as it echoed round the bay; there was no risk of the French envoy leaving unnoticed. Captain Jouglas then gave orders to hoist the English colours on *La Perle* and to fire a twenty-one gun salute. These resounding exchanges were only recorded in the English archives: Mornay could hardly permit himself, in his last Moroccan report, to praise this dashing salute, he who, from the outset, had filled his correspondence with constant animosity towards the British and the 'English agent': any compliment he now made would seem suspicious and would suggest that he had been wrong all along.

After a ten-day stop-over in Oran from **Wednesday 13 June** and scarcely three days in Algiers from **Monday 25 June**, the mission set sail for Toulon. Both Mornay and Desgranges were proud of having successfully concluded a mission considered at the outset to be problematic. In Oran the French envoy gave his support to the military commander of the region, Pierre Boyer: 'We other Europeans may accuse him of extreme severity, but unfortunately in those countries clemency has no credit.'

From his arrival in Tangier, Delacroix had rejected this type of reference and dismissed the clichés through which the diplomat had constantly seen the Arabs, Moors and Jews. He was grateful to the Count for having included him in the expedition, but soon recognized the gulf which separated their views. Of much the same age, these two young people may have shared similar ambitions but they certainly did not react to their new surroundings in the same manner. The diplomat was imperious and scornful, whereas the artist was attentive and impassioned. His curiosity was always accompanied by tolerant attentiveness: '*O tempora!* Is this the price we pay for civilisation, and the happiness of wearing a round hat instead of a burnous?'

La Perle drew alongside Toulon on **Thursday 5 July**. Once again due to the quarantine regulations, the delegation had to stay in a 'wretched paddock in which a donkey couldn't graze'. The port's lazaretto which looked out onto 'three cemeteries' was 'a real purgatory'. What could one do in a

40 - Group of Moroccans against a Background of Crenellated Ramparts,
grey and brown wash,
15.9 x 20.2 cm.
Département des Arts graphiques, Louvre, Paris.

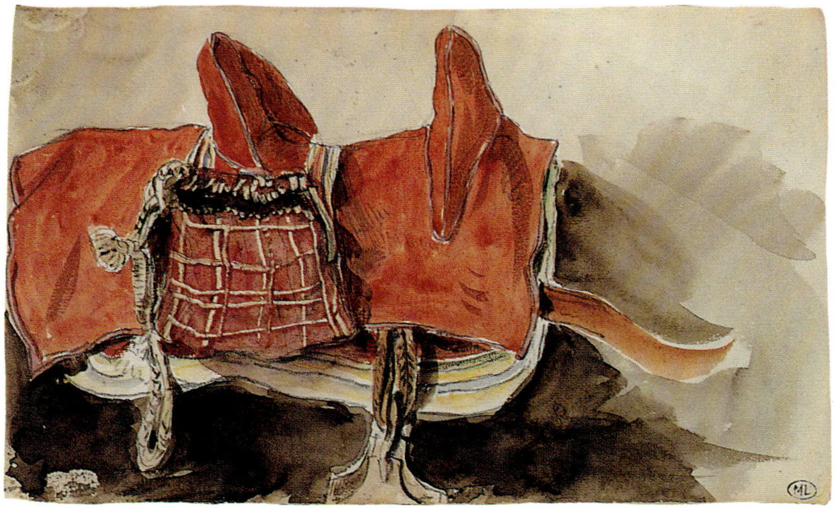

41 - Moroccan Album: the saddle given to the Count de Mornay,
pencil and watercolcur.
Département des Arts graphiques, Louvre, Paris (RF 39050, fol. 52v).

frightful place where, in addition, one was 'treated as a prisoner and an African'? Delacroix used this period of detention to his advantage by throwing himself into his work. A building which first had to be 'purged of a century's filth' with a 'stone slab on which autopsies are performed', was designated as a studio. The artist wanted to prepare some souvenirs for his companions in memory of their experiences together. He painted eighteen large watercolours for Mornay (see cat. nos 51 to 57), who could rediscover, in the brilliant and humorous series, the highlights of the voyage, such as the encampment near El-Ksar el-Kebir, the stop-off point near Tangier and the fantasia outside the gates of Meknes. There were also the comic moments which had cheered the Count on the route, such as the performances of the Gnaouas (fig. 42) and the travelling players, which helped to rid Mornay of any lingering bad memories. Finally, there was a gallery of portraits including the emperor Moulay Abd al-Rahman, Ettayeb Biaz, Mohammed Ben Abou and the Benchimol family, proudly represented by a portrait of Abraham and a watercolour of his wife Saada with their daughter Preciada (see p. 179).

On **Friday 20 July**, *La Perle* went into dry dock for repairs while Delacroix, Mornay, Desgranges, Ferrary and the two valets were already squeezed into a coach on its way to Paris. Jouglas had remitted to the Admiralty the summary of expenses incurred by the passengers on board, one thousand five hundred francs and fifty centimes, chargeable to the Ministry of Foreign Affairs. They had unanimously agreed to omit Delacroix's name. With 'skilful' accounting the artist's expenditure was incorporated into the estimated expenses of the 'official' members of the delegation.

On his return to Paris, Delacroix, consciously or not, followed the dominant trends of the century. In his day glory depended on painting 'great themes' from antiquity or mythology.

From 1832, however, Delacroix's genius was imbued with the land of Morocco. He leafed through his Moroccan notes, each entry an invitation to a new image. The pages of descriptions and sketches reminded him the spectacles, rituals and timeless traditions which were revealed at every step, in a country where 'there is less of the Turkish alloy . . . and the vanities that fret our minds . . . '.

The discomfort of the journey on horseback and the life on the road had forceably altered the conditions in which the artist worked. A new freedom was born (fig. 43) and colours poured out with tenderness or anxiety beyond the rigid limits, reaching the innermost soul of the work and preserving the emotional potential and symbolic force of the subject. In his hasty sketches and watercolours, Delacroix explored far beyond the picturesque, the folkloric and the anecdotal, uniting the image of a country, a population and a period of Moroccan life which progressed nobly and without artifice.

Then there was the light in that country, sunlight, blinding or faint, the flashing rhythm of the primary and complementary colours of its rays; in this incandescent world, red shook green, yellow faded next to indigo and intense metallic blues stood out in white or grey rain. The landscapes, topped by a transparent glow, kept watch in the heart of the furnace or stretched out on the infinite horizons.

In Morocco, Delacroix had composed a new palette which rippled with colour and flowed with audacity and generosity between apparently dislocated forms, until logic and instinct were united in the vital animation of a final brushstroke.

From Tangier to Meknes, whether in the shade of a hundred-year-old fig tree or a giant palm tree, in the Swedish consulate garden or leaning against a sun-baked wall in the 'glare and the reflected light from the houses, which are all painted white', Delacroix intoned a poem of liberty. Through his drawings, writings and attentive eye, he was able to express his Moroccan passions in a blazing cavalcade hung on picture rails throughout the world (fig. 44). He compared these Moorish splendours with the scenes he encountered in Seville and Cádiz. During brief stays in Oran and Algiers he searched for sensuous sources and with the *Women of Algiers* (see p.115) found 'the silent power which speaks first to the visual sense, then takes hold of all the faculties of the soul'.

To capture 'the striking sublimity that lies all about one here and staggers one with its reality', Delacroix had a creed: 'start by sketching large, with a broom if necessary . . . finish with a needle', an aesthetic message confirmed with the passage of time and which was heard and used by all successive artistic movements. Monet, Renoir, Seurat, Matisse, Picasso . . . all drank from this source of innovation.

Morocco had been the 'catalytic element which forced Delacroix to develop his art by revealing to him his own genius'. Delacroix's perception of the country, its contrasts and the diversity of its population, bore the mark of tolerance and humility.

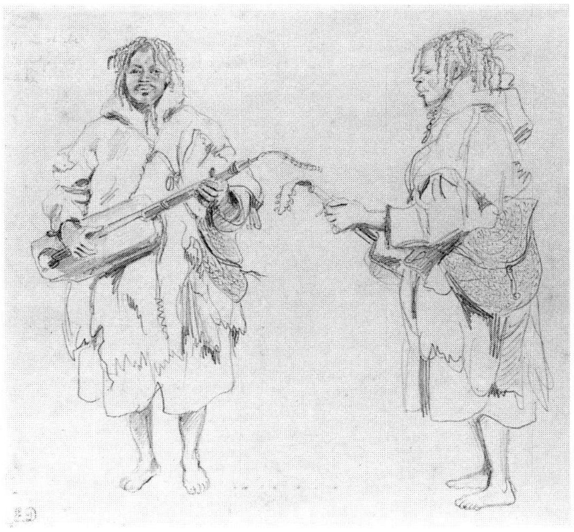

42 - Two Gnaouas Musicians,
pencil,
23.5 cm x 27.4 cm.
Département des Art graphiques,
Louvre, Paris.

43 - North African and Spanish Album: notes and sketches made during the journey from Meknes to Tangier,
ink and watercolour.
Département des Arts graphiques, Louvre, Paris (RF 1712 bis, fol. 31v–32r).

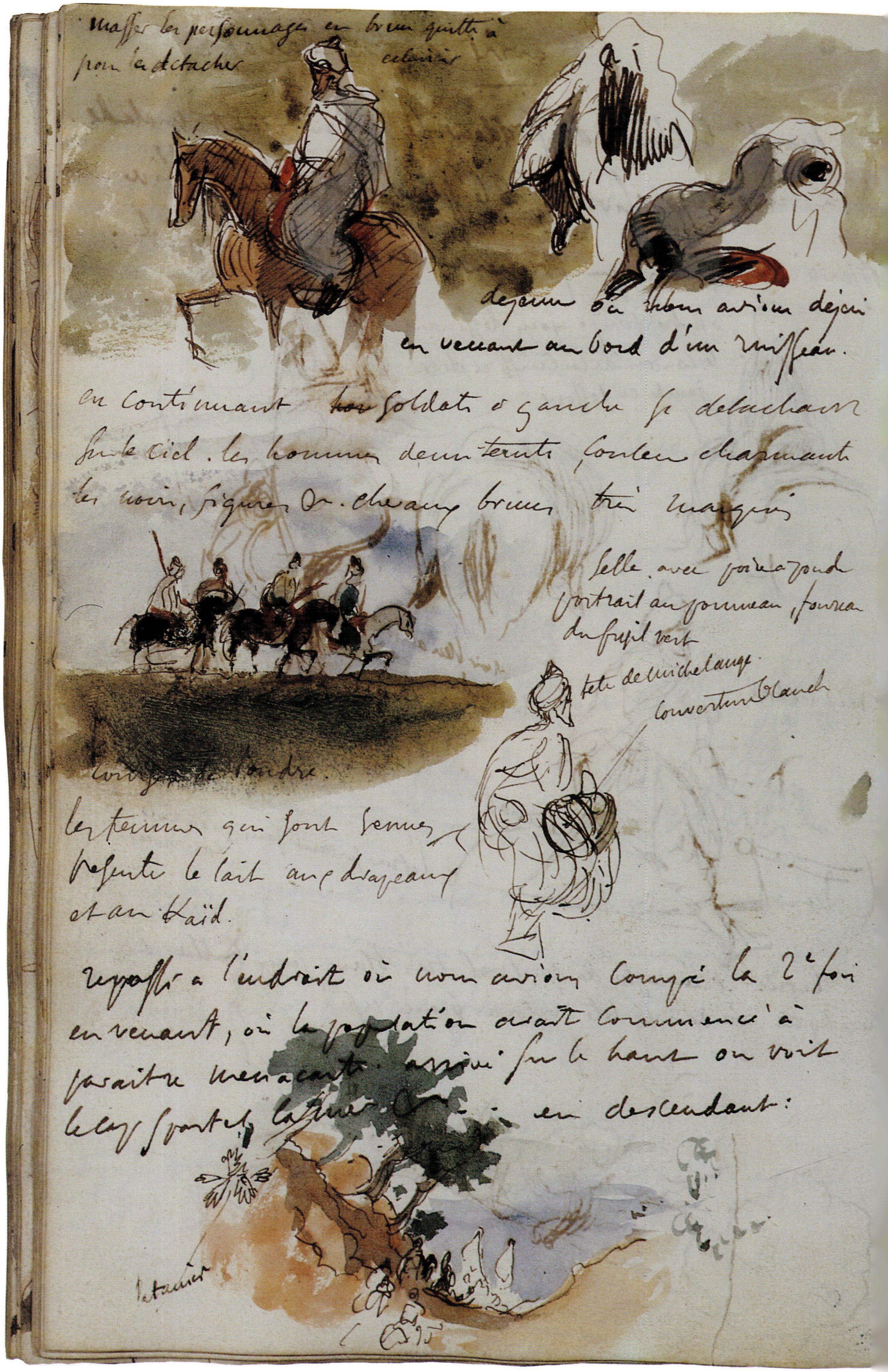
masser les personnages en brun quitte à éclaircir
pour les détacher
déjeuné où nous avions déjà
en venant au bord d'un ruisseau.
en continuant les soldats à gauche se détachant
sur le ciel. les hommes demi teintés couleur charmante
les noirs, figures &c. chevaux bruns très maigres
selle avec point à fond
pourtrait au pommeau, fourreau
du fusil vert
tête de Michelange
couverture blanche
Coups de poudre.
les femmes qui sont venues
présenter le lait aux drapeaux
et au Kaïd.
repassé à l'endroit où nous avions campé la 2e fois
en venant, où la population avait commencé à
paraître menaçante. arrivé sur le haut on voit
le cap Spartel, la mer ... en descendant:
latanier

Vaste plaine marécageuse, très détrempée ~~au~~ au premier voyage; très sèche à présent. drapeaux

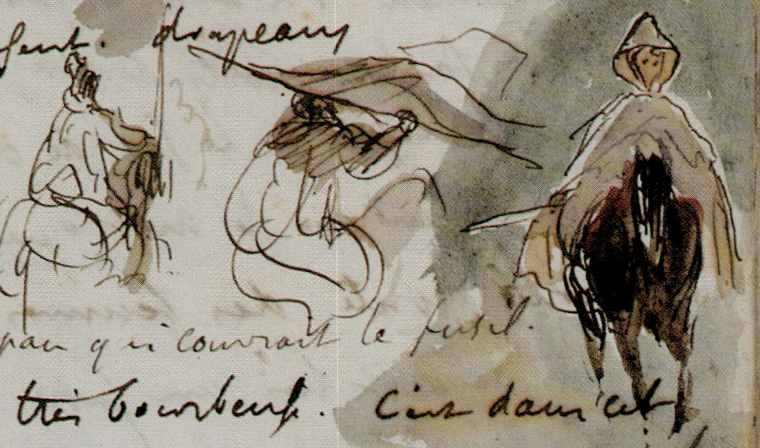

hommes éclairés par derrière
burnous transparent autour
de la tête, de même que le pan qui couvrait le fusil.

Il y a aussi une petite rivière très bourbeuse. C'est dans cet endroit où nous avons vu courir la poudre pour la 1re fois au 1er voyage.

Commencé à monter la montagne où est la forêt de lièges. Source charmante à droite qui serpente depuis le haut. Fleurs en profusion. rochers isolés comme des Contreb[illegible] [illegible]. Manteau rouge en montant [illegible]

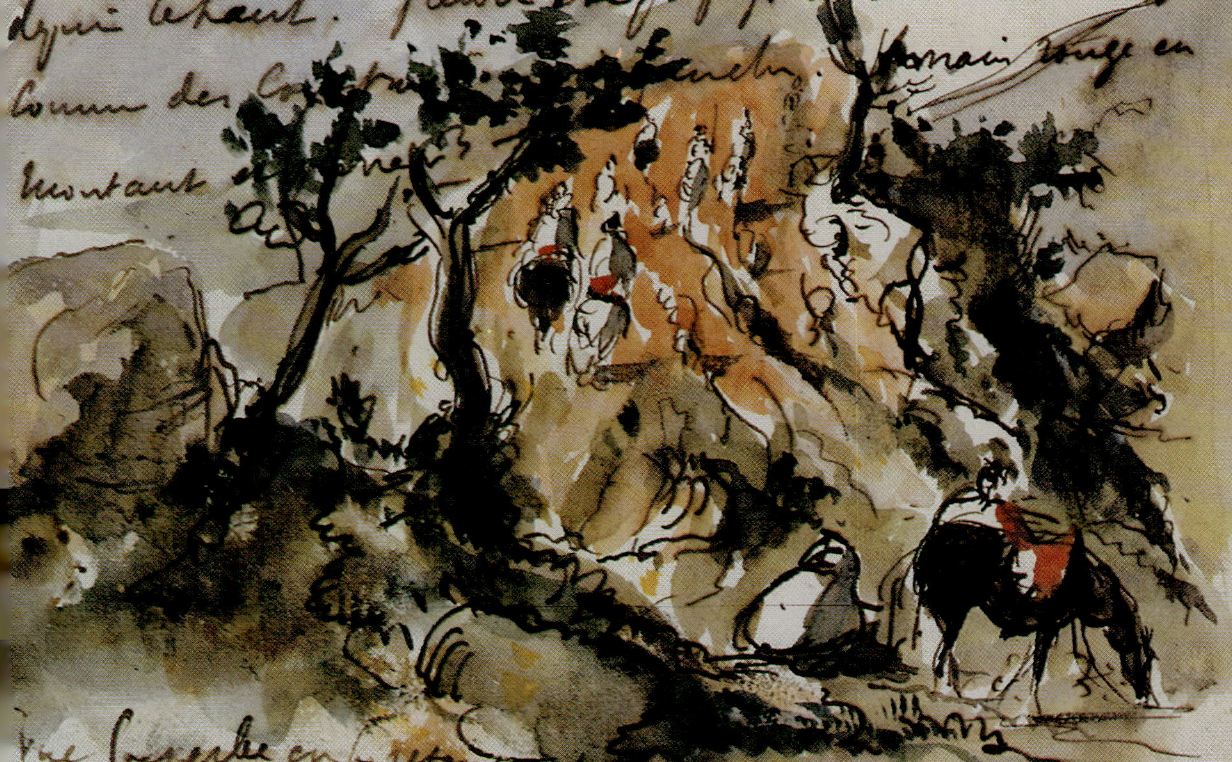

Vue superbe en se retournant.

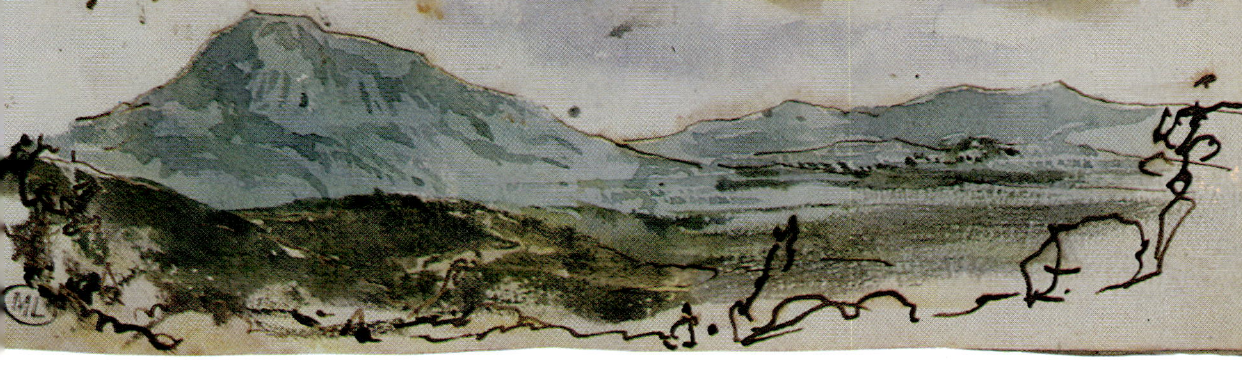

His spirit shines forth under the blazing skies and follows a people whom he accompanies in their splendour and their simplicity. He illuminates a land of 'grace and beauty . . . where the rainbow of liberty . . . gleams as brightly as in our own fair country . . . '.

Delacroix's Moroccan experience is still a beautiful reality.

Maurice Arama

44 - Arab Horseman Giving a Signal,
1851,
oil on canvas,
55 x 46 cm.
The Chrysler Museum, Norfolk, VA.
Gift of Walter P. Chrysler, Jr.

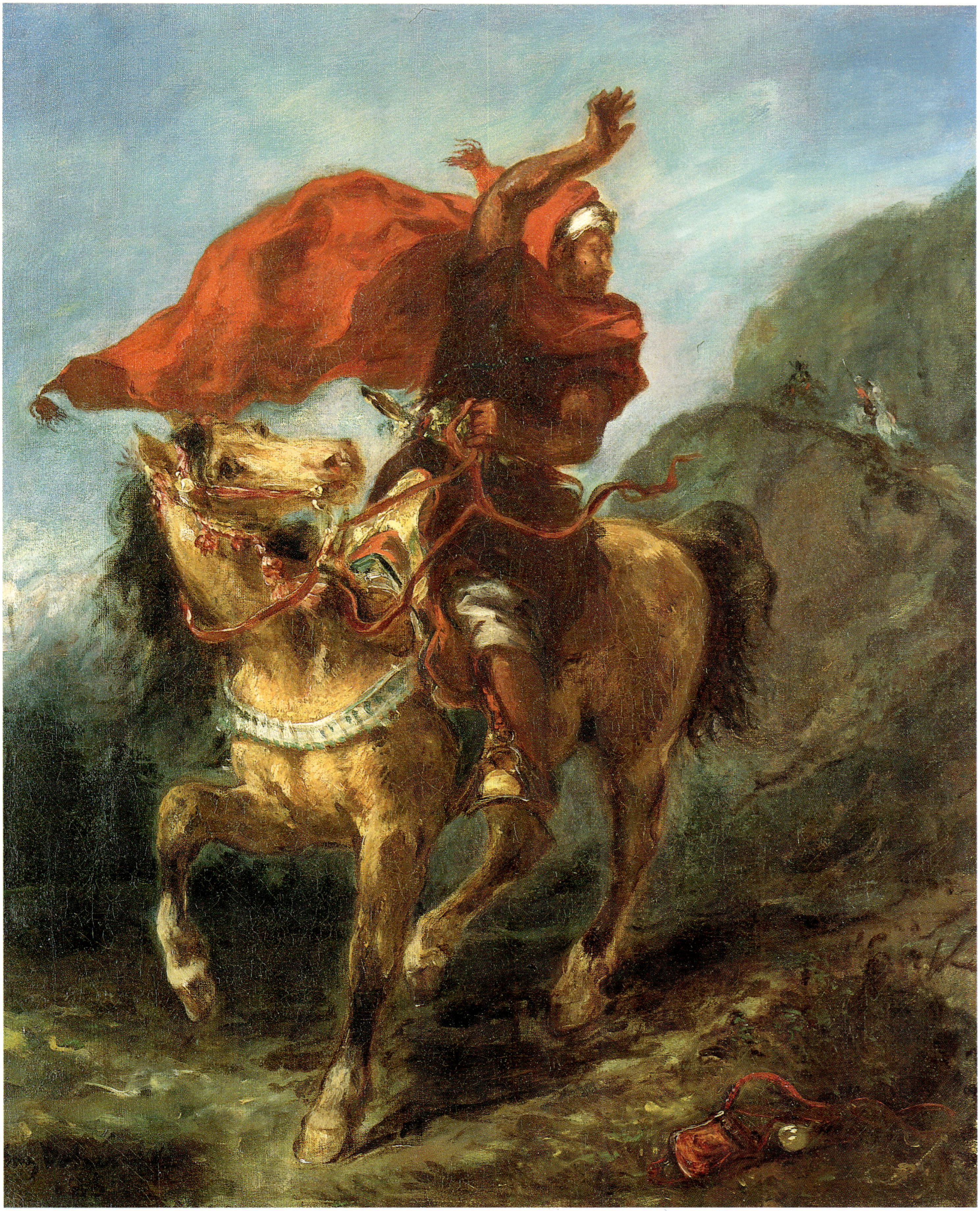

The Influence of the Journey on Delacroix's Art

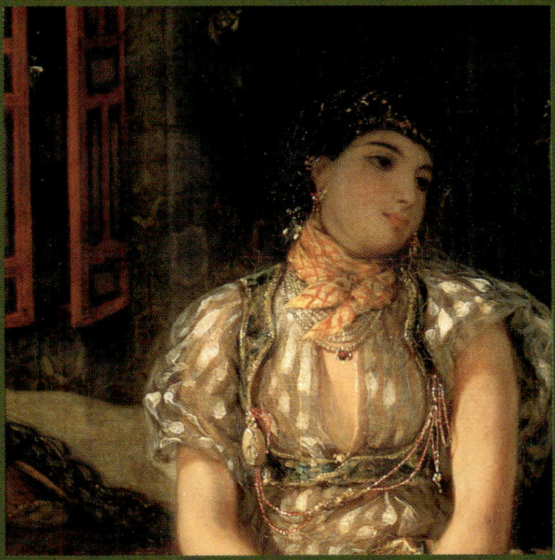

The Influence of the Journey on Delacroix's Art

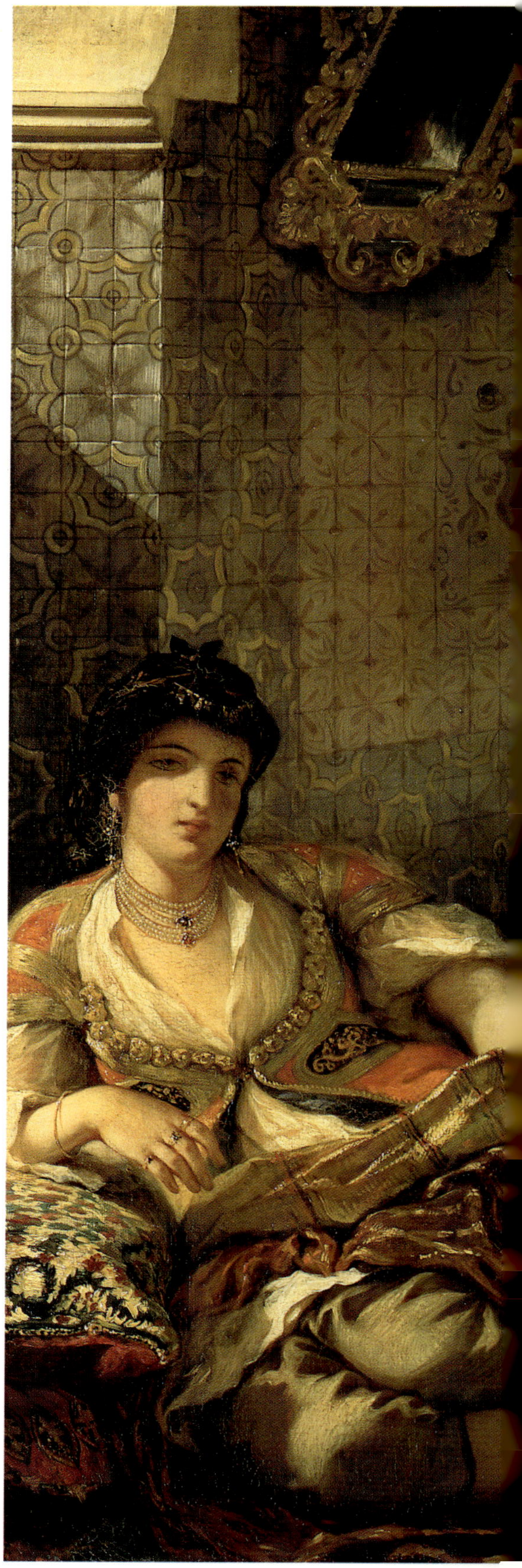

Delacroix's journey to North Africa in 1832 was arguably the most important single even in his life in terms of the influence it had on his art. Unlike the more classically inclined masters of his age, David, Ingres, Corot, he never spent a formative period in Rome, in fact was never to visit Italy; and unlike them he had established a formidable reputation with four major Salon paintings and a number of official commissions before undertaking the journey, which was to prove as significant for his development as the Roman sojourn had been for these other artists. He was in Tangier on his thirty-fourth birthday. Corot, the latest developer among the others, was five years younger when he first went to Rome.

The most obvious influence of the journey is iconographic: it provided Delacroix with subjects of pictures to last a lifetime, indeed several lifetimes, for did he not write to Armand Bertin from Meknes, 'At every step one sees ready-made pictures which would bring fame and fortune to twenty generations of painters.'[1] Apart from imaginary hunt scenes (about fifteen in all) and mural paintings with Moroccan motifs, he found time to paint approximately eighty pictures with North African themes, including such famous masterpieces as the *Women of Algiers* (fig. 1), the *Jewish Wedding* (see p. 68) and the *Sultan of Morocco and his Entourage* (cat. no. 84), shown at the Salons of 1834, 1841 and 1845 respectively. Between 1834 and 1859 he sent fourteen more to the Salons, three of which were rejected by the jury. Two of his last paintings were of Moroccan subjects—*An Arab Camp at Night* (see p. 89) and *Arabs Skirmishing in the Mountains* (fig. 6), both dated 1863. He also, of course, produced countless works on paper—drawings, watercolours, pastels—many of them highly finished pieces that rank in quality with the smaller easel paintings and on occasion surpass them in sensitivity or in richness of colour.

Concomitant with his new interest in North African subject-matter, there is a marked increase in documentary realism as well as in accurate observation of natural lighting effects in the first major painting based on his direct experience of the Arab world, the *Women of Algiers* (fig. 1). Having hitherto been acquainted only vicariously with exotic lands, through prints or paintings, Romantic literature and contact with widely travelled relatives or a friend such as

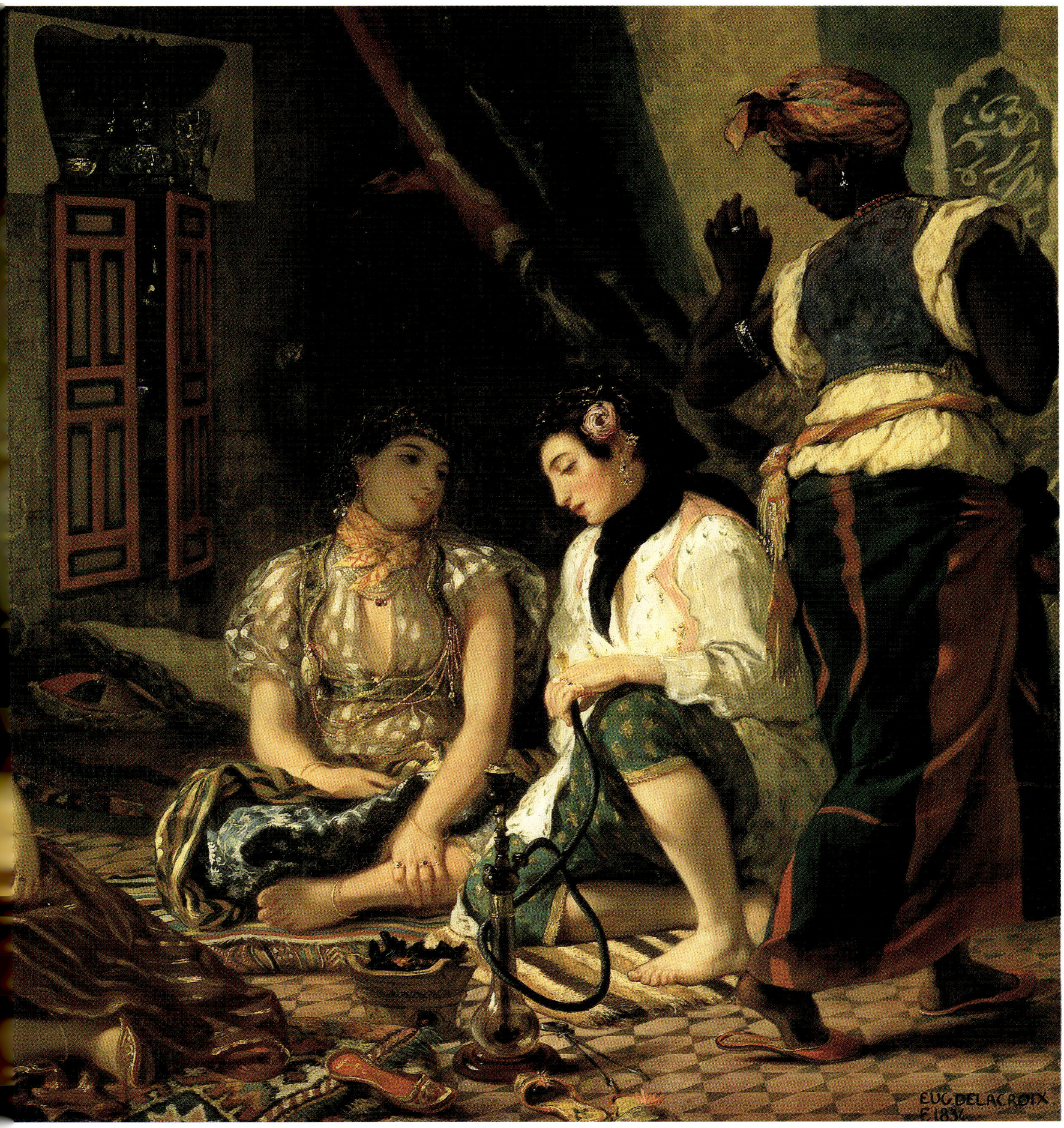
EUG. DELACROIX
F. 1834

Monsieur Auguste, Delacroix was overwhelmed by the wealth of unfamiliar sights that unfolded before him in Morocco. He feared that on his return to Paris he could not hope to recapture the vitality and striking aspects of the scenes he had witnessed. He expressed his misgivings in a letter to Pierret from Tangier: 'I'm even sure that the considerable sum of curious information that I shall bring back from here will be of little use to me. Away from the land where I discovered them, such particulars will be like trees torn from their native soil; my mind will have forgotten its impressions, and I shall disdain to give a cold and imperfect rendering of the living and striking sublimity that lies all about one here, and staggers one with its reality.' It is not surprising, therefore, to find Delacroix preoccupied with documentary accuracy, with getting the details of costume and ornament right, as he struggled for the first time to transmute his assortment of 'curious information' into a major work of art. Pieced together from studies he had made on the spot and from costumes and accessories he had brought back with him, the *Women of Algiers* is sufficiently accurate in detail to have been used by an ethnographic museum in Paris in our day to illustrate the dress of the period. Perhaps influenced also by the intensity of the light in North Africa, which he found to have a special brilliance and animating effect, he also pays meticulous attention in the *Women of Algiers* to reproducing the modifications of local colours by light—in contrast to the much more arbitrary colouring in the *Death of Sardanapalus*, for example, a painting inspired by literature, not by real life.

But the *Women of Algiers* is more, much more, than the sum of its carefully observed details. While it is largely documentary in intent and 'Romantic' in spirit, it is nevertheless classical in the supple monumentality of the forms and the grandeur of the design derived from the Venetian Renaissance—classical in the sense that Delacroix once defined the Antique: 'A skilful breadth of form combined with a feeling of life.' And here we touch on what was perhaps the most profound influence of the North African journey on Delacroix's vision: it enabled him to find a synthesis between the classical tradition, in which he had been educated and trained as a painter, and exotic orientalism, to which he was drawn by temperament. Not only did he not go to Rome but in a celebrated pronouncement, contained in a letter to Auguste Jal from Tangier, he declared defiantly: 'Rome is no longer to be found in Rome.' In North Africa he discovered a living antiquity, which he set against what he saw as the contrived antiquity of the neo-classicists based on a superficial imitation of antique sculpture. It is a recurrent theme in his letters home and he is reported to have cried on being introduced into the household of the women of Algiers, 'It is beautiful! It is like the age of Homer!' To Pierret he wrote: 'Imagine, my friend, what it is to see lying in the sun, walking about the streets . . . , figures like Roman consuls, like Cato or Brutus, not even lacking that disdainful look which those rulers of the world must have worn.' And in the letter to Jal: 'I have Romans and Greeks on my doorstep: it makes me laugh heartily at

Page 113:
Women of Algiers in their Apartment (detail),
Louvre, Paris.

Preceding page:
1- Women of Algiers in their Apartment,
1834,
oil on canvas,
1.80 x 2.29 m.
Louvre, Paris.

1
The translations of the extracts from Delacroix's letters are from Stewart, 1971.

David's Greeks, apart, of course, from his sublime skill as a painter. I know now what they were really like; their marbles tell the exact truth, but one has to know how to interpret them, and they are mere hieroglyphs to our wretched modern artists.'

The *Sultan of Morocco and his Entourage* (cat. no. 84) is an ideal example of the synthesis of the diverse elements comprised in Delacroix's artistic vision of North Africa. Conceived on a heroic scale, it is fitting that it should be the largest of the Moroccan pictures, for it represents the central event of the Count de Mornay's mission, his reception by the Sultan at Meknes—without the Count, however, who had long since been posted to a cooler zone, as Minister Plenipotentiary in Stockholm, and whose presence in the picture would have diminished its timeless quality as well as being rather irrelevant for the Salon public of 1845: his role as emissary of the King of France had paled into insignificance next to that of the artist who had attended the audience as a humble observer. The picture is ostensibly no less documentary in intent than the *Women of Algiers*: it was described, not quite accurately, in the Salon catalogue as reproducing 'exactly the ceremonial audience which

2 - Women of Algiers in their Apartment,
1849,
oil on canvas,
0.84 x 1.11 m.
Musée Fabre, Montpellier.

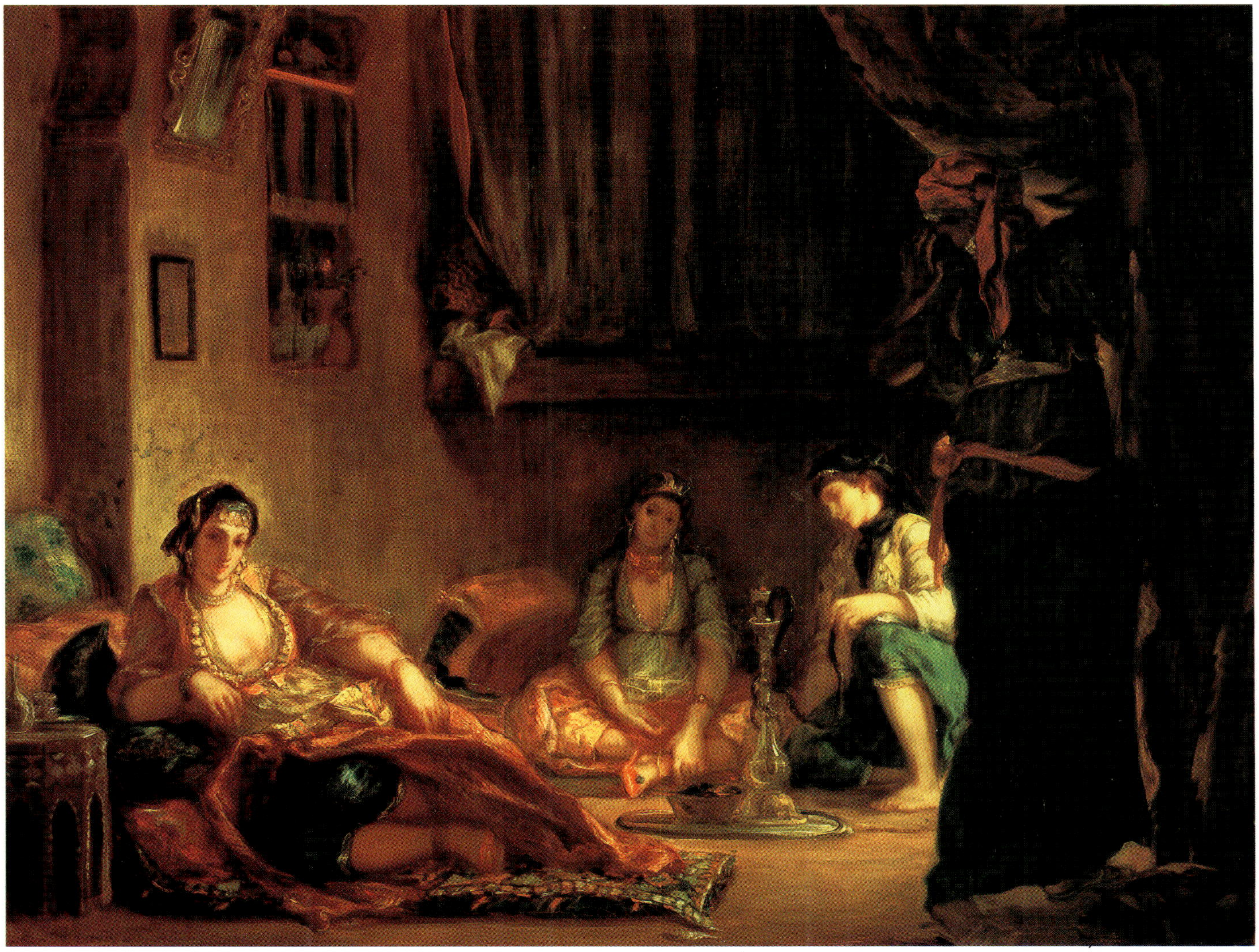

the author attended in March 1832.' Yet it far transcends mere reportage and also makes nonsense of the artificial opposition between classicism and romanticism so beloved by French critics of the nineteenth century. It combines in perfect harmony a subject and a mastery of colour and atmosphere that we think of as characteristic of romanticism with the best qualities of the French classical and Italian Renaissance traditions: clarity of design with majestic figures in bold relief foiled by a grand architectural setting (upgraded from the 'gateway, mean and without ornament' of the real scene), calm dignity allied to forceful draughtsmanship. For the first time a European artist has paid tribute to an Islamic potentate in a work of art that bears comparison, in scale and *gravitas*, to Titian's equestrian portrait of the Catholic emperor Charles V. It is, moreover, a personal, uncommissioned homage, although Delacroix may well have had good reason to suppose that his picture would be acquired by the State, as in the event it was.

In the face of the matchless beauty of the *Women of Algiers,* which some might regard as a perfect illustration of Delacroix's belief that 'Beauty is truth idealized', it seems unduly modest of him to have noted in October 1853: 'I began to make something tolerable of my African journey only when I had so far forgotten the trivial details as to recall in my pictures just the striking and poetic side of the subject; up to that time, I had been haunted by the passion for accuracy that most people mistake for truth.' Yet without necessarily agreeing with him or knowing at precisely what point he abandoned his quest for accuracy, it is easy to see, by comparing variants of the same subject, what he meant. For instance, in the second version of the *Women of Algiers* (fig. 2), shown at the Salon of 1849, there is a drastic reduction of ornamental detail and a more atmospheric, more delicately nuanced handling of light and colour, a softening of the light and of tonal contrasts, which creates a most poetic effect of lethargic reverie. It is as though Delacroix were recalling the scene through a tinted veil of memory.

Much detail is also eliminated in the two later, small versions of the *Sultan of Morocco* (fig. 3), of 1856 and 1862, and the severe monumentality of the original is relaxed. In the last variant particularly there is a sense of agitation in contrast to the noble calm of the large picture and a vibrancy in the brushwork giving the impression that Delacroix's hand was quivering with emotion as he sought to evoke 'the striking and poetic side' of the momentous occasion.

A comparable development is to be found in pictures containing more action, such as those of an Arab practice that fascinated Delacroix and which he had frequent opportunities to observe: the fantasia or *course de poudre*. In his first full treatment of the subject, the watercolour for the Count de Mornay's commemorative album, *Fantasia outside Meknes* (cat. no. 53), the horses run neck-and-neck and he relies largely on the English sporting print convention of the so-called 'flying gallop' (horses in mid-air with all four legs stretched out) to

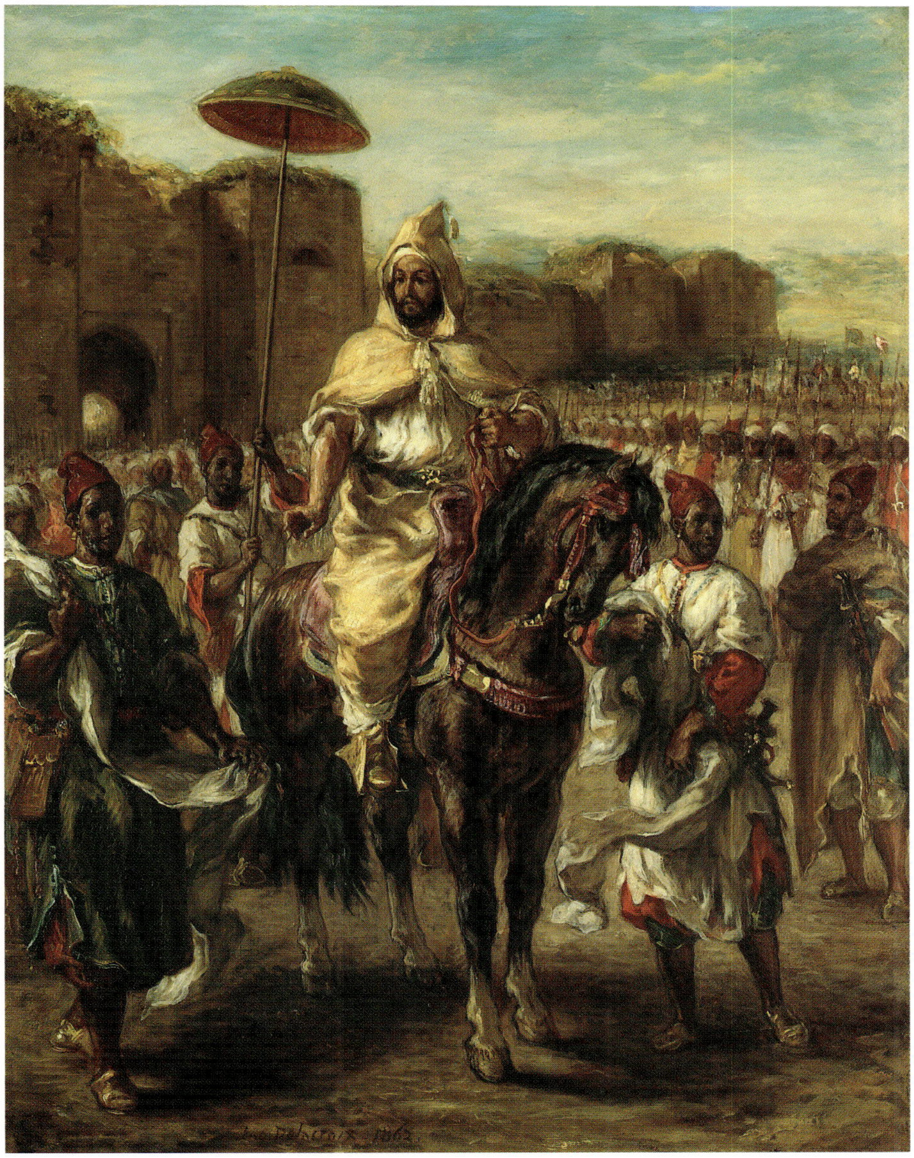

3 - Moulay Abd al-Rahman, Sultan of Morocco,
1862,
oil on canvas,
69 x 65 cm.
Bührle Foundation, Zurich, Collection E.G.Bührle.

convey a sense of speed. He has produced a sort of Arab Derby. This is followed, in 1832 and 1833, by two paintings (see cat. no. 58 and p. 88) which do not radically differ from it in conception, though the illusion of speed is enhanced somewhat by the introduction of a contrast of arrested motion in the foreground—a seated figure in one case, an Arab reining in his mount in the other. Nothing in these early versions quite prepares us for the wonderful explosion of energy in the *course de poudre* entitled *Moroccan Military Exercises* (fig. 4) in the Salon catalogue of 1847. Here, as careless of conventional gallops as of military alignment, and with a breathtaking vigour and freedom of facture, Delacroix catches horsemen dashing pell-mell across the full width of the canvas, one having half galloped out of it so frantic is their charge. Gautier caught the spirit of it well when he remarked in his review of the Salon: 'One has to be quick to get a look at this picture, for it gallops past.' Here, if anywhere, Delacroix disregarded trivial details and remembered only the striking aspects of his journey. Yet it is worth noting that, despite this ability to sacrifice detail in order to depict thrilling action with maximum effect in a picture meant to be seen by the public, he retained his more objective, analytical interest in individual items of Islamic dress or ornament long after his return to Paris. As late as 1851, for instance, he made for its own sake a detailed study in pastel

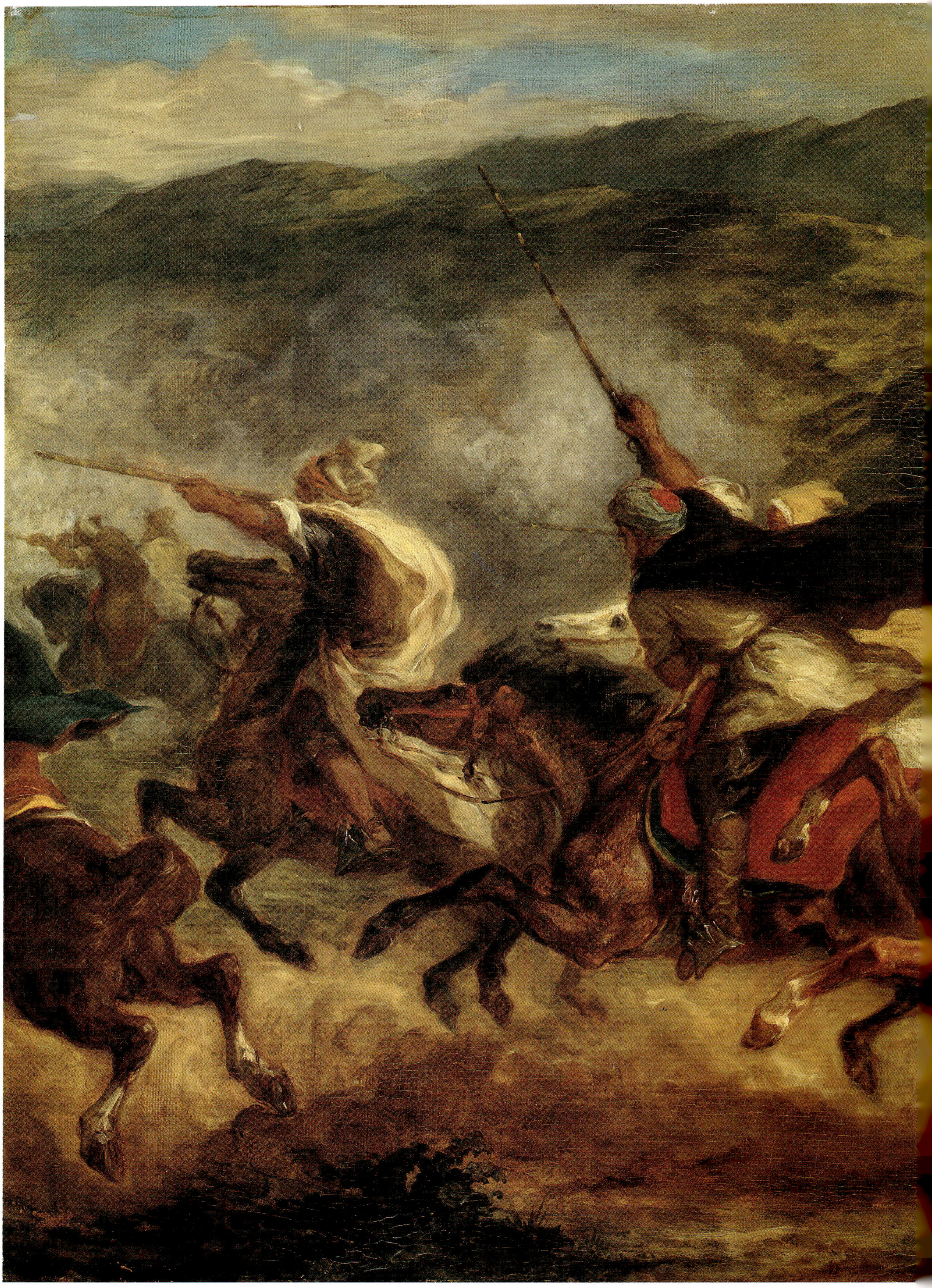

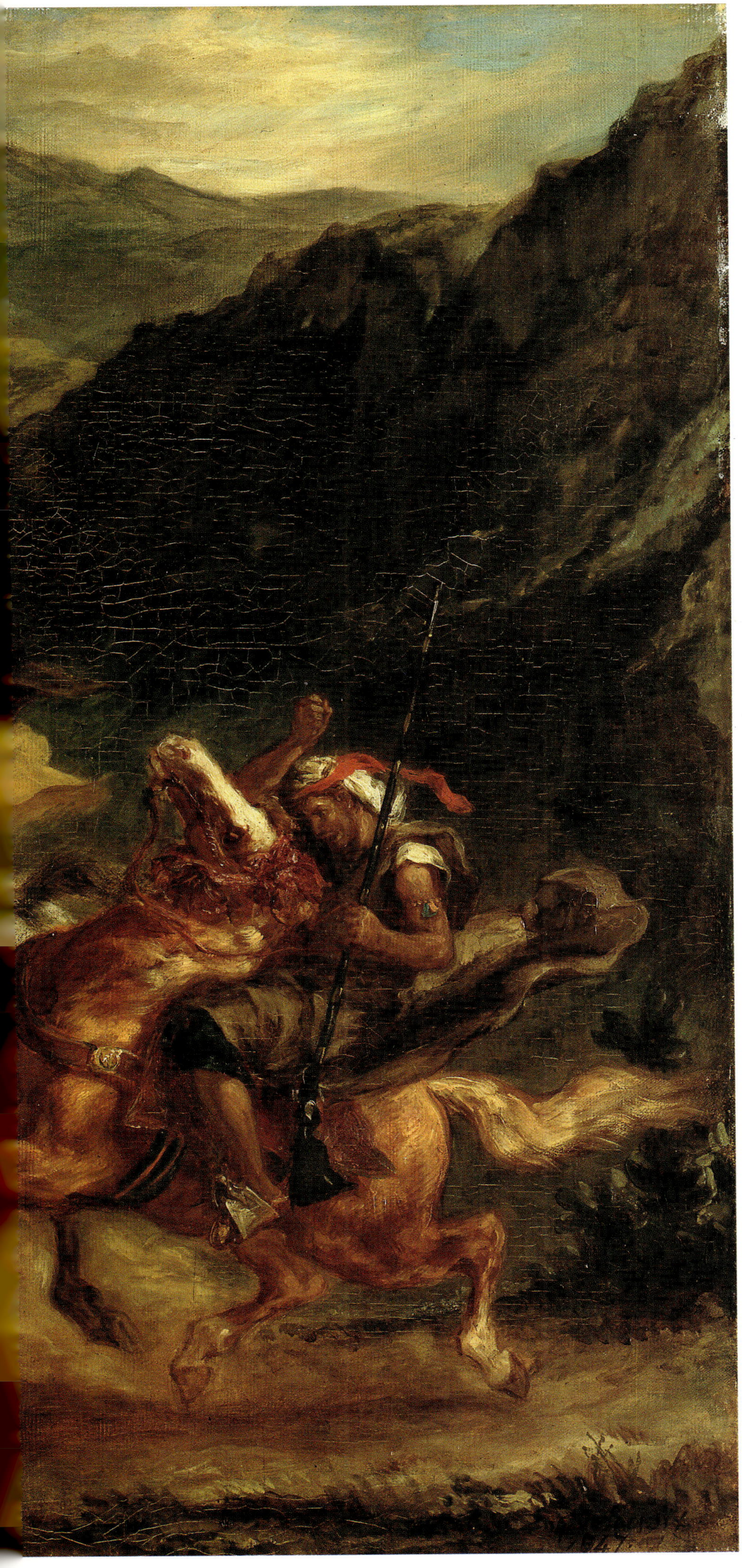

4 - Moroccan Military Exercises,
1847,
oil on canvas,
66 x 82 cm.
Sammlung Oskar Reinhart, Winterthur,
'Am Römerholz'.

of a colourful striped *gandoura* lent to him by his friend Charles Cournault, who had bought it in Algiers; and no earlier than the 1840s he took tracings of other Arab artefacts such as ceramic tiles from sketches made by Cournault in North Africa.

If Delacroix may have cried 'It is beautiful! It is like the age of Homer!' on seeing the Algerian women at home, his very personal conception of the Homeric was by no means limited to the languorous charms of the harem. For him the Homeric in art consisted primarily in grasping the essence of a subject, not necessarily a classical one, and conveying it with dramatic and telling, sometimes ferocious detail so as to fire the imagination and remind us that we are sentient beings made of flesh and blood, not hieroglyphs. Thus he considered Rubens (and no doubt himself) truly Homeric, the 'Homer of painting' he called him, whereas Ingres was Homeric only in pretension because in copying externals he failed to capture the true spirit of antique art. In this special sense another variant on the theme of the fantasia, the *Collision of Arab Horsemen* of 1843/4 (fig. 5), might be seen as Homeric, and certainly Rubensian. Here Delacroix focuses on a moment of high drama as two horsemen collide, singling them out and enlarging them in relation to the main body of cavalry, which plays a secondary role. He had witnessed such an incident during a *course de poudre* en route from Tangier to Meknes, noting in a sketch-book at the time: 'The two riders who collided: the one whose horse's rump touched the ground.' And earlier he had been spell-bound by a furious battle between two Arab horses which had thrown their riders, describing it in a letter to Pierret from Tangier: 'Two of these horses fell out with one

6 - Arabs Skirmishing in the Mountains,
1863,
oil on canvas,
92 x 74 cm.
National Gallery of Art, Washington. Chester Dale Fund.

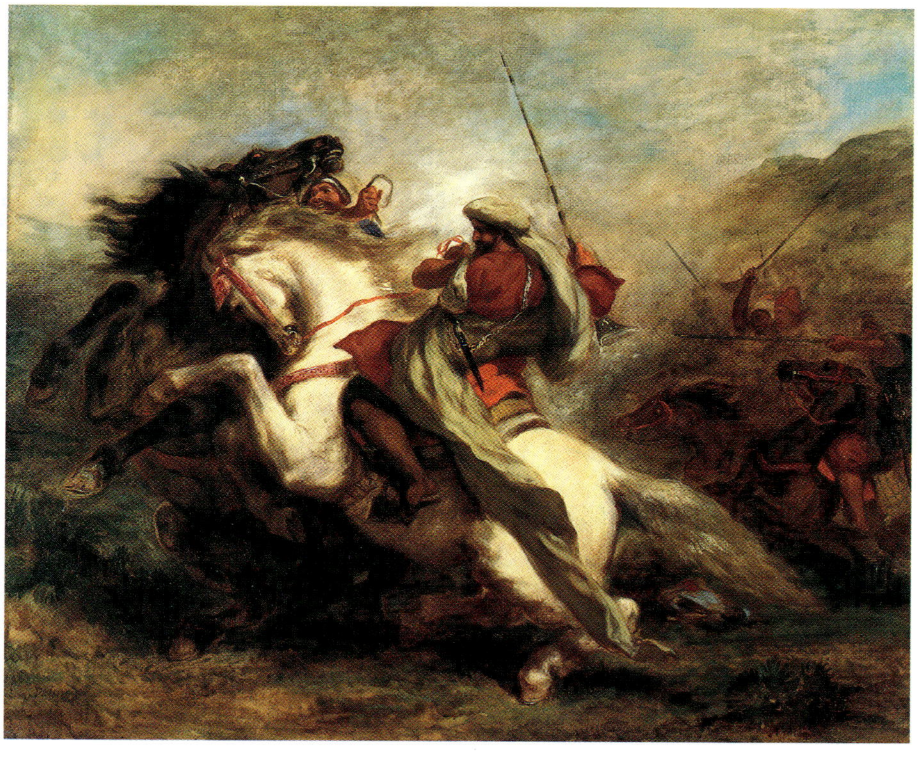

5 - Collision of Arab Horsemen,
1843/4,
oil on canvas,
81 x 99 cm.
The Walters Art Gallery, Baltimore.

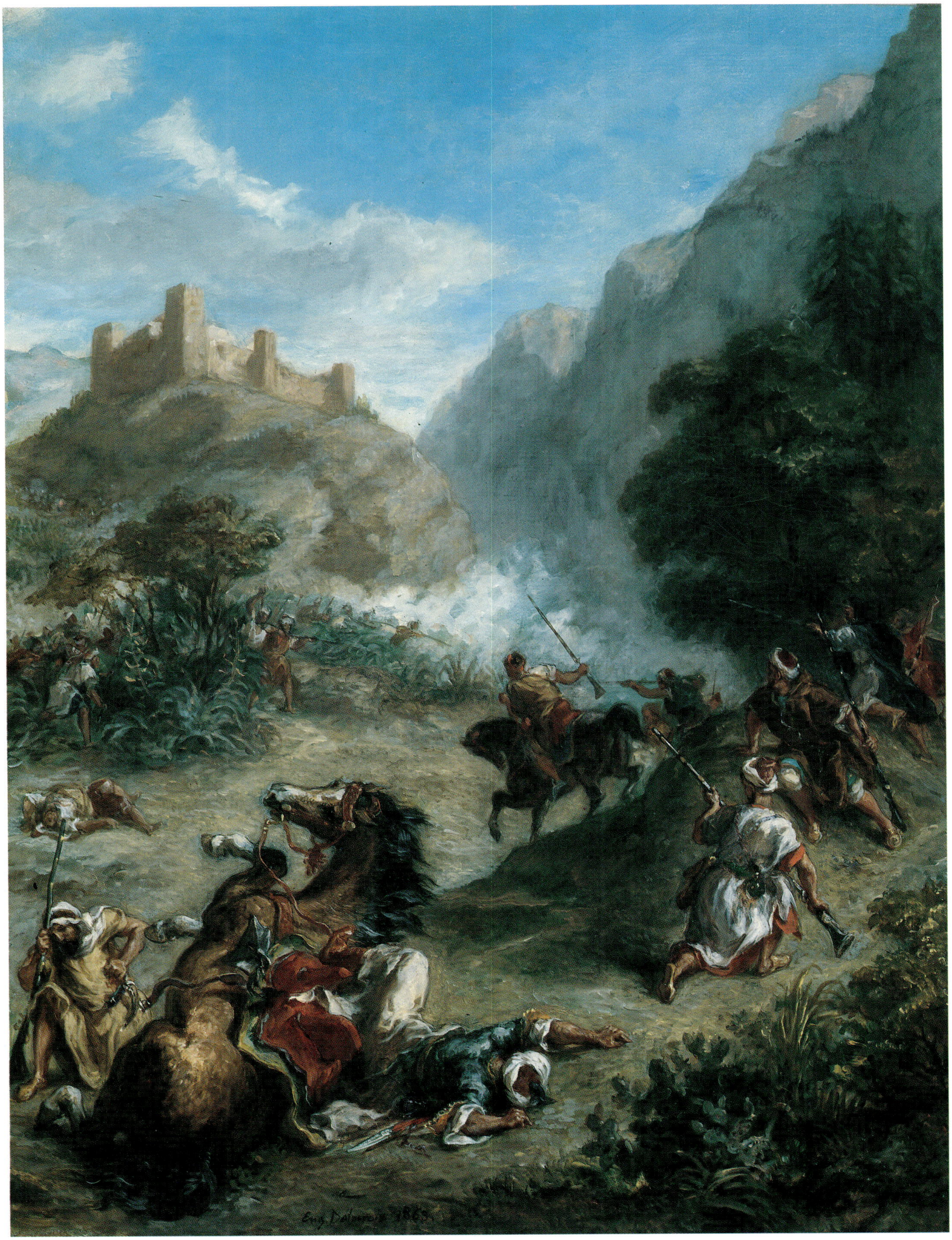

another, and I witnessed the fiercest battle you can imagine: all the furies invented by Gros and Rubens are tame in comparison.' (This combat was to provide the main inspiration for *Arab Horses Fighting in a Stable* dated 1860 (cat. no. 102). In an exhibition notice for the first of the two versions of the *Collision*, painted in 1833/4, Delacroix explained that in fantasias 'the horses often carry off their riders and fight one another when they collide.' While composing his picture, Delacroix no doubt turned over in his mind mixed recollections of the two real-life clashes that he had written about, and of Rubens. Now, instead of distributing all his horsemen parallel to the picture plane, as in the earlier *Fantasias*, he places the foremost of the two main horses thus, but the other is foreshortened and set diagonally in depth. This arrangement appears to be an adaptation of the similar contrast between parallelism and the oblique in the two prancing horses in Rubens's *Rape of the Daughters of Leucippus*, of which he was to make a copy from a print a few years later and which had evidently influenced him earlier, in a different way, in the *Death of Sardanapalus*.

If the *Fantasias* are based more or less faithfully on actual scenes witnessed by Delacroix, his last painting on a North African theme, *Arabs Skirmishing in the Mountains* (fig. 6), for which he was paid just four months before he died, appears, like his various pictures of Arabs hunting or being mauled by large cats, to be almost pure fantasy, though it clearly reflects direct knowledge of Arab dress and equipment. He seems never to have witnessed such a scene of carnage and in this instance to have invented the striking aspects of his journey. But he may have imagined it from a conversation he had with Amin Bias, who explained when they crossed the river Sebou by boat that as a matter of policy bridges were not built, 'in order to make it easier to arrest thieves, to levy taxes and to apprehend rebels.'

As in many of his later pictures on themes other than Moroccan, he devotes a large area of the canvas to the landscape and reduces the scale of the figures in relation to it. Thus they are less individualized than in many of the earlier works: most of those in the foreground turn away from the viewer, and the band in the middle distance, rendered with a sketchy touch, is largely absorbed into the vegetation and the smoke of battle. On the whole, specific detail and striking motifs are subsumed under the overall effect of colour, line and brushwork.

Despite the presence of a cactus or two, it may be wondered how far the flora is truly representative of North Africa and whether the towering background of rocks and fortress evokes an identifiable spot in Morocco (several critics at the Salon of 1859 doubted whether the local landscape was faithfully reproduced in *The Banks of the River Sebou* (cat. no. 100), one of them, Mathilde Stevens, seeing in it 'a Normandy-like Africa'). However far Delacroix's conception of the Arab world may have evolved from fact to romantic fiction in this, his final vision of the kingdom of Morocco, it is pleasing to imagine that, looking back thirty-one years to that fateful trip as he put the finishing touches to it, he may have been happy to reflect, in Homeric mood, that he 'comme Ulysse a fait un beau voyage'.

Lee JOHNSON

Chronicle of an Adventure

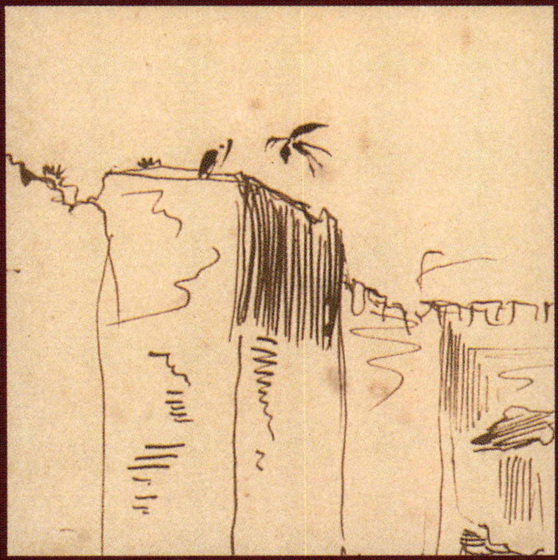

Chronicle of an Adventure

From what we know of Delacroix's character, we are inclined to believe that as soon as he received confirmation of his departure for Morocco, the artist took particular care to take with him everything that would be necessary for his work. The country he was about to discover would certainly not be able to supply him with paper of all sizes, pencils, pencil holders, writing cases, quills, brushes, inks and colours. Although we only dispose of scant information regarding the preparations for his departure (see the letter addressed to the stockist of art materials, Haro, 4 December 1831; *Correspondance*, I, p. 296), we can, nevertheless, imagine the aspect and contents of the artist's luggage by consulting the archives of some of his colleagues who, like him, travelled in North Africa or in the Middle East.[1] One thing is certain, and that is that he bought sketch-books of various forms and sizes. Of the seven which figured in the sale of Delacroix's studio in 1864, four remain intact: the three albums in the collection of the Louvre and the one in the collection of the Musée Condé, Chantilly. One of the Louvre albums (inventory RF 9154) is oblong, *à l'italienne* (perfect for landscape sketches), while the two others are the size of a small book (the Chantilly album with a red cardboard cover, and the famous album donated to the Louvre by Philippe Burty, inventory RF 1712 bis, fig. 2), whereas the fourth, modestly covered with green paper, resembles a pocket diary (inventory RF 39050, fig. 1).

The question of whether Delacroix took more than seven albums with him still remains unanswered; no documentation has emerged to give us new evidence on the subject. On the other hand, it is probable that the three missing albums have been split up (what sacrilege!). Current research, not only on the Louvre collections, but also based on inventories of drawings in private collections in France and abroad, has brought to light similarities in the paper and format between these individual drawings and the above-mentioned albums. Even if one takes into account alterations made when the pages were mounted and framed (until quite recently collectors did not hesitate to trim off the edges of a page to make it square), the convergence of all the available data may one day permit the reconstitution of one or more of these precious albums.[2]

Page 27:
Ramparts and Three Sketches of Arabs (detail),
see cat. no. 9.

1 - Moroccan Album,
pencil, brown ink and watercolour, album page: 16.5 x 9.8 cm. Département des Arts graphiques, Louvre, Paris (RF 39050, fol. 7v–8r).

2 - North African and Spanish Album,
brush, brown ink and watercolour, album page: 19.3 x 12.7 cm. Département des Arts graphiques, Louvre, Paris. (RF 1712 bis, fol. 25v–26r).

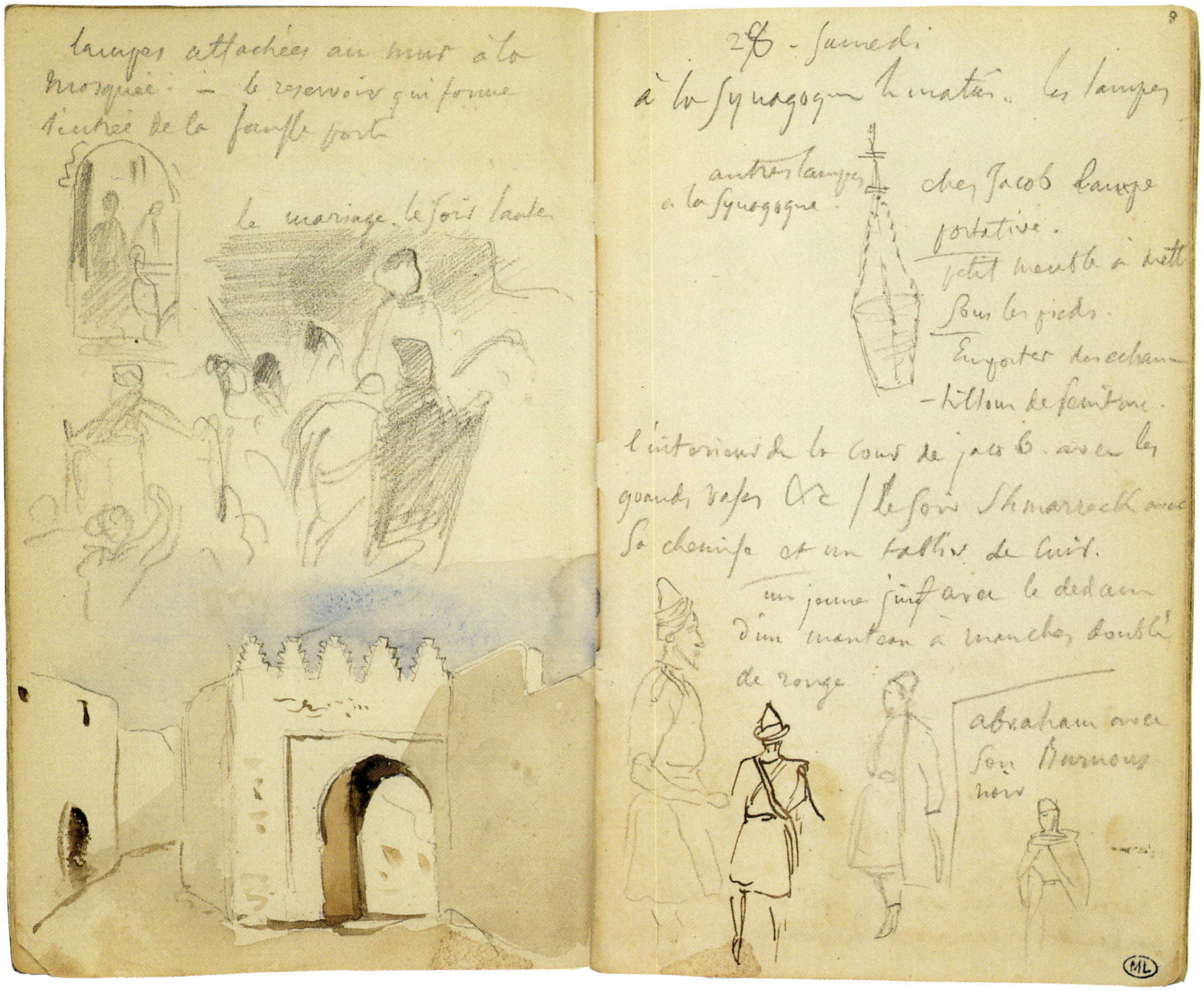
lampes attachées au mur à la mosquée — le reservoir qui forme l'entrée de la fausse porte
28 — Samedi
à la synagogue le matin. Les lampes
autres lampes à la synagogue
chez Jacob lampe portative.
Emporter des echantillons de ceinture.
l'intérieur de la cour de Jacob avec les grands vases &c / le soir Shmarrech avec sa chemise et un tablier de cuir.
un jeune juif avec le dedans d'un manteau à manches doublé de rouge
abraham avec son Barnous noir

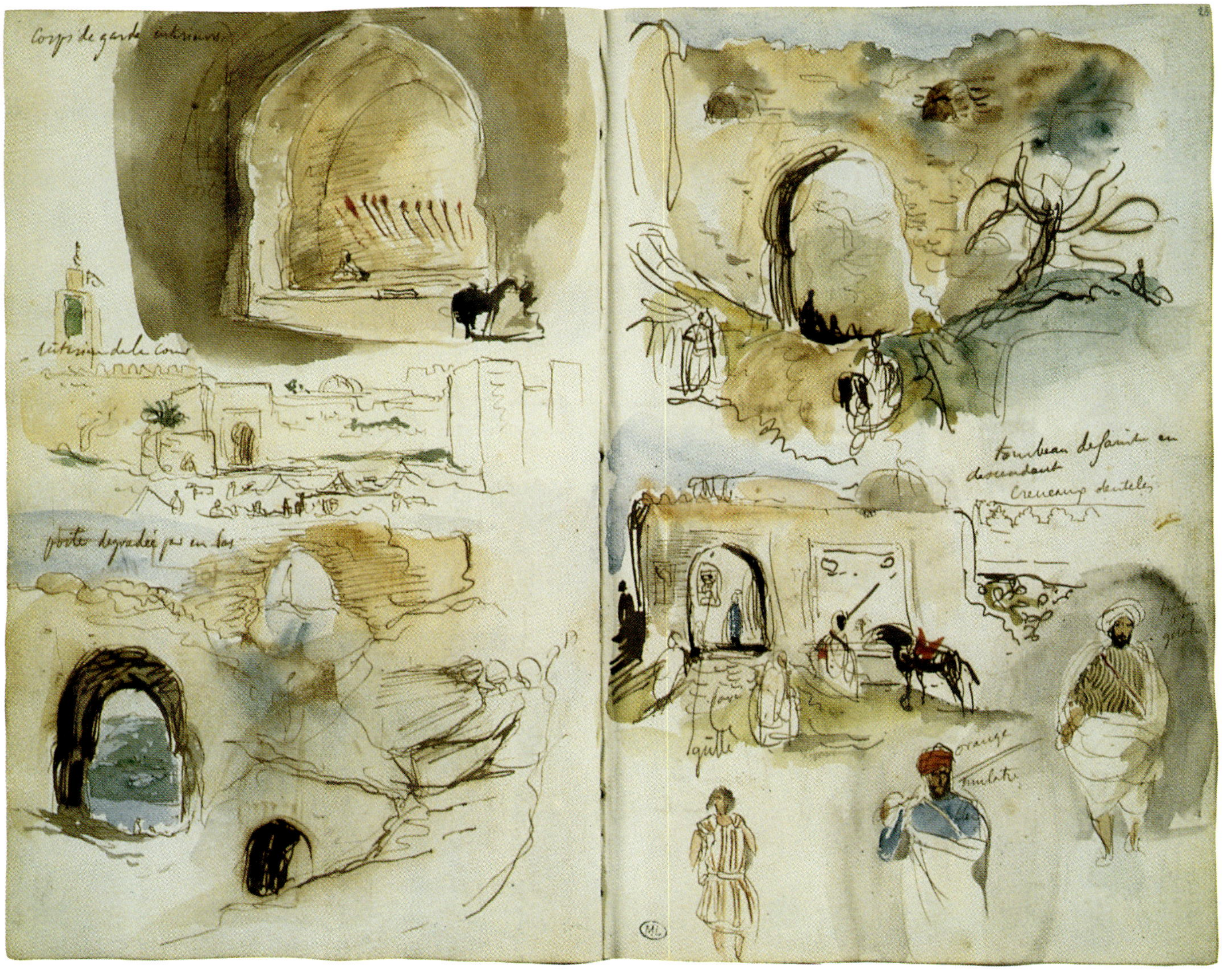
Corps de garde intérieur
porte degradée par en bas
tombeau de saint en descendant
creneaux dentelés
orange

According to the catalogue of the posthumous sale, about one thousand pages of sketches executed during the Moroccan voyage were found in Delacroix's studio at the time of his death (that is to say one sixth of the total number of drawings, pastels and watercolours put up for sale). These included studies of individual figures or groups, various events, landscapes, architectural details, studies of interiors, costumes etc., in other words, as Philippe Burty so rightly pointed out, a 'series of unique studies, both brilliant and scrupulously precise, of styles and costumes, of events and landscapes, notes that he made daily either against the pommel of his saddle or in an Arab's tent, in the streets of Meknes or in Abd al-Rahman's palace, his intention being to compile an illustrated account of his voyage on his return. Among this population which had not as yet been spoiled by European civilisation, he discovered thousands of aspects of antiquity. The voyage made an indelible impression on him and inspired several of his masterpieces. . . . ' (foreword to the catalogue of the sale following the death of Eugène Delacroix, 22–27 February 1864, p. XIII).

In addition to Burty's concise and sensitive commentary, we wish to quote an extract from André Joubin's preface for the exhibition, *Voyage de Delacroix au Maroc*, organized in Paris at the Musée de l'Orangerie in 1933, to celebrate the centenary of Delacroix's journey: 'Imagine Delacroix in 1832 . . . Then suddenly transport this young man from his studio in the gloomy rue des Fossés Saint-Germain to Algeciras or Tangier harbour, into a typical Mediterranean landscape, and into the liveliest, brightest, most picturesque and colourful of worlds that grace our planet! This oriental life with its turmoil of colours and the magic and rhythm of its forms is a veritable revelation for this somewhat intellectual artist, more inclined to search for a vision of the world through self-reflection than in the spectacle of the outside world. The result of this shock is to be found in the thousands of pages he brought back from this voyage . . . watercolours adorned with all the radiance of this wonderful country; rust-coloured landscapes enhanced by the proximity of the azure-tinted sea, women with strange costumes in dazzling colours, noble, serious Moroccan figures of proud deportment, petulant horses playing or fighting like children, and finally houses, dilapidated cottages or palaces and crenellated ramparts which evoke a land of legends and dreams. One should also admire the hasty pen and ink drawings executed at a street corner or against the pommel of his saddle while travelling, in order to capture a particular movement, a costume, a harness or an architectural detail.'

The first part of the current exhibition presents a selection of pages from the albums in which the artist noted all his discoveries from the moment he set foot in Tangier. The dates of some of them prove that Delacroix seems rapidly to have overcome the first day's bewilderment, which he confessed to his friend Jean-Baptiste Pierret on 25 January 1832: 'We landed in the midst of the strangest crowd of people. The Pasha of the city received us, surrounded

1

Dominique Vivant Denon (1747–1825), engaged in the Egyptian expedition, portrayed himself by the ruins of Hieraconpolis, sketching on a large sheet of paper with a portable folding stool next to him. In his work Voyage dans la Basse et la Haute Égypte, *he makes it clear that only the preservation of his drawings and diary was of any importance to him: 'I never let my portfolio out of my sight, I took it with me everywhere and at night it served as a pillow . . .' (vol. II, pl. 54 bis 2).*

In the correspondence of Nestor L'Hôte (1804–42), who accompanied the archeologist Champollion to Egypt, there are some indications as to the materials that the young artist used for his official surveys as well as for his own watercolours. 'I have several albums, but I forgot to bring ones with well-stuck, thick, white vellum paper for watercolours which are the best for making rapid studies of light and tone and which portray the real nature of this country in the most pleasant fashion . . . I would like two or three albums, one with sixty

by his soldiers. One would need to have twenty arms and forty-eight hours a day to give any tolerable impression of it all . . . At the moment I'm like a man in a dream, seeing things he's afraid will vanish from him.'[3] The first drawing dated *16 février* (16 February) is anything but a hasty sketch and is one of a series of figures whose faces and costumes are portrayed with great care, although some details are more cursory (see cat. nos 1–4, 14, 17 and 18). On the other hand, the page dated *8 mars* (8 March) (cat. no. 5) contains some much simpler, half-finished sketches exactly like the small drawings found throughout the famous Louvre albums. This is most probably a page taken from an album and the date indicates that Delacroix had started his famous journey on horseback two days earlier. But what about the Chicago drawing (cat. no. 8) dated *3 avril, Méquinez* (3 April, Meknes)? Do the larger dimensions (18.4 x 26.9 cm) also correspond to the size of an album page? There is no proof of this, even though the drawing scarcely differs in style from the one in Stockholm.

It has become popular to point out the progressive transformation which supposedly took place in Delacroix's notes and drawings over the six months he spent in North Africa. The first stay in Tangier is said to be characterized by a feverish, disorderly accumulation of a mass of information which then undergoes a more methodical organization, particularly during his stay in Meknes. On the return journey to Tangier, along the same route and with the same festivities, Delacroix would have had ample time to refine his approach towards a henceforth more familiar country and civilisation. But no matter how attractive this analysis appears, it loses some of its logic when one examines the large number of drawings available for our appreciation. Admittedly there was an initiation period, and there were of course numerous obstacles which made the artist's first immersion in this unknown world somewhat difficult, but his visual acuity coupled with his astounding draughtsmanship would normally have enabled him to overcome all these difficulties. During his stay in Morocco, Delacroix in fact used two complementary and parallel styles. The first is composed of signs, a sort of code, derived from manuscript notes, to serve in the case of an eventual lapse of memory. Examples of this can be seen in this exhibition in some of the drawings lent by the Nationalmuseum of Stockholm (cat. nos 5, 6, 11; fig. 3) and by the Louvre (cat. nos 9, 12, 30, 32, 44). Making fine, rapid sketches in pen or pencil, he only recorded the details essential to his comprehension: pointed bonnet, fold of a burnous, slippers or jewels (for a costume); profile of a nose, direction of a glance, movement of an arm or a leg (for a figure); wall or roof arris (see illustration p. 127), mosaic decoration on a staircase (fig. 4), door panelling (for architecture); the line of a crest of mountains or cut-off angles of aloes (for the landscapes). . . . The second style is more painstaking and reveals a perfect understanding of the harmony between line and colour, without ever producing a static, rigid image (cat. nos 20 and 22). From his first days in Morocco,

sheets of at least six by eight inches; the others approximately seven or eight inches and containing about sixty sheets each. . . . I also need two or three large badger-hair brushes, not quite as thick as a little finger and of proportionate length (Alph. Giroux, rue du Coq-Saint-Honoré in Paris)', (letter to his parents, Alexandria, 14 September 1828; cf. D. Harlé and J. Lefebvre, Sur le Nil avec Champollion. Lettres, journaux et dessins inédits de Nestor L'Hôte. Premier voyage en Égypte, 1828–1832, *Orléans–Caen, 1993, pp. 56–7).*

Antoine-Alphonse Montfort (1802–1884) travelled through Palestine for several months (December 1837–May 1838) and shared, when necessary, the rough life-style of the nomads. When he decided to spend the month of February 1838 in the Mar Saba monastery in particularly wild country: 'He left Jerusalem . . . on foot; his only weapons were his brushes, his only luggage his easel and paints, loaded onto a donkey driven on ahead of him by its owner' (L. de Laborde, 'Un artiste dans le désert', Revue française, *XI, March 1839, pp. 199–200).*

2 *R. Penzone,* Les Dessins de Delacroix au musée du Louvre: examen du support à l'aide des méthodes de la codicologie moderne, *DEA d'Histoire de l'Art contemporain, Université de Paris- Sorbonne, Paris IV, 1991.*

3 *Letter to Pierret, 25 January 1832; collection of the Louvre.* Correspondance, *I, p. 307; Stewart, p. 181.*

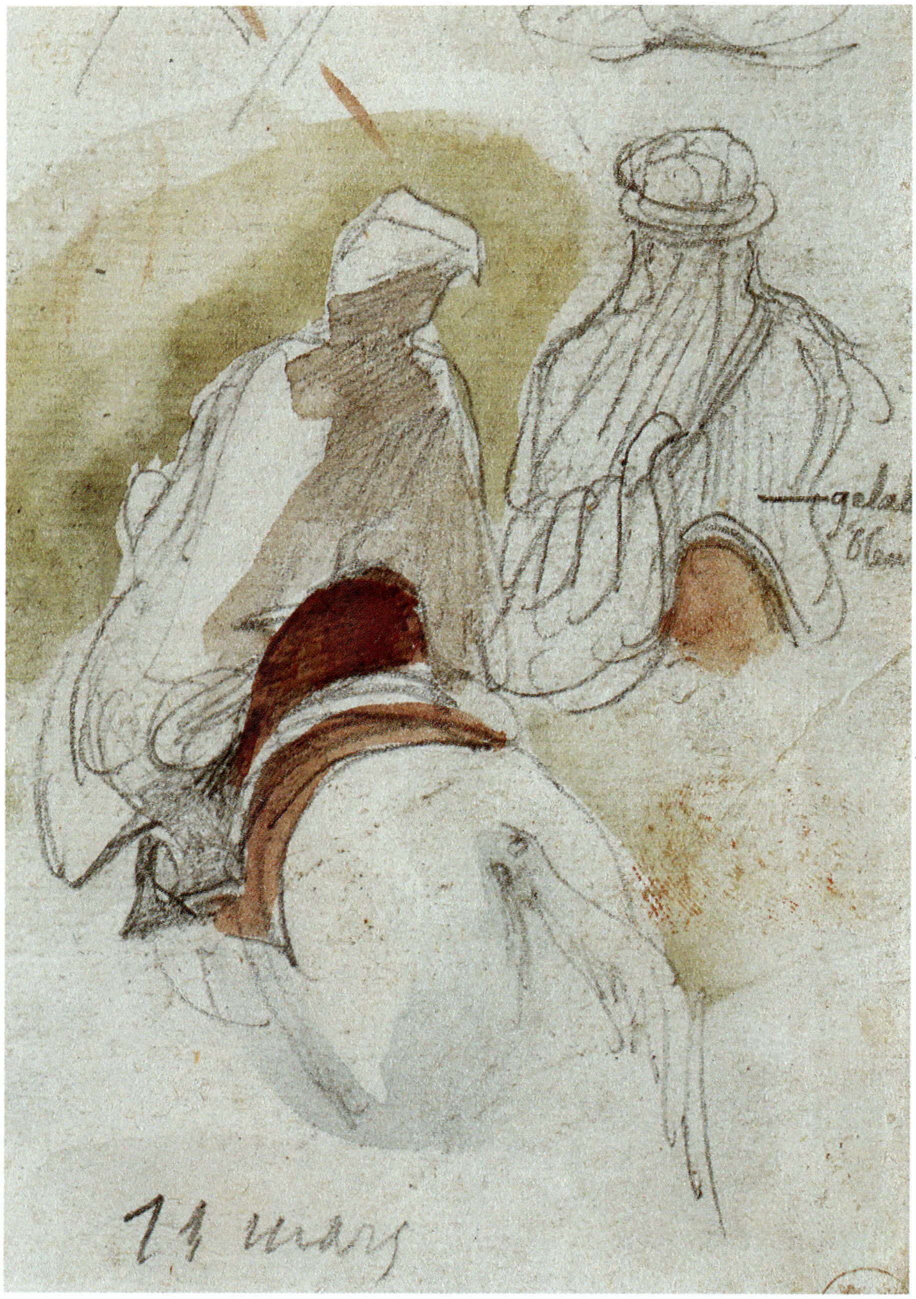

3 - Studies of Arabs on Horseback
(detail),
see cat. no. 6.

Delacroix was confronted with the living image of antiquity and at the same time with the sudden revelation of the magical colours and the brilliant light which enhanced and transformed the world around him (cat. no. 39). The imposed quarantine provided him with the opportunity to meditate, without being disturbed, on this unique discovery and to reflect on the best way of portraying it. It is the general opinion, never corroborated, that it was during this quarantine that the artist executed or finished the eighteen watercolours for the Count de Mornay, seven of which are presented in this exhibition (cat. nos 51 to 57). Each one is a small visual souvenir of one of the most important episodes of the voyage, notably the fantasias, or of individuals who played an important role in the negotiations between the French and the Moroccans, such as Benchimol, Biaz and Ben Abou, not forgetting of course the portrait of the Sultan of Morocco surrounded by his imperial guard.

On his return to France and up until his death, Delacroix never ceased to look for inspiration in this infinite source of new forms, colours and compositions. The third part of the exhibition presents some particularly revealing examples of this phenomenon of transformation, fruit of a prodigious imagination which allowed Delacroix constantly to renew his North African imagery from his stock of vivid memories. For six months he had been unable to set up an easel, but on his return to Paris he more than made up for the frustration he must have endured. From 1832 to 1863 he produced no less than sixty-five paintings (see Lee Johnson's *Critical Catalogue,* 1986) and this figure does not even include those pictures which cannot be traced. The most famous Moroccan painting, which constitutes the centre-piece of this exhibition, is of course the large portrait of the Sultan of Morocco, exhibited at the 1845 Salon and now in the Musée des Augustins in Toulouse (cat. no. 84). It is the most finished and most imposing work among the individual and group portraits which mark Delacroix's work during the thirty years which follow his return from Morocco. The artist made two replicas of it, smaller in size and somewhat different in style and conception.

At the Salon of 1833, Delacroix only ventured to exhibit three watercolours, (no. 636, *Arab Guardroom;* no. 637, *Jewish Family, Moroccan Costumes* and no. 638, *Costumes from the Kingdom of Morocco*), whereas at the 1834 Salon he presented three oil paintings. Two of them were accepted (no. 496, *A Street in Meknes,* cat. no. 59; no. 497, *Women of Algiers in their Apartment,* Louvre), but the third one was less successful in the eyes of the jury (*Collision of Arab Horsemen,* cat. no. 68). At the Salon of 1835 , the artist was able to present *Arabs of Oran* (no. 557; Johnson, 1986, no. 357, pl. 172), then at the 1838 Salon, he showed three works, the first of which can no longer be traced (no. 456, *A Courtyard in Morocco,* see cat. no. 13; no. 457; *The Fanatics of Tangier,* Minneapolis Institute of Arts; and no. 458, *Moroccan Chieftain,* cat. no. 69). The following year, the jury's selection was less in his favour and they excluded *Arab Soldier by a Grave,* as well as *Encampment of Arab Mule-drivers* (cat. nos 71 and 74).

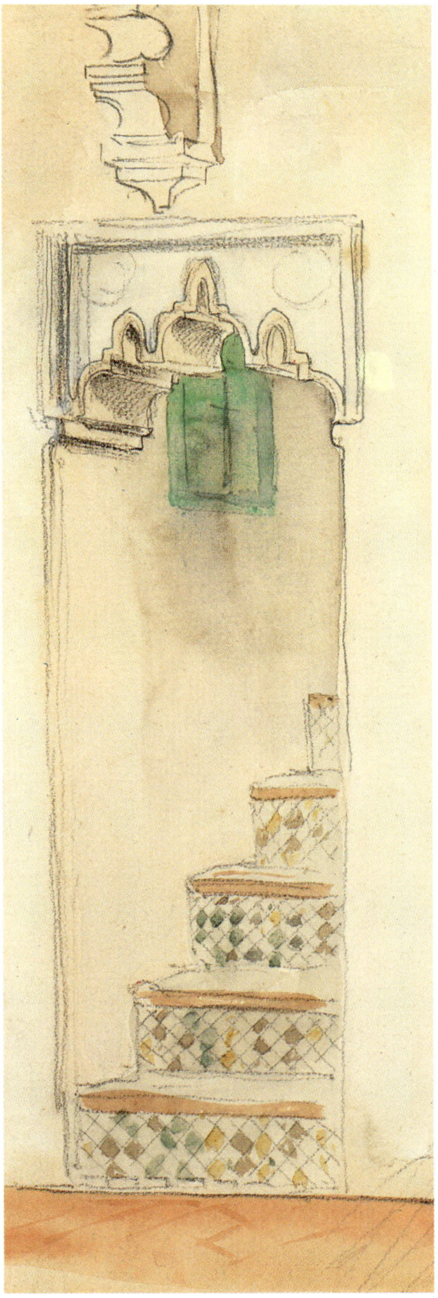

4 - Doors and Bay-windows in an Arab House (detail),
see cat. no. 44.

The situation was, however, quite different at the Salon of 1841, where Delacroix presented the *Jewish Wedding* (Louvre), and again in 1845, the year which marked the success of the large portrait of the *Sultan of Morocco* (cat. no. 84). Two years later, three works were passed by the vigilant jury, *Moroccan Military Exercises* (Oskar Reinhart collection, Winterthur), *Soldiers Sleeping in a Guardroom* (von der Heydt Museum, Wuppertal, see p. 97) and *Jewish Musicians from Mogador* (Louvre). However, at each of the two subsequent Salons, Delacroix only presented a single work: in 1848 *Arab Players* (Musée des Beaux-Arts, Tours, see. p. 80), and in 1849 *Syrian Arab with his Horse* (Johnson, 1986, no. 348, pl. 161). In the Universal Exhibition of 1855, Delacroix had a room reserved for his works where, in addition to the *Women of Algiers*, the *Jewish Wedding* and *The Fanatics of Tangier*, already known to the public, the artist presented a new painting, *Arab Family* (Johnson, 1986, no. 395, pl. 205).

For his final participation in the Salon, in 1859, Delacroix once again included a Moroccan work, *The Banks of the River Sebou* (cat. no. 100) among the eight pictures he exhibited. But his African works did not stop there, and in fact subjects derived from his voyage continued to haunt his imagination for the rest of his life. Occasionally the artist contented himself with a subject he had already depicted, as in 1862 with a second version of *Arab Chieftain* exhibited at the 1838 Salon, or again a final variation of *The Sultan of Morocco* (Bührle Foundation, Zurich). Often, however, the subject was completely new, as in the case of *Horses at a Trough* (cat no. 103), or *The Collection of Arab Taxes*, also known as *Arabs Skirmishing in the Mountains* (National Gallery of Art, Washington; see p. 123) which Delacroix executed in the year he died, at the same time as *Arab Camp at Night* (Szépmüvészeti Muzéum, Budapest, see p. 89).

One day Delacroix confided to Théophile Silvestre, 'Morocco made a great impression on me. All these emotions deeply moved me; I could only express them if my heart possessed a language. This country's aspect will always remain fixed in my mind, the men and women of this beautiful, strong race will be present in my memory as long as I live. It is through them that I really found the beauty of antiquity . . . ' (*Histoire des Artistes vivants*, Paris, pp. 65–6). Looking over the paintings and drawings which testify to what extent the artist was imbued with Moroccan images, one realizes that the peaceful scenes, pretexts for admirable compositions illustrating man and nature in perfect harmony (*Arab Chieftain, Arab Players, On the Road*, etc., see p.103) predominate, while the violent, warlike scenes centred around contests or combats (*Fantasias, Fanatics of Tangier, Collision of Arab Horsemen, Arab Horses Fighting in a Stable*) are less common, despite the fact that there are a great many references to these in the sketch-books and letters. This was most certainly a deliberate choice and is not really surprising considering how particular the artist was about which details he selected when recording a scene. Once back in France, although Delacroix did not systematically avoid referring to the prodigious repertoire of forms and colours he had accumulated during the six months, he nevertheless tended to use only the essential from the images recorded, which could then serve as a springboard for his imagination to create works where the actual memory is transformed by an increasingly lyrical vision. For the vivid luminosity of North Africa had modified his palette. Having discovered the effects created between colours, the trick of complementarity and the problem of reflections, Delacroix started to use a new technique consisting in the juxtaposition of brushstrokes which he called *flochetage* (flocking) (fig. 5), which enabled him to portray 'the illusion of movement' and the sparkle of reflections.

Many of the artists from Delacroix's day, and those who followed after him, were inspired by the Orient. Théodore Chassériau (1819–1856), for example, that 'Indian who studied in Greece and who, with the pure beauty of Phidias and an Athenian elegance, linked the mysterious and the sad with a certain savage grace and an indefinable oriental languor . . . ' (Théophile Gautier); other exponents were Alexandre Decamps (1803–1860), who travelled in Asia Minor, Alfred Dehodencq (1822–1882), Adrien Dauzats (1804–1868) and Eugène Fromentin (1820–1876), whose 'judicious, powerful and well-controlled' painting, as Baudelaire noted in 1859, 'evidently derives from Eugène Delacroix'; or again Gustave Guillaumet (1840–1887), Léon Belly (1827–1877) and even, more recently, Auguste Renoir and Henri Matisse. Not one of them, however, managed to produce that same 'rich, happy or melancholy impression' on the soul which so fascinated Charles Baudelaire, the profound impression of a voyage which gave Delacroix the opportunity to 'study at leisure both man and woman in their independence and native originality of movement, and . . . comprehend antique beauty in the sight of a race pure of all base-breeding and adorned with health and the free development of its muscles' (*Salon of 1846*). This was coupled with a particular magnetism issuing from 'the colourist's special power, from the perfect concord of his tones and from the harmony which is pre-established in the painter's brain, between colour and subject-matter' (*Universal Exhibition, 1855*). For Delacroix's genius resides in this intense expression of colour, which '*thinks for itself*, independently of the objects which it clothes. Further, these wonderful *chords* of colour often give one ideas of melody and harmony, and the impression that one takes away from his pictures is often, as it were, a musical one' [ibid.].[4] More than the discovery of a country and a race, it is the revelation of light and of its multiple effects on form and colour which constitutes the key to Delacroix's voyage from January to June 1832, a voyage of adventure and initiation.

Arlette Sérullaz

Page 136:
5- Arab Chieftain reclining on a Carpet (detail),
see cat. no. 15.

4

Art in Paris 1845–1862, *Selected writings by Charles Baudelaire, translated and edited by Jonathan Mayne, Phaidon Press, 1965, pp. 55, 141, 184.*

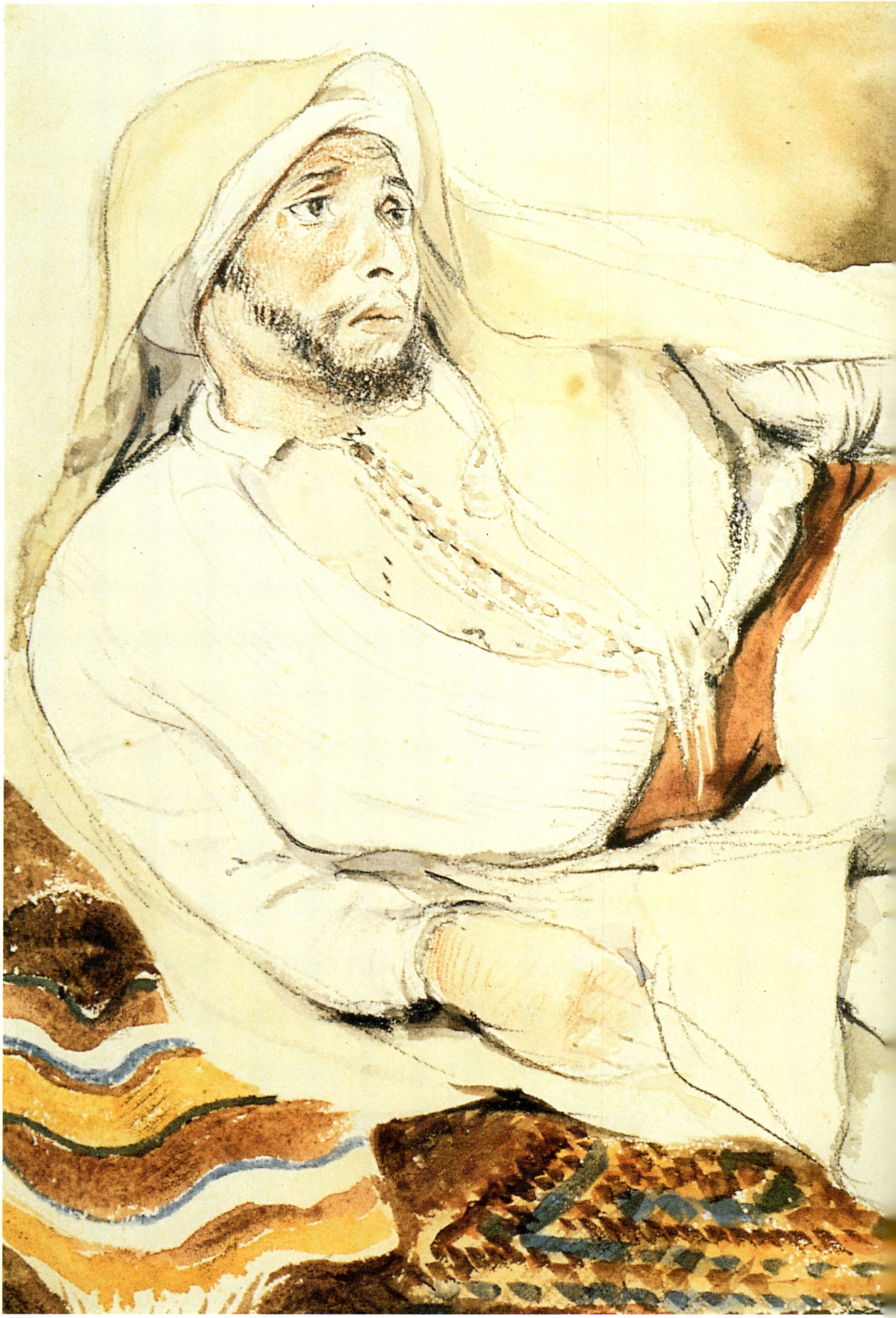

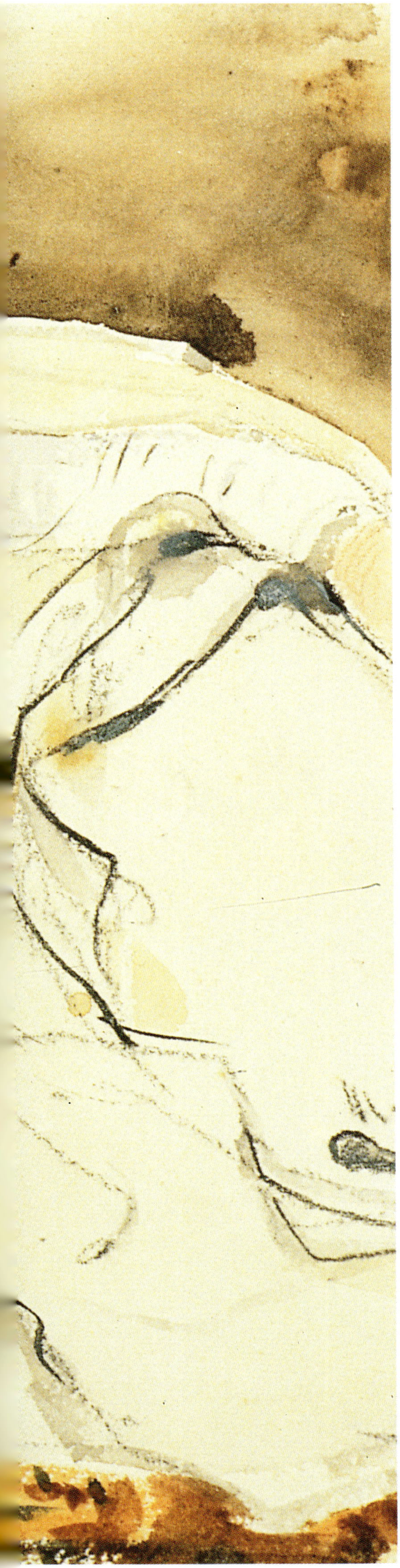

Notes for use of the catalogue

The catalogue has been divided into three sections.

The first section consists of a selection of forty-nine drawings and the only painting executed by Delacroix during his stay in North Africa. The dated works precede the undated works, which have been grouped by subject.

The second section is devoted to the watercolours offered by Delacroix to the Count de Mornay. The order and French titles of these works are the same as those used in the original catalogue of the Mornay sale.

The third section includes the paintings, engravings and drawings executed after 1832. They are arranged in chronological order. Those paintings originally exhibited in the Salons have been identified by the original French titles that appeared in the Salon catalogues, accompanied by an English translation.

The bibliography has been limited to the publications devoted to Delacroix's voyage to North Africa, museum catalogues and to the descriptive catalogues of the paintings and drawings. Only monographic exhibitions have been listed.

English titles for the oil paintings have been taken from Lee Johnson's *The Paintings of Eugène Delacroix*, Oxford, 1986. The editors of the English edition would particularly like to thank Mr Johnson for his generous collaboration and his suggestions for the English translations of the titles of works on paper.

Discovering Morocco

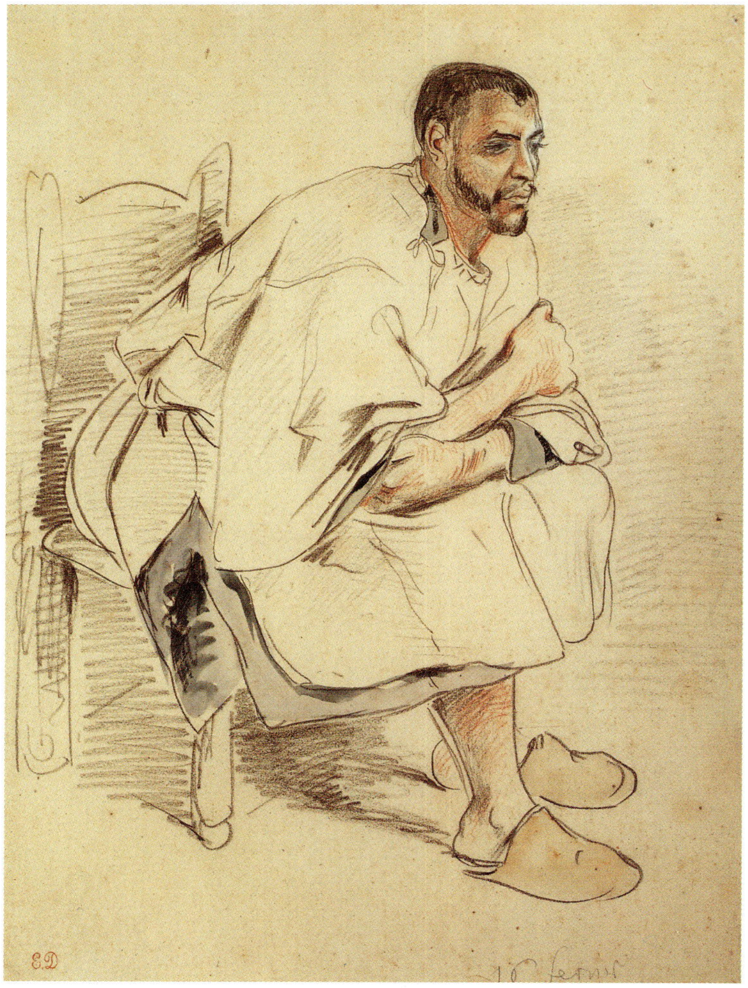

A SEATED MOOR
Maure assis
1

Lead pencil and red chalk with watercolour
36.5 x 30 cm
Dated lower right in pencil: 16 février
Nationalmuseum, Stockholm (NM 71/1915)

PROVENANCE:
Delacroix Studio, marked lower left (L.838 a); sale, Paris, 22–27 Feb. 1864, lot 529, to M. Planté; Alfred Robaut; Winkler & Magnusson; acquired by the Nationalmuseum in Stockholm in 1915.

BIBLIOGRAPHY:
Robaut, 1885, no. 1589; Sérullaz, 1967, p. 405, no. 3, pl. 41; Bjurström, 1986, no. 1501, repr.

EXHIBITIONS:
Paris, 1885, no. 390(?); Stockholm, 1981, no. 4.

Delacroix arrived in Tangier on 25 January 1832. Two days later, having paid the customary visits demanded by protocol, he was able to start visiting the town. This he usually did in the company of Abraham Benchimol, the French consulate dragoman since 1820, or with Abraham's nephew, David Azencot. While feverishly recording the first details which caught his eye in his little green-covered album (Département des Arts graphiques, Louvre, inventory RF 39050), Delacroix began to make a collection of more elaborately worked images. There were apparently no noteworthy events on 16 February, on which date the Count de Mornay wrote to Paris to recommend M. Delaporte to the Minister. Nothing therefore indicates the circumstances in which Delacroix was able to draw this Moorish figure, whose pensive expression is accentuated by the artist's somewhat rare association, found only during the Moroccan period (see nos 14 and 15), of lead pencil and red chalk. The same figure appears in a drawing which was formerly part of the Edward M.M. Warburg collection, New York, and the Louvre owns two pen and ink sketches for the head of this figure, one of which is on tracing paper (inventory RF 9587 and RF 9588; Sérullaz, 1984, II, nos 1734 and 1735, repr.). In the catalogue of the posthumous sale, two other studies were entitled *Mountain Berber* (*Berbère des montagnes*) (22–27 Feb. 1864, nos 527 and 528).

JEWISH WOMAN
IN TRADITIONAL DRESS
Femme juive en costume de fête
2

Watercolour and pencil drawing
25 x 19 cm
Dated at top right in pencil: 28 fr (February).
Private collection. Courtesy of the Galerie Schmit, Paris

PROVENANCE:
Delacroix Studio, marked lower right (L.838 a); sale, Paris, 22–27 Feb. 1864, lot 555, to Alfred Sensier; Georges Aubry; sale, Paris, 11 Mar. 1933, lot 64, repr.

BIBLIOGRAPHY:
Joubin, 1930, pl. 10; Dumur, 1988, p. 40 repr.

Starting from a rapid outline in pencil, Delacroix delicately and lightly applied a few touches of colour, mainly to the young woman's hair and jewellery, in this case long pendants, hanging down on her forehead, which were attached to a headband decorated with cabochons. 'The Jewesses are quite lovely', he wrote to his childhood friend Jean-Baptiste Pierret, on 25 January 1832, 'I'm afraid it will be difficult to do more than paint them: they are real pearls of Eden' (*Correspondance*, I, p. 307; Stewart, p. 181). In the years 1838–40 this watercolour probably served as inspiration for the composition of the painting alternately entitled *The Jew of Algiers* (*Le Juif d'Alger*), *Jewish Merchant in Algiers* (*Marchand juif à Alger*) or *Jewish Merchant from Morocco* (*Marchand juif du Maroc*) (collection R. Lopez, Paris; Johnson, 1986, no. 363, pl. 180) in which a Jewish woman can be seen standing on the right, in a pose fairly similar to the one portrayed here.

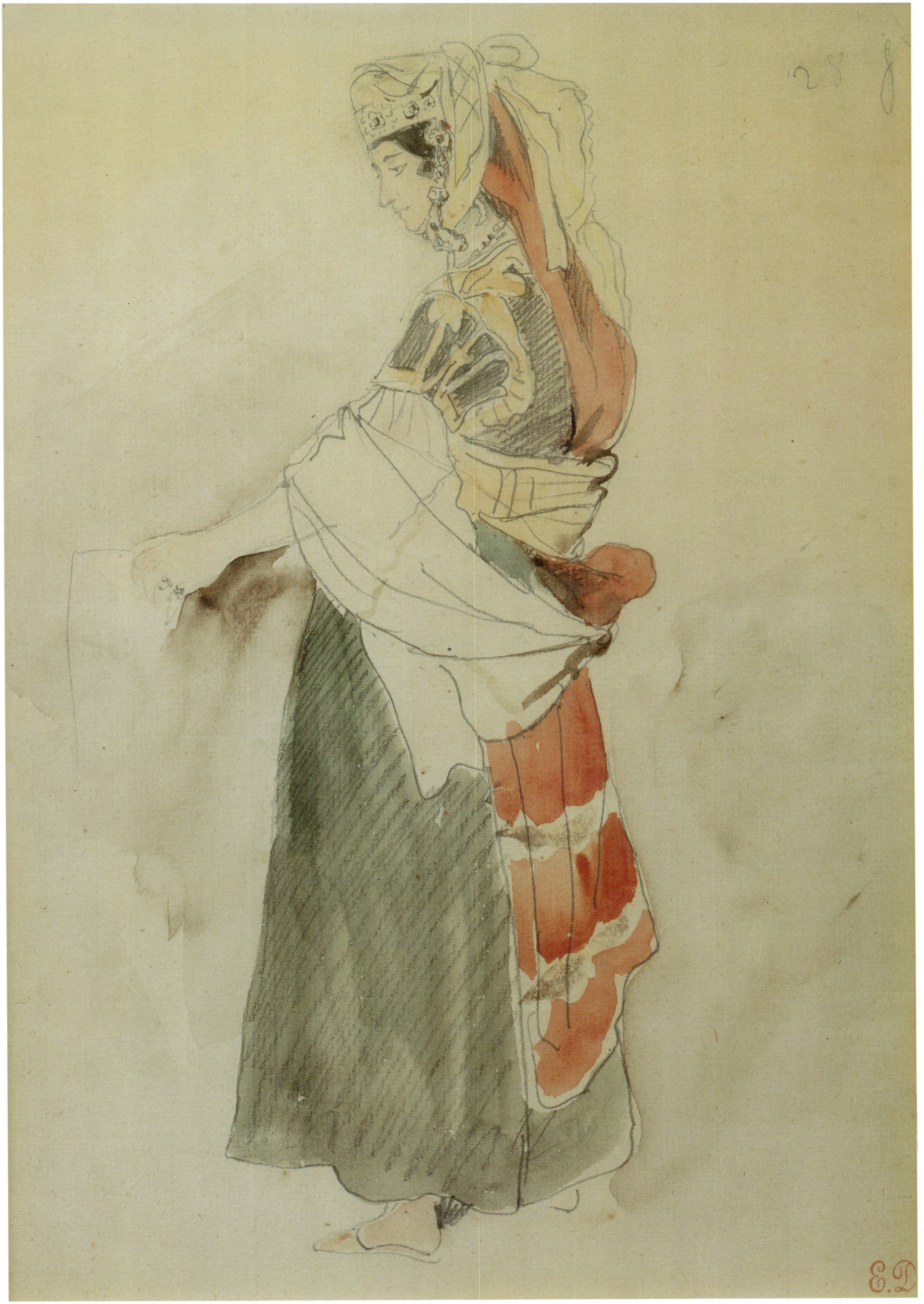
E.D

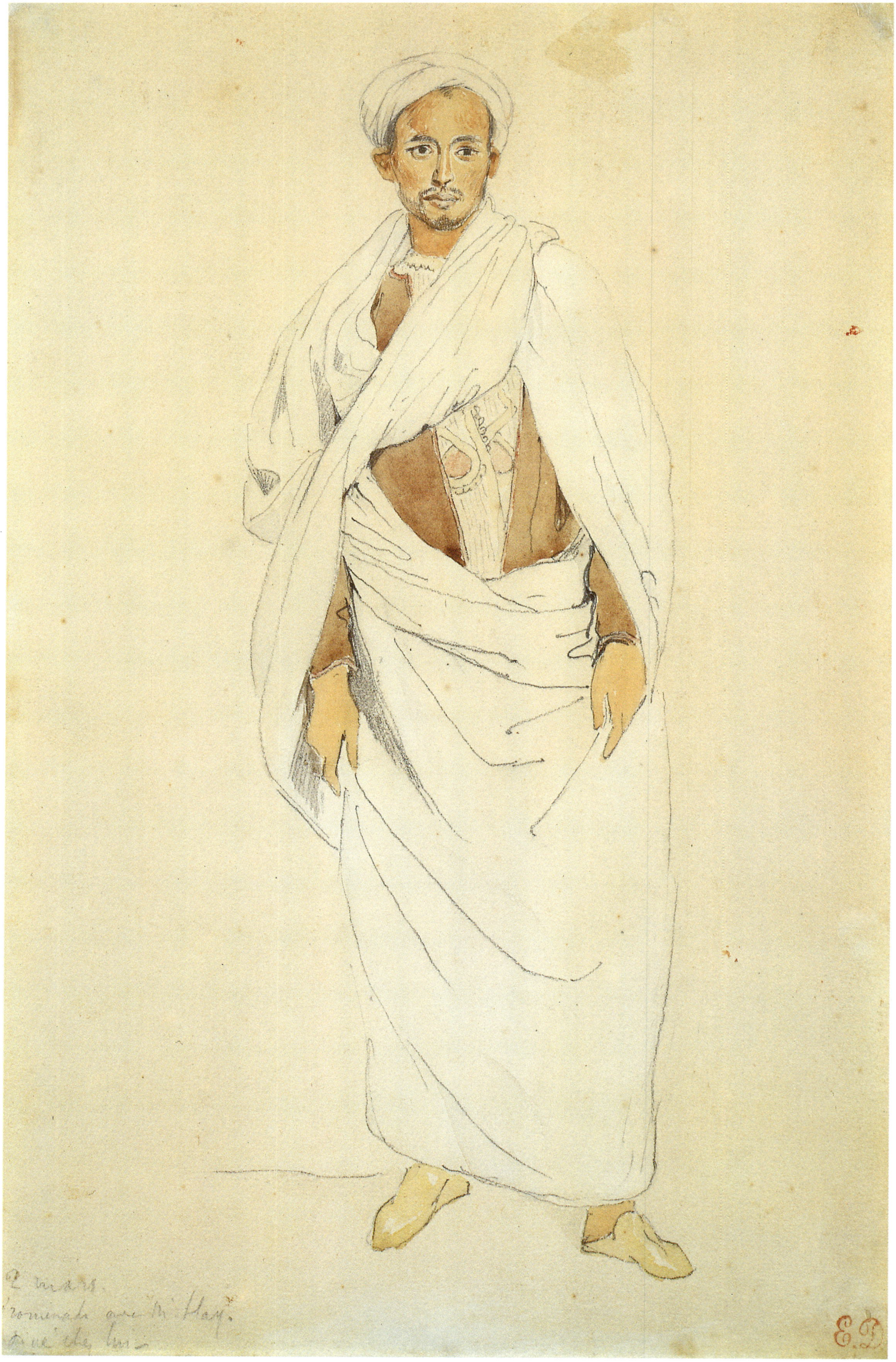
2 mars.
romenade avec M. Hay.
chez lui

MOROCCAN FROM TANGIER STANDING
Marocain de Tanger debout
3

Watercolour and pencil drawing
27 x 18 cm
Dated lower left in pencil: 2 mars—promenade avec Mr. Hay—diné chez lui
Private collection

PROVENANCE:
Delacroix Studio, marked lower right (L.838 a); sale, Paris, 22–27 Feb. 1864, one of lots 543 to 547, to Pierre Andrieu; Edgar Degas; sale, Paris, 26–27 Mar. 1918, lot 113, to Marcel Guérin.

BIBLIOGRAPHY:
Dumur, 1988, p. 49, repr.

EXHIBITIONS:
Paris, 1925, no. 41; Paris, 1930, no. 302; Paris, 1933, no. 20; Zurich, 1987, no. 34; Frankfurt, 1987–1988, no. H 18, repr.

Detained in Tangier longer than expected due to the death of Moulay Meimoun, the Moroccan emperor's brother, the French mission was able to attend the funeral of the Danish general consul, Peter Schousboë, which took place on 2 March. This obligation did not prevent Delacroix from taking a walk in the company of the British consul, Edward Drummond-Hay, renowned for his passion for horses, even the most unmanageable. This walk, mentioned on fol. 23 recto of the small green album (Département des Arts graphiques, Louvre, inventory RF 39050), is remembered in a pencil sketch of ruins, (at the beginning of the album which Delacroix mainly used during the journey from Tangier to Meknes, the stay in Meknes and the return to Tangier; Département des Arts graphiques, Louvre, inventory RF 1712 bis, fol. 3 recto) as well as in two studies in this exhibition of a Moroccan wearing a white turban and a brown open jacket over an embroidered shirt, one with and one without his white burnous (see following number).

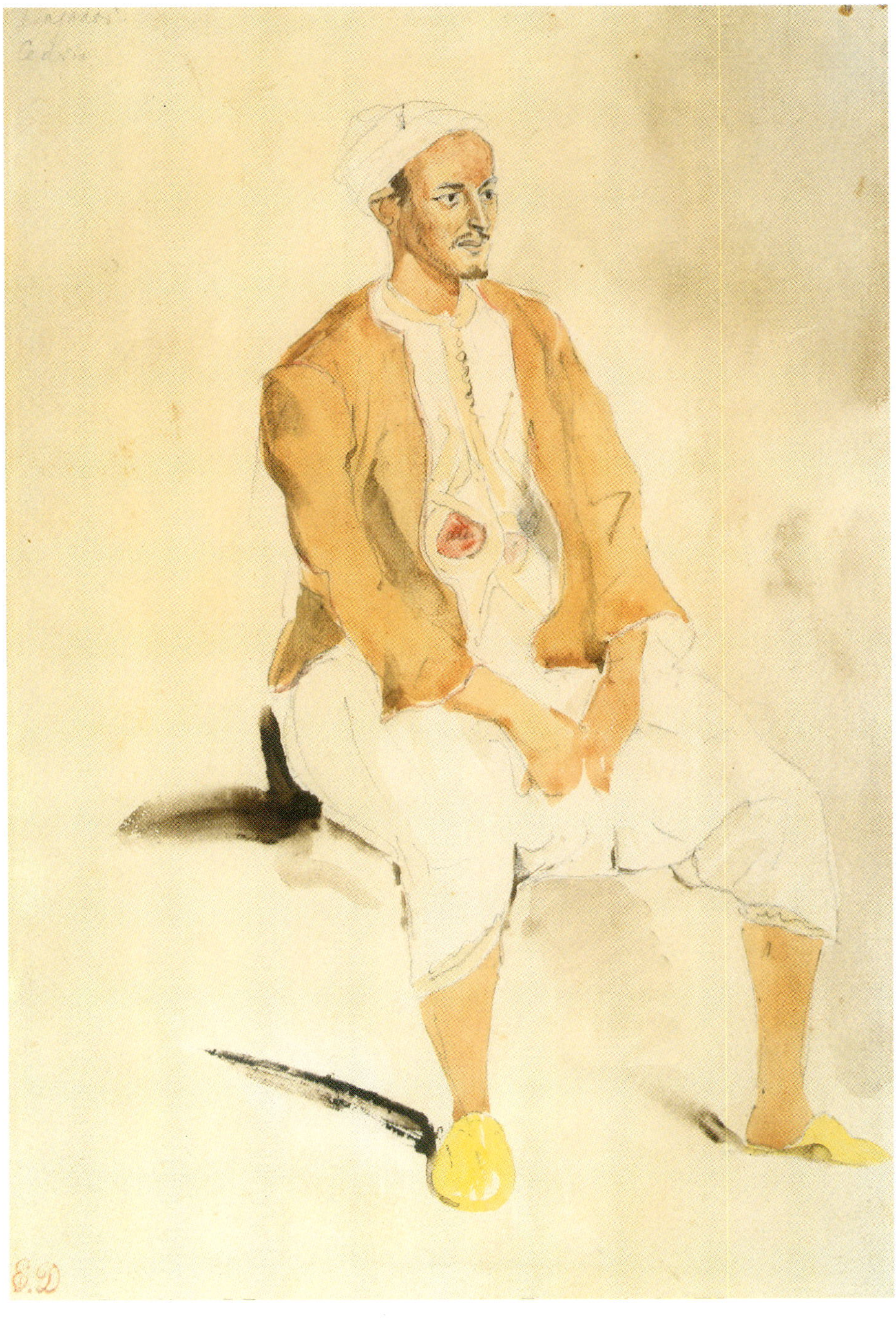

A MAN OF TANGIER
Marocain de Tanger assis
4

Watercolour and pencil drawing
26.6 x 18.6 cm
Annotated in Delacroix's hand, in pencil, top left: Bajador—Cedria (?)
The Thaw Collection. Courtesy of the Pierpont Morgan Library, New York

PROVENANCE:
Delacroix Studio, marked lower left (L.838 a); sale, Paris, 22–27 Feb. 1864, included in lots 543, to 547, to Alfred Robaut; P.-A. Chéramy; sale, Paris 14–15 Apr. 1913, lot 98, to Marcel Guérin; Hector Brame.

BIBLIOGRAPHY:
Robaut, 1885, no. 425, repr.

EXHIBITIONS:
Paris, 1925, no. 40; Paris, 1930, no. 301; Paris, 1933, no. 21; Brussels, 1936, no. 93; Brussels, 1986, no. 83, repr.

Although Delacroix's annotation is difficult to interpret, this figure is nevertheless clearly the same as the one represented in the previous drawing. Admittedly there is no burnous, but the rest of the costume is identical, as is the form of the head and the shrivelled right ear. According to Maurice Arama, the note at the bottom of folio 23 recto in the small green-covered album, referred to in the preceding entry: *l'homme au château, soldat tunique courte, culotte blanche comme les juifs*, corresponds to the two drawings exhibited here.

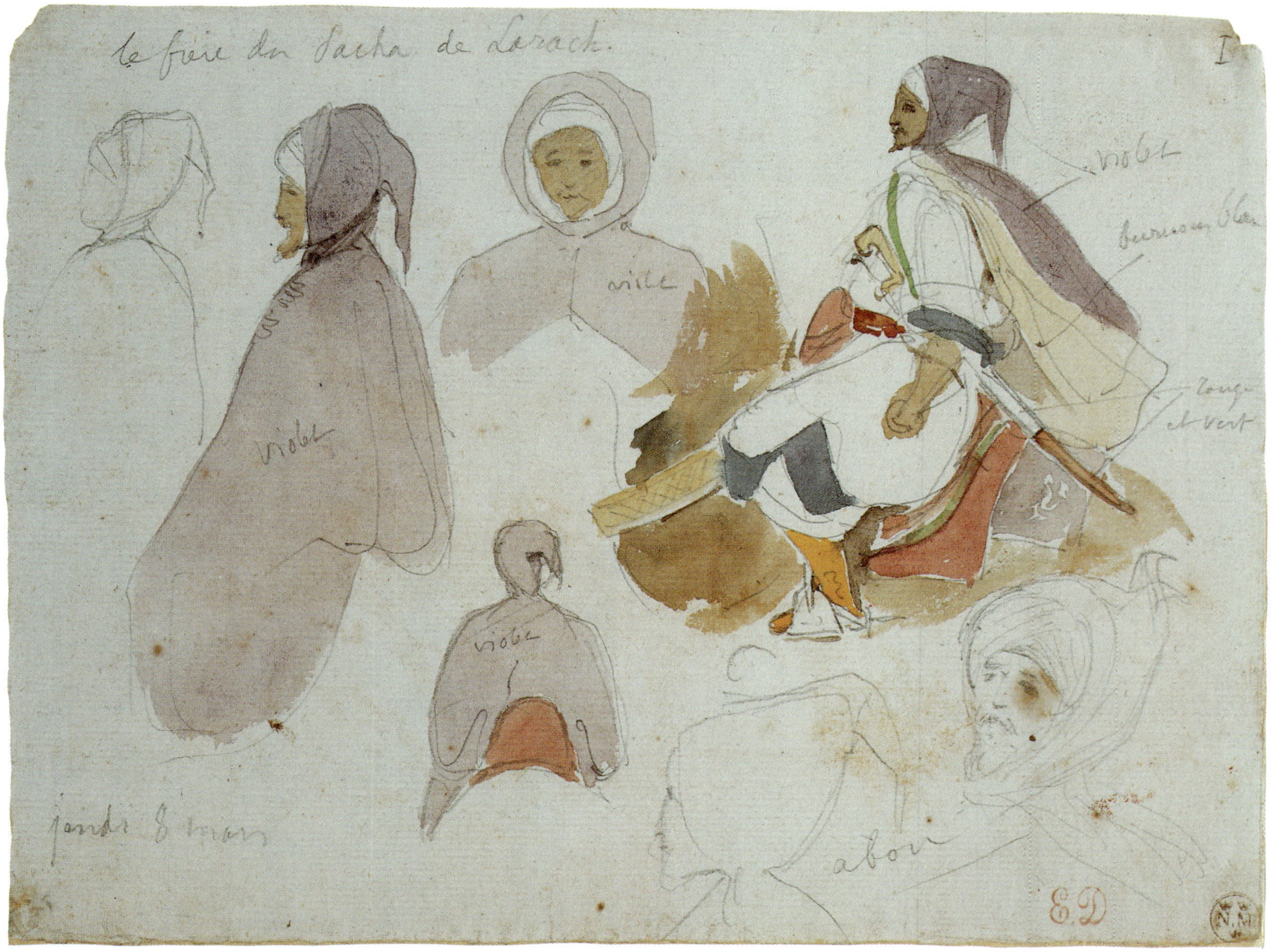

SEVEN SKETCHES OF ARABS
Études d'Arabes à cheval
5

Pencil and watercolour
15.5 x 21.3 cm
Dated lower left in pencil: jeudi 8 mars *and annotated in Delacroix's hand, top:* le frère du pacha de Larach*: bottom:* violet*; centre:* violet—violet*; right:* violet—burnous blanc—rouge et vert*; lower right:* abou.
Nationalmuseum, Stockholm (NM 65/1949)

PROVENANCE:
Delacroix Studio, marked lower right (L.838 a); sale, Paris, 22–27 Feb. 1864, possibly included in lots 571 or 572, to Alfred Robaut; Marcel Guyot; acquired by the Nationalmuseum of Stockholm in 1949.

BIBLIOGRAPHY:
Sérullaz, 1967, p. 405, no. 4, pl. 42 a; Bjurström, 1986, no. 1502, repr.

EXHIBITIONS:
Stockholm, 1981, no. 3.

This sketch is characteristic of the manner in which Delacroix organized his repertoire of forms and colours. Considering the dimensions, it is possible that it was formerly part of an album, of a similar size to the one in the Louvre, once in the collections of the artist Adrien Dauzats, Eugène Lecomte and Étienne Moreau-Nélaton (Département des Arts graphiques, Louvre, inventory RF 9154).

Having left Tangier on 5 March 1832, the French mission arrived on 8 March at El-Ksar el-Kebir, which Delacroix noted in his album, gallicizing it to Alcassar-El-Kébir. In the lower right-hand corner is the rapidly sketched head of Sidi Mohammed Ben Abou, who, with 120 soldiers, guaranteed the protection of the French convoy. According to custom, the visitors were escorted by the Pasha of Tangier, Sidi Larabi Saïdi, as far as the border of his province. Each pasha was obliged to accompany the mission on the territory under his authority, so the Pasha of Larache, Abdeslam Es-salaoui, had taken over since the previous day.

This detail figures in a letter from the Count de Mornay addressed to the Count Sebastiani from Meknes on 23 March 1832: 'Having arrived in the territory of the province of Garbe, the Pasha of Tangier left me and put me in the hands of the brother of the Pasha of Larache, who came to meet me with four hundred cavalrymen.' (Arama, 1992, VI, p. 227.)

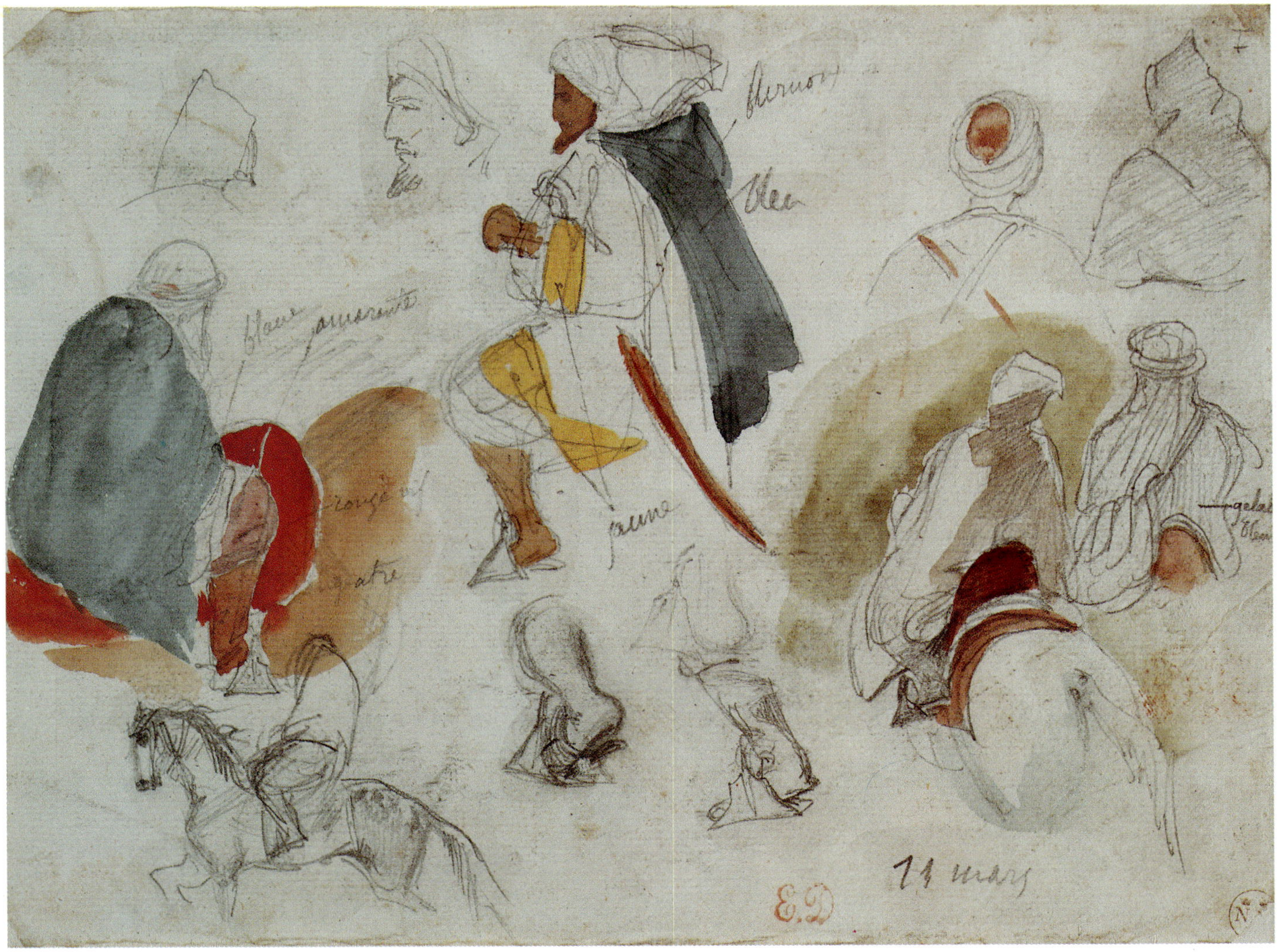

STUDIES OF ARABS ON HORSEBACK
Études d'Arabes à cheval
6

Pencil and watercolour
15.5 x 21.6 cm
Dated lower right in pencil: 11 mars *and annotated in Delacroix's hand, left:* blanc—amarante—rouge vif—rougeâtre; *centre:* burnous—bleu—jaune; *far right:* gelabia—bleu
Nationalmuseum, Stockholm (NM 66/1949)

PROVENANCE:
Delacroix Studio, marked lower right (L.838 a); sale, Paris, 22–27 Feb. 1864, possibly included in lots 571 or 572, to Alfred Robaut; Marcel Guyot; acquired by the Nationalmuseum of Stockholm in 1949.

BIBLIOGRAPHY:
Sérullaz, 1967, p. 405, no. 5, pl. 42 b; Bjurström, 1986, no. 1503, repr.

EXHIBITIONS:
Stockholm, 1981, no. 2.

On 11 March 1832, Delacroix noted in his album: 'At the Sebou river, at the El-Aïtem passage. For three days now we have been followed by a sherif from Fez, a friend of Biaz, who insists that we give him a present.' (Département des Arts graphiques, Louvre, inventory RF 1712 bis, fol. 12 verso.)

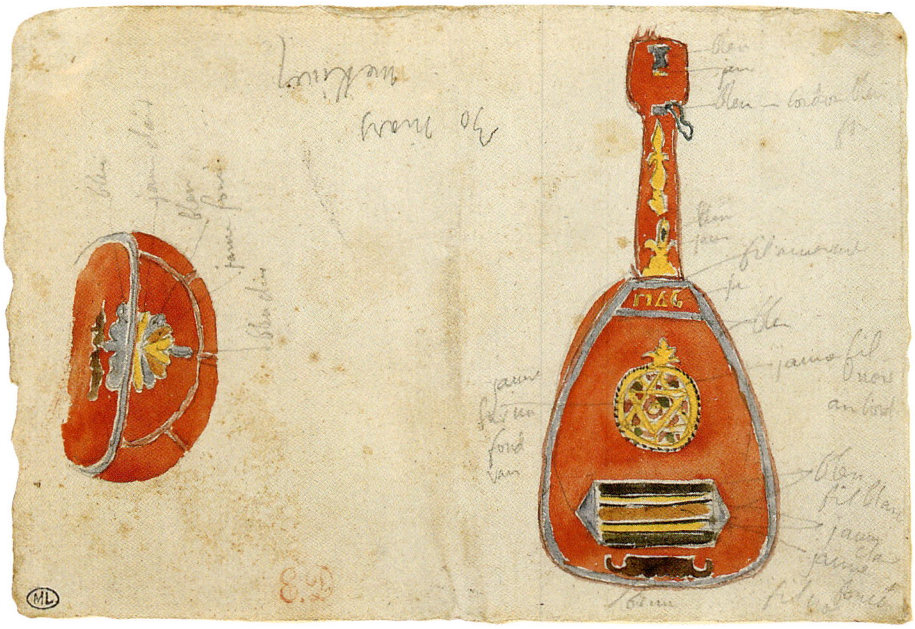

TWO STUDIES
OF AN ARAB *AOUD*
Deux études d'aoud arabe

7

Watercolour and pencil drawing
10.9 x 15.8 cm
Dated in pencil on the reverse side of the sheet: 30 mars—Mekinez
Annotated in Delacroix's hand, in pencil, the length of the instrument: bleu—jaune—bleu—cordon bleu fon[*cé*]—bleu—jaune—file amarante—ja[*une*]—bleu—jaune fil noir au bord—bleu fil blanc—jaune clair—jaune foncé—fil noir—brun—jaune sur fond ver[*t*]—bleu—jaune clair—bleu—jaune foncé—bleu clair
Département des Arts graphiques, Louvre (RF 10102)

PROVENANCE:
Delacroix Studio, marked lower centre (L.838 a); sale, Paris, 22–27 Feb. 1864, probably included in lot 571, to Étienne Moreau-Nélaton; bequeathed to the Louvre in 1927 (L.1886 a).

BIBLIOGRAPHY:
Robaut, 1885, no. 1629, repr. p. 419; Sérullaz, 1984, II, no. 1684, repr.

On 30 March, the emperor sent some Jewish musicians from Mogador to the French mission. 'They are the best in all the empire' Delacroix noted (Louvre album; RF 1712 bis, fol. 22 verso), and fifteen years later he portrayed the scene in a little painting exhibited at the 1847 Salon (Louvre, see p. 101). Heedful of the slightest detail, the artist could not fail to be interested in the instruments used by the musicians, which produced very different sounds to those used to play the music of Rossini or Cimarosa to which his European ear was accustomed.

He therefore carefully noted each decorative element of this *aoud* (a sort of lute), red in colour, with marquetry designs and a medallion in the shape of a five-point star. The Musée Delacroix contains several musical instruments which the artist brought back from his stay in Morocco.

FOUR SKETCHES
OF ARAB MEN
Quatre études d'Arabes

8

Pencil, pen, brown ink and watercolour
18.4 x 26.9 cm
Dated lower right in pencil: 3 avril—Méquinez
The Art Institute, Chicago (1960.822)

PROVENANCE:
Delacroix Studio, marked lower left (L.838 a); sale, Paris, 22–27 Feb. 1864, possibly included in lots 571 or 572, to Baron Vitta; Francis H. Hardy; donated by Mrs Francis H. Hardy by 1960 to the Art Institute of Chicago in memory of her husband.

BIBLIOGRAPHY:
Arama, 1987, p. 193, repr. (whereabouts unknown); Dumur, 1988, p. 74, repr.

This work in fact consists of three studies of the same man in a white burnous, covered by a dark blue burnous, most probably one of the emperor's soldiers, with a *moghazni* on the left recognizable by his red pointed bonnet. (Delacroix also portrayed a *moghazni* about to saddle his horse, in the painting in this catalogue, see no. 97, from Budapest). There is no entry in the artist's notes alluding to 3 April.

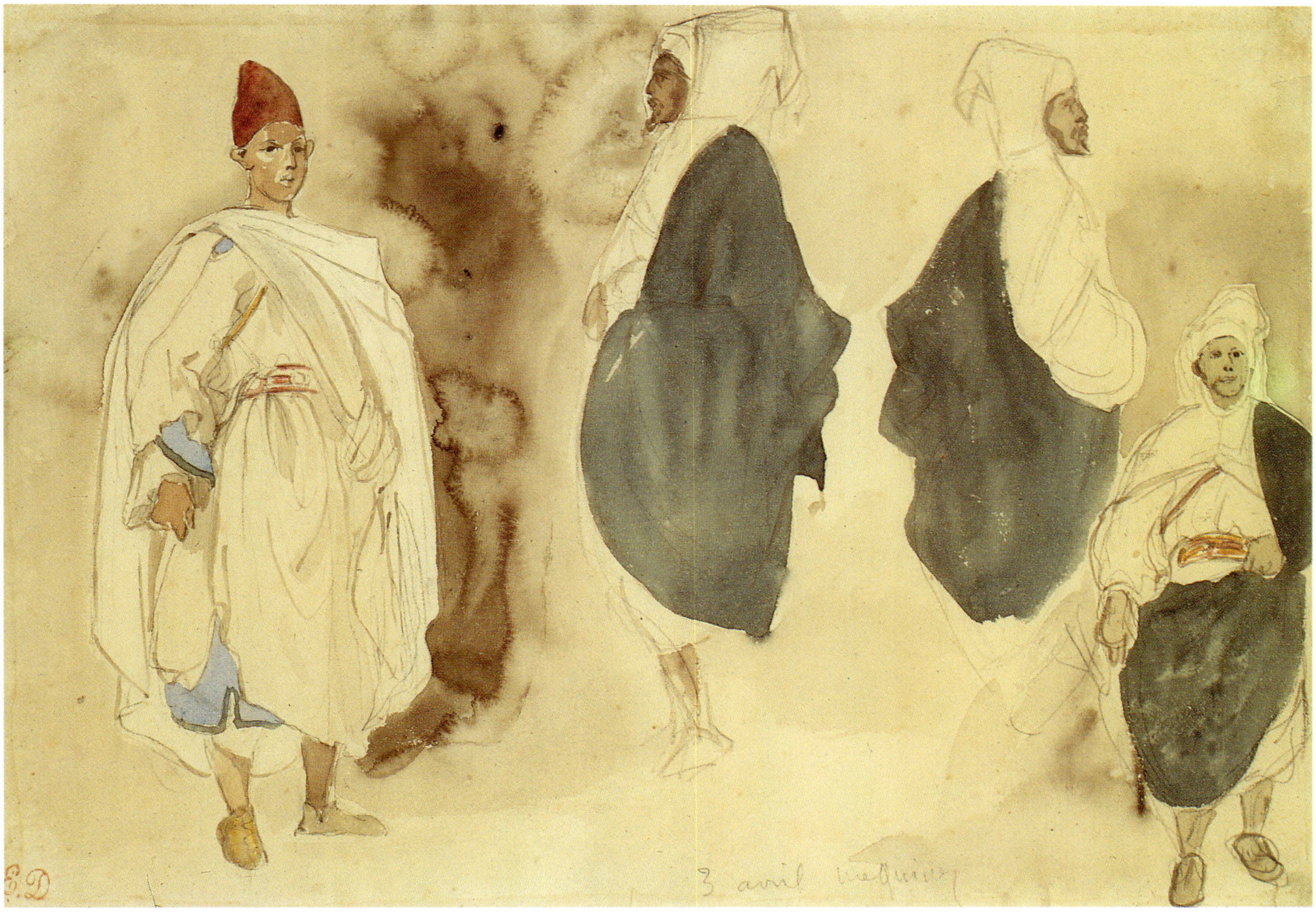

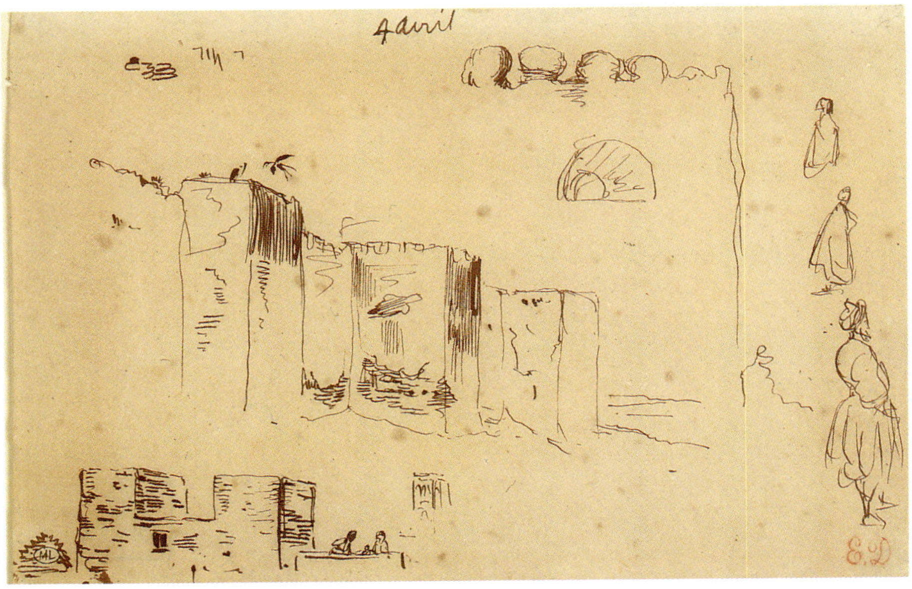

RAMPARTS AND THREE SKETCHES OF ARABS
Remparts d'une ville et trois croquis d'Arabes
9

Pen and brown ink
12.8 x 20 cm
Dated at top centre, in pen: 4 avril
Département des Arts graphiques, Louvre (RF 10079)

PROVENANCE:
Delacroix Studio, marked lower right (L.838 a); sale, Paris, 22–27 Feb. 1864, to Étienne Moreau-Nélaton; bequeathed to the Louvre in 1927 (L.1886 a).

BIBLIOGRAPHY:
Robaut, 1885, possibly included in lot 1632; Sérullaz, 1984, II, no. 1522, repr.; Dumur, 1988, p. 74, repr.

Delacroix spent his last day in Meknes walking around the town and beyond the ramparts. Naturally there was no shortage of opportunities for drawing, as testified by this rapid pen and ink sketch of a section of the ramparts, with three small silhouettes of Arabs along the right edge. Below, two minute figures lean on a wall, propped up on their elbows.

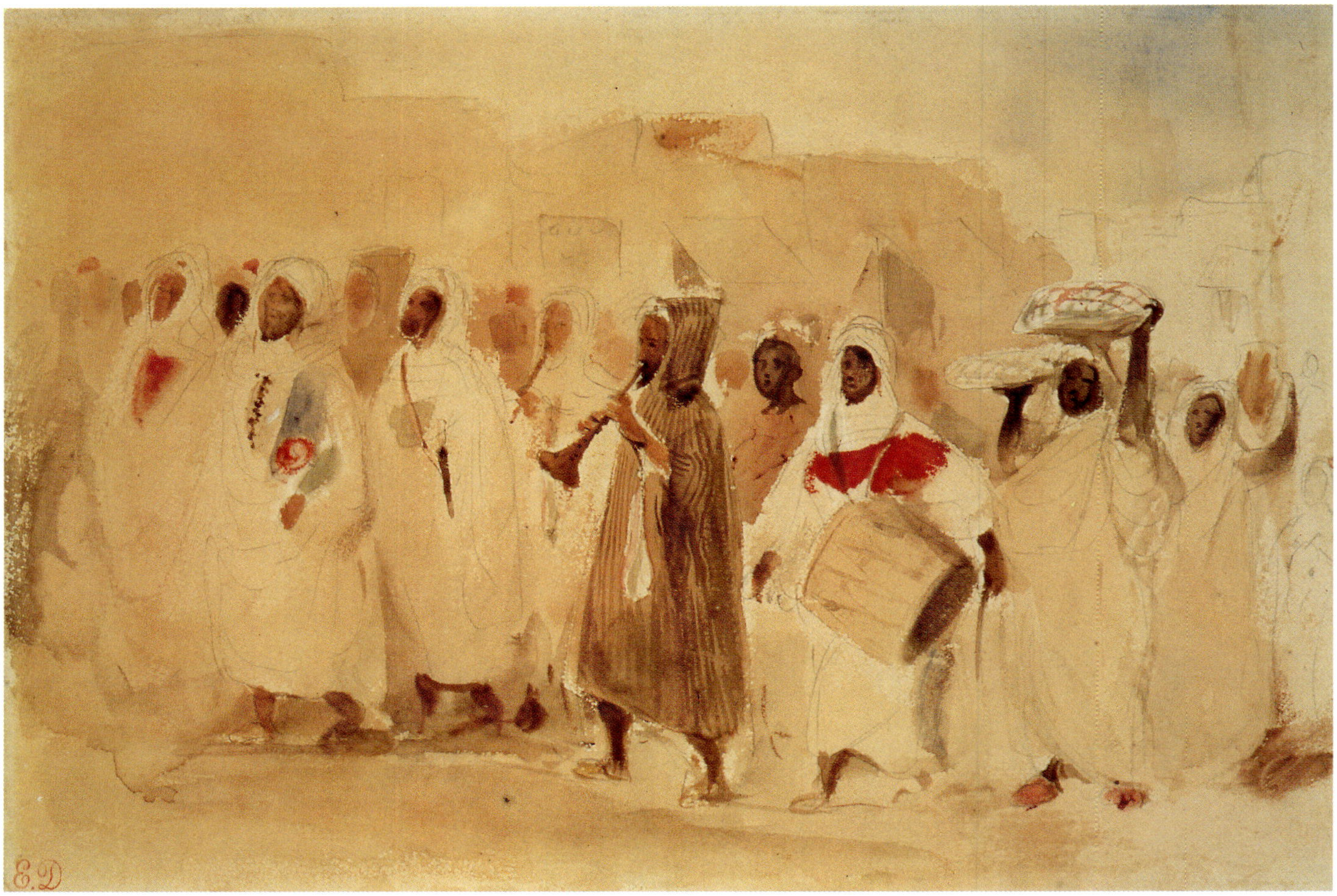

PROCESSION IN TANGIER
Procession à Tanger
10

Watercolour and pencil drawing
18.3 x 27.2 cm
Private collection

PROVENANCE:
Delacroix Studio, marked lower left (L.838 a); sale, Paris, 22–27 Feb. 1864, lot 517, to Cavé; Tony Mayer; Jean Cau; sale, Paris, 16 Dec. 1993, lot 33, repr.

BIBLIOGRAPHY:
Robaut, 1885, no. 1600.

Maurice Arama has associated this watercolour, catalogued at the posthumous Delacroix sale under the title *Procession of Musicians in Mogador (Procession de musiciens à Mogador)*, which belonged to the sadly missed Jean Cau, with the scene described by Delacroix in the album of his voyage during the second stay in Tangier: 'Yesterday, 27 April, a procession with a band (drums and oboes) passed under our windows. A young boy who had just finished his schooling was being ceremoniously escorted round the town. He was surrounded by singing schoolfellows, and his parents and teachers. People ran out from their shops to congratulate him.' (Wellington, p. 53; Département des Arts graphiques, Louvre, RF 1712 bis, fol. 33 recto.)

This quick sketch has been enhanced by a few touches of watercolour in warm tones which capture perfectly the luminous and dusty atmosphere. In the centre, the dark brown striped burnous worn by the *gaita* player (a sort of wooden clarinet) contrasts with the rest of the figures, who seem to melt into the ochre ramparts.

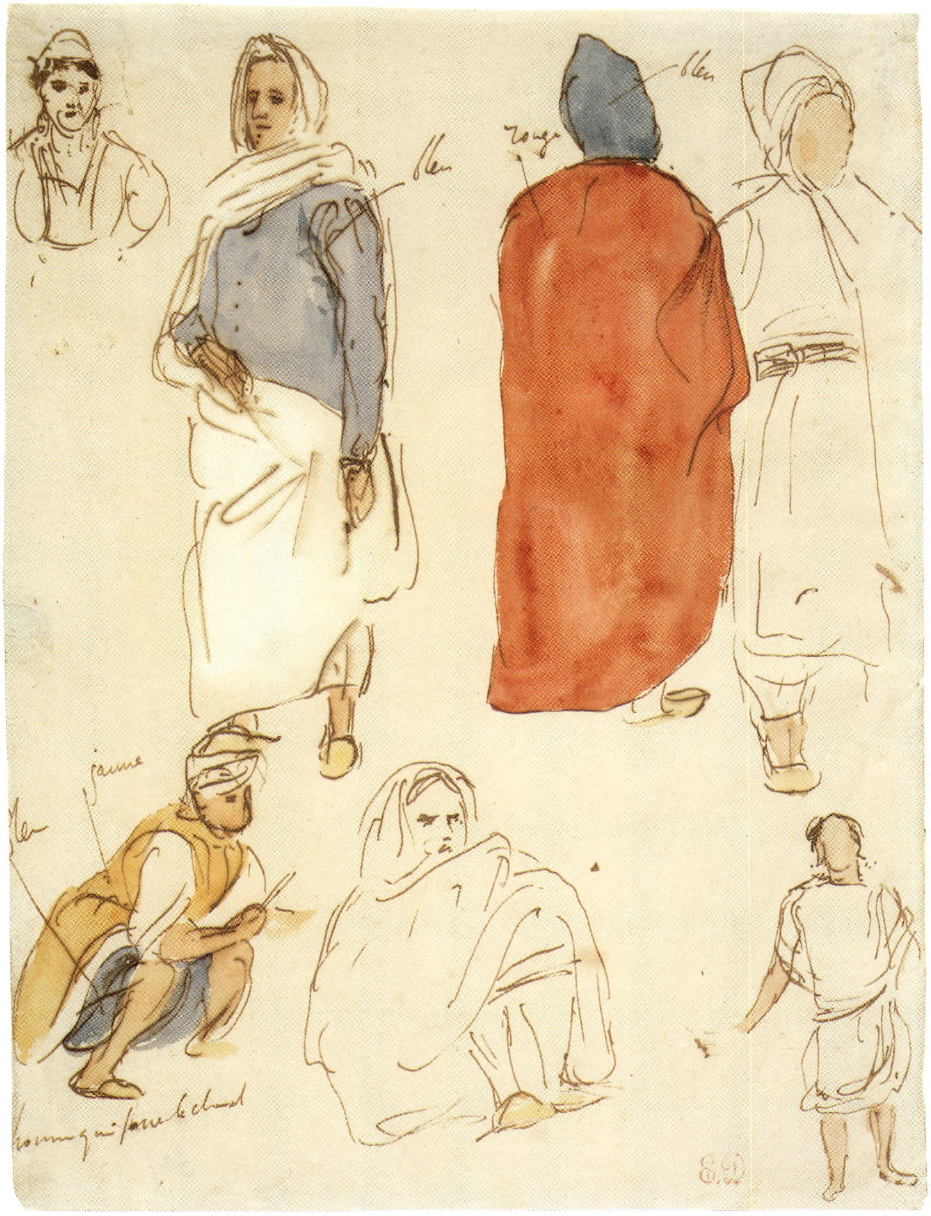

SEVEN SKETCHES OF ARABS
Sept études d'Arabes
11

Pen, brown ink and watercolour
25.1 x 19 cm
Annotated in Delacroix's hand, in pen and brown ink, top: bleu—rouge—blue;
lower left: blue—jaune—l'homme qui ferre le cheval
Nationalmuseum, Stockholm (42/1920)

PROVENANCE:
Delacroix Studio, marked lower right (L.838 a); sale, Paris, 22–27 Feb. 1864, possibly included in lots 571 or 572, to W. Hansen; acquired by the Nationalmuseum in Stockholm in 1920.

BIBLIOGRAPHY:
Sérullaz, 1967, p. 405, no. 6, pl. 43; Bjurström, 1986, no. 1504, repr.

EXHIBITIONS:
Stockholm, 1981, no. 1.

Stylistically close to the drawings which fill the pages of the small album which Delacroix mainly used during the first stay in Tangier (Département des Arts graphiques, Louvre, inventory RF 39050), these rapidly executed pen sketches show his attentiveness when observing the picturesque crowds in the streets. A few notes indicating the colours rapidly assimilated by the artist's eye were sufficient to enable Delacroix to reproduce them in watercolour: intense red, blue and yellow ochre.

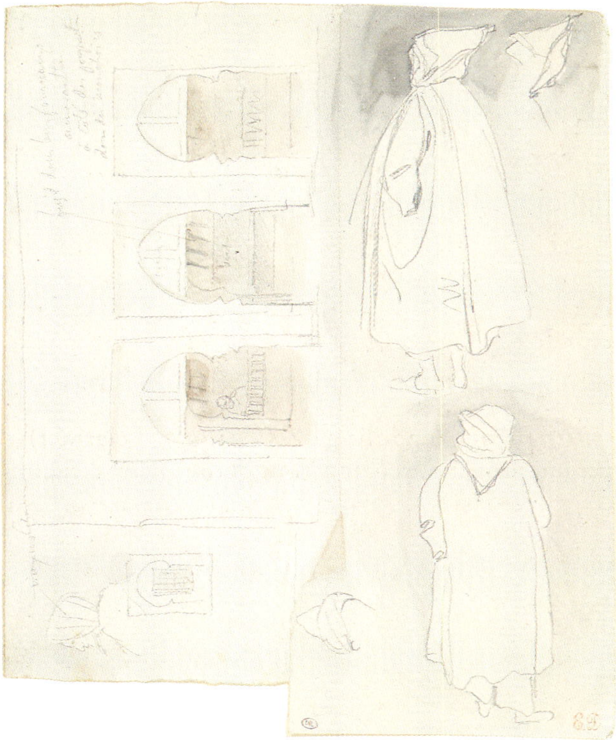

STUDIES OF ARABS AND OF ARCHITECTURE
Études d'Arabes et d'architecture
12

Pencil and watercolour
26 x 22 cm
On two adjacent pages, irregularly cut.
Annotated top left on the bias, in Delacroix's hand, in pencil: vieux mouchoir—fusils dans leurs fourreaux amaranthe à côté des paquets dans des mouchoirs—vert—vert
Département des Arts graphiques, Louvre (RF 10085)

PROVENANCE:
Delacroix Studio, marked lower right (L.838 a); sale, Paris, 22–27 Feb. 1864, included in lots 571 or 572; Étienne Moreau-Nélaton; bequeathed to the Louvre in 1927 (L.1886 a).

BIBLIOGRAPHY:
Robaut, 1885, part of nos 1629 or 1632; Sérullaz, 1984, II, no. 1584, repr.

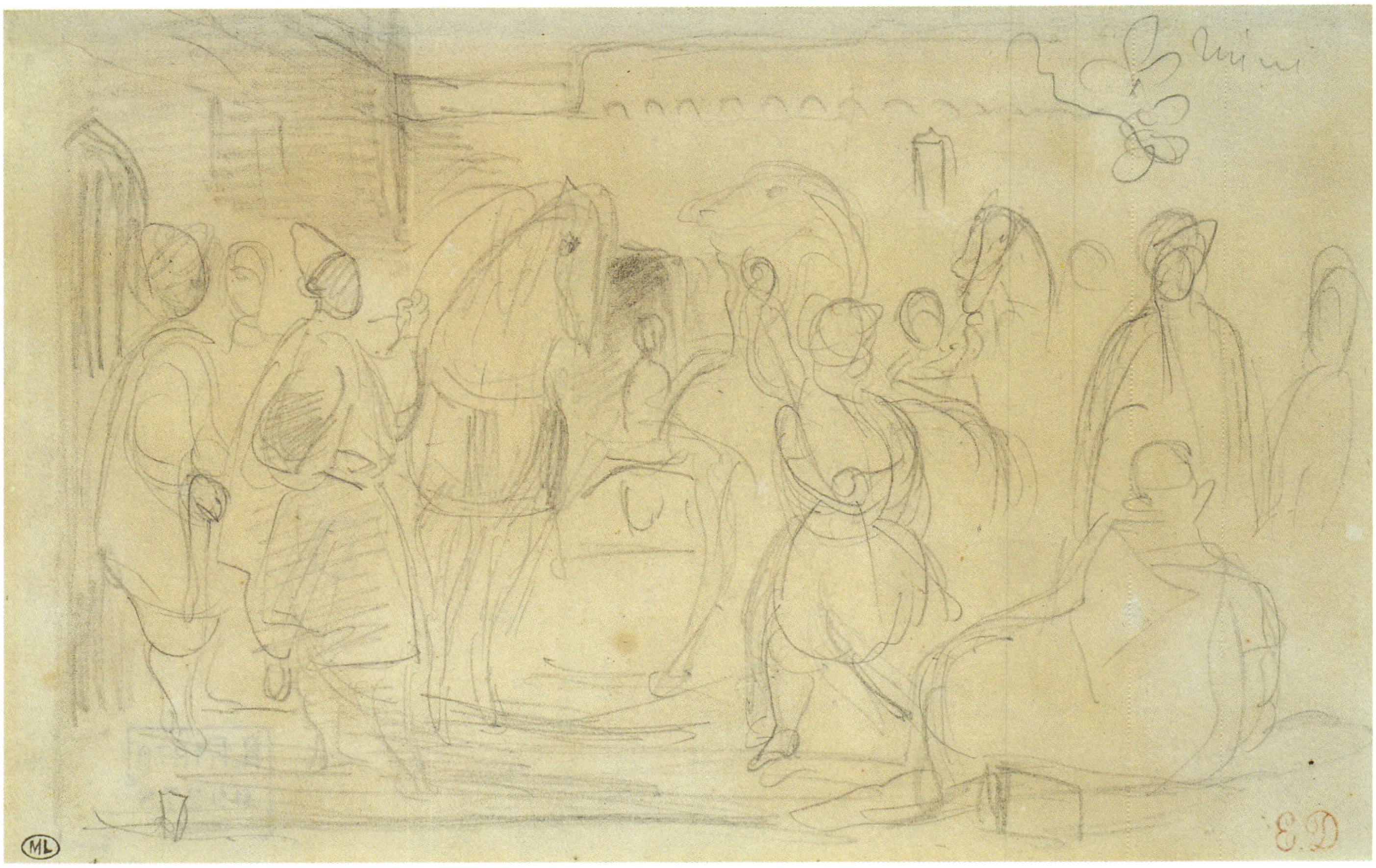

ARAB MARKET AND HORSES
Marché arabe aux chevaux
13
Pencil
13.2 x 21.1 cm
Annotated in Delacroix's hand in pencil: ruines
Département des Arts graphiques, Louvre (RF 9278)
PROVENANCE:
Delacroix Studio, marked lower right (L.838 a); sale, Paris, 22–27 Feb. 1864, probably included in lot 571, to Arosa; sale, Paris 27–28 Feb. 1864, lot 165 bis, to Dr Suchet; possibly sale, Paris, 30–31 Jan. 1905, included in lot 150, to Étienne Moreau-Nélaton; bequeathed to the Louvre in 1927 (L.1886 a).
BIBLIOGRAPHY:
Robaut, 1885, no. 1631, repr.; Sérullaz, 1984, II, no. 1576, repr.
EXHIBITIONS:
Paris, 1930, no. 325; Paris, 1982, no. 224.

It was from this drawing, which he considerably modified, that Delacroix composed the painting presented at the 1838 Salon, entitled *A Courtyard in Morocco (Intérieur d'une cour dans laquelle des soldats marocains ont amené des chevaux)* (Johnson, 1986, no. 354, pl. 167). The most noteworthy change is on the right-hand side of the composition: Delacroix has substituted the seated figure seen from behind, wrapped in a burnous, with a crouching soldier planting pickets in the ground to fetter the horses, according to the Arab custom.

STUDY OF AN ARAB
Étude d'Arabe assis
14
Lead pencil, with red and white chalk
31 x 27.4 cm
The British Museum, London (1968–2–10–24)
PROVENANCE:
Delacroix Studio, marked lower left (L.838 a); sale, Paris 22–27 Feb. 1864, lot 536, to Bornot; M. Bornot's son-in-law, M. Porlier by 1877; César Mange de Hauke; bequeathed to the British Museum in 1965.
BIBLIOGRAPHY:
Robaut, 1885, no. 392.

The same figure, seen facing with arms crossed, appears in a technically identical drawing in the Louvre (inventory RF 5633; Sérullaz, 1984, II, no. 1597, repr.). According to the catalogue of the posthumous Delacroix sale (Paris, 22–27 Feb. 1864, lot 536), the artist also made a third half-length study of the figure, entitled *Arab dressed in a striped burnous* (*Maure vêtu d'un burnous rayé*).

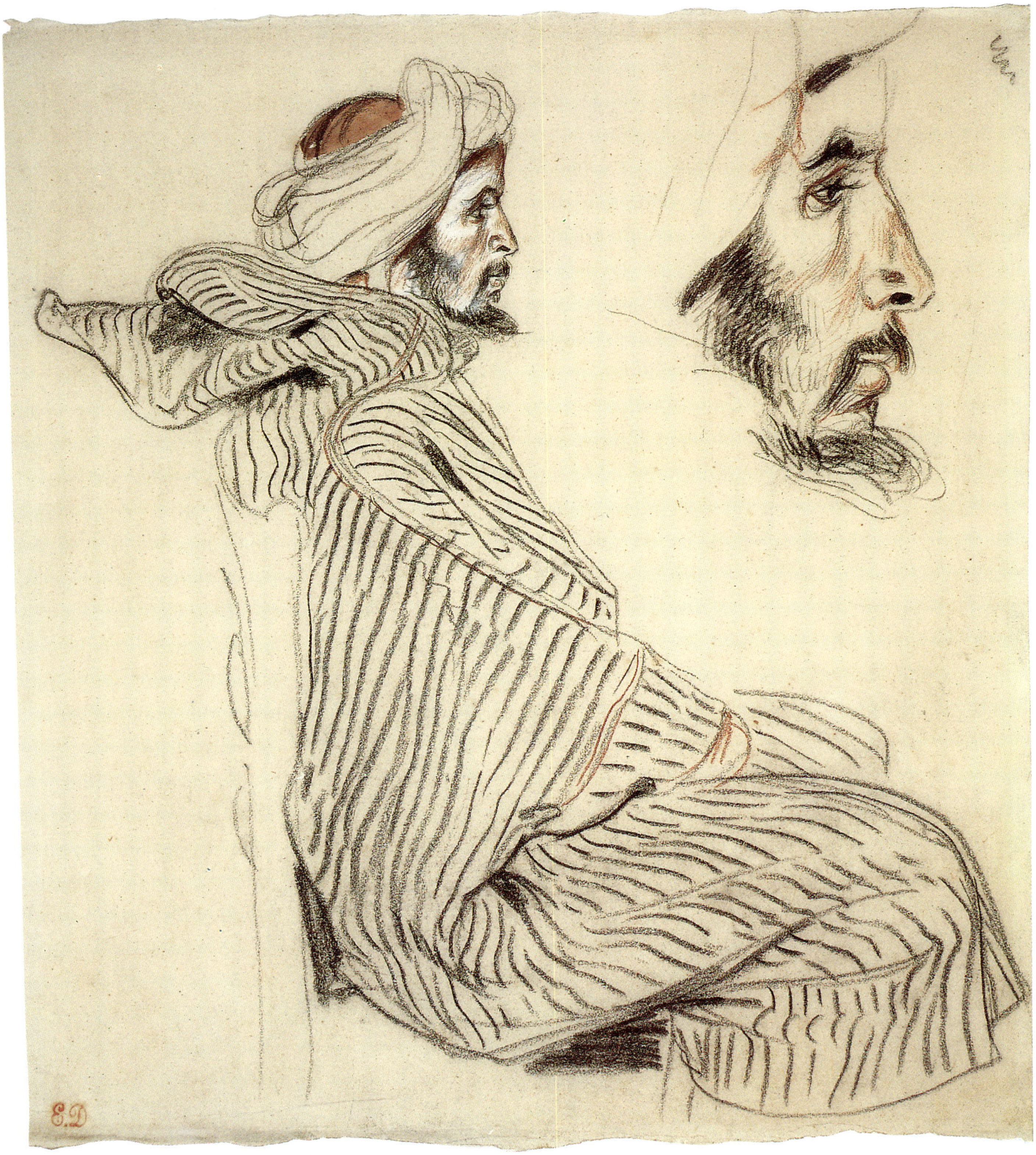

ARAB CHIEFTAIN RECLINING ON A CARPET
Chef arabe couché sur un tapis
15

Watercolour, red chalk and lead pencil drawing
19 x 27.4 cm
On the reverse side, study of the head of the same figure, in pencil.
Département des Arts graphiques, Louvre (RF 23 323)

PROVENANCE:
Delacroix Studio, marked lower right (L.838 a); sale, Paris, 22–27 Feb. 1864, lot 526, to Philippe Burty; sale, Paris, 2–3 Mar. 1891, lot 63, to P.-A. Chéramy; sale, Paris, 5–7 May, 1908, lot 302, to Raymond Koechlin; bequeathed to the Louvre in 1933 (L. 1886 a).

BIBLIOGRAPHY:
Robaut, 1885, no. 417, repr.; Joubin, 1930, pl. 26; Sérullaz, 1984, II, no. 1606, repr.; Arama, 1987, p. 184–5, repr.; Arama, 1992, VI, p. 149, repr.

EXHIBITIONS:
Paris, 1885, no. 245; Paris, 1925, no. 63; Paris, 1930, no. 304; Paris, 1933, no. 62; Paris, 1934, no. 48; Brussels, 1936, no. 94; Zurich, 1939, no. 180; Basel, 1939, no. 184; Paris, 1963 (1), no. 44, pl. VIII; London-Edinburgh, 1964, no. 122, pl. 59; Kyoto-Tokyo, 1969, no. A 4, repr.; Paris, 1982, no. 191.

This is one of the most famous Moroccan watercolours in the Louvre, due both to the extremely imposing model and to the admirable rendering of the colourful designs of the carpet on which he is reclining.

The dazzling whiteness of the costume stands out in contrast to the delicate brown moiré background and the vivid colours of the carpet, produced by the famous *flochetage* (flocking), which Delacroix later used for the cushions on which the women are reclining in the *Women of Algiers* (Louvre, see p. 115).

Several sketches of the head of this Arab were found on a page of studies of heads in pen and ink, dated in another hand (?) *2 9bre* (sale, Hôtel Drouot, Paris, 22 June 1981, lot 173, repr.).

Maurice Arama has identified the person portrayed as the commander of the cavalry of Tangier, Sidi Mohammed Ben Abou Ben Abdelmalek, who was responsible for escorting the French delegation as far as Meknes.

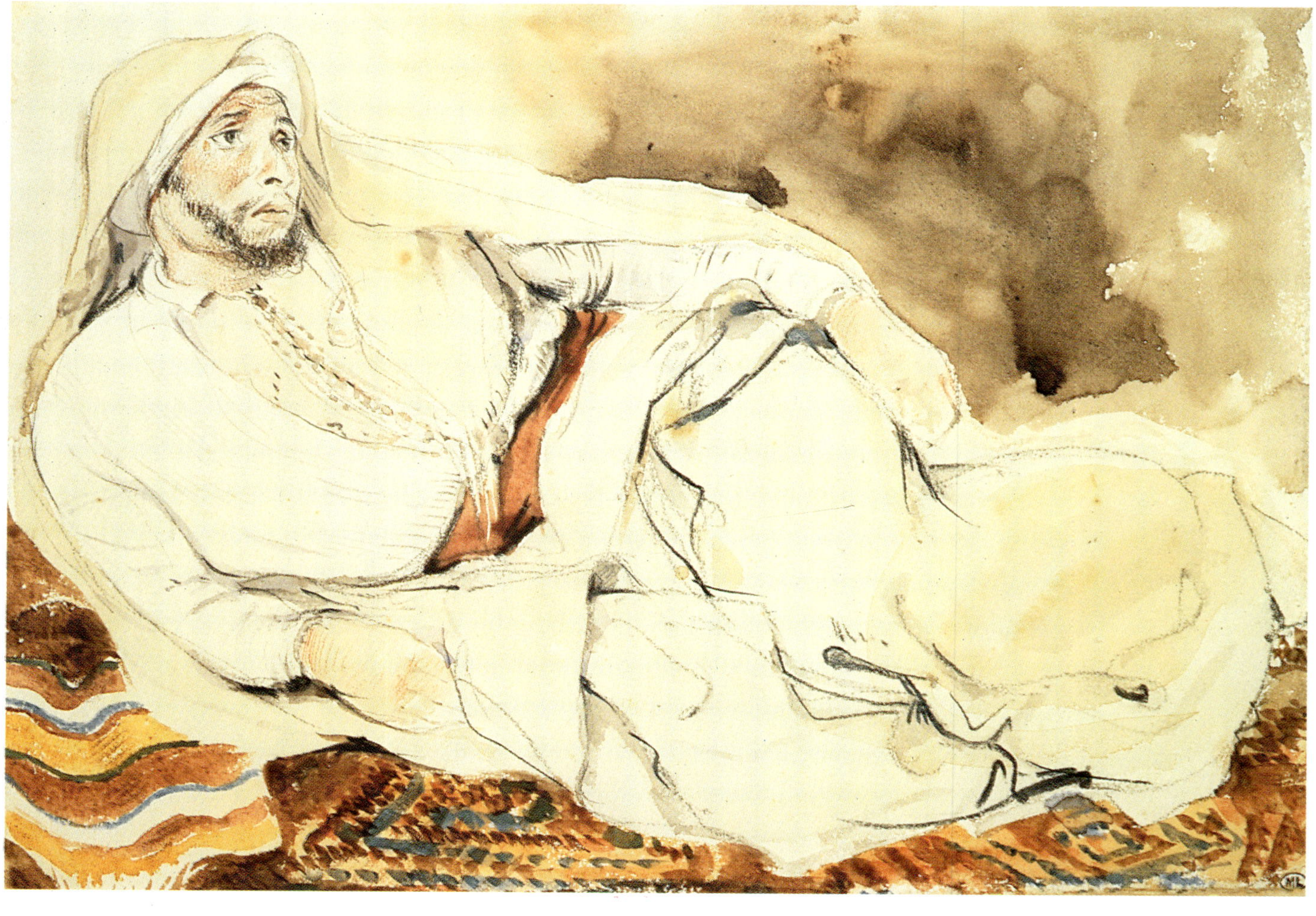

YOUNG ARAB
IN HIS APARTMENT
Jeune Arabe dans son appartement
16

Watercolour and pencil drawing
19 x 29.8 cm
Département des Arts graphiques, Louvre
(RF 4874)

PROVENANCE:
Delacroix Studio, marked lower right (L.838 a); sale, Paris, 22–27 Feb. 1864, lot 521, to Count Arnaud Doria; sale, Paris, 8–9 May 1899, lot 262, to Léon-Michel Lévy; Edgar Degas; sale, Paris, 26–27 Mar. 1918, lot 113, repr., to Paul Leprieur, sale, Paris, 21 Nov. 1919, lot 40; bought by the Société des Amis du Louvre and donated to the museum (L.1886 a).

BIBLIOGRAPHY:
Robaut, 1885, lot 418; Joubin, 1930, pl. 27; Sérullaz, 1963, no. 172, repr.; Sérullaz, 1984, II, no. 1605, repr.; Arama, 1987, pp. 176–7, repr.; Arama, 1992, VI, p. 160, repr.

EXHIBITIONS:
Paris, 1885, no. 259; Paris, 1930, no. 298; repr. Album, p. 37; Paris, 1933, no. 64; Paris, 1934, ex cat.; Zurich, 1939, no. 183; Basel, 1939, no. 181; Paris, 1963, no. 173.

According to Maurice Arama, this watercolour, along with the one following, possibly represents one of the sons of the Pasha of Tangier, Sidi Larabi Saïdi.

As usual, Delacroix tested, along the left-hand edge of the page, the colours that he intended to use—in this case for the designs of the wall hangings and the carpet. The calculated lay-out of the composition contrasts ingeniously with the apparent nonchalance of the model. The intense black of the gun sets off the cream coloured costume, while its diagonal position balances the piece of material which frames the picture in the background.

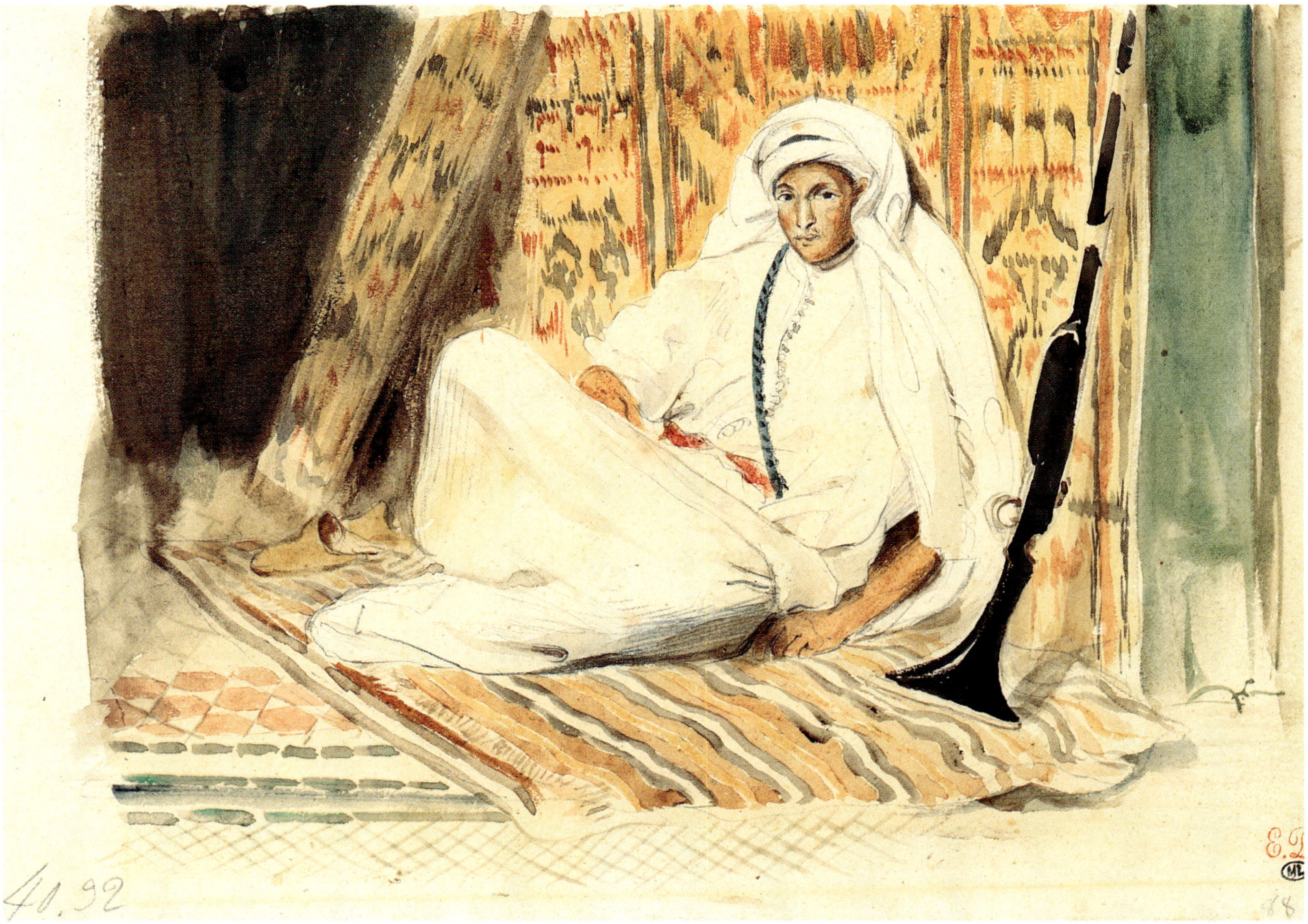

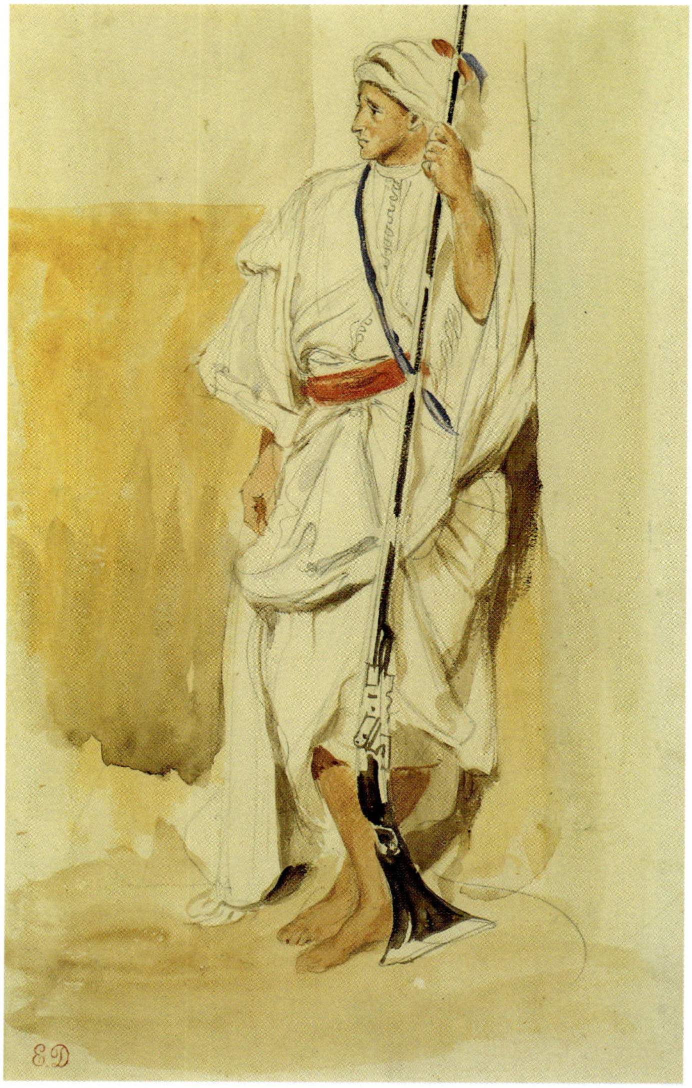

YOUNG ARAB STANDING WITH A RIFLE
Jeune Arabe debout tenant un fusil noir
17

Watercolour and pencil drawing
31 x 19.5 cm
Private collection. Courtesy of the Galerie Schmit, Paris

PROVENANCE:
Delacroix Studio, marked lower left (L.838 a); sale, Paris, 22–27 Feb. 1864, lot 524.

BIBLIOGRAPHY:
Robaut, 1885, no. 1587.

Once again, one can appreciate the ease with which Delacroix depicts, in a few pencil strokes and a few touches of watercolour, the noble simplicity of Arabs, taken by surprise while resting or in semi-activity. Their costumes never failed to astonish the artist: 'Their dress is quite uniform and very simple, and yet the various ways of arranging it confer on it a kind of beauty and nobility that leaves one speechless.' (Letter to Duponchel, Tangier, 23 February 1832, *Correspondance*, I, p. 314; Stewart, p. 185).

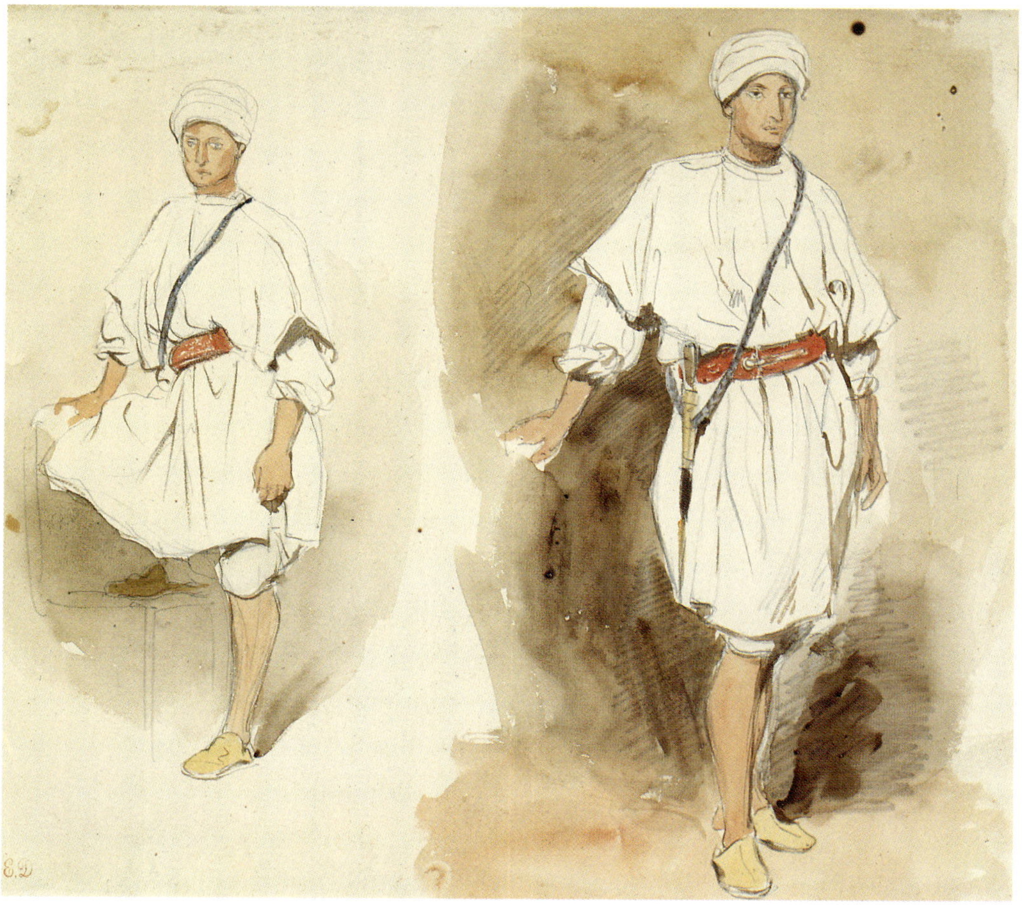

TWO VIEWS OF A YOUNG ARAB
Deux études d'un jeune Arabe
18

Watercolour and pencil drawing
29.6 x 34.4 cm
The Baltimore Museum of Art. Nelson and Juanita Greif Gutmann Collection (BMA 1976.27)

PROVENANCE:
Delacroix Studio, marked lower left (L.838 a); sale, Paris, 22–27 Feb. 1864, lot 531, to M. Gariel (according to Robaut); sale, Palais Galliera, Paris, 16 Mar. 1972, lot 6, repr.; with S. Maison, Hazlitt, Gooden and Fox, London, 1976; acquired by the Baltimore Museum in 1976.

BIBLIOGRAPHY:
Robaut, 1885, no. 1590.

Here Delacroix was only really interested by the costume, which he recorded with his usual exactitude. The almost invisible pencil marks trace the outlines in their simplest form and the watercolour accentuates the various features of the costume: the white gandoura reaching down to the hem of the short trousers, tightly held in by a bright red belt,

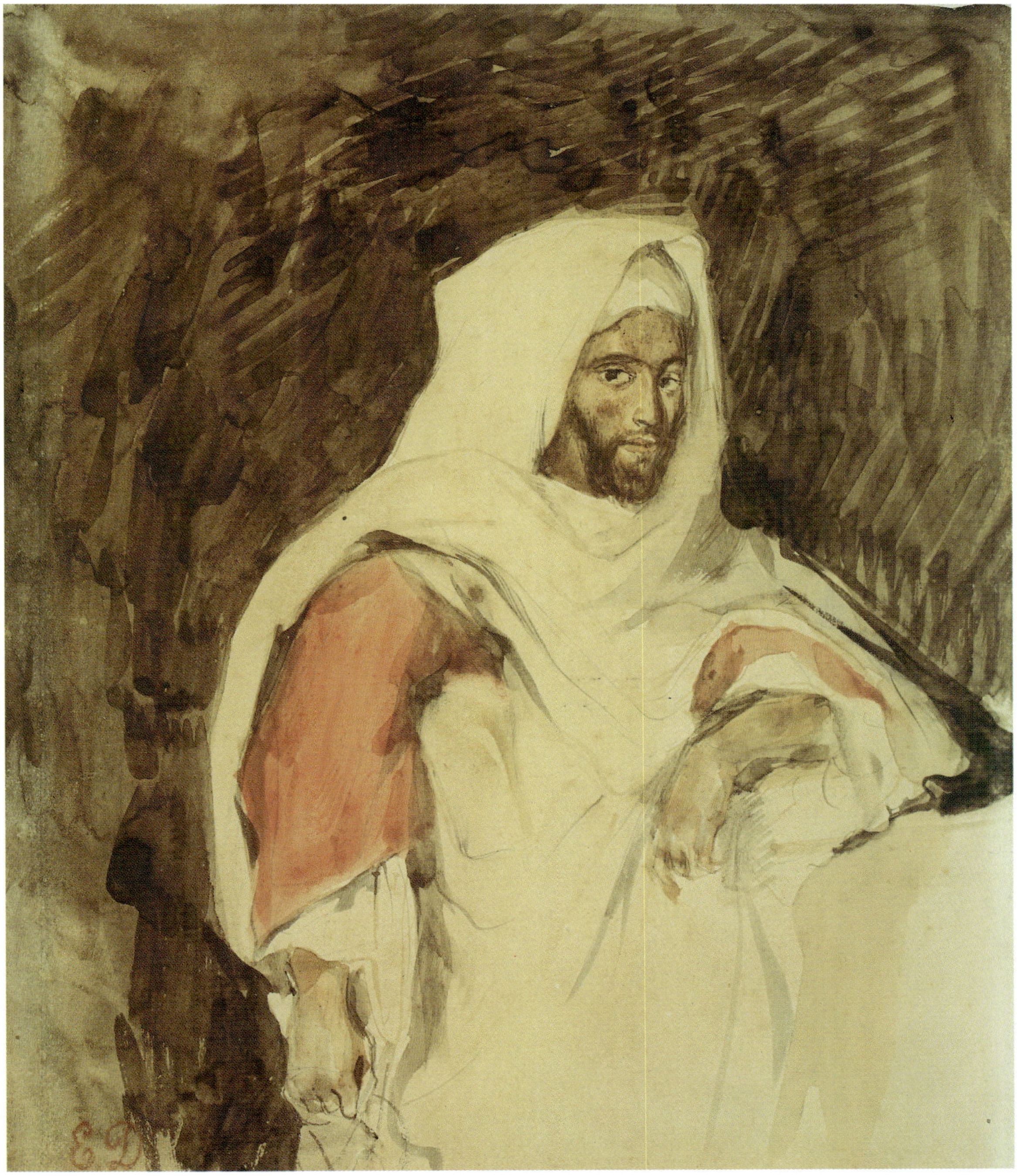

the dagger held into a sash by a narrow plaited cord, and the yellow slippers.

It might well be Caddour, the guardian of the French consulate in Tangier, who is portrayed in this work, especially if one compares the study on the left with a drawing in the album which belonged to Baron Vitta, reproduced by Maurice Arama (1992, VI, p. 249).

MOROCCAN CHIEFTAIN
Chef marocain
19

Watercolour and pencil drawing
16 x 13.7 cm
Private collection

PROVENANCE:
Delacroix Studio, marked lower left (L.838 a); sale, Paris, 22–27 Feb. 1864, lot 437, to Paul Huet; Dr Viau; Alfred Daber.

BIBLIOGRAPHY:
Robaut, 1885, no. 1570; Arama, 1992, VI, p. 147, repr.

EXHIBITIONS:
Zurich, 1987 (1), no. 31, repr.

Maurice Arama has identified the sitter as Sidi Mokhtar el-Jamaï, minister of the emperor of Morocco in charge of decrees. He was one of the protagonists in the negotiations conducted with the Count de Mornay, which resulted in the audience of 22 March 1832. Sidi Mokhtar el-Jamaï appears on the left of Moulay Abd al-Rahman in the painting of the Musée des Augustins, Toulouse (see no. 84).

SEATED ARAB
Marocain assis
20
Watercolour and pencil drawing
14.8 x 11.4 cm
Musée des Beaux-Arts, Dijon (DG 233)
PROVENANCE:
Delacroix Studio, marked lower right (L.838 a); sale, Paris, 22–27 Feb. 1864, to Louis Rouart; Georges Aubry; Pierre Granville; donated to the Musée des Beaux-Arts, Dijon in 1969.
BIBLIOGRAPHY:
Lemoine, 1976, no. 86, repr.; Arama, 1992, VI, p. 148 repr.
EXHIBITIONS:
Paris, 1933, no. 150; Zurich, 1939, no. 154; London, 1952, no. 57; Paris, 1953, no. 21; Bordeaux, 1963, no. 104.

According to Maurice Arama, this sketch is a portrait of Ben Abou, commander of the Tangier cavalry (see no. 56). The 'fragmented' yellow-ochre watercolour touches used by Delacroix make the piece of material in the foreground appear to vibrate.

YOUNG ARAB SEATED BY A WALL
Jeune garçon assis à l'angle d'un mur
21
Watercolour and pencil drawing
18.4 x 13.2 cm
Musée Carnavalet, Paris (D.7947)
PROVENANCE:
Delacroix Studio, marked lower left (L.838 a); sale, Paris, 22–27 Feb. 1864, lot 432, to Maracquau; M. Cassagnade; bequeathed to the Musée Carnavalet in 1947.
BIBLIOGRAPHY:
Robaut, 1885, no. 1568.
EXHIBITIONS:
Zurich, 1987 (1), no. 40, repr.

The model's costume suggests he might be the young David Azencot, Abraham Benchimol's nephew. (M. Arama)

MOROCCAN CHIEFTAIN
Chef marocain
22
Pencil and watercolour
29 x 20.5 cm
Private collection
PROVENANCE:
Delacroix Studio, marked lower right (L.838 a); sale, Paris, 22–27 Feb. 1864, possibly included in lots 571 or 572.
BIBLIOGRAPHY:
Robaut, 1885, no. 412.

This is one of the numerous studies of Arab notables draped in their white burnouses whom Delacroix admired from the first glance, overwhelmed by their noble aspect, comparable, he noted, to that of the ancient Greek or Roman heroes.

Apart from a few changes in detail, this figure seems to correspond to a little pen and ink sketch illustrating the letter Delacroix wrote to his friend Jean-Baptiste Pierret from Tangier on 29 February 1832. Next to the sketch he writes: 'All of them in white like Roman senators or Greeks at the Panathenaean festival.' (*Correspondance*, I, p. 319; Stewart, p. 188; the letter is in the collection of the Louvre).

ARAB DANCER
Danseur arabe
23
Pen and brown ink
19 x 15.4 cm
Museum Boymans-Van Beuningen, Rotterdam (F.II.82)
PROVENANCE:
Franz W. Koenigs, marked lower right (L.1023 a); donated to the Boymans-Van Beuningen Museum in 1940.
BIBLIOGRAPHY:
Hoetink, 1968, no. 101, repr.
EXHIBITIONS:
Bremen, 1964, no. 204.

Maurice Arama suggests that this drawing is related to a note Delacroix wrote on 16 April 1832: 'The negroes who came to dance at the consulate and in the town' (Département des Arts graphiques, Louvre, inventory RF 39050, fol. 24 recto). In this case, the study exhibited here should also be associated with the double study, now in the Louvre, of a black musician playing the *tanbûr*, one of the renowned musicians and dancers from the Gnaouas brotherhood who were in Tangier at that date (inventory RF 23324; Sérullaz, 1984, no. 1596, repr, see p. 107).

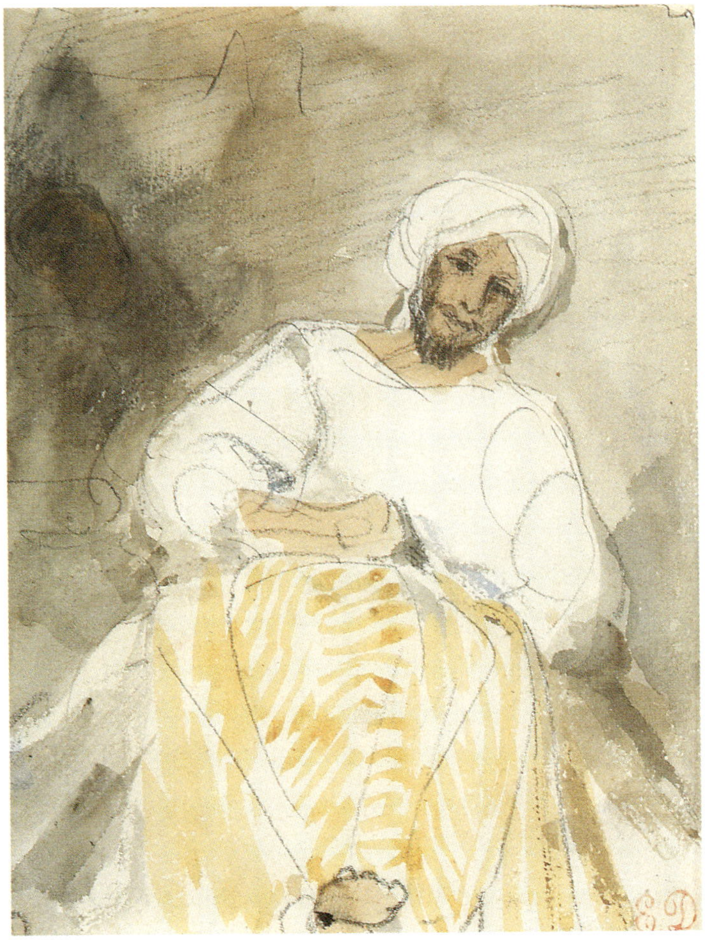

20

22

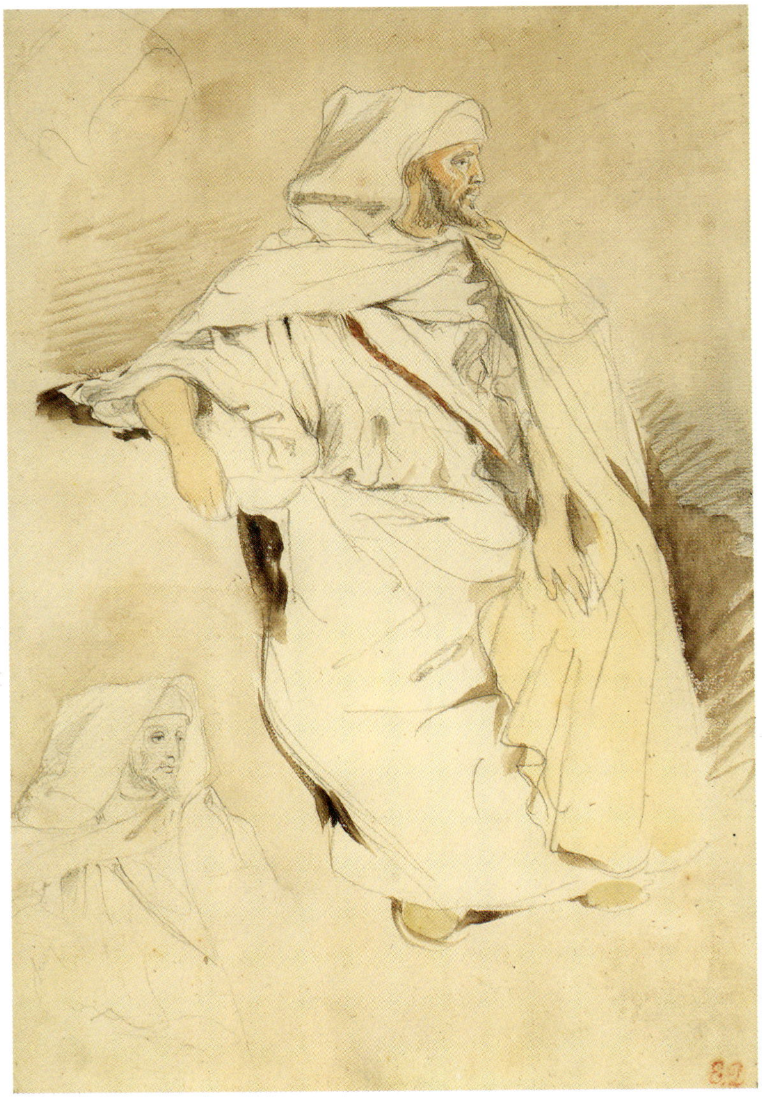

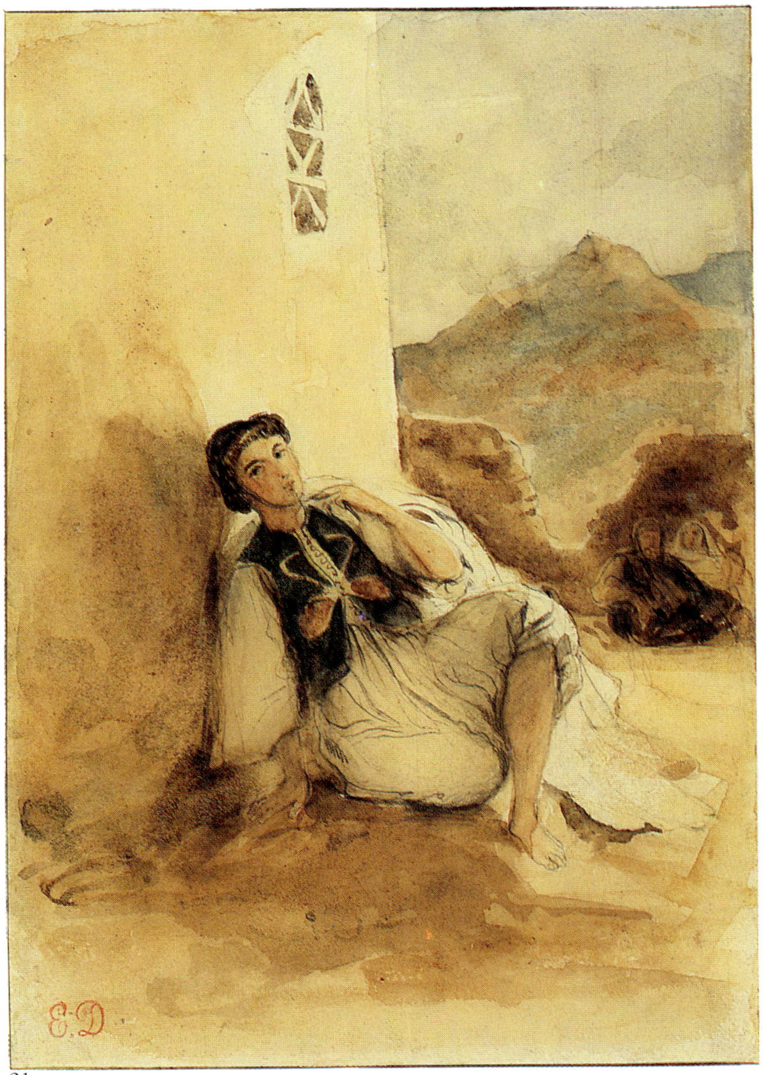

21

23

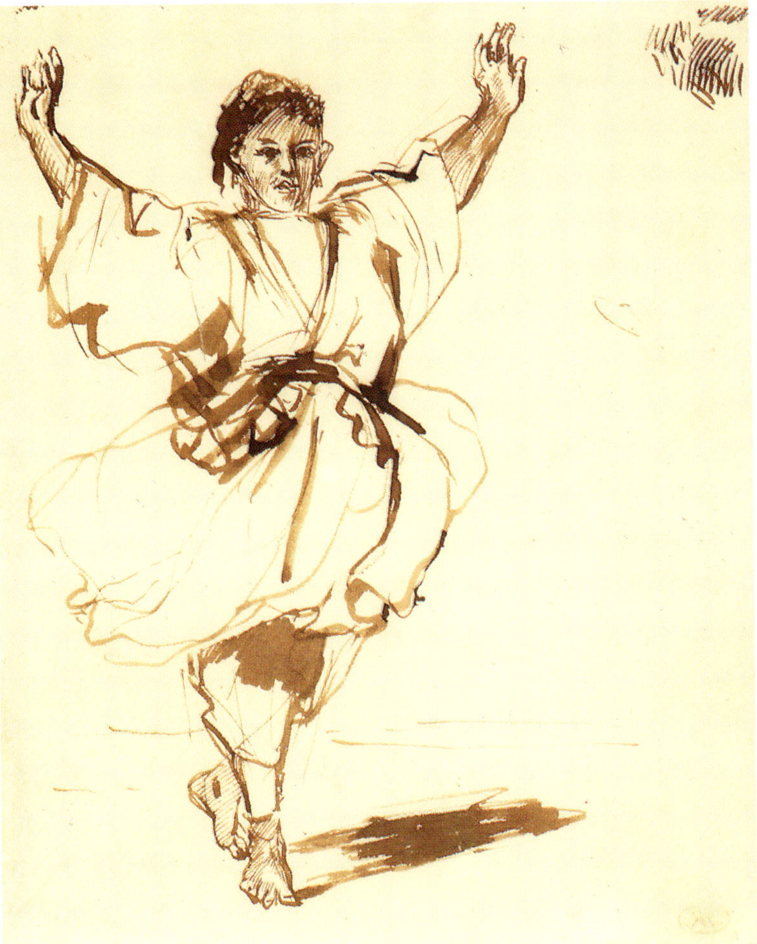

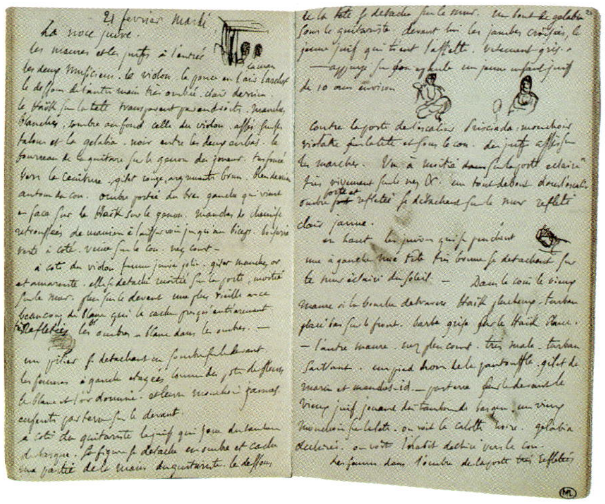

Not in exhibition:
Moroccan Album:
description of the Jewish wedding, Département des Arts graphiques, Louvre (RF 39050, fol. 20 v–21r).

JEWISH BRIDE OF TANGIER
Mariée juive de Tanger
24

Watercolour and pencil drawing on beige paper
28.8 x 23.7 cm
Département des Arts graphiques, Louvre
(RF 4614)

PROVENANCE:
Delacroix Studio, marked lower right (L.838 a); sale, Paris, 22–27 Feb. 1864, lot 553, to Roger Galichon; bequeathed to the Louvre in 1918 (L.1886 a).

BIBLIOGRAPHY:
Robaut, 1885, no. 1622; Joubin, 1930, pl. 12; Sérullaz, 1963, no. 152, repr.; Sérullaz, 1984, II, no. 1588, repr.; Arama, 1987, p. 156–7, repr.; Dumur, 1988, p. 45, repr.

EXHIBITIONS:
Paris, 1930, no. 318; repr. Album, p. 38; Paris, 1933, no. 13, pl. XIII; Paris, 1934, no. 38; Brussels, 1936, no. 91; Paris, 1963, no. 153; Berne, 1963–4, no. 139; Bremen, 1964, no. 187; London-Edinburgh, 1964, no. 120; Paris, 1982, no. 197.

This fine watercolour depicts the Jewish wedding attended by Delacroix, the details of which he feverishly noted in his little green notebook (Département des Arts graphiques, Louvre, RF 39050, fols. 20 verso to 22 verso). He recorded all the costume details during the event, and later transcribed them, without allowing the abundance of ornament to spoil the overall composition. He noted, for example, the mitre (*jemar*) around the bride's forehead, retaining the long blue veil reaching down to the ground, the double headband on which the earrings composed of large rings and pendants (the famous 'ram' or *khras kbach* earrings) were fastened, the necklaces (*el aguila*), the brooches on the bust and the belt folded lengthwise. In an article published in the *Magasin Pittoresque* in January 1842, Delacroix refers several times to the behaviour required of a Jewish bride throughout the various wedding rituals. Contrary to her companions, she is obliged to appear indifferent to everything taking place around her: 'When the last day arrives that the bride will spend at her parent's house . . . they put a sort of mitre on her head composed of numerous scarves superimposed in such a way that only a small part of each is visible. She is seated on a table against the ramparts as motionless as an Egyptian statue. . . . Elderly women paint her cheeks and forehead with cinnabar or henna, or blacken her eyelids with kohl.'

The catalogue of the posthumous Delacroix sale included five other studies of costumes worn by the Jewish bride (Paris, 22–27 Feb. 1864, nos 557 to 561).

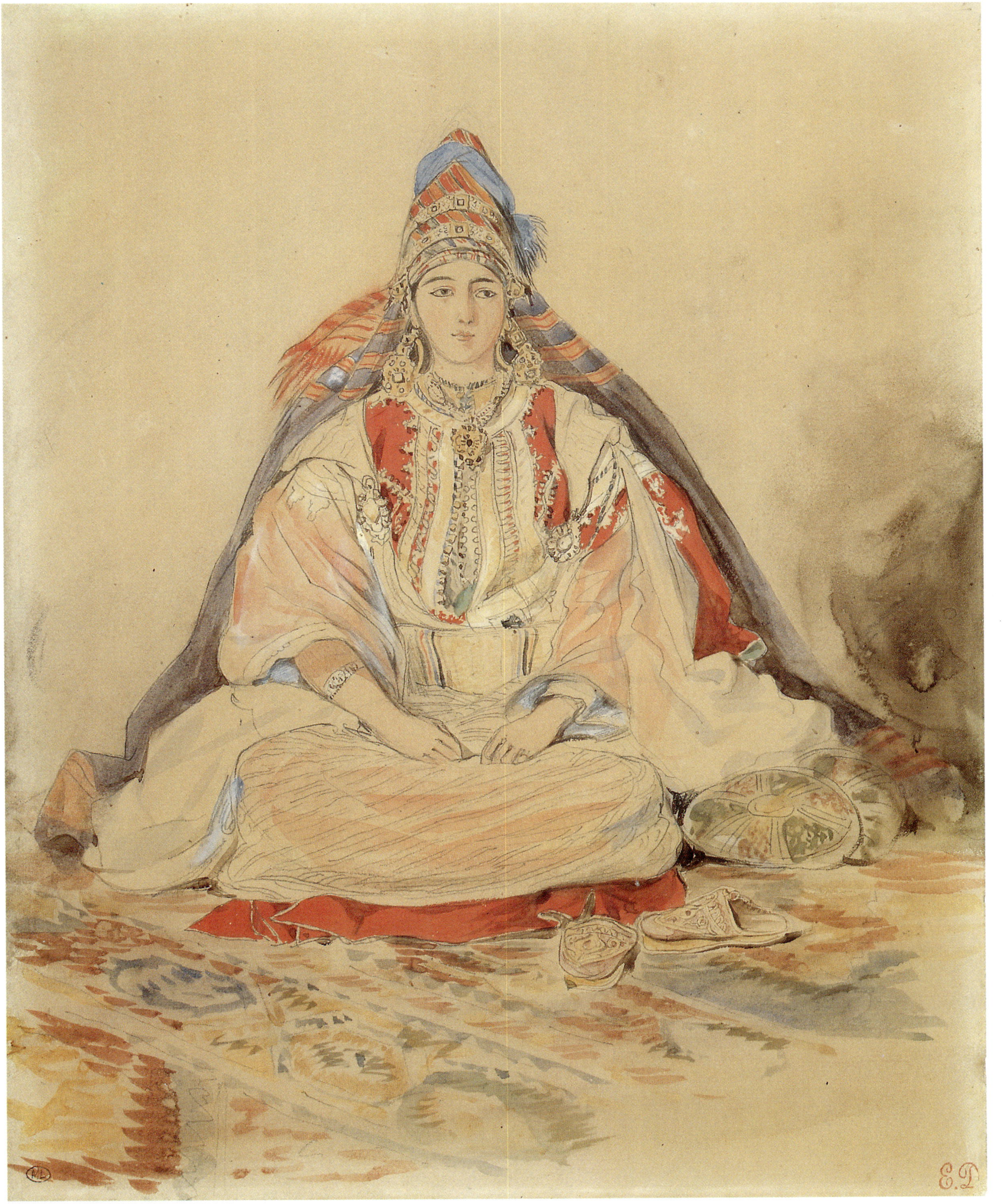

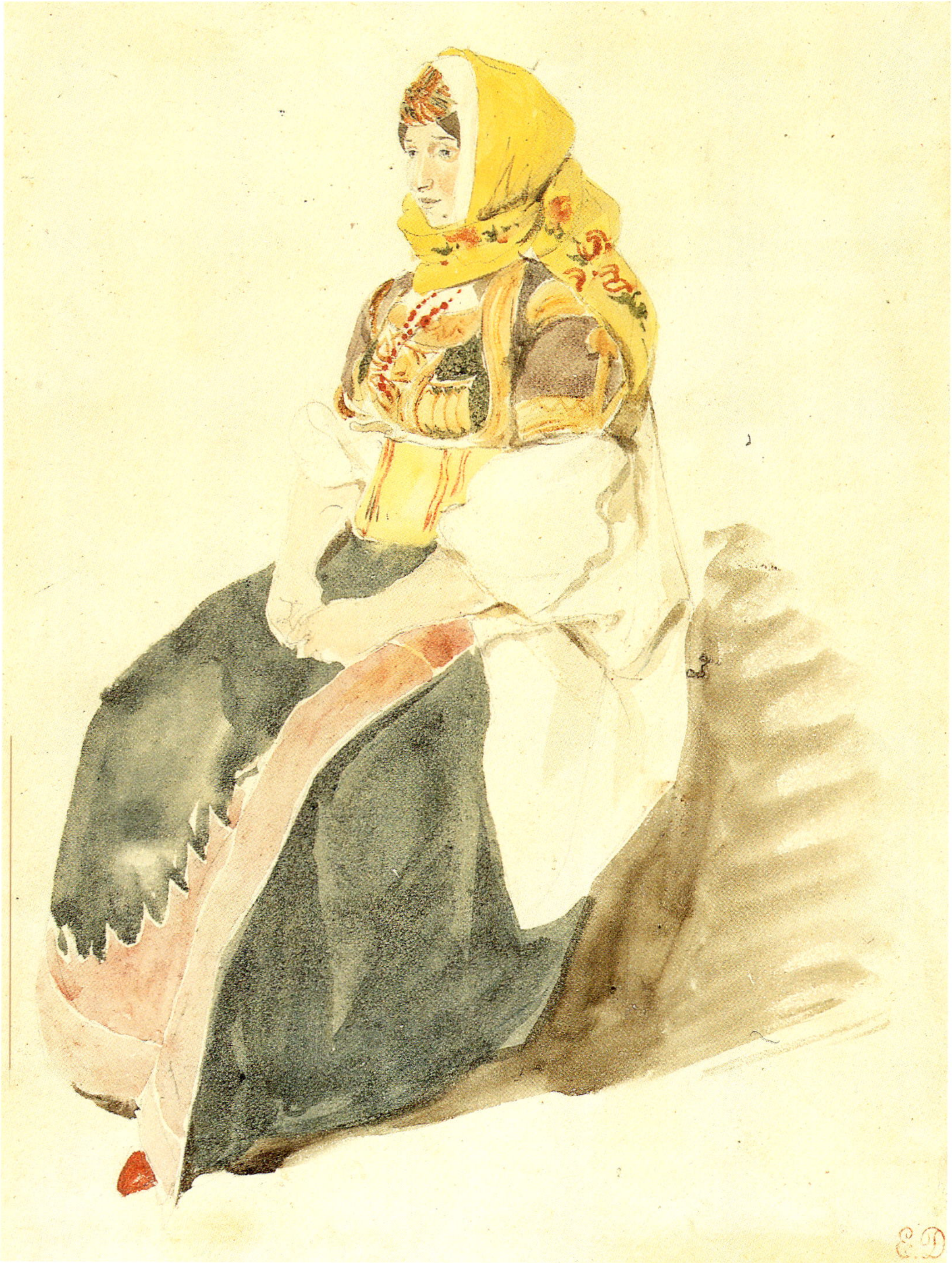

SEATED JEWESS FROM MOROCCO
Juive marocaine assise
25

Watercolour and pencil drawing
25.3 x 19.4 cm
Musée Fabre, Montpellier (15.1.18)

PROVENANCE:
Delacroix Studio, marked lower right (L.838 a); sale, Paris, 22–27 Feb. 1864 lot 562(?) to Barbet de Jouy(?); Georges d'Albenas; bequeathed to the Musée Fabre, Montpellier in 1915.

BIBLIOGRAPHY:
Robaut, 1885, no. 1519 or 1620; Sérullaz, 1963, no. 308, repr.; Arama, 1987, p. 43, repr.

EXHIBITIONS:
Paris, 1963, no. 311; Frankfurt, 1987–8, no. H 29, repr.

Delacroix used this study for his painting exhibited at the 1841 Salon, *Jewish Wedding in Morocco (Noce juive dans le Maroc)* (Louvre, see p. 68). She is portrayed on the opposite side, on the far left of the picture, sitting near the doorway in the shade of the gallery.

The simplicity of the green and pink material of the skirt contrasts with the gleaming embroidery of the blouse and with the hair-style, all of which Delacroix portrayed in a restricted range of colours: green, golden yellow and pink with brownish shadows. The bright red detail on the slipper matches the stippled vermilion of the embroidery at the top of the drawing.

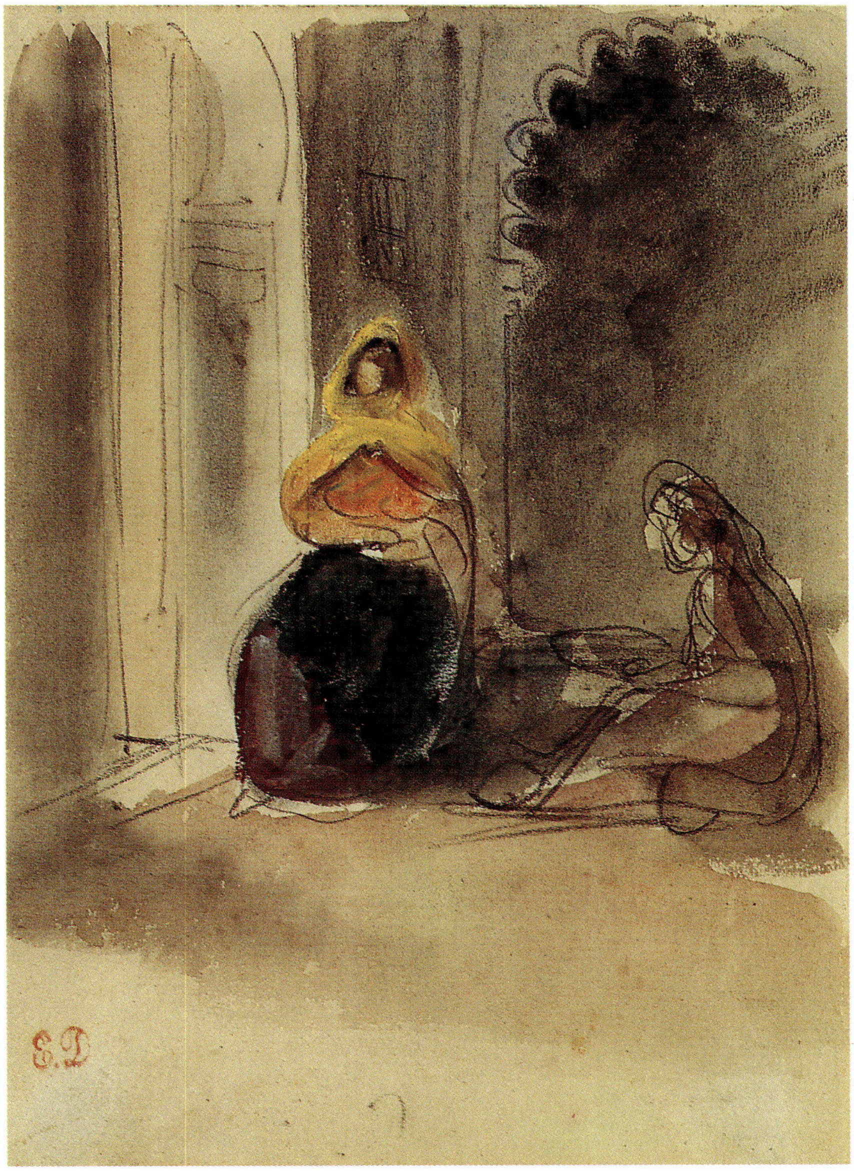

BACKS OF A SEATED MOORISH WOMAN AND AN ARAB IN A BURNOUS
Mauresque assise et Arabe en burnous vu de dos
26

Pen and brown ink
18.3 x 29.5 cm
Private collection. Courtesy of the Galerie Schmit, Paris

PROVENANCE:
Frédéric Villot; sale Paris, 11 Feb. 1865, lot 38, to D. David Weill.

EXHIBITIONS:
Paris, 1933, no. 143, repr. (left-hand drawing).

Delacroix noted in his journal that unimportant details should be eliminated, but that important ones responsible for the legibility of the theme should, on the contrary, be stressed. Here, in the case of the young Jewess seated on the left, he uses firmer strokes of the pen for the ankle and arm bracelets, the rings and earrings, thus emphasizing the model's 'femininity' and sensuality.

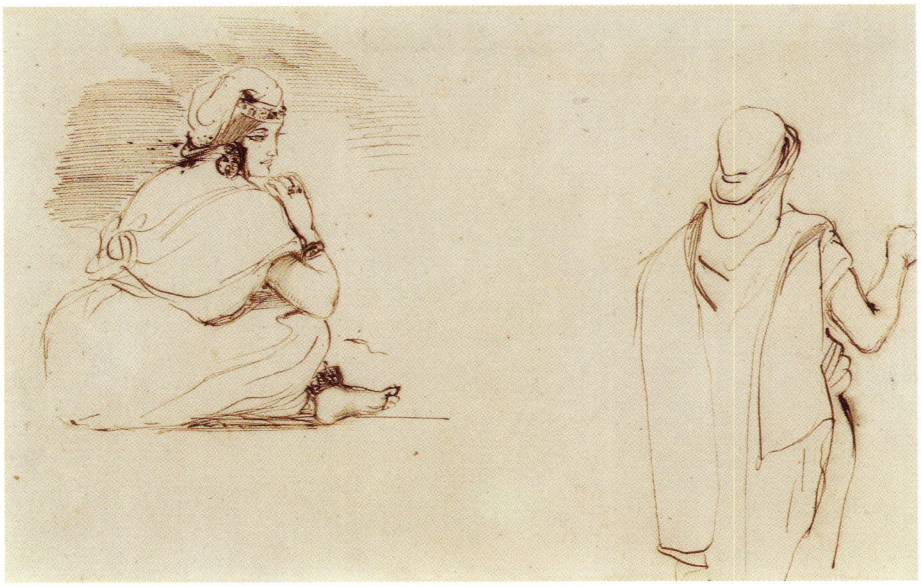

JEWISH WOMAN IN HER APARTMENT
Femme juive dans son appartement
27

Watercolour and pencil drawing
19 x 13.8 cm
Private collection

PROVENANCE:
Delacroix Studio, marked lower left (L.838 a); sale, Paris, 22–27 Feb. 1864, possibly part of nos 571 or 572.

Exhibited here for the first time, this interior scene must have been sketched, according to Maurice Arama, during the second half of Delacroix's stay in Morocco (between mid-April and 10 June 1832).

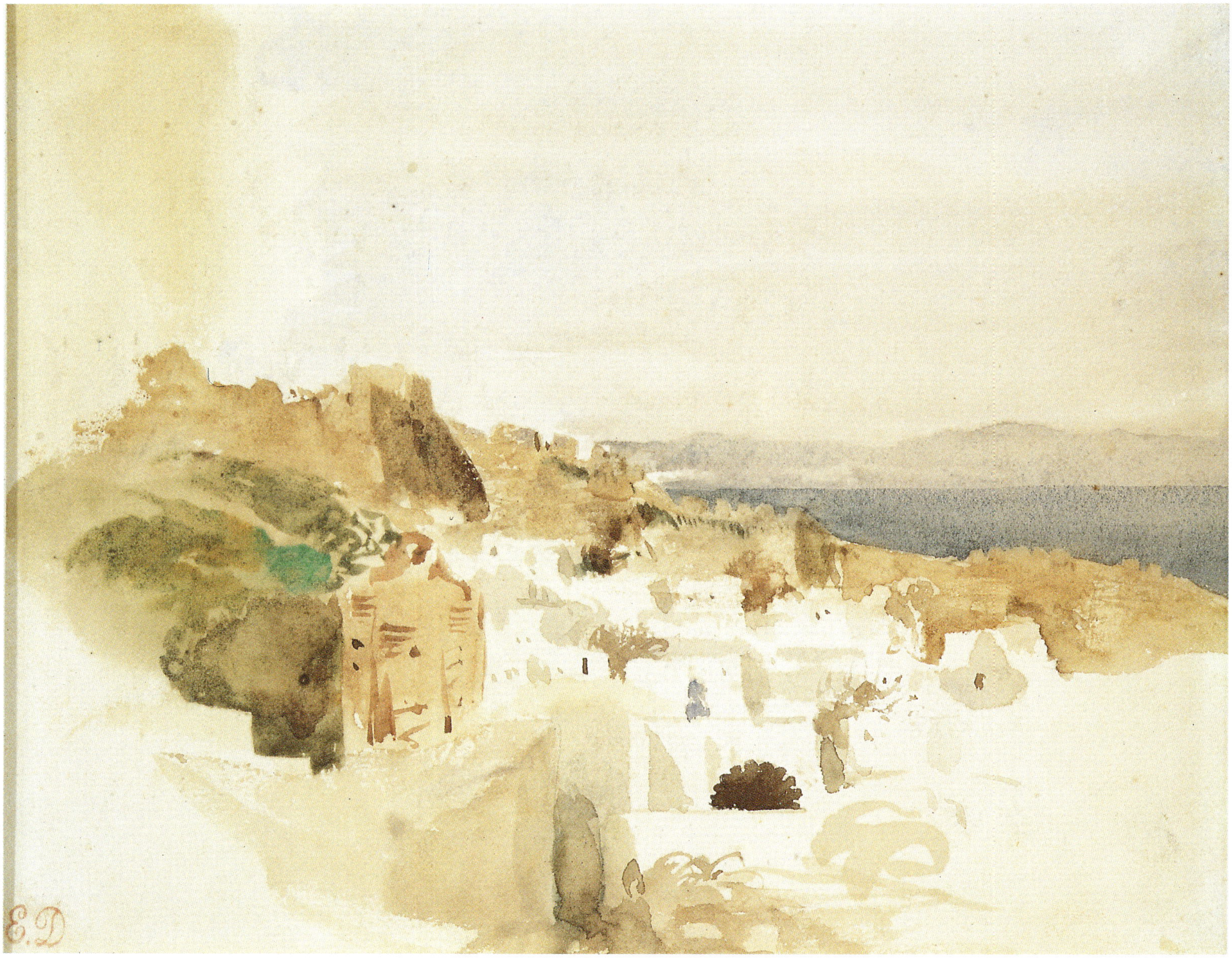

VIEW OF TANGIER
Vue de Tanger
28

Watercolour
16 x 20.5 cm
Musée des Beaux-Arts, Dijon (DG 702)

PROVENANCE:
Delacroix Studio, marked lower left (L.838 a); sale, Paris, 22–27 Feb. 1864; with P. Prouté in 1966; Pierre Granville; donated to the Musée des Beaux-Arts, Dijon in 1969.

BIBLIOGRAPHY:
Lemoine, 1976, no. 85, repr.

EXHIBITIONS:
Zurich, 1987 (1), no. 33; Frankfurt, 1987–8, no. H 11, repr.

In this watercolour, the areas of white paper purposely left blank enable the artist to suggest the luminosity of the scene through the contrast they provide with the brown and green areas of colour. The uniform blue of the sea and the hills in the background herald certain views of L'Estaque painted by Cézanne, in which the density of the sea is evoked in a similar fashion.

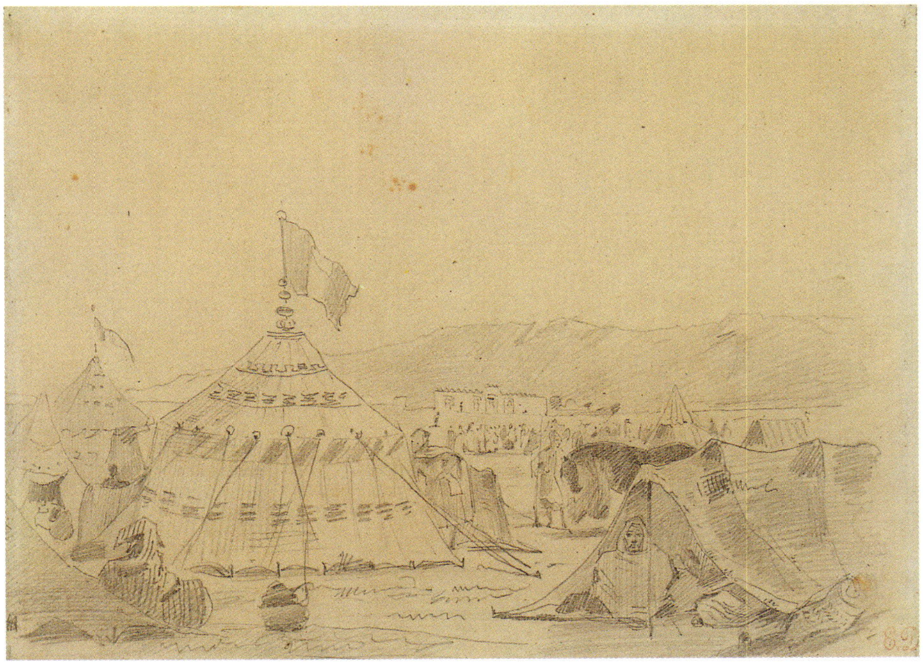

ENCAMPMENT AT EL-KSAR EL-KEBIR
Campement à El-Ksar el-Kébir
29

Pencil on tracing paper
17.6 x 24.7 cm
Département des Arts graphiques, Louvre
(RF 9261)

PROVENANCE:
Delacroix Studio, marked lower right (L. 828 a); sale, Paris, 22–27 Feb. 1864, included in lots 571 or 572, to Étienne Moreau-Nélaton; bequeathed to the Louvre in 1927 (L. 1886 a).

BIBLIOGRAPHY:
Robaut, 1885, part of nos 1629 or 1632; Sérullaz, 1963, no. 157; Sérullaz, 1984, II, no. 1640, repr.; Dumur, 1988, p. 53, repr.

EXHIBITIONS:
Paris, 1930, no. 324; Paris, Orangerie, 1933, no. 32; Paris, 1963, no. 157; Paris, 1982, no. 149.

This drawing is a study for the watercolour of the same subject in the album offered by Delacroix to the Count de Mornay (see pp. 178 to 187). It was on 8 March 1832 that the French mission arrived at El-Ksar el-Kebir, the ancient Roman Oppidum Novum. In his brown album, Delacroix noted on this date: ‘Climbed a hill and went into a pretty wood of green oaks called [blank], went into the valley of [blank] where the army of D. Sebastien was defeated.’ (Département des Arts graphiques, Louvre, RF 1712 bis, fol. 9 verso.) It was indeed not far from El-Ksar el-Kebir that the so-called ‘Battle of the Three Kings’ took place on 4 August 1578, opposing the armies commanded by don Sebastian, king of Portugal and his ally Moulay Mohammed, known as el-Motaouakir, the dethroned king of Morocco, with the army of the Sultan Abd el-Malek. The Moroccans were victorious but the three kings lost their lives.

ENCAMPMENT IN MOROCCO
Campement au Maroc
30

Watercolour, gouache and pencil drawing
9.5 x 16 cm
Annotated in Delacroix's hand in pencil, top centre: couleur—poussière; above: vert jaune doré
Département des Arts graphiques, Louvre
(RF 4772)

PROVENANCE:
Delacroix Studio, marked lower right (L.838 a); sale, Paris, 22–27 Feb. 1864, to Paul Leprieur; donated to the Louvre in 1921.

BIBLIOGRAPHY:
Sérullaz, 1984, II, no. 1641, repr.

EXHIBITIONS:
Paris, 1933, no. 31; Zurich, 1939, no. 187; Basel, 1939, no. 189; Paris, 1963 (1), no. 38; Paris, 1982, no. 176.

As in the case of the watercolour exhibited at no. 32, it is likely that this work originally formed part of an album. It probably corresponds to one of the stages of the journey between Tangier and Meknes.

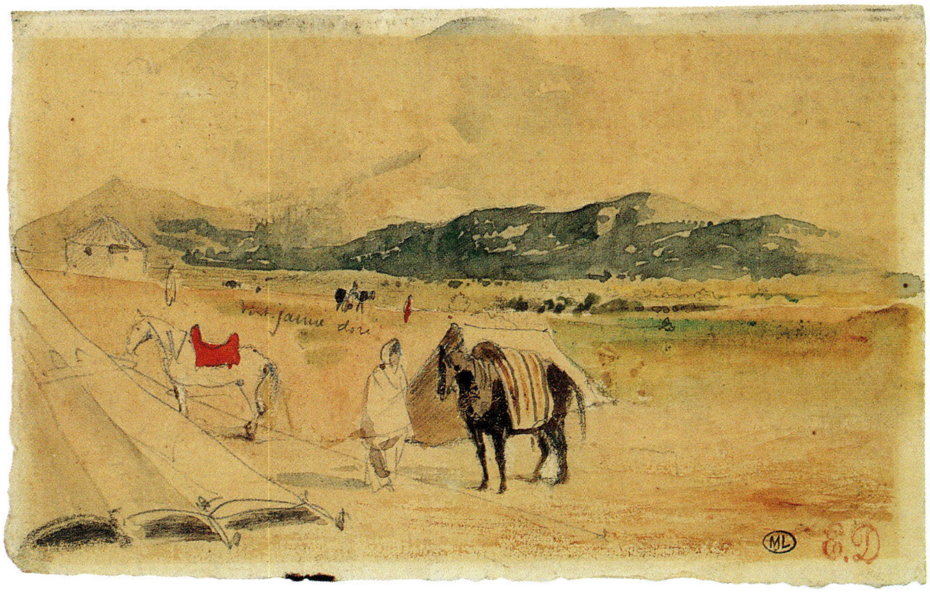

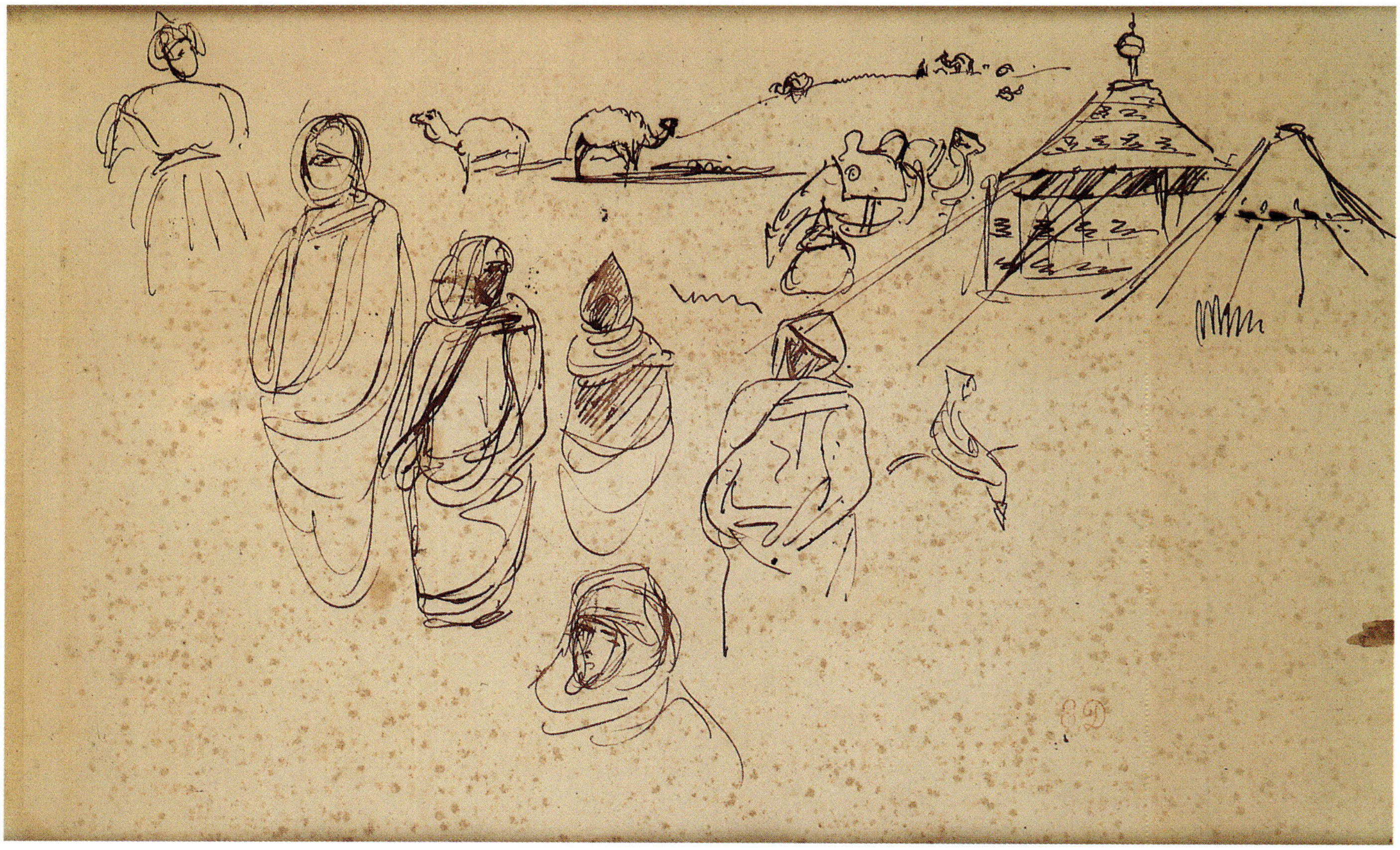

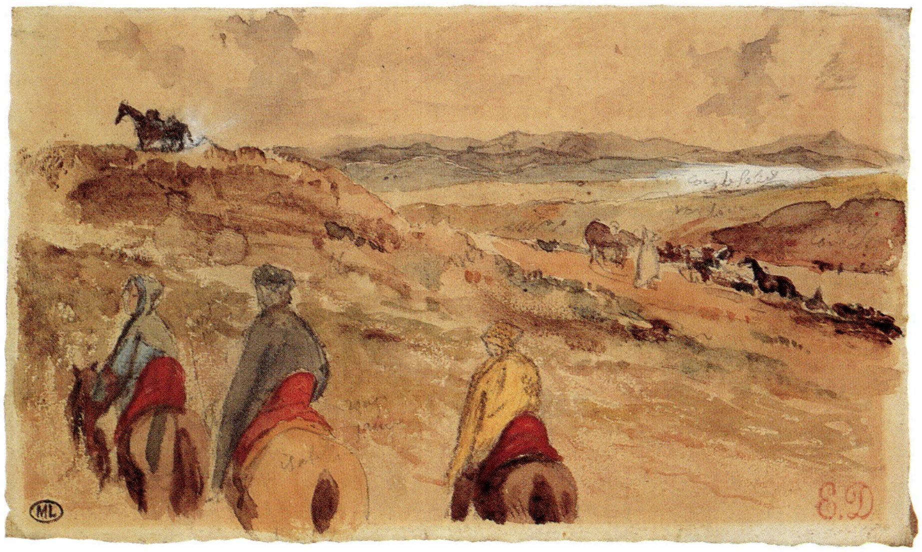

MOROCCAN ENCAMPMENT
Campement marocain
31

Pen and brown ink
18.7 x 30.6 cm
Private collection

PROVENANCE:
Delacroix Studio, marked lower right (L.838 a); sale, Paris, 22–27 Feb. 1864, included in lots 571 or 572.

Maurice Arama has suggested that this drawing was probably executed around 14 March 1832, during the stop near the Zerhoun, before the convoy's arrival in Meknes.

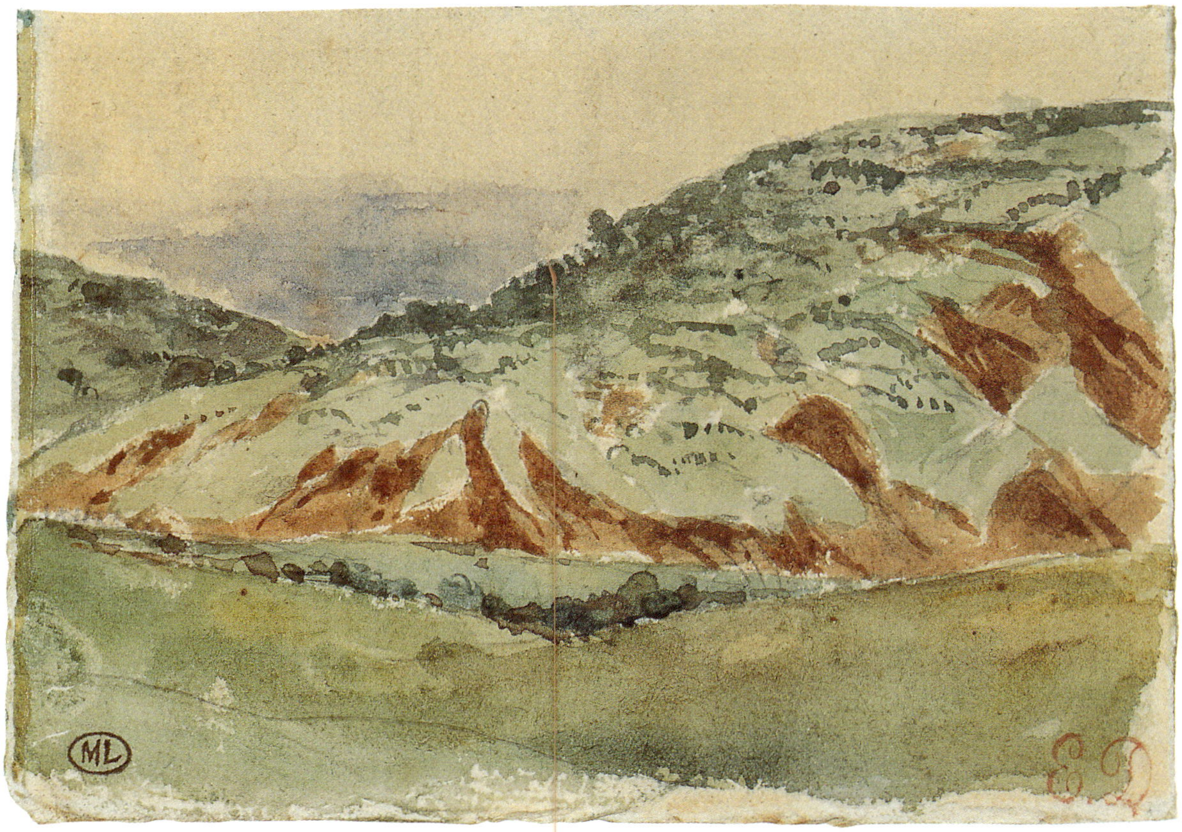

ON THE ROAD
En route
32
Watercolour, gouache and pencil drawing
9.3 x 15.9 cm
Annotated in Delacroix's hand in pencil: cou[p] de soleil—ver[t] [or lavé?]—cou[p] de soleil—bleu—rouge—jaune—isabelle
Département des Arts graphiques, Louvre (RF 4771)

PROVENANCE:
Delacroix Studio, marked lower right (L.838 a); sale, Paris, 22–27 Feb. 1864, probably included in lots 572 or 663, to Étienne Moreau-Nélaton; bequeathed to the Louvre in 1927 (L.1886 a).

BIBLIOGRAPHY:
Sérullaz, 1984, II, no. 1642, repr.

EXHIBITIONS:
Paris, 1933, no. 33; Zurich, 1939, no. 186; Basel, 1939, no. 190; Paris, 1963 (1), no. 39; Paris, 1982, no. 175.

Most probably a page torn out of an album of sketches, this little watercolour, enhanced by a few touches of bright red, evokes some of the climbs Delacroix made with the French mission on the outgoing and return journeys between Tangier and Meknes.

MOROCCAN LANDSCAPE WITH WOODED HILLS
Paysage du Maroc avec des collines boisées
33
Watercolour and pencil drawing
7.5 x 10.8 cm
Département des Arts graphiques, Louvre (RF 9263)

PROVENANCE:
Delacroix Studio, marked at lower right (L.838 a); sale, Paris, 22–27 Feb. 1864, possibly included in lots 572 or 663, to Étienne Moreau-Nélaton; bequeathed to the Louvre in 1927 (L.1886 a).

BIBLIOGRAPHY:
Robaut, 1885, possibly part of nos 1632 or 1643; Sérullaz, 1963, no. 155, repr.; Sérullaz, 1984, II, no. 1637, repr.

EXHIBITIONS:
Paris, 1930, no. 329; Paris, 1933, no. 29; Paris, 1963, no. 156; Paris, 1982, no. 211.

This watercolour evokes the atmosphere with great sensitivity, with its dominant tones of harmonious greens and browns and the background 'bathed' in a hazy light. It prefigures the watercolours painted in the same style, but done much later, in 1855, at Les Eaux-Bonnes, where the artist succeeded in portraying with very simple means the magnificence of the Pyrenean mountains and the mist that sometimes envelops them. This watercolour may have been executed on Thursday 15 March after Zerhoun, as it is similar to one of the pages of the album in the Louvre (inventory RF 1712 bis, fol. 16 recto, see p. 90).

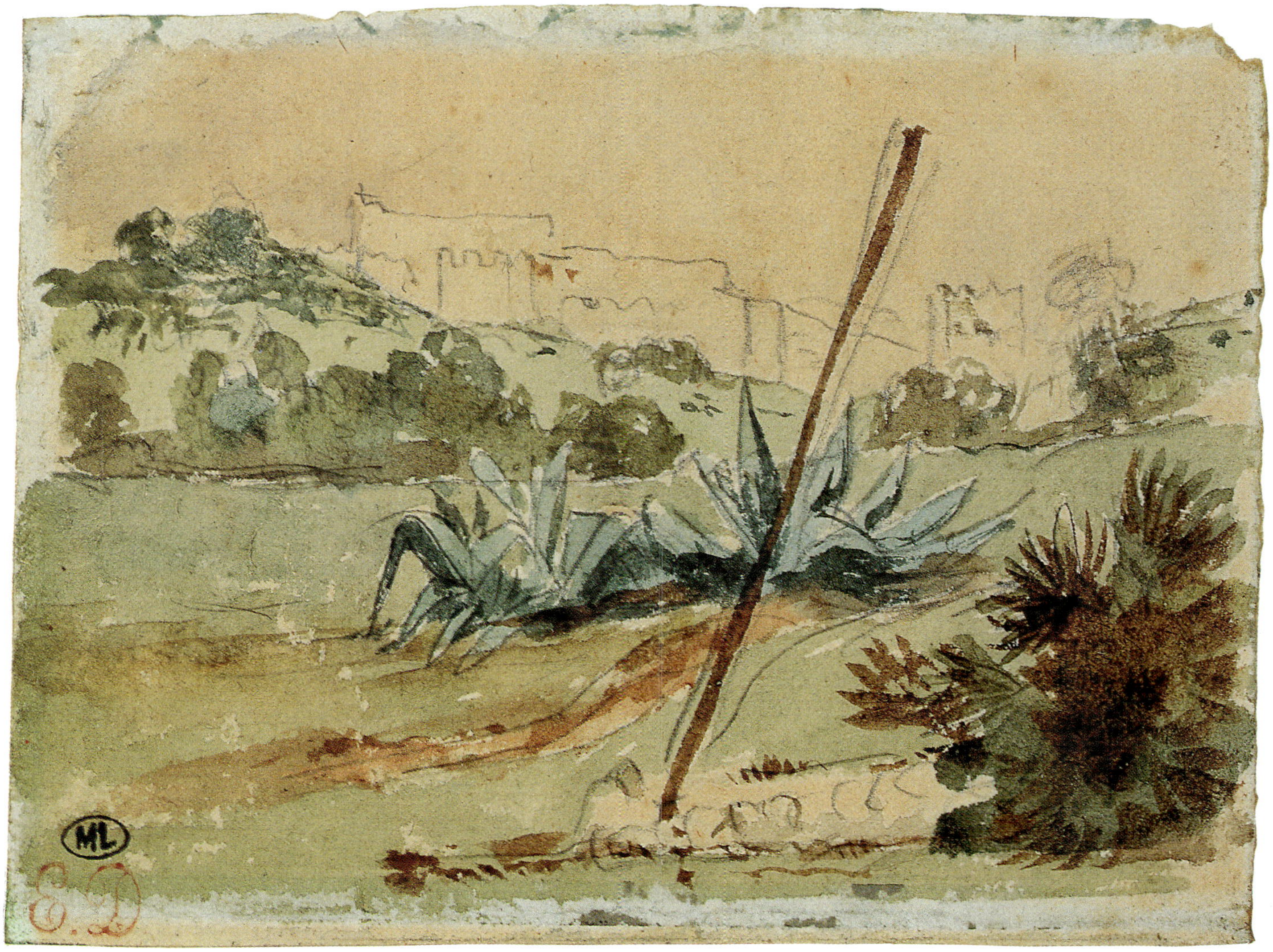

LANDSCAPE WITH ALOE AND RAMPARTS IN THE BACKGROUND
Paysage avec des aloès et des remparts au second plan
34

Watercolour and pencil drawing
8 x 10.8 cm
Département des Arts graphiques, Louvre (RF 9262)

PROVENANCE:
Delacroix Studio, marked at lower left (L.838 a); sale, Paris, 22–27 Feb. 1864, possibly included in lots 572 or 663, to Étienne Moreau-Nélaton; bequeathed to the Louvre in 1927 (L.1886 a).

BIBLIOGRAPHY:
Robaut, 1885, possibly part of nos 1632 or 1643; Sérullaz, 1963, no. 154, repr.; Sérullaz, 1984, II, no. 1636, repr.; Arama, 1987, p. 136, repr.

EXHIBITIONS:
Paris, 1930, no. 328; Paris, 1933, no. 28; Paris, 1963, no. 155; Paris, 1982, no. 210.

This watercolour was most probably executed on the outskirts of Tangier and, like the preceding drawings, was originally part of an album of sketches.

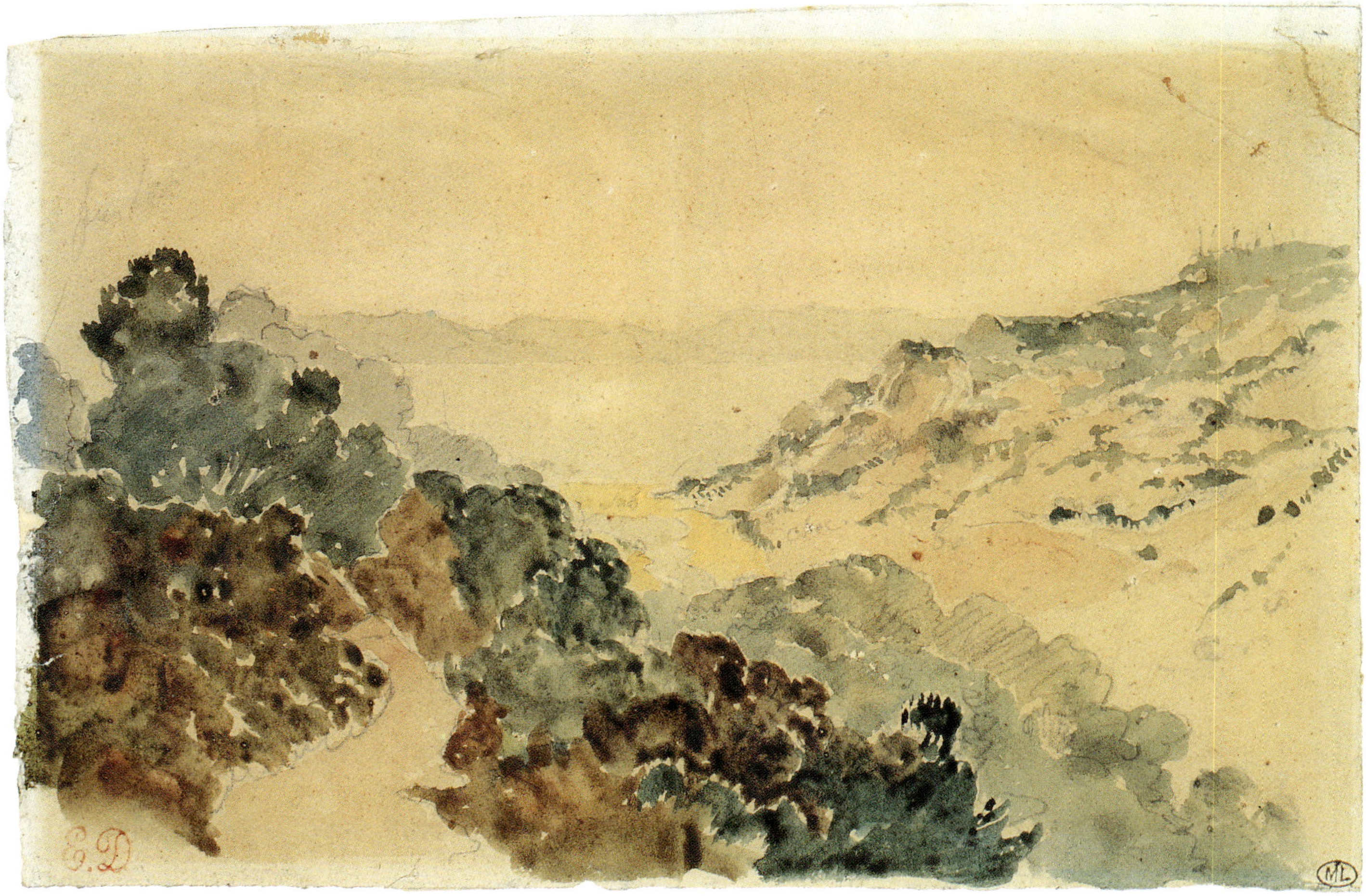

MOROCCAN COASTAL LANDSCAPE WITH WOODED HILLS
Paysage marocain avec collines boisées en bord de mer
35

Watercolour and pencil drawing
12.6 x 19.2 cm
Annotated in Delacroix's hand, in pencil, centre: gris—sab[*le*]—br[*un*].
Département des Arts graphiques, Louvre (RF 9757)

PROVENANCE:
Delacroix Studio, marked lower left (L.838 a); sale, Paris, 22–27 Feb. 1864, possibly included in lot 572, to Étienne Moreau-Nélaton; bequeathed to the Louvre in 1927 (L.1886 a).

BIBLIOGRAPHY:
Robaut, 1885, possibly part of no. 1632; Sérullaz, 1963, no. 156, repr.; Sérullaz, 1984, II, no. 1635, repr.

EXHIBITIONS:
Paris, 1963, no. 475.

The landscape in the foreground, more detailed than in the middle distance, is reminiscent of Corot's small painting executed during his first trip to Italy in 1826: *The Bridge at Narni* (Louvre). The background of sea and hills seems to be drowned in the mist.

THE RAMPARTS AT MEKNES
Les remparts de Meknès
36

Pastel
10.5 x 18 cm
Private collection

PROVENANCE:
Delacroix Studio, marked lower left (L.838 a); sale, Paris, 22–27 Feb. 1864, possibly included in lots 571 or 573; sale, Paris, 17 Nov. 1982, no. 25, repr.

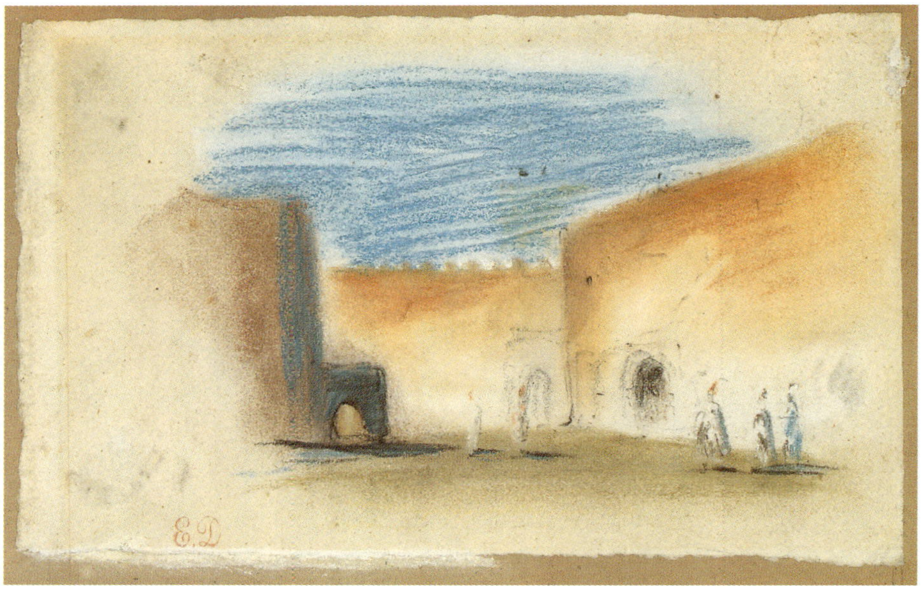

View of a section of the walls near the entrance to the palace—in luminous yellow-ochre—with a few silhouettes and an intensely blue sky. This little pastel illustrates the evolution of Delacroix's vision; henceforth he is increasingly preoccupied by the question of light.

On the right is the silhouette of one of the *moghaznis* of the imperial guard, recognizable by his red bonnet.

LANDSCAPE OUTSIDE MEKNES
Paysage aux environs de Meknès
37

Watercolour and pencil drawing
16.5 x 11.6 cm
Annotated in Delacroix's hand, in pencil, top: ouvrir [?] la fouta autour [*illegible word*] sur la tête—la veste de toile
Musée de la Ville de Poitiers et de la Société des Antiquaires de l'Ouest, Poitiers (882.1.349)

PROVENANCE:
Delacroix Studio, marked lower right (L. 838 a); sale, Paris, 22–27 Feb. 1864, possibly included in lot 572, to Babinet; bequeathed to the Musée des Beaux-Arts, Poitiers in 1882.

BIBLIOGRAPHY:
Robaut, 1885, possibly part of no. 1632; Sérullaz, 1963, no. 175 repr.

EXHIBITIONS:
Paris, 1963, no. 177.

According to Maurice Arama, Delacroix must have executed this watercolour after his arrival in Meknes, taking into account the pencil note in his brown album dated 1 April 1832: 'Saint's tomb descending crenellated ramparts.' (Département des Arts graphiques, Louvre, inventory RF 1712 bis, fol. 26 recto, see p. 129.)

PANORAMIC VIEW OF THE COUNTRYSIDE AROUND MEKNES
Vue panoramique des environs de Meknès
38

Watercolour
15.7 x 27.6 cm
Musée de la Ville de Poitiers et de la Société des Antiquaires de l'Ouest, Poitiers (882.1.348)

PROVENANCE:
Delacroix Studio, marked lower left (L.838 a); sale, Paris, 22–27 Feb. 1864, possibly included in lot 572, to Babinet; bequeathed to the Musée de Poitiers in 1882.

BIBLIOGRAPHY:
Robaut, 1885, possibly part of no. 1632; Sérullaz, 1963, no. 161 repr.

EXHIBITIONS:
Paris, 1963, no. 161.

Beyond an area deliberately left blank, the Meknes ramparts stand out against the sombre foothills of the Zerhoun. Considering the extreme confusion of the French mission's arrival in Meknes, greeted by a multitude of *jeux de poudre*, the shouting of the crowd and the deafening din of the musicians on horseback, it is difficult to imagine that Delacroix was able to paint this subtle watercolour during the official tour of the ramparts. It seems more probable that it was executed during the course of one of the walks he took after the imperial audience, between 1 and 5 April 1832.

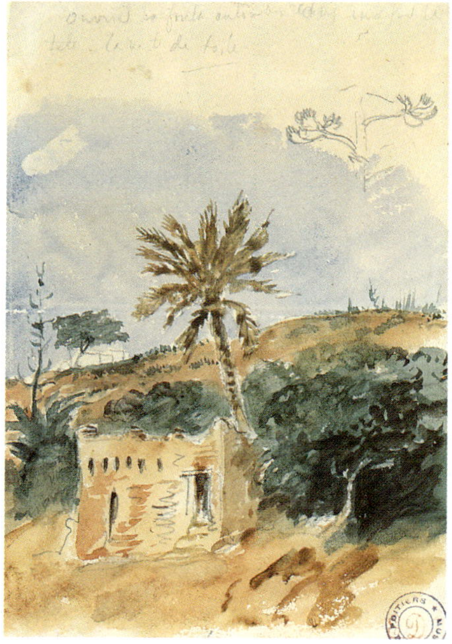

HOUSE IN TANGIER
Maison à Tanger
39

Watercolour and pencil drawing
21.5 x 27.5 cm
Collection Jan et Marie-Anne Krugier. Courtesy of Galerie Jan Krugier, Geneva

PROVENANCE:
Delacroix Studio, marked lower left (L.838 a); sale, Paris, 22–27 Feb. 1864, lot 567, to Charles Diéterle. Sale, 15 Oct. 1991, lot 22, repr.

BIBLIOGRAPHY:
Robaut, 1885, no. 1642.

EXHIBITIONS:
Paris, 1933, no. 155, repr.

'I am really in a most curious country' Delacroix wrote to his friend Jean-Baptiste Pierret on 8 February 1832. 'My health is good but I am a little anxious about my sight. Although the sun isn't very strong yet, the glare and the reflected light from the houses, which are all painted white, tire my eyes excessively.' (*Correspondance*, I, p. 310; Stewart, p. 183). Despite this handicap, apparently rapidly overcome, Delacroix, from his arrival in Tangier until the end of his stay in Morocco, never ceased to admire, down to the smallest detail, the houses and palaces that he was sometimes able to visit. The nine drawings exhibited here (see nos 40 to 47) illustrate that the artist was as sensitive to the architecture bathed in light, as he was to the splendour of the interior decoration, the colours of which he never failed to note down.

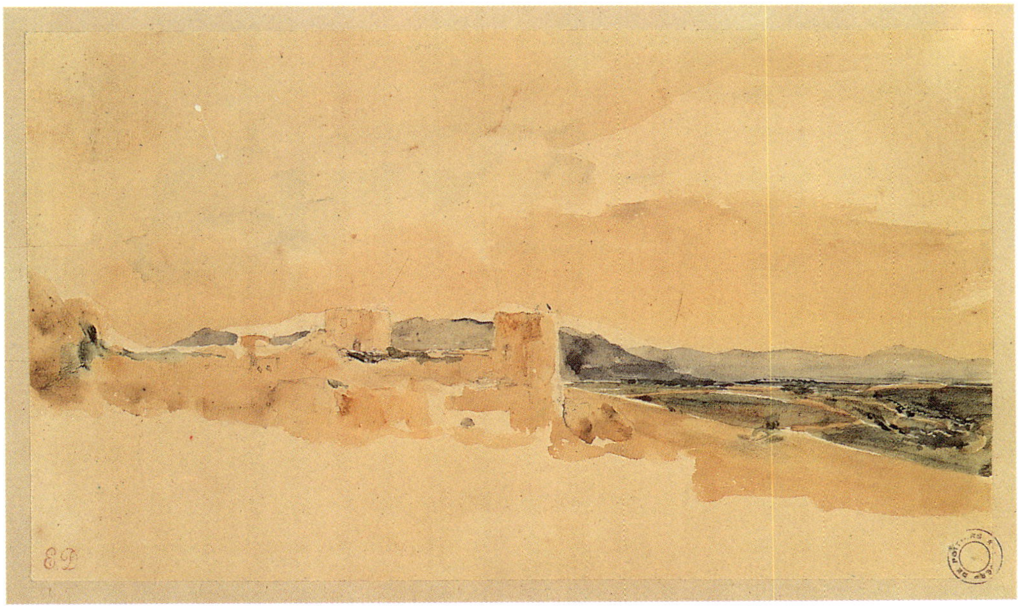

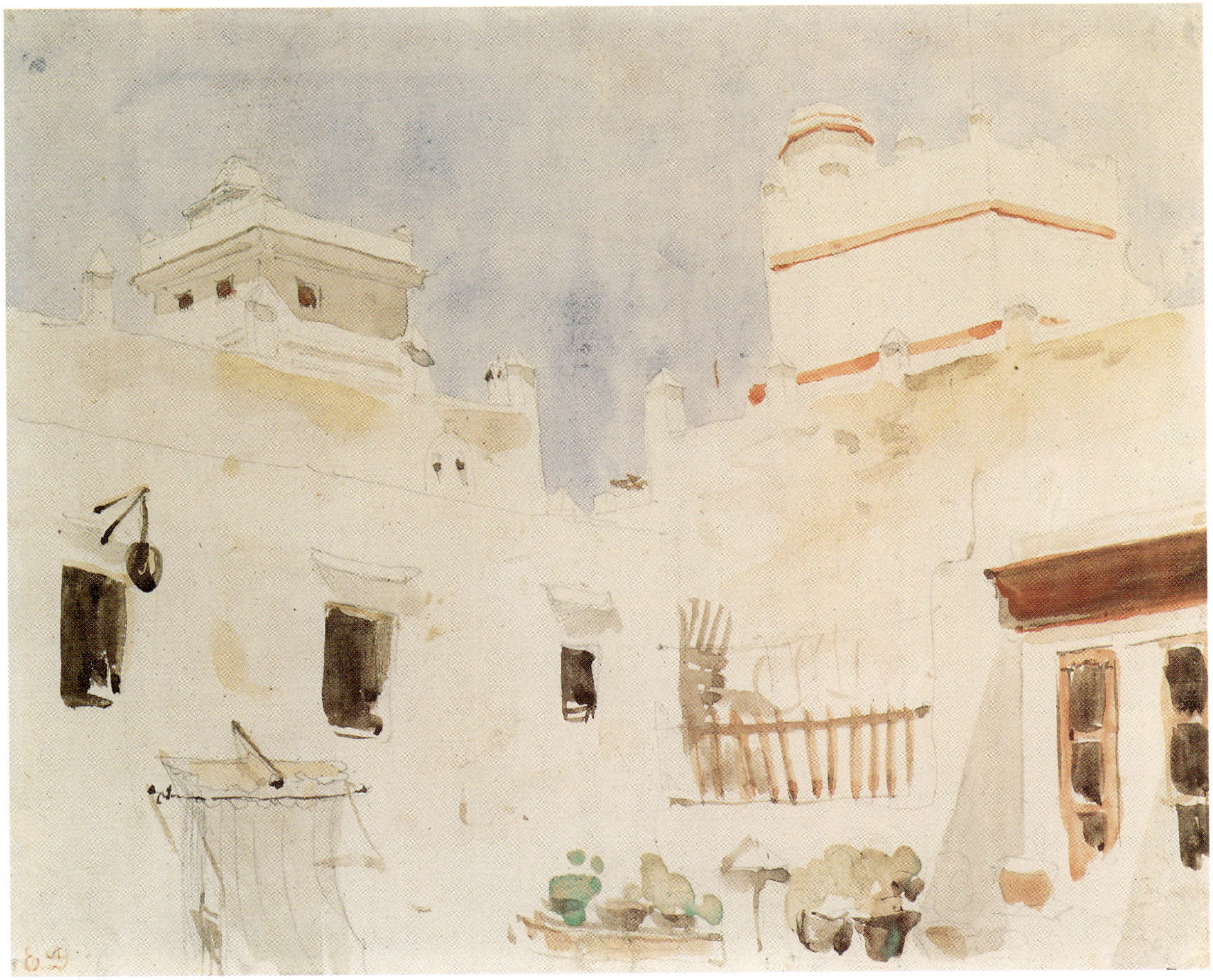

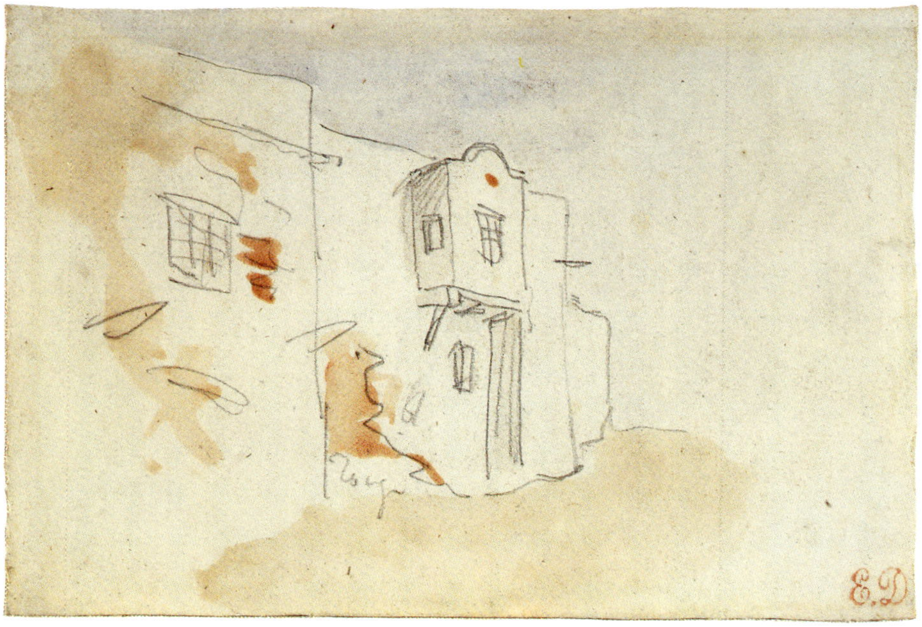
E.D

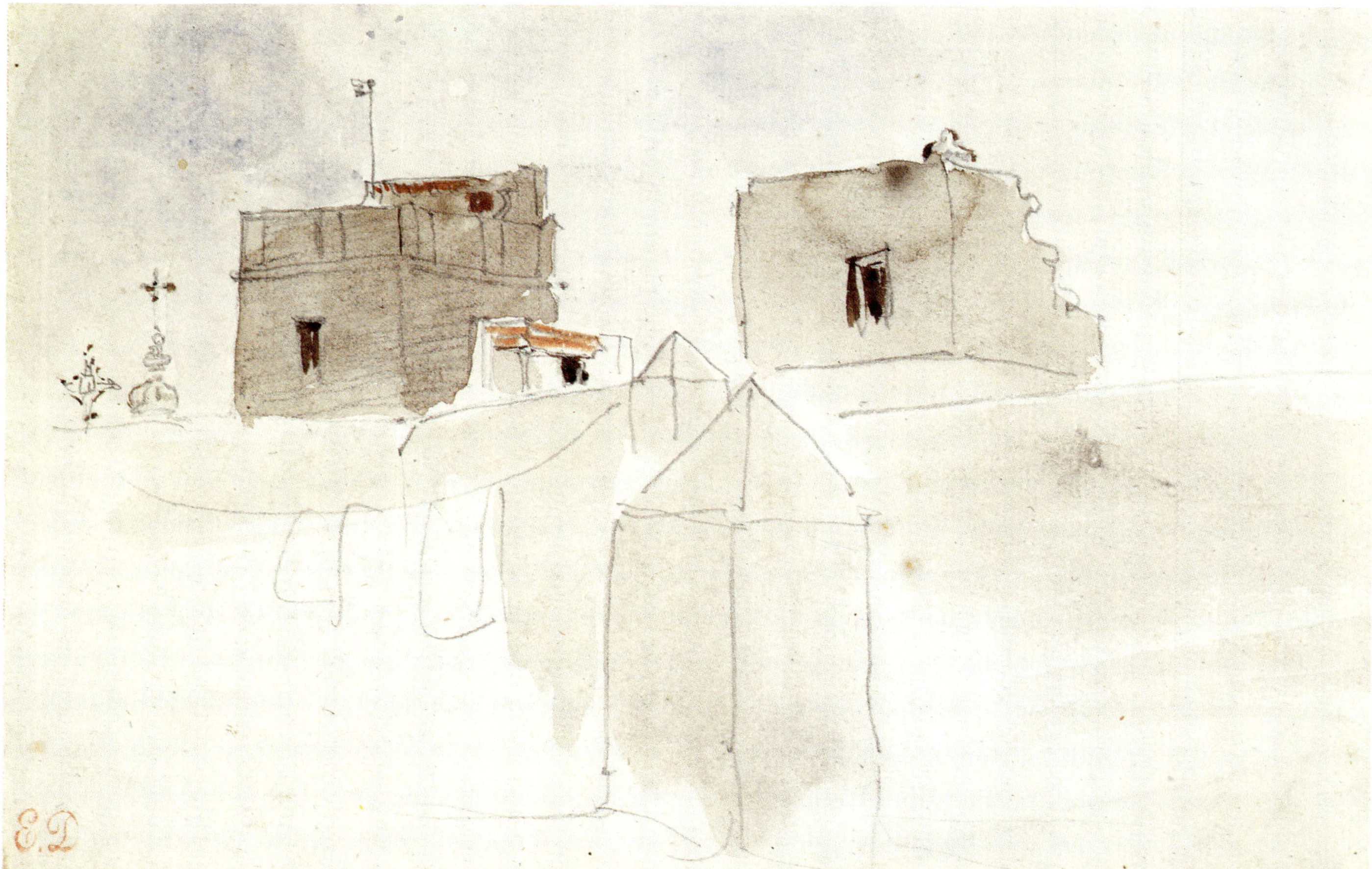
E.D

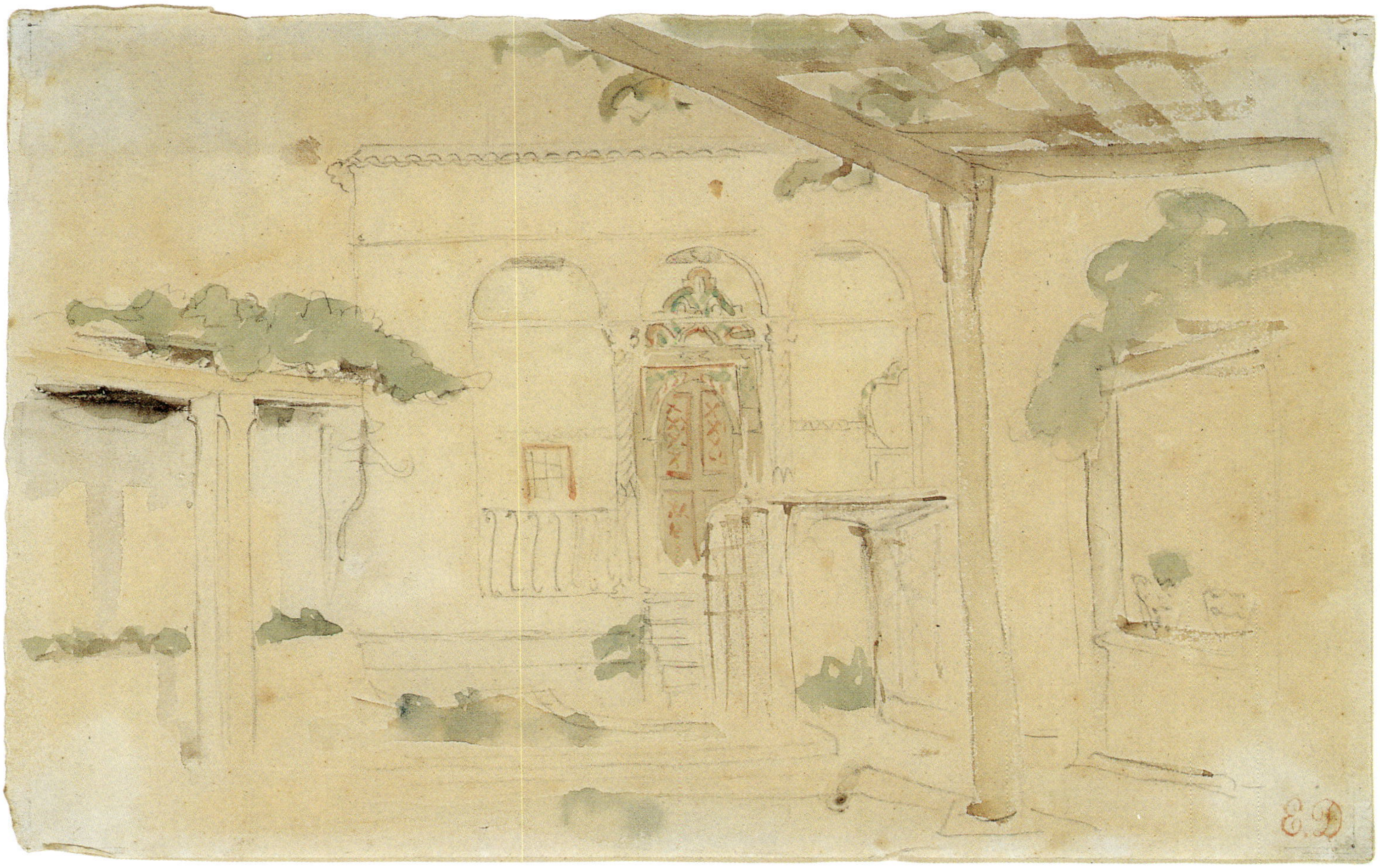

FRONT OF A HOUSE IN TANGIER
Façade d'une maison a Tanger
40

Pencil and watercolour
10.1 x 15.6 cm
Annotated in Delacroix's hand, in pencil, lower centre: bl[anc]—rouge
Huguette Bérès, Paris

PROVENANCE:
Delacroix Studio, marked lower right (L.838 a); sale, Paris, 22–27 Feb. 1864, possibly part of no. 572.

See the preceding number.

TWO MOROCCAN HOUSES WITH TERRACES
Deux maisons marocaines à terrasse
41

Pencil and watercolour
13.5 x 21 cm
Huguette Bérès, Paris

PROVENANCE:
Delacroix Studio, marked lower left (L.838 a); sale, Paris, 22–27 Feb. 1864, possibly part of no. 572.

See no. 39.

MOROCCAN COURTYARD
Cour marocaine
42

Watercolour and pencil drawing
13.5 x 22 cm
Private collection

PROVENANCE:
Delacroix Studio, marked lower right (L.838 a); sale, Paris, 22–27 Feb. 1864, possibly part of no. 572.

EXHIBITIONS:
Paris, 1973 (no cat.).

According to Maurice Arama, this is probably a corner of the royal palace at Meknes, which Delacroix visited after the French delegation's audience with Moulay Abd al-Rahman. See no. 39.

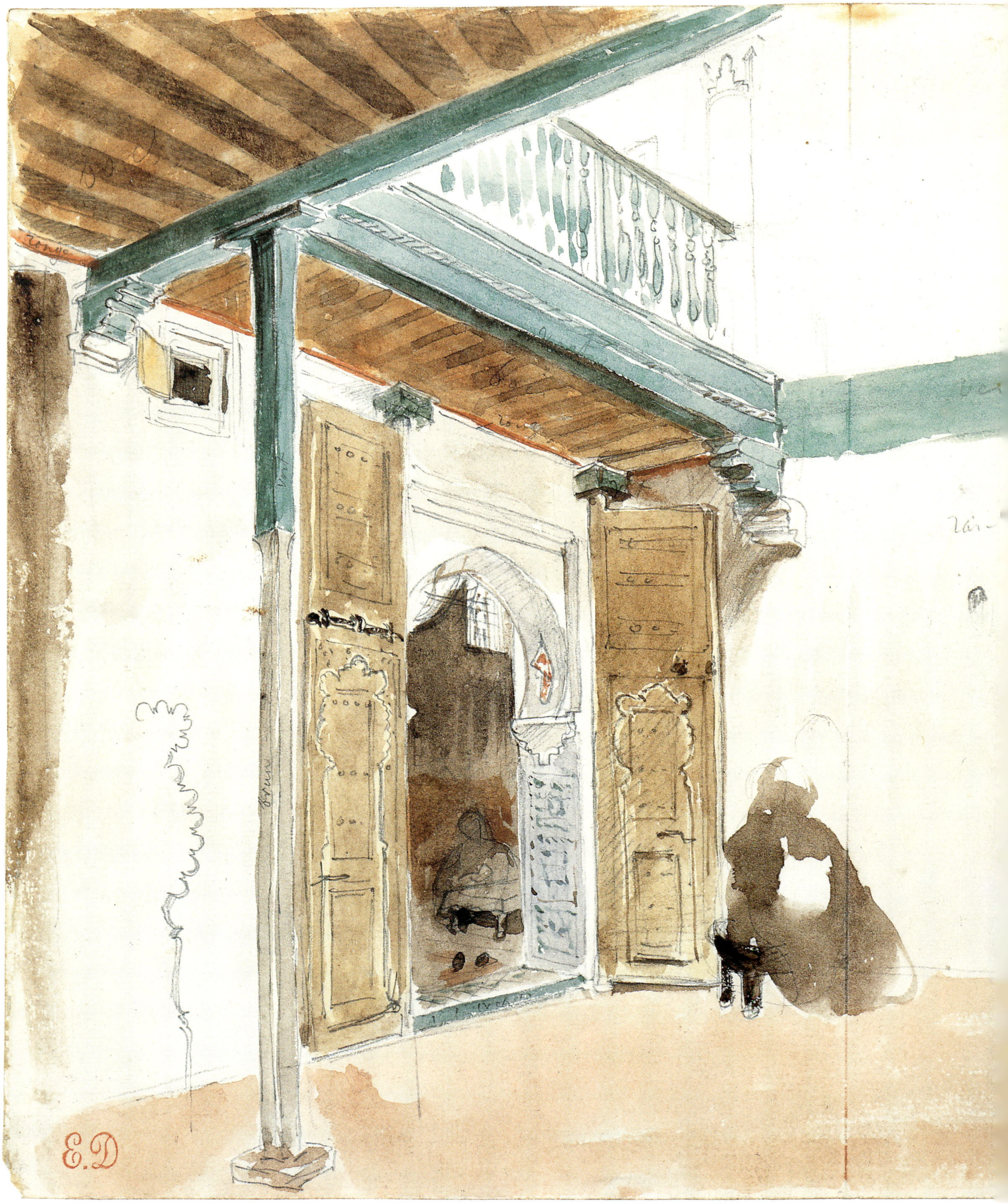

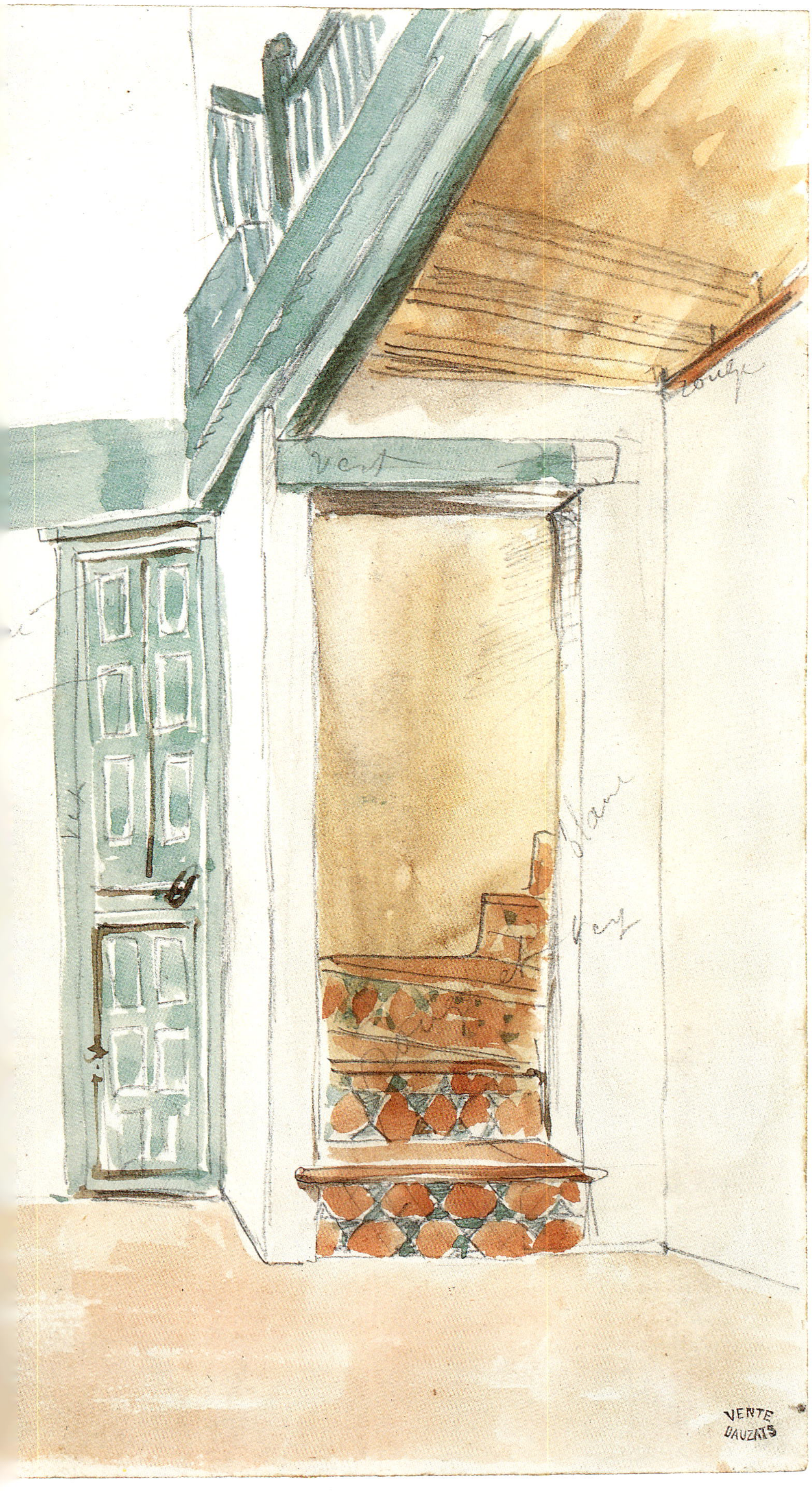

A COURTYARD IN TANGIER
Une cour à Tanger
43

Watercolour and pencil drawing
20.7 x 29.4 cm
Annotated in Delacroix's hand in pencil, top centre: vert—raie blanc; *right:* rouge—vert—blanc—vert
Département des Arts graphiques, Louvre (RF 3375)

PROVENANCE:
Delacroix Studio, marked lower left (L.838 a); sale, Paris, 22–27 Feb. 1864, lot 565, to Adrien Dauzats, marked lower right; sale, Paris, 1–4 Feb. 1869, lot 388, to Victor Chocquet; sale Paris, 1–4 July 1899, lot 115, to Étienne Moreau-Nélaton; donated to the Louvre in 1907 (L.1886 a).

BIBLIOGRAPHY:
Robaut, 1885, no. 1636; Guiffrey-Marcel, 1909, no. 3465, repr.; Joubin, 1930, pl. 15; Sérullaz, 1963, no. 307, repr.; Sérullaz, 1984, II, no. 1664, repr.; Arama, 1987, p. 152, repr.; Dumur, 1988, p. 46, repr.

EXHIBITIONS:
Paris, 1930, no. 405; Paris, 1933, no. 14; Paris, 1963, no. 310; Paris, 1982, no. 206.

Somewhat curiously, this watercolour, which is described in the catalogue of the posthumous Delacroix sale as *Study of Interior used for the 'Jewish Wedding' (Étude d'intérieur ayant servi pour la 'Noce juive')* lost its identity five years later at the Dauzats sale where it figured under the title of *Courtyard of an Arab Dwelling (Cour d'habitation arabe).* This occurred yet again at the sale of the Chocquet collection where it was recorded as *Courtyard in an Arab House (Cour intérieure de maison arabe).* But when Étienne Moreau-Nélaton located it, probably at this sale, the well-informed collector had no difficulty in connecting it with the painting *The Jewish Wedding*, exhibited at the 1841 Salon (Louvre, see p. 68). Apart from one or two details, the architectural organization of the painting is identical in both works, with the staircase on the right, the gallery with its green painted ramp and the curved door on the left. The lighting, however, is quite different: in the final composition the dazzling light reflected by the white walls is replaced by alternating sunlight and shadow, in perfect harmony with the groups of figures.

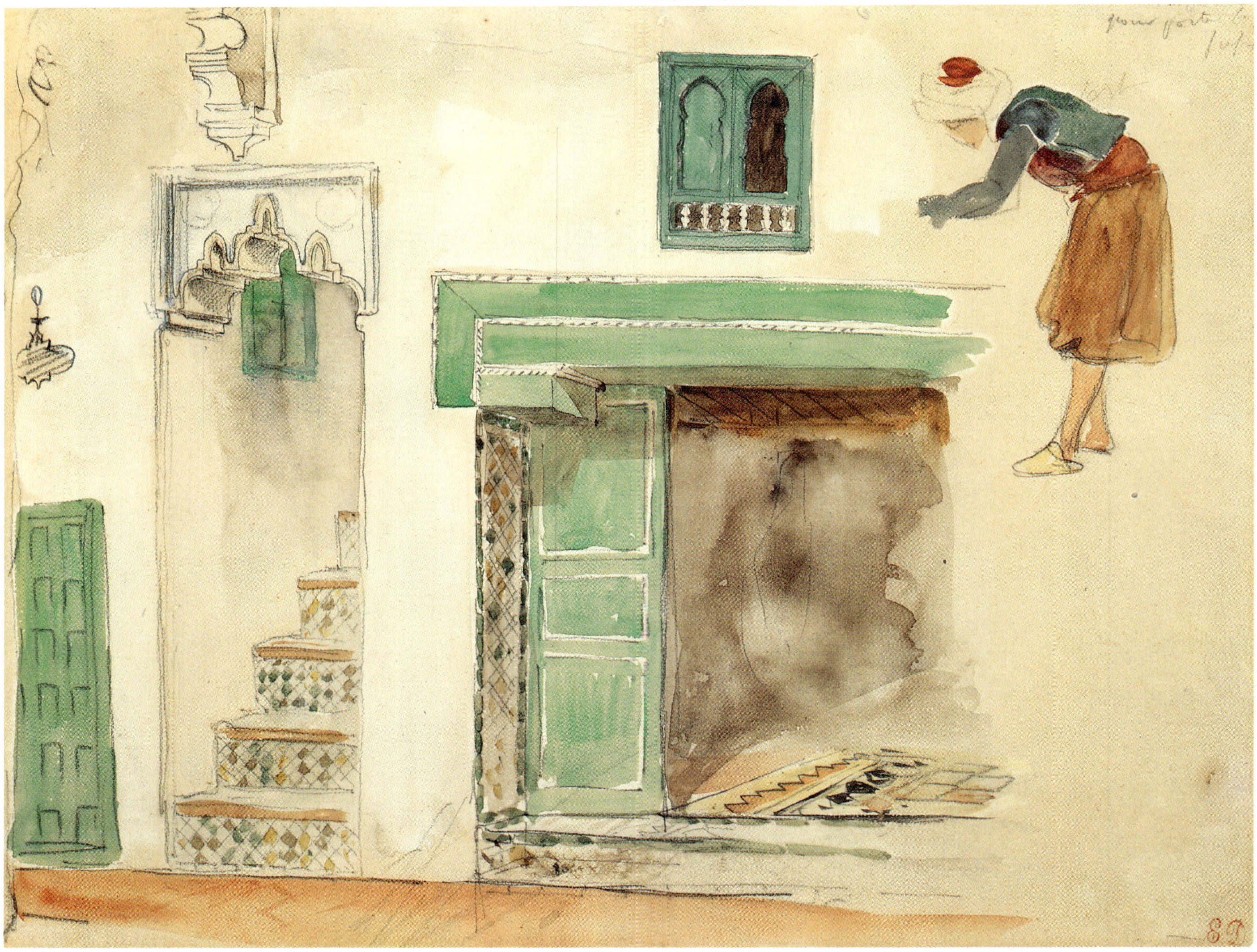

DOORS AND BAY-WINDOWS IN AN ARAB HOUSE
Portes et baies d'une maison mauresque
44

Watercolour and pencil drawing
23.5 x 31.3 cm
Annotated in Delacroix's hand, in pencil, top right:
pour porter le [*illegible word*]—vert
Département des Arts graphiques, Louvre
(RF 9265)

PROVENANCE:
Delacroix Studio, marked lower right (L.838 a); sale, 22–27 Feb. 1864, possibly part of no. 572, to Étienne Moreau-Nélaton; bequeathed to the Louvre in 1927 (L.1886 a).

BIBLIOGRAPHY:
Robaut, 1885, possibly part of no. 1632; Sérullaz, 1984, II, no. 1665, repr.

EXHIBITIONS:
Paris, 1930, no. 335; Paris, 1933, no. 161; Paris, 1937, no. 32; Paris, 1939, no. 6; Paris, 1963(1), no. 52; Paris, 1982, no. 204.

Delacroix skilfully applied his colours over a freely sketched pencil outline, choosing with great precision the various tones of green which enhance the simplicity of the architecture and the mosaic decoration.

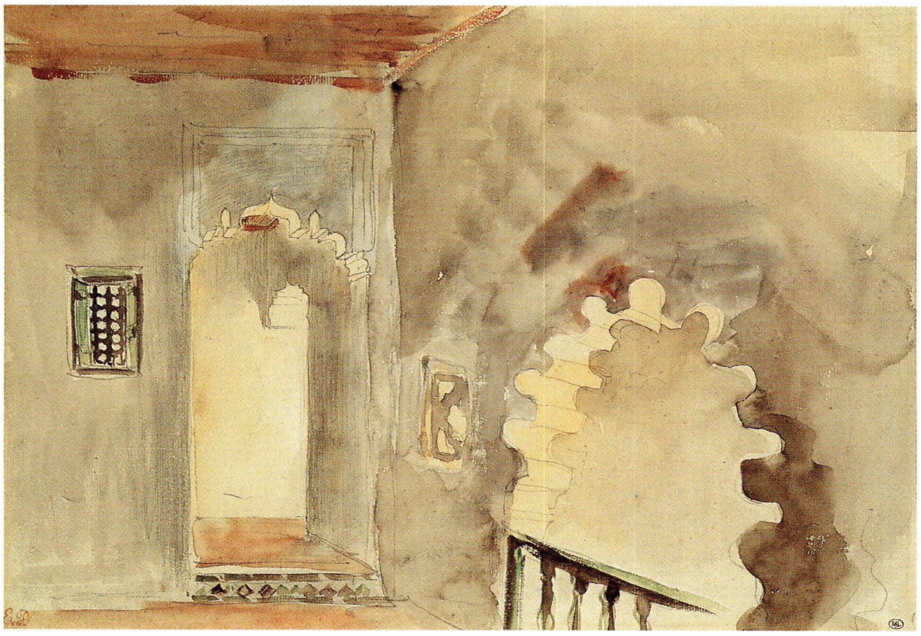

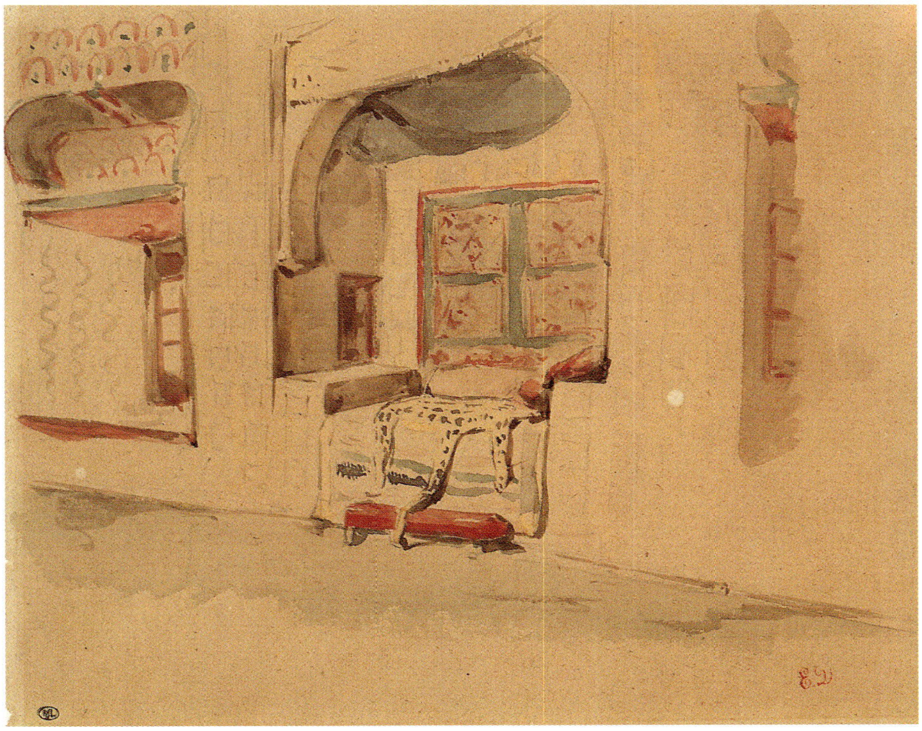

BAY-WINDOWS IN AN ARAB INTERIOR
Baies dans un intérieur mauresque
45

Watercolour and pencil drawing
23.9 x 34.2 cm
On the reverse side, pencil sketch of a door, scarcely visible.
Département des Arts graphiques, Louvre (RF 9266)

PROVENANCE:
Delacroix Studio, marked lower left (L.838 a); sale, Paris, 22–27 Feb. 1864, possibly included in lot 572, to Étienne Moreau-Nélaton; bequeathed to the Louvre in 1927 (L.1886 a).

BIBLIOGRAPHY:
Robaut, 1885, possibly part of no. 1632; Sérullaz, 1984, II, no. 1674, repr.

EXHIBITIONS:
Paris, 1930, no. 336; Paris, 1933, no. 162; Paris, 1937, no. 10; Paris, 1939, no. 19; Paris, 1963(1), no. 53; Paris, 1982, no. 205.

Conceived in much more sombre colours than the previous watercolour, this work is nonetheless remarkable for the movement in the shadows which encircle the serrated bay-windows.

ARAB INTERIOR WITH ALCOVE
Intérieur marocain avec une alcôve
46

Watercolour and pencil drawing
21.2 x 26.8 cm
Département des Arts graphiques, Louvre, Paris (RF 4526)

PROVENANCE:
Delacroix Studio, marked lower right (L.838 a); sale, Paris, 22–27 Feb. 1864, possibly included in lot 572, to Edgar Degas; 2nd sale, Paris, 15–16 Nov. 1918, included in lot 131; bought by the Société des Amis du Louvre and given to the museum (L. 1886 a).

BIBLIOGRAPHY:
Robaut, 1885, possibly part of no. 1632; Joubin, 1930, pl. 16; Sérullaz, 1963, no. 174, repr.; Sérullaz, 1984, II, no. 1675, repr.

EXHIBITIONS:
Paris, 1933, no. 160; Zurich, 1939, no. 163; Basel, 1939, no. 200; Paris, 1963, no. 176; Kyoto-Tokyo, 1969, no. A 7 repr.; Paris, 1982, no. 202.

See no. 39.

INTERIOR OF A HOUSE IN TANGIER WITH OPEN DOOR
Intérieur de maison à Tanger avec une porte ouverte, à droite
47

Pencil and watercolour
20 x 15.5 cm
Annotated lower right in Delacroix's hand, in pencil: v[ert]—br[un]—brun—br[un]
Huguette Bérès, Paris

PROVENANCE:
Delacroix Studio, marked lower right (L.838 a); sale, Paris, 22–27 Feb. 1864, possibly included in lot 572.

See no. 39.

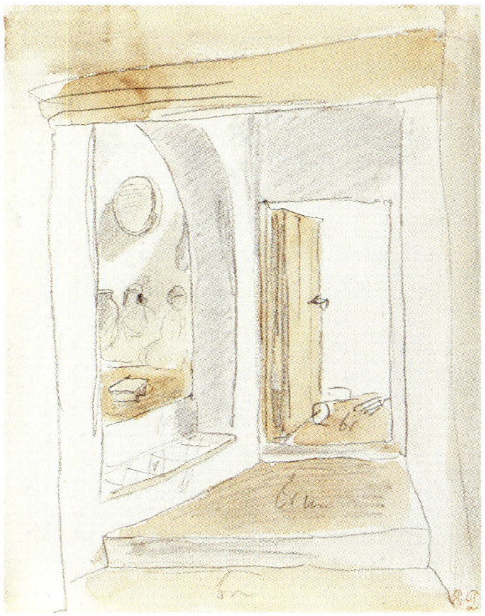

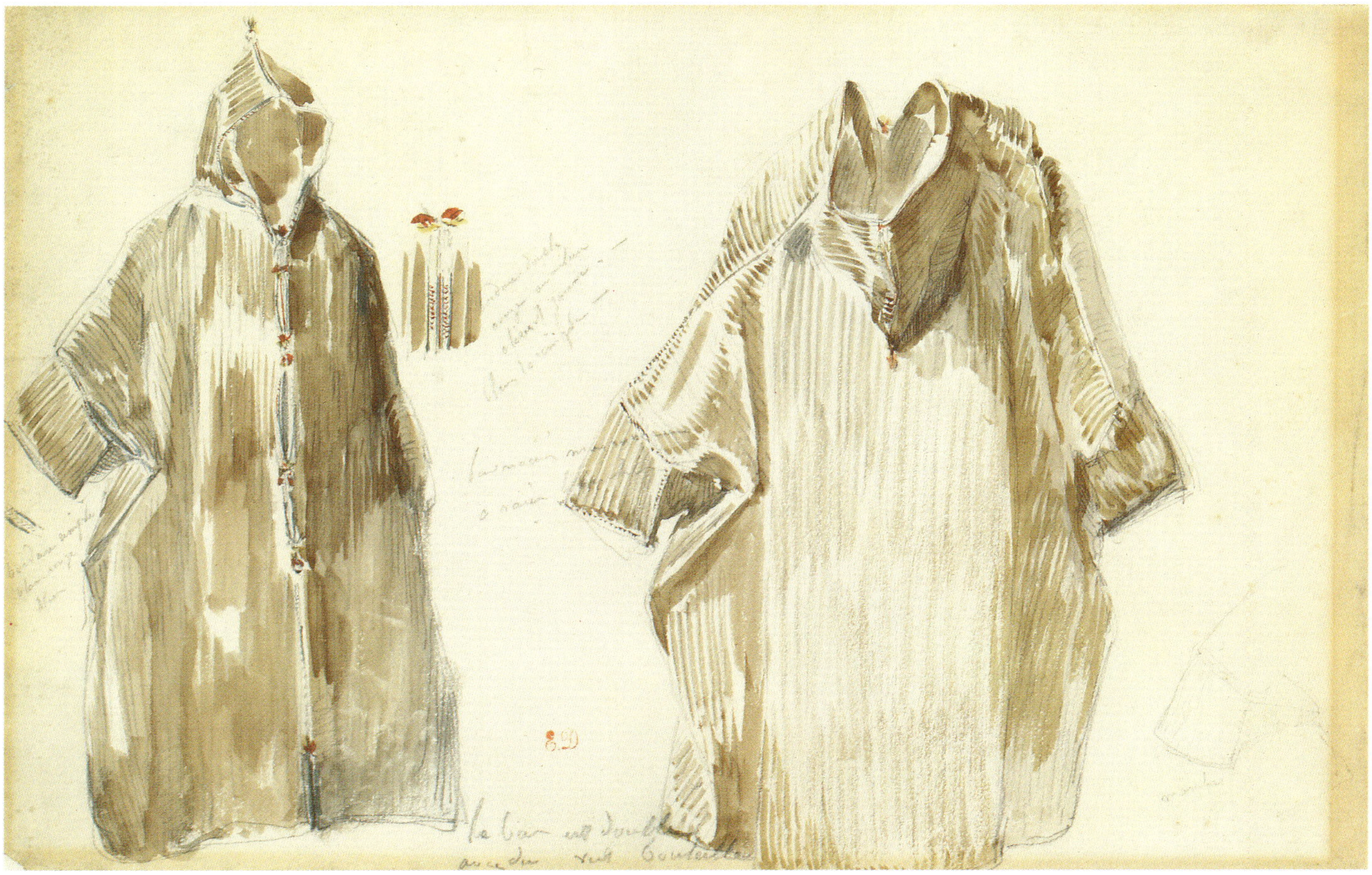

TWO STUDIES OF *MECHLA*
Deux études de *mechla*
48

Watercolour and pencil drawing
25 x 39.3 cm
Annotated in Delacroix's hand, in pencil, left: bordure simple—blanc rouge—bleu; *centre:* bordure double—rouge au milieu—[*an illegible word*] jaune—bleu la remplace; *above:* burnous marron à raies blanchâtres(?) *lower centre:* le bas est doublé—avec du vert bouteille
Musée des Arts Décoratifs, Paris (21 153 A).

PROVENANCE:
Delacroix Studio, marked lower centre (L. 838 a); sale, Paris, 22–27 Feb. 1864, possibly included in lot 571, to Edgar Degas; sale, Paris, 15–16 Nov. 1918, included in lot 129; bought by the Musée des Arts Décoratifs at this sale.

BIBLIOGRAPHY:
Dumur, 1988, p. 39, repr.

EXHIBITIONS:
Paris, 1933, part of no. 170.

The *mechla*, a coarse wool jellaba, seemed to Delacroix 'like a bag in which holes have been cut for the arms and which has a hood, which makes the wearers look somewhat like Carthusian monks' (letter to Félix Guillemardet, 'overlooking Tangier, 24 January 1832', *Correspondance*, V, p. 157). Concerned with recording the exact shape and appearance of the *mechla*, the artist noted in his little album, as soon as he arrived in Tangier on 26 January 1832, during the visit to the kasbah, 'Sometimes there is some red on the facings and hood of the brown-striped *mechla*' (Département des Arts graphiques, Louvre, inventory RF 39050, fol. 6 verso).

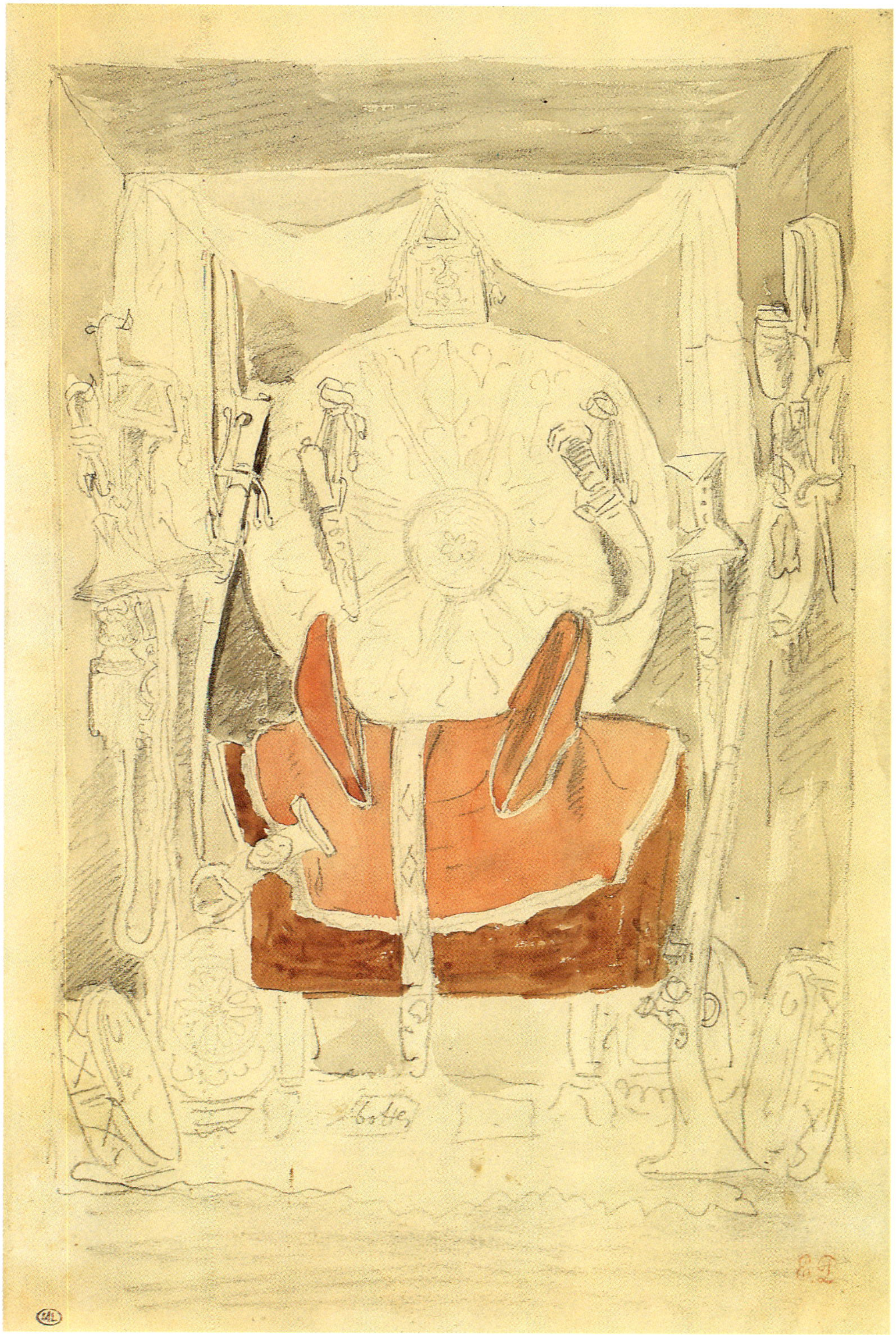

DISPLAY OF ARAB WEAPONS AND TROPHIES
Panoplie et trophées arabes
49

Pencil, watercolour and grey wash
31 x 21 cm
Annotated in Delacroix's hand in pencil: bottes
Département des Arts graphiques, Louvre
(RF 10050)

PROVENANCE:
Delacroix Studio, marked lower right (L.838 a); sale, Paris, 22–27 Feb. 1864, possibly included in lot 572, to Alfred Robaut; Étienne Moreau-Nélaton; bequeathed to the Louvre in 1927 (L.1886 a).

BIBLIOGRAPHY:
Robaut, 1885, possibly part of no. 1632; Sérullaz, 1984, II, no. 1683, repr.

EXHIBITIONS:
Paris, 1933, no. 169; Paris, 1982, no. 217.

On the reverse side of the page, Alfred Robaut indicated that a trophy such as this one embellished the famous tent-apartment of the Count de Mornay, rue de Verneuil, but this could also be a drawing executed in Morocco. Deliberately left unfinished, the study draws attention to the impressive red and brown saddle placed in front of a large circular tray, flanked here and there by rifles, sabres and curved daggers or *khanjar*. At top centre there is a little metallic box which was used to stock gunpowder and on the ground are several musical instruments (*bendir*).

ARAB HORSEMAN PRACTISING A CHARGE
Cavalier arabe chargeant
50

Oil on canvas
14 x 21 cm
Signed and dated lower right: Eug. Delacroix 1832
Private collection

PROVENANCE:
Probably executed in Tangier, destined for Jacques Denis Delaporte; remained in his family until 1961; Galerie Daber, Paris, 1962; Mme Jourdan.

BIBLIOGRAPHY:
Johnson, 1986, no. 349, pl. 163; Arama, 1987, p. 209, no. 3, repr.

EXHIBITIONS:
Berne, 1963–4, no. 34.

Unknown when the various less recent publications devoted to Delacroix appeared, this little painting, the dimensions of which correspond to the format of many of the artist's drawings, was exhibited for the first time in Paris in 1962 at the Galerie Daber entitled *Moroccan Horseman Practising a Charge (Cavalier marocain chargeant)* (exhibition cat., *Peinture 1830–1940. Œuvres de Delacroix à Maillol*, no. 4).

The name inscribed in pen on the stretcher reminds us that the work belonged to the family of Jacques Denis Delaporte (1777–1861), put

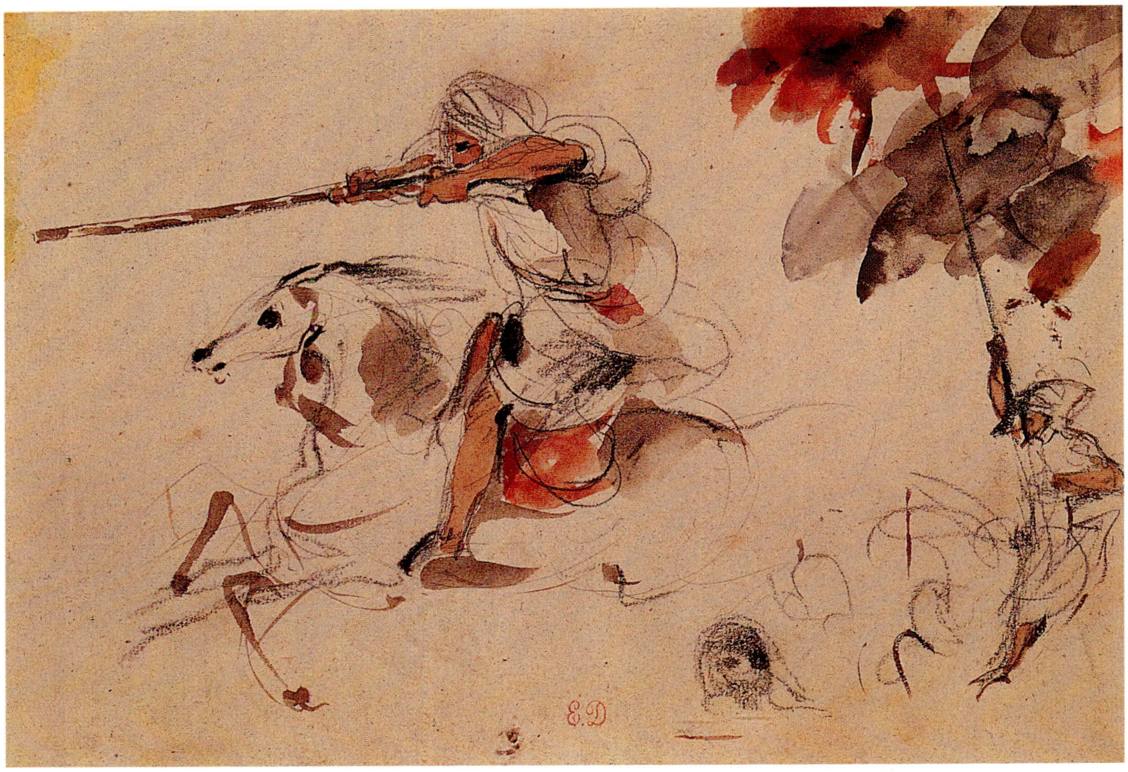

Not in exhibition:
Study of a Horseman Practising a Charge (Étude de cavalier chargeant), *watercolour and pencil drawing. Location unknown.*

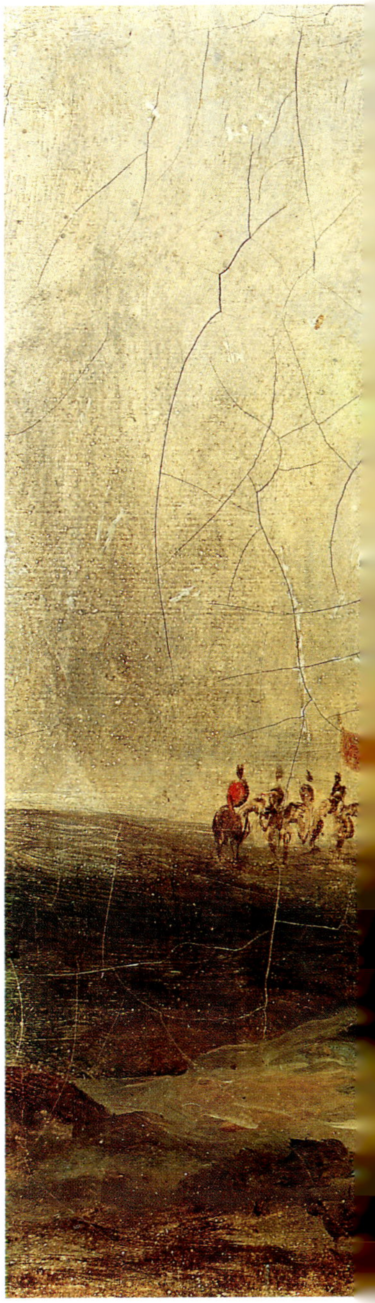

provisionally in charge of the consulate after the death of Édouard Sourdeau in 1829. Unfortunately, we do not know in what circumstances Delaporte received this painting. It is generally thought that this is one of only two paintings that Delacroix actually executed during his Moroccan visit (the second being the portrait of Mme Delaporte, today in the Musée des Beaux-Arts, Algiers). It remains to be discovered whether Delacroix gave it to Delaporte when still in Morocco, or subsequently, during one of their meetings in Paris, recorded in the artist's journal. On 24 January 1849, Delacroix notes: 'At M. de Laporte's home: he was pleased to see me again', and on 10 April 1850: 'M. Delaporte came to see me. He is extremely interesting. He knows and remembers so much. He spoke of the 'Horses of the Sun' (concerning the ceiling of the Galerie d'Apollon), of their various attributions and he even knew the colour of each of them. He talked to me about Morocco: Biaz fell out of favour as governor of Fez. When among the tribes, he saw sheiks imposing a tax and calculating the amount for each person with little pebbles *(calculi)* or shells.'

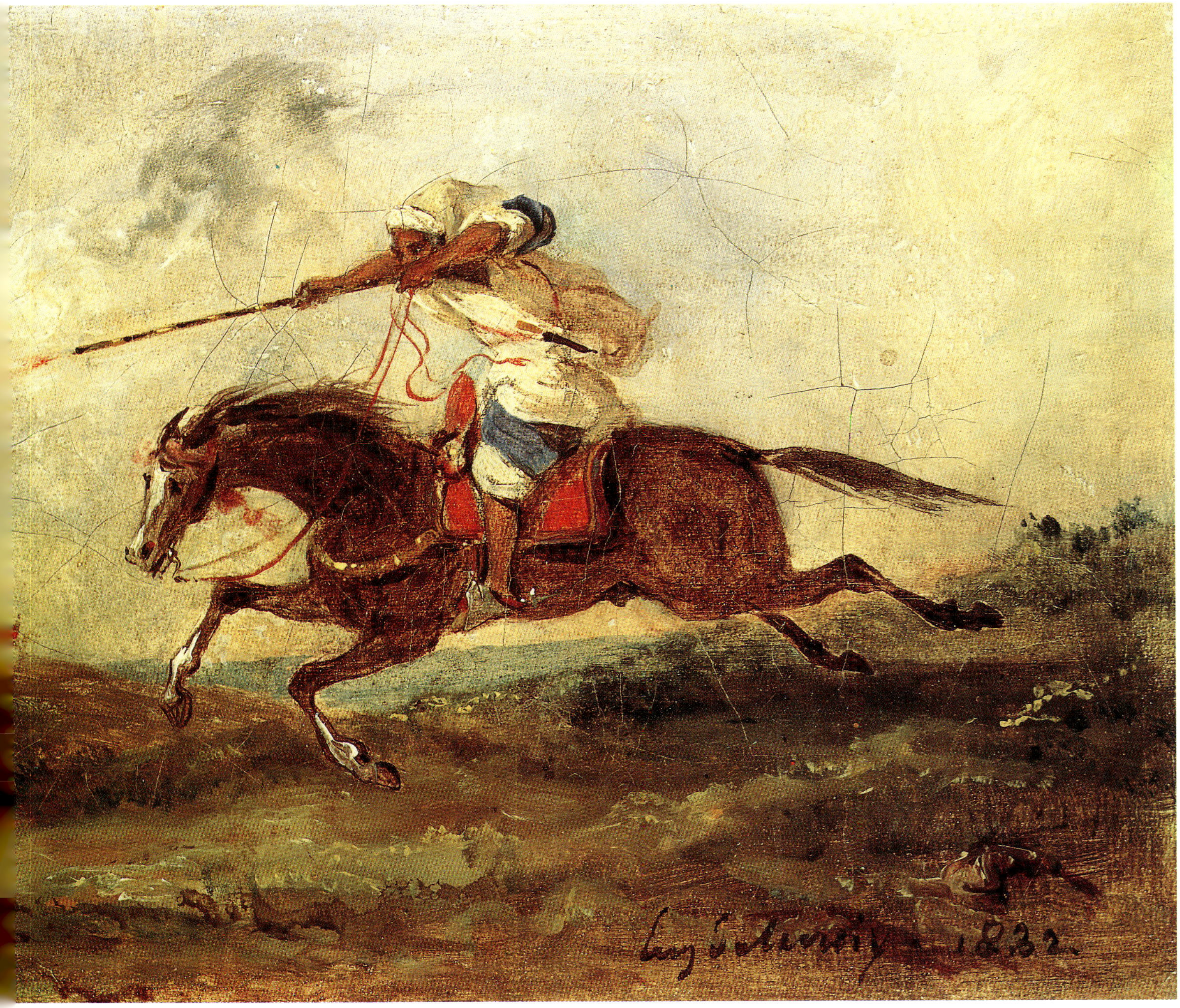

The Count de Mornay album

1- The Wife and Daughter of Abraham Benchimol
Watercolour and pencil drawing, 22.3 x 16.2 cm.
The Metropolitan Museum of Art, New York, Bequest of Walter C. Baker, 1971.

The eighteen watercolours that Delacroix gave to the Count de Mornay, as a souvenir of the six months spent together in Morocco, were unfortunately sold separately in the public auction held on 29 March 1877, at the same time as two of Delacroix's paintings (nos 1 and 2 in the sale): *Charles V at the Monastery of Saint Yuste* and *Interior* (portrait of the Count de Mornay and of the Prince Demidoff; this painting was destroyed during the the first world war). At present, only eleven of them have been located, seven of which are exhibited here (see nos 51 to 57). The four watercolours which were unable to be loaned to us are in the Fogg Art Museum, Cambridge (no. 5 in the Mornay sale; fig. 3), the Metropolitan Museum of New York (nos 6 and 10 in the Mornay sale) (figs 1 and 2) and in the County Museum of Art, Los Angeles (no. 20 in the Mornay sale). No. 15, *Moulay Abd al-Rahman, Emperor of Morocco,* has been lost since 1953, when Elie Lambert reproduced it in his study of the painting exhibited at the 1845 Salon (p. 40, no. 13, pl. X). The scene of the *Fanatics in Tangier* (no. 11 in the Mornay sale), appeared in the Baron Vitta sale (Galerie Charpentier, Paris, 15 Mar. 1935, no. 2, repr.) but its current whereabouts is unknown.

In 1885 when Alfred Robaut compiled his catalogue of *L'Œuvre complet d'Eugène Delacroix,* the notes transmitted by Mme Adolphe Moreau, whose husband had attended the sale, enabled him to give details of each of the eighteen compositions, but he was unable to produce all the accompanying illustrations (Robaut, 1885, nos 494 to 511). In 1909, when the facsimile albums of the Louvre and the Musée Condé were published, Jean Guiffrey used the information gathered by Philippe Burty before the auction to compile a description of each of the watercolours (Guiffrey, 1909, pp. 185–95). Until the missing pages are found, these two publications make it possible to get an idea of this famous album which, it is generally thought, was put together by Delacroix during the enforced quarantine period in the Toulon lazaretto from 5–20 July 1832: 'My dear friend, I have already been in quarantine for two days and an entire fortnight will be deadly boring. For entertainment, when I disembark, there is a treeless enclosure where thistles serve as bushes. I have a little room where I can come and complete my drawings in the daytime.' This phrase from a letter addressed to Frédéric Villot from Toulon on 7 July 1832 (*Correspondance,* I, p. 334) has always been considered as an allusion to the watercolours destined for the Count de Mornay, but, to our knowledge, there is no other document which upholds this supposition. Neither is it known how Mornay reacted on receiving this gift, the presentation of which has unfortunately never been recorded. Below is the list drawn up from the catalogue of the Mornay sale according to the titles given therein:

3 *Encampment outside the Town of Aliassar-el-Kebir (El-Ksar el-Kebir) on the Battlefield where the Infante don Sebastian of Portugal lost his life* / Campement devant la ville d'Aliassar-el-Kébir sur le champ de bataille où périt l'Infant don Sébastien de Portugal

4 *View of Tangier and its Port* / Vue de la ville et de la rade de Tanger

5 *An Arab Woman and her Servant on the Banks of a River* / Une Mauresque avec sa servante au bord d'une rivière (fig. 3)

6 *An Arab Man and Woman on their Terrace* / Un Maure et une Mauresque sur leur terrasse (fig. 2)

7 *Abraham Benchimol, Dragoman to the French Consulate* / Abraham Benchimol, drogman du Consul de France

8 *A Black Slave-girl fetching Water* / Une Négresse esclave venant chercher de l'eau

9 *Amin Biaz, Minister of Finance and Foreign Affairs* / Amin-Biaz, ministre des finances et des affaires étrangères

10 *The Wife and Daughter of Abraham Benchimol* / La femme et la fille d'Abraham Benchimol (fig. 1)

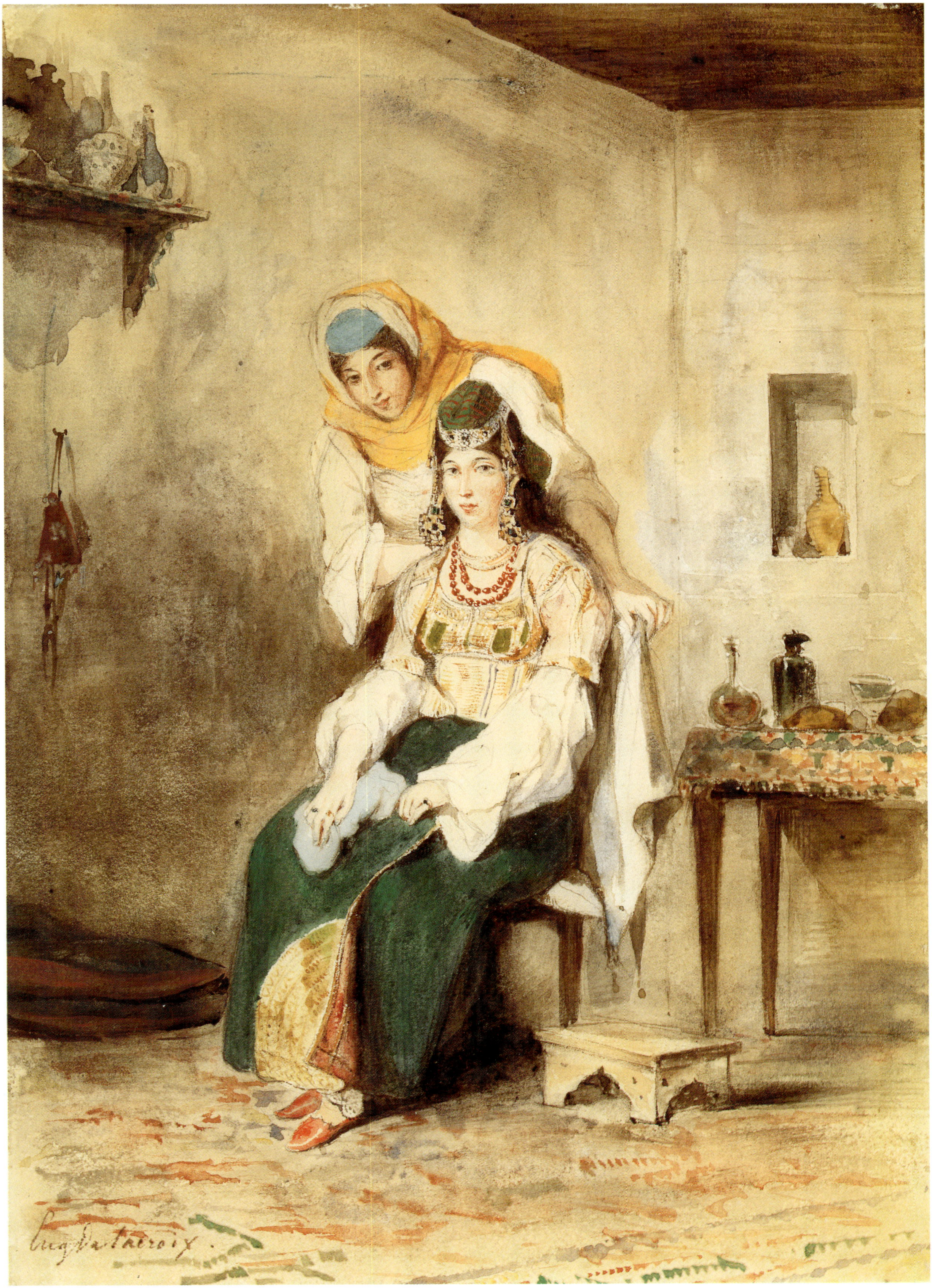

2- An Arab Man and Woman on their terrace,
watercolour and pencil drawing, 13.7 x 18.8 cm.
The Metropolitan Museum of Art, New York, The Mr & Mrs Henry Ittleson Jr. Purchase Fund, 1963.

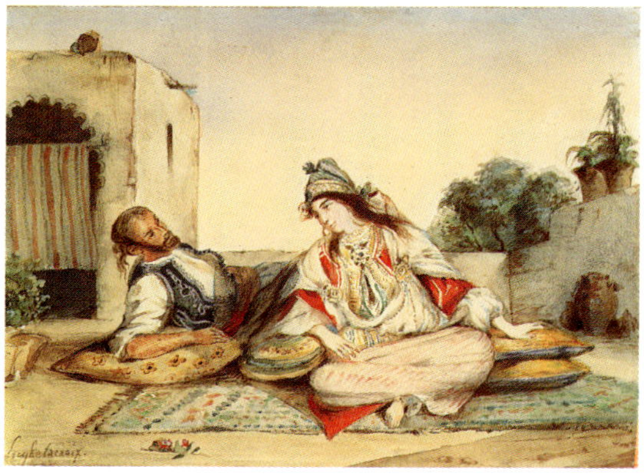

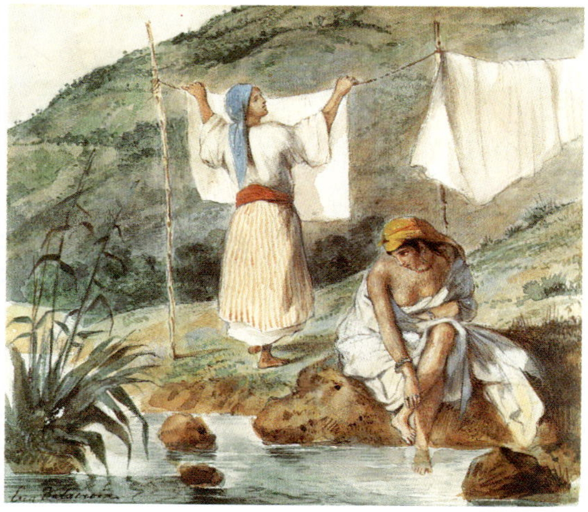

3- An Arab Woman and her Servant on the Banks of a River,
watercolour and pencil drawing, 16 x 18.3 cm.
Harvard University Fogg Art Museum, Cambridge, Bequest of Granville L. Winthrop.

11 *Fanatics in Tangier* / Une scène de convulsionnaires à Tanger
12 *Blacks dancing in a Street in Tangier* / Danse de nègres dans une rue à Tanger
13 *Arab Horsemen resting outside Tangier* / Halte de cavaliers arabes aux environs de Tanger
14 *A Fantasia or* Jeux de la Poudre *outside the Gates of Meknes* / Une Fantasia ou jeu de la poudre devant la porte d'entrée de la ville de Méquinez
15 *Moulay Abd al-Rahman, Emperor of Morocco* / Mouley-Abd-er-Rhaman, empereur du Maroc
16 *Soldiers sleeping in a Guardroom* / Soldats endormis dans un corps de garde
17 *Arabs at a Market* / Arabes sur un marché
18 *Ben Abou, Military Chief* / Le caïd Ben-Abou, chef militaire
19 *A Coulouglis and an Arab seated in front of their Home* / Un Coulouglis et un Arabe assis devant la porte de leur maison
20 *Travelling Players* / Comédiens ambulants

The dimensions given in the catalogue indicate an almost equal quantity of tall formats (26 x 18 cm approx.) and wide ones (20 x 23 cm approx.), with an occasional square format (16 x 16 cm). Specific episodes during the various stages of the journey alternate with portraits of the Moroccan protagonists and scenes from daily life. As Philippe Burty so rightly pointed out, all the compositions in this 'magnificent and delightful album of watercolours . . . had previously been recorded by Delacroix on site in pen or pencil in his sketch-books'. (Burty, 1877, p. 54; this chapter reproduces an article by Burty published in the *Gazette des Beaux-Arts* in 1865, entitled 'Eugène Delacroix au Maroc', pp. 144–54). Moreover, a certain number of them were reproduced as paintings or engravings. *Encampment outside the Town of Aliassar-el-Kebir* (*El-Ksar el-Kebir*) (see no. 74, the version refused by the 1839 Salon), the scene of *Fanatics in Tangier* (two pictures, one dated 1838, Minneapolis Institute of Arts, the other 1857, Art Gallery of Ontario, Toronto (see pp. 72 and 75), *Fantasia* (see no. 58, the painted version in the Musée Fabre in Montpellier), *Moulay Abd al-Rahman* (which Delacroix incorporated in the painting presented at the 1845 Salon; see no. 84), *Soldiers sleeping in a Guardroom* (two pictures dated 1846 and 1847, von der Heydt Museum, Wuppertal and Musée Condé, Chantilly), the *Portrait of Ben Abou* (the corresponding etching is exhibited at no. 67) and the *Travelling Players* (the picture painted in 1848 is today in the Musée des Beaux-Arts, Tours; see p. 80).

Of the ten buyers who attended the sale, only two proved to be particularly enterprising: M. Féral bought *An Arab Man and Woman on their Terrace, Abraham Benchimol* and *Arabs at a Market*, while L. Gauchez bought *Blacks dancing in a Street in Tangier, Fantasia* and *Travelling Players*. The others limited their intervention to one or two purchases: M. Goupil—*Arab Woman and her Servant* and *Moulay Abd al-Rahman*, Alfred Hartmann—*Fanatics in Tangier* and *Arab Horsemen resting outside Tangier*, M. de Bourdesoulle—*Ben Abou, Military Chief* and *A Coulouglis and an Arab seated in front of their Home*. M. de la Valette, the Duke de Vicence, M. Hecht, the Duke de Gramont and M. de Sourdeval purchased, respectively, *View of Tangier, Black Slave-girl fetching Water, The Wife and Daughter of Abraham Benchimol, Amin Biaz* and *Soldiers sleeping in a Guardroom*. The first watercolour, *Encampment outside the Town of Aliassar-el-Kebir*, was withdrawn from the sale, there being no buyer at 420 francs.

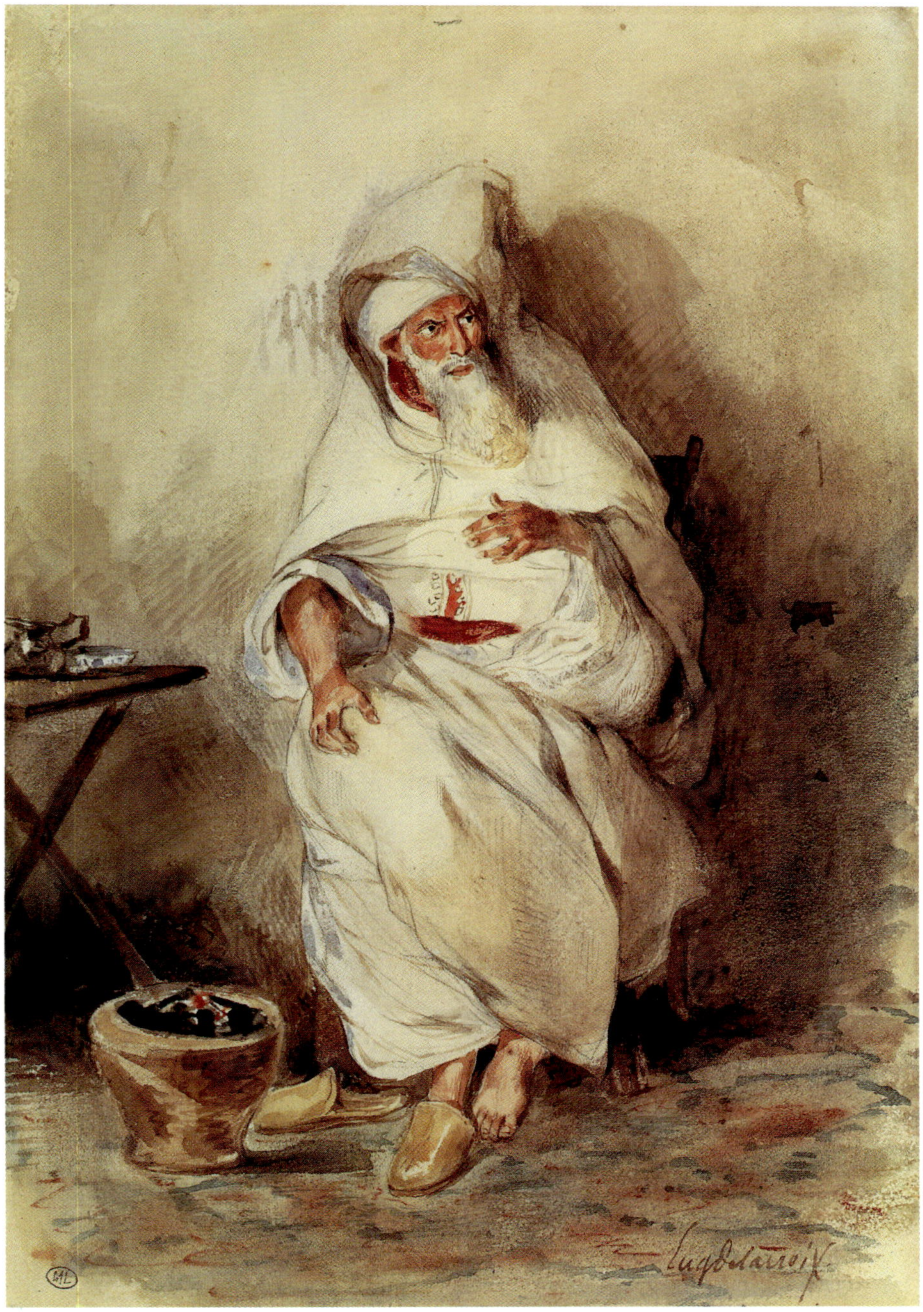

AMIN BIAZ, MINISTER OF FINANCE AND FOREIGN AFFAIRS

Amin Bias, ministre des finances et des affaires étrangères

51

Watercolour and pencil drawing
23.4 x 16.6 cm
Signed lower right in paint: Eug. Delacroix
Département des Arts graphiques, Louvre
(RF 4612)

PROVENANCE:
Gift from the artist to Count Charles de Mornay; Count Charles de Mornay; sale, Paris, 29 Mar. 1877, lot 9, to the Duke de Gramont; P.-A. Chéramy; sale, Paris, 5–7 May 1908, lot 307, to Roger Galichon; bequeathed to the Louvre in 1918 (L.1886 a).

BIBLIOGRAPHY:
Robaut, 1885, no. 501; Sérullaz, 1963, no. 169, repr.; Sérullaz, 1984, II, no. 1607, repr.; Arama, 1987, p. 217, no. 6; Dumur, 1988, p. 38 repr.

EXHIBITIONS:
Paris, 1930, no. 295; Paris, 1933, no. 107; Paris, 1934, no. 36; Paris, 1937, no. 11; Paris, 1963, no. 169; Kyoto-Tokyo, 1969, no. A 3 repr.; Paris, 1982, no. 193.

Sidi Ettayeb Biaz occupied the post of customs officer (*amin*) in Tangier at the time of Delacroix's visit with Count de Mornay's diplomatic mission. Having learned that Biaz would accompany them to the emperor, Mornay hastened to warn Paris: 'It is generally believed that this civil servant will be designated to deal with the negotiations under the watchful eye of his sovereign . . . As wily as a Moor can be, and that's saying a great deal, he is usually responsible for the negotiations with Europeans. His excessive love of money has sometimes conflicted with his religious principles and his hatred of Christians.' (Tangier, 4 March 1832; Arama, 1992, VI, p. 211). The negotiations, which began on 24 March, ended, after eleven meetings, on 4 April, when Biaz brought Mornay a letter from Moulay Abd al-Rahman for the French king Louis-Philippe.

Delacroix had noted in his little green album, the details of the costume worn by Biaz, at their first meeting in Tangier on 26 January: 'Very wide haik on his head. White turban above a piece of amaranth material which hung down on his chest. Dark blue burnous crossed over his chest, without the hood up. Legs crossed. When we met him, he was on a grey mule. His legs were quite visible. A little of his coloured breeches. Saddle covered at front and back by scarlet material. A red band encircled the hindquarters of the horse and hung down. Similarly, the red bridle, or rather the belly.' (Département des Arts graphiques, Louvre, inventory RF 39050, fol. 2 verso and 3 recto; three sketches of Biaz on horseback and in a squatting position complete the description.)

In the luminous portrait offered to the Count de Mornay, the suspicious, wily character of Biaz is captured in the scrutinizing glint in his eyes.

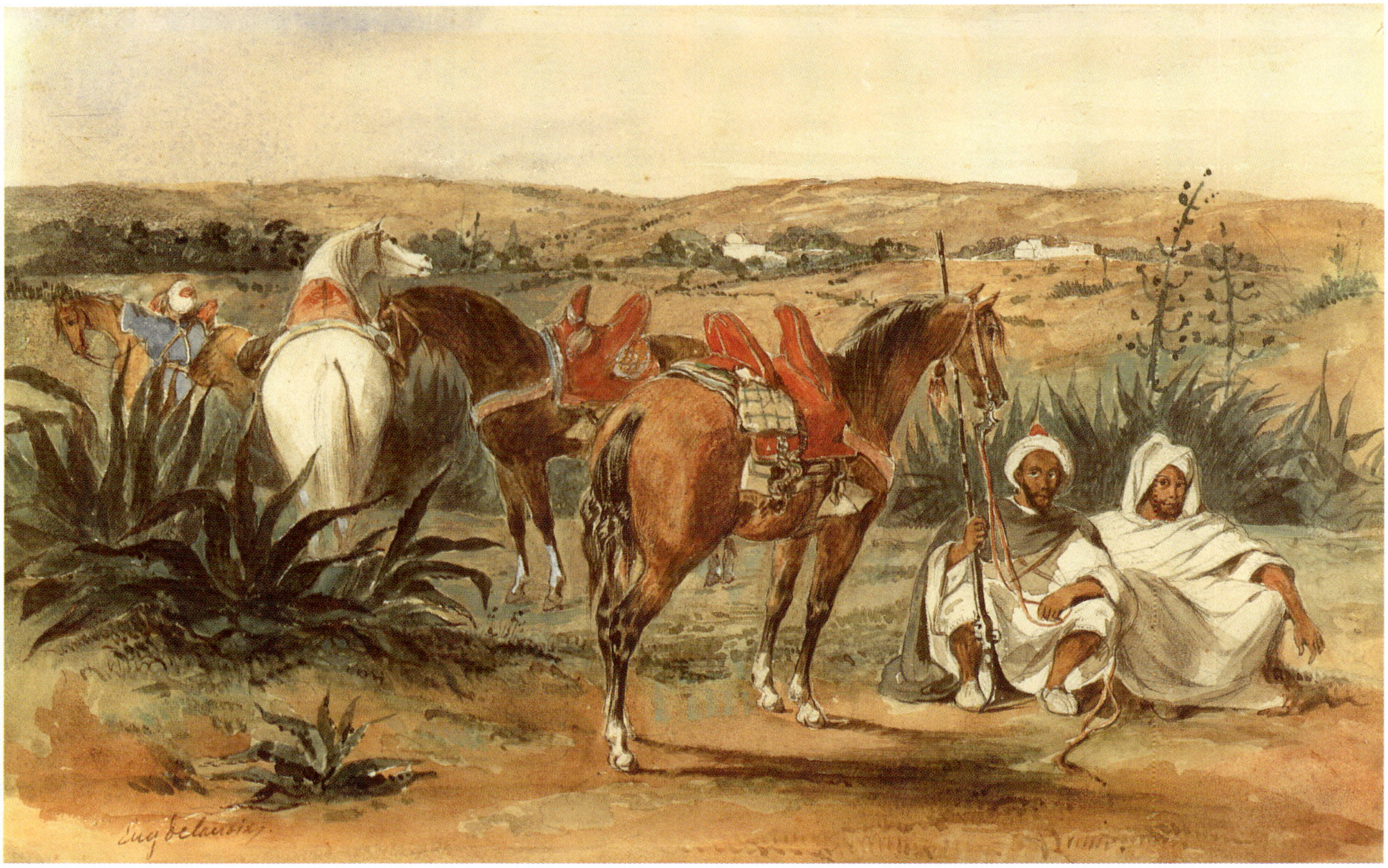

ARABS AND HORSES NEAR TANGIER
Halte de cavaliers arabes aux environs de Tanger
52

Watercolour, gouache and pencil drawing
16.7 x 26.5 cm
Signed lower left in paint: Eug. Delacroix
Achenbach Foundation for Graphic Arts, The Fine Arts Museums of San Francisco (1951.35)

PROVENANCE:
Gift from the artist to Count Charles de Mornay; Count Charles de Mornay; sale, Paris, 29 Mar. 1877, lot 13, to Alfred Hartmann; Jacques Seligmann & Co., New York, 1951; bought at that date by the California Palace of the Legion of Honour, Mildred Anna Williams Fund.

BIBLIOGRAPHY:
Robaut, 1885, no. 504; Arama, 1987, p. 217, no. 9; Dumur, 1988, p. 43, repr.

EXHIBITIONS:
Oakland, 1963, no. 10, pl. VII; London-Edinburgh, 1964, no. 126, pl. 68.

This watercolour has no direct connection with any episode described by Delacroix in his notes made during the journey from Tangier to Meknes. It probably sums up the observations made by the artist during the organization of the night camps on the various stages of the journey. It is very close in style, but without the same animation, to the Louvre watercolour depicting a *Fantasia* (see following number).

A FANTASIA
OR *JEU DE LA POUDRE*
OUTSIDE THE GATES
OF MEKNES
Une fantasia ou jeu de la poudre devant la porte d'entrée de la ville de Méquinez

53

Watercolour and pencil drawing
15.6 x 27.2 cm
Signed lower right in paint: Eug. Delacroix
Département des Arts graphiques, Louvre (RF 3372)

PROVENANCE:
Gift from the artist to the Count Charles de Mornay; Count Charles de Mornay; sale, Paris, 29 Mar. 1877, lot 14, to L. Gauchez; Adolphe Moreau; Étienne Moreau-Nélaton; donated to the Louvre in 1907 (L.1886 a).

BIBLIOGRAPHY:
Robaut, 1885, no. 505, repr.; Guiffrey-Marcel, 1909, no. 3452, repr.; Sérullaz, 1963, no. 189, repr.; Sérullaz, 1984, II, no. 1571, repr.; Arama, 1987, p. 217, no. 10; Dumur, 1988, p. 61, repr.; Arama, 1992, VI, p. 154, repr.

EXHIBITIONS:
Paris, 1930, no. 323; Paris, 1933, no. 104, pl. XV; Paris, 1937, no. 27; Paris, 1963, no. 191; Paris, 1982, no. 219.

The galloping riders firing their rifles mask the ramparts which surround the city of Meknes. Yet in the background, on the right, silhouetted against the nearby Zerhoun, one can make out the gate of Bab Berdaïn with its colourful porcelain decoration similar to another of the town gates, Bab el-Khemis, which Delacroix sketched at the bottom of one of the pages of his brown-covered album (Département des Arts graphiques, Louvre, inventory RF 1712 bis, fol. 25 recto, see p. 93).

The *courses de poudre,* which the artist witnessed several times between Tangier and Meknes, provided him with a subject for four paintings on his return to France. The first two are included in this exhibition (see nos 50 and 58). The third one (see p. 88), dated 1833, is in the Städelsches Kunstinstitut, Frankfurt, and the fourth (see p. 120), dated 1847, is in the Oskar Reinhart collection, Winterthur (Johnson, 1986, nos 353 and 376, pls 165 and 192). Also inspired by the *jeux de poudre,* but concentrating on the confrontation of the two riders, are the two versions of the *Collision of Arab Horsemen* (private collection, Paris, and Walters Art Gallery, Baltimore, see p. 122; Johnson, 1986, nos 355 and 367, pls 168 and 169) which Delacroix also represented in an etching (see no. 68).

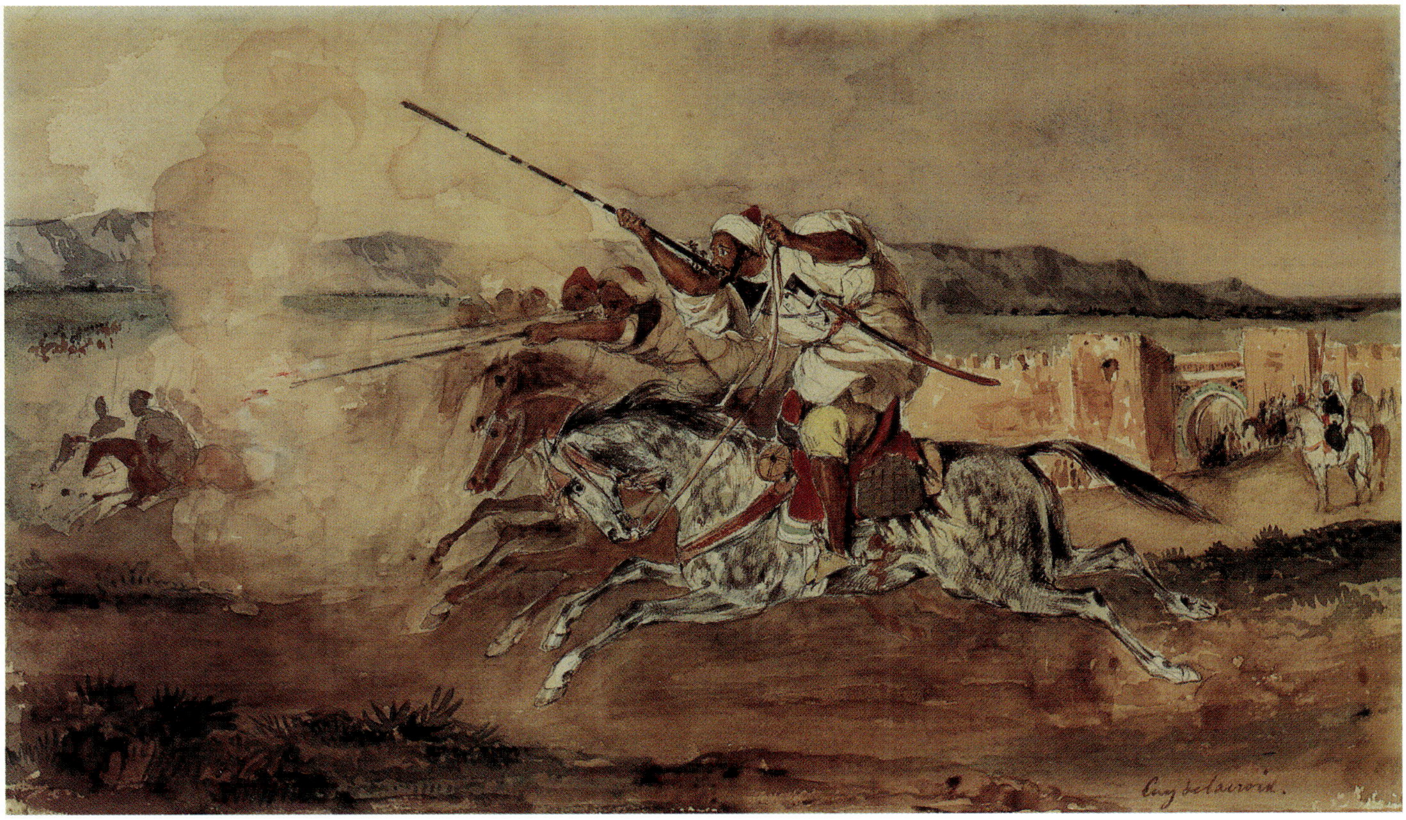

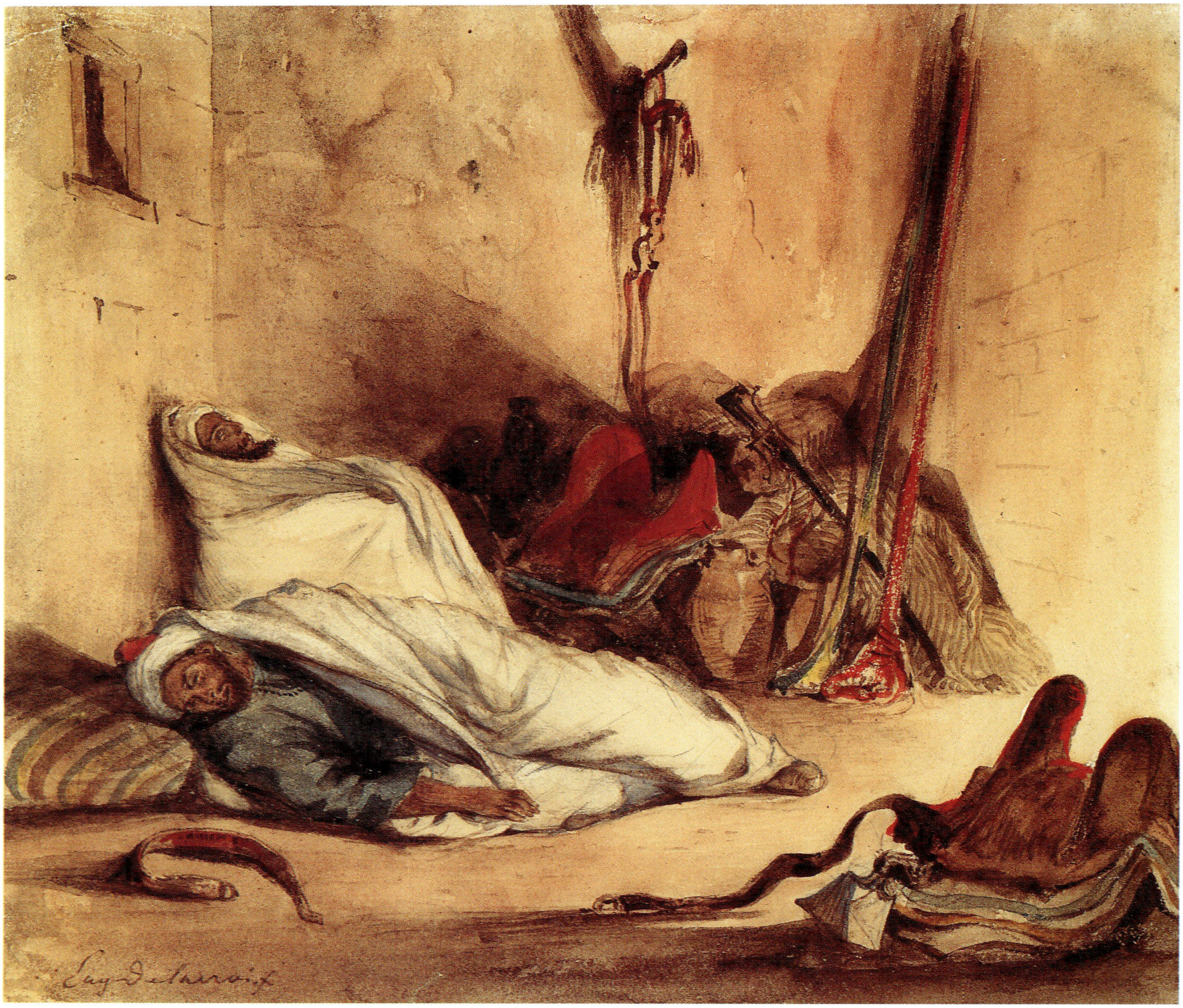

SOLDIERS SLEEPING IN A GUARDROOM
Soldats endormis dans un corps de garde
54

Watercolour and pencil drawing
16 x 19 cm
Signed lower left in pen: Eug. Delacroix
Private collection

PROVENANCE:
Gift from the artist to the Count Charles de Mornay; Count Charles de Mornay; sale, Paris, 29 Mar. 1877, lot 16, to M. de Sourdeval; Tony Mayer; sale, Paris, 3 Dec. 1957, lot 42, repr.

BIBLIOGRAPHY:
Robaut, 1885, no. 507; Johnson, 1986, p. 187; Arama, 1987, p. 217, no. 12.

This subject inspired three watercolours and two paintings by the artist. The watercolour given to the Count de Mornay differs considerably from the one exhibited at the 1833 Salon (Oskar Reinhart collection, Winterthur), which is of larger dimensions and presents four soldiers instead of two. On the other hand, a third watercolour, as yet untraced, the broad outlines of which can be imagined thanks to Robaut's illustration (1885, no. 492), seems nearer to the composition destined for Mornay. In 1846, Delacroix undertook a first painting which he exhibited the following year at the Salon entitled *Guardroom at Meknes* (*Corps-de-Garde à Méquinez*) (von der Heydt Museum, Wuppertal; Johnson, 1986, no. 374, pl. 184, p. 97). In the same year, 1847, he returned to this subject in a work of practically identical dimensions commissioned by

M. de Cailleux, the Director of Museums, on behalf of the Duke d'Aumale (the painting is now in the Musée Condé, Chantilly; Johnson, 1986, no. 375, pl. 185).

The indirect lighting (probably a lamp on the floor hidden by the saddle in the foreground on the right), which illuminates the two white forms of the sleeping soldiers, also sets off to advantage the various details of their equipment, provisionally abandoned in an apparent disorder: red saddle, rifles, sabre, pitchers, striped jellabas. In the two oil versions, not only is the format changed, but Delacroix opts for more contrasted lighting and more intense colours, so as to accentuate the nocturnal character of the scene and heighten its strange atmosphere.

ARABS AT A MARKET
Arabes sur un marché
55

Watercolour
12 x 18 cm
Signed lower right in paint: Eug. Delacroix
Private collection

PROVENANCE:
Gift from the artist to the Count Charles de Mornay; Count Charles de Mornay; sale, Paris, 29 Mar. 1877, lot 17, to Féral; Alexandre Benois and others; sale, Paris, 20 Mar. 1985, Paris, p. 19, repr.

BIBLIOGRAPHY:
Robaut, 1885, no. 508; Johnson, 1986, p. 170; Arama, 1987, p. 217, no. 13.

EXHIBITIONS:
Zurich, 1987 (1), no. 39, repr.; Frankfurt, 1987–8, no. H 19 repr.

Delacroix used this scene for an etching in 1833 (see no. 60), then again in 1834 for a painting, signed and dated, which was exhibited in the 1835 Salon (Johnson, 1986, no. 357, pl. 172), and finally in 1837 for a watercolour (see no. 70). An unfinished wash drawing, probably begun during the stop at Oran on 20 June 1832, may have been the starting point for the composition. The artist slightly modified the image from one version to the next, moving certain objects or substituting new ones, sometimes ageing the faces or enhancing the landscape with aloes and a distant chain of mountains.

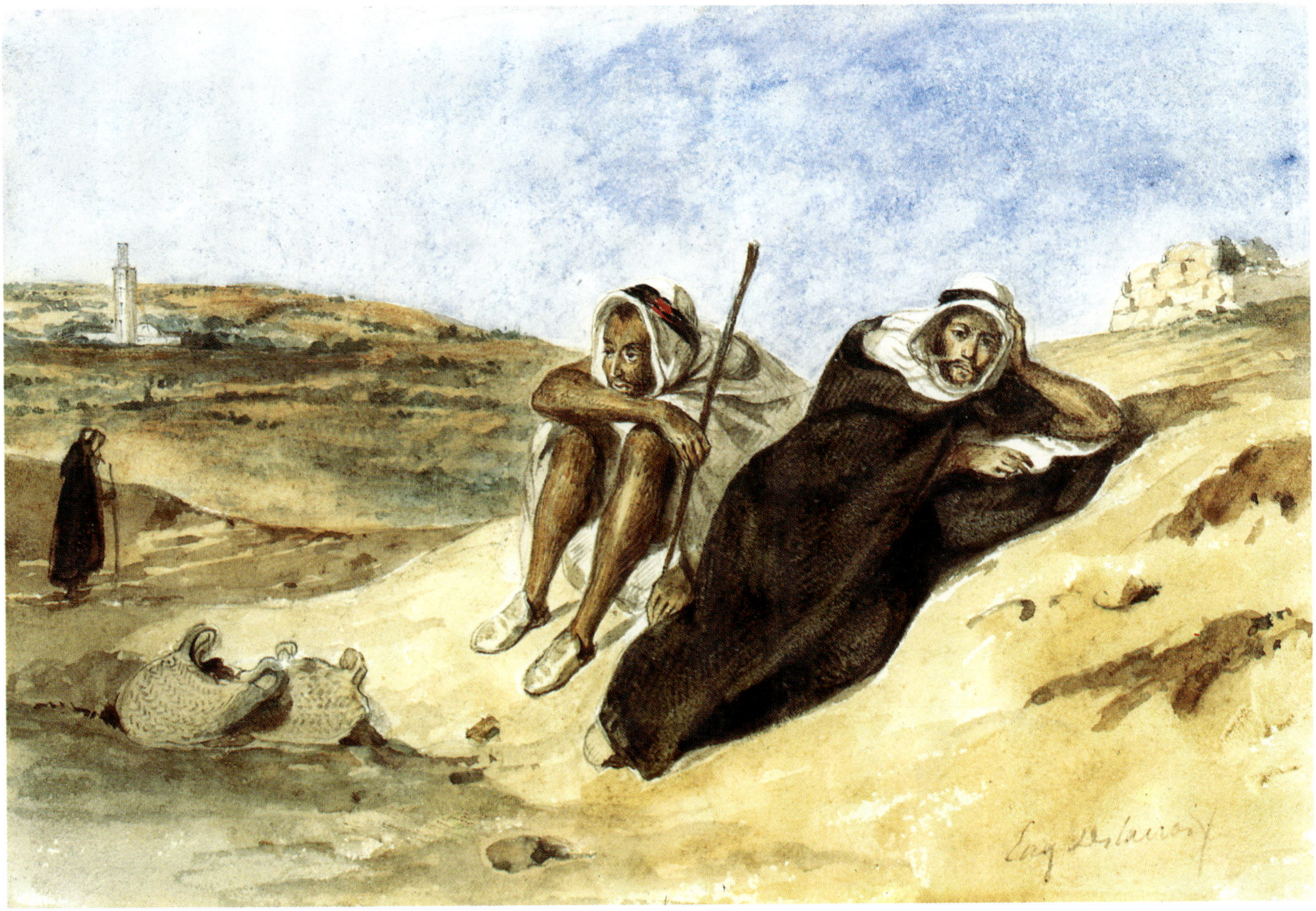

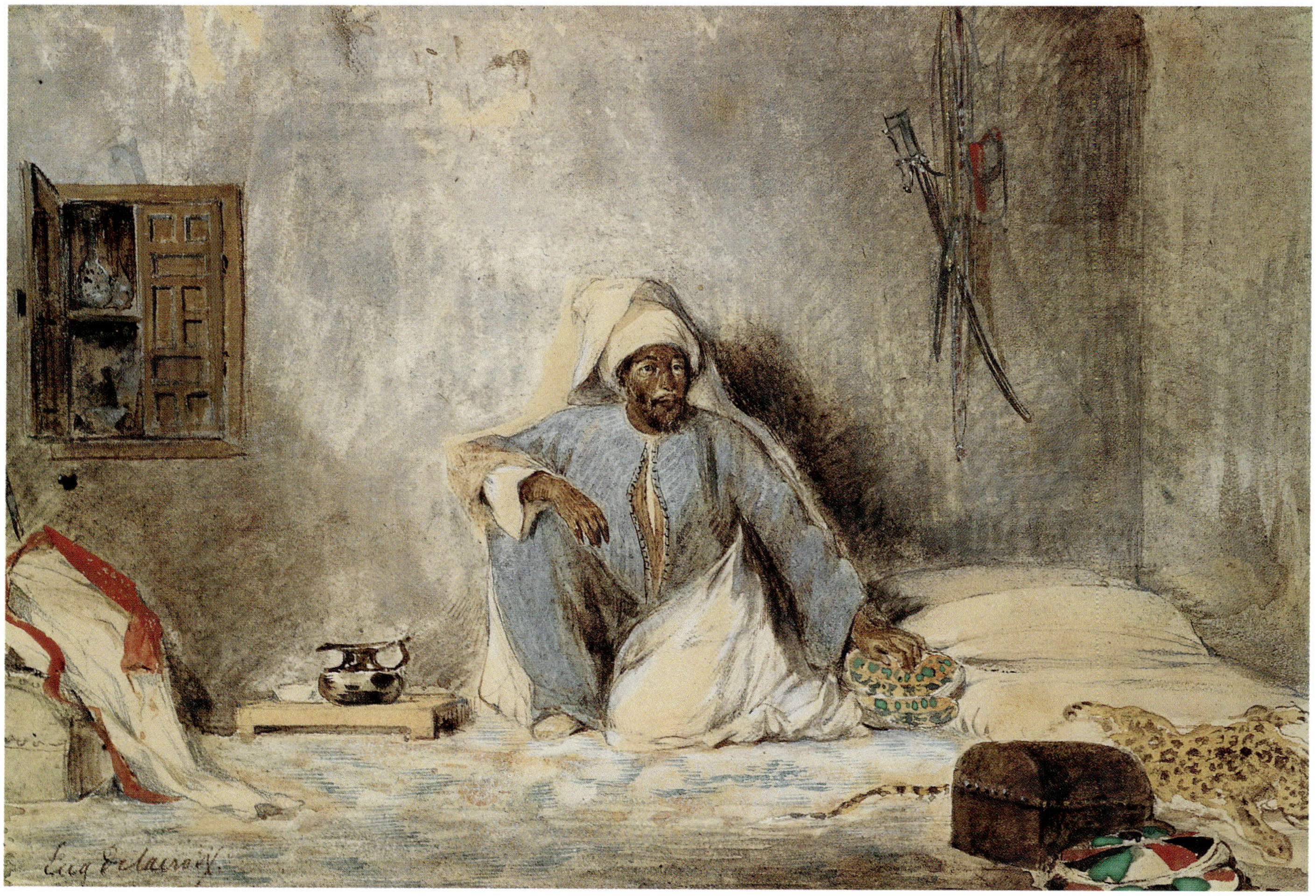

A MILITARY CHIEF IN HIS HOME
Un Caïd, chef militaire dans sa maison
56

Watercolour and pencil drawing
15.4 x 20.7 cm
Signed lower left in pen: Eug. Delacroix
Private collection

PROVENANCE:
Gift of the artist to Count Charles de Mornay; Count Charles de Mornay; sale, Paris, 29 Mar. 1877, no. 18, to M. de Bourdesoulle; Count de Mailly-Châlons; Countess de Mailly-Châlons.

BIBLIOGRAPHY:
Robaut, 1885, no. 509; Arama, 1987, p. 217, no. 15.

EXHIBITIONS:
Paris, 1933, no. 106.

The model is Sidi Mohammed Ben Abou Ben Abdelmalek (see no. 15). This watercolour, with its dazzling colours, was the inspiration for an etching made by Delacroix in 1833 (see no. 67). Contrary to the indications given by Robaut, the artist made very few changes to this later version.

This work, of the same provenance as the following watercolour, was shown in the Orangerie in 1933, as part of the exhibition celebrating the centenary of Delacroix's journey to Morocco. Sixty years later, the current exhibition provides a rare occasion for it to be admired once again.

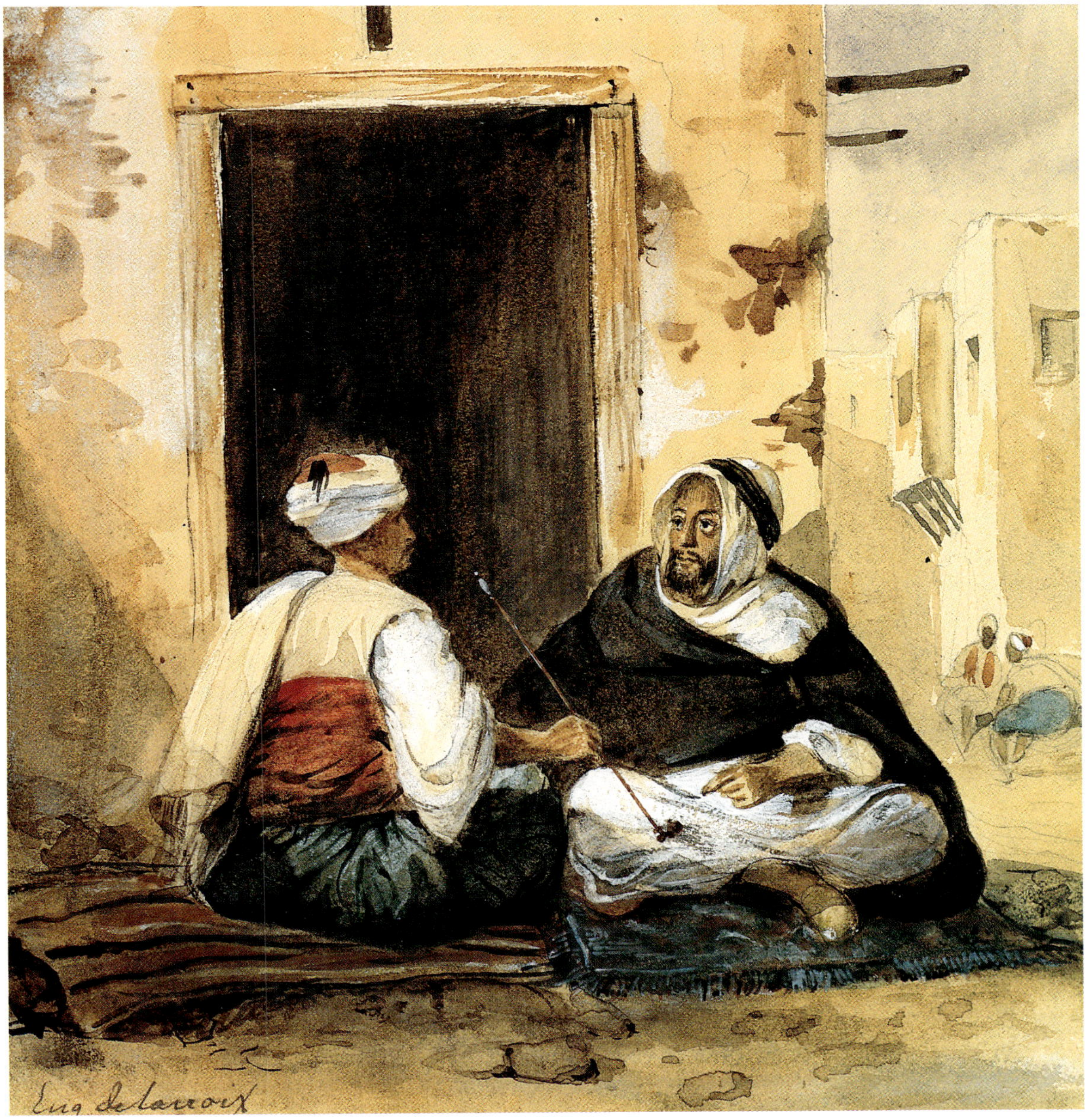

A COULOUGLIS AND AN ARAB
Un Coulouglis et un Arabe
57

Watercolour, gouache and pencil drawing
16 x 16 cm
Signed lower left in pen: Eug. Delacroix
Private collection

PROVENANCE:
Gift of the artist to Count Charles de Mornay; Count Charles de Mornay; sale, Paris, 29 Mar. 1877, no. 19, to M. de Bourdesoulle; Count de Mailly-Châlons; Countess de Mailly-Châlons.

BIBLIOGRAPHY:
Robaut, 1885, no. 510; Arama, 1987, p. 217, no. 18.

EXHIBITIONS:
Paris, 1933, no. 105.

A pencil sketch related to this watercolour was included in the posthumous Delacroix sale in 1864 (catalogued by Robaut, 1885, no. 612).

Delacroix took the subject up once again in 1834, this time adding a third figure, in a small painting catalogued in the sale of the Jacob de Vos collection (Amsterdam, 23 May 1889, no. 39) as *Three Natives Seated by a Doorway* (*Orientaux assis à la porte d'une maison*) (Johnson, 1986, no. 358, pl. 173).

The scene represents two men seated on the ground in front of the doorway of a house, an Arab and, in front of him, with his back turned to the viewer, a Turk smoking a long pipe. In his *Introduction et description des albums conservés au Louvre, au musée Condé et dans les collections Étienne Moreau-Nélaton et de Mornay* (Paris, 1909, pp. 194–5, no. 19), Jean Guiffrey explains: 'A Coulouglis is the son of a Turk and a Moor . . . The scene takes place at Oran. The other Muslims in Morocco, the third religious subdivision, do not smoke.'

The Moroccan Legacy

MOROCCAN MILITARY EXERCISES
Exercices militaires des Marocains
58
Oil on canvas
59 x 73 cm
Signed and dated lower centre:
Eug. Delacroix 1832
Musée Fabre, Montpellier (868.1.37)
PROVENANCE:
Count Charles de Mornay; sale, Paris, 18 Jan. 1850, lot 119, to Alfred Bruyas; donated to the Musée Fabre, Montpellier in 1868.
BIBLIOGRAPHY:
Robaut, 1885, no. 408; Sérullaz, 1963, no. 187, repr.; Johnson, 1986, no. 351, pl. 164; Arama, 1987, p.114–16 repr. 209 no. 2; Arama, 1992, VI, p. 81, repr.
EXHIBITIONS:
Montpellier Salon, 1860, no. 77; Paris, 1864, 2nd edit. supplement, no. 300; Paris, 1930, no. 62; Paris, 1963, no. 189.

In his presentation of the Bruyas collection, Théophile Silvestre gave a lyrical description of the Montpellier painting: 'It is as though the gunpowder *speaks* as the riders sweep by, one by one, in a whirlwind crowned by a torrent of blazing, smoky, powdery clouds; a sort of atmospheric apotheosis intensifying this painting's impact as it flies by in a flurry of marvellous visions.

The gunfire turned the atmosphere into a furnace, the excited cries of the savage riders, upright on their stirrups, lent wings to these horses—drinkers of air and gunpowder, sharper than gunpowder, faster than air, burning space and burned by the sun. Impetuously they fly into the fire like dragons and hippogriffs, all of which compels our admiration for Delacroix's fantastic excess.

Here is the artist's unforgettable impression of a Morocco which was to inspire many of his masterpieces, among which this painting is by no means unimportant' (*La Galerie Bruyas par Alfred Bruyas avec le concours des écrivains et des artists contemporains. Introduction par Théophile Silvestre*, Paris, 1876, p. 273).

During his stay in Morocco, Delacroix witnessed several *courses de poudre* on the journey from Tangier to Meknes. At each stage of the journey the mission was welcomed with a fantasia, which the artist described, depending on his humour or the weather, in more or less detail. The Count de Mornay also mentions them in his correspondence: 'Large detachments of cavalry and infantry assembled all along my route to act as escort and to perform the *jeux de poudre,* a military exercise which is used for grand occasions or in honour of important dignitaries. The Christians, for whom these marks of consideration are performed, run a certain risk, as the Moors like to aim at their faces to see if they panic' (letter dated 23 March 1832, Meknes; Arama, 1992, VI, pp. 213–15).

On Delacroix's return from North Africa, these captivating *courses de poudre* inspired one watercolour (see no. 53) and four paintings, executed between 1832 and 1847. The Montpellier version corresponds to some of the notes made by the artist on 6 March 1832: 'Tribe following us; disorder, dust, preceded by cavalry. *Courses de poudre*, horses in the dust, sun behind. The arms pulled up for speed' (Département des Arts graphiques, Louvre, RF 1712 bis, fol. 7 verso).

The 1833 version in the Städelsches Kunstinstitut, Frankfurt (Johnson, 1986, no. 353, pl. 165; see p. 88) is reminiscent of the watercolour offered to the Count de Mornay (see no. 53), with the exception of a new architectural element. When Delacroix used this subject again in 1847 (Oskar Reinhart collection; Johnson, 1986, no. 376, pl. 192; see p. 120), he gave it a more grandiose and violent interpretation, using the whole width of the canvas to portray the riders in a frenzied gallop against a majestic background of mountains.

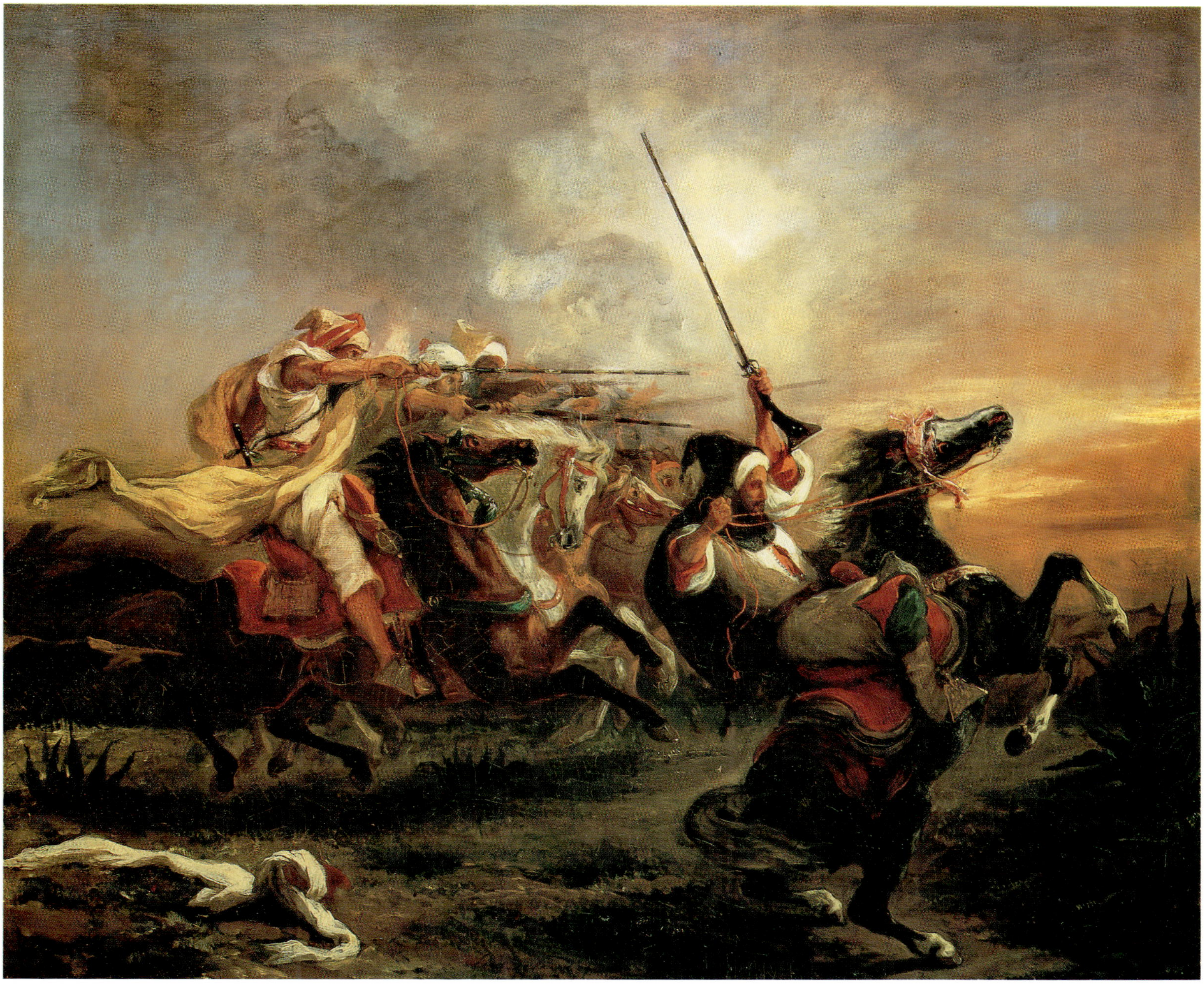

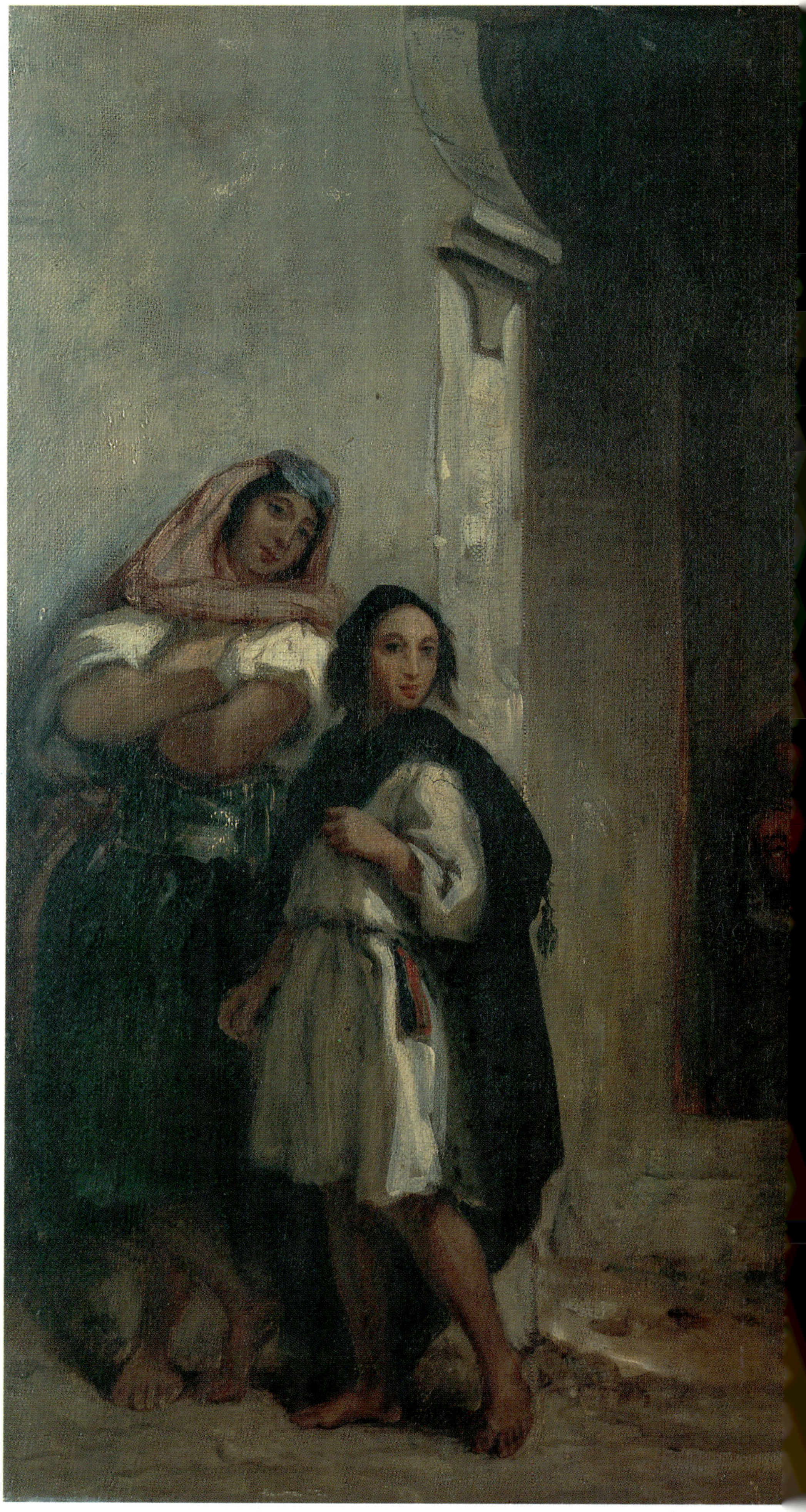

A STREET IN MEKNES
Une rue à Mékinez
59

Oil on canvas
46.3 x 64.5 cm
Signed and dated lower right:
Eug. Delacroix 1832
Albright-Knox Art Gallery, Buffalo (49:4)

PROVENANCE:
Robert de Flers; Bernheim-Jeune, Paris; Wolf Ebenrod, Germany; Fine Arts Association, New York; acquired in 1948 by the Albright-Knox Art Gallery, Buffalo, Elizabeth H. Gates and Charles W. Goodyear Funds.

BIBLIOGRAPHY:
Robaut, 1885, no. 551; Sérullaz, 1963, no. 200, repr.; Johnson, 1986, no. 352, pl. 166; Arama, 1987, p. 103, repr. (detail), 209, no. 8, repr.; Arama, 1992, VI, p. 88, repr.

EXHIBITIONS:
1834 Salon, no. 496; Toronto-Ottawa, 1962–3, no. 6, repr.; Paris, 1963, no. 200; London-Edinburgh, 1964, no. 29; Kyoto-Tokyo, 1969, no. H–13, repr.

Exhibited at the 1834 Salon, two years after it was executed, this small painting was eclipsed by the *Women of Algiers* (Louvre; see p. 115) and so comments on it are rare. Contrary to the critics, who reproached the artist for his 'excess of facility', and 'extreme negligence', attention should be drawn to the skilfully depicted atmosphere and the careful balance of the composition with its alternating areas of light and shadow. The memories of walks in the town, particularly in the Jewish quarter, start to bear fruit with this work.

Anxious to avoid a picturesque, anecdotal style, Delacroix portrays a woman and a young boy leaning against a dazzling, sun-drenched wall and an Aïssaoua crouching on the ground, deep in meditation. In the centre, in the shadowy light, one can just discern a figure squatting on the steps. The only decorative element is the little openwork aperture at top right.

'*A Street in Meknes* distinguishes itself by its dazzling, diaphanous light and the poses of the figures which appear simple and natural. It is a good study; it needed very little more to make it into a good painting', commented Gustave Planche in the *Revue des Deux Mondes*, 1 April 1834 (vol. 2, p. 58).

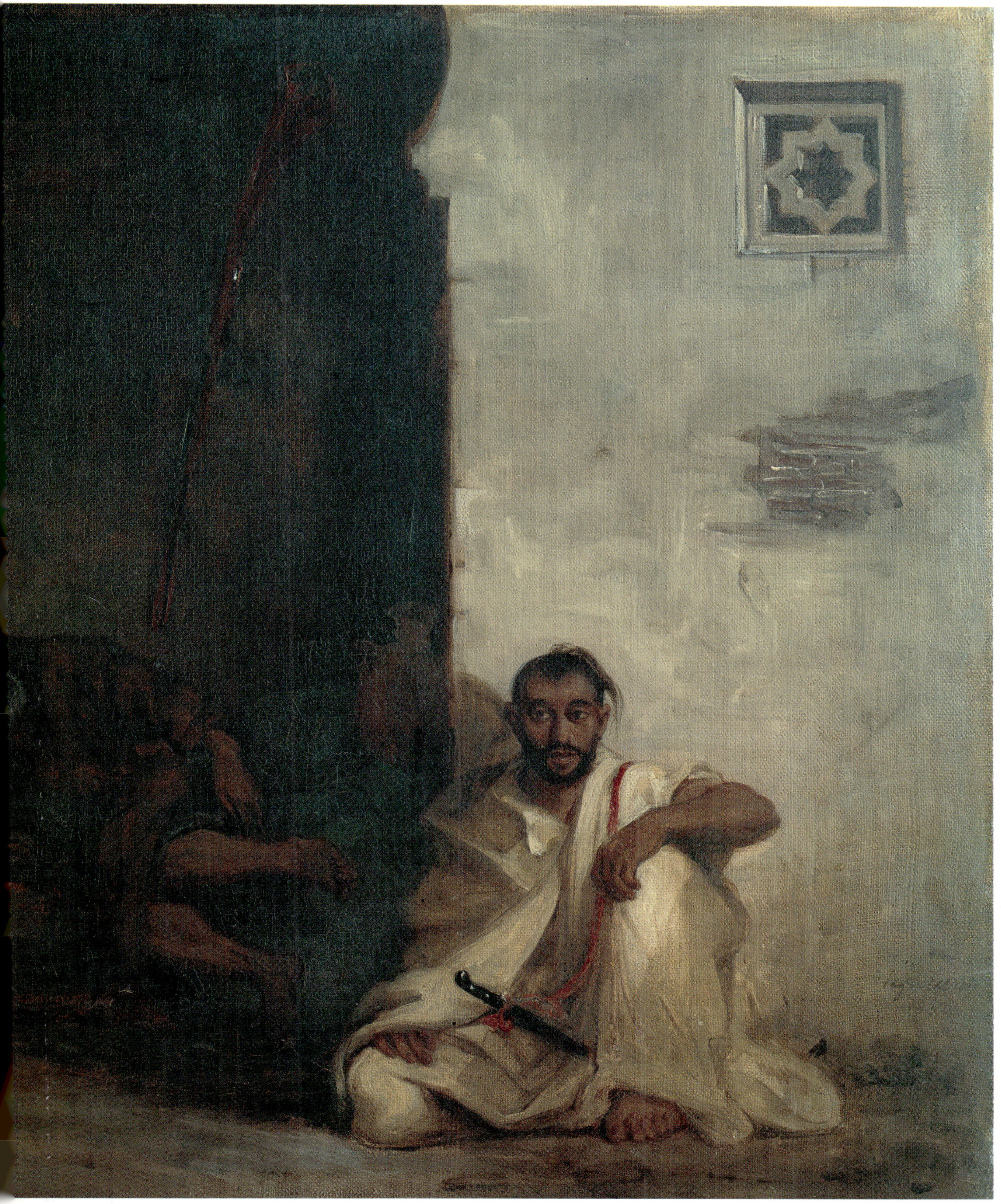

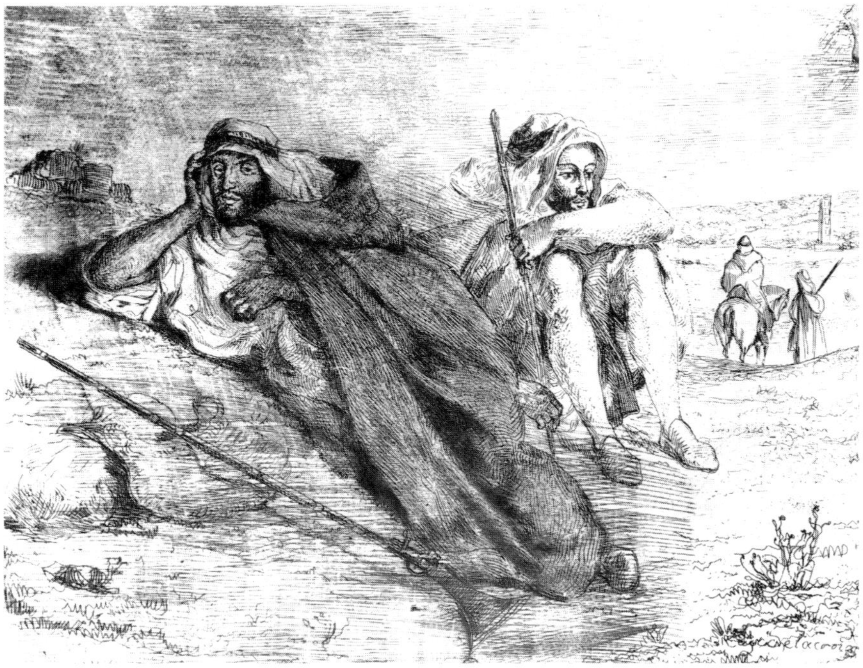

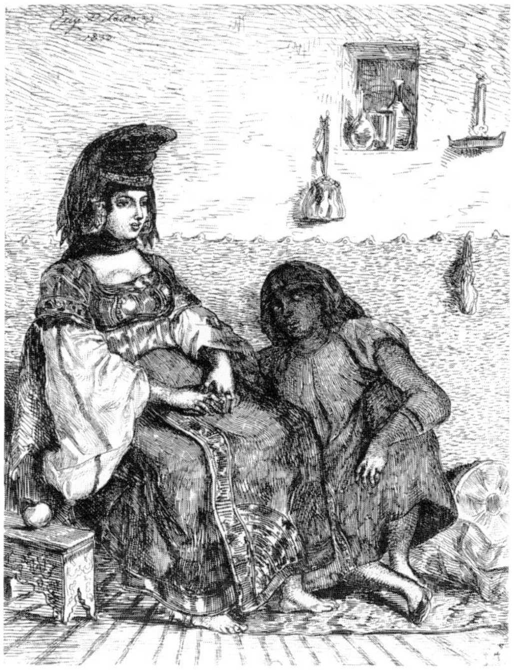

ARABS OF ORAN
Arabes d'Oran
60

Etching
17. 3 x 21.4 cm
1st print
Signed lower right: Eug. Delacroix.
In the margin, lower centre: Arabes d'Oran.
Bibliothèque Nationale, Paris
(DC 183n rés.t.1)

PROVENANCE:
Étienne Moreau-Nélaton; bequeathed to the Bibliothèque Nationale, Paris, in 1927.

BIBLIOGRAPHY:
Robaut, 1885, no. 462; Delteil, 1908, no. 20. 1.

EXHIBITIONS:
Paris, 1933, no. 241.

L. Delteil (op. cit.) has listed six prints of this etching. The image of the watercolour offered to the Count de Mornay (see no. 55), has been reversed and some details changed. Delacroix has replaced one of the baskets by a rifle, and the Arab in the middle distance, who walks forward leaning on a stick, has been replaced by two Arabs seen from behind, one of whom is on horseback. While the landscape remains largely the same, the smaller dimensions of the engraving highlight the costumes and the poses of the two travellers. A nielloed copperplate of this work exists in the Cabinet des Estampes, Bibliothèque Nationale, Paris.

JEWESS OF ALGIERS
Juive d'Alger
61

Etching
20.8 x 15.3 cm
2nd print
Signed and dated top left: Eug. Delacroix / 1833.
Bibliothèque Nationale, Paris (DC 183n rés.t.1.)

PROVENANCE:
Étienne Moreau-Nélaton; bequeathed to the Bibliothèque Nationale, Paris in 1927.

BIBLIOGRAPHY:
Robaut, 1885, no. 461; Delteil, 1908, no. 18, repr.

This is the second of the four prints catalogued by L. Delteil (op. cit.).

In Bordeaux in 1852, Delacroix exhibited a painting of the same subject, described as follows: 'A Jewess at Home with a Moorish Woman (Moroccan dress)', two versions of which exist, both belonging to American collectors (Johnson, 1986, nos 388 and 389, pls 196 and 197). One of them (Johnson, 1986, no. 388) is fairly similar to the engraving, while the other one presents a variation in the pose of the soubrette who carries a tray with a coffee pot which, in this work, is visible in the niche.

WOMAN OF TANGIER HANGING OUT LAUNDRY
Femme de Tanger étendant du linge
62

Pen and ink autography
30.5 x 24.8 cm
Signed lower left: Eug. Delacroix
Bibliothèque Nationale, Paris (DC 183n rés.t.5)

PROVENANCE:
Étienne Moreau-Nélaton; bequeathed to the Bibliothèque Nationale, Paris, in 1927.

BIBLIOGRAPHY:
Robaut, 1885, no. 476; Delteil, 1908, no. 95, repr.

EXHIBITIONS:
Paris, 1933, no. 242.

The Louvre owns a pencil drawing, most probably executed during the second stay in Tangier (12 April–early May 1832), which served as starting point for this autography. Tradition has it that it was while making this sketch that Delacroix was assailed by the husbands of the washerwomen, who, nervous about being observed and sketched, had called them over (Département des Arts graphiques, inventory RF 9258; Sérullaz, 1984, II, no. 1573, repr.).

A watercolour of a similar subject, but reversed and with certain variations, is in the collection of the Fogg Art Museum, Harvard University, Cambridge; it was one of the eighteen watercolours given by Delacroix to the Count de Mornay (see p. 180, fig. 3).

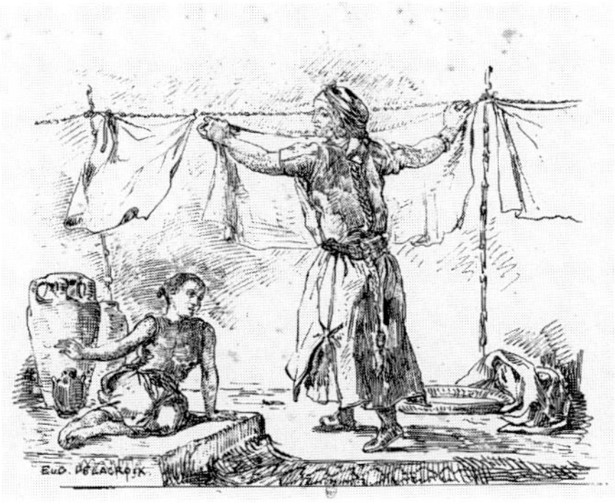

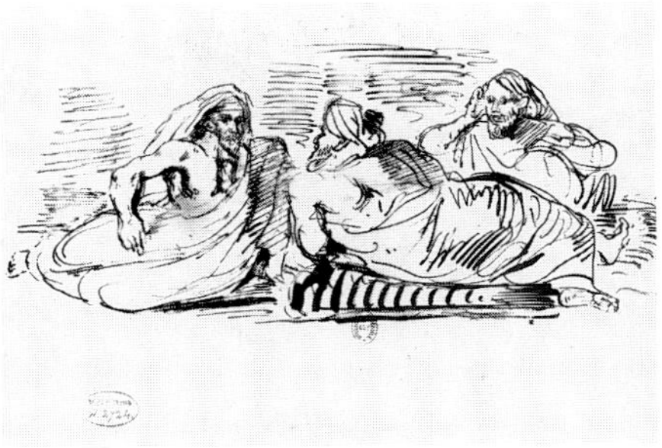

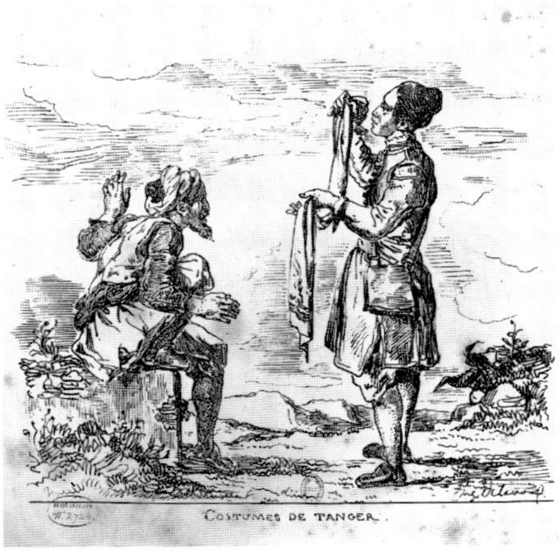

The technique of *autography* consists in transferring a drawing executed on *autographic paper* (paper coated with glue) with *autographic ink*, or a lithographic pencil, onto a lithographic stone. The illustrated side of the paper is applied to the stone and dampened. Strong pressure from the press causes the ink to adhere to the stone (cf. A. Béguin, *Dictionnaire des termes techniques*, in M. Melot, *Histoire d'un art. L'Estampe*, Geneva, 1981, p. 244).

Delacroix used this technique for some of his engravings of Moroccan subjects destined for publication (see the following numbers).

CONVERSATION BETWEEN ARABS RECLINING ON CUSHIONS
Arabes causant étendus sur des coussins
63

Pen and ink autography
25 x 12 cm
2nd print
Bibliothèque Nationale, Paris (DC 183n rés.t.5)

PROVENANCE:
Étienne Moreau-Nélaton; bequeathed to the Bibliothèque Nationale, Paris in 1927.

BIBLIOGRAPHY:
Robaut, 1885, no. 471; Delteil, 1908, no. 98, repr.

EXHIBITIONS:
Paris, 1933, no. 240.

See the preceding number. The theme of Arabs in conversation recurs many times in Delacroix's paintings, drawings and engravings after 1832.

COSTUMES FROM TANGIER
Costumes de Tanger
64

Pen and ink autography
23 x 19 cm
Signed lower right: Eug. Delacroix
Bibliothèque Nationale, Paris (DC 183n t.5)

PROVENANCE:
Étienne Moreau-Nélaton; bequeathed to the Bibliothèque Nationale, Paris in 1927.

BIBLIOGRAPHY:
Robaut, 1885, no. 465; Delteil, 1908, no. 94, repr.

EXHIBITIONS:
Paris, 1933, no. 237.

'In the countryside a young Jewish merchant, standing, unfolds a strip of material that he seems to be offering to an elderly Moor with a long beard, seated opposite him on a stone'. According to Robaut (op. cit.), this composition was the basis for a painting sold at the Hôtel Drouot in 1873, but no trace of this work has been found.

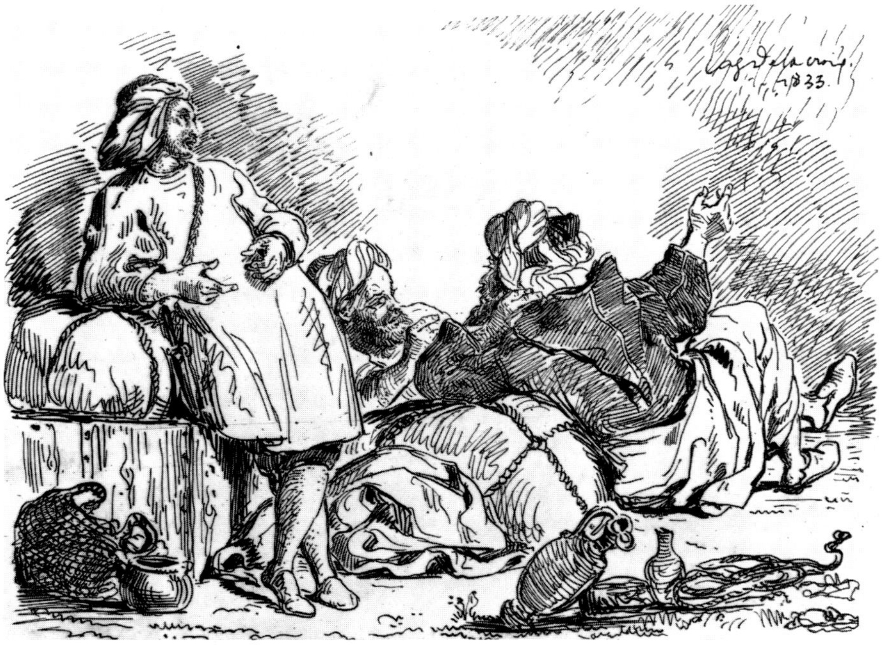

MULE-DRIVERS FROM TETUAN
Muletiers de Tétuan
65

Pen and ink autography
26.2 x 18.9 cm
Signed and dated at top right:
Eug. Delacroix /1833
Bibliothèque Nationale, Paris (DC 183n rés. t. 5)

PROVENANCE:
Étienne Moreau-Nélaton; bequeathed to the Bibliothèque Nationale in 1927.

BIBLIOGRAPHY:
Robaut, 1885, no. 475; Delteil, 1908, no. 96, repr.

EXHIBITIONS:
Paris, 1933, no. 235.

A pencil sketch of the same subject, with some variations, has been catalogued by Robaut (1885, no. 474). The figure standing on the left, propped up on his elbows, is taken directly from a pencil sketch on a page in the Louvre (Département des Arts graphiques, Louvre, inventory RF 10 084; Sérullaz, 1984, II, no. 1572, repr.). On the same page, the half-length figure in the foreground was almost certainly used for the Arab seated on the right.

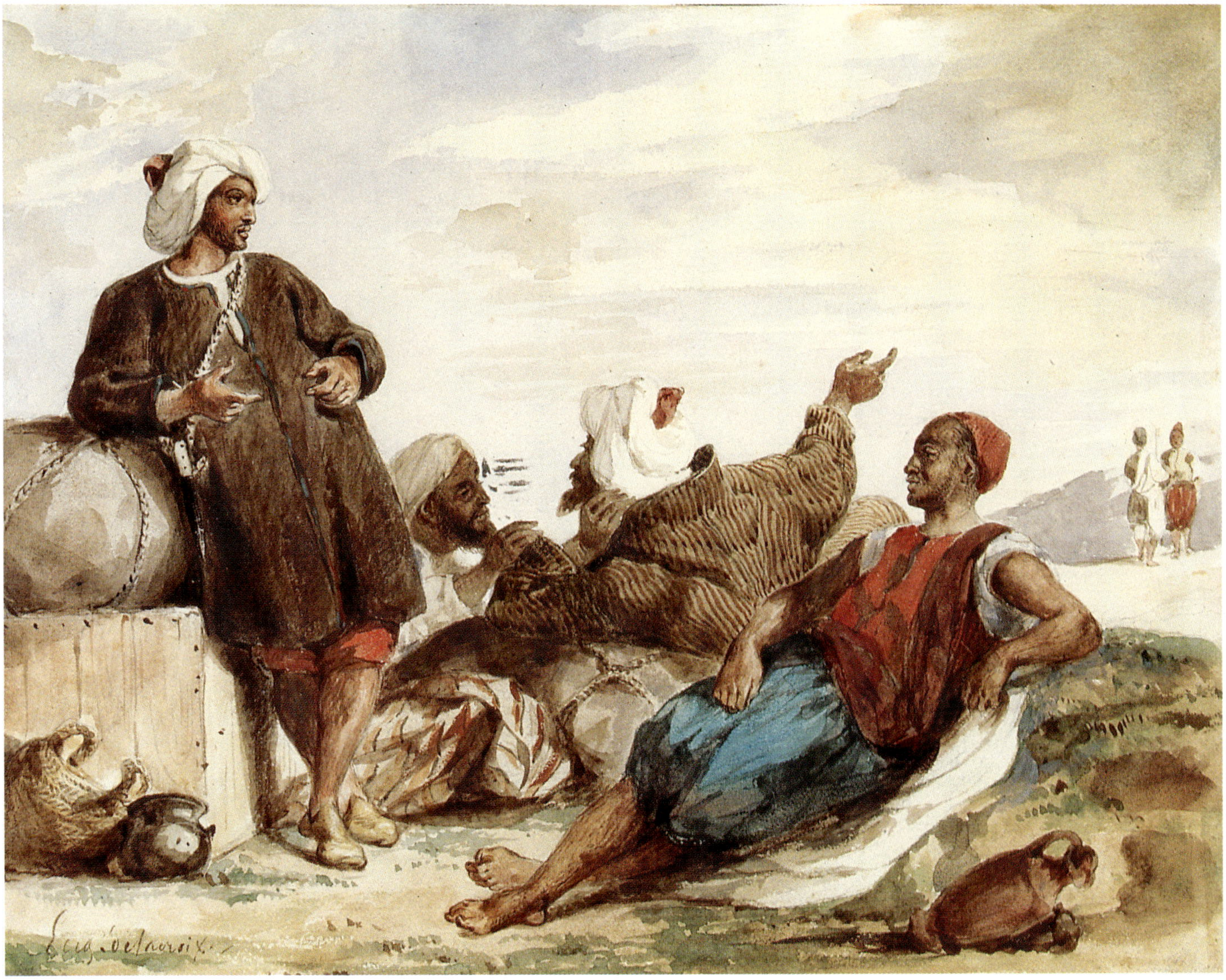

MULE-DRIVERS FROM TETUAN
Muletiers de Tétuan
66

Watercolour
25.2 x 32.5 cm
Signed lower left in paint:
Eug. Delacroix
Musée Archéologique Municipal, Laon (989.85)

PROVENANCE:
Original collection

This watercolour seems to have escaped the curiosity of the Delacroix historians until now. Clearly derived from the autography catalogued under the preceding number, this version contains a fourth figure in the foreground on the right, whose dress, composed of a red tunic over a carmine waistcoat and bright blue baggy breeches (*saroual*), contrasts with the general harmony of the scene. This work is a fine illustration of the interest Delacroix took in the characteristics of Arab dress, which he systematically asked Abraham Benchimol to explain to him.

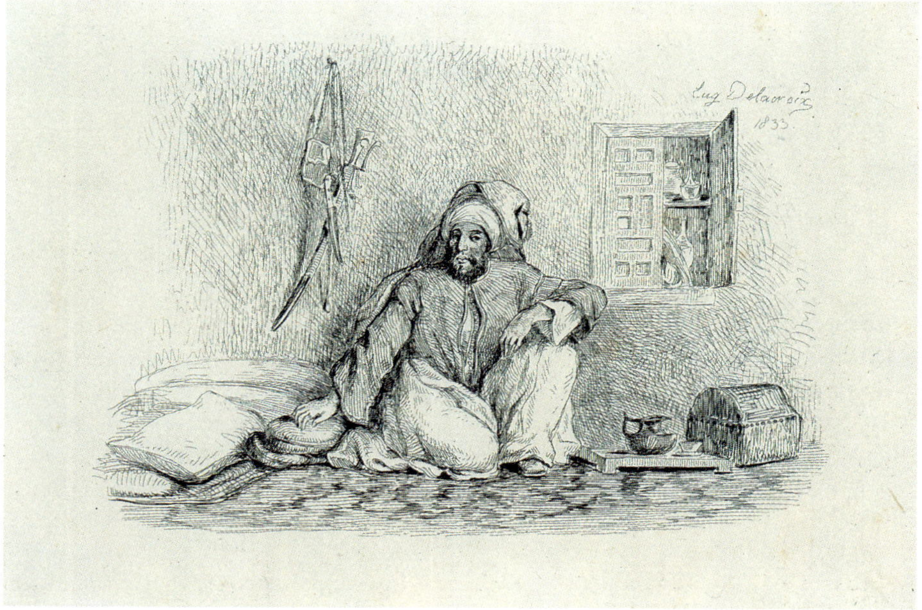

MOHAMMED BEN ABOU,
ARAB CHIEFTAIN OF MEKNES
Le Caïd Mohammed-Ben-Abou
(Chef Maure à Meknez)
67

Etching
11 x 17 cm
1st print avant la lettre
Signed and dated at top right, above the small cupboard: Eug. Delacroix 1833
Musée Eugène Delacroix, Paris (MD.SAD.34-5)
PROVENANCE:
Alfred Robaut; Baron Joseph Vitta; Société des Amis de Delacroix.

In the catalogue of the posthumous sale (Paris, 22–27 Feb. 1864, lot 694) this etching is given the title *Arab Chieftain at Meknes (Chef maure à Méquinez).* It in fact represents the Tangier cavalry commander squatting on a pile of carpets. His coffee has been placed on the floor on a small board.The reversed drawing, which Delacroix used for the execution of his etching, also figured in his posthumous sale (Paris, 22–27 Feb. 1864, lot 452). There was also a portrait of Ben Abou in the album of watercolours offered to the Count de Mornay (see no. 56). According to A. Moreau (*Delacroix et son œuvre*, Paris, 1873), Delacroix expressly asked the engraver Louis-Pierre Henriquel-Dupont (1797–1892) to make the plate.

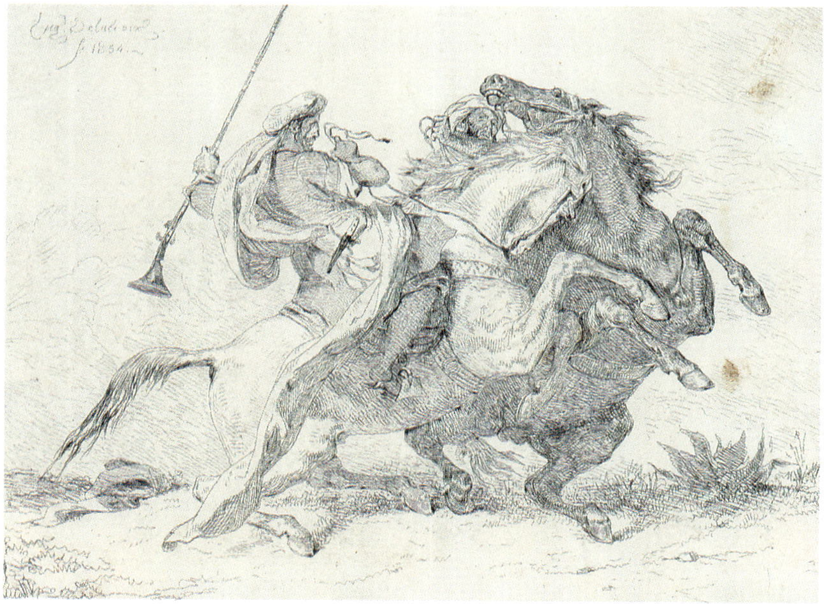

COLLISION
OF ARAB HORSEMEN
Rencontre de cavaliers maures
68

Etching
18.4 x 25.1 cm
Signed and dated top left:
Eug. Delacroix/f. 1834
Musée Eugène Delacroix, Paris (MD.SAD.34-2)
PROVENANCE:
Baron Joseph Vitta; Société des Amis de Delacroix.

Three copies of this engraving figure in the catalogue of the posthumous sale (Paris, 22–27 Feb. 1864, lot 697). The composition consists of the reversed image of a painting which was refused at the 1834 Salon (Johnson, 1986, no. 355, pl. 168) and which evokes an incident Delacroix witnessed on 6 March, soon after leaving Tangier: '*Courses de poudre* on the plain facing the river—The two riders who collided: the one whose horse's rump touched the ground' (Département des Arts graphiques, Louvre, RF 1712 bis, fol. 7 recto). When Delacroix sent the painting to Nantes, for an exhibition held in the spring of 1839, he recounted to Charles Leroux: 'Their military exercises consist of launching their horses at full speed and then bringing them abruptly to a halt once they have fired a rifle shot. The horses often carry off their riders, and fight one another when they collide' (*Correspondance*, II, p. 38). The artist executed a replica of this work which is now in the Walters Art Gallery, Baltimore (Johnson, 1986, no. 367, pl. 169, see p. 122).

MOROCCAN CHIEFTAIN RECEIVING TRIBUTE
Le Kaïd, chef marocain
69

Also known as Moroccan Chieftain visiting a Tribe (Chef marocain visitant une tribu) or The Offering of Milk (L'offrande du lait).
Oil on canvas
0.98 x 1.26 m
Signed and dated lower right:
Eug. Delacroix / 1837
Musée des Beaux-Arts, Nantes (892)

PROVENANCE:
Sold by Delacroix to the Musée de Nantes following an exhibition held in Nantes in 1839.

BIBLIOGRAPHY:
Robaut, 1885, no. 647 and p. 489; Sérullaz, 1963, no. 257, repr.; Johnson, 1986, no. 359, pl. 174; Arama, 1987, p. 118–19, no. 4, repr.; Arama, 1992, VI, p. 93, repr.

EXHIBITIONS:
1838 Salon, no. 458; Paris, 1864, no. 3; Paris, 1930, no. 84, repr. Album, p. 52; Paris, 1933, no. 180, repr.; Zurich, 1939, no. 326, repr.; Basel, 1939, no. 225, repr.; Paris, 1963, no. 261; Berne, 1963–4, no. 42; Paris, 1973, no cat.; Zurich, 1987, no. 49, repr. p. 158.

'He is at the head of a troop of soldiers. Inhabitants from the surrounding country come to pay him tribute along his route. A woman offers him a jug of milk. He dips his finger into it and then lifts to his lips.' (Description in the 1838 Salon catalogue).

The offering of milk, to which the artist alludes on several occasions in his notes, was a symbol of welcome and peace. On 9 April 1832, during the halt at El-Ksar el-Kebir, Delacroix attended one such ceremony (Département des Arts graphiques, Louvre, RF 1712 bis, fol. 30 recto and 31 verso), but there is nothing to indicate when this work was executed. *The Moroccan Chieftain* is mentioned only once in a list of pictures drawn up in 1843 with the note: 'in Nantes' (*Journal,* III, p. 374). The painting was bought after its exhibition in Nantes, in 1839, probably organized by Charles Leroux, judging by the letter Delacroix sent him on 26 May 1839: 'The two paintings that you saw in my studio and that I wanted to include in the Nantes exhibition, were despatched the day after your kind visit. I have suggested the note that could be included with the price of both of the paintings . . . *Moroccan Chieftain.* Price: 1,200 francs. The chieftain, the head of a troop of cavalry: men and women from the country offer him a large jug of milk as a sign of hospitality. According to custom, the chief dips the tip of his finger into the milk and puts it to his lips. The same ceremony takes place for the standard-bearers' (*Correspondance,* II, p. 38). On June 20, Delacroix addressed the members of the commission of the Nantes exhibition: 'Gentlemen, I have received the letter in which you propose to acquire my painting representing *A Moroccan Chieftain* for the sum of 1,000 francs, and despite the reduction in the price I had fixed for this work, you show such a flattering eagerness to exhibit it in your Museum, that it is with great pleasure that I accept your request. I know that the Musée de Nantes houses many beautiful masterpieces. I will therefore be very honoured to occupy a small place there' (Johnson, 1986, p. 171).

Flapping in the wind, the three flags, white, red and blue, add an unexpected flash of colour to the composition, which inspired the following commentary from A.T. (Tardieu) (*Le Courrier Français,* 22 March 1838): 'In these three works (*The Chieftain, Horses in a Courtyard* and *The Fanatics of Tangier*) in the style of a sketch with extremely bold brushwork, the particular talent of M. Delacroix, that of a colourist, is clearly evident. In the composition *The Fanatics of Tangier,* there is a strangeness which Delacroix's critics will seize upon, but the powerful colour in *The Chieftain* should be sufficient to disarm them and to inspire a certain indulgence towards one of the most original and probably one of the most incorrigible artists of our day.' Delacroix is unequalled in his portrayal of the rider and his noble mount. The principal group is slightly off centre, leaving a clear view of the landscape as far as the horizon. Only a goat, on the extreme right, provides an intimate touch to the majestic scene. In 1862, Delacroix executed a considerably smaller and very different version of this work (Johnson, 1986, no. 416, pl. 225).

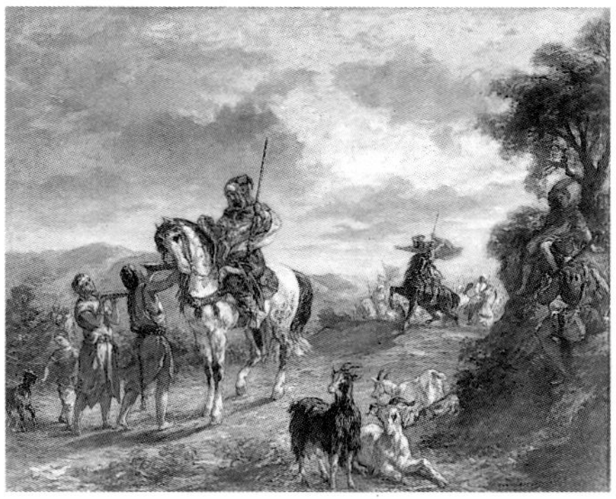

Not in exhibition:
Moroccan Chieftain with Sheperds (Le caïd Marocain acceptant l'hospitalité des pasteurs),
oil on canvas.
Private collection.

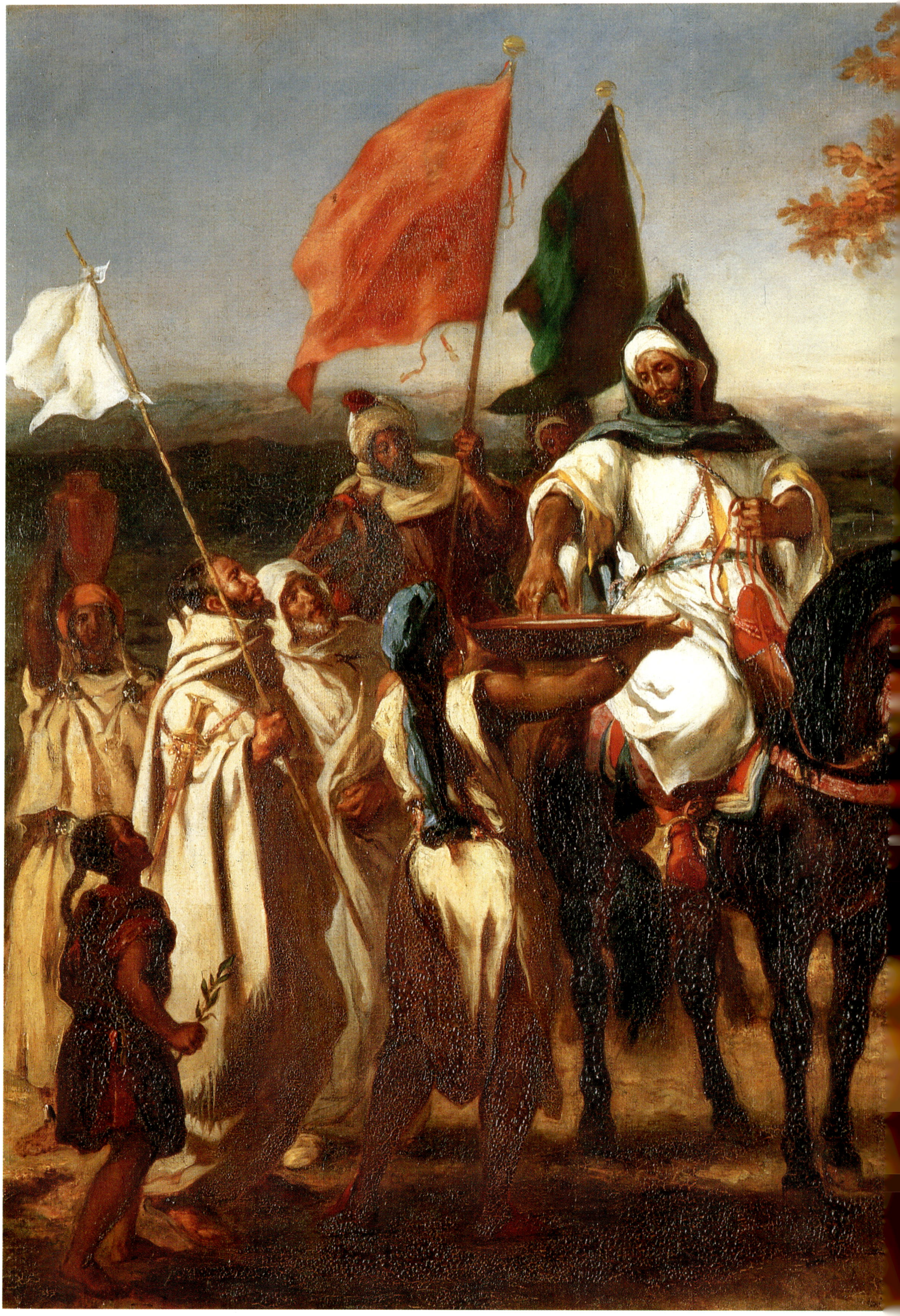

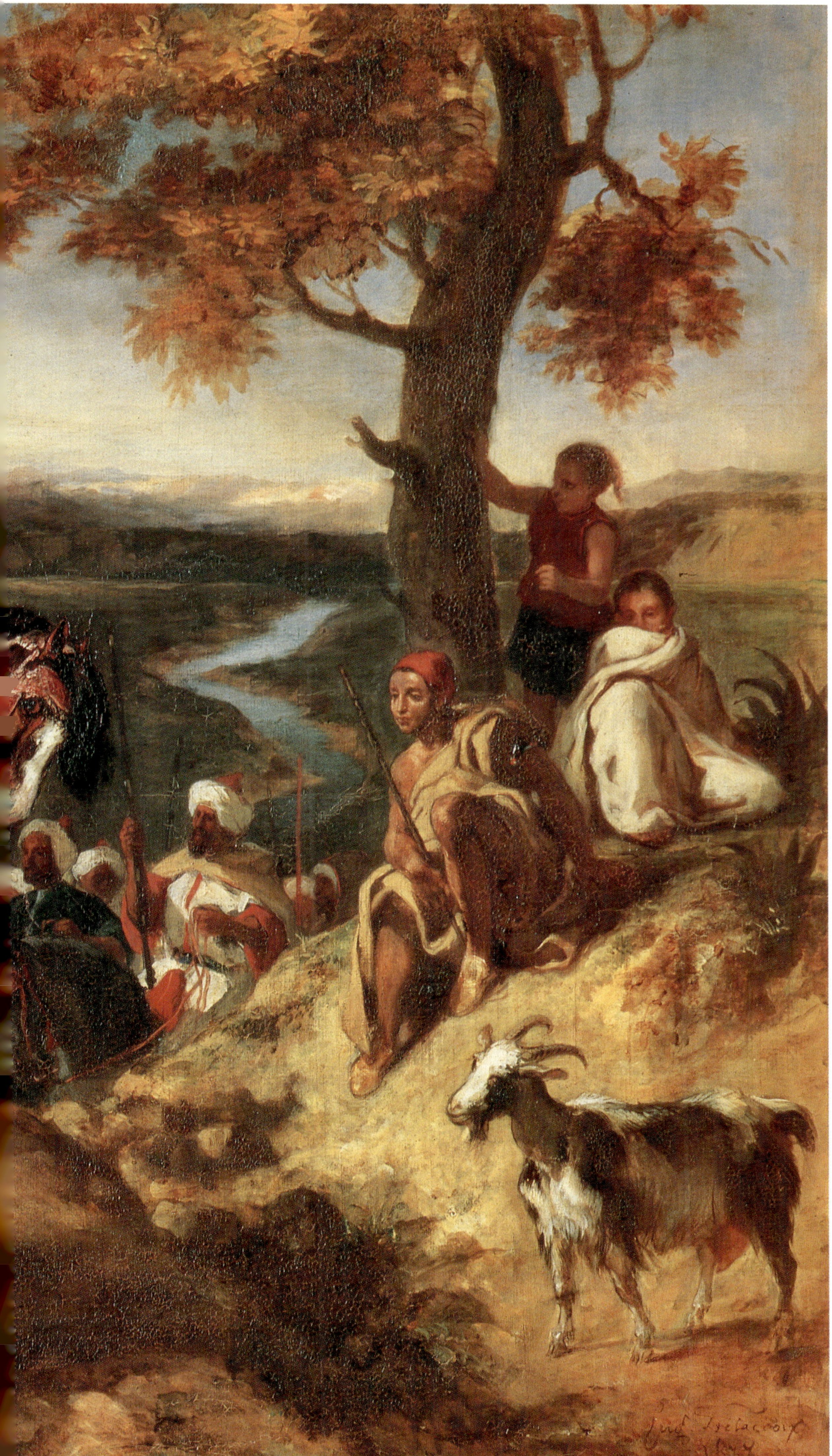
Eug. Delacroix

ARABS OF ORAN
Arabes d'Oran
70

Watercolour and pencil drawing
11.5 x 19 cm
Signed and dated lower right in paint:
Eug. Delacroix 1837
Private collection. Courtesy of the Galerie Schmit, Paris

PROVENANCE:
V. Goldschmidt; J. Diéterle.

BIBLIOGRAPHY:
Johnson, 1986, p. 170.

EXHIBITIONS:
Paris, 1930, no. 600(?); Paris, 1973, no cat.; Zurich, 1987 (1), no. 49; Frankfurt, 1987–8, no. H 21 repr.

The final transformation of a subject first painted in 1832 (see no. 55), this watercolour retains the essential elements in a noticeably modified landscape, scattered with aloes and closed in by a distant chain of mountains. The objects on the ground, a basket, small green and brown jugs and a bundle wrapped in red and green striped material, held together by a stick, bring a colourful note to the grass-covered ground. This is in total contrast to the watercolour offered to the Count de Mornay, conceived in a harmony of luminous pale ochre tones evoking a hot sunny day.

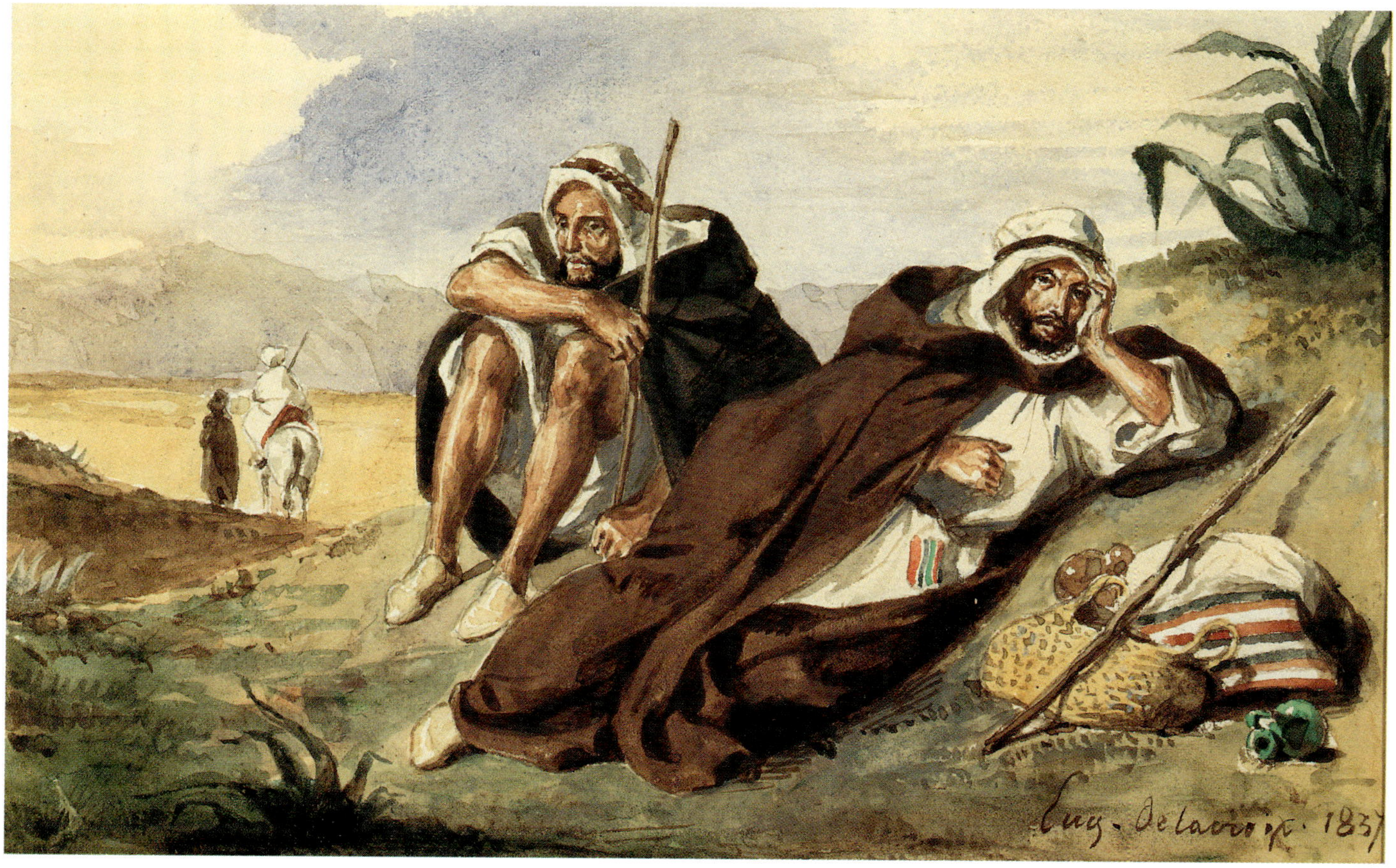

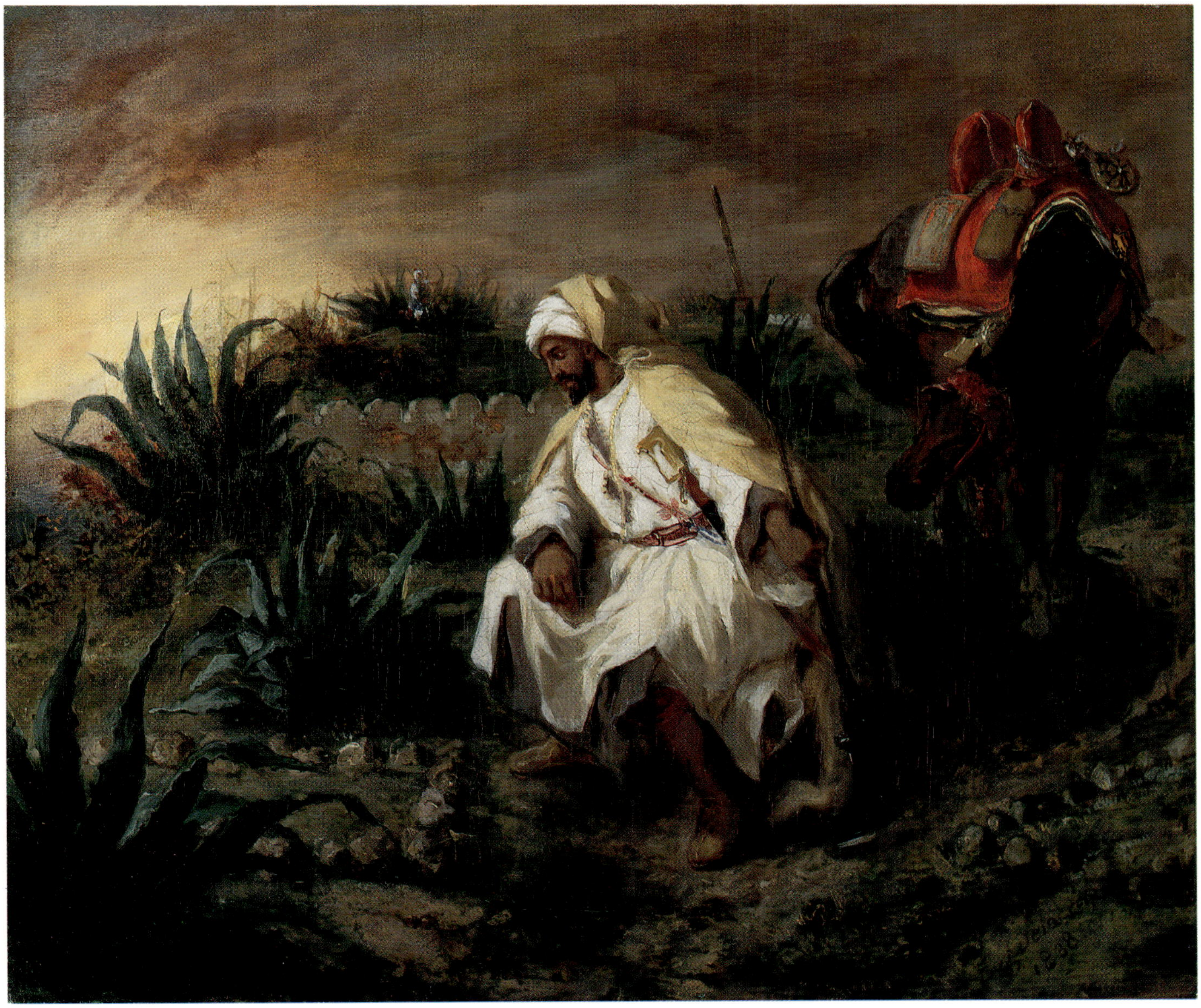

ARAB SOLDIER BY A GRAVE
Guerrier près d'un tombeau
71

Oil on canvas
47.3 x 56.2 cm
Signed and dated lower right: Eug. Delacroix / 1838
Museum of Art, Hiroshima

PROVENANCE:
Duke of Orleans, deceased in 1842; Duchess of Orleans; sale, Paris, 18 Jan. 1853, lot 21, to Bouruet; Aubertot, by 1864; Count de Lambertye; sale, Paris, 7 Dec. 1868, lot 18; Amédée Larrieu, by 1869; with MM. Vanderdonckt, Le Roy, Francis Petit, by 1874; Boussod, Valadon et Cie, then Secrétan, by 1881; Arnold, Tripp & Co., by 1884; again Boussod, Valadon et Cie, by 1894; Montaignac, by 1895; Society of American Art, New York; sale, 25 Apr. 1895, lot 140; George Harding, Chicago, by 1930; sale, Sotheby's, New York, 20 Oct. 1976, lot 12, to Eugene V. Thaw, New York; Artemis Fine Arts, London; bought by the Nichido Gallery, Tokyo in 1978; Museum of Art, Hiroshima, since 1980.

BIBLIOGRAPHY:
Robaut, 1885, no. 663; Johnson, 1986, no. 362, pl. 175; Arama, 1987, p. 110–111, repr., 210 no. 13, repr.

EXHIBITIONS:
Paris, 1864, no. 136.

A. Moreau (*E. Delacroix et son œuvre*, Paris, 1873) was the first to suggest that the person represented here was none other than Mohammed Ben Abou, although when it was presented to the jury at the 1839 Salon—who refused it—the painting was registered under the title of *Arab Soldier by a Grave (Guerrier près d'un tombeau)*. Among the works executed in the 1840s, Delacroix mentions a *Ben Abou by a Grave (Ben-Abou auprès d'un tombeau)* (*Journal*, III, p. 372). The critic Eugène Bareste, disappointed at not seeing the painting in the Salon, publicly expressed his regrets: 'The first painting to be refused, or rather the one we saw the first, belongs to the Duke of Orléans . . . This small painting . . . portrays an *Arab Soldier by a Grave* ...Oh! how you would curse the jury for having deprived you of this canvas, if you knew of its beauty. Maybe these gentlemen found the colours in this painting too crude, too green, too clashing, and the position of the Arab ungraceful, but are these small faults enough to warrant a refusal? And the magnifying glasses of these powerful lords must have been very dull to have hidden the calm, religious, touching expression of this man in the desert. Are their eyes, weakened not by work, but by age, like those of the gospel: for they did not see all that is beautiful, rich and well-executed in the horse which lowers its head as if to kiss the hand that his master offers him?' (*La Revue du XIXe siècle*, II, pp. 233–4).

See no. 67, an engraved portrait of Ben Abou.

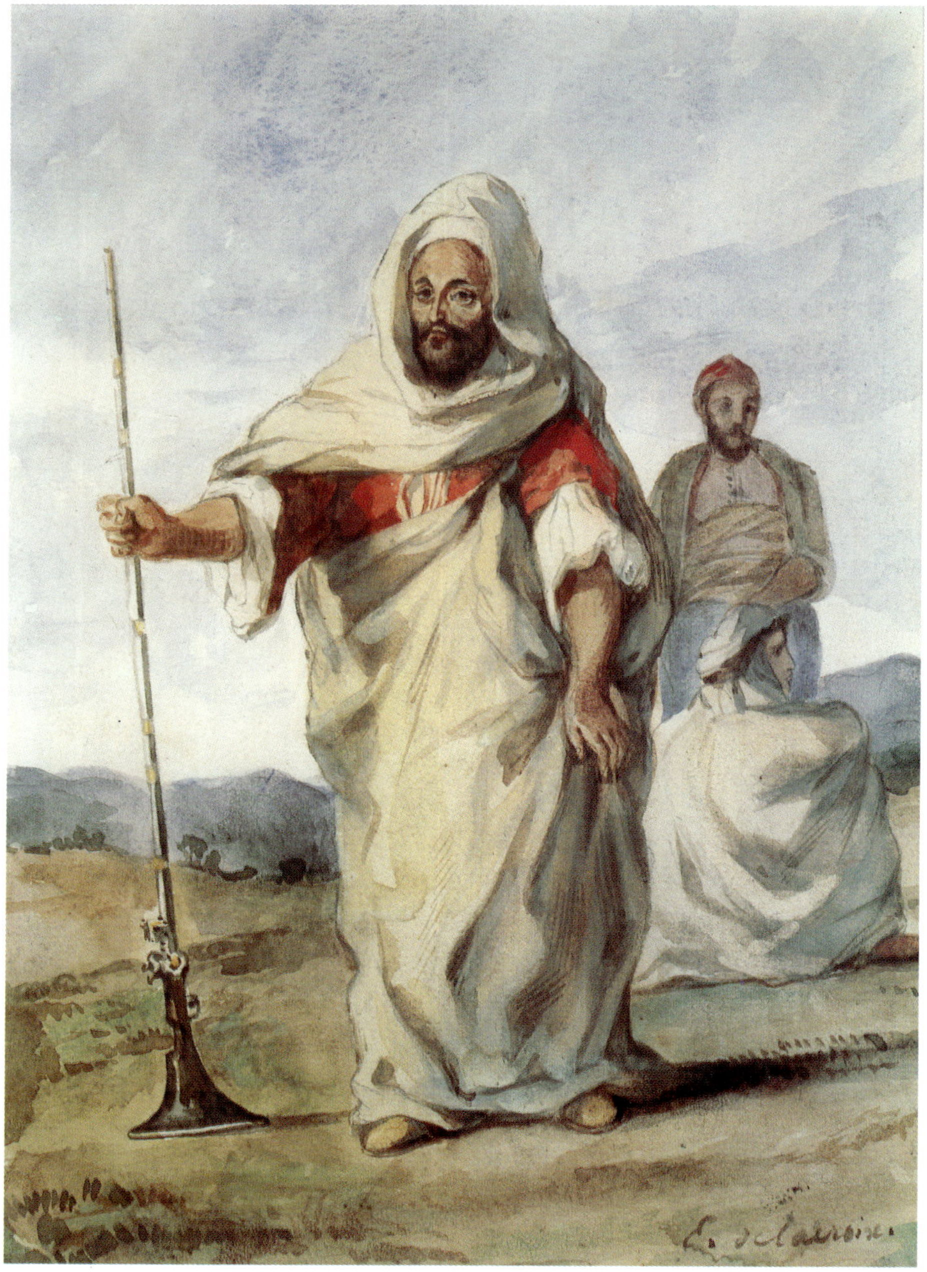

ARAB CHIEFTAIN WITH A RIFLE
Chef Arabe tenant un fusil
72

Watercolour and gouache
22 x 15.8 cm
Signed lower right in point: E. Delacroix
Private Collection

PROVENANCE:
Sale, Paris, 5 May 1986, no. 29, repr.

This watercolour is a variation of another watercolour, signed and dated *1834*, sold in Paris on 30 June 1950 (no. 2, repr.), and also of a small picture which figured in the posthumous Delacroix sale under the title: *Moroccan Chieftain (Chef marocain)* (whereabouts unknown; Paris, 22–27 Feb. 1864, no. 71; Johnson, 1986, no. 363, pl. 179). During 1834, the artist seems to have executed several studies, in paint or watercolour, of similar figures; a picture signed and dated in the same year, represents an Arab standing by the sea, who, according to Maurice Arama, is probably Mokhtar el-Jamaï (Johnson, 1986, no. 361, pl. 178; sale, Sotheby's, New York, 26 May 1994, no. 52, repr.).

STANDING ARAB, WEARING A TURBAN AND A BURNOUS
Arabe debout, coiffé d'un turban et drapé dans un burnous
73
Watercolour and pencil drawing
29.5 x 15.5 cm
Jan and Marie-Anne Krugier Collection. Courtesy of the Galerie Jan Krugier, Geneva

PROVENANCE:

Delacroix Studio, marked lower right (L.838 a); sale, Paris, 22–27 Feb. 1864, possibly included in lots 571 or 572; sale, Paris, 8 Apr. 1989, no. 4, repr. (under the title Souvenir of a Journey, the Oriental *(*Souvenir de voyage, l'oriental*).*

See the preceding number.

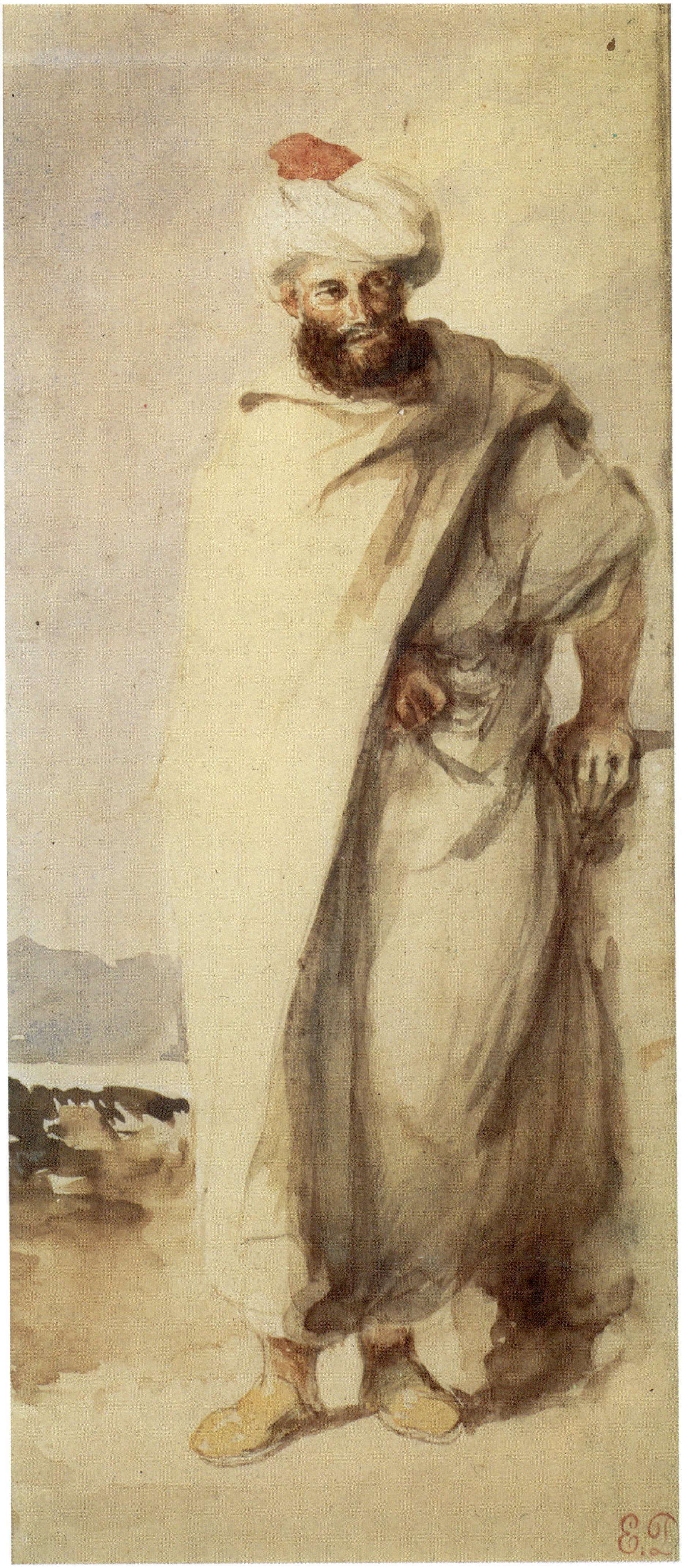

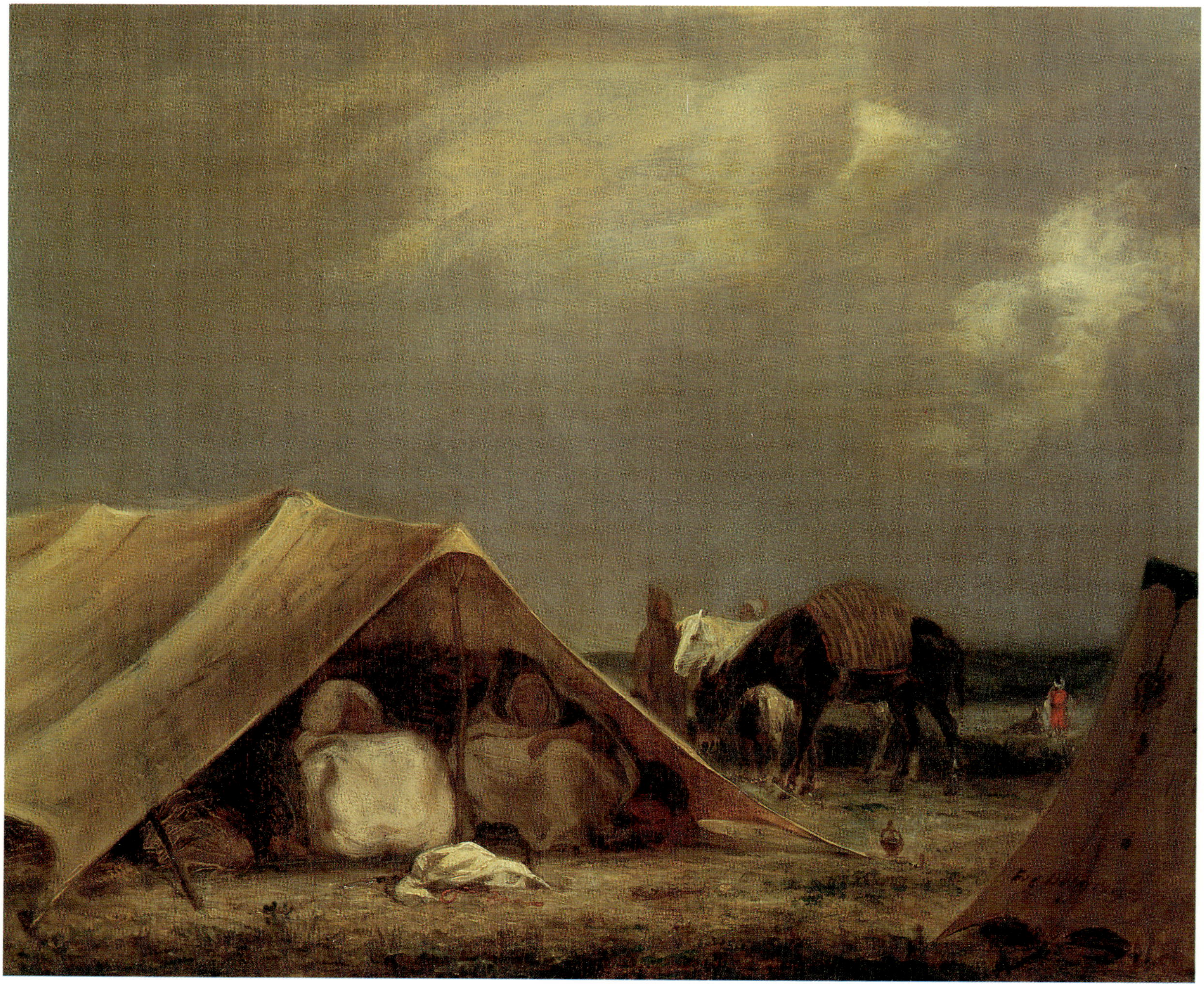

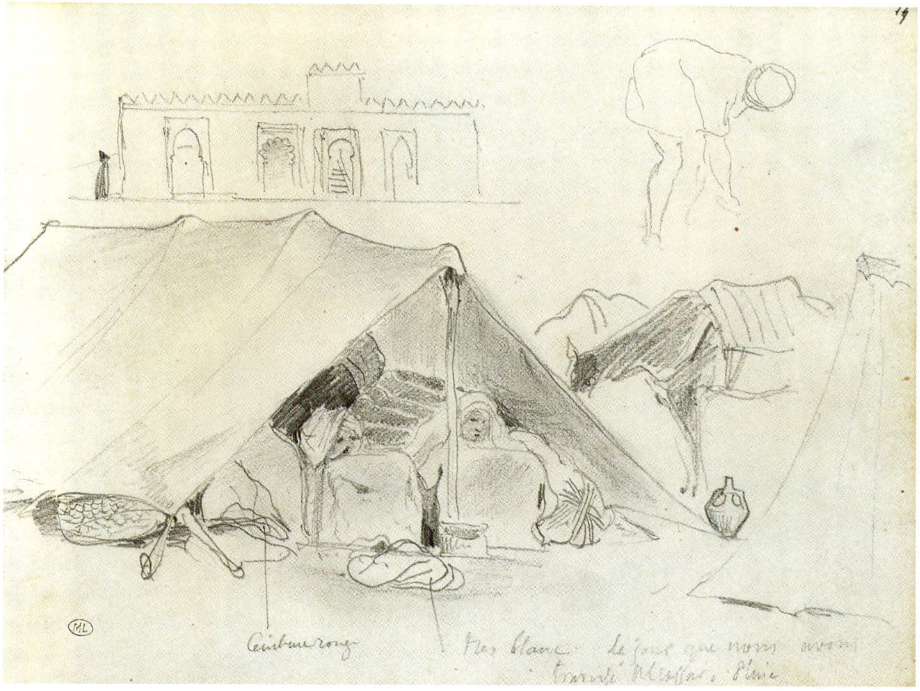

ENCAMPMENT OF ARAB MULE-DRIVERS
Campement au Maroc
74

Oil on canvas
38.1 x 46.3 cm
Signed lower right: Eug. Delacroix
Milwaukee Art Museum, Milwaukee
(M. 1960–46)

PROVENANCE:
G. Arosa; sale, Paris, 25 Feb. 1878, lot 33, to Pinart; Charles Maniez, Valenciennes; sale, 2 Dec. 1918, lot 13, repr., to Countess Venturini; Van Dienen Galleries, New York, by 1930; Julius Weitzner, by 1935; Mr and Mrs Theodore Ball, New York; donated to the Milwaukee Art Center in 1960.

BIBLIOGRAPHY:
Robaut, 1885, no. 688; Johnson, 1986, no. 364, pl. 178; Arama, 1987, p. 210, no. 16, repr.; Arama, 1992, VI, p. 40, repr.

EXHIBITIONS:
Paris, 1864, no. 25; Chicago, 1930, no. 22; Toronto-Ottawa, 1962–3, no. 9; Bordeaux, 1963, no. 24; Regina, 1975, no. 10.

In the 1840s, Delacroix made a list of works (*Journal*, III, p. 372, suppl.) which included '*Mule-drivers from Tetuan camping, grey weather*', a composition directly inspired by a pencil sketch on a page of the landscape album in the Louvre (Département des Arts graphiques, inventory RF 9154, fol. 19 recto), and annotated: 'The day we crossed Alcassar. Rain.' This particular detail drew the attention of the critic P. Haussard who, writing in *Le Temps* in 1839, affirmed, having seen the painting and deploring its exclusion from the Salon: 'This modest little painting has originality and a wonderful sentimental charm. The artist was in Africa the day of this flood, and, hidden under a tent, he sketched the two Moroccan mule-drivers.' The jury of the 1839 Salon refused the painting, probably disconcerted by the dominant moonlight, only broken by the touch of red on the silhouette standing in the background on the right. Although Eugène Bareste (*La Revue du XIXe siècle*, II, p. 234) also considered 'the little Turk's red garment...too bright', he nevertheless regretted the jury's ostracism of 'a charming little sketch' of gracious composition and harmonious colours.

Not in exhibition:
Moroccan Album:
study of an encampment,
Département des Arts graphiques, Louvre.
(RF9154, fol.19r).

STUDY FOR THE SULTAN OF MOROCCO
Étude pour le Sultan du Maroc
75

Pencil, pen and brown ink
19.4 x 30.8 cm
Annotated in Delacroix's hand, in pen and in pencil, top: voir van Thulden—faire les dessins dans l'atelier de Villot à cause du jour qui vient d'en haut. faire un grand tableau—moines au réfectoire par exemple ou dans la grande salle de Séville que j'ai dessinée
Département des Arts graphiques, Louvre (RF 9386)

PROVENANCE:
Delacroix Studio, marked lower centre (L.838 a); sale, Paris, 22–27 Feb. 1864, probably included in lot 351, to Alfred Robaut; Étienne Moreau-Nélaton; bequeathed to the Louvre in 1927 (L.1886 a).

BIBLIOGRAPHY:
Robaut, 1885, probably part of no. 1742; Lambert, 1953, no. 16, pl. XIII; Sérullaz, 1984, I, no. 363, repr.; Johnson, 1986, under no. 369; Arama, 1992, VI, p. 164, repr.

On 22 March 1832, during the audience granted to the Count de Mornay by the emperor of Morocco, Delacroix did not have much time to record the progress of the ceremony, but he just managed to make a hasty sketch in the notebook which he always kept with him and recorded the main events during or after the reception: 'From the gateway, which is mean and without ornament, there came at short intervals small detachments of about eight or ten negro soldiers in pointed caps, who lined up to right and left, then two men carrying lances, then the king, who rode towards us and drew rein when he was quite close.' (Wellington, p. 52; Département des Arts graphiques, Louvre, inventory RF 1712 bis, fol. 19 verso, see p. 96).

Thirteen years later, having supplied several pen and ink sketches to *l'Illustration*, including one of Moulay Abd al-Rahman on horseback flanked by two *moghaznis* on foot, Delacroix exhibited a painting of imposing dimensions at the Salon, for which he had made numerous preliminary studies, in pencil, pen and ink or wash, some of which are presented here (see nos 76 to 79 and 81 to 83). Grouping them together, one can follow the progress of the artist's conception, starting from a precise illustration of the event and ending with a ceremonial portrait of the sovereign, surrounded by the various Moroccans who conducted the negotiations. It is difficult, however, to ascertain in what order these studies were executed. Elie Lambert suggested a possible order (in 1953) which was criticized by Maurice Sérullaz on the grounds of the impossibility of distinguishing sketches executed in Morocco, either on site or from memory, from the preliminary studies effected for the painting show at the 1845 Salon. Lee Johnson proposes a different order, but does not include all the drawings related to the painting. As regards the drawing in this exhibition, Lee Johnson suggests, on account of the group of figures just above the little pencil drawing, that it was probably executed around 1833, at the time when Delacroix learned that he was to be commissioned to decorate the Salon du Roi at the Palais Bourbon.

STUDIES FOR THE SULTAN OF MOROCCO
Études pour le Sultan du Maroc
76

Pen and brown ink
19.5 x 30 cm
Annotated in pen in Delacroix's hand: Eugène
Département des Arts graphiques, Louvre (RF 9391)

PROVENANCE:
Delacroix Studio, marked lower right (L.838 a); sale, Paris, 22–27 Feb. 1864, probably included in lot 351, to Alfred Robaut; Étienne Moreau-Nélaton; bequeathed to the Louvre in 1927 (L.1886 a).

BIBLIOGRAPHY:
Robaut, 1885, probably part of no. 1742; Lambert, 1953, no. 17, pl. XIII; Sérullaz, 1963, no. 341, repr.; Sérullaz, 1984, I, no. 362, repr.; Johnson, 1986, under no. 369; Arama, 1992, VI, p. 164, repr.

EXHIBITIONS:
Paris, 1963, no. 347; Paris, 1982, no. 155

On the right, Delacroix has sketched the silhouettes of the Count de Mornay, Abraham Benchimol and the kaid Mohammed Ben Abou, recognizable by the sabre hanging at his left side. The word *Eugène,* inscribed above an oval, no doubt indicates the place the artist occupied during the ceremony. Mokhtar el-Jamaï faces front, surrounded by various other figures. The three male and female studies from the nude have no connection with the scene of the audience and are probably related to the decoration of the Salon du Roi in the Palais Bourbon, for which Delacroix was commissioned in 1833.

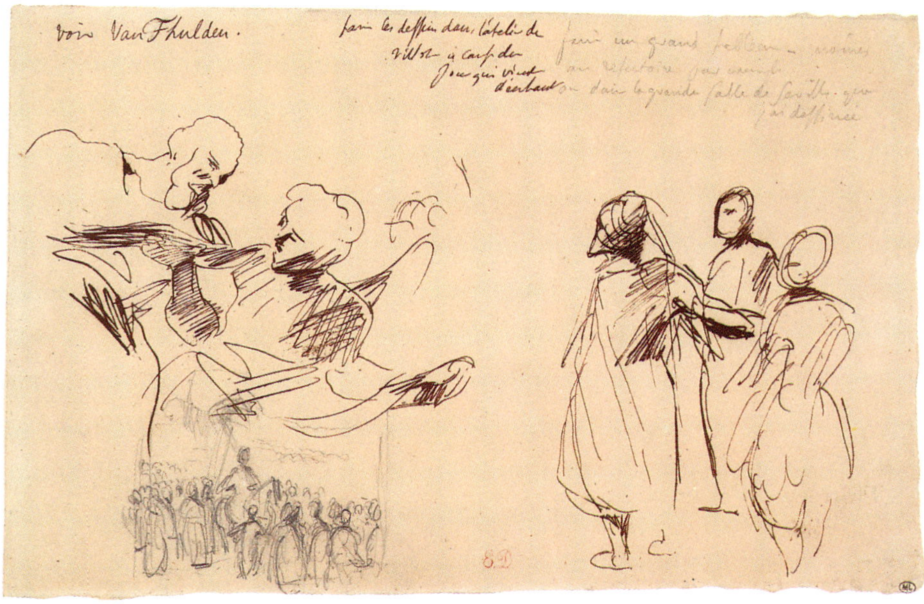

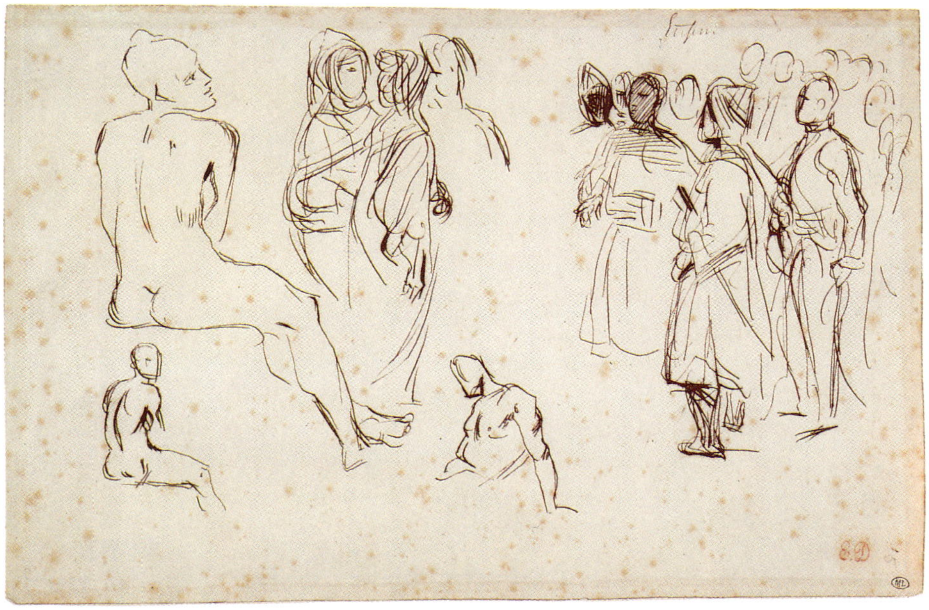

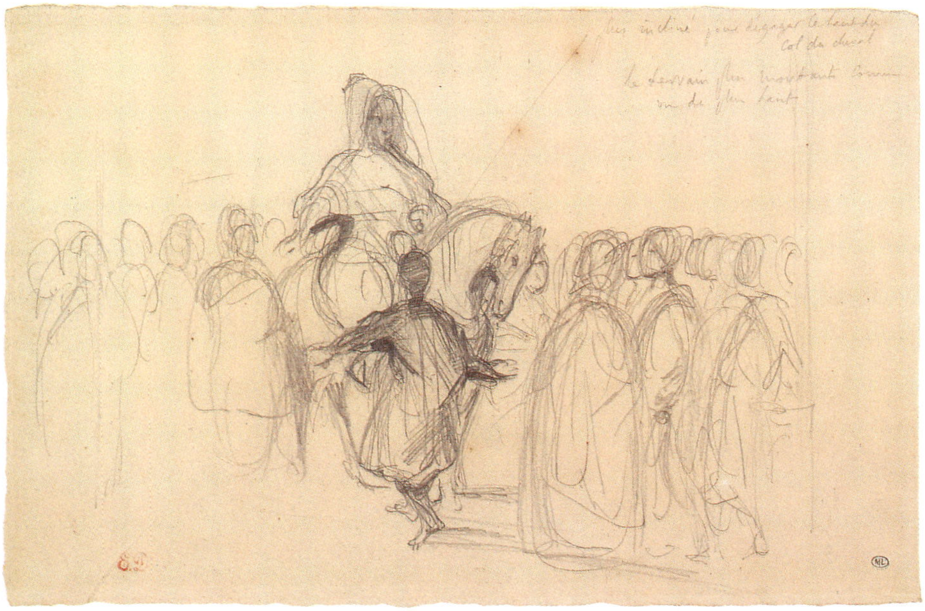

STUDY FOR THE SULTAN OF MOROCCO
Étude pour le Sultan du Maroc

77

Pencil
19.8 x 30.7 cm
Annotated in Delacroix's hand in pencil, top right:
plus incliné pour dégager le haut du col
du cheval—Le terrain plus montant comme vu
de plus haut
Département des Arts graphiques, Louvre
(RF 9383)

PROVENANCE:
Delacroix Studio, marked lower left (L.838 a) sale, Paris, 22–27 Feb. 1864, probably included in lot 351; Alfred Robaut; Étienne Moreau-Nélaton; bequeathed to the Louvre in 1927 (L.1886 a).

BIBLIOGRAPHY:
Robaut, 1885, probably part of no. 1742; Lambert, 1953, no. 14, pl. XI; Sérullaz, 1963, no. 346, repr.; Sérullaz, 1984, I, no. 359, repr.; Johnson, 1986, under no. 369; Dumur, 1988, p. 118, repr.

EXHIBITIONS:
Paris, 1930, no. 436; Paris, 1933, no. 220; Paris, 1951, no. 14; Paris, 1963, no. 341; Paris, 1982, no. 153.

This is probably one of the first sketches for the painting. The figures are spread out horizontally on one level. Facing the emperor, against the light, is Abraham Benchimol. The annotations at the top of the page indicate that Delacroix felt the need to modify this project.

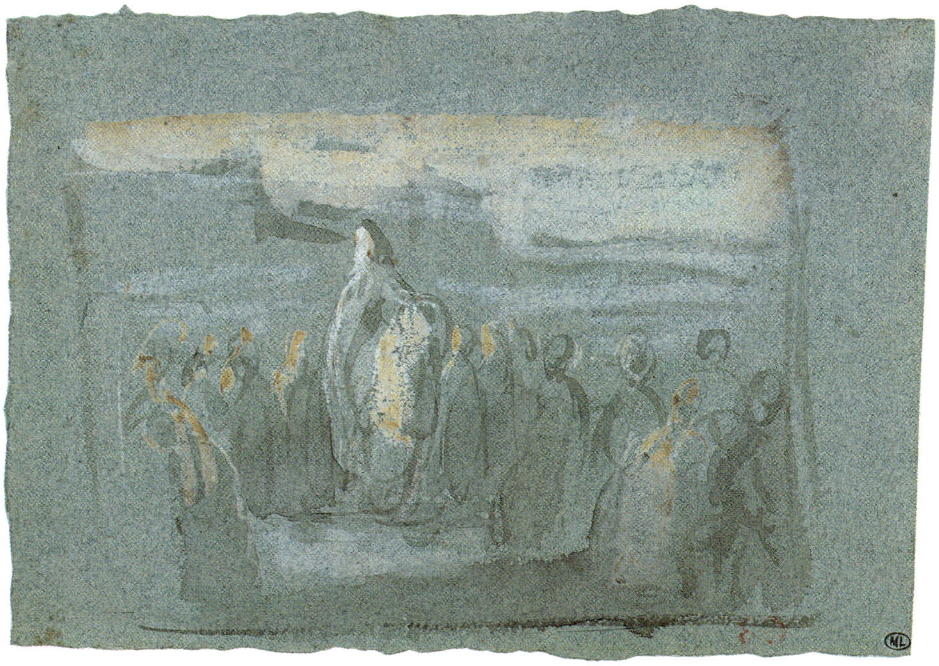

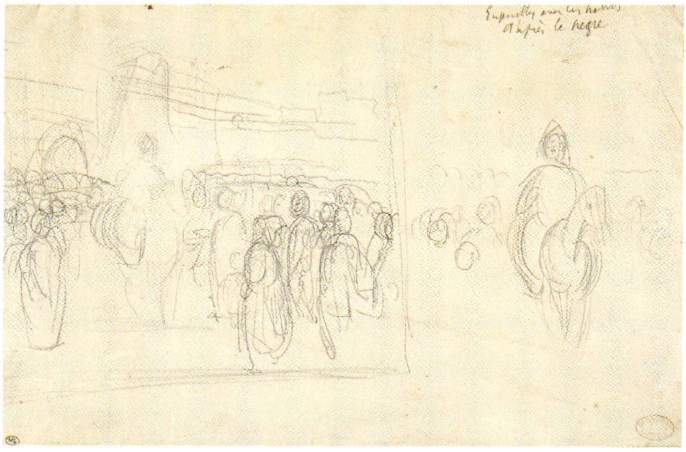

STUDY FOR THE SULTAN OF MOROCCO
Étude pour le Sultan du Maroc
78

Grey wash and gouache on blue-tinted paper
14.7 x 20 cm
Département des Arts graphiques, Louvre
(RF 9381)

PROVENANCE:
Delacroix Studio, marked lower right (L.838 a); sale, Paris, 22–27 Feb. 1864, probably included in lot 351, to Alfred Robaut; Étienne Moreau-Nélaton; bequeathed to the Louvre in 1927 (L.1886 a).

BIBLIOGRAPHY:
Robaut, 1885, probably part of no. 1742; Sérullaz, 1963, no. 348, repr.; Sérullaz, 1984, I, no. 361, repr.; Johnson, 1986, under no. 369.

EXHIBITIONS:
Paris, 1930, no. 437; Paris, 1963, no. 351; Paris, 1982, no. 156.

This rapid study was made in order to determine the positioning of the groups in the final composition. The way the image is framed and the disposition of light and shadow are similar to the painted sketch in the Musée des Beaux-Arts, Dijon (see no. 80).

STUDY FOR THE SULTAN OF MOROCCO
Étude pour le Sultan du Maroc
79

Pencil
19.5 x 30.5 cm
Annotated in Delacroix's hand, in pen, top right:
ensemble avec les habits d'après les nègres
Département des Arts graphiques, Louvre
(RF 22 970)

PROVENANCE:
Darcy, marked lower right (L. 652 F); Cailac; acquired by the Louvre in 1932.

BIBLIOGRAPHY:
Sérullaz, 1963, no. 345, repr.; Sérullaz, 1984, I, no. 358, repr.; Johnson, 1986, under no. 369.

EXHIBITIONS:
Paris, 1963, no. 344; Paris, 1982, no. 152.

This rapid sketch of the general composition, includes, on the right, a schematic silhouette of the emperor on horseback, alone. The layout of the scene is in a squarer, less horizontal format than the other studies.

THE SULTAN OF MOROCCO
Le Sultan du Maroc
80

Oil on canvas
31 x 40 cm
Musée des Beaux-Arts, Dijon (DG 86)

PROVENANCE:
Delacroix Studio, red wax seal at the back of the stretcher; sale, Paris, 22–27 Feb. 1864, lot 137, to Adrien Dauzats; Louis de Planet, following an exchange with Dauzats for another Delacroix painting; remained in the Planet family until 1952; Pierre Granville; donated to the Musée des Beaux-Arts, Dijon in 1969.

BIBLIOGRAPHY:
Robaut, 1885, no. 1744; Lambert, 1953, no. 21, pl. XVI; Sérullaz, 1963, no. 336, repr.; Lemoine, 1976, no. 96, repr.; Johnson, 1986, no. 369, pl. 182; Arama, 1987, p. 120 repr., 209 no. 9 repr.; Dumur, 1988, p. 121, repr.; Arama, 1992, VI, p. 183, repr.

EXHIBITIONS:
Paris, 1963, no. 340; Berne, 1963–4, no. 36; Bremen, 1964, no. 32; Paris, 1973, no cat.; Zurich, 1987, no. 58, repr.

This little sketch, with its dazzling colours and vigorous brushwork, gives a general idea of Delacroix's original conception of the composition, illustrating the reception given to the French diplomatic mission by the emperor of Morocco in front of the Meknes ramparts. The French delegation, presented by Abraham Benchimol, faces the group which includes the emperor and his ministers and advisers, and stands out half in the light, half in the shade.

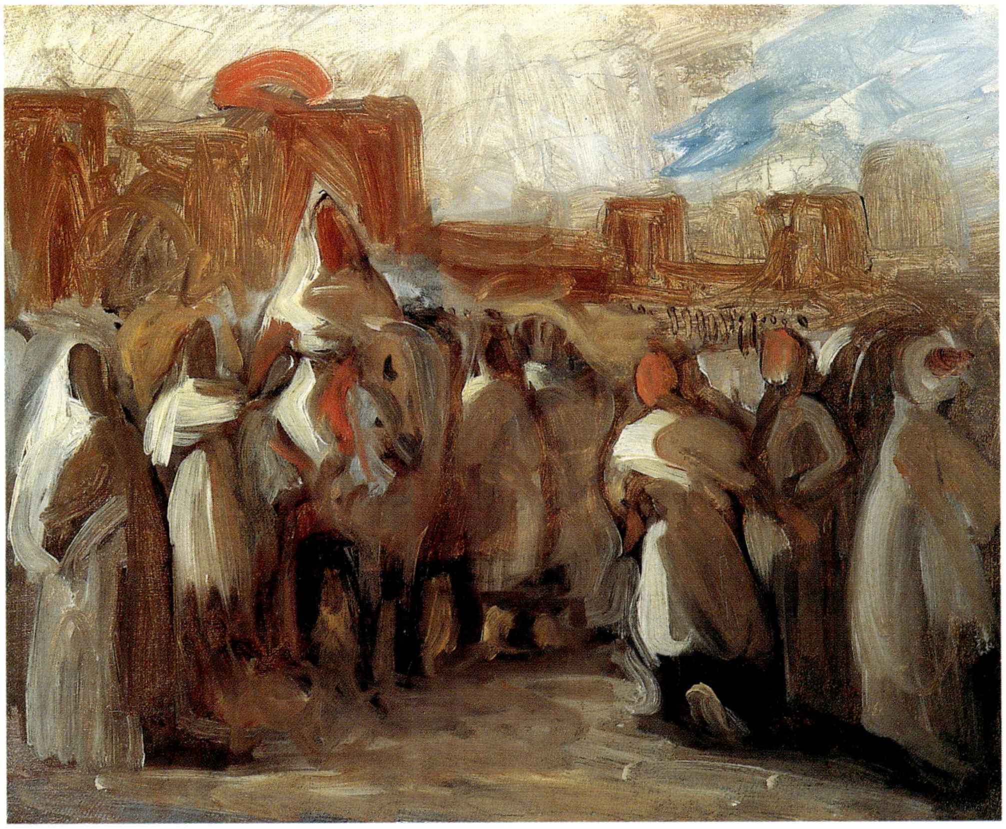

STUDY FOR THE SULTAN OF MOROCCO
Étude pour le Sultan du Maroc

81

Brown wash on grey-blue paper
20 x 21 cm
Private collection

PROVENANCE:
Delacroix Studio, marked lower centre (lot 838 a); sale, Paris, 22–27 Feb. 1864, probably included in lot 351, to M. Gobin.

BIBLIOGRAPHY:
Johnson, 1986, under no. 369; Arama, 1992, VI, p. 182, repr.

EXHIBITIONS:
Paris, 1933, no. 221.

This rapid wash sketch, in an almost square format, portrays the figure of the emperor on horseback, slightly left of centre. On the right, seen from the back and facing a tightly gathered group, is Abraham Benchimol, who is making the presentations.

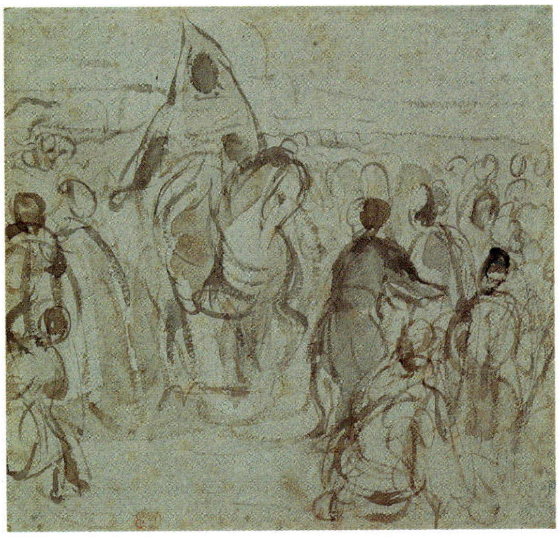

STUDY FOR THE SULTAN OF MOROCCO
Étude pour le Sultan du Maroc

82

Pen and brown ink
20.1 x 29.8 cm
Département des Arts graphiques, Louvre (RF 9389)

PROVENANCE:
Delacroix Studio, marked lower left (L.838 a); sale, Paris, 22–27 Feb. 1864, probably included in lot 351, to Étienne Moreau-Nélaton; bequeathed to the Louvre in 1927 (L.1886 a).

BIBLIOGRAPHY:
Robaut, 1885, probably part of no. 1742; Sérullaz, 1984, II, no. 365, repr.; Arama, 1992, VI, p. 180, repr.

Study for Moulay Abd al-Rahman and one of his servants (*moghazni*).

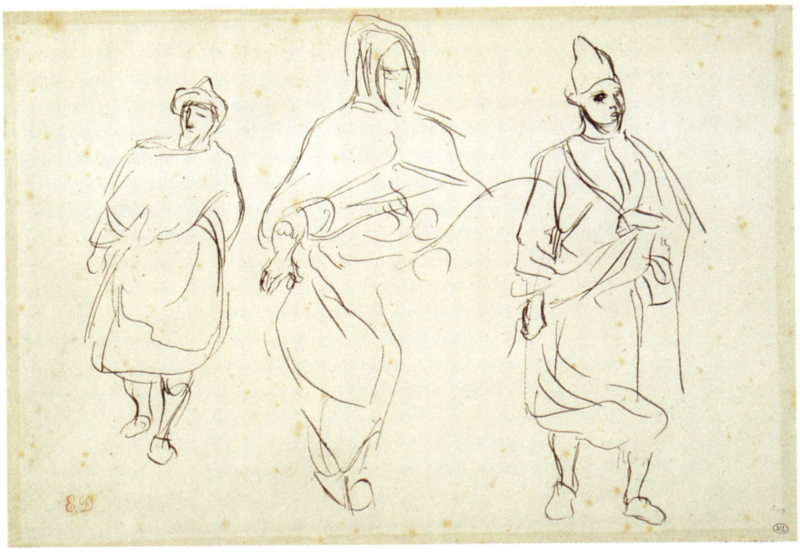

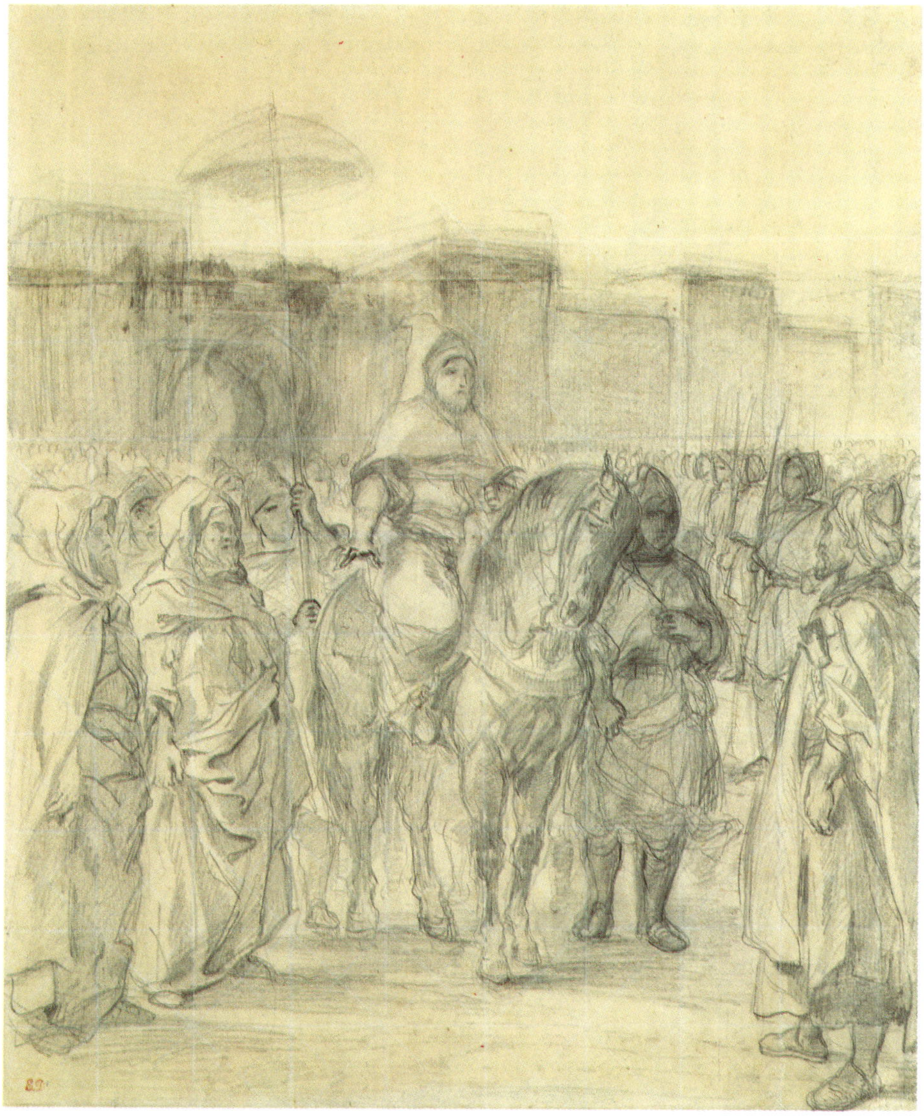

STUDY FOR THE SULTAN OF MOROCCO AND HIS ENTOURAGE
Étude d'ensemble pour le Sultan du Maroc
83

Lead pencil and graphite. Squared in white chalk
59.8 x 49.7 cm.
The Metropolitan Museum of Art, New York (61.202)

PROVENANCE:
Delacroix Studio, marked lower left (L.838 a); sale, Paris 22–27 Feb. 1864, possibly included in lot 351; Arosa; sale, Paris, 27 Feb. 1884, no. 131, to Dr Suchet-Péreire; sale, Paris, 4 June 1937, no. 1; New York, 1961, aquired by the Metropolitan Museum of Art, Rogers Fund.

BIBLIOGRAPHY:
Robaut, 1885, no. 1711; Sérullaz, 1963, no.349, repr.; Johnson, 1986, under nos 369 and 370, p. 183; Arama, 1987, p. 22 repr., 216; Arama, 1992, VI, p. 186, repr.

EXHIBITIONS:
Paris, 1963, no. 343; New York, 1991, no. 44, repr.

This large study, carefully squared in white chalk, must have been executed a short time before the Musée de Toulouse painting, from which the French diplomatic mission is also excluded. Mokhtar el-Jamaï and Mohammed Ben Abou remain in this work, el-Jamaï on the left of the emperor, Ben Abou on the extreme right. For the canvas formerly in the Norton Simon Foundation in Pasadena there exists a pencil drawing of the entire scene (sale, Paris, 22 Nov. 1985, lot 31, repr.; private collection, New York).

THE SULTAN OF MOROCCO AND HIS ENTOURAGE
Muley-Abd-err-Rhahmann, sultan du Maroc, sortant de son palais de Méquinez, entouré de sa garde et de ses principaux officiers
84

Oil on canvas
3.84 x. 3.43 m
Signed at dated lower centre, left:
Eug. Delacroix 1845
Musée des Augustins, Toulouse (Ro 67)

PROVENANCE:
Given to the Musée de Toulouse by order of the Ministry of the Interior, in replacement of the Marc-Aurèle (Musée des Beaux-Arts, Lyon) formerly acquired by decree on 24 June 1845, for the same price.

BIBLIOGRAPHY:
Journal, I, p. 140–1; III, p. 432; Correspondance, I, p. 323; II, pp. 212, 213, 219, 233, 238; IV, p. 277, note 1; V, p. 177–8; Robaut, 1885, no. 927; Lambert, 1953, no. 1, pl. I; Sérullaz, 1963, no. 335, repr.; Johnson, 1986, no. 370, pl. 183; Arama, 1987, p. 121 repr., 211 no. 21, repr.; Dumur, 1988, p. 117, repr.; Arama, 1992, VI, p. 187, repr.

EXHIBITIONS:
1845 Salon, no. 438; Paris, 1885, no. 218; Paris, 1930, no. 114, repr. Album, p. 63; Paris, 1963, no. 339; Zurich, 1987, no. 59, repr.

The catalogue of the 1845 Salon, where the painting caused a sensation, contained a long explanation of the subject, summarized below: 'The painting reproduces exactly the ceremonial audience which the author attended in March 1832, when he accompanied the King's diplomatic mission to Morocco. At the right of the Emperor are two of his ministers, the nearest one is Mokhtar, his favourite, and the other is Amin Biaz, the customs officer. The foremost figure with his back to the spectator is the kaid Mohammed Ben Abou, one of the most respected military commanders. . . . The Emperor, strikingly mulatto, wears a string of mother-of-pearl beads around his arm; he is astride a barb of tall stature, typical of that race. On his left is a page who waves a piece of material from time to time to chase off the insects. The sultan is the only person on horseback.' This description gave the visitors to the Salon the impression that they were looking at a faithful representation of the famous audience of 22 March.

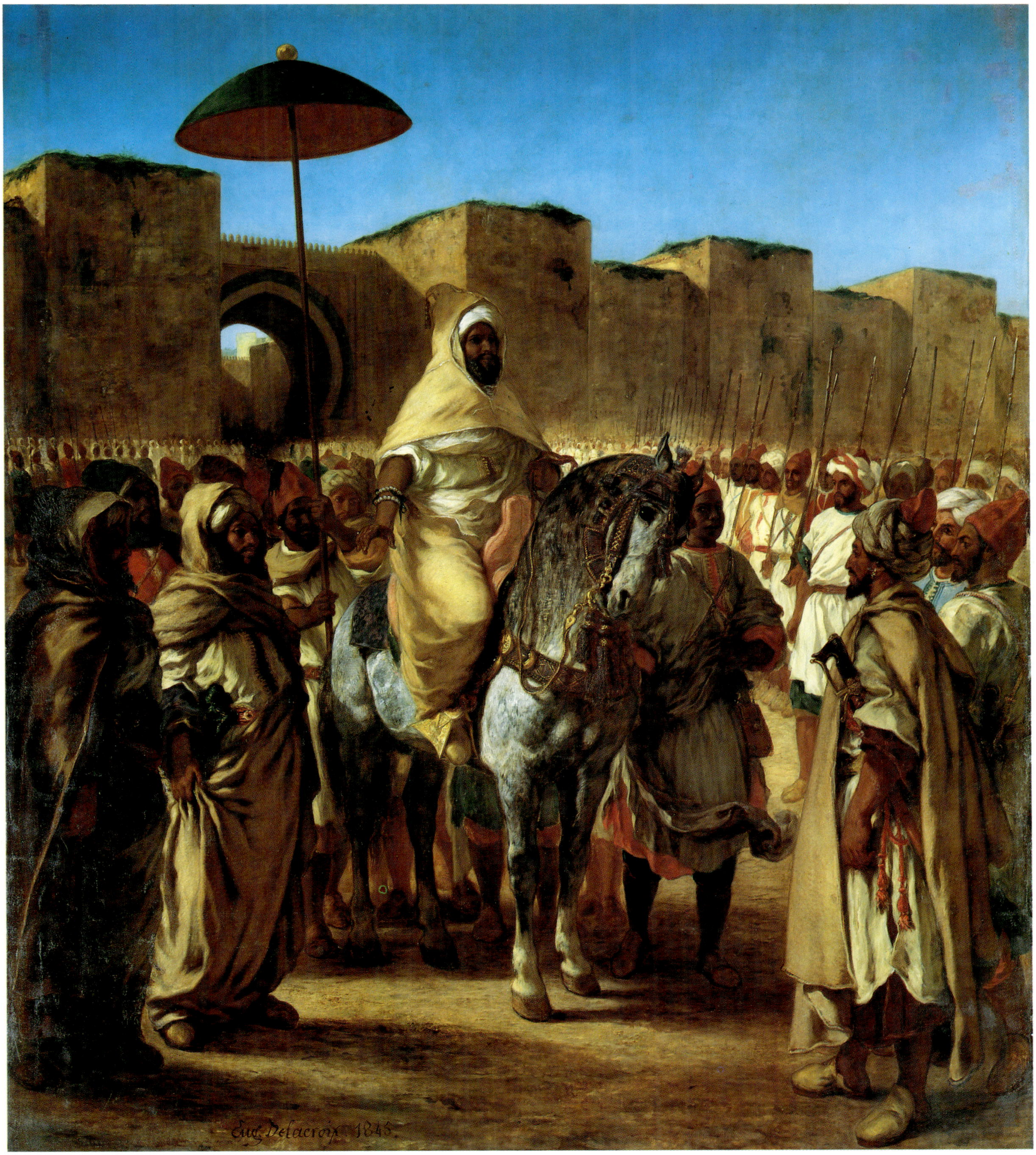

And why should they have doubted this, since they were reminded that the artist had attended in person? And yet . . .

Admittedly, Delacroix had memorized the ceremony in great detail, and he had made care to note the most significant aspects (Département des Arts graphiques, Louvre, inventory RF 1712 bis, fols. 19 and 20), but thirteen years had passed since then. After his return to France, the more he explored the idea, the more the project changed. All the preliminary sketches currently recorded (see nos 75 to 82) testify to these transformations. At the outset, the composition was in a horizontal format, like a vast frieze, and was to include both the French and Moroccan protagonists, as well as the dense crowd, which mingled with the imperial guard. Delacroix's main problem concerned the positioning of the principal figures, starting with the emperor himself. From one page to the next, the artist sketches alternative positions for the Count de Mornay, Abraham Benchimol, the kaid Mohammed Ben Abou and Mokhtar el-Jamaï. Those where the emperor is present (see nos 75-79 and 81-83) prove that, little by little, the artist felt the need to organize his composition around the monarch, the key figure in the scene. This imposed a change of format, eventually entailing the elimination of the French group. Only minor changes were made between the comprehensive squared drawing in the Metropolitan Museum, New York (see no. 83) and the final composition in oil. Instead of a picturesque illustration of the highly coloured ceremony, Delacroix decided on a monumental portrait, composed in a large triangle with Moulay Abd al-Rahman's head positioned symbolically at its apex. The rounded parasol and its slightly oblique line, soften the various vertical lines in the composition, conceived in a dazzling harmony of colours: red head-dresses, dark green parasol and red lining against a resolutely blue sky and white and pale ochre costumes. 'This painting is so harmonious, despite the splendour of the tones', exclaims Baudelaire, 'that it seems grey like nature, grey like the atmosphere in summertime when the sun spreads its twilight of shimmering dust over each object.' (*Salon de 1845*, p. 357). Thoré goes even further: 'The general tone is so harmonious that at first glance this dazzling, varied painting seems sober. Therein lies M. Delacroix's incomparable talent for blending the richest and most varied tones, like musicians who use the complete range of notes. . . . M. Delacroix has attained a supreme degree in art, that of portraying magnificence and grandeur in simplicity' (*Le Constitutionnel*, 18 March 1845).

On the whole, the painting met with a favourable reception from the critics. Even if he found that the draperies were creased, Arsène Alexandre recognized that 'one cannot deny the character, truth and grandeur of this canvas' (*L'Artiste*, 6 April 1845, p. 211). In turn, Charles Blanc praised '[the] background and [the] sky which are of a rare beauty, an unattainable beauty for anyone who is not a colourist. The eye naturally seeks repose in the pleasant tone of these solid ramparts of Meknes: they are superb walls which would impress even Decamps himself . . . and it is pleasant to follow their grave silhouette against the vigorous but not garish sky. The moss and grass covering these imposing ramparts softens their profile' (*La Réforme*, 26 March 1845).

As for Eugène Pelletan, his first impression transported him 'into another dimension. The sky is of a deep, strong blue, a magnificent cover for a land loved by the sun. A limpid, warm atmosphere inhabits this painting and renders all the shadows translucent.' In his opinion the work's main qualities lie in, 'The strong impression of the place . . . drawn from nature, assimilated by the artist's imagination and reflected beyond it. The other merit of this composition is that it is well constructed. The horizontal and vertical lines give the scene all its gravity, but they are skilfully diversified so as to avoid all rigidity and symmetry' (*Démocratie pacifique*, 24 March 1845).

In 1856 Delacroix executed a smaller version of this subject (65 x 55 cm), which has not been traced since its sale by the Norton Simon Foundation in Pasadena (Johnson, 1986, no. 401, pl. 210). He used the same subject in 1862 (Bührle Foundation, Zurich; Johnson 1986, no. 417, pl. 211; see p. 119). In both these cases, the figure of the emperor has been brought forward and the advisers and ministers have been excluded.

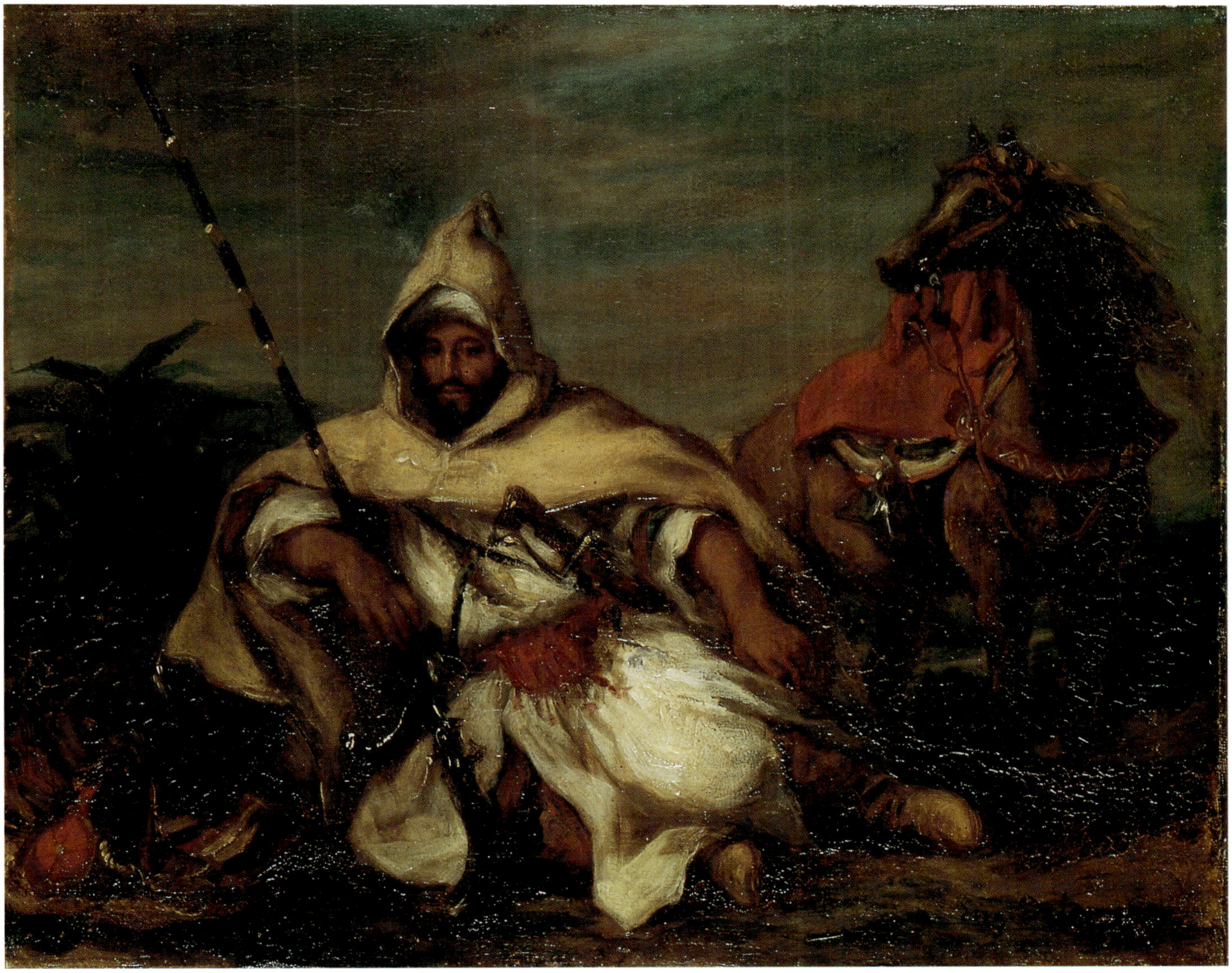

ARAB SOLDIER SEATED AND HIS HORSE
Soldat marocain assis près de son cheval
85

Oil on canvas
32 x 41 cm
Signed and dated lower right:
Eug. Delacroix / 1845
Musée des Beaux-Arts, Bordeaux
(Bx E: 401 / Bx M: 7197)

PROVENANCE:
General Charles Delacroix, the artist's brother, deceased 31 December 1845 in Bordeaux; given by Delacroix in 1846 to the town of Bordeaux according to his brother's will.

BIBLIOGRAPHY:
Correspondance, II, p. 263; Robaut, 1885, no. 1046; Johnson, 1986, no. 371, pl. 175; Arama, 1987, repr. at top pp. 4-5, 211 no. 20, repr.

EXHIBITIONS:
Paris, 1933, no. 183; Kyoto–Tokyo, 1969, no. H–20, repr.

This painting, with a few variations, depicts the same subject as a signed watercolour executed in 1833, later engraved by Frédéric Villot in 1845. Here a single horse replaces the group formed by two Arabs and a horse, originally visible on the right-hand side in the background of the watercolour.

Delacroix probably gave this canvas to his brother, Charles-Henri, Baron de l'Empire, field marshall and Prince Eugène's aide-de-camp, when passing through Bordeaux, in either July or August 1845, on his way to or from a season at Les Eaux-Bonnes in the Pyrenees.

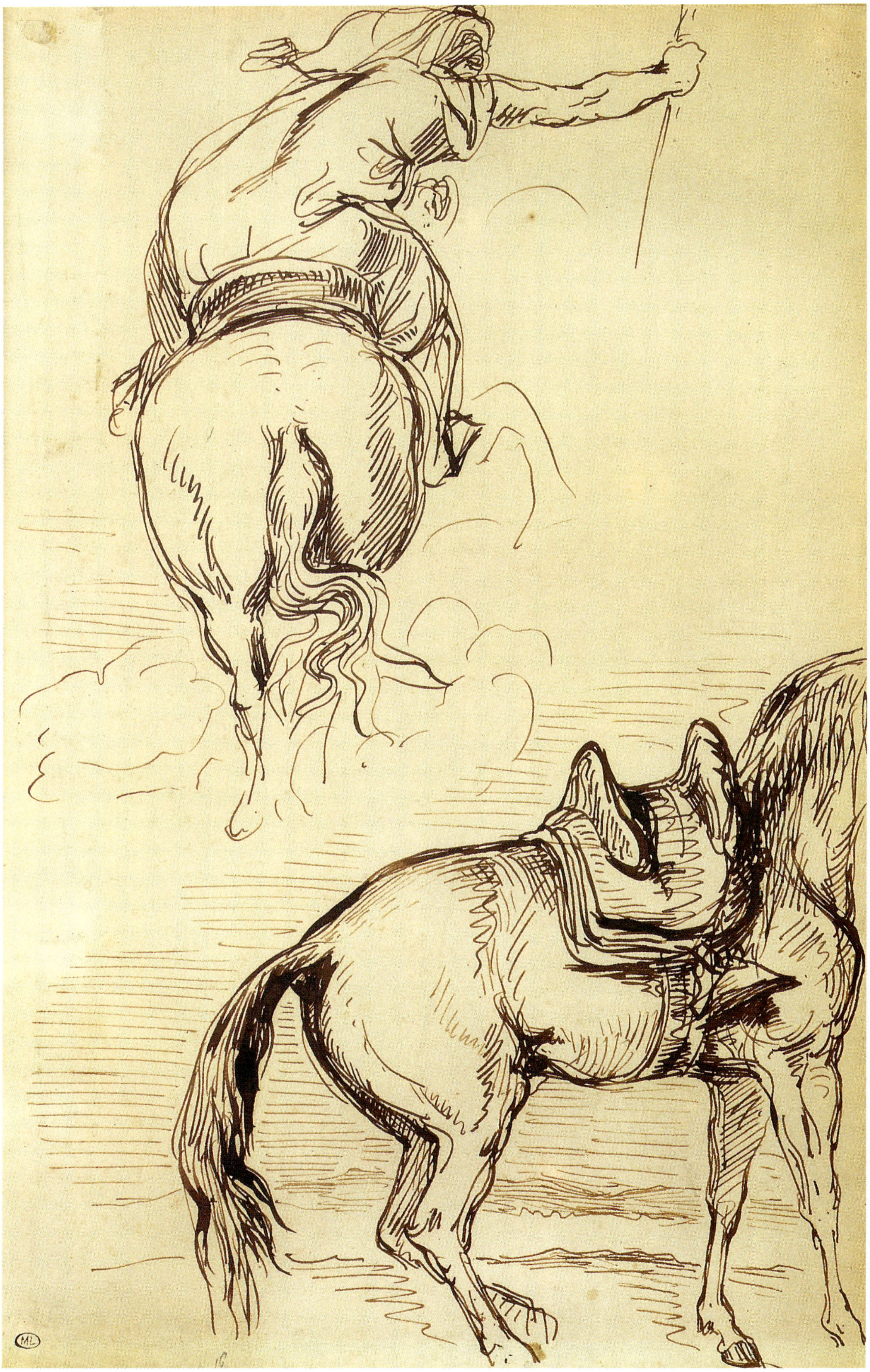

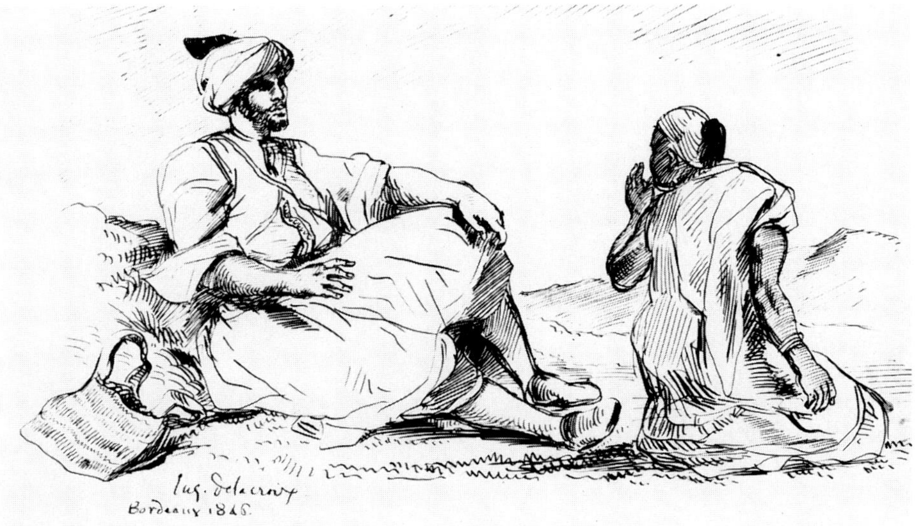

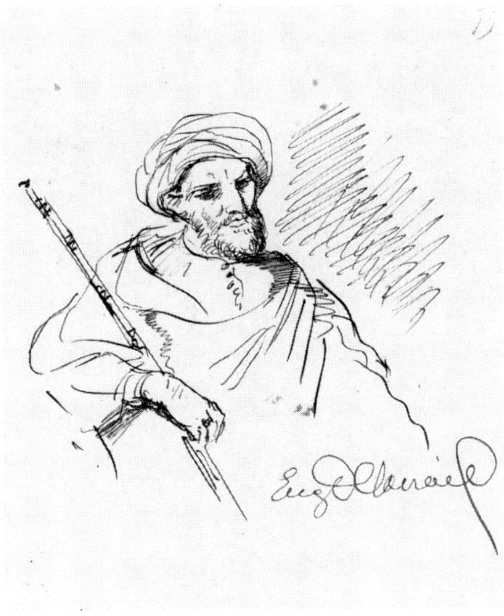

TWO SEATED ARABS
Deux Arabes assis
86

Pen and brown ink
21 x 33 cm
Signed and dated lower left:
E. Delacroix/Bordeaux 1846
Musée des Beaux-Arts, Bordeaux (1982–7.1)

PROVENANCE:
Bought by the Musée des Beaux-Arts of Bordeaux in 1982.

Warned about the deterioration of his brother Charles-Henri's state of health, Delacroix left Paris on 27 December 1845, but only arrived in Bordeaux just after the general had passed away. Heir to his brother's estate, the artist spent the whole of January in Bordeaux settling the necessary formalities. One of the two pictures he gave to the town, in conformity with his brothers wish, was an *Arab Soldier Seated and his Horse* (see no. 85). It is hardly surprising, therefore, that the artist, once again, took up a Moroccan theme in this drawing.

BACK OF ARAB AND HORSE TURNED TO THE RIGHT
Cavalier arabe vu de dos et cheval tourné vers la droite
87

Pen and brown ink
32.1 x 21.1 cm
Département des Arts graphiques, Louvre (RF 10474)

PROVENANCE:
Étienne Moreau-Nélaton; bequeathed to the Louvre in 1927 (L.1886 a).

BIBLIOGRAPHY:
Sérullaz, 1984, II, no. 1725, repr.

This firm-handed drawing was probably inspired by the memory of a *course de poudre*, but executed quite some time after Delacroix's voyage in North Africa (1832).

HALF-LENGTH PORTRAIT OF AN ARAB
Arabe vu à mi-corps
88

Pen and brown ink
18 x 21.5 cm
Signed in pen, bottom: Eug. Delacroix
Private collection. Courtesy of Brame & Lorenceau, Paris

This decorative study corresponds stylistically to a page of studies in the Louvre (Département des Arts graphiques, Louvre, inventory RF 9279; Sérullaz, 1984, II, no. 1721, repr.).

ARABS PLAYING CHESS
Marocains jouant aux échecs
89

Oil on canvas
46 x 55.5 cm
Signed lower left: Eug. Delacroix
National Gallery of Scotland, Edinburgh
(NG 2190)

PROVENANCE:
Arsène Houssaye, by 1848; probably given back to Delacroix, who sold it to the art dealer Weill in 1849; Baron Dejean; Garnier; with Durand-Ruel, 1872; Salomon Goldschmidt; sale, 17 May 1888, lot 30, to Arnold, Tripp & Co.; L. Crist Delmonico; Secrétan; Nickerson, Chicago; acquired in 1900 by the Art Institute of Chicago who sold it in 1931; Joseph Stransky, New York, by 1934; Wildenstein, New York, by 1952; Nathan, Zurich; with Reid and Lefevre, London; acquired in 1957 by the National Gallery of Scotland.

BIBLIOGRAPHY:
Journal, I, p. 236; Robaut, 1885, no. 598; Johnson, 1986, no. 379, pl. 187; Arama, 1987 p. 211, no. 25, repr.

EXHIBITIONS:
Paris, 1864, no. 163; Chicago, 1930, no. 20; Paris, 1930, no. 74; London-Edinburgh, 1964, no. 44; Zurich, 1987, no. 66 repr.

From 1848 this painting was often known as *Arabs playing Chess in Jerusalem (Joueurs d'échecs à Jérusalem)* due to the title given to the engraving made by Ferdinand Lefman which appeared in *L'Artiste*. In his *Journal*, however, Delacroix mentions a painting that was he was already working on at Champrosay in July 1847, entitled *Arabs playing Chess* (*Journal*, I, p. 236). On 13 March 1849 he mentions *Men playing Chess (Hommes jouant aux échecs)*, sold to the art dealer Weill (*Journal*, I, p. 277). The Aïssaoua on the right bears a strong resemblance to the one sitting, also on the right, in *A Street in Meknes* (see no. 59). There are several allusions to draughts players in the notes Delacroix took while in Morocco (Département des Arts graphiques, Louvre, RF 39050, fol. 17 recto), and on a page of studies for *The Sultan of Morocco* (inventory RF 9390) the artist notes: 'The mad Negress of Oran with Men playing Draughts'; Sérullaz, 1984, I, no. 364, repr.). This work is a particularly poetic expression of memories of buildings bathed in sunlight.

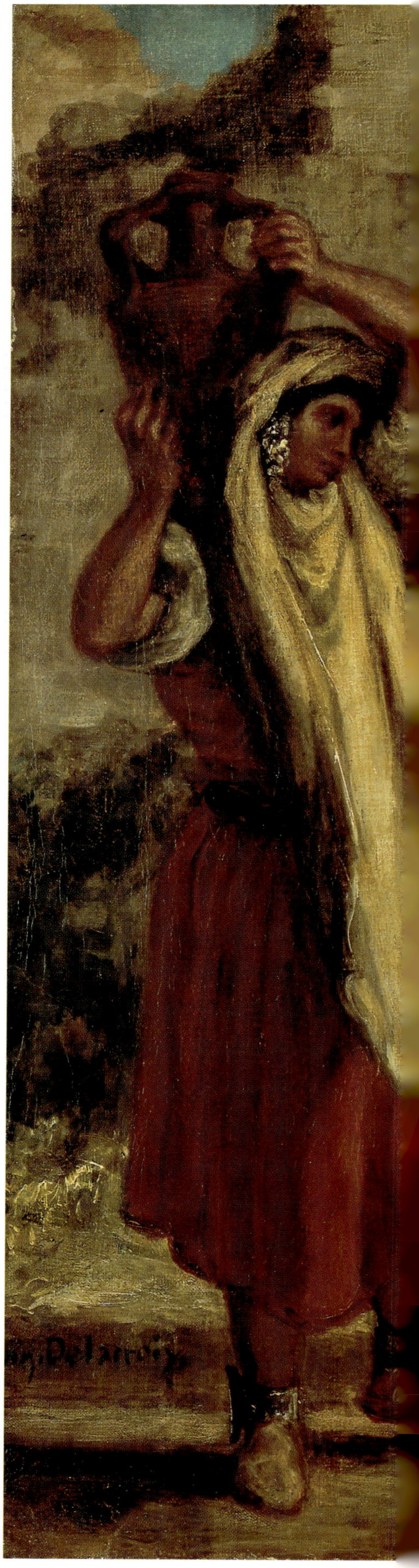

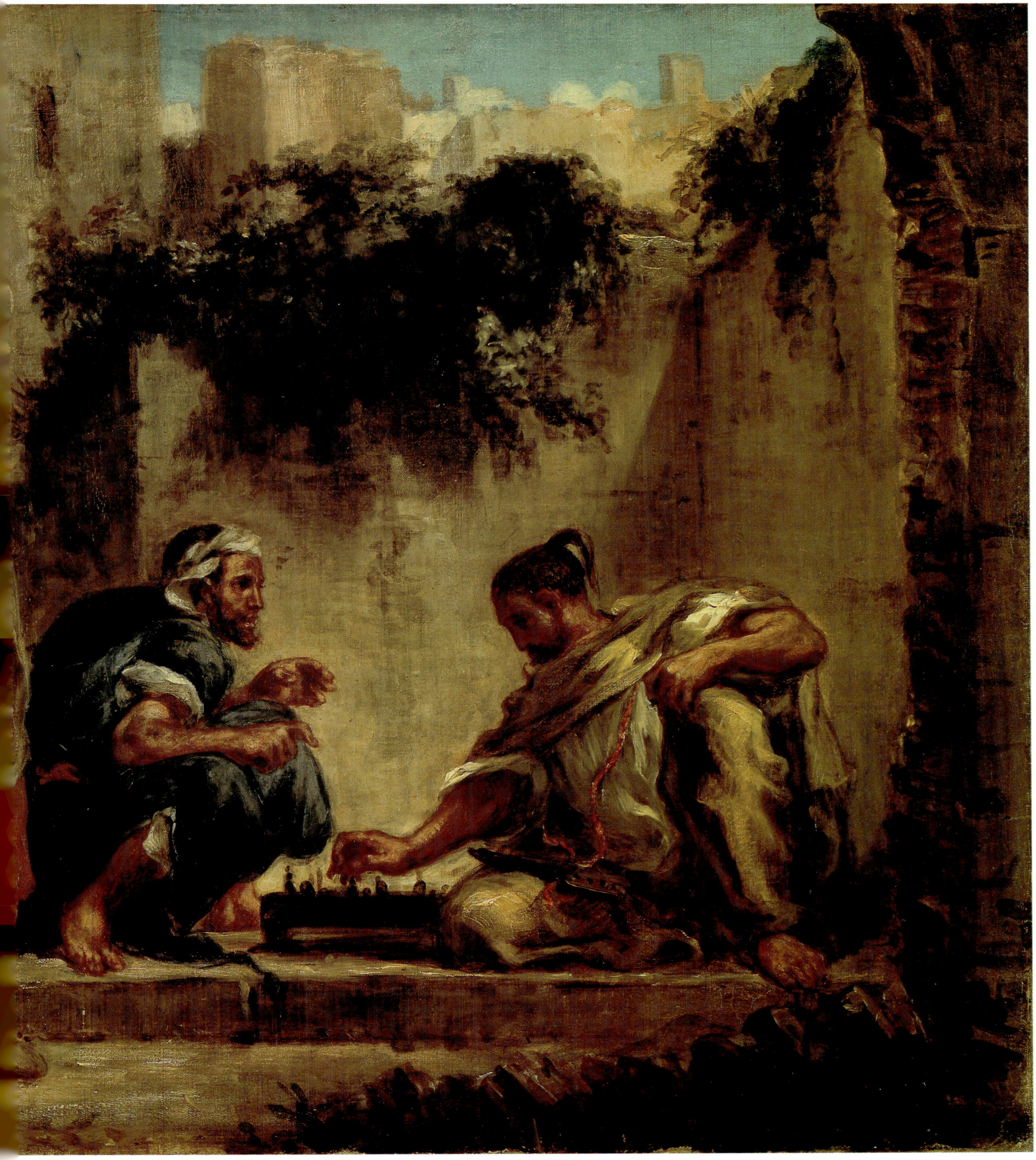

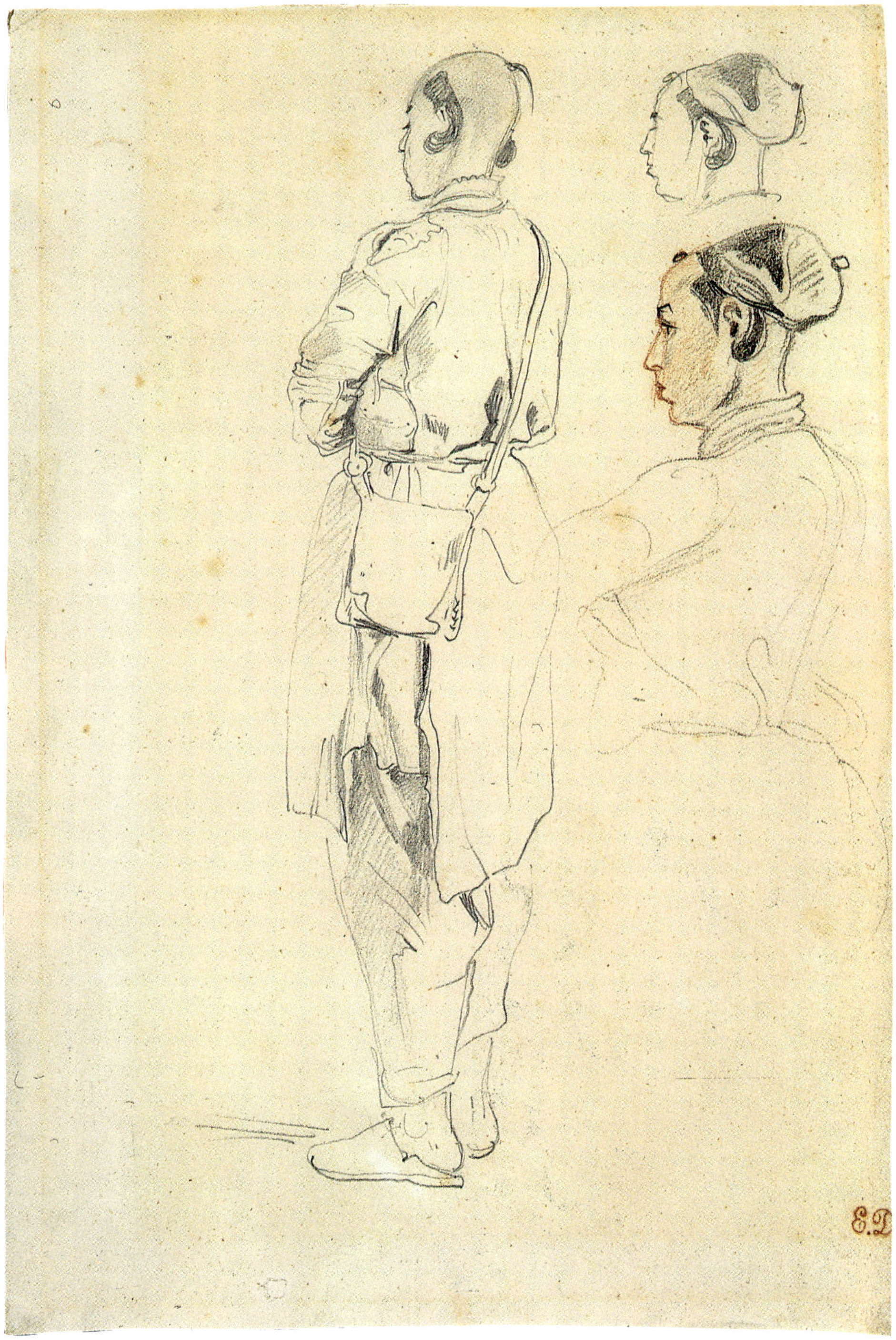

STUDIES OF A YOUNG JEW STANDING
Études d'un jeune juif debout

90

Pencil, Conté crayon and red chalk
31.5 x 21 cm
Musée des Beaux-Arts, Tours (48–2–1)

PROVENANCE:
Delacroix Studio, marked lower right (L.838 a); sale, Paris, 22–27 February 1864, possibly included in lots 571 or 572, to Marcel Guérin; bequeathed to the Musée des Beaux-Arts, Tours in 1948.

BIBLIOGRAPHY:
Sérullaz, 1963, no. 391, repr.

EXHIBITIONS:
Paris, 1963, no. 393.

The figure of this adolescent also appears on the extreme right-hand side of the painting exhibited at the 1848 Salon, *Arab Players (Comédiens et bouffons arabes)*, unfortunately unavailable for this exhibition (Musée des Beaux-Arts, Tours). The scene described in the Salon catalogue does not seem to correspond to a precise episode in Delacroix's stay in Morocco: 'There are two of them and they are acting a sort of parade in the open air outside the gates of a city. They are surrounded by Moors or Jews, seated or standing, who have stopped to listen to them.' The work derives from a watercolour, signed and dated *1836*, in the Bührle Foundation, Zurich: under a sky full of dark clouds, the artist has grouped all the protagonists of the scene in the manner of an antique frieze. This work is one of the finest illustrations of the harmonious coexistence of the various communities living in Morocco during this period.

LIONESS MAULING AN ARAB
Lionne déchirant la poitrine d'un Arabe

91

Etching
27 x 15 cm
1st print avant la lettre
Signed and dated lower left:
Eug. Delacroix / 1849
Bibliothèque Nationale, Paris (DC 183n rés.t.5)

PROVENANCE:
Étienne Moreau-Nélaton; bequeathed to the Bibliothèque Nationale, Paris, in 1927

BIBLIOGRAPHY:
Robaut, 1885, no. 1095; Delteil, 1908, no. 25, repr.

EXHIBITIONS:
Paris, 1933, no. 245, repr.

This engraving illustrates a theme, particularly dear to Delacroix in the years 1840 to 1855, that of the combat between an Arab and a wildcat, which was to inspire the *Lion Hunt*, exhibited at the 1855 Universal Exhibition, and numerous variations on the same theme.

The subject, inversed and with certain modifications, is the same as in a painting exhibited at the 1848 Salon (Nasjonal Galleriet, Oslo; Johnson, 1986, no. 178, pl. 11). A second version (whereabouts unknown) executed at about the same time, emphasized a more bloodthirsty aspect of the scene by portraying the overpowered Arab with his legs overhanging a precipice. Delacroix also painted the fatal confrontation between an Arab and a lion in a watercolour (private collection).

LIONESS MAULING AN ARAB
Lionne déchirant la poitrine d'un Arabe
92
Etching
13 x 27 cm
2nd print, sanguine
Signed and dated lower left:
Eug. Delacroix / 1849
Musée Eugène Delacroix, Paris (M.D. 1992–5)
PROVENANCE:
Maurice Moiroud; donated by Mme Maurice Moiroud in 1992 in memory of her husband.

See the preceding number.

The second print of this engraving was published in *L'Artiste* (the stamp of the review is visible lower left and the title appears in capital letters at top centre).

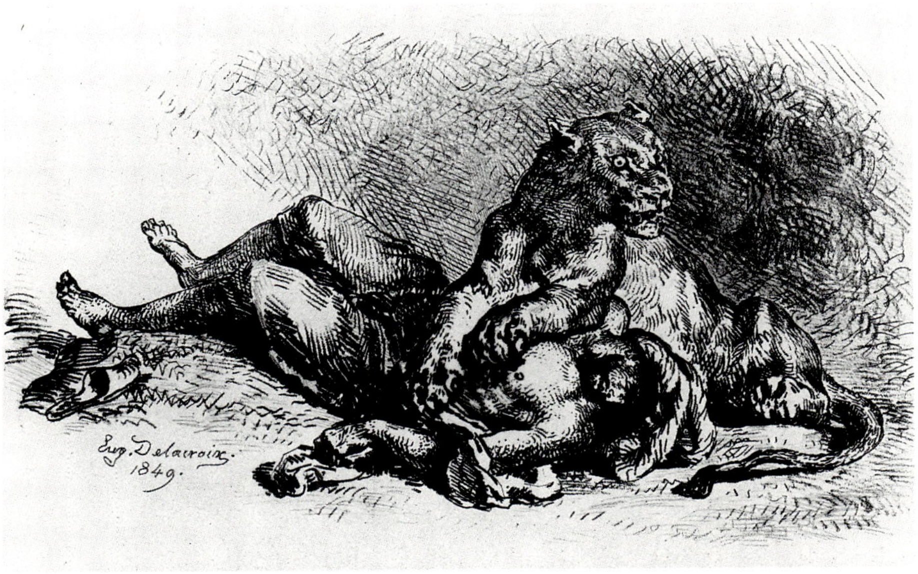

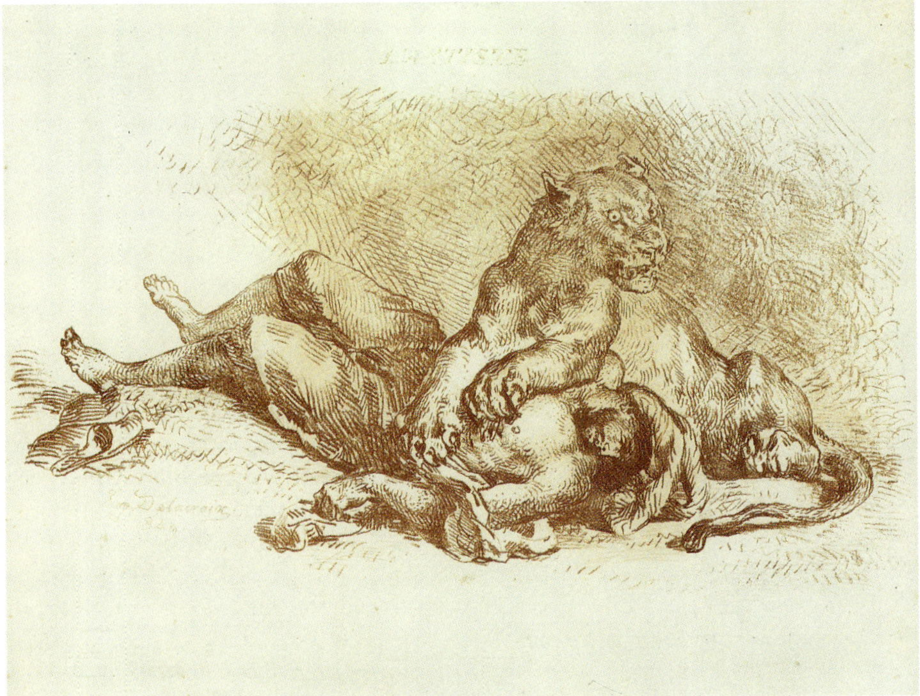

ARAB RIDING A REARING HORSE
Cavalier marocain au galop
93
Pen and brown ink
32.5 x 21 cm
Private collection
PROVENANCE:
Delacroix Studio, marked lower right (L.838 a); sale, Paris, 22–27 Feb. 1864, lot 419, to M. de Laage; Félix Faure; sale, Paris, 27 Mar. 1992, lot 3.
BIBLIOGRAPHY:
Robaut, 1885, no. 1105; Arama, 1987, p. 84 repr., 217.

Alfred Robaut (op. cit.) catalogued this drawing as dating from 1849 and grouped it with two other cavalry studies. The first, technically similar to this one, represents an *Arab Horseman Crossing a River (Un Cavalier arabe passant un gué)*; it was engraved on zinc for *l'Illustration* in September 1846. The second is a pencil sketch of an Arab rider climbing a hill. Like the drawing in this exhibition, *Arab Horseman Crossing a River* was bought in the posthumous Delacroix sale by Baron de Laage (no. 420 of the catalogue; now in a private collection).

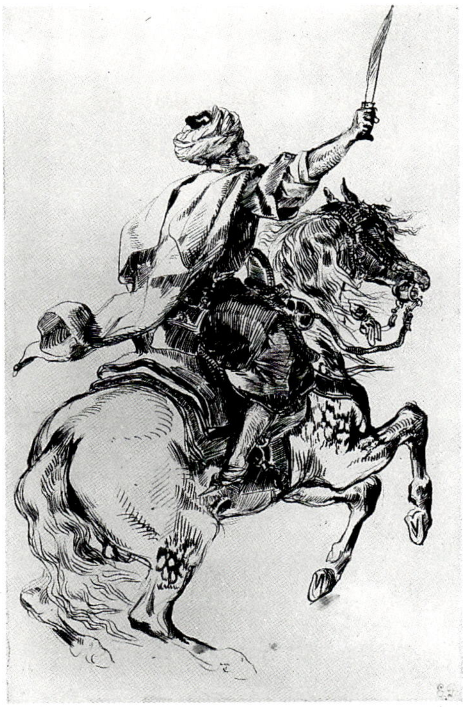

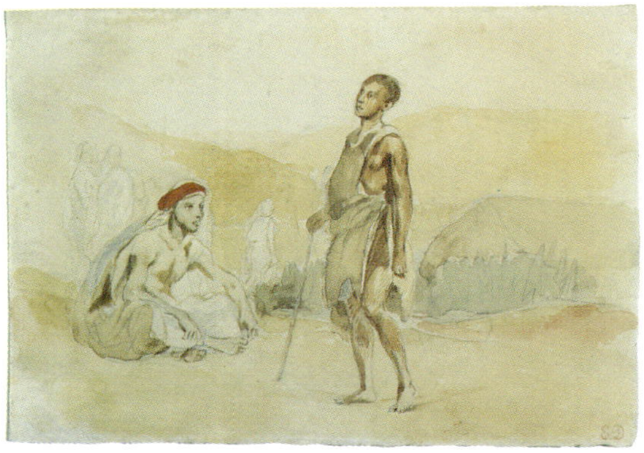

SEATED ARAB
Arabe assis

94

Oil on canvas
43.5 x 44 cm
Private collection. Courtesy of the Galerie Schmit, Paris

PROVENANCE:
Gift of the artist to an employee of Haro's, M. Tripart; André Joubin, by 1930; Countess de Lenclos, by 1952.

BIBLIOGRAPHY:
Journal, I, pp. 331, 424; II, p. 437; Johnson, 1986, no. 385, pl. 191; Dumur, 1988, p. 100, repr.

EXHIBITIONS:
Paris, 1930, no. 140, repr. Album, p. 76; Paris, 1933, no. 188; London, 1952, no. 37.

The unfinished aspect of this painting makes it impossible to give it a precise date, even if it is mentioned several times in Delacroix's *Journal* in the year 1850. Lee Johnson has pointed out the similarity of the pose to that of an Arab seated in the background of the watercolour reproduced left.

Not in exhibition:
Moroccans in the Countryside (Marocains dans la campagne),
watercolour and pencil drawing.
The Cleveland Museum of Art,
Mr and Mrs Lewis B. Williams Collection

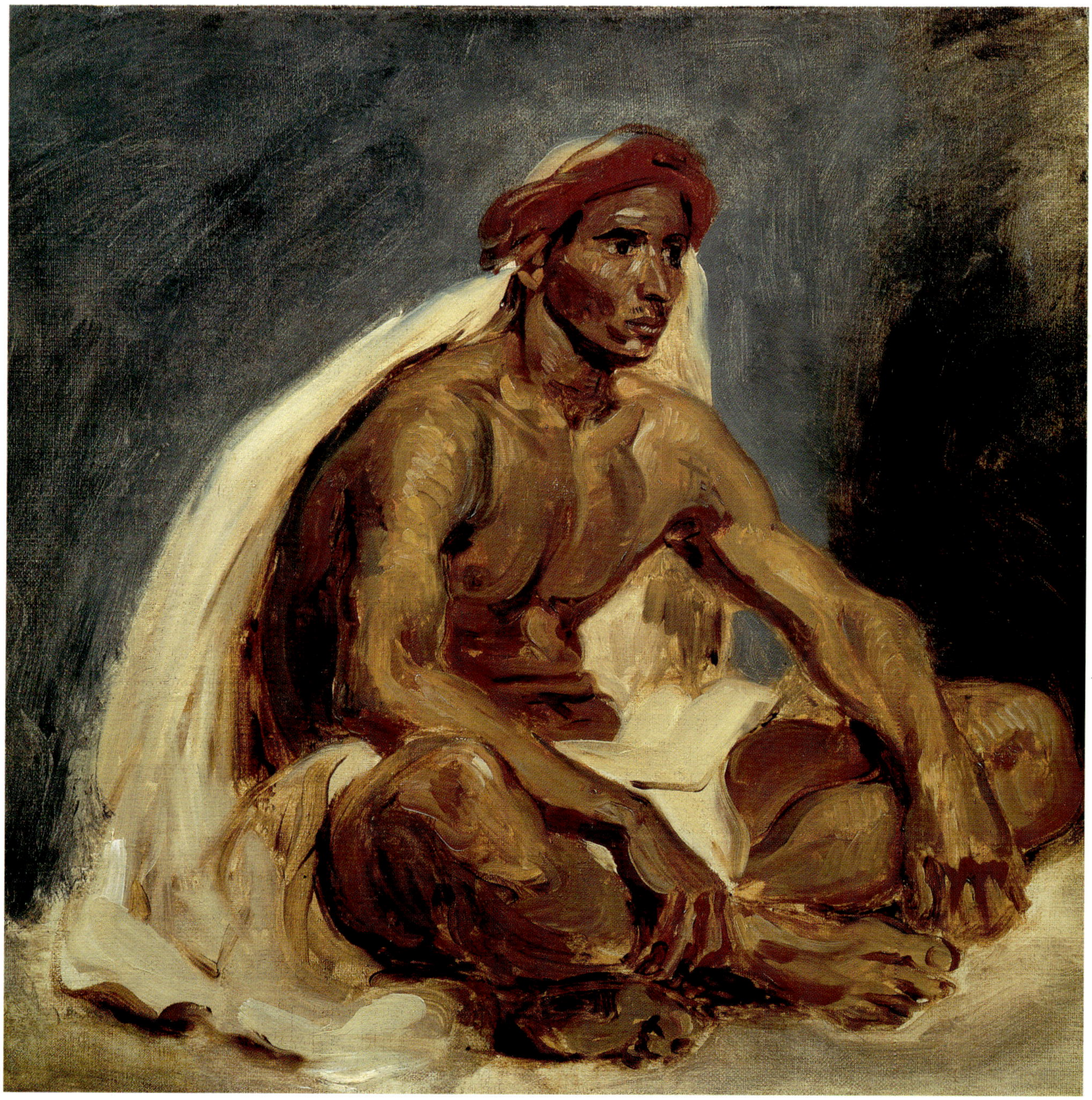

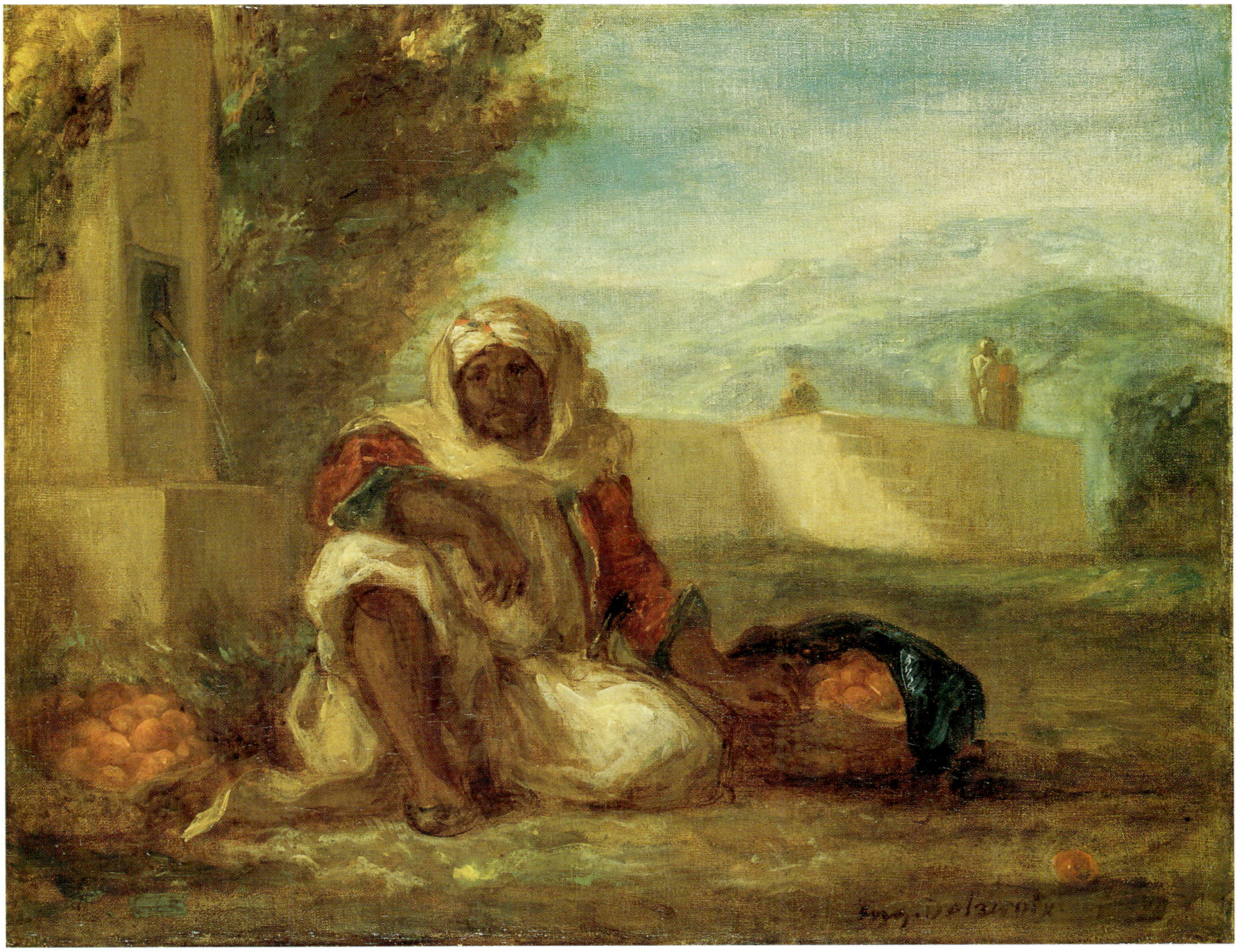

AN ORANGE-SELLER
Un marchand d'oranges
95

Oil on canvas
27.5 x 35.5 cm
Signed lower right: Eug. Delacroix
Kunsthaus, Zurich (2475)

PROVENANCE:
Sold by Delacroix to the art dealer Weill in 1853; Mme Thattet, friend of Alfred de Musset; Mme F. ; sale, Paris, 11 May 1892, no. 32; with Tempelaere in 1897; Edouard Martel; Bernheim-Jeune then Georges Petit, Jan. 1899; M.P. Peytel, by 1930; acquired in 1939 by the Kunsthaus, Zurich.

BIBLIOGRAPHY:
Robaut annotated, no. 1565 bis; Johnson, 1986, no. 392, pl. 202; Arama, 1987, p. 106, repr., 212 no. 32, repr.; Dumur, 1988, p.105, repr.

EXHIBITIONS:
Paris, 1930, no. 61; Paris 1933, no. 176; Zurich, 1939, no. 320; Berne, 1963–4, no. 35; Bremen, 1964, no. 31.

As Lee Johnson has suggested, this painting probably corresponds to the painting of the *Orange-Seller* which figures, without any other details, in a list of four paintings Delacroix sold to the art dealer Weill in 1853 (*Journal*, I, p. 502). This is one of the rare compositions in which the artist abandons the haughty, armed Arab figures in favour of an intimate, calm portrait, bathed in a golden light, which gives the scene a poetic atmosphere tinged with melancholy. A pastel of the same subject was included in the posthumous Delacroix sale (Robaut, 1885, no. 1605).

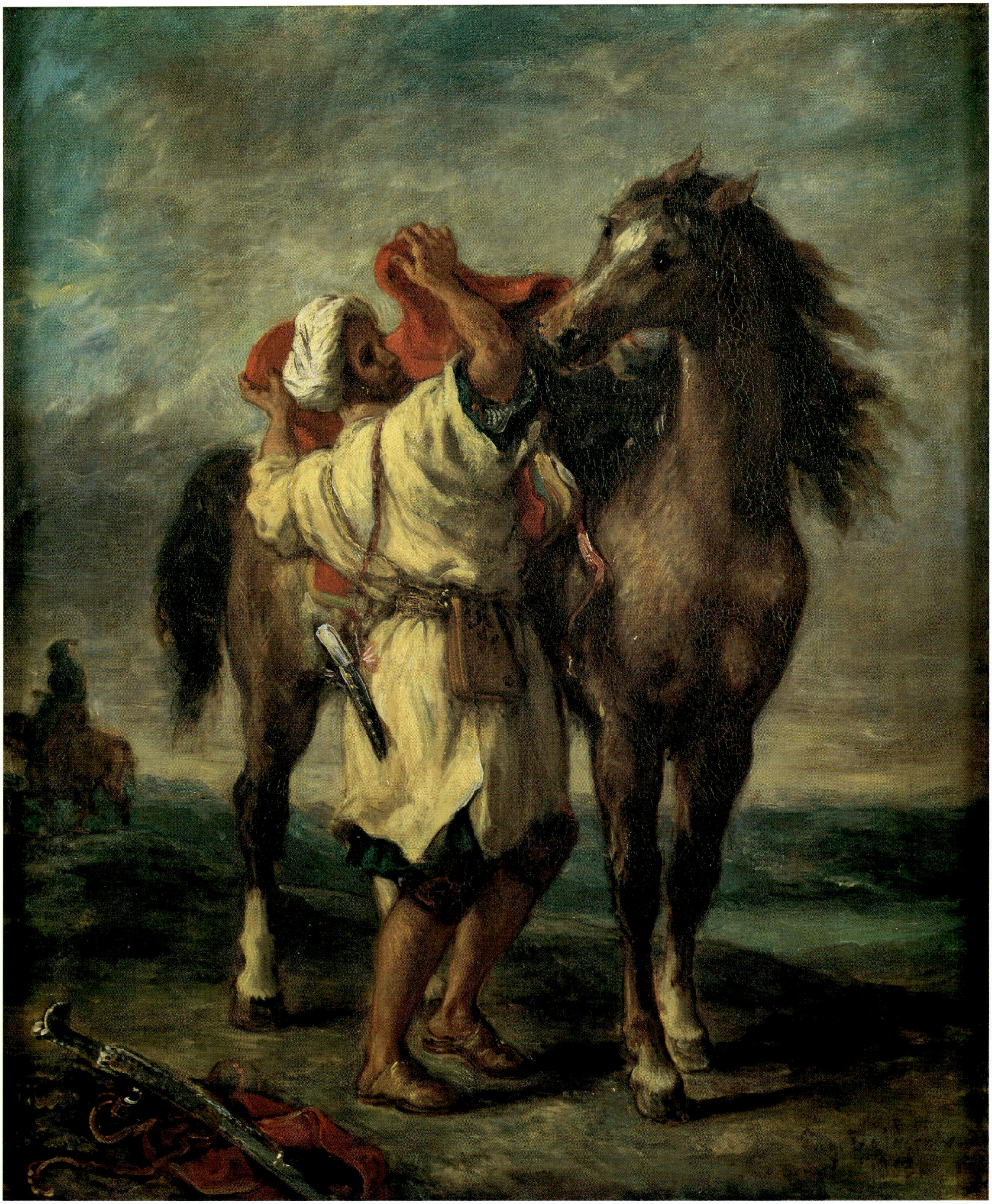

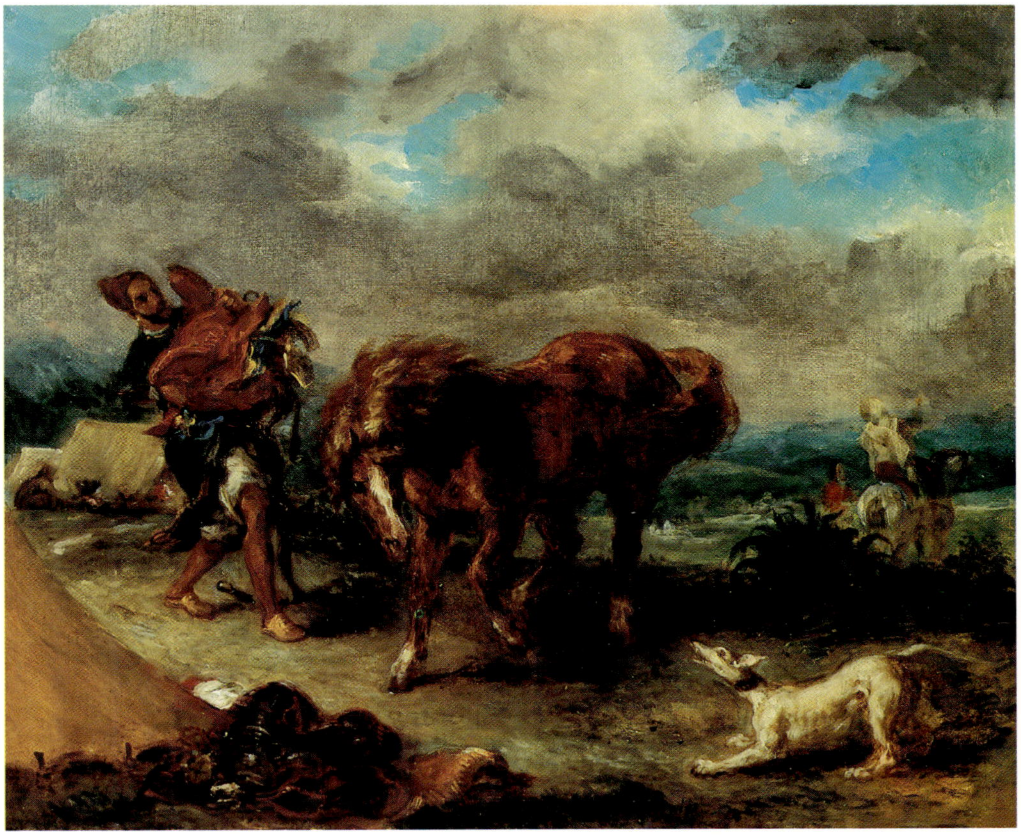

ARAB SADDLING HIS HORSE
Arabe sellant son cheval
96

Oil on canvas
56 x 47 cm
Signed and dated lower right: Eug. Delacroix / 1855
Hermitage Museum, St Petersburg (3852)

PROVENANCE:
Kucheleff-Besborodko; bequeathed to the Museum of the Academy of Fine Arts, St Petersburg, 1862; transferred to the Hermitage in 1922.

BIBLIOGRAPHY:
Sérullaz, 1963, no. 475, repr.; Johnson, 1986, no. 398, pl. 207; Arama, 1987, p. 125 repr., 213 no. 41, repr.

EXHIBITIONS:
Paris, 1963, no. 470; London-Edinburgh, 1964, no. 201.

No document has ever elucidated the circumstances in which this painting came to be in Russia during Delacroix's lifetime. Stylistically, the work corresponds to a series of paintings representing Arabs either about to mount a horse, saddling it, or on horseback, in each of which the figure is situated in a more or less detailed landscape (Johnson, 1986, nos 384, 386, 387, 396; pl. nos 193, 194, 195, 206). A pen drawing of the same subject was included in the posthumous Delacroix sale (no. 418; private collection).

ARAB ABOUT TO SADDLE HIS HORSE
Arabe s'apprêtant à seller son cheval
97

Oil on canvas
50 x 61.5 cm
Signed and dated lower centre: 1857 Eug. Delacroix
Szépmüvészeti Muzéum, Budapest (385 3)

PROVENANCE:
Soultzener, 1885; Antony Roux; sale, Paris, 19 May 1914, lot 14; acquired in June 1914 by the Budapest Museum, courtesy of Bernheim-Jeune.

BIBLIOGRAPHY:
Journal, II, pp. 449, 461, 475; Robaut, 1885, no. 1317; Sérullaz, 1963, no. 489, repr.; Johnson, 1986, no. 404, pl. 209; Arama, 1987, p. 214, no. 54, repr.; Arama, 1992, VI, p. 104, repr.

EXHIBITIONS:
Paris, 1885, no. 205; Paris, 1930, no. 174, repr. Album, p. 92; Paris, 1963, no. 485; Zurich, 1987, no. 107, repr.

See the preceding number. Delacroix began this painting, depicting a *moghazni*, in the spring of 1856 at Champrosay. He was still working on it in October, but the exact date of its completion is not known.

MOROCCAN TROOPS FORDING A RIVER
Passage du gué
98
Pencil
19 x 24 cm
Musée des Beaux-Arts, Dijon (DG 554)
PROVENANCE:
Delacroix Studio, marked lower right (L.838 a); sale, Paris, 22–27 Feb. 1864; Pierre Granville; donated to the Musée des Beaux-Arts, Dijon.
BIBLIOGRAPHY:
Lemoine, 1976, no. 100; Johnson, 1986, p. 205.

Study for cat. no. 99 below.

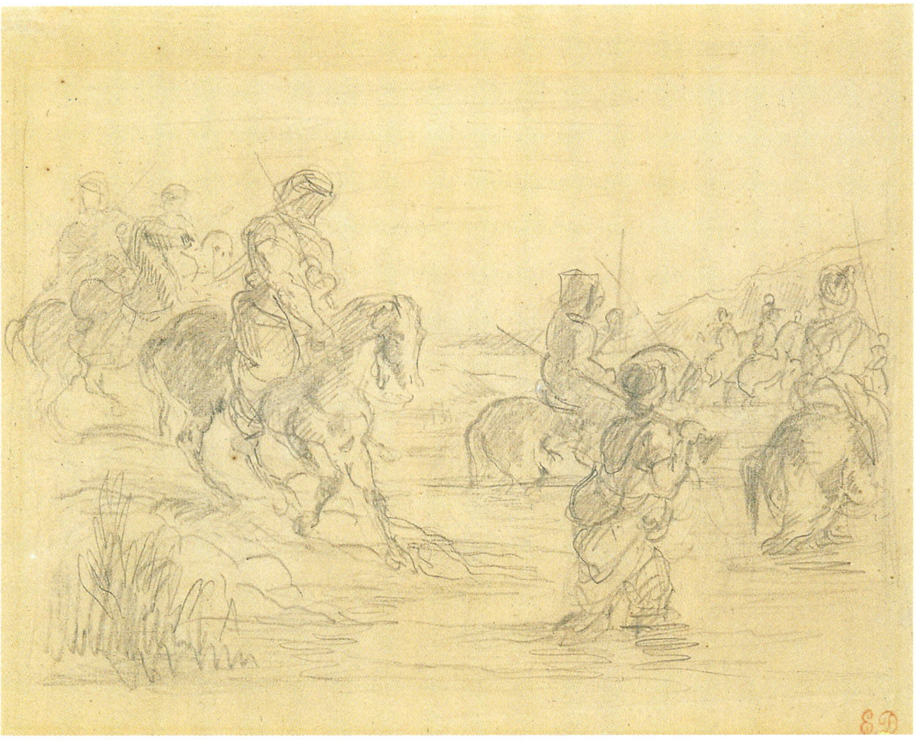

MOROCCAN TROOPS FORDING A RIVER
Le passage du gué
99
Oil on canvas
60 x 73 cm
Signed and dated lower left: Eug. Delacroix 1858
Musée d'Orsay, Paris (RF 1987)
PROVENANCE:
Commissioned from Delacroix by Count Anatole Demidoff, Prince of San Donato, by 1856 (?); sale, Paris, 21 Feb. 1870, lot 27, to Petit; Edouard Kums, Antwerp; sale, 17 May 1898, lot 5, to Isaac de Camondo; bequeathed to the Louvre in 1908, entered the collection in 1914.
BIBLIOGRAPHY:
Journal, II, p. 442; Robaut, 1885, no. 1347; Johnson, 1986, no. 406, pl. 215; Arama, 1987, p. 123 repr., 214 no. 50, repr.; Arama, 1992, VI, p. 56, repr.
EXHIBITIONS:
Paris, 1930, no. 176; Paris, 1933, no. 200; Paris, 1951, no. 6; Bordeaux, 1963, no. 54, repr.; Paris, 1967, no. 8.

In this painting, Delacroix recalls the fording of the rivers on their outgoing and return journeys from Tangier to Meknes. On 9 March 1832, he noted in his dark-brown sketch-book 'Left the Alcassar camp late. . . . Arrived at the river bank. Tall trees at the edge of the river. Dangerous descent', and the next day: 'Crossed the river Emda which meanders in the form of the figure three.' On 5 April, having left Meknes, the mission crossed the same river again. On 7 April they had to cross the 'Wharrah river' (*oued Ouerrha*), 'not deep', Delacroix noted. On 11 April they forded 'a little muddy river' (*oued Mharhar)* (Département des Arts graphiques, Louvre, RF 1712 bis, fol. 10 verso, 11 recto and verso, 28 recto, 29 recto).

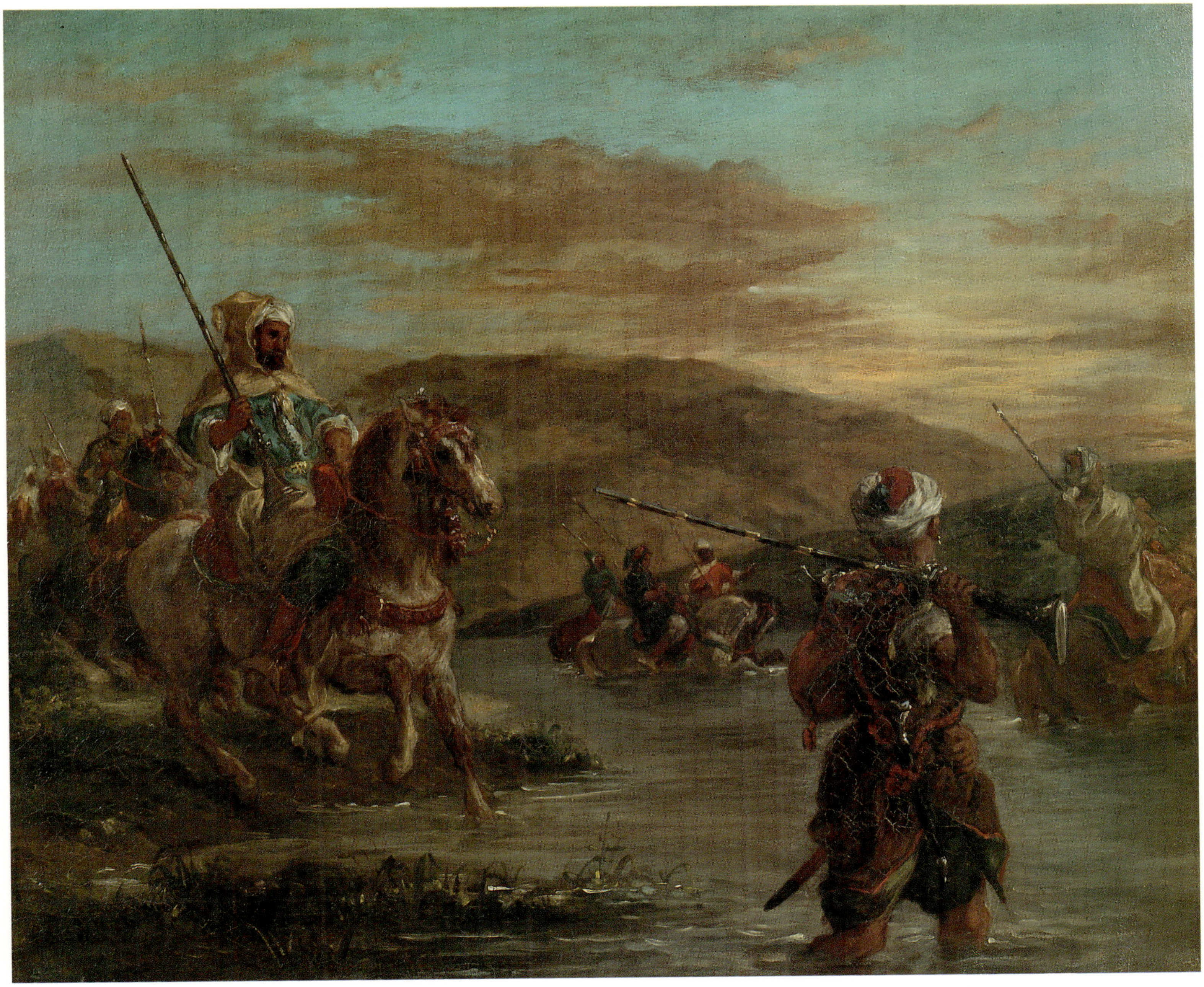

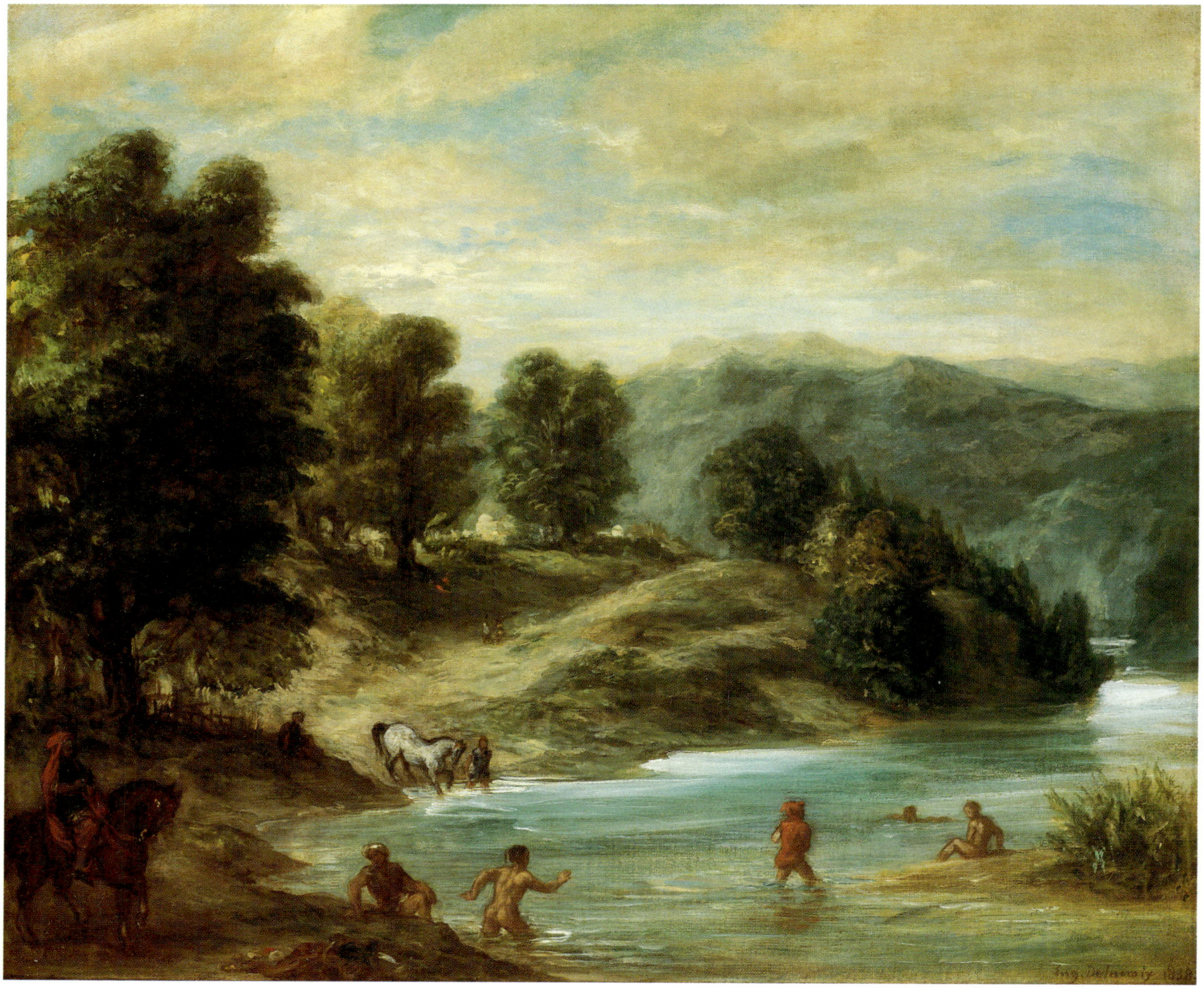

THE BANKS
OF THE RIVER SEBOU
Les bords du fleuve Sébou
(Royaume de Maroc)
100

Oil on canvas
48.9 x 59.7 cm
Signed and dated lower centre:
Eug. Delacroix 1858
Artemis Group, London

PROVENANCE:
Marquis du Lau; sale, Paris, 5 May 1869, lot 8, to Fould; sale L., 14 May 1873, lot 24, to Alfred Robaut; Constant Dutilleux; sale, 26 Mar. 1874, lot 11, to Malinet; Arnold, Tripp & Cie, by 1886; Théodore Revillon, by 1888; Mme Albert Esnault-Pelterie, in her family until about 1950; deposited in the Philadelphia Museum of Art until 1968.

BIBLIOGRAPHY:
Robaut, 1885, no. 1346; Johnson, 1986, no. 407, pl. 216; Arama, 1987, p. 214 no. 48.

EXHIBITIONS:
1859 Salon, no. 826; Paris, 1885, no. 138; Paris, 1930, no. 178, repr. Album, p. 96.

This painting, as pointed out by Lee Johnson, has not been seen in France since the exhibition held in Paris in 1930 in commemoration of the centenary of Romanticism. The subject, which may seem far from Delacroix's works of Moroccan inspiration, nonetheless corresponds to an incident which occurred on 12 March during the journey from Tangier to Meknes, and which the artist noted in his sketch-book: 'Crossed the Sebou in the morning—Ridiculous embarkation. The horses trying to get away and being beaten to get into the boats. Naked men driving the horses in front of them.—Biaz told us while crossing with us that they do not build bridges in order to make it easier to arrest thieves, to levy taxes and to apprehend rebels.' (Département des Arts graphiques, Louvre RF 1712 bis, fol. 13 verso and 14 recto.)

Disconcerted by the gloomy light issuing from the left and the sombre green tones of the trees, some of the 1859 critics were not at all impressed by the strangeness of the work. Théophile Gautier wrote in the *Moniteur universel* (21 May 1859): 'We would have had serious doubts as to the authenticity of *The Banks of the River Sebou* if we did not already know that the artist had actually made the voyage to Morocco. It is difficult to recognize the African countryside in this cabbage-coloured landscape, in these grassy river banks, in these Northern trees, in this river similar to the Seine or the Marne, in which children bathe and splash around.' Maxime Du Camp provoked the artist's admirers in the following terms: 'What will they think of this impossible, soapy, monochromatic landscape entitled *The Banks of the River Sebou*?

The colour itself has gone; grey, pallid tones have replaced that praiseworthy harmony in the name of which one indulgently forgave so many shocking imperfections!' (Salon de 1859, Paris, pp. 32–3). In more measured terms, Paul Mantz admitted his astonishment in *La Gazette des Beaux-Arts*: '*The Banks of the River Sebou* is an interesting example of Delacroix's landscape studies . . . It has a luminous but somewhat strange perspective due to the overaccentuated blue tone. Should I tell you? Well, this little painting, of little significance in the work of the master, reminded me of Rubens's landscapes' (Salon de 1859, p. 137).

VIEW OF TANGIER FROM THE SEASHORE
Vue de Tanger prise de la côte

101

Oil on canvas
81 x 99 cm
Signed and dated lower left:
Eug. Delacroix / 1858
The Minneapolis Institute of Arts, Minneapolis (49.4)

PROVENANCE:
Painted for the art art dealer Tedesco; with Salomon Goldschmidt in 1860; sale, Paris, 17 May 1888, lot 31, to Fanien; with Boussod, Valadon & Cie by Mar. 1892; James J. Hill, St Paul, Minnesota; his widow; his daughter Mrs E.C. Lindley, New York, his daughter; bequeathed to the Minneapolis Institute of Arts in 1949, in memory of her father.

BIBLIOGRAPHY:
Journal, II, p. 462, 464; Robaut, 1885, no. 1348; Johnson, 1986, no. 408, pl. 218; Arama, 1987, p. 215, no. 57, repr.

EXHIBITIONS:
Paris, 1860, suppl. no. 348; Toronto-Ottawa, 1962–3, no. 23, repr.; London-Edinburgh, 1964, no. 66, repr.

According to the notes in his *Journal*, it was during the summer of 1856 that Delacroix undertook this painting, destined for the art dealer Tedesco. On 8 July, Delacroix mentions that he has started a *Tangier Seascape* (*Paysage de Tanger au bord de la mer*) for Tedesco. The artist alludes to it a second time on 15 August describing it as *The Coast at Tangier (Bord de mer à Tanger)* but there is no further mention of the painting, so it is not known when exactly Tedesco received it. For this composition, as Lee Johnson notes, the artist used a pencil sketch of fortified ramparts at the summit of a hill (Département des Arts graphiques, Louvre, inventory RF 10112; Sérullaz, 1984, II, no. 1632, repr.). A study more directly connected with the painting is also in the Louvre (Département des Arts graphiques, Louvre, inventory RF 9513; Sérullaz, 1984, I, no. 467, repr.).

Commenting on the exhibition held in 1860, in the boulevard des Italiens, Théophile Gautier took particular interest in this painting which he called *Seascape on the African Coast (Marine des côtes d'Afrique)*: 'A grim path leads up the rock, and a hot sky, soft and luminous, spreads like an antique velarium over this strong, wild, yet peaceful landscape. It is remarkable that the turbulent Delacroix succeeds so well in portraying the impassive serenity of the Orient' (*Le Moniteur universel*, 15 March 1860).

Delacroix executed several paintings of Moroccan inspiration for the art dealer Tedesco. In addition to *View of Tangier from the Seashore*, he sold him *The Moroccan Blacksmith (Maréchal ferrant)* (A.K. Solomon collection, USA; Johnson, 1986, no. 391, pl. 200), *Horses coming out of the Sea (Les Chevaux sortant de la mer)* (private collection, Los Angeles; Johnson, 1986, no. 393, pl. 204), *Horses at a Trough* (see no. 103), *An Arab Camp at Night* (Szépmüvészeti Muzéum, Budapest; Johnson, 1986, no. 418, pl. 226, see p. 89) and *The Collection of Arab Taxes (La Perception de l'impôt Arabe)* (National Gallery, Washington; Johnson, 1986, no. 419, pl. 227, see p. 123).

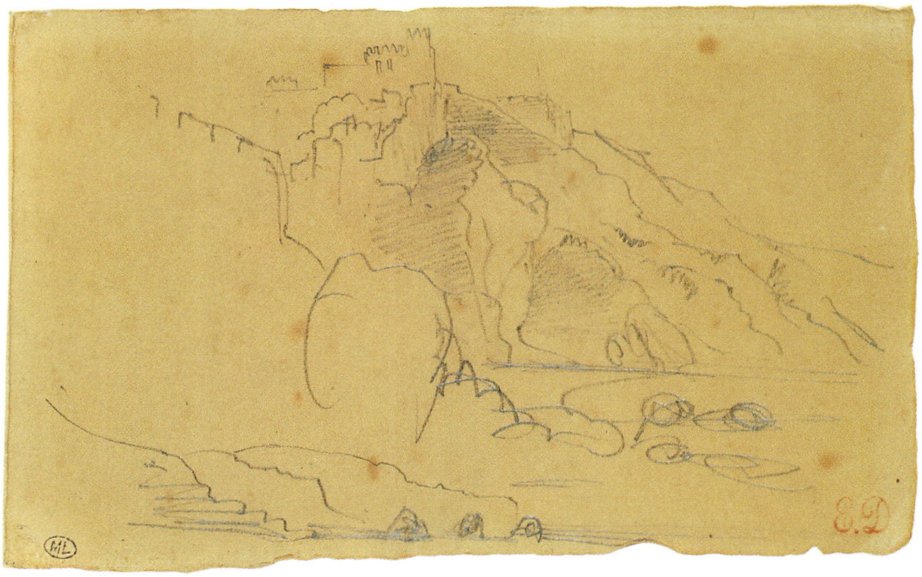

Not in exhibition:
Ramparts at the top of a Hill (Murailles fortifiées au sommet d'une colline),
pencil.
Département des Arts graphiques, Louvre (RF 10112).

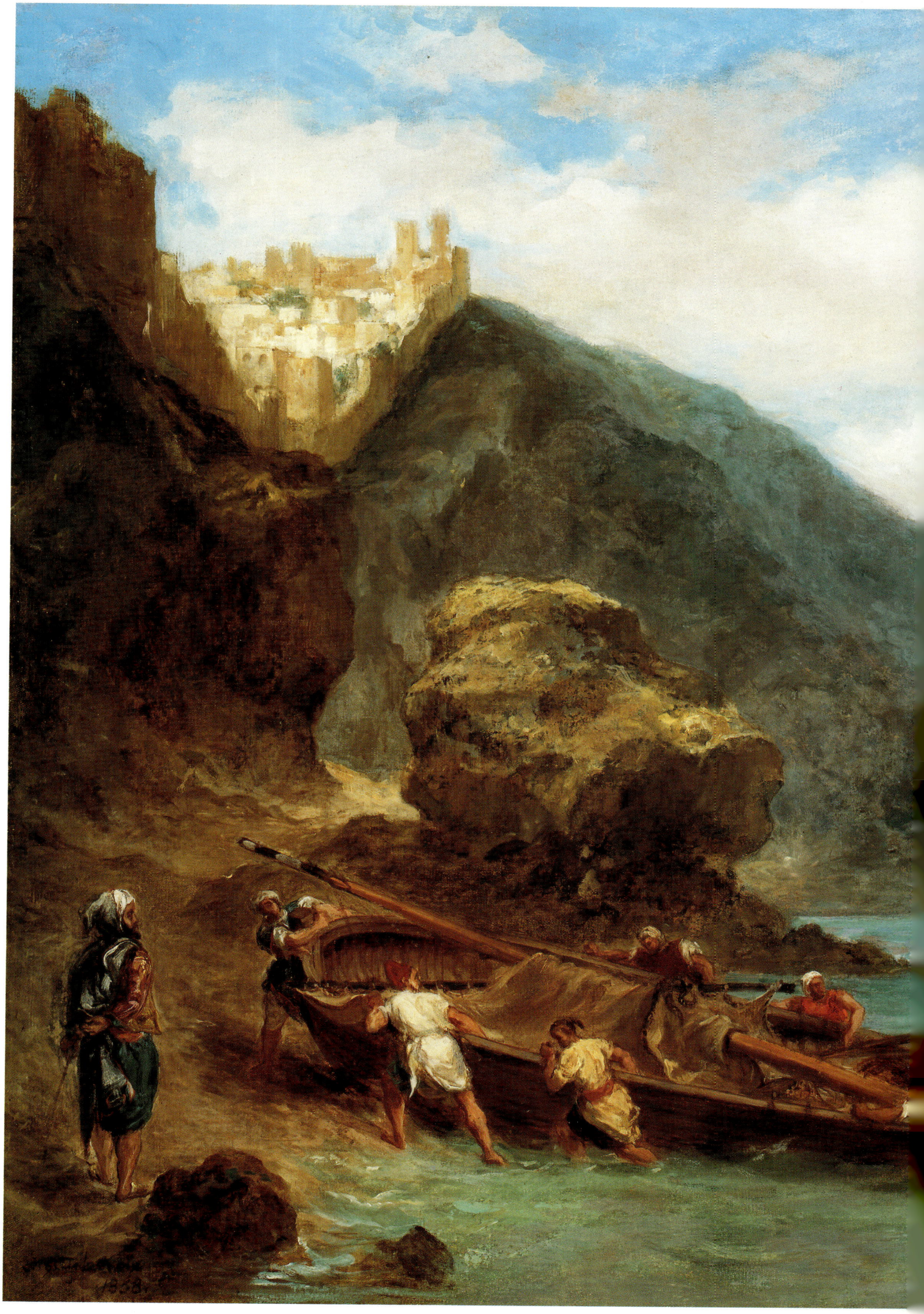

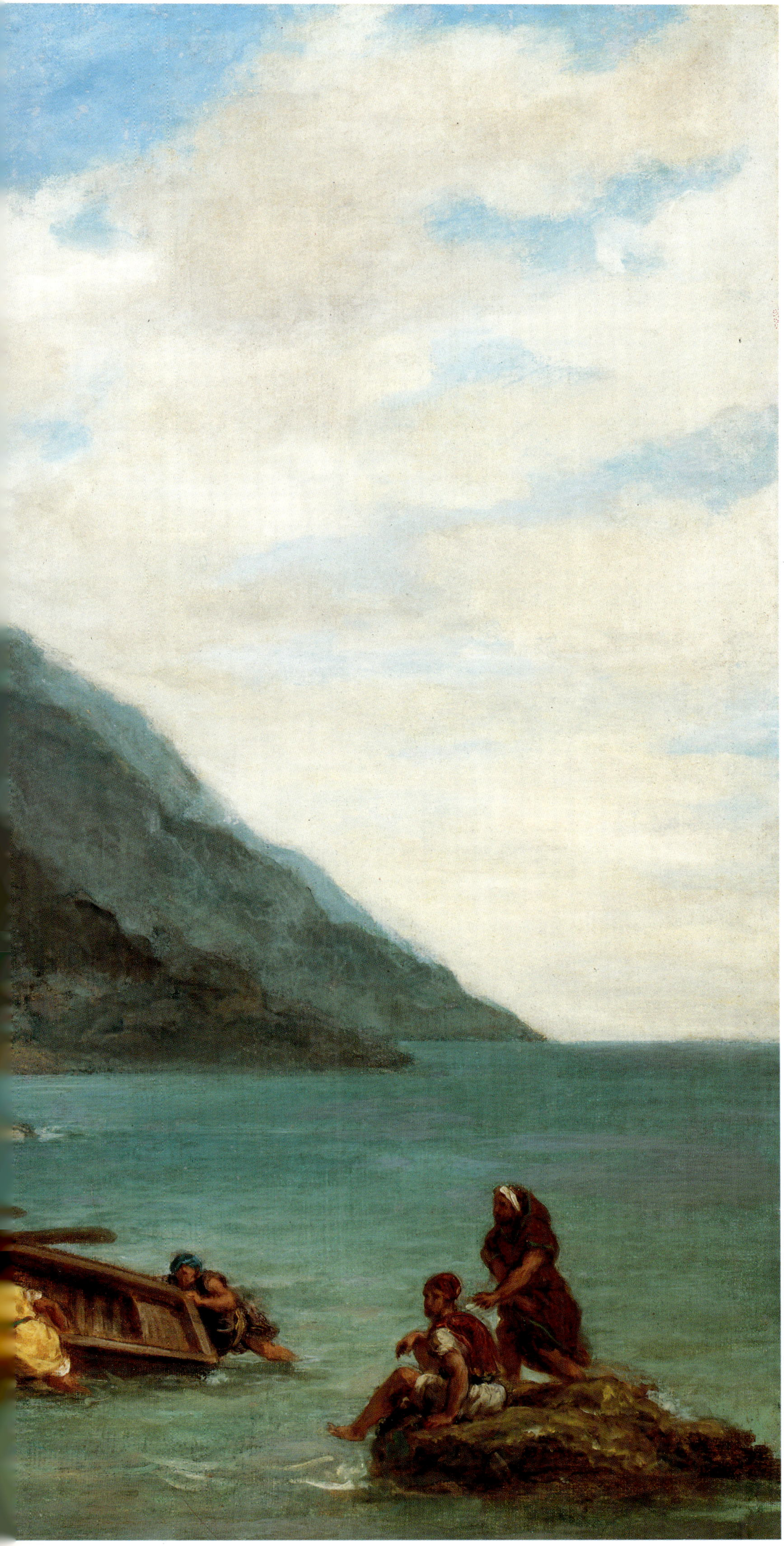

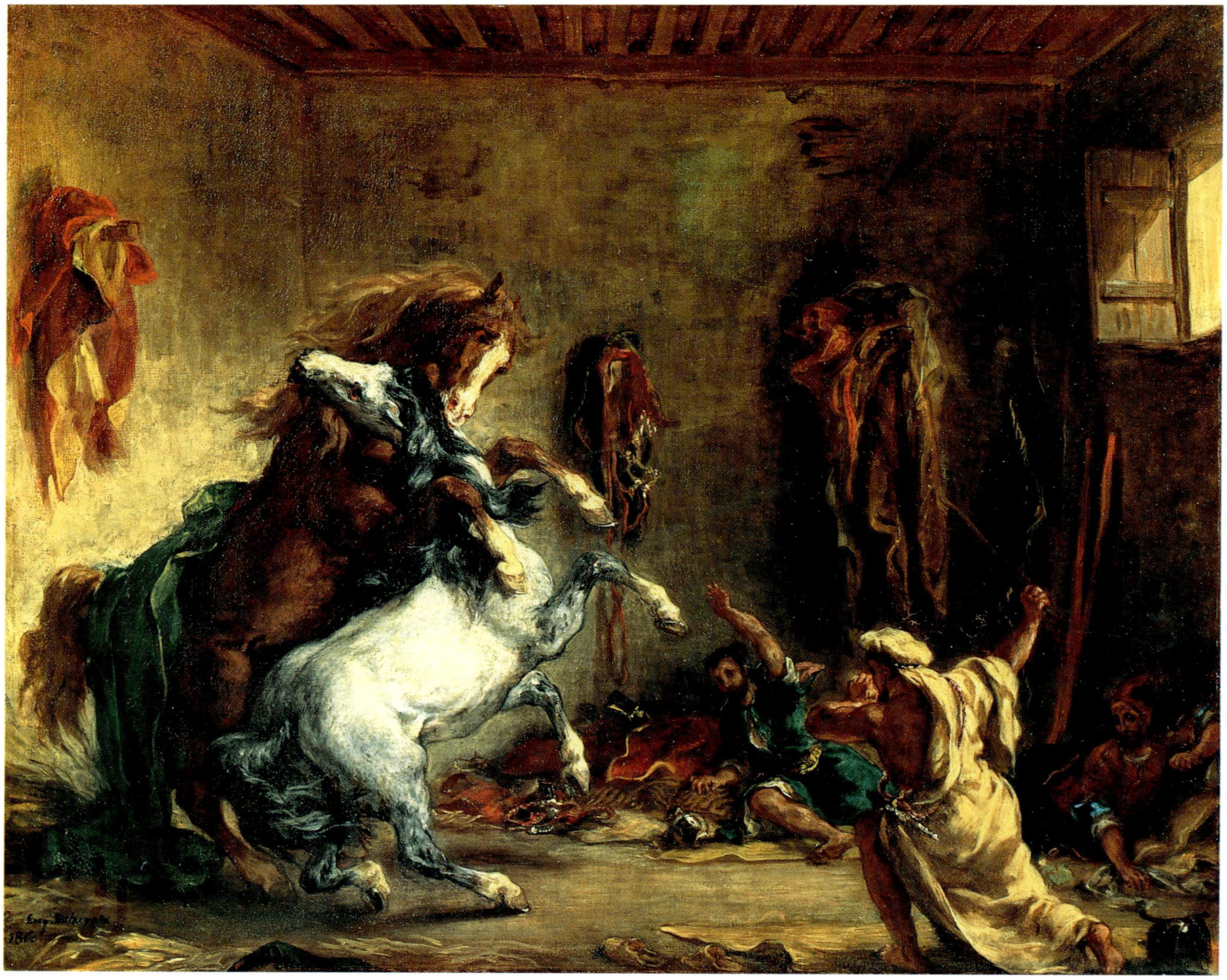

ARAB HORSES FIGHTING IN A STABLE
Chevaux se battant dans une écurie
102

Oil on canvas
64.6 x 81 cm
Signed and dated lower left:
Eug. Delacroix / 1860
Musée d'Orsay, Paris (RF 1988)

PROVENANCE:
Painted for the art art dealer Estienne; M.A.. and M. E..; sale, Paris, 12 Feb. 1872, lot 13, to Durand-Ruel; John Saulnier, Bordeaux, by 1873; Charles Hayem, by 1885; Isaac de Camondo; bequeathed to the Louvre in 1908, received in 1911.

BIBLIOGRAPHY:
Journal, II, pp. 203, 449; III, p. 90, 167, 291, 292; Robaut, 1885, no. 1409; Johnson, 1986, no. 413, pl. 223; Arama, 1987, p. 215 no. 57, repr.

EXHIBITIONS:
Paris, 1885, no. 96; Paris, 1930, no. 190; Paris, 1933, no. 201; Paris, 1945, no. 11; Paris, 1946, no. 11; Venice, 1956, p. 535, no. 39.

The origin of this painting is in an incident which occurred during a walk around Tangier on 29 January 1832, which was to leave an unforgettable impression in the artist's memory: 'The scene of the fighting horses. From the very beginning they reared up and fought with a fury that made me tremble for their riders, but magnificent for painting. I am sure that I have witnessed a scene as extraordinary and fantastic as anything that Gros or Rubens could have imagined. Then the grey got his head over the other horse's neck, and it seemed an eternity before he could be made to release his hold. Mornay managed to dismount. While he was holding it by the head, the black reared up furiously. They other went on fiercely biting it from behind. In the midst of the struggle the consul fell off.' (Wellington, pp. 49–50; Département des Arts graphiques, Louvre, inventory RF 39050 fol. 10 verso and 11 recto). From two small and hasty sketches, Delacroix, assisted by his notes and a prodigious imagination, entirely reconstituted the savage confrontation of the two mounts, watched by three Arabs, powerless, who are relegated to the right-hand side of the painting, the violence of which is accentuated by the lighting. In his *Histoire des Artistes vivants* (Paris, 1855, pp. 65–6) Théophile Silvestre recounts that Delacroix often spoke of his pleasure in discovering the beauty of the Arabian horses in Morocco: 'Under their native sky, they have a particular pride and energy which they lose when they find themselves in a different climate; quite frequently they throw their riders violently in order to engage in combats which last for hours: they bite each other like tigers and nothing can separate them; the raucous, inflamed breath coming from their scarlet nostrils with a sound like an engine, their scant, blood-coated manes, their ferocious jealousy, their mortal rancour: everything within them, their attitudes and character, crescendoes into poetry.' On 19 June 1854, Delacroix mentions this subject as being one of several of his Moroccan projects (*Journal*, II, p. 203) but he appears only to have started it two years later (*Journal*, II, p. 449). The painting was completed on 14 June 1860 (*Journal*, III, p. 292).

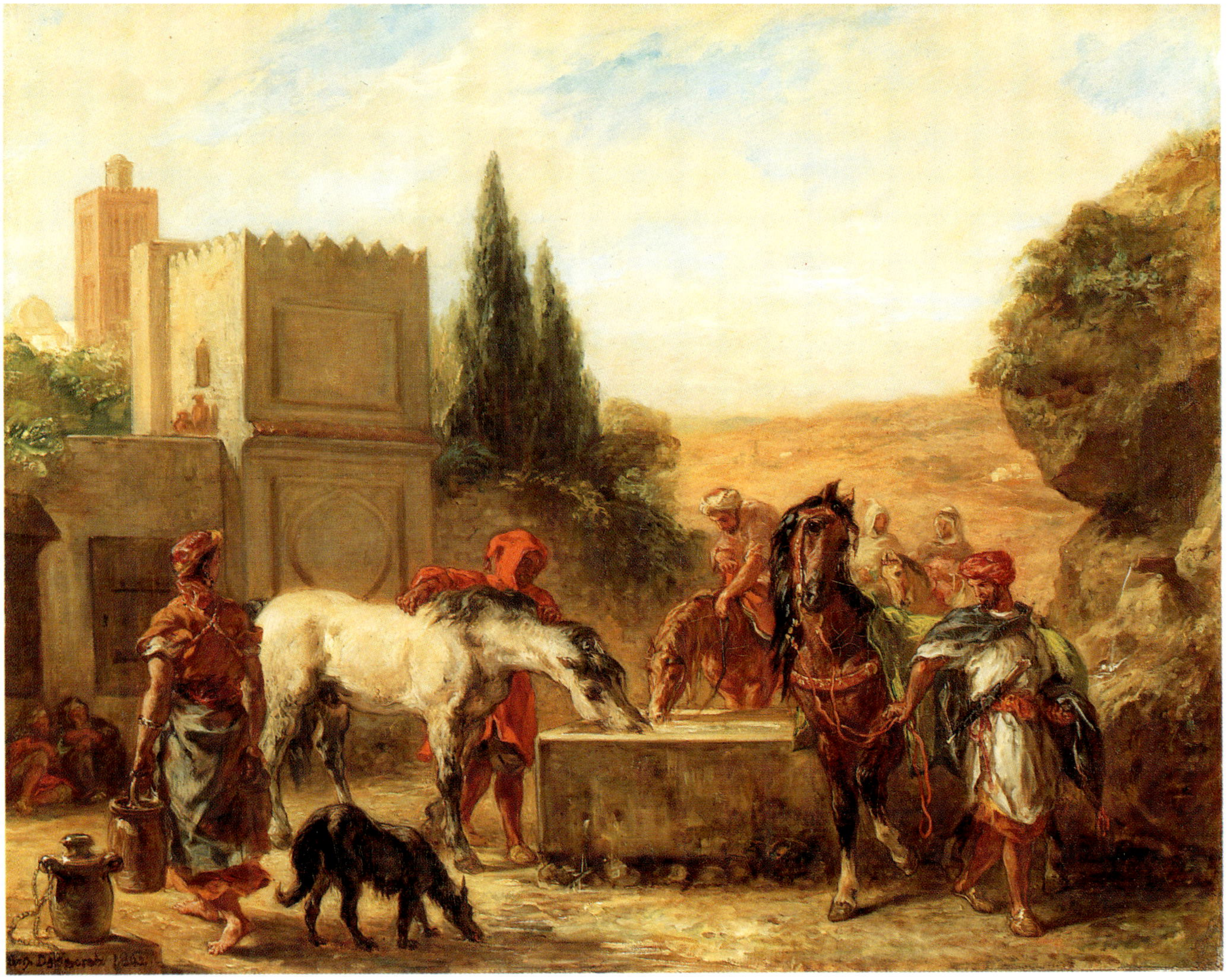

HORSES AT A TROUGH
Chevaux à l'abreuvoir
103

Oil on canvas
76 x 91 cm
Signed and dated lower left: Eug. Delacroix 1862
Philadelphia Museum of Art, Philadelphia (W.50–1–2)

PROVENANCE:
Sold by Delacroix to the art art dealer Tedesco, 6 Oct. 1862; sale, Paris, 23 Apr. 1866, lot 14, to Khalil Bey; sale, Paris, 16 Jan. 1868, lot 21, to Constant Say; Countess de Tredern, née Say; Bernheim-Jeune; Boussod, Valadon et Cie; Georges Petit, by 1911; Baillehache, by 1916; Prince of Wagram, Germany, by 1921; Étienne Bignon, by 1930; Marcel Kapferer, by 1931; Chester Beatty, London, by 1939; with Paul Rosenberg, New York, by 1950; acquired by the Philadelphia Museum of Art for the W.P. Wilstach Collection.

BIBLIOGRAPHY:
Journal, II, p. 462; III, p. 292; Robaut, 1885, no. 1442; Johnson, 1986, no. 415, pl. 224; Arama, 1987, p. 215 no. 63, repr.

EXHIBITIONS:
Paris, 1930, no. 197 A.

Delacroix used themes inspired by his memories of Morocco until the very end of his life, whether it be for *Arab Horses fighting in a Stable* (see no. 102), *Chieftain visiting a Tribe (Kaïd visitant une tribu)* (1862, private collection; see cat. no. 69), or *The Sultan of Morocco* (1862, Bührle Foundation, Zurich; see no. 84 and p. 119) or *Arabs Skirmishing in the Mountains* (1863, National Gallery of Art, Washington; Johnson, 1986, no. 419, pl. 227, see p. 123). Although the scene portrayed here does not seem to correspond to any particular annotation in the sketch-books from 1832, it must nevertheless come from a specific scene. Based on a pencil sketch (private collection), Delacroix considerably modified his composition, integrating buildings which block the horizon on the left. Due to its restrained, somewhat melancholy atmosphere, its classical composition and the warm harmony of the predominant tones of sombre red, green and brown, this painting is among the most refined of Delacroix's later works.

On 6 October 1862, Delacroix signed a receipt for the art dealer Tedesco: 'I received from Monsieur Tedesco the sum of *two thousand francs* in payment of a painting representing a horse trough in Morocco' (Bibliothèque Nationale, Département des manuscrits, nouv. acq. fr. 24019; quoted in Johnson, 1986, p. 210).

DELACROIX AND HIS ERA

Delacroix

1798 Born in Charenton-Saint-Maurice

1805 Death of Delacroix's father

1815 Enters Guérin's Studio

1816 Accepted into the École des Beaux-Arts

1822 *The Barque of Dante*

1824 Delacroix exhibits *The Massacre at Chios* at the Salon

1827 Exhibits *The Death of Sardanapalus*

1830 *Liberty Leading the People*, exhibited at the 1831 Salon

1831 Receives the Légion d'Honneur

1832 Moroccan Journey

1833 Salon du Roi in the Palais Bourbon

1834 *The Women of Algiers in their Apartment*

1838–1847 Library of the Palais-Bourbon

1840 *The Justice of Trajan*

1840–1846 Library of the Palais du Luxembourg

1845 *The Sultan of Morocco*

1846 Made Officer of the Légion d'Honneur

1850–1851 Decorates the ceiling of the Apollo Gallery in the Louvre

1852–1854 Decorates the Salon de la Paix in the Hôtel de Ville

1855 Success at the Universal Exhibition – Made Commander of the Légion d'Honneur

1857 Elected to the Institute

1861 Inauguration of the Chapel of the Holy Angels in Saint-Sulpice, began in 1850

1863 *An Arab Camp at Night*—13 August 1863 Dies in Paris

1864 Sale of the contents of the artist's studio

1865 Retrospective at the Ecole des Beaux-Arts

Literature

1801 F.R. de Chateaubriand: *Atala*

1804 É.Pivert de Sénancour: *Oberman*

1812 Byron: *Childe Harold's Pilgrimage*, translated into French in 1819

1813 Byron: *The Giaour*, and *The Bride of Abydos*

1814 Sir Walter Scott: *Waverley*

1819 Sir Walter Scott: *Ivanhoe*

1820 A. de Lamartine: *Méditations poétiques*

1822 V. Hugo: *Odes*

1826 A. de Vigny: *Poèmes antiques et modernes*

1827 J.W.L. Goethe: *Faust*, (translated by Nerval)

1829 V. Hugo: *Les Orientales*

1830 Stendhal: *Le Rouge et le Noir*

1831 V. Hugo: *Notre-Dame de Paris*

1832 G. Sand: *Indiana*

1834 H. de Balzac: *Séraphita*

1835 V. Hugo: *Les Chants du Crépuscule*

1836 A. de Musset: *Les Confessions d'un enfant du siècle*

1838 V. Hugo: *Ruy Blas*

1840 P. Mérimée: *Colomba*

1843 T. Gautier: *Tra los montes*

1844 A. Dumas: *The Three Musketeers*

1846 W.P. Thackeray: *Vanity Fair*

1848 A. Dumas fils: *La Dame aux Camélias*

1850 C. Dickens: *David Copperfield*

1851 G. de Nerval: *Voyage en Orient*

1853 T. Gautier: *Constantinople*

1854 J.A. Barbey d'Aurevilly: *L'Ensorcelée*

1856 V. Hugo: *Les Contemplations*

1857 C. Baudelaire: *Les Fleurs du Mal*
G. Flaubert: Madame Bovary

1859 E. Fromentin: *Une Année dans le Sahel*

1862 G. Flaubert: *Salammbô*

1863 C. Baudelaire: *The Painter of Modern Life*

Painting

1799 David: *Rape of the Sabine Women*
1801 Girodet: *Ossian greeting the shadows of French Heroes*
1804 Gros: *The Pest-house at Jaffa*
1805 - 1807 David: *Coronation of Napoleon*
1806 Gros: *The Battle of Aboukir*
1810 Girodet: *The Cairo Revolt*
1812 Géricault: *Charge of the Cavalry Officer*
1814 Goya: *The Third of May*
1819 Géricault: *The Raft of the Medusa*
1824 Ingres: *Vow of Louis XIII*
1827 A. Scheffer: *Souliote Women*
1834 Daumier: *La Rue Transnonain*
1835 Delaroche: *The Assassination of the Duke de Guise*
1836 Rude: *La Marseillaise (Departure of the Volunteers)*
1842 Courbet: *Self-portrait with Black Dog*
1844 Turner: *Rain, Steam, Speed*
1845 Chassériau: *Ali-Ben-Hamet, Kalif of Constantine*
1847 Couture: *Romans in the Period of Decadence*
1853 Chassériau: *Tepidarium*
1855 Courbet: *The Painter's Studio*
1862 Ingres: *Turkish Bath*
1863 Manet: *Déjeuner sur l'herbe* (exhibited at the Salon des Refusés)

Music

1803 Beethoven: The 'Eroica' Symphony
1813 Rossini: *The Italian Girl in Algiers*
1815 Schubert: *The King of the Aulnes*
1816 Rossini: *The Barber of Seville*
1817 Schubert: 'Death and the Maiden' Quartet
1822 Schubert: The Unfinished symphony
1824 Beethoven: Ninth Symphony
1830 Berlioz: 'Symphonie Fantastique'
1836 Chopin: The 'Grande Polonaise'
1837 Donizetti: *Lucia di Lammermoor*
1839 Berlioz: *Romeo and Juliet*
1846 Berlioz: *La Damnation de Faust*
1847 Verdi: *Macbeth*
1850 Liszt: *Mazeppa*
1851 Schumann: *Manfred*
1853 Verdi: *La Traviata*
1859 Wagner: *Tristan and Isolde*
1861 Wagner: *Tannhaüser*: scandal at the Paris Opera

Politics

1798 Napoleon's Egyptian Campaign
1802 Napoleon elected consul for life
1804 Coronation of Napoleon
1812 Napoleon's Retreat from Russia
1815 Hundred Days Restoration of Napoleon
1820 The assassination of the Duke de Berry
1825 Coronation of Charles X
1826 Missolonghi falls to the Turks
1827 Battle of Nazarin (defeat of the Turks and Egyptians)
1830 Louis-Philippe becomes King of the French
1837 The Fall of Constantinople
1847 The defeat of Abd el-Kader
1848 February revolution and declaration of the Second Republic
1851 *Coup d'état* by Louis-Napoleon Bonaparte
1852 Napoleon III becomes Emperor
1854 Crimean War
1859 Italian War of Liberation
1861 Beginning of American Civil War
1862 Mexican Expedition
1864 Creation of the First International in London

Short Titles: Literature

Arama, 1987
M. Arama, *Le Maroc de Delacroix*, Paris, 1987

Arama, 1992
M. Arama, *Eugène Delacroix. Le voyage au Maroc.* Facsimile of the sketchbooks from the Musée du Louvre and the Musée Condé in Chantilly, supplemented by two volumes of notes and documents, Paris, 1992, 6 vols, box collection

Bjurström, 1986
P. Bjurström, *French Drawings, Nineteenth Century*, Stockholm, 1986

Correspondance
General correspondence of Eugène Delacroix published by André Joubin, Paris, 1936–1938, 5 vols. (I, 1804–1837; II, 1834–1849; III, 1850–1857; IV, 1858–1863; V, supplement and indexes)

Delteil, 1908
L. Delteil, *Le Peintre-Graveur illustré. III. Ingres–Delacroix*, Paris, 1908

Dumur, 1988
G. Dumur, *Delacroix et le Maroc*, Paris, 1988

Guiffrey–Marcel, 1909
J. Guiffrey and P. Marcel, *Inventaire général des dessins du musée du Louvre et du musée de Versailles, École Française*, vol. IV (Corot - Delacroix), Paris, 1909

Hoetink, 1968
H. R. Hoetink, *Franse Tekeningen uit de 19e Eeuw. Catalogus van de verzameling in het Museum Boymans-Van Beuningen*, Rotterdam, 1968

Johnson, 1982
L. Johnson, 'Delacroix's Road to the Sultan of Morocco', *Apollo*, CXV, 1982, 186–9

Johnson, 1986
L. Johnson, *The Paintings of Eugène Delacroix. A Critical Catalogue*, III, IV, 1832-1863 (Movable Pictures and Private Decorations), Oxford, 1986

Joubin, 1930
A. Joubin, *E. Delacroix. Voyage au Maroc. 1832. Lettres, Aquarelles et Dessins*, Paris, 1930

Journal
Le Journal d'Eugène Delacroix. Avant-propos de Jean-Louis Vaudoyer, de l'Académie française. Introduction et notes par André Joubin, Paris, 1960, 3 vol. (I, 1822-1852 ; II, 1853-1856 ; III, 1857-1863)

Lambert, 1953
E. Lambert, *Histoire d'un tableau. L'Abd Er Rahman Sultan du Maroc de Delacroix*, Paris, 1953

Lemoine, 1976
S. Lemoine, *Musée des Beaux-Arts de Dijon. Donation Granville. Catalogue des peintures, dessins. Tome 1. Œuvres réalisées avant 1900.* Dijon, 1976

Robaut, 1885
A. Robaut, *L'œuvre complet de Eugène Delacroix, peintures, dessins, gravures, lithographies*, Paris, 1885

Robaut annotated
A. Robaut, *L'œuvre complet de Eugène Delacroix, peintures, dessins, gravures, lithographies*, Paris, 1885. Copy annotated by the author, Département des Estampes et de la Photographie, Bibliothèque Nationale de France

Sérullaz, 1963
M. Sérullaz, *Mémorial de l'exposition Eugène Delacroix organisée au musée du Louvre à l'occasion du centenaire de la mort de l'artiste*, Paris, 1963

Sérullaz, 1967
M. Sérullaz, 'Unpublished drawings by Eugène Delacroix at the Nationalmuseum, Stockholm ', *Master Drawings*, 1967, vol. V, n° 4, 404-6

Sérullaz, 1984
M. Sérullaz, *Musée du Louvre. Cabinet des Dessins. Inventaire général des dessins. Ecole française. Dessins d'Eugène Delacroix 1798-1863*, Paris, 1984, 2 vol.

Stewart, 1971
Eugène Delacroix: Selected Letters, 1813-1863, edited and translated by Jean Stewart, London, 1971

Wellington, 1980
The Journal of Eugène Delacroix, a selection edited with an introduction by Hubert Wellington. Translated by Lucy Norton. Phaidon, Oxford, 1980

Short Titles: Exhibitions

Basel, 1939
Eugène Delacroix (1798–1863), Kunsthalle, Basel, 1939

Berne, 1963–1964
Eugène Delacroix, Kunstmuseum, Berne, 1963–1964

Bordeaux, 1963
Delacroix, ses maîtres, ses amis, ses élèves, Bordeaux, 1963

Bremen, 1964
Eugène Delacroix, 1798–1863, Kunsthalle, Bremen, 1964

Brussels, 1986
Ingres–Delacroix, Palais des Beaux-Arts, Brussels, 1936

Brussels 1986
Ingres et Delacroix, Dessins et aquarelles, Palais des Beaux- Arts, Brussels, 1986

Chicago, 1930
Delacroix, The Art Institute of Chicago, 1930

Frankfurt, 1987–1988
Themen und Variationen. Arbeiten auf Papier, Städtische Galerie im Städelschen Kunstinstitut, Frankfurt, 1987–1988

Kyoto-Tokyo, 1969
Exposition Delacroix, Municipal Museum, Kyoto; National Museum, Tokyo, 1969

London, 1952
Eugène Delacroix (1798–1863), Wildenstein, London, 1952

London-Edinburgh, 1964
Delacroix, Royal Academy of Arts, London; Royal Scottish Academy, Edinburgh, 1964

New York, 1991
Eugène Delacroix (1798–1863), Paintings, Drawings and Prints from North American Collections, The Metropolitan Museum of Art, New York, 1991

Oakland, 1963
Drawings, Watercolors and Prints by Eugène Delacroix, Mills College, Oakland, 1963

Paris, 1864
Exposition des œuvres d'Eugène Delacroix, Société Nationale des Beaux-Arts, Paris, 1864

Paris, Ecole des Beaux-Arts, 1885
Exposition Eugène Delacroix au profit de la souscription destinée à élever à Paris un monument à sa mémoire, École des Beaux-Arts, Paris, 1885

Paris, 1925
Aquarelles et dessins de Delacroix, Galerie Dru, Paris, 1925

Paris, Louvre, 1930
Centenaire du Romantisme. Exposition Eugène Delacroix, Louvre, Paris, 1930

Paris, 1933
Delacroix au Maroc, Orangerie, Paris, 1933

Paris, 1934
Exposition de peintures et de dessins d'Eugène Delacroix, Atelier d'Eugène Delacroix, 6 rue de Furstenberg, Paris, 1934

Paris, 1937
Tableaux, aquarelles, dessins, gravures, lithographies provenant du Musée du Louvre, des donations Étienne Moreau-Nélaton, Baron J. Vitta ou prêtés par divers amateurs, Appartement et Atelier d'Eugène Delacroix, 6 rue de Furstenberg, Paris, 1937

Paris, 1937 (1)
Exposition du 26 novembre au 18 décembre 1937 de Peintures, Aquarelles et Dessins par Eugène Delacroix (1798-1863), Maurice Gobin, Paris, 1937

Paris, 1939
Tableaux, aquarelles, dessins, gravures, lithographies provenant du legs Étienne Moreau-Nélaton au Musée du Louvre, de la donation du baron J. Vitta et de dons et prêts de divers amateurs, Appartement et Atelier d'Eugène Delacroix, 6 rue de Furstenberg, Paris, 1939

Paris, 1945
Chefs-d'œuvre de Delacroix (1798-1863), Atelier Delacroix, Paris, 1945

Paris, 1946
Chefs-d'œuvre de Delacroix (1798-1863), Atelier Delacroix, Paris, 1946

Paris, Atelier, 1951
Delacroix et l'orientalisme de son temps, Société des Amis d'Eugène Delacroix. A l'Atelier du Maître, 6 rue de Furstenberg, Paris, 1951

Paris, 1963
Delacroix, Louvre, Paris, 1963

Paris, 1963 (1)
Delacroix, Dessins, Cabinet des Dessins, Louvre, Paris, 1963

Paris, 1967
Delacroix, son atelier et la critique d'art, Atelier Delacroix, Paris, 1967

Paris, 1973
Delacroix et la peinture libérée, Musée Delacroix, Paris, 1973 (no catalogue but with a list of works loaned by private collectors published in *La Revue du Louvre et des Musées de France*, 1973-6, p. 366)

Paris, Louvre, 1982
Revoir Delacroix, Cabinet des Dessins, Louvre, Paris, 1982

Regina, 1975
Eugène Delacroix 1798–1863, Norman MacKenzie Art Gallery, University of Regina (Saskatchewan), 1975

Stockholm, 1981
Delacroix' Lejonjackter, Nationalmuseum, Stockholm, 1981

Toronto-Ottawa, 1962–1963
Delacroix, The Art Gallery of Toronto, Toronto; The National Gallery of Canada, Ottawa, 1962–1963

Venice, 1956
28th Venice Biennial, 1956

Zurich, 1939
Eugène Delacroix, Kunsthaus, Zurich, 1939

Zurich 1987
Eugène Delacroix, Kunsthaus, Zurich, 1987

Zurich, 1987 (1)
Eugène Delacroix. Zeichnungen, Aquarelle, Graphik, Kunsthaus, Zurich, 1987

Glossary

Aïd el-Kebir: known as *Aïd el-adha* in literary Arabic. Ceremony commemorating the sacrifice of Abraham. This feast-day is celebrated sixty days after Aïd el-Fitr which marks the end of the month of Ramadan
Aïn: a spring
Aïssaoua: traditional religious brotherhood of Sufism, founded by the Saint Sidi Mohammed Ben Aïssa, whose tomb is in Meknes; one of the orders in which music plays a significant spiritual role
Amin: administrator, finance employee, head of a trade association
Aoud: lute
Balgha: Moroccan slipper
Ben: son of
Bendir: drum
Bit el-mal: treasury
Burnous: hooded wool cape
Canoun: brazier
Commander of the Faithful: monarch's formal title
Columns of Hercules : the European Mount Calpe (Rock of Gibraltar) and the African Rock of Abyla, which demarcate the Straits of Gibraltar and were considered as the extremities of the universe by the Ancients
Dar ech-Cheraa: law courts
Dar el-Maghzen: state house
Dragoman: former term for official interpreters in the orient
Fantasia/Course de Poudre/Laab el Barode: Arabian cavalry display
Fellah: peasant
Gaita (Ghayta): clarinet
Gandoura: sleeveless tunic
Gnaoua: religious brotherhood of African origin, whose rituals revolve around music, dancing and trance
Haik: piece of material in which women drape themselves
Jellaba: hooded male robe
Kaid: tribal chief, army commander, urban administrator
Kasbah: citadel or fortified sector of a town
Kbir: tall
Khaima: A tent
Khanjar: dagger
Kif: mixture of tobacco and Indian hemp
Koubba : sanctuary, dome
Ksar: 1) fortified village 2) castle, palace
Moor: term applied to Berbers
Mechla: jellaba made of coarse wool
Mechouar (Mashwar): palace courtyard where official receptions and military parades take place
Mellah: Jewish quarter
Moghazni: guard, civil servant
Moussem: fair, annual pilgrimage to a saint's tomb
Oued: waterway, river
Oulema: A doctor of law, Muslim theologian
Pasha: title given to the head of a province
Rebec: very simple violin, similar to a *rebab*
Saroual: wide trousers
Sherifian: pertaining to a sherif, descendant of the prophet Mohammed
Sidi: honorary title preceding the christian and family name
Souk: market, bazaar; *socco* in Spanish
Sultan: the supreme authority
Tanbûr: drum

Index

Picture Credits

Albright-Knox Art Gallery, pp. 190-1
Maurice Arama, pp. 63-4
Artephot / A. Held, p. 48
Artephot / Faillet, p. 49
Artothek / U. Edelmann, p. 88
© 1994, The Art Institute of Chicago (All rights reserved), p. 145
The Baltimore Museum of Art, p. 152
Michèle Bellot, pp. 159, 162
Bibliothèque Nationale de France, pp. 192, 193, 194, 219
Patrick Boyer, p. 218
The British Museum, p. 149
Bulloz, p. 35
Camerarts, N.Y., p. 140
The Chrysler Museum, p. 111
The Cleveland Museum of Art, p. 220
Cliché Ville de Nantes / Musée des Beaux-Arts / H. Maertens, pp. 198-9
P. Cumming Ass. Ltd, p. 226
Dénes Józsa / Courtesy administrative council of the Szèpmüvèzsèti Muzeum, Budapest, pp. 89, 223
Winnie Denker / Patrimoine 2001 / Fondation " La Caïda ", p. 222
Walter Dräyer, p. 119
(All rights reserved), p. 155
Edimedia, pp. 50, 176
Courtesy E. V. Thaw & Co, New York, pp. 141, 202
The Fine Arts Museum of San Francisco, p. 182
Courtesy of the Fogg Art Museum / Rick Stafford, p. 180
Courtesy Galerie Jan Krugier, Geneva, pp. 167, 203
Courtesy Galerie Nathan, Zurich, pp. 153, 185
Courtesy Galerie Schmit, Paris, pp. 139, 152, 159, 200
Gallery of Ontario / Brenda Dereniuk, p. 75
Giraudon, pp. 34, 197, 211
Tom Haartsen, p. 177
Hiroshima Museum of Art, p. 201
Courtesy Huguette Bérès, Paris, pp. 168, 173, 219
Kunsthaus, Zurich, couverture, pp. 31, 221
Philippe Maillard, pp. 37, 84, 87, 93, 94, 96, 99, 104, 166, 169, 186, 187, 196, 209, 219, 227
© 1994, The Metropolitan Museum of Art, pp. 179, 180, 210
Milwaukee Art Museum, p. 204
The Minneapolis Institute of Arts, pp. 72–3, 77, 228–9
Musée des Arts Décoratifs / L. Sully – Jaulmes, Paris, p. 174
Musée des Beaux-Arts, Bordeaux, pp. 213, 215
Musée des Beaux-Arts, Dijon ; donation Granville, pp. 24, 155, 160, 209, 224
Musée des Beaux-Arts, Tours, pp. 80–1
Musée Boymans-van Beuningen, p. 155
Musée Fabre, pp. 117, 158
Musée Fabre / Frédéric Jaulmes, pp. 2-3, 46, 189
Musée de Grenoble, p. 91
Musée de Laon, p. 195
Musée de Poitiers / Ch. Vignaud, pp. 166, 167
Musées de la Ville de Paris, © by SPADEM 1994, p. 155
Museum of Art, Rhode Island School of Design, p. 103
© 1994, National Gallery of Art, Washington, p. 123
National Gallery of Scotland, pp. 217–18
Nationalmuseum, Stockholm, pp. 132, 138, 142, 143, 147
Philadelphia Museum of Art / Graydon Wood, p. 231
Christian Poite, p. 184
Réunion des musées nationaux, pp. 20, 29, 33, 36, 38, 39, 41, 42, 45–7, 51, 53, 55, 57, 58, 60, 65, 67, 68-70, 74, 76, 85-7, 90, 92-6, 98, 101, 102, 106-109, 113, 115, 127, 129, 133, 136, 148, 150, 151, 156, 161, 165, 170–3, 175, 181, 183, 205, 208, 225, 230
R.M.N. / Michèle Bellot, pp. 44, 48, 144, 145, 147, 157, 161–4, 173, 207–9, 214
Sammlung Oskar Reinhart, pp. 120–1
Philippe Sebert, p. 146
Studio Lourmel, p. 215
Studio Lourmel / J.-M. Routhier, p. 220
© Succession H. Matisse / Giraudon, p. 27
Von der Heydt Museum, Wuppertal, p. 97
The Walters Art Gallery, pp. 16, 122

This exhibition was made possible by :

MAROC
OFFICE NATIONAL MAROCAIN DU TOURISME

الخطوط الملكية المغربية
royal air maroc

مؤسسة التعريف بالمغرب
FONDATION CONNAISSANCE DU MAROC